COVERING
AMERICA

A Narrative History of a Nation's Journalism

———— ★ ————

Christopher B. Daly

University of Massachusetts Press
Amherst and Boston

LC 2011050381
ISBN 978-1-55849-911-9

Designed by Sally Nichols
Set in Minion Pro
Printed and bound by Thomson-Shore, Inc.

Library of Congress Cataloging-in-Publication Data

Daly, Christopher B.
Covering America : a narrative history of a nation's journalism / Christopher B. Daly.
p. cm.
Includes bibliographical references and index.
ISBN 978-1-55849-911-9 (cloth : alk. paper)
1. Journalism—United States—History. 2. Press—United States—History. I. Title.
PN4855.D36 2011
071'.3—dc23
2011050381

British Library Cataloguing in Publication data are available.

This book is dedicated to

Jim Fishel

—a great friend to American journalism
and a dear friend to me.

Contents

Preface
A Note on Methods

——◆——

ACENTRAL THEME OF this book is that in order to understand the news business, it is important to understand the news *as a business*. I have tried to pay attention, first and foremost, to the economics of this field. The fundamental fact about the news business in America is that it has been conducted, overwhelmingly, as a private enterprise. Whether for-profit or not, the institutions that engage in mass communication have been almost entirely in private hands, separate from the government. But while they operate as businesses, the news media are not *merely* businesses. The practice of journalism is, at one and the same time, a business and a vocation; it is a cultural enterprise lodged inside a business enterprise. More often than not, the result has been an uneasy relationship between news and business. In the history of journalism there is a recurring tension between the contents of the news and the forms of business that produce them, between what have been referred to as the "sacred" and the "profane" sides of the news field. In step with changes in the larger economy, the business model for journalism has changed over the last three centuries. From a small-scale shop to a factory-sized corporation to a global conglomerate, the news business *as a business* has kept pace with broader trends. That process has in turn created a recurring set of crises in which the values of journalism have come into conflict with the values of business. In each ensuing crisis, a change in the economics of news has led to a change in the definition of news itself. From the "penny press" of the 1830s to the "yellow journalism" of Hearst and Pulitzer in the 1890s, and from the pioneering of the broadcast networks by David Sarnoff and William Paley in the 1920s to the building of giant media behemoths like Time Warner and News Corp., journalists and executives have continually been forced to redefine the relation between the "business side" and the "news side" of the news business. It has been a contested terrain. Each new phase of journalism history contains within itself the seeds of its own destruction and renewal.

Common metaphors for the press (and, since the twentieth century, "the media") are the lens or the mirror. The news media allow us to "see" our society, or the media "reflect" our society. For all their popularity, however, these metaphors were never adequate and are sometimes downright misleading. The media are not neutral instruments; they are made up of people who have their own motives, both economic and non-economic. While individual media are distinct, they also combine to create a complex institution whose power waxes and wanes relative to the power of others. The media interact with those other institutions. To take one example, news is the oil that allows the wheels of capitalism to turn; without information about prices, you cannot have a continental market. The media do not make capitalism perfectly efficient, but they make it what we might call "efficient enough."

The news media also make the system of representative democracy possible. As Federalist No. 10 pointed out, citizens of a continent-sized nation cannot possibly manage their own affairs directly; they rely on elected officials to do that for them. In order for the people to learn about those elected officials (to acquire what John Adams called the "divine right to that most dreaded and envied kind of knowledge, I mean of the characters and conduct of their rulers"), the people need information. The news media also serve as a watchdog, barking at the smell of corruption and biting the ankles of the malefactors. In the process, the media can be seen as powerful institutions in their own right, assessing the performance of other powerful institutions. The media do not succeed in keeping our democracy perfectly honest, but it may be "honest enough."

The media do not stand still. They are usually in flux, and once in a while, one of those forms goes extinct. More often, new ones are added to the scene, resulting in a proliferating array. Like organisms, media outlets evolve, in no particular direction, as a result of differential rates of success in adapting to their environments, which they can sometimes also shape, as a beaver shapes a stream into a pond. As in the process of natural selection, we can see "older" forms coexisting alongside newer ones, just as the crocodile and the hummingbird do. And occasionally a journalistic form passes into oblivion, as did the colonial era master-apprentice model. Like scientists trying to understand a living system, we need to examine both the organisms and the environment. The journalism environment is shaped by many forces and trends: the availability of capital, the emergence of new technology, the framework of broadcast regulation, the policies of the Post Office, and many more that are taken up in this book. The evidence suggests that the history of journalism in America is an open-ended process of recurrent disequilibrium. There are inevitable shocks to the prevailing media system. Sometimes these are internal, such as the rise of a new philosophy of news. Usually they are external, such as the collapse of the shop system of printing or the introduction of a new technology, like steam. Such external shocks require or enable change in other areas, such as in the business model of news or the sociology of news. That dynamic of change is the story of *Covering America*.

If we think in evolutionary terms, all news institutions can be said to live, flourish, or fail in a particular environment. That environment has certain features—

economic, social, and cultural. Those media outlets that adapt well are rewarded with larger audiences, more advertising, higher profits, and the other things that allow them to persist as a life form. Those that don't adapt to their environment die out. At the same time, there are environmental niches that allow "mutants" to persist, occupying a special slot. That is why not all the media have to be *exactly* the same all the time. Occasionally the environment changes, as when literacy becomes widespread, radio is invented, people start commuting to work, or other options arise for people's free time. Such changes in the broader society create shocks that propel changes throughout the whole media system.

At times, news outlets manage to shape their environment. The media stimulate literacy; they advertise themselves; they make themselves useful. In some cases news organizations can be seen to have grown to gargantuan proportions, like dinosaurs, only to go extinct. Greeley's *Tribune,* Pulitzer's *World, McClure's* magazine, CBS Radio, *Life* magazine—all were considered in their day to be absolutely indispensable, state-of-the-art resources that intelligent people would rely on forever. But all are gone. They could not adapt to change.

In many cases, when the idea of evolution is borrowed from biology and adopted in some other field, it takes on an implication that Darwin never intended, that is, that evolution somehow implies progress. This has nothing to with the original Darwinian idea of adaptation to the environment, which is the only true test of "fitness." It is a strict test, but there is no particular direction or purpose to it. If the salinity of the ocean changes, for example, some species will adapt sooner and better than others; that does not make them somehow "better fish." It just means that they passed that particular test. When the next change comes along, today's winners may be very poorly suited to the new situation. And so it is in the evolution of the news media.

This book is the result of extensive research. For the media of earlier periods, I have relied on archives, libraries, and microfilm. This book also reflects research conducted in the memoirs, journals, notes, and papers of the major actors as well as copious reading, listening, and viewing of the actual work product of three centuries of American journalism. During the years that this project has been under way, I have benefited from a revolution in the availability of source materials, thanks to many digitization efforts. These have put vast amounts of historical material within practical reach, not only for scholars but also for students and for the general reader as well. At the same time, this book is also a work of interpretation and synthesis. It draws on the research of several generations of scholars, and I am indebted to them.

Although the practice of journalism is central to the experiences of most Americans, when it comes to writing the general histories of the United States, journalism is oddly missing, muted, or understated. The historic press or the modern media pop up here and there, but often as an unruly guest. Historians make generous use of the media as evidence, but they too often overlook the role of the media in shaping the course of other institutions. In this book I make an implicit argument for assigning journalism a central role in our nation's history. In my view, the history of journalism is as important as military history, or political history, or social history. Indeed, it is possible to read this book as a general history of America from a journalistic perspective. Doing so alters our view of how change is brought about and how traditions are conveyed. We can see the issues of race, class, and gender in a new light, even as we see the ways in which journalism has sometimes let us down. *Covering America* is not intended as either a celebration or a denunciation; it is a critical study that combines an insider's knowledge with an outsider's skepticism.

I must also admit a shortcoming: the focus of this book is on *American* topics. When my attention wanders overseas, as it does in chapter 9, for example, it is because I am following American journalists in their travels abroad. It would, of course, be desirable to expand the focus to include an international and comparative perspective, but that, alas, was beyond the scope of this project.

In the growing field of journalism history, there are a number of schools of thought. One tradition emphasizes the question of whether journalism is an accurate reflection of society or a distorting lens. Other books of journalism history take a biographical approach, usually admiring a single person or family but not situating them within the larger story. Some historians of journalism focus on the development of the field from the "primitive" press of the eighteenth century to the "modern" media of the twenty-first century. Some emphasize the public service role of journalists, who stand on guard as the "watchdogs" of society, especially when they keep an eye on government. Some historians see journalism as a field that swings between poles of rectitude and licentiousness (or "tabloid"-ism). In other versions, journalists are players in the class struggle or in party politics. In *Covering America,* I present a narrative that tells the story of a recurrent, dynamic tension or dialectic involving the business of news and the philosophy of journalism.

In reading this book, you may find it helpful to keep in mind some key patterns. In my thinking about the major periods in American journalism history, I have devised an approach that tracks closely the changes in the basic business model of the news media (for a list of these periods, see the Appendix). The use of periodization in the study of history is intended as an aid to organizing data and thinking about them, but it is important not to overstate the case. Historical periods are, of course, artificial. People did not pay them any mind as they lived through them. Historical periods are also artificially neat. In the great, messy human experience that makes up the entirety of history, things rarely change all at once or once and for all. Real historical change is always uneven and often ambiguous, but if we are going to think about it in useful ways, we must engage in the challenge of deciding when things are more alike and when things are more different. Readers are invited to join in.

In this book I look at changes in the practice of journalism in America over time. How have individuals from within the field brought about innovation? How did journalists create change within the news business? How did they make change outside their own field, influencing everything from politics and war to fashion and other fields? Equally important, how have people and institutions changed journalism from outside the field (the White House, the military, the stock market)? There are two questions that I return to again and again in *Covering America:* How does journalism change, and how does the practice of journalism *cause* change?

I have tried to focus consistently on patterns of change in the field of journalism along several key dimensions:

> ECONOMICS, which entails the question of where resources come from and how they get allocated, both in society and in individual enterprises
>
> TECHNOLOGY, which I examine in its social context and not as a separate, autonomous "change agent" acting upon people
>
> PHILOSOPHY, by which I mean the multiple theories or definitions of news and the rationales for each
>
> POLITICS, which I define broadly as the relationships of power that exist in society, between individuals, and among institutions
>
> SOCIOLOGY, which I take to mean the study of people in groups, such as the changing audience for news and the changing journalistic workforce

In all of these areas I have shaped the narrative to highlight changes in each of the major periods—and in a few cases across those periods as well. These themes are deeply embedded in the narrative and inform the entire book.

COVERING
AMERICA

Introduction

Journalism is the first rough draft of history.
—Philip Graham, 1963

ON AN EARLY SPRING NIGHT in 1722, a young man hurried along the narrow streets of Boston, trying not to be seen. He was not a spy or a thief. He only wanted to be a writer. Just sixteen years old, Ben Franklin was hoping to get his writing published for the first time, and he had chosen a risky, roundabout route to do so. He had waited until dark, and it was darker still in the shadows of the close-set shops, sheds, barns, and houses along Milk Street. Young Ben was skulking around the shop of the *New-England Courant,* one of several newspapers that had sprung to life in the previous two decades or so in Boston, then the biggest city and busiest port among England's colonies in North America. The newspaper was printed and edited by Ben's older brother James, who would certainly not publish anything that he knew came from the pen of such a youngster. So Ben took his manuscript and slid it under the door, anonymously. With that furtive gesture, Ben Franklin launched a career—one that would shape not only his own astonishing life but also the direction of one of the central institutions in American life, the newspaper. In that moment Ben Franklin took a step out of provincial obscurity and began to let loose a torrent of words and ideas that would help mold journalism and, in the process, America itself.[1]

In his own telling of the tale many years later, Franklin recalled that while he was still a young and unhappy apprentice in his brother's print shop, he had been in the habit of eavesdropping on the literary men who would stop by and praise James

Franklin for the clever things that were appearing in the *Courant*. "Hearing their Conversations," Ben later wrote, "I was excited to try my Hand among them. But being still a Boy, & suspecting that my Brother would object to printing any Thing of mine in his Paper if he knew it to be mine, I contriv'd to disguise my Hand."[2]

The next morning Ben got to work early. He made sure he was already in the shop when his brother showed up and discovered the unsolicited submission. Soon the shop filled with James's friends, and the printer showed them the new manuscript while Ben worked nearby, awaiting their judgment on his work. "They read it," he recollected, "commented on it in my hearing, and I had the exquisite Pleasure, of finding it met with their Approbation."

At this very moment of blissful discovery, several of the defining characteristics of American journalism are evident. To begin with, there is the setting itself—a print shop. Printing was already a business in colonial days, organized along the lines of any other town-based, moneymaking enterprise. Although closely regulated by the Crown and its agents, printing was always separate from the British government and operated as a business in private hands. Second, Franklin was entering the field under typical circumstances: he was very young, and he had virtually no training. For better or worse, journalism has always been a field open to youth and raw talent. Finally, Franklin himself noted the "exquisite Pleasure" he felt at having his work accepted for publication. That pleasure is real. It is a feeling that, I trust, all published authors will recognize, and it remains a driving force behind the practice of journalism today as much as it was three hundred years ago. It is the same allure that would propel so many of the journalists who followed Franklin to great heights of self-sacrifice, enterprise, and genius, as well as to occasional depths of depravity and deceit.

At the time Ben Franklin was launching his first career, the practices now commonly referred to as *journalism* rested on certain assumptions—at least in the English-speaking colonies of North America.[3] Paramount among these was the economic idea that journals carrying news would be produced mainly by printers. These printers were masters of a traditional craft based on hand power whose technology had not changed much since the invention of movable type in the fifteenth century. Printers worked in a stable form of enterprise known as the shop, which was the most common way of organizing the kinds of trades that took place in cities and towns. In a shop, a master directed the work of a journeyman and an apprentice. In terms of philosophy, or a set of guiding principles, the printers who published journals in Ben Franklin's day operated on the assumption that they had better not rock the boat, finding it expedient not to challenge either the Crown or the clergy. In social terms, printers assumed that their field was one in which literate white men served customers who were themselves literate white men. Over the next three centuries, every one of these assumptions would be set aside or turned on its head. This book tells the story of how people—not just white men but also women, minorities, immigrants, and others—brought about those changes and, in that messy process of innovation and experiment, created the contemporary news media.

Throughout the history of America, journalism has played a central part. From providing the forum for the Founders' early debates over independence and self-government to ferreting out corruption in high places, from organizing the major political parties to helping form and strengthen communities, journalism has filled an indispensable role. America was, as Lincoln said, "a new nation," founded on a continent known as the New World. America was a place where settlers began with no definite traditions, filled with rootless and restless people who made up a nation as they went along. Most arrangements had to be improvised, beginning with the relationship to the native peoples, the uses of unfamiliar plants and animals, and the unusual project of very different people trying to live together—native and immigrant, slave and free, literate and illiterate. Americans pieced together a culture that is marked by innovation, tinkering, and experiment. It is a country that has long been characterized by mobility and diversity with little to hold it together. It is a place where timely information could have great value, where the right to free expression has been treasured (if not always honored), and where people and markets have regularly rewarded the novel and the unprecedented. America is a place where the question is always being asked: "What's new?"

Journalism is central to the very idea of America. It has been practiced here since before the beginning of our existence as a country. It was instrumental in creating the new nation called the United States in the late eighteenth century. From that time on, first as "the press" and later as "the media," journalism has been at the heart of the American story. The ready access to information, the robust discussion of what John Adams called "the characters and conduct of their rulers," and the roar of partisan debate and invective: all of these aspects of the "public sphere" have served Americans as much as the natural resources of the continent's rivers, fields, and forests. Indeed, it is difficult to conceive of America without journalism. Newspapers were Ben Franklin's first field of endeavor, and they were Jefferson's remedy for the threat of tyranny. Newspapers served to strengthen the slave trade, then helped to end it. Newspapers conducted some of the earliest examples of the exposé and forced ugly truths into the open, leading to reforms of such evils as tainted meat, child labor, lynching, and public corruption. With the coming of photography, radio, and television, the broader array of enterprises known as "the news media" have only become larger, more pervasive, and more controversial. From battlefield dispatches to stock tables, from trivia and cartoons to hoaxes and hatred, the news media have brought enlightenment and caused grave concern. That is the story of *Covering America*.

This book arrives at a time of crisis and opportunity in American journalism. When I began this undertaking in late 2001, the traditional media were still quite prosperous. In fact, many of them were setting annual records for sales, profits, and reach. Then, with dramatic suddenness, the bottom seemed to fall out. Readers will find the roots of that crisis explained in this history. As *Covering America* also shows, this is not the first convulsive change that journalism has passed through. In the 1830s, to take perhaps the most dramatic case, the news business faced another existential challenge when the upstart penny press challenged not just the older business model but the very meaning of news. In later periods, too, the death knell has sounded for journalism, first with the rise of popular mass newspapers in the nineteenth century, then with the introduction of radio in the 1920s, and again with the advent of television in the 1950s. The old guard has regularly rung the alarm bells and warned of destruction. Somehow, journalism—the business of supplying news and views about recent matters of wide interest—has always survived, thanks to a process that is examined in these pages in great detail. I completed *Covering America* in early 2011, believing that the great enterprise of delivering news will survive and perhaps prosper. That is not to say that all of the existing news institutions will make it into the digital future. That seems unlikely. But I am quite optimistic about the future of *news,* which appears to be going through a rebirth. At a time when the practice of journalism is under siege from so many quarters, it is worthwhile to recall its long tradition of service to humanity.

Across the centuries, American journalism has meant many things to many people. The term "journalism" encompasses a variety of activities and approaches that can usually be distinguished from one another. Rather than trying to impose a fixed definition, I use the term broadly, to embrace several major themes.

The advocacy tradition. From its earliest days, journalism has been a calling that involves using rhetoric, evidence, and invective to persuade an audience. Inherited from England, this is one tradition explored in this book. Readers will encounter (or rediscover) Tom Paine, William Lloyd Garrison, Frederick Douglass, Rachel Carson, Gloria Steinem, and others—all united in the belief that their role as journalists was to *change* the world.

The reporting tradition. Dating from the nineteenth century, this type of journalism emphasizes the search for facts and, ultimately, truth. Reporting is an empirical inquiry, similar in spirit to the disciplines of science or history. *Covering America* tells the stories of the great journalists in the reporting or documentary tradition, from Mathew Brady to Nellie Bly, from Marguerite Higgins to Ernie Pyle, and from Earl Caldwell to Katharine Graham. These writers, photographers, and publishers, along with many others introduced in these pages, have sought to understand the world so they can *describe* it.

The exposé tradition. Time and again, journalists have uncovered wrongdoing, corruption, and abuse, believing (perhaps naïvely) that if only the American people were fully informed, they would righteously demand reform. This book explores that work, too, from Ida B. Wells and her campaign against lynching, to the "muckrakers" of the early twentieth century, to the takedown of Charles Ponzi and the exposure of the Watergate scandal. These journalists have carried out investigations that identified the rotten apples and improved life for others. They have practiced journalism to *reform* the world.

In discussing all of these major traditions, this book tracks great changes over time. One of the most important is the broadening of the franchise in American journalism. Initially newspapers in the colonies were written by members of the white male elite for other members of their own social circle. Almost from the beginning, however, more Americans began staking their claims. From the emergence of the early women printer-editors of the eighteenth century to the founding of the first black newspaper in America in the early nineteenth century, journalism has gradually undergone a slow revolution in terms of race, class, and gender. Eventually the practice of journalism expanded to embrace a multilingual ethnic press, a large labor press, feminist magazines, gay media, and a host of other initiatives all aiming to serve the needs of a multitude of communities. Over the course of three centuries, the ranks of those who own the media—as well as those who have the power to determine their contents—have expanded, in part because an expanding audience forced those changes. In addition to some of the most familiar names in American journalism, this book acknowledges and incorporates the stories of those who had to fight their way into media that were often closed to them. *Covering America* presents the slow, uneven, and often frustrating pace of that change.

Journalism is a big tent. In addition to reporting about the latest events, journalism encompasses pursuits in allied fields such as the writing of memoirs, much of the writing about travel and nature, and criticism of the arts and other fields, as well as many kinds of explanatory and service-minded materials. In the face of so many variations, I take an inclusive approach. In writing or speaking about journalism, there is a tendency to use the word "media" in the singular, as if the entire field of communications were a single entity. After studying the varying modes of newsgathering and dissemination over the past three hundred years, I find it far more useful to keep in mind that "media" is a multitude of different "mediums." At the same time, it is important to note that *Covering America* is a book about the *news* media; it does not extend to entertainment media such as Hollywood films or the dramas and comedies found on television. This book is also not a history of advertising or public relations, although it does pay attention to the relationship between those fields and journalism.

Above all, this book is a narrative. It attempts to inform readers about the broad scope of journalism in America, but it is not an encyclopedia; it does not include every fact, detail, or episode. I have chosen narrative as my storytelling strategy for several reasons—for its aesthetic appeal, its explanatory power, its tonal range, and its rhythmic flexibility. At its heart, a narrative shows people engaged in struggle over time. I was drawn to the men and women who appear in these pages because they were *innovators;* that is, they brought change of some kind to the practices of the news business. As such, they are consistently interesting people. They are also occasionally humorous and sporadically heroic. Moreover, a great many of them are political progressives, although that was hardly the case with most journalists most of the time, especially among the owners. Because so much of the focus of this book is on innovation, I have necessarily located most of the action in America's media capital. For almost two centuries, there has been one city that has dominated not just newspapers and magazines but also book publishing, radio, television, and the advertising that pays for so many of those other enterprises: New York City, and in particular midtown Manhattan. I recognize, of course, that many noteworthy things happened elsewhere, but in a work of this scale and focus, it is impossible to describe them all. In addition, many interesting people and events have been left out of my narrative on the grounds that their experiences were simply additional examples and did not drive the story forward. My effort to focus on innovation provided another surprise: the amount of material I had to devote to the coverage of war. Throughout our history, war has tested the institutions of American journalism to the utmost, and it has usually forced a change in the relationship between the government and the media as a whole.

Some readers may be disappointed not to find more discussion of the issue of objectivity or bias. In my view, objectivity is one of the great bugaboos of American journalism. Although many people outside the news business complain that a given news story or journalist is not "objective," most journalists either reject objectivity as a goal or question whether it is even achievable. It is worth keeping in mind that in several of the great journalistic traditions, objectivity plays no part whatsoever. All of the journalists working in the advocacy tradition are proudly and frankly biased, as are those in the reform tradition. There are no neutral, detached observers there. Even among those in the reporting tradition, there is debate over whether objectivity is actually possible. In my experience, working journalists almost never discuss objectivity; they are far more likely to ask whether a given piece of work is fair and thorough and leave it at that.

At the same time, it must be admitted that many journalists *are* biased. That does not make them bad people, or even bad journalists. Most journalists, for example, are biased in favor of the underdog, for understandable reasons. The fact is, little boys and girls do not lie in bed at night dreaming of upholding the status quo. They do not want to grow up to be Goliath; they want to be David. They don't want to be the Sheriff of Nottingham; they want to be Robin Hood. They want to comfort the afflicted. Sure, the sheriff has a role in the system, which ultimately provides order. But any kid can see that the system is rotten and needs a merry band of adventurers to challenge it. So there is a natural leaning in journalism toward the subversive. In the long run, most journalists believe, the public is best served by the kind of journalists who notice that the emperor has no clothes and are willing to say so. In short, most journalists are biased in favor of novelty, fairness, and a good story.

In the interest of full disclosure, I should share a few personal details. Over the course of my career I have had a foot in two camps: journalism and history. I spent more than twenty years making my living as a professional journalist, first as a reporter and editor at the Associated Press and later as the New England correspondent for the *Washington Post*, and like many journalists I also wrote freelance articles for magazines. On the basis of those experiences, I have tried to bring the insider's view and voice to this book. At the same time, I have aimed to bring the discipline of the scholarly historian. I was trained as a historian in graduate school, then returned to the academic life more than two decades later. In my career as a professor, my major scholarly focus for more than a dozen years now has been the history of journalism.

Finally, let me frankly admit my own bias, which pervades this book: I am sympathetic to those who have risen to immense challenges—the great reporters and investigators, the great polemicists and reformers. I am hostile to all those who have tried to interfere with them or jail them, and I am against all those who have corrupted, cheapened, or disgraced journalism. I am biased in favor of the First Amendment specifically and in favor of free inquiry and free expression generally. I am opposed to censorship and intimidation. I crave the light of free inquiry, and I stand with all who seek the truth.

PART ONE

The Press, 1704–1920

———— ★ ————

CHAPTER 1

Foundations of the American Press, 1704–1763

FRANKLIN AND HIS CONTEMPORARIES

Printers are educated in the Belief, that when Men differ in Opinion, both Sides ought equally to
have the Advantage of being heard by the Publick; and that when Truth and Error have fair
Play, the former is always an overmatch for the latter.
—Benjamin Franklin, 1731

WHEN YOUNG BEN FRANKLIN was learning the printer's trade in the early eighteenth century, the business of putting out a newspaper was still a new one in North America. As the early settlers along the Atlantic coast started establishing their farms and towns, they brought with them a cultural inheritance from Europe. Among English speakers, that legacy included newspapers such as those that were already flourishing in London by the late seventeenth century.[1] During the first decades of settlement and well into the 1600s, the colonists found themselves much too busy with more pressing matters to bother publishing newspapers of their own. Even before they had newspapers, however, colonists had ways of acquiring information, points of view, and ideas. They could visit their neighbors or see them in their village. They could go to church and hear the weekly sermon, or they could read collections of sermons, which were among the earliest forms of printed matter in the colonies. They could read or hear an official proclamation. They might subscribe to a London newspaper. And thanks to the growing reach of the postal system, they could also receive letters from distant parts.[2] By the late 1600s, one colonist was ready to try adding something else to the mix. On September 25, 1690, there appeared in Boston a new publication, bearing the rather comprehensive title

PUBLICK OCCURRENCES
Both FORREIGN and DOMESTICK.

The publisher was Benjamin Harris, who clearly had in mind creating a newspaper of the sort that had existed for decades in European capitals and trading centers such as Amsterdam, Paris, and London. But Harris had made one critical mistake: he had failed to get permission from the royal authorities. For most of the years since 1538, English law had required that all printed matter be issued under license, or "by authority" of the Crown, and this obligation naturally extended to those English people who happened to be living abroad in the colonies.[3]

Harris was not only lacking in authority but also lacking in tact. His *Publick Occurrences* touched on a number of sensitive subjects, starting with his criticism of England's allies, the Iroquois Indians, calling them "those miserable Salvages, in whom we have too much confided." He went on to suggest, impertinently, that some of France's troubles could be traced to the fact that Louis XIV was having sex with his own daughter-in-law, or as Harris put it, that the King *"used to lie with the Sons Wife."*[4] At the very start of the long relationship between journalism and the government, it was clear who had the upper hand. And so, after only a single edition of *Publick Occurrences,* Harris was shut down and his newspaper banned.[5] His swift punishment shows that the royal governor of Massachusetts had plenty of power to suppress thought by censoring the press and would not hesitate to do so.[6] Harris has thus always appeared in histories of American journalism with an asterisk next to his name, since historians dispute whether his one-time publication meets the definition of a newspaper.[7] But without doubt, he was the first to give it a try.

Fourteen years passed before anyone dared try again to publish a newspaper in America. During this period, around the end of the seventeenth century, the English colonists were gradually strengthening their ties to one another. From their beginnings the colonies had been oriented eastward toward London rather than north and south toward their neighbors. Until well into the eighteenth century it was much easier for a letter—or for that matter a person—to go from Boston to London than from Boston to, say, Philadelphia or Richmond or Charleston. By degrees, however, the colonists built roads and turnpikes, dug canals, and established a postal service. In a piecemeal way, they created and strengthened the ties running north and south that began to bind the colonies to one another.

In the history of American journalism, one of the most significant of these ties was the development of a postal service. From the start, postal delivery allowed residents along the Atlantic seaboard to exchange personal and political news through private letters. At the same time, the beginnings of postal service gave rise to an important new position in society—that of the colonial postmaster. A royal appointee in most cases, the postmaster in any colony had the opportunity to see the people who sent letters and to talk to them as they visited his shop to send or pick up mail. What's more, many letters were opened in the course of

1.1 THE FIRST SUCCESSFUL NEWSPAPER IN AMERICA was the *Boston News-Letter,* a weekly founded in 1704 by Postmaster John Campbell. As it proclaimed, it was "published by authority" because it had official approval.

—*American Antiquarian Society.*

transit, and so the postmasters became masters as well of all sorts of information that was being posted. They also got to read the newspapers arriving from Europe, even before their ultimate recipients did. Thus, in each of the growing port cities, the postmaster was one of the best-informed people in his area. Such knowledge of other people's affairs was a precious resource in the colonies, where most people got essentially all of their information through face-to-face exchanges. Most of the time, news was personal and local, involving births and deaths, sick cows and burned barns, and whatever other gossip might be making the rounds. But a postmaster could be counted on to know more than his neighbors—to know the prices of things in other colonies, or the fate of distant empires. For this reason, it is no surprise that some postmasters would find a way to peddle the news that was coming their way.

One of those postmasters, John Campbell, was in charge of the mail in Boston. He followed the custom of many other postmasters by periodically writing, in longhand, a summary of the most noteworthy items of information that passed through his post office and circulating that newsletter to a small group of friends. Eventually, drawing on models that he would have been familiar with from his years in London, Campbell took the next logical step and started having his letters printed. In 1704, Campbell launched the first successful English-language newspaper in the New World. He called it the *Boston News-Letter*. Starting with his very first edition, on April 24, Campbell took pains to note on the front page that his *Boston News-Letter* was "Published by Authority" (fig. 1.1). Unlike Benjamin Harris, Campbell was a member of the local establishment, so he was well acquainted with the duty to seek official approval for circulating any printed material. In moving his newsletter to print, he was able to expand his distribution, but only a bit. By all accounts, Campbell never sold more than a few hundred copies per issue, and he cannot have made much money at it. Nevertheless, he and his successors managed to keep publishing the *News-Letter* for many years.[8]

Editorially, Campbell's approach was straightforward: he wrote for a small audience of his fellow social elites, and he shunned coverage of any matters that might offend the local authorities. For the most part he filled his paper with stories that he lifted from London newspapers—supplemented by letters from his friends, news of the comings and goings of ships, public announcements, and some paid advertising.[9] Such materials were easy to come by, cheap to gather, and sure not to upset. Almost all of his readers were, by necessity, white men. There were others who could read, of course, in eighteenth-century Boston, owing to the colony's origins as a destination for Protestant settlers, for theirs was a faith that valued literacy. But most people would have found little of concern to them in the *News-Letter*. It was aimed principally at those men who engaged in business (especially shipping), who paid taxes, and who took part in running the colony's affairs. Most of these men knew one another, and they probably knew a fair proportion of the people who figured in the stories that Campbell printed.

In 1704, as newswriting conventions were just being established, most items in a newspaper read like letters. They were discursive, they took a lot for granted, and they assumed that the reader would continue reading to the end. Often the contents of a newspaper would include many actual letters, sent to the postmaster-editor or to his friends, and they would be printed because they were so informative. The early papers also contained a regular flow of proclamations from the

Crown or the provincial authorities, always conveying a one-way message from those at the top of the social hierarchy to those below.

For the next fifteen years, Campbell enjoyed a monopoly over the newspaper business in the English colonies in America. But in 1719 a rival entered the field, again in Boston. As the largest city in the English colonies of North America, Boston was the natural birthplace for such ventures, and it remained an important center of publishing until it was overtaken in the nineteenth century by New York. Starting in 1719, readers in Boston could choose between Campbell's *News-Letter* and the new *Boston Gazette*. In short order a newspaper started up in Philadelphia, and over the next twenty years another dozen newspapers would appear in the colonies.[10] In 1721 Boston got its third paper, the *New-England Courant*, published by a young printer named James Franklin.

During the colonial period, most newspapers continued to be produced by people who were not journalists. Although many of the earliest founders were postmasters, in time the most common arrangement was for a printer to become a newspaper editor as a sideline to the other work of his print shop. Printing had been one of the earliest trades to be established in the English colonies. Indeed, there was a printer in Massachusetts as early as 1638, just eight years after the founding of the colony at Boston.[11] The first press was established in Cambridge, primarily to meet the needs of the new college (which would later be named Harvard). Eventually there were a number of presses in several colonies, all imported at considerable cost. At the start, and for many decades to come, their major purpose was to serve a Protestant population, among whom it was expected that adults would read the Bible and other religious materials. Those colonial-era presses were kept busy printing psalm books, sermons, and the like,[12] supplying a population in which the ability to read was remarkably widespread (especially given the scarcity of reading matter and the challenges of tiny typeface and minimal interior lighting).

The bulk of most printers' output was in the form of pamphlets, collections of sermons, hymnals, and other printed material but did not initially include many book-length works. From the printer's point of view, the problem with printing most jobs was that the work was rather episodic. A "job printer" might get an order, set his letters, and print a certain number of copies of the edition, only to wait weeks or months for another order. What the printer needed was steady work, the kind that would justify his expensive investment in a press and a supply of metal type by keeping them fully engaged, as well as providing a steady source of income and employment for the printer's children or apprentices. Colonial printers got some relief through the demand for printing sermons, which were delivered weekly, and they embraced another literary form that also supplied steady work: the almanac. In an agricultural society the almanac was a valuable aid, with its tables of planting times and phases of the moon, and its advice to farmers. To the printer the almanac was valuable because it was, by its very nature, regularly in need of replacement.

Best of all, though, was a newspaper, which was—by definition—*constantly* in need of replacement. As a business proposition, what could be better? A newspaper must appear regularly, and it is contents are highly perishable. Unlike a book, it has little shelf life. At first, newspapers were published once a week (the first daily paper would not appear in the United States until 1783), which was about all that the cumbersome hand-powered presses of the early eighteenth century could handle. In nearly all cases, customers were expected to subscribe for a year at a time, and most of them came to the printer's shop to pick up their copy, thus providing potentially valuable foot traffic into the shop. Many printers seized upon this opportunity by adding another sideline: the sale of stationery. In the colonial setting, then, most newspapers were primarily business ventures run by men who were skilled at the physical production of printed matter and quite content to fill the pages of the public prints with whimsy, recycled news from distant lands, poetry, essays on all manner of topics, and the occasional bit of original information about local occurrences. Most of that material was brought to the print shop—in the form of other newspapers, letters, or gossip—or else it was conjured out of the wit and imagination of the printer himself. Printers did not typically go out looking for information; material came to them.

As a business, a colonial print shop was a sole proprietorship; that is, the master printer owned the entire operation. Usually this included the shop itself, along with extra rooms in the rear and upstairs, where the members of the household lived. That household also included an apprentice—a young boy or teenager who was legally bound to the master in exchange for being taught the trade. In addition, many print shops would include a journeyman printer—a young man who had acquired most of the tricks of the trade but had not saved up enough money yet to open his own shop—who was paid a wage and who usually lived somewhere else. In terms of physical capital, the master's key holdings were the press, a stock of paper, and the printer's precious set of metal letters, which would have been made in a foundry in England. When it came to putting out a newspaper, the man with the title of printer embodied nearly all the skills and duties that would later fill a factory-sized newspaper plant: publisher, editor, compositor, pressman, writer, reporter, ad salesman, circulation manager. The shop was a strict hierarchy in which the master ruled. The colonial-era printer put all of his abilities and capital into the operation; he bore all the risks; and he reaped all of the profit, whatever there might be.

In the eighteenth century and well into the nineteenth, the process of printing was exacting, tedious, dirty, and smelly.[13] A printer began with content, usually written out in longhand. The first step was to set that material into type (fig. 1.2). To do so, a printer would stand at a high table. Above the table were two large wooden boxes called cases, the one on top holding all the capital letters (hence

1.2 COLONIAL-ERA PRINTERS worked in shops such as the one depicted here. At left, a compositor chooses letters from the upper case or lower case. At center, a printer checks the contents, while at right an assistant pounds the metal letters into place. At rear, pages can be seen hanging to dry.
—*Library of Congress.*

the term "uppercase") sorted alphabetically, along with numerals and decorative elements, and the lower case holding the other letters (hence, "lowercase"). The printer would hold a small metal tray, called a compositor's stick, in one hand; with the other he would select the letters of each word one by one and place them into the composing stick until he filled a line of type, adjusting with tiny metal blanks to make each line the same length. Then he would transfer the line to a shallow tray called a "galley," which was surrounded by a rectangular "chase" that resembled a frame around a picture. After the galley was filled with letters and corrected, it could be locked with the chase to hold all the letters and columns snugly in place. The printer would then check it for accuracy, which required yet another skill: the ability to read upside down and backwards, since the metal type was a negative image of the version that would ultimately appear on the paper. Next the printer had to apply ink to the metal chase. Printers typically brewed their own ink from a combination of lampblack, tree sap, and linseed oil. (Printing presses, sets of type, and most kinds of paper all had to be imported. Only ink could be made entirely in the colonies, from materials readily at hand.) The ink had to be applied carefully with an "ink beater," a tool with a wooden handle that resembled a big ball on a stick. The rounded end was covered in leather and sheathed with a layer of sheep's wool. If the ink was to be applied smoothly, it was important that the sheepskin be just the right consistency. To achieve the perfect pliancy, the pelts had to be soaked in a bucket filled with urine. Each day they had to be wrung out by hand, dried, then returned to the bucket of pee—a task that always fell to the apprentice (poor devil!).

Once the chase was properly inked, the printer or his journeyman would prepare the paper, which was made of linen rags. The paper was inserted into a frame called a tympan, positioned just above the inked chase. The paper would then have to be pressed down against the chase. To make a firm impression, the tympan had to be lowered under pressure, supplied by a heavy, weighted platen. To lower the platen, the printer had to swing a long, horizontal arm and then, using his own muscle power, raise it again. Only at this stage could the paper be lifted off the chase. Because inks did not dry instantly, the damp sheet would have to be carried across the shop and laid over a rope strung like a clothesline. Once the ink was dry, the paper could be folded and stacked until the subscribers stopped in to pick up their copies. At the end of a press run, the ink was cleaned off the type with lye, the chase was unlocked, and all the letters were removed, sorted one by one, and put back into their proper place in the compositor's cases. On a good day, a colonial-era printer could hope to produce more than one hundred sheets.

As for the contents, the newspapers of the era varied widely, but there were several common themes. Most newspapers included information—usually old, often wrong—about developments from far away, especially Europe and the Caribbean. Those stories were generally reprinted verbatim from newspapers in Europe; in a sense, the American printers were aggregating news gathered by others without paying for it. In some cases a printer would continue the unbroken thread of publication of material from a European newspaper even if a ship arrived with newer information, so that colonial readers would not miss any developments. In a world with limited information, even stories that were months old were still new if no one had heard about them yet. Newspapers were frequently posted in public places such as markets and taverns so customers could peruse them, and some printers left a page blank for readers to write their own comments by hand.

The "public prints" also carried plenty of information of interest to merchants, ship captains, and others involved in the vast Atlantic trading system, including offers of slaves for sale. In addition, papers routinely carried news about oddities such as lightning strikes, baby goats born with two heads, meteor showers, and the like. Such strange occurrences were often presented for more than their ability to astonish; they were framed as occasions for readers to reflect on how these signs and portents revealed God's providence, and many were explicitly presented as episodes of divine wrath.[14] Another common type of item involved reports of public executions; these were usually quite gruesome and might include descriptions of rather leisurely procedures designed to torture the miscreant before sending him (or her) to meet the Creator. In describing such burnings, hangings, and stranglings, the newspapers were advancing the social purpose of public executions, which was to caution and intimidate the general population against a life of depravity. In addition, newspapers offered a grab bag of poetry, quips, jokes, and whatever else came to the printer's mind. In that sense, dipping into a newspaper three hundred years ago was not entirely different from doing so today: you never knew what you might find there.

It was just such an operation that became the livelihood of James Franklin and the proving ground of his young brother Ben.

* * *

THE FIGURE OF BENJAMIN FRANKLIN holds a place of the first order in American memory, and in no field more than journalism.[15] It is flattering to the practice of journalism to claim Franklin as a founder, but it is also a claim with a fair amount of justification. Journalism was Franklin's first career and the one in which he initially made his mark in the wider world. It was also a field that helped shape Franklin as a person skilled in expressing himself to a wide audience and as someone who was deeply engaged in the affairs of his city, his colony, and ultimately the world. However much the practice of journalism may have shaped Franklin, it is clear that Franklin also shaped the field of American journalism. He not only mastered its techniques and worked to improve the business model but also gave the field its philosophical foundation. It was Franklin who best articulated the view that journalists serve the public by presenting controversial material in their pages and should be thanked for going to the trouble, not sued, suppressed, or hanged. For that alone, generations of American journalists have owed Franklin a debt. What's more, Franklin was awfully good company, and he remains so, even across the span of more than two centuries. Tongue in cheek, mind open, he continues to engage us. Even more than any of his remarkable contemporaries, the image he so carefully cultivated embodies the spirit of his age: inquisitive, practical, but always with at least the trace of a smile upon his lips. Most of the time he repays his readers with a wink, a jest, or a poke in the ribs. Among his many gifts to posterity is a marvelous clarity of expression in service to a first-rate mind. In this he left American Journalism perhaps its greatest legacy: a model to emulate.

Benjamin Franklin was born in 1706 in Boston, in a modest home opposite the city's Old South Church, at the tail end of a long line of Franklin children. He was the youngest son and the fifteenth child of Josiah Franklin.[16] His father, who had moved with his first wife, Anne, from his home in the English Midlands in 1683, settled in Boston and became a chandler, making candles and soap in the growing port city. Benjamin, born to Josiah and his second wife, Abiah, grew up in a home full of brothers and sisters, half-brothers and half-sisters, in a rented house on Milk Street. The house was just a few blocks from the waterfront, a bustling seaport and a center of shipbuilding. At age eight Ben was enrolled in the town's grammar school (now known as Boston Latin School, the oldest public school in America), where he excelled. His father briefly placed him in a school that specialized in arithmetic and writing, but according to one biographer, "numbers proved mystifyingly perverse, and the experiment was canceled."[17] At age ten Ben was drafted into the family's chandlery business, making soap, dipping candles, and running errands.

In terms of his character, Franklin points the way for many future journalists by combining the great qualities of curiosity and a hunger for reading. Later in life he would remark, "I do not remember when I could not read."[18] In his autobiography he wrote: "From a Child I was fond of Reading, and all the little Money that came into my Hands was ever laid out in Books. Pleas'd with the Pilgrim's Progress, my first Collection was of John Bunyan's Works, in separate little Volumes. I afterward sold them to enable me to buy R. Burton's Historical Collections."[19] In this way Franklin could exercise not only his great love for books but also his shrewdness in turning over his modest supply of capital, using one book to get another. "This Bookish Inclination at length determin'd my Father to make me a Printer, tho' he had already one Son, (James) of that Profession."[20]

It was not so simple. First, Josiah put Ben to work in his shop, tending the vats of candles and soap. Ben appears to have hated it. Instead the boy had "a Hankering for the sea," and he might well have shipped out aboard one of the many ships leaving the port of Boston. To head off such a fate, his father stepped in and decided to install Ben in the print shop run by his older brother. Ben recalled later that he held out as long as he could but eventually "signed the Indentures"—the papers that bound him to his brother James. Ben was twelve and now legally obligated to serve his brother until the age of twenty-one. Under the laws of indenture, James was obligated to teach Ben the art of printing, which he did. There was nothing in the law to prevent him from beating his young apprentice, and he did that too. "In a little time I made great Proficiency in the Business, and became a useful Hand to my Brother," Ben recounted later in his *Autobiography*. And, looking on the bright side, he observed that he "now had Access to better Books."[21] Of this happy circumstance he took full advantage, buying and borrowing books as fast as he could. Although he had only about two years of formal schooling, Franklin would end his life ranking among a handful of the best-educated, most knowledgeable people in the world, celebrated by all the learned societies and decorated with international honors. His learning was both wide and deep, and he appears to have used books to continue his self-education throughout his long life. Around this time, he recounts, he also became a vegetarian. With the money he saved by not buying meat, he found that he could buy even more books, and from them he taught himself such useful things as mathematics, rhetoric and grammar, navigation, and the Socratic method.

After four years of learning the printer's trade, submitting to his brother while carrying out his own program of self-improvement, Ben felt ready to take the step from printer's apprentice to writer. That was how he decided, at age sixteen, to present the first of his anonymous manuscripts, signed "Silence Dogood." Determined as he was to make something of himself, his anxiety must have been great as he pushed his first essay under the door of the shop, then hurried back to work in the morning so he would not miss his brother's reaction. By his own account, Ben felt that "exquisite Pleasure" of seeing his writing meet with the approval of others. Not only that, but James and his friends were stumped about the writer's identity.

It was a common practice in the newspapers of the time for a writer to use a nom de plume, or pseudonym, that would protect the author's identity. Sometimes this was done to disguise the fact that nearly all the items in a newspaper were written by the same person, or it might be done to protect a critic from the wrath of the authorities. In Boston alone, readers could encounter the works of such masked authors as "Harry Meanwell" or "Abigail Afterwit."[22] In any case, Ben adopted the pen name of "Silence Dogood," a pointed and richly ironic name for someone who was, after all, setting out, if not to do good, at least to make noise.

Along with his pen name, the teenage city boy adopted an entire literary persona. (Thus it must be admitted that at least this one beam in the foundation of American journalism is crooked, that is, based on a hoax—not the most auspicious basis for an industry devoted to truth and candor.) Silence Dogood was a country widow, a woman who had been married to a minister and had given birth to three little Dogoods. In her first few epistles to the *Courant,* Dame Dogood gave few hints of her true identity. "I would not willingly displease any [readers]," she wrote, adding, "I never intend to wrap my Talent in a Napkin."[23] Like many of the items that appeared in newspapers of the day, these writings were literary essays, from which Franklin emerges as a playful, arch observer, using dreams, invented characters, poetry, and an array of poses to explore all sorts of topics, from the shortcomings of the education to be had at Harvard College to the rules for a good marriage.

In 1723, during his first year as Silence Dogood, Franklin took his writing career a step further. He used the pages of the *Courant,* now writing under a different pen name (he signed his piece "A, B, C & c."), and with his brother's knowledge, to propound his first statement of journalistic philosophy. This came in the form of a set of rules or editorial guidelines, probably meant as a satirical commentary on the punitive attitudes of the Massachusetts authorities, who had briefly jailed James for his own impertinent writings.[24] In his "Rules for The New-England Courant," Franklin—using one of his favorite literary devices, the numbered list—wrote:

1. In the first place, then, Whatever you do, be very tender of the Religion of the Country.
2. Take great care that you do not cast injurious Reflections on the Reverend and Faithful Ministers of the Gospel. . . .
3. Be very careful of the reputation of the People of this Land in general.
4. By no means cast any Reflections on the Civil Government, under the Care and Protection of which you live. . . .
5. We advise you to avoid Quotations from prophane and scandalous authors. . . .
6. In writing your Courants, we advise you carefully to avoid the Form and Method of Sermons, for that is vile and impious in such a Paper as yours. . . .
7. Be very general in your Writings, and when you condemn any Vice, do not point out particular Persons.[25]

In laying out these rules, Franklin may appear terribly cautious, especially for a young man. After all, the basic message (if Franklin can ever be taken at face value) is: Don't rock the boat. He is urging the newspaper to be diligent in pleasing all and offending none. In the Boston of his day, that may have been a practical approach, given the power of the royal governors to censor and suppress papers that gave offense. But in any case, it would not be Franklin's last word on the subject of how to run a newspaper.

In his own early columns Franklin tried to follow his "Rules," sticking to themes that were almost entirely apolitical. In an essay on drunkenness, for example, the sixteen-year-old Benjamin—still writing undetected as "Dogood"—observes that moderate drinking is probably, on the whole, a good thing. " 'Tis true, drinking does not *improve* our Faculties, but it enables us to *use* them." He goes on to argue, however, that excessive drinking is to be avoided: "Enjoyment is not to be found by Excess in any sensual Gratification; but on the contrary, the immoderate Cravings of the Voluptuary, are always succeeded with Loathing and a palled Appetite. What Pleasure can the Drunkard have in the Reflection, that, while in his Cups, he retain'd only the Shape of a Man, and acted the Part of a Beast." He concludes with an astonishing list of synonyms and phrases to describe being drunk, ranging from *boozey, cogey, tipsey, fox'd, merry,* and *mellow* to *fuddl'd, groatable,* and *feavorish,* to being *Confoundedly cut, Among the Philistines,* and *In their Altitudes.*[26]

By 1724, Ben had had enough of his apprenticeship and decided to flee. Granting that he was perhaps at fault himself for being "too saucy & provoking," he also faulted his brother for "the Blows his Passion too often urg'd him to bestow on me." Finding life under his brother's rule intolerable, Franklin sold his precious books to raise some cash, then bribed a ship captain into letting him board a vessel bound for New York. Ben was just seventeen and, in his words, "with very little Money in my Pocket."[27] In taking this step, Franklin was establishing another pattern for American journalists: the decision, while still young, to head to the big city to seek one's fortune.

Through a series of misadventures, Franklin ended up not staying very long in New York. Instead, after a detour to London, he landed in Philadelphia, where he arrived tired, hungry, and devoid of any resources beyond the clothes on his back, one puffy roll, and the contents of his pockets—"a Dutch Dollar and about a Shilling in Copper."[28] But Franklin, the embodiment of pluck, was not to be defeated. By working hard and making useful social connections, he quickly made his way in the growing city. By late 1729, when Ben was just twenty-three, he had amassed enough capital and influence to buy a part interest in a newspaper being published in Philadelphia, the *Pennsylvania Gazette.* Soon he owned it outright. In one of his first issues, Franklin took a step that many new editors have taken: he printed a direct address to the readers. First, Franklin struck a note of deep humility, noting that "to publish a good News-Paper is not so easy an Undertaking as many People imagine it to be." With that in mind, he laid out what he considered the proper credentials for anyone who proposed to run a good paper:

> The Author . . . ought to be qualified with an extensive Acquaintance with Languages, a great Easiness and Command of Writing and Relating Things cleanly and intelligibly, and in a few Words; he should be able to speak of War both by Land and Sea; be well acquainted with Geography, with the History of the Time, with the several Interests of Princes and States, the Secrets of Courts, and the Manners and Customs of all Nations.[29]

That about sums it up, as much today as in 1729. In making such a list, Franklin was, of course, striking a double pose, at once arrogant and humble. It was terribly arrogant to suppose that anyone would master such a roster of disciplines. But Franklin was shrewd enough not to leave the matter there. He went on to note that such men are quite rare in such a remote part of the world as the colony of Pennsylvania, then expressed the hope that he, as editor, "could make up among his Friends what is wanting in himself."[30]

Applying his tremendous determination and exploiting his growing network of useful acquaintances, Franklin managed to secure a contract as the official printer for the colony of Pennsylvania in 1730. This was a business plum, and one that helped secure the financial success of the *Gazette*. Franklin was busy printing the newspaper and writing his usual wide variety of items for it—everything from observations of the aurora borealis, to reporting on hangings, to advice on marriage, to speculation as to why horses stay in their stalls when their barns catch fire. About this same time he also moved in with his common-law wife, Deborah Read, and acknowledged a son, William, born to another woman.[31] As if all that were not enough, Franklin was also becoming immersed in the public affairs of his adoptive city.

In 1731, Franklin wrote one of the most extraordinary documents in the history of American journalism, one of the bedrock statements of its philosophy. By this time his thinking had evolved far beyond his initial attempt to outline a set of rules for his brother's *New-England Courant*—the advice he had proposed, while still a teenage apprentice, that the paper should offend no one. Now, after several more years' experience, Franklin took another look at the whole issue. In response to several letters from readers who were angry with him about an item he had printed, Franklin replied in his "Apology for Printers," which appeared in his *Gazette* on June 10, 1731. As he so often did when trying to address a topic systematically, Franklin used numbered paragraphs to marshal his argument:

> I request all who are angry with me on the Account of printing things they don't like, calmly to consider these following Particulars

1. That the Opinions of Men are almost as various as their Faces; an Observation general enough to become a common Proverb, "So many Men so many Minds."

2. That the Business of Printing has chiefly to do with Mens Opinions; most things that are printed tending to promote some, or oppose others.

By establishing himself as a voice of reason and stating propositions that are obviously true, Franklin is, of course, laying the groundwork for his argument. He goes on:

3. That hence arises the peculiar Unhappiness of that Business, which other Callings are no way liable to; they who follow Printing being scarce able to do any thing in their way of getting a Living, which shall not probably give Offence to some, and perhaps to many; whereas the Smith, the Shoemaker, the Carpenter, or the Man of any other Trade, may work indifferently for People of all Persuasions, without offending any of them: and the Merchant may buy and sell with Jews, Turks, Hereticks, and Infidels of all sorts, and get Money by every one of them, without giving Offence to the most orthodox, of any sort; or suffering the least Censure or Ill-will on the Account from any Man whatever.

Here the argument really takes off. Franklin makes the point that the practice of journalism, *as a business,* necessarily and inevitably involves the presentation of controversial views. That is, the printer is not like the shoemaker because the printer traffics in *ideas,* not things, and ideas are bound to upset at least some of the readers at least some of the time. Then, echoing English ideas about press liberty, he continues:

5. Printers are educated in the Belief, that when Men differ in Opinion, both Sides ought equally to have the Advantage of being heard by the Publick; and that when Truth and Error have fair Play, the former is always an overmatch for the latter: Hence they chearfully serve all contending Writers that pay them well, without regarding on which side they are of the Question in Dispute.

Here, then, is the key proposition: the public should let truth and error have "fair play," confident in the power of truth to win out in the end. That was a radical and quite modern idea, because for most of human history, "Truth" had been the responsibility of the powerful, such as the pope or the king, and not a matter to be left to the hazards of battle against "Error." But in Franklin's view, truth could be trusted to prevail on its own. In this scheme, the role of the printer is to be a sort of referee who sees to it that different parties to a dispute have their turn to make a case. The printer therefore should be *dis*interested (although certainly not *un*interested) when his paper is airing views on the great issues of the day. The

printer should not take sides but should be an honest broker, providing a forum
for the disputants. In fact, Franklin observes, readers should expect to find ideas
in print that not only offend the readers but also offend the printer himself. If
printers confined their pages exclusively to ideas they agreed with, then readers
would gain exposure only to "what happen'd to be the Opinions of Printers" and
would never have the chance to evaluate other points of view. Later in the "Apology" he offers some further observations:

> 8. That if all the People of different Opinions in this Province would
> engage to give me as much for not printing things they don't like, as I
> can get by printing them, I should probably live a very easy Life; and
> if all Printers were every where so dealt by, there would be very little
> printed.

Ultimately, in spite of all the troubles that go with printing, Franklin takes a stand:
"I consider the Variety of Humours among Men, and despair of pleasing every
Body; yet I shall not therefore leave off Printing. I shall continue my Business. I
shall not burn my Press and melt my Letters."[32]

In his "Apology," written not long after the founding of the newspaper trade in
the English-speaking New World, Franklin puts forward the elements of a philosophy of journalism that has shaped the field in America down to the present day.
Franklin is asking readers not to identify the views that appear in his newspaper
with its owner. Instead, the newspaper is to be the marketplace of ideas, where various opinions battle it out. In this view, Franklin is echoing the famous argument
made a century earlier by the English poet John Milton, in his speech to Parliament
in favor of the "liberty of unlicensed printing," in which the poet had argued that
liberty does not consist of a perfect and static unity of thought but instead involves
a dynamic process of continual testing, criticizing, and re-forming of ideas and
institutions.[33]

In his version, Franklin advances the argument by proposing that the printer—
and, by implication, any author or editor—should not be merely *tolerated* by society.
No, the printer is a valuable public servant, doing everyone a favor by providing
the forum in which truth and error can have "fair play." What Franklin was defending was a concept often called an "open press." In such a system, the printer-editor
was expected to open his pages to competing points of view, just as a ship captain
would be expected to transport goods for all sorts of customers, provided only that
the customer could pay the freight, or just as a coachman would be expected to
carry passengers of all different persuasions, rather than, say, just Tories or Masons
or Englishmen. It is significant that Franklin was arguing not that each *journalist* or
each *article* should be neutral, but only that the newspaper as a whole should be. He
assumed that each contributor would have a point of view; hence his remark about
"so many Men, so many Minds."

Whatever its origins, the simple but powerful idea that truth and error ought to have "fair play" is one that took root among colonial printers and later genera-tions of newspaper editors, no doubt because of its obvious practical utility. It applied equally well to printer-editors, who were becoming the most common newspaper owners, and to "job printers," who did not publish their own material but only printed the work of others. And it is an idea with an enduring appeal to the present day.[34]

It is not surprising that Franklin should make such an "apology" for printers, given his circumstances. Working in a diverse colony such as Pennsylvania—with its fundamental conflict between the proprietary Penn family and everyone else, overlaid with growing ethnic and religious tensions among English and Ger-mans, Quakers and Moravians, whites, blacks, and natives—Franklin had con-cluded that conflict was inevitable. Given that fact, how could a printer hope to operate? Lacking the power to resist the other powers in society who might want to shut him down, the printer needed some grant of immunity, a special status that would allow him to flourish. At a minimum, Franklin was making the case to his fellow colonists: If you don't like the news, please don't shoot the messenger.

Besides, he adds with a wink, printers have no choice but to publish opinions, for who will pay them *not* to print?

The central idea expressed in Franklin's "Apology" also had immediate political and legal implications. In the 1730s Pennsylvania and the rest of the colonies were under British rule; indeed the inhabitants were, in the eyes of many of them, Englishmen who just happened to be living at a greater remove from London than, say, those in Dorset or Edinburgh, but no less English. One difference be-tween them and their countrymen that struck a growing number of the colonists was that they lacked representation in Parliament, but otherwise they considered themselves ordinary subjects of the Crown and the beneficiaries of traditional English common law. Unfortunately for printers of newspapers, that legacy in-cluded the legal doctrine of "seditious libel," under which English and colonial printers could be accused of a crime if they printed materials that offended, criti-cized, or insulted the government or its officials. Franklin was quite familiar with this doctrine; after all, his own brother, James, had been imprisoned on just such a charge in Boston.

In 1735 the most celebrated case of seditious libel of the colonial period unfolded in New York. John Peter Zenger, a recent immigrant from Germany, was a printer who had been enlisted to publish a newspaper, the *New York Journal,* as an outlet for the political views of a faction headed by James Alexander. Zenger was approached by enemies of the royal authorities to print an article critical of New York governor William Cosby. It was Alexander who wrote the offending material, but it was Zenger who printed it and who was arrested and tried. While he was awaiting trial, Zenger spent nine months in jail. During that time, his sons and his wife, Anna, gamely took over his duties, making Anna Zenger one of the first women to run a print shop in America. Several other remarkable women

1.3 **BENJAMIN FRANKLIN CREATED THIS CARTOON,** first printed in the *Pennsylvania Gazette* on May 9, 1754, to urge colonists to unite to resist the French and their native allies. It is one of the earliest examples of an editorial cartoon in the American press.

—*Library of Congress.*

also took up printing in the eighteenth century, and about a half dozen published newspapers of their own, even as the trade remained almost exclusively for white men.[35]

The charge that Anna's husband was facing—seditious libel—was defined under English law as any sort of publication that criticized or undermined the government or its officers. It was a doctrine of long standing, and it had been used many times against printers, both in England and, as of 1704, in colonial America as well. The case against Zenger appeared to be particularly straightforward: the material was in fact critical of the governor, and Zenger had in fact published it. Under English law, that should have been that.

But Zenger, with help from his fellow printer Ben Franklin, had gotten himself a Philadelphia lawyer, Andrew Hamilton (an uncle of the illustrious Alexander Hamilton). When Zenger's case was called, attorney Hamilton pressed a daring defense. He argued to the jurors that they should acquit Zenger because the material at issue was true. This was an unorthodox defense, to say the least. According to English law, anyone who came into court and insisted that an allegedly libelous statement was true was committing a fresh offense, compounding the original libel by repeating it in public. Unlike private libel, seditious libel involved the added element of a challenge to authority and, ultimately, to the social order itself. To come into court and repeat the calumny was bad enough, but to insist on the rightness of the insult was anathema and a further provocation. Nevertheless, Hamilton pressed on and appealed to the jurors as the guardians of the people's liberty: "The question before the court and you, gentlemen of the jury, is not of small nor private concern, it is not the cause of a poor printer, nor of New York alone, which you are now trying. No! It may in its consequence affect every freeman that lives under a British government on the Main of America. It is the best cause. It is the cause of liberty." Disregarding the judge's instructions on the plain meaning of the law, the jurors voted, after just ten minutes of deliberation, to find Zenger not guilty. Supporters hoisted the aging attorney and carried him off to the Black Horse Tavern to celebrate. The next day, the printer was freed from jail.[36]

The Zenger case is often hailed as a milestone on the triumphant American march to freedom. It was in fact a milestone, but it is important to qualify that celebration in two respects. First, as for the triumphant march to freedom: if there is such a procession, it walks a crooked street and sometimes makes its progress backward. As later generations discovered, government agencies, the military, churches, courts, corporations, and other powerful institutions have regularly attempted to limit press freedom since the country's founding, and they have succeeded more often than most Americans like to admit. As for Zenger, his case had negligible *legal* impact, involving as it did the action of a single jury in a single case in a remote outpost of the British Empire. It had none of the force of an act of Parliament, and it created no precedent that other English courts were bound to follow. Authorities in England continued to press cases of seditious libel, such as the notorious prosecution of the radical journalist and politician John Wilkes in 1763.[37] Nevertheless, the Zenger case did have an important *political* impact in the American colonies. Most immediately, it sent a message to every other colonial governor up and down the Atlantic coast: juries could no longer be counted on to convict. After 1735 not a single governor pressed a charge of seditious libel. Zenger's case had at least one more important impact: it was often cited during the 1780s in the debate over the need to protect press freedom in drafting the new Constitution and Bill of Rights.

For the time being, American printers could celebrate along with Zenger. They would not have to worry about facing charges of seditious libel (at least not until their own government yielded to the temptation to jail troublesome editors a mere two generations later). The way was now open to a bolder approach.

Franklin, meanwhile, was flourishing. In his role as a printer, he adopted two additional solutions to the basic business problem he faced, which was how to keep his shop busy: he joined the ranks of publishers of almanacs, and he invented two new "characters." Under the pseudonyms "Poor Richard" and "Father Abraham," Franklin instructed and amused thousands of readers. He brought out his first almanac in 1732, no doubt hoping to capitalize on the immense popularity of the almanacs already being printed. By one estimate, sales of almanacs in America outstripped all other types of books combined in the seventeenth and eighteenth centuries.[38] Like his rivals, Franklin filled his almanac with practical advice, promising in an advertisement in his own *Gazette* that readers would find in the almanac "the Lunations, Eclipses, Planets' Motions and Aspects, Weather, Sun and Moon's rising and Setting, High Water &c., besides many pleasant and witty Verses, Jests and Sayings."[39] In such a competitive market, Franklin became immensely popular, largely on the strength of his "witty Verses, Jests and Sayings." After all, most of the information in the almanacs of the day was essentially the same, which is hardly surprising, since most almanac publishers stole freely from one another. In Franklin's case, his great facility for inventing jokes, aphorisms, and the like served him well. It is from the almanacs, in the voice of Poor Richard, that many of Franklin's sayings have endured and in some cases entered the language. Some of his sayings are justly famous:

> "Early to bed, early to rise . . . "
> "God helps them that help themselves."
> "Don't throw stones at your neighbours', if your own windows are glass."

Others deserve to be better known than they are:

> "Three may keep a Secret, if two of them are dead."
> "Fish & Visitors stink in 3 days."
> "God heals, and the Doctor take the Fees."

At the same time, his newspaper was thriving, and Franklin was becoming the most influential printer in the colonies. To some extent he benefited from the fortunate circumstance of his location. Philadelphia was nearly the midpoint of English settlement along the Atlantic seaboard, so it was natural for a Philadelphia paper to circulate the most widely. What's more, Philadelphia was a rapidly growing city, a fact that each year brought Franklin more readers, more advertisers, and more news. In addition, Franklin knew just about everyone worth knowing in Pennsylvania and, as the years went on, in other colonies as well. Finally, Franklin benefited as a journalist from one of his many other activities: in 1736 he was appointed clerk of the Pennsylvania Assembly and thus became one of the best-informed people in the colony. All of these circumstances—along with his immense gifts of drive, wit, and thrift—combined to put him in the front ranks of the field.

So it came as a bit of a surprise when in 1748, at the age of forty-two and at the height of his accomplishment as a printer, Franklin retired from the business. Happily for the rest of humanity, he decided that he had established himself sufficiently to leave off printing and devote himself to his many other interests: science, diplomacy, and public affairs. Franklin did, however, manage to keep his hand in journalism in a way and, in so doing, became something of a venture capitalist to boot. His way of staying involved in the newspaper trade was to "sponsor" other young men as printers in various colonies, providing them with the capital they needed to set up a shop in return for a third of the future profits, thus ensuring himself a tidy regular income over the coming decades (fig. 1.3).[40]

Franklin also lived on in the practice of American journalism in one other, more indirect way. In 1771, at the age of sixty-five, he began writing his *Autobiography*, for the ostensible purpose, he declared, of providing a moral roadmap for his son. It is unclear what impact the book had on its intended audience, but the *Auto-*

biography went on to have an astounding career. Remaining continuously in print for more than two hundred years, it has achieved an extraordinary inspirational status. It played a special role in American journalism, as it was read by many of those who followed Franklin into the field in the following decades and centuries. Among them were James Gordon Bennett (see chapter 3), who read the book as a lad in Scotland, and William Lloyd Garrison (see chapter 4), who read it as a boy in Newburyport, Massachusetts, as did many others who followed Franklin into the printer's trade.

By the midpoint of the eighteenth century, just as Franklin was leaving the field, the practice of journalism in America was well launched. There were more than a dozen newspapers up and down the coast—from Boston to New York to Philadelphia and in smaller cities such as Annapolis and Williamsburg—operating as private businesses run by printer-editors, each one navigating the legal and political shoals of colonial life.[41] For the most part they were modest in their business success and, perhaps because they were so small compared to the power of the Crown and all its agents, they were without exception cautious in their approach to politics. The printers had, in other words, adapted to their environment. In the English colonial setting, that environment offered a limited freedom to make money, combined with the constant threat of censorship. And yet these printers also managed to shape that environment. One of the ways they did that was by challenging the empire directly, as the newspaper printer Zenger had done. Another way was to adopt an important new tactic: the anonymous political pamphlet. In the next few years a new species of journalism—and a new kind of journalist, the pamphleteer—would appear on the American scene. Indeed, these new journalists would be largely responsible for seeing to it that there came to be a country called America.

Ben Franklin lived to be eighty-four but never really retired. In the year before his death, while serving as president of the Pennsylvania Society for Promoting the Abolition of Slavery, he sent a petition to the new Congress opposing slavery; sent copies of his Autobiography *to friends in England and France; achieved membership in the Russian Imperial Academy of Sciences; and observed in a letter, "In this world, nothing can be said to be certain except death and taxes." The next year, during the first term of President George Washington, Franklin again petitioned Congress against slavery and the slave trade.*

On April 17, 1790, Ben Franklin—polymath, patriot, and printer—died at home in bed.

CHAPTER 2

Printers Take Sides, 1763–1832

What do we mean by the Revolution? The war? That was no part of the Revolution; it was only
an effect and consequence of it. The Revolution was in the minds of the people, and this was effected,
from 1760 to 1775, in the course of fifteen years before a drop of blood was shed at Lexington.
The records of 13 legislatures, the pamphlets, newspapers in all the colonies, ought to be consulted during
that period to ascertain the steps by which the public opinion was enlightened and informed.
—John Adams to Thomas Jefferson, 1815

A popular government, without popular information, or the means of acquiring
it, is but a Prologue to a Farce or a Tragedy; or, perhaps both.
—James Madison to W. T. Barry, 1822

THE FATE OF NORTH America and all its peoples—whether they spoke English, French, or Spanish; Mandinka or Yoruba; Navajo or Cherokee; Creole, German, or Russian—was decided on September 13, 1759, when General James Wolfe and his British troops sneaked up the cliffs of Quebec and defeated the French forces under the Marquis de Montcalm. There was no mention of the momentous event in the next day's newspapers along the Atlantic seaboard, although the journalists of the day were hardly to blame, since there were no journalists present to see it. From the moment of Wolfe's victory, a succession of British ministers embarked on a policy to squeeze the colonies financially to make them pay for the years of war that had brought those colonies security. To make the colonies pay, authorities in London imposed a series of harsh new laws; those economic and political measures in turn propelled some colonists to seek independence, with consequences for the entire world.

The peace settlement between the French and the English, expressed in the Treaty of Paris of 1763, set the American colonies on a collision course with the full array of English power—the king, his ministers, and Parliament—making a war for independence almost inevitable. The conflict was fundamental: the Crown saw Wolfe's military victory as a signal that the time had come to begin extracting wealth from those colonies, which for more than a century had been primarily an expense and a burden. Many English colonists saw Wolfe's military victory in

The TIMES are
Dreadful
Doleful
Dismal
Dolorous, and
DOLLAR-LESS.

Thursday, October 31. 1765.   NUMB 1195.

THE
PENNSYLVANIA JOURNAL;
AND
WEEKLY ADVERTISER.

EXPIRING: In Hopes of a Resurrection to LIFE again.

I am sorry to be obliged to ac-quaint my read-ers that as the Stamp Act is feared to be obligatory upon us after the *first of November* ensuing (The Fatal To-morrow), The publisher of this paper, un-able to bear the Burthen, has thought it expedient to stop awhile, in order to deliberate, whether any methods can be found to elude the chains forged for us, and escape the insup-portable slavery, which it is hoped, from the last representation now made against that act, may be effected. Mean while I must earnestly Request every individual of my Subscribers, many of whom have been long be-hind Hand, that they would immediately dif-charge their respective Arrears, that I may be able, not only to support myself during the Inter-val, but be better prepar-ed to proceed again with this Paper whenever an opening for that purpose appears, which I hope will be soon. WILLIAM BRADFORD.

nearly the opposite terms: with the victory, they reasoned, it should be less costly in the future to maintain the American colonies, not more so. Without the French and their native allies harassing them in trans-Appalachia, many English settlers were hoping for an increase in freedom. What they got instead was less freedom, because the king and Parliament were now trying to make the colonies pay, which necessitated a policy of legal and political crackdowns that aggravated this conflict sharply and repeatedly. These repressive actions were the fuel that fed the repeated flare-ups through the 1760s and 1770s that American schoolchildren once memo-rized: the Stamp Act, the Townsend Act, the Intolerable Acts.

If conflict between England and the colonies was inevitable after 1763, it was not at all obvious that a campaign for the independence of the colonies should also entail a second, even more ambitious goal: the establishment of a repub-lic. The truly radical idea behind the American rebellion—the one for which it deserves the name "revolution"—was that the colonists were proposing to break away from the king *and not replace him.* Before this time, Europeans had seen plenty of separations and realignments of boundaries, but in every case some king or emperor, some pope or cardinal, some prince or duke eventually claimed the top spot in a society that remained hierarchical. That is, when change came to societies before 1776, it was widely assumed that the natural, vertical order of society itself would not change. In the American case, the colonists were propos-ing a world turned upside down, a world with a flatter and broader franchise than anyone had seen since classical antiquity, a world with no kings and no hereditary titles at all. That was the great radical idea behind the Revolution, and it was the idea that took root in the pre-Revolutionary pamphlets. It is there, in that furious burst of polemic, argument, and debate, that we must look, as John Adams suggested, to see how ordinary people became history-making radicals.[1]

Around 1760 the printer-editors who ran most of the newspapers in the colonies began to adopt a new philosophy of journalism, one that would have lasting consequences. In fits and starts, editors abandoned the principle of an "open press" and began to take sides themselves in the great issues that were coming to dominate public discourse in the colonies. In place of the open press, printers started to assert their belief in a "free press," which could mean different things to different people. The distinction was not a neat or formal one, and some printers used both terms more or less interchangeably. Moreover, not all the printer-editors of newspapers in the colonies moved in the same direction, or at the same pace. But the trade was never the same again.

One of the key reasons for this change was the new environment that followed Wolfe's success in 1759. With the British victory over the French, the stable political structure of the previous 140 years in North America suddenly began to shake. People were questioning what it meant to be an English subject in this setting. Radicalized by the stamp tax, some printers in the American colonies quickly evolved into a new species of journalist, the writer or editor who is an *advocate* for a cause or party, the journalist whose goal is not just to keep his press busy but to change the world. The earlier ideal of an open press gave way to a new conception, a "free" press, in which editors would be free to take sides (fig. 2.2). If readers wanted other points of view, they would have to buy another printer's paper and compare them. In the free press system, society is still served by a contest of ideas, but individual editors are no longer required to open their pages to all shades of opinion. Instead, the press *as a whole* can be counted on to provide the forum for debate.

Most colonists, however, stopped short of embracing the full meaning of a free press. What they usually meant by freedom of the press was freedom for the press they agreed with. With the use of boycotts, threats, and mob violence, they did not hesitate to suppress those printer-editors who dared to offend them and their neighbors. By the time of the final break in 1776, patriots would not tolerate loyalists and vice versa.[2] And once the shooting started, neither the rebels nor the British army tolerated any dissenting press in the areas they controlled.[3] Press freedom thus began its career in America in a crabbed, tactical crouch, not in a bold, expansive stance.

* * *

THERE WAS NO GREATER EXEMPLAR of the new advocacy style of journalism than Thomas Paine, a man both praised and damned as the greatest troublemaker of his age. Paine was something of a latecomer in taking up the pen in the cause of liberty. He did not even emigrate to the colonies from England until near the end

2.2 PAUL REVERE
PORTRAYED THE BOSTON
MASSACRE in this image,
intended to inflame popular
opinion in the colonies against
London. Versions were reprinted
in the *Boston Gazette* and other
patriot newspapers.
—*Library of Congress.*

of 1774. When he took up his pen, he was joining a debate that had been raging for more than a decade in the colonies, taking place in newspapers and pamphlets. By 1776 these writers and printers would evolve into a distinct new category, but only after a long process that began as a trickle of protest and grew into a torrent of polemic.

Hundreds upon hundreds of pamphlets, broadsides, and newspaper articles were printed in the colonies between 1760 and 1776. These publications provided the intellectual setting and the "public sphere" where the debate over independence took place.[4] They—and their authors—emerged to play a role that was at least as important as that of established newspapers in giving expression to the growing political crisis. Between 1760 and 1776, the number of newspapers being published in the colonies more than doubled, from fewer than twenty to more than forty.[5] At the outbreak of hostilities, seven decades after the first American newspaper had appeared, there were forty-two papers being regularly printed in the mainland colonies. Most were published weekly, and they remained concentrated in port cities such as Boston, Newport, New York, and Savannah; but more newspapers kept opening in the interior, in settlements such as Hartford and Worcester. The papers were "crowded with columns of arguments and counter-arguments appearing as letters, official documents, extracts of speeches and sermons."[6] Especially at the start of this period, in the early 1760s, many of those newspaper printer-editors managed to remain above the fray personally, following the ideal laid out by Franklin in the 1730s. Indeed, most printers still operated on the principle that "liberty of the press" meant that printers should keep their presses open to all comers.

In addition to newspapers, there were "broadsides"—single sheets jammed with type that were well suited to being posted in public places like taverns and marketplaces. But perhaps most important were the pamphlets, a format that proved to be perfectly adapted to the new situation. These were, according to one historian, "booklets consisting of a few printer's sheets, folded in various ways so as to make various sizes and numbers of pages, and sold—the pages stitched together loosely, unbound and uncovered."[7] It was important that they be cheap to make, because the goal of their authors was to reach the largest possible audience, and they rarely cost more than a shilling or two—much less than a regular newspaper subscription.

The authors of the pamphlets—the pamphleteers—were not professional writers, nor were they printers. They were lawyers, farmers, ministers, merchants, and in some cases men whose true identities were and are still unknown. It was a well-established practice for writers to use pen names, as Franklin had done, even when writing on noncontroversial subjects. With the coming of conflict with England and the fear of reprisals by the authorities, the pamphleteers resorted almost exclusively to writing under a nom de plume (or, after hostilities broke out, what might be considered a nom de guerre). Particularly popular were names that evoked the ancient republics of Athens and Rome, such as Cato or Centinel. Thanks to that adaptive cloak of camouflage, the pamphleteer had one great advantage over the printer: he could boldly state the most provocative claims against the Crown and not have to fear any penalties. A printer was in a different spot. Because he had a regular place of business, a heavy metal press, and a crew of helpers, a printer who put the same sort of material into his newspaper could be easily tracked down, intimidated, and even punished. "A newspaper is to a pamphlet or a broadside as a store is to a peddler," one historian has observed. "It is an established business with a reputation to uphold and an investment to protect."[8] The pamphleteers amounted to the nation's first version of an underground press, a guerrilla counterpart to the established newspapers.[9]

For their part, many printers tried to hold a middle ground, but most found that increasingly difficult to do as each new crisis unfolded. The experience of one of them, the Massachusetts printer Isaiah Thomas, illustrates the difficulties. In the summer of 1770 the young Thomas enlisted a partner and launched a newspaper in Boston called the *Massachusetts Spy*. At first he hoped to appeal to readers on both sides—the loyalists, known as Tories, as well as the incipient rebels, known as Whigs or patriots. But in the rapidly polarizing environment of early 1770s Boston, he failed in that goal. Thomas, who was also the first historian of American journalism, later recalled: "A number of gentlemen supplied [the *Spy*] with political essays. . . . For a few weeks some communications were furnished by those who were in favor of the royal prerogative, but they were exceeded by the writers on the other side; and the authors and subscribers among the tories denounced and quitted the *Spy*. The publisher then devoted it to the cause of his country, supported by the whigs, under whose banner he had enlisted."[10] In other words, the printer followed his readers into overt partisanship rather than leading them there. Although personally sympathetic to the cause of independence, Thomas was not prepared to take sides until he found that, in business terms, neutrality was now a losing proposition. Other printers followed suit, often under direct threats from patriot groups such as the Sons of Liberty. Still other printers took a different tack: they would allow partisans with whom they agreed to use their press to produce their pamphlets under cover of night, provided they were gone in the morning.

As the number of pamphlets kept increasing, so did the radicalism of their rhetoric. A striking quality of the writing was its high-mindedness. Adopting pen names from classical antiquity, many authors quoted extensively from Greek and Roman authorities, making arguments that presupposed a grounding in history, philosophy, and literature—not to mention fluency in Latin, French, and ancient Greek. A central theme of their writings was the discovery of a threat to the traditional liberties enjoyed by the colonists as Englishmen. They often located that threat in a "corrupt" conspiracy aimed at reducing them to a condition of slavery. The tyrant in those scenarios was variously identified as the king, his ministers, or Parliament, but by the mid-1770s these were all blurring into one, and a growing number of colonists were coming to see England itself as the threat. To the Tories and Tory printers in the colonies, these ideas were not only wrong but also quite dangerous; sometimes the radical patriot press incited mobs in Boston and other cities to take direct action against loyalist figures such as Lieutenant Governor Thomas Hutchinson of Massachusetts or to wreck the offices of Tory newspapers. As partisan feelings grew hotter, a printer on the wrong side of public opinion could find his newspaper boycotted, vandalized, or destroyed altogether.[11]

Into this setting came the greatest polemicist of the age. Thomas Paine arrived in Philadelphia—by then the biggest city in the colonies and a hotbed of radical thought—on November 30, 1774. Paine, who was thirty-seven at the time, was not at first a terribly impressive figure. Born in Thetford in the English county of Norfolk, he was the son of a Quaker who made a living by farming and by making corsets.[12] Young Tom went to grammar school for seven years, but his father would not allow him to study Latin.[13] As a result, he spent a great deal of time reading Shakespeare and Milton, who became models of clear, plain English for Paine. At age thirteen he was apprenticed to his father, turning whalebones into stays for ladies' corsets. Later on, Tom left home and met with a series of setbacks.

He married, but his wife died. He opened his own corset shop but soon closed it. He went to work as a tax collector, an experience that showed him the worst features of English life as he attempted to collect taxes from the rural poor. Paine's own life, meanwhile, turned ever more miserable. He was fired from tax-collecting and took up teaching at a private academy in London. Then he got reinstated as a tax collector, moved back to the countryside, and married again. In the early 1770s Paine became active in Whig politics and led a campaign to improve the pay of tax collectors. That, too, failed, and he was fired again. In 1774 he moved back to London, where a friend introduced him to a visiting colonist—none other than Benjamin Franklin. With a letter of introduction from the great Franklin, Paine decided, according to one biographer, to "seek a new beginning in America."[14] Jobless, nearly penniless, and separated from his second wife, Paine set sail in October. On the way he fell ill and almost died.[15]

In Philadelphia, his life began to turn. Making the most of his slim resources, Paine started writing essays for the *Pennsylvania Magazine* and was invited to become its editor in February 1775. He met and became friends with several advocates of independence, including the prominent doctor Benjamin Rush and the astronomer David Rittenhouse, as well as the visiting Massachusetts lawyer and radical John Adams. After a few months, Paine left the magazine but continued writing. As he was well aware, British troops were now fighting—and killing—colonists in Massachusetts and northern New York, and as the fateful year 1775 drew to a close, arguments were raging between those colonists who favored separation from England and those still inclined toward reconciliation. Paine joined the fray, writing a pamphlet of his own.

That pamphlet was titled *Common Sense,* and it shook the world. It appeared on January 10, 1776, first on the streets of Philadelphia. Addressed "to the inhabitants of America," it was unsigned, but its author would not remain obscure for long. The impact of this particular pamphlet, out of the hundreds then circulating, was unprecedented. It spread quickly throughout the colonies, rapidly going through several editions. Paine himself later estimated that some 150,000 copies were sold in 1776, although that number seems high. But since each copy was likely to be passed around a few times or posted in a tavern or other public place, *Common Sense* was seen by perhaps a quarter of a million people. At the time, the entire population of the colonies was about 2 million. If we subtract slaves, children, and illiterate adults (although the essay was sometimes read aloud, too), Paine appears to have come to the attention of almost everyone in the colonies who could read. That is not to say that they all agreed with him—far from it. But it represents a degree of penetration into popular awareness that is almost without rival.[16]

For the time being, all that Paine would say about himself was that he belonged to no party (which was, of course, not strictly true, since he was at least a sympathizer with the faction supporting independence). While its author remained anonymous, the pamphlet expressed a doctrine that was unmistakable. Paine embraced republicanism—the idea that people can govern themselves without a hereditary or religious authority—and made it the centerpiece of *Common Sense*. He launched a direct assault on England's "constitution," a term that had come to mean essentially the traditional, unwritten English way of allocating power between segments of society and between institutions of power such as the Crown and Parliament. He went on to offer arguments in favor of separating the colonies from England immediately, calling for "an open and determined declaration for independance."[17]

At the heart of the matter was the issue of republicanism. Like many political philosophers before him, Paine asked: What is the social order? Where does it come from? How should it be organized? In many settings, merely raising these questions could be considered an act of insurrection or sedition, and it could be quite risky. For many English subjects, questioning the legitimacy of the monarchy had been known to lead to imprisonment, torture, or death. The reason was that the core idea of republicanism was flatly at odds with the traditional response to the question of civil society, which held that society belongs to a single person, usually infused with divine authority and religious backing, who dictates by right to others. In the English setting it was widely believed that a state of nearly perfect harmony had been achieved once the power of the monarch had been "balanced" by the constitutional arrangement that made Parliament a counterweight to the Crown. In the normal course of politics, English theorists argued over the proper degree of that balance, or disagreed about whether the Crown was corrupting Parliament, or vice versa.

What Paine was proposing (along with some other colonial radicals) was to take the entire English system—the monarchy, the nobility, the hereditary status of titles, the primogeniture system of landownership—and throw it all overboard in favor of a fresh start. That was a powerful new idea.[18] Originally, of course, the proponents of this liberating clean sweep envisioned that its gifts would extend only to literate, propertied white men, not to women of any class, not to Africans, not to the native peoples, nor to many other inhabitants of the colonies.[19] Even so, in comparison to what existed, this idea was a call for nothing less than a new kind of society. That was the great project contained in *Common Sense*.

In his pamphlet Paine plunged straightaway into a direct assault on the institution of the monarchy itself. In his view the monarchy, when stripped of all its ermine robes and gilded scepters, consisted of naked power, plain and simple. Inquiring into the origins of kings, Paine wrote, "It is more than probable, that could we take off the dark covering of antiquity, and trace them to their first rise, that we should find the first of them nothing better than the principal ruffian of some restless gang."[20] As for the founder of the institution of the British monarchy, Paine had little good to say about him in particular: "A French bastard landing with an armed banditti, and establishing himself king of England against the consent of the natives, is in plain terms a very paltry rascally original."[21] So much for William the Conqueror.

Paine's other great theme in *Common Sense* was independence. Paine was all for it. With equal passion he attacked the arguments in favor of reconciliation, which was still a very popular option for colonists hoping to avoid a final rupture with England. Striking a pose of sweet reason, Paine begins this section of the pamphlet by declaring, "I offer nothing more than simple facts, plain arguments, and common sense." With that disarming rhetorical device, he unleashes an array of homespun metaphors and similes. "The sun never shined on a cause of greater worth," he writes of independence, dismissing all the arguments put forth before April 19, 1775, when the first shots were fired, as being "like the almanacks of the last year; which, though proper then, are superceded and useless now." Remaining England's colony, he warns, would only drag America into an endless series of conflicts with England's many European enemies, even though the colonies were made up of peoples from all over Europe. Besides, Paine argues, England started the bloodshed and would be certain to extract some revenge. Finally, Paine lets loose his biggest guns:

> Ye that tell us of harmony and reconciliation, can ye restore to us the time that is past? Can ye give prostitution its former innocence? Neither can ye reconcile Britain and America. The last cord is now broken.
>
> . . .
>
> O ye that love mankind! Ye that dare oppose, not only the tyranny, but the tyrant, stand forth! Every spot of the old world is overrun with oppression. Freedom hath been hunted round the globe. Asia, and Africa, have long expelled her. —Europe regards her like a stranger, and England hath given her warning to depart. O! receive the fugitive, and prepare in time an asylum for mankind.[22]

With such stirring words, Paine's *Common Sense* provided a kind of tipping point in the colonial debate. Just six months after it appeared, Paine got his "declaration for independance" (fig. 2.3).

Part of the reason for Paine's tremendous success lay in his style. It was not only bold and heroic but also quite readable. Many of the authors of other pamphlets wrote in a much more scholarly, lawyerly fashion, larding their prose with chunks of Latin and invoking arcane authorities. Elite members of the rebel cause like Jefferson and Adams had read their classics and their English Enlightenment thinkers, and they carried on a debate largely among themselves. What Paine added was a prose style that could reach the masses of literate artisans and others of middling ranks among the small farmers and city dwellers, without whom it would be impossible to carry out a revolution. Paine, whose own background was in the artisan class, achieved this by dispensing with the trappings of learned disputation. He demanded nothing more of his readers than an acquaintance with the Bible, and he used Latin only sparingly.[23] For the rest, he offered reason, everyday analogies, and fiery appeals to a better future for all.

Heeding his own call to arms, Paine next enlisted in the patriot cause himself. Just after July 4 he joined the Pennsylvania militia and became an aide-de-camp to General Nathanael Greene at Fort Lee, New Jersey. When British forces arrived to crush the rebels, Paine joined the "Continental" troops serving under General George Washington as they began falling back across New Jersey. Late that year Paine published another brilliant burst of revolutionary rhetoric with his pamphlet *The American Crisis, Number 1,* which appeared first in Philadelphia on December 19 and was widely reproduced. Paine opened with some of the most stirring phrases in American history:

> These are the times that try men's souls: The summer soldier and the sunshine patriot will, in this crisis, shrink from the service of his country; but he that stands it NOW, deserves the love and thanks of man and woman. Tyranny, like hell, is not easily conquered; yet we have this consolation with us, that the harder the conflict, the more glorious the triumph. What we obtain too cheap, we esteem too lightly.

Disdaining those "sunshine patriots," he called on his readers to stand by the army in the darkness of the bitter winter. He went on to inform them that he had been an eyewitness as the army "marched" (he avoided the more accurate term "retreated") from New Jersey to Pennsylvania and that Washington and his men were facing grave challenges. On the one hand, Paine wanted Americans to know that the army was short of men and supplies. On the other hand, he wanted to leave the impression that, so far, the soldiers were bearing it all "with a manly and martial spirit" and could prevail, but only if the states would quickly send reinforcements. "Up and help us," he pleaded. "Lay your shoulders to the wheel."[24] Paine went on to attack the Tories still in their midst, calling them cowards and pointing out that the British had abandoned New England because that region's patriots had fought the troops so hard and expelled most of the region's loyalists.

With his access to the troops Paine was, of course, in a position to write a full and factual account of the military situation. He might have reported that men were defecting from this army faster than new recruits were showing up. He might have reported that Americans had met with defeat after defeat—at Quebec, at Charleston, at Long Island, at Lake Champlain, at Fort Washington in Manhattan, at Fort Lee. He might have reported that Britain had sent the largest armed fleet in the world into New York Harbor almost unopposed. He might have reported that British General William Howe had far more experience than General Washington had and about twice as many men. This Paine did not do. His goal, after all, was not to help his readers *know* things; he wanted them to *feel* things, in hopes that they would *act* on those feelings. So he marshaled such facts as can be found in *The American Crisis* very carefully, while freely dispensing passion and poetry with his skillful pen. He also offered his readers the wildest speculation, predicting that "a single successful battle next year will settle the whole," unsupported by any facts at all.[25]

With Paine's help, Washington made it through that winter and then through the next, even more desperate winter, holed up at Valley Forge, where the winter soldiers suffered brutally from a lack of everything but snow, and where some four thousand soldiers out of an army of twelve thousand were rendered unfit for service. Nowhere was the one decisive victory that Paine had predicted. Undaunted, he continued to use his pen for the cause, turning out thirteen installments of *The Crisis* as well as other articles and pamphlets.

Like Paine, many newspaper editors embraced the patriot cause and remained steadfast throughout the long war. Others, however, took their chances by supporting the Crown. One of them, James Rivington, who published the *New York Gazetteer,* found it expedient to flee the city when the rebels got the upper hand, only to return when British troops expelled the rebels from New York and its environs. At least one newspaper editor found another survival tactic. While Philadelphia was serving as the home for the rebel Continental Congress, publisher Benjamin Towne used his *Evening Post* to support the cause of independence; when British forces occupied the city, he simply closed his newspaper and reopened as a loyalist sheet. He soon denounced the patriot press for its "glaring falsehoods"—and who would know better than he?[26]

Meanwhile, as the war dragged on, Paine came to see the military situation in a new light. He used his second installment of the *Crisis* series to write an open letter to Lord Howe, taunting the British general and warning him that his position was hopeless. In that letter Paine demonstrated his grasp of the power of guerrilla tactics in the prosecution of a war to throw off colonial power, pointing out that the British troops could easily occupy this city or that town, but Howe could never hope to occupy *every* city and every town at the same time. Paine compared the war to a game of checkers, in which the American side would always keep one jump ahead of total annihilation. Indeed, he wrote, "we have the advantage . . . because we conquer by a drawn game, and you lose by it."[27] In other words, Washington and his men did not even need a big victory; all they had to do was outlast the British.

And so they did. To the great surprise of perhaps everyone but Tom Paine, the raggedy Continental Army survived long enough to defeat one of the world's great powers, or at least (with the help of the French fleet) to force a settlement. During the six years of fighting, from the battles of Lexington and Concord in 1775 to the surrender of Cornwallis at Yorktown in 1781, the Revolution brought a host of changes to American society, including the practice of journalism. The Revolution brought not just the extinction of the Tory press but the virtual elimination of any neutral press at all. By the end of the war, most surviving newspapers had become thoroughly politicized and converted to the cause of liberty.[28]

Although he was hardly alone, Paine represented the vanguard of this movement. In Paine, American journalism found a full-throated partisan. He had no taste for neutrality, and he was no printer either. Paine was a new kind of journalist in America: the full-time political writer. "In America," according to biographer Eric Foner, "Paine was the first professional pamphleteer, the first writer to have the single-minded goal of stirring public opinion."[29] Where did that leave printers? In the coming decades, the figure of the colonial printer who did every job himself, from gathering news to writing it to printing it, would split into separate callings. The roles of reporter, writer, and editor would come to dominate the newsroom, while printers were subordinated to inky backrooms. But at the dawn of America, printers still held their traditional status in the newspaper field.

Printers not only aided the Revolution but also were aided by it in turn. They emerged from the nation-building process in a greatly improved position—in fact, in an exalted status with protections written into the Bill of Rights unlike those enjoyed by any other trade or profession except the clergy. Many printers continued to take sides in political matters well after the Revolution. Indeed, once politicized, American editors worked to place themselves at the heart of the new system of party politics, and they managed to remain important political players for the rest of the nineteenth century.[30] Yet within a few years some members of the generation of Founders turned against the press and sharply curtailed the liberty of printers, going so far as to put some of them in jail. Thus almost from the start in the history of this country a paradox arose: the journalist was at once honored and condemned, welcomed and imprisoned.

In shaping the early American press, no one played a greater role than Thomas Jefferson. Although he was never a printer, publisher, or journalist himself, Jefferson was active both on stage and off in defining "the liberty of the press" and in building the network of newspapers that would support his emerging political party. At the outset of his career, the young Jefferson was in agreement with his older friend Franklin about the importance of an unfettered press. Writing from Paris, for example, in 1787, Jefferson penned these memorable words: "Were it left to me to decide whether we should have a government without newspapers, or newspapers without a government, I should not hesitate a moment to prefer the latter."[31] Then Jefferson went beyond Franklin. He came to believe—and to advocate publicly—that a free press is not merely something to be tolerated in society but an essential element in any plan for an enduring republic. In Jefferson's thinking, liberty of the press is not only good for printers and their readers but indispensable as well for the proper functioning of a republican government as a whole, because only a free press can arm the people to protect their liberties against the grasping, aggressive nature of centralized power.

These ideas were on Jefferson's mind and in circulation among his political allies when delegates assembled in 1787 in Philadelphia for a Constitutional Convention. It had been four years since the Treaty of Paris formally settled the conflict between Britain and its former colonies, and in that period of experience under the Articles of Confederation, some Americans—at least among the elites—had concluded that the system was not working, particularly in terms of national finance. They feared that they might have traded tyranny for chaos. So, acting on a vote taken by the confederation's Congress, delegates from all thirteen states gathered in Philadelphia. They convened on May 25 and promptly agreed to close the proceedings to the press.[32] Jefferson was not a member of the convention because he was serving the young country as minister to France. But his allies from Virginia such as James Madison and from other states used the mail to inform Jefferson of developments at home and to learn about his views, which they pressed at the convention.

In terms of the future of journalism, the Constitutional Convention of 1787 was perhaps most noteworthy for what it did *not* do: it made no positive statement of press freedom. Instead, it fell to Jefferson's allies to take up that cause. Since the convention had lacked a direct popular mandate, the Constitution that it proposed had to be submitted to the states for ratification, which was the occasion for a debate over the nature of the new government—a noisy public debate that raged throughout 1787 and into 1788. Naturally that debate took place in the newspapers.[33] In the broadest terms, the battle over ratification pitted defenders of the proposed new federal Constitution as written (people who became known as "federalists") against their critics. Spearheading the federalist campaign was the brilliant Alexander Hamilton of New York, supported by John Jay of New York and James Madison of Virginia. Leading the campaign against the draft version of the Constitution was Jefferson, working through anti-federalist allies at home while still serving in France. At the core of their dispute was a difference over the concept of a good government: Hamilton favored a government that, by collecting taxes, has the resources for large projects such as chartering a national bank and encouraging manufacturing. Jefferson, by contrast, believed that government should do as little as necessary and thought that America's best hope lay in an agrarian future (including the necessary evil of slavery). In this debate Hamilton and Jefferson established one of the central fault lines in American politics, and the new nation's press generally lined up on one side or the other.

On the matter of press freedom, Jefferson was adamant. When drafting the constitution of his home state of Virginia in 1776, he had made sure to protect freedom of the press—except in cases of private libel. In the debate over the federal Constitution, both in the closed convention and in the public debate during the ratification period, the "liberty of the press" was one of many specific issues that were raised. It is important to see the press freedom debate in context among the broader issues—paramount among them a cluster of ideas that might fall under the heading of "federalism" in the sense of the balance of power between the existing states and the new central government which the Founders were creating. Another was the balance of power between the legislative, executive, and judicial branches of the national government. But uppermost in the minds of the Revolutionary generation was the problem of how to secure the long-run victory of republicanism, in the sense of self-government through elections, over tyranny. How to banish the tyrant, not only for a season but for all time?

Some of the leaders in the patriot movement began to see an answer in a free press. As early as 1765, John Adams had written, "Liberty cannot be preserved without a general knowledge among the people, who have a right . . . and a desire to know; but besides this, they have a right, an indisputable, unalienable, indefeasible, divine right to that most dreaded and envied kind of knowledge, I mean of the characters and conduct of their rulers."[34] Where else would the people get knowledge about the character and conduct of their rulers but from the press?

In Jefferson's thinking, the idea of a free press became one of the central elements in any effective program to banish tyranny. If the people were to govern themselves, they would need information. In a preamble to his 1778 "Bill for a More General Diffusion of Knowledge," Jefferson put it plainly: "Experience hath shewn, that . . . those entrusted with power have, in time, and by slow operations, perverted it to tyranny; and it is believed that the most effectual means of preventing this would be, to illuminate, as far as practicable, the minds of the people at large."[35] How would the people at large get such information and illuminate their minds? Certainly not from the government itself, not even from an officially licensed or approved press. No, the only solution lay in a free and independent press, despite its potential for mischief.

As a political matter, Jefferson and his supporters pressed for a Bill of Rights throughout 1787 and 1788, during the debate over ratification, and they threatened to vote against ratifying the Constitution if they did not get a written set of safeguards. Such criticisms prompted Hamilton to fire back. This he did, with help from James Madison and John Jay, in a celebrated series of essays that appeared in newspapers in New York City and were reprinted by federalist editors elsewhere. Writing under the pen name "Publius," Hamilton and his colleagues wrote eighty-five essays in all (which later generations would collect under the heading *The Federalist Papers*).[36] In these extended arguments, the federalists reasoned that there was no need for a Bill of Rights because the new government would have only those powers enumerated to it by the Constitution. Besides, Hamilton declared, the liberties of the people are ultimately dependent on the will of the people at large and could not be secured by a few sentences. For his part, Jefferson, with his deep distrust of government, insisted that power must be checked.[37] In the end, rather than slaughter each other, these two revolutionary factions compromised: the federalists got their Constitution, and the anti-federalists got a promise that they could pursue their Bill of Rights.

In April 1789, assembling in New York City, the new Congress of the United States finally rounded up a quorum and met for the first time to set about organizing the new government. Madison took the lead in forcing the Federalists to live up to their promises and adopt a Bill of Rights.[38] Initially he proposed amending the Constitution line by line. Instead, he gathered all the proposals for amendments that had been suggested and introduced them systematically into the House. After much debate, twelve emerged and were sent to the states for ratification.[39] With the vote by Virginia in favor, the Bill of Rights was adopted on December 15, 1791.

For journalists, the most important provision in the Bill of Rights (and the only section of the entire Constitution that most journalists can recite) is the one on press freedom. It famously states,

CONGRESS SHALL MAKE NO LAW
... ABRIDGING THE FREEDOM
... OF THE PRESS.

With those eleven words, the Founders established the fundamental charter for the practice of journalism in America. As a matter of law, what the First Amendment created was a limitation on *governmental* action; it is aimed at the Congress and does not prevent any *private* efforts to limit individual freedom of the press, such as through a boycott or a buyout. In legal terms, the First Amendment is a bar to "prior restraint." That is, it says that the government cannot do what the king and his ministers had done in censoring and shutting down presses. Henceforth printers would be free to print what they wished. But that was not the end of it. Not even Jefferson construed the First Amendment as absolute license for people to print anything they liked *with no consequences.* For printers, there might well be consequences.[40] The whole matter of private libel suits, for example, was left untouched by the First Amendment. This view was clearly expressed during the Pennsylvania convention called to debate ratification when a pro-ratification delegate, James Wilson, rose to challenge a previous speaker: "I presume it was not in the view of the honorable gentleman to say there is no such thing as a libel, or that the writers of such ought not to be punished. The idea of the liberty of the press, is not carried so far as this in any country—what is meant by the liberty of the press is, that there should be no *antecedent restraint* upon it; but that every author is responsible when he attacks the security or welfare of the government, or the safety, character and property of the individual."[41]

Freedom of the press is a principle long enshrined in American life, but it is an ideal that has often been honored in the breach—one that is neither as popular nor as uncomplicated as it seems. It is a principle whose meaning has often been in the eye of the beholder. Many Americans endorse freedom of the press for ideas they agree with but will happily suspend it for others. And as later generations would discover, despite the simple and sweeping language of the First Amendment, there were many situations in which Congress, the president, or the courts would find reasons and ways to limit press freedom. Within a decade of the adoption of the First Amendment, Federalist prosecutors would be putting Republican editors in jail for publishing their views.

What is important to keep in mind is that the First Amendment expresses something fundamental about our entire society. It is not like a law or regulation that applies to a particular industry, like automobile mileage efficiency standards or USDA meat inspections. Those regulations are intended to address specific, transient problems. The First Amendment is basic. It expresses rights that reach beyond the press as an industry to the people themselves. The press is empowered by the First Amendment to discover facts and to articulate arguments not for its own benefit but for the benefit of the public as a whole. In order for them to govern themselves, the people must have reliable information. The press freedom asserted in the First Amendment is therefore a trust placed in the press on behalf of the broader society. The rights expressed in it belong to all Americans.

*   *   *

FOLLOWING THE ADOPTION OF THE Bill of Rights, how did the young nation's press use its new freedom? Did America's journalists serve the republic with balanced, fair-minded factuality and restraint? Even to pose such a question is perhaps to answer it. The fact is that the leading practitioners of the press fairly ran amok, trafficking in rumors and half-truths, and—when those ran short—printing pure invective. Federalist editors took aim at Republican office-holders and at the Republican journalists who supported them; the Republicans fired right back. It was quite a brawl.

With the creation of the new national government in 1789, the first president, the heroic Virginia planter and soldier George Washington, soon became a focus of press attention. It is not quite right to think of Washington as a focus of *reporting,* however, since the idea of sending a full-time gatherer of facts to the capital city to report on the government was still some decades off. But George Washington was certainly the focus of abundant press *commentary,* as editors flexed their new freedoms and attempted to provide what John Adams, who was now serving as Washington's vice president, had referred to as the people's "divine right" to know about their rulers' characters and conduct. While many editors heaped praise on the new president, hailing him as the epitome of the selfless citizen-soldier, others looked at him askance. Washington and Adams were no longer revolutionaries criticizing the king but were now the embodiment of executive power themselves. They'd moved from the back of the tavern, where a dart thrower winds up to hurl his dart, right into the bull's-eye, and they found that they did not like being the target. Washington came under attack almost immediately from Republican editors who favored Jefferson. They criticized Washington for any signs of "monarchical" tendencies, and they found him far too pro-British, especially as they were becoming more pro-French under the influence of the French Revolution. The attacks kept coming.

In any case, Washington had other problems as he struggled to carry out the Founders' ideal of a government that acted on "the public good" rather than the narrow demands of one faction. As it turned out, the country that Washington was trying to preside over did in fact have real, persistent divisions. He needed to look no further than his own cabinet. In striving for a unity government, Washington had decided to bring both of the two great antagonists, Hamilton and Jefferson, into his administration—Hamilton as the first secretary of the treasury and Jefferson (newly returned from France) as the first secretary of state. Almost immediately, the two cabinet members started arguing. Hamilton pressed his case for a program advancing the urban agenda of trade, finance, and manufacturing, while Jefferson countered with a rural agenda based on agriculture and self-reliance. Around these two forceful and articulate young men, the first two American political parties eventually formed. But it was a gradual process, in which newspaper editors on both sides played leading roles. Without any of the apparatus of the modern parties—polling, fund-raising, advertising, and the like—there was no institution in American society around which partisans could mobilize other than the newspaper. At first the parties lacked everything—headquarters, membership lists, candidates, even names of supporters—so it fell to political editors to keep like-minded readers informed. Those editors provided the essential link between the office-holding leaders like Jefferson or Hamilton and their backers far from the capital.

Many of the Founders had hoped that America would never have permanent political parties. They envisioned a system in which wise and virtuous public servants discerned the "public good," then implemented it. This was sustainable only as long as there was a single, external public enemy: the British Crown and its military. During the Revolution, many local conflicts within the colonies were necessarily postponed or suppressed under the banner "Join or Die." After the victory, however, the fault lines in the new American society were quickly exposed: free and slave, urban and rural, manufacturing and agriculture, large state and small state. Those conflicts now came to the forefront, and it became clear that there were deep divisions in the new nation. Inevitably these conflicting points of view would find their champions, and around them would grow political parties. Those supporting Hamilton became known as Federalists; those backing Jefferson were first called anti-Federalists and later Republicans.

The editors and readers of most newspapers in the 1790s and early 1800s were thus responsible for creating what has been called "the party press," or a system of "newspaper politics." It was seen as normal and natural that editors would have strong partisan loyalties and that they would turn their newspapers into political engines. For most editors, that meant favoring their friends and never letting up on their enemies. Washington felt the lash of partisanship, and so did Adams. One of their chief tormentors was a young man named Benjamin Franklin Bache, editor of a newspaper called the *Aurora,* located in Philadelphia, which became the seat of the federal government after New York, until the creation of the new District of Columbia in December 1800. Bache, a grandson of Ben Franklin, typified the partisan spirit of his age. Bache tormented President Washington, denouncing the president for his "apish mimickry of Kingship," to the point where Bache probably figured in Washington's decision to retire from public life, a step Washington said was due to "a disinclination to be longer buffeted in the public prints by a set of infamous scribblers."[42] In any case, Bache scribbled a rude sendoff to Washington after the first president made his famous farewell address in 1796. While the Federalist press heaped praises on Washington for his statesmanship, Bache fired away: "If ever a nation was debauched by a man, this American nation has been debauched by Washington. If ever a nation has suffered from the improper influence of a man, the American nation has suffered from the influence of Washington. . . . Let his conduct then be an example to future ages. Let it serve to be a warning that no man may be an idol."[43] When Adams succeeded Washington as president the following spring, Bache tweaked the stout Federalist by referring to Adams as "His Rotundity." Such attacks occasionally made Bache himself the subject of hostile fire from Federalist prints like the *Gazette,* published by William Cobbett, an editor so prickly that he called himself "Porcupine." "Nobody believes [Bache]," proclaimed Cobbett. "He knows that all the world knows and says he is a liar; a fallen wretch, a vessel formed for reprobation; and, therefore, we should always treat him as we would a TURK, a JEW, a JACOBIN, or a DOG."[44]

Even Jefferson, the patrician planter, was not above party politics; he just chose to work behind the scenes. Jefferson considered editing a newspaper to be beneath his station; instead he recruited others to found newspapers that would support his ideas (and ultimately himself as well). Beginning as early as 1791, he helped persuade Philip Freneau to come to the capital in Philadelphia to start up a paper that would be critical of the administration, especially Hamilton. Federalists were also busy establishing a supportive press, and were even more successful. By one estimate, well over half the papers in the country were staunchly Federalist. Reflecting and amplifying the upsurge in politics, many new newspapers were founded in the 1790s, including an increasing number of daily papers—the first daily having been launched in Philadelphia in 1783. By 1790 there were ninety-two newspapers (including eight dailies), and by 1800 there were 234 (including twenty-four dailies). Most of the new ones were openly partisan, which indicates that the upsurge in new titles was not the spontaneous result of the workings of the marketplace alone; there were many hidden hands sponsoring newspapers in all the states.

Beginning around 1790 and continuing through most of the nineteenth century, newspapers were closely involved in partisan politics. In the decades before government took responsibility for conducting elections, newspapers frequently printed ballots, which readers would take to the polling place. Naturally a newspaper aligned with one political party would print a straight party-line ballot for its readers. But perhaps the most significant link between the papers and the parties was economic. The state and federal governments were important sources of subsidies that could make or break a newspaper's fortunes. In some cases these subsidies were nonpartisan. All newspapers, for example, enjoyed discounted postal rates, beginning with the Postal Act of 1792, which included free exchanges of papers from one editor to another. More often, though, subsidies were granted to particular newspapers as rewards after a political victory. The most significant of these was the awarding of contracts for the government's printing business. Until the establishment of the Government Printing Office around the time of the Civil War, all federal printing was contracted out, and the business was distributed as a political plum, part of the "spoils of victory." Jefferson himself offered such a contract to Freneau to do the printing for the State Department. In addition, victors in the political wars—at both the state and federal levels—had patronage jobs at their disposal to use as rewards, and many of these were given to partisan printers, especially the position of postmaster.

In the thick of all these party-building maneuvers involving the partisan press was Thomas Jefferson. Again and again, evidence suggests that Jefferson, like many of the other Founders, was working hard to promote himself and his views, sometimes using allies such as Madison as his agent and often enlisting an editor as his cat's-paw. In one case, though, the cat turned on Jefferson and mauled him. That was Jefferson's experience with one of the most vicious and dangerous of all the partisan writers and editors: the hard-drinking Scottish immigrant James Thomson Callender, perhaps the ultimate example of the partisan polemicist and scandalmonger, a mutant offshoot of the new species of journalist.

Callender seemed to have had a knack for finding trouble. Born in Scotland in 1758, he worked for a while as a clerk; when he got fired, he took up the cause of Scottish nationalism, quickly becoming a militant.[45] In 1792 he was charged with sedition. Hunted by the Edinburgh deputy sheriff, Jimmy Callender skipped out on his trial, bade farewell to his wife and four children, and fled to America. He arrived in Philadelphia in May 1793—alone and (like Franklin and Paine before him) nearly penniless. Within months he was offered a job reporting on the debates in Congress for the *Philadelphia Gazette.* He was sacked from that post in February 1796 after his boss discovered that Callender was also working anonymously as a freelance writer for Bache's staunchly Republican newspaper the *Aurora.*

By now Callender's family had crossed the Atlantic and joined him. Struggling to make ends meet, he moved his family onto Philadelphia's docks and began drinking heavily.[46] At the time, of course, most Americans drank what we would consider prodigious amounts of alcohol, from sunup to sunset. With a shortage of clean drinking water, most people drank beer, hard cider, or whiskey as part of their daily diet. Even in that setting, those in the newspaper trade were known to have an especially strong thirst,[47] and among them Callender's was perhaps the most unquenchable of all. Nevertheless, he managed to make himself useful to the Republican cause, writing pamphlets in support of Jefferson and his allies. In July 1797, Callender tackled one of the stars of the Federalist camp, Treasury Secretary Alexander Hamilton. In a lengthy pamphlet Callender revealed that Hamilton had transferred money to a convicted swindler named James Reynolds, insinuating that Hamilton and Reynolds were scheming to speculate in Treasury certificates, which were under Hamilton's supervision.[48] The accusation forced Hamilton to reply, which he did, denying the charges of financial chicanery. But in order to explain the money transfers, he had to confess that he was having an affair with Reynolds's wife, Maria. The money he was transferring to Mr. Reynolds was blackmail money, intended to keep him from telling the story of Hamilton's liaison with Mrs. Reynolds. Callender was unimpressed with the explanation, and in a follow-up article he mocked Hamilton: "The whole proof . . . rests upon an illusion. 'I am a rake, and for that reason I cannot be a swindler.' "[49] In any case, the damage was done. Politically Hamilton was now dead.

Hamilton's disgrace naturally improved the standing of Jefferson, who encouraged Callender in his slashing style of journalism and became something of a father figure to the younger man; the next year, Callender temporarily replaced Bache as editor of the *Aurora.* At the time, the Republicans were pro-French on account of their sympathy for the antimonarchical, democratic spirit of the

French Revolution. Jefferson, who had spent much of the 1780s in Paris serving as the American minister to France, had seen the earliest phase of the Revolution firsthand. When he returned to America late in 1789 and joined the Washington administration, he was seeking ways to support the French. By 1797, when Callender's exposé of Hamilton was published, Jefferson was the closest thing the Republicans had to a national leader—which was somewhat awkward, since he was serving as vice president under the Federalist John Adams.

Adams, not surprisingly, viewed the French with alarm, especially the radicals. He and other Federalist leaders were soon preparing to go to war with France if need be. The fever rose in the spring of 1798 with the publication, at the instigation of the Republicans, of the notorious "XYZ" letters, which revealed attempts by the French to extort funds from American envoys. The publicity proved terribly damaging to the Adams administration. As Jefferson tried to prevent a war between the United States and France, the press vilified him for his troubles as a traitor and a coward. He resigned the vice presidency and retreated to Monticello. In the clamor for war, Congress chose (not for the last time) to make things worse. The Federalists, showing more concern for security than for liberty, decided to snuff out any popular support for France. In July, Adams signed the Sedition Act, which had passed narrowly on a straight party vote in Congress. The new law raised the specter, for the first time since the Zenger trial more than sixty years earlier, of making it a crime to express certain ideas.[50]

The Sedition Act of 1798 did not impose prior restraint on printers, and it did allow truth as a defense in court, but it also imposed heavy fines and jail terms on anyone who conspired to oppose the government, who promoted riots, or who published "any false, scandalous and malicious writing" against the government or its elected officials. In other words, the expression of banned ideas was now a crime—just as it had been under English law for centuries—through a new federal law applying to every journalist in America. It was promptly used to bring indictments against fifteen Republican editors, and ten of them were convicted.[51] Among the first editors to be indicted was none other than the man wielding the poison pen at the Aurora, Benjamin Franklin Bache, who was arrested and slapped in jail. While he was still awaiting trial, Bache expired of yellow fever. As for Jimmy Callender, he took the passage of the Sedition Act as his cue to go into hiding and fled to Virginia—only to end up serving six months in jail for sedition there.

For Jefferson, the Federalists' handling of the Sedition Act was intolerable. He believed that its passage violated the Constitution and that its implementation violated all decency. While staying away from the national capital, Jefferson swung into action behind the scenes. He helped Republicans in Virginia and Kentucky draft resolutions in which the people of those two states declared, in effect, that the Sedition Act was null and void because it was not permitted by the Constitution. This is an idea that may strike modern readers as eminently plausible, but it was one that had not even occurred to the U.S. Supreme Court, which had yet to declare any act of Congress unconstitutional. (The high court did not discover that power until 1803 in *Marbury v. Madison.*) Among other reasons, Jefferson argued that the Sedition Act was a flat contradiction of the plain language of the First Amendment because Congress was clearly abridging the freedom of the press. At the same time, Jefferson spent much of 1799 and 1800 actively seeking the presidency and cultivating newspaper editors, who naturally shared his revulsion over the Sedition Act.

By a wide margin Jefferson defeated Adams in the popular vote in the election of 1800 but only narrowly survived a series of maneuvers that sent the election to the House. In March 1801, Jefferson was sworn in as president (and promptly ceased all communication with Adams). In many ways, the election of 1800 was a watershed in American history. It marked the first peaceful transfer of power from one party to another. The significance was perhaps even greater than that of the election of 1796, in which Washington made the magnificent gesture of voluntarily relinquishing the presidency and thus set the stage for the peaceful transfer of power to an unrelated person. But when Adams was forced to yield to his bitter rival Jefferson, he set the country on a course of peaceful transfers of power that has made the United States the envy of much of the world. The election of 1800 was also a watershed in another respect: it marked the arrival of the partisan newspaper editor as the backbone of the country's developing political system.[52]

As for the Sedition Act, it had been enacted with an expiration date of March 3, 1801, and Jefferson and his supporters decided to let it die. Americans would not have a sedition law for another 120 years. Some of the credit for decriminalizing the publishing of attacks on government certainly belongs to Jefferson. He could have revived the act, ordered up a fresh round of trials of Federalist editors, and thus begun a cycle of tit-for-tat punishment of the press. Instead, he helped enlarge the zone of legal protection in which the press could operate freely, which was a significant change. Some of the credit also belongs to the Republican editors, who showed little appetite for a perpetuation of such attacks, which they knew would harass their Federalist brethren and, eventually, themselves as well.[53] For their own reasons, they helped ensure that the First Amendment would mean, at a minimum, that no more editors from either side would be locked up. They would all be free to continue their bombardments.

In the aftermath of his victory in the election of 1800, Jefferson faced many decisions, including the novel political question of how many positions on the federal payroll should be taken away from their Federalist occupants and turned over to Republicans.[54] One of those who came calling after the election was none other than James Callender, who had his eye on the postmaster position in Richmond. Callender must have felt that he had an abundantly justified claim to some of the spoils of office. After all, he had done everything the party could ask; he had kneecapped Hamilton, the brightest star in the opposition camp, and he had even served time in jail for the Republican cause. Jefferson, however, was unmoved. Callender was hardly the well-born talented sort that Jefferson thought should be serving in his administration, and the president sent him away empty-handed.

Callender set out to get even. He promptly switched parties, and in February 1802 he went into partnership with a Federalist editor in running the *Richmond Recorder*. Callender assigned himself the job of bringing down Jefferson. Acting on the basis of rumors that he had picked up from anonymous sources, he let fly in print with the accusation that Jefferson had engaged in sexual relations with one of his slaves, later identified as Sally Hemings.

> It is well known that the man, whom it delighteth the people to honor, keeps and for many years has kept, as his concubine, one of his slaves. Her name is SALLY. The name of her eldest son is Tom. His features are said to bear a striking though sable resemblance to those of the president himself. . . .
>
> By this wench Sally, our president has had several children. There is not an individual in the neighbourhood of Charlottesville who does not believe the story, and not a few who know it.[55]

The Federalist press had what it was looking for. The story was repeated, sometimes accompanied by lurid speculation about the "black Venus" at Monticello. In the two centuries since then, Callender's assertion has become the focus of intense debate, both among Jefferson and Hemings family descendants and among historians. Recent DNA studies have tended to vindicate Callender's reporting and strongly indicate that the story is almost certainly true—that this founding father found a way to father more than one branch of his family.[56]

As for Callender, he was nearly finished. Having set the bar in the practice of scandal-mongering about the sex lives of presidents, his own life quickly went downhill. In December he was the victim of a public beating and again succumbed to his great thirst. The following summer, in July 1803, during another of his periods of heavy drinking, James Callender was found floating in Virginia's James River, dead at age forty-five.

Jefferson, meanwhile, was experiencing a loss of faith in press freedom. With his election, Jefferson moved into the bull's-eye of the partisan dartboard. Now it was his turn to face attacks from the Federalist press, including those coming from a new paper in New York City called the *Post,* founded by his political rival Hamilton in 1801. In his private correspondence, Jefferson often complained bitterly about his treatment by the newspapers. By the time of his second inaugural address in March 1805, Jefferson was coming to view the press as a menace to decency itself. "During the course of this administration," he complained, "and in order to disturb it, the artillery of the press has been levelled against us, charged with whatsoever its licentiousness could devise or dare. These abuses of an institution so important to freedom and science, are deeply to be regretted." Plainly exasperated, he allowed himself the political luxury of speculating publicly about whether new state or federal laws might be needed to rein in the press:

> No inference is here intended, that the laws, provided by the state against false and defamatory publications, should not be enforced; he who has the time, renders a service to public morals and public tranquility, in reforming these abuses by the salutary coercions of the law. . . .
>
> But the experiment is noted, to prove that, since truth and reason have maintained their ground against false opinions in league with false facts, the press, confined to truth, needs no other legal restraint;
>
> The public judgment will correct false reasonings and opinions, on a full hearing of all parties; and no other definite line can be drawn between the inestimable liberty of the press and its demoralizing licentiousness.[57]

Even while still serving as president, Jefferson found time to engage in press criticism. In 1807, late in his second term, he corresponded with a Republican named John Norvell, who had written to the president to inquire about starting another new Republican newspaper. Jefferson saw the issue darkly:

> Nothing can now be believed which is seen in a newspaper. Truth itself becomes suspicious by being put into that polluted vehicle. . . . I will add, that the man who never looks into a newspaper is better informed than he who reads them; inasmuch as he who knows nothing is nearer to truth than he whose mind is filled with falsehoods & errors. . . .
>
> Perhaps an editor might begin a reformation in some such way as this. Divide his paper into 4 chapters, heading the 1st, Truths. 2d, Proba-bilities. 3d, Possibilities. 4th, Lies. The first chapter would be very short.[58]

Clearly, Jefferson had abandoned his earlier hope that newspapers would serve the nation as the guardians of the people's liberty. His comments radiate a sense of an immense sadness and regret, coming from a man who fought for a free press but perhaps later wished that he had not, who fought against the formation of political parties but later led one, who fought to secure his good name only to find it constantly in jeopardy in such a putrid and mendacious vehicle as a newspaper.

At the same time, there was much that could have been said in favor of the American press during this period. The country's printers had rallied to the cause of liberty and sustained the people in rising up against the greatest power in the world. The newspaper trade—both commercial and partisan—was a growing and thriving business enterprise, spreading with the post-Revolutionary peace and employing more and more hands while reaching more and more eyes. The traditional job of the printer was splitting into specialized roles of writing, editing, and typesetting. Editors were establishing themselves as key figures in the emerging two-party political system. And press freedom, while constantly in jeopardy, was the official law of the land. Newspapers, however, were still in their infancy. The means of physically producing a newspaper had not changed significantly in centuries. Newspaper editors had yet to devise most of the features later used to aid readers; there were still no bylines, no photographs, no big headlines. Most newspapers did not engage in reporting. Instead they relied on a system of "exchanges" that had arisen during the colonial era and became formalized in the Post Office Act of 1792, which allowed every printer of newspapers to send one copy of his paper to every other printer.[59] Each editor could then lift items from other papers and insert them, often without giving credit, into his own columns. For these reasons, what newspapers lacked in the early nineteenth century, above all, was something most modern readers would recognize as *news*. Soon, though, a rising generation of editors would change American newspapers almost beyond recognition.

Following his success in the War for Independence, Tom Paine continued his career as a polemical writer. Destitute at war's end, Paine struck a series of deals in order to get compensated, including a grant from Congress of an abandoned Tory estate in New Rochelle, New York. So desperate was Paine for money that he was once even accused of the ungentlemanly practice of "writing for hire." Like Franklin, he pursued a career as an inventor, working on smokeless candles and iron bridges.

More great accomplishments lay ahead. Paine went to France, took up the cause of the Revolution, and defended it in his book Rights of Man *(1791), only to find himself jailed by one faction. In his ultimate campaign, he undertook an attack on religion itself in his great work* The Age of Reason. *A heavy drinker, Paine managed to live to age seventy-two. He died on his New Rochelle farm in 1809.*

CHAPTER 3

Putting the News in Newspapers, 1833–1850

I am in earnest—I will not equivocate—I will not excuse—I will not retreat a single inch
—AND I WILL BE HEARD!
—William Lloyd Garrison, 1831

Business is business—money is money. . . . We permit no blockhead to interfere with our business.
—James Gordon Bennett, 1836

D EEP CHANGES WERE COMING. Without any program or ultimate purpose guiding them, a number of people, acting independently during the first decades of the nineteenth century, came up with inventions or made new social arrangements that, taken together, had the effect of setting the stage for the creation of the modern newspaper. From those separate and uncoordinated acts there arose a major manufacturing industry, a vessel of popular culture, and a pervasive institution that changed the flow of information, broke down barriers of isolation, and—sometimes—challenged the powers that be. After 1833, the newspaper became the key element in a web of mass production, mass consumption, and mass communication that has come to characterize life in America. If we live in a media age, it is because of decisions made, struggles fought, and power wielded in the crucial period before the Civil War.

The conditions that made it possible for people to make that change were many. In the early nineteenth century, America held out a measure of promise to its inhabitants—provided they were white and male and not indentured to someone else. It was a country where land was comparatively cheap, and labor, especially skilled labor, was comparatively dear. It was one of the few countries in all of world history up to that point where the mass of people were not kept miserable by some form of serfdom. "Americans do not use the word *peasant*. They do not use the word because they do not possess the idea," the French nobleman Alexis de Tocqueville observed after his travels in America during 1831–32.[1] As he saw, America was a place where people (not equally, but generally) were a valuable resource. In this setting, however, the flow of information was still rather spotty. America had more newspapers than any other country on earth, and thanks to the Post Office, they could be delivered to even the rudest new cabin in the farthest reaches of the frontier.[2] But those newspapers that arrived in the mail had some serious limitations: most were published weekly, so their contents were not as timely as they might be, and they usually had a near-exclusive focus on one of two topics—commerce or party politics.

The changes in newspapers built on changes occurring elsewhere. According to the sociologist Michael Schudson, these conditions can be grouped into a few categories.[3]

In terms of *technology,* change was finally coming to the printing trade. In the early nineteenth century, steam power was applied to the printing press, a step that burst through the physical limitations of hand-powered printing (fig. 3.1). When each page had to be literally pressed against the inked tablet of metal letters by hand, no printer could hope to make more than a few hundred impressions a day, so no newspaper could plan to sell more than that number. With steam, however, presses could run off thousands of copies. At the same time, the price of paper was beginning to fall (it would fall even further with the development of papermaking processes based entirely on wood pulp later in the nineteenth century), and it was becoming easier, cheaper, and faster to move people and things around the country. One legacy from the colonial experience was a transportation network that had originally centered on London. After the coming of independence, Americans addressed the huge task of uniting the states by crossing the many rivers and mountains with a system of roads, canals, and rails that would constitute a truly continental network of transportation and communication. During the early nineteenth century, progress was rapid, but the starting point was quite basic. In 1830 there were just twenty-three miles of railroad track in all of the United States. Ten years later there were three thousand miles, and by 1860 there were ten times that number.[4] With the advent of the railroads, news reports could travel quickly back to newspaper offices for inclusion in the paper, and the finished product could be delivered much faster to distant points.

Another indispensable condition for newspaper growth was *cultural.* In the United States, the portion of the population that was white and free was probably the most literate in the world. More people could read and write with each passing year, especially with the spread of free public schooling. More young boys were taught than young girls, and there is evidence that more people were taught to read than to write.[5] But the United States was probably the first country on earth where it was considered normal for adults to be able to read. As members of Protestant churches (as most were), Americans were expected to be able to read Scripture; as

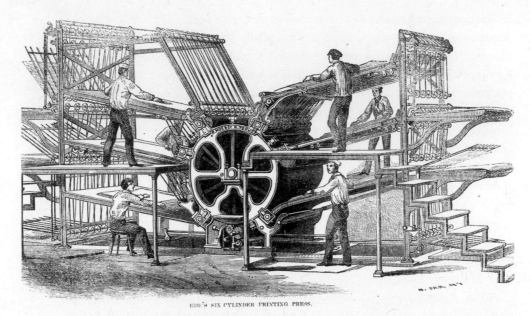

HOE'S SIX CYLINDER PRINTING PRESS.

3.1 STEAM POWER CHANGED PRINTING by greatly speeding up the process, making possible the mass-circulation daily papers that emerged in big cities in the nineteenth century. This press was made by the Hoe company, founded in New York in 1803 and long an innovator in the manufacture of printing presses. Encyclopedia Britannica, *History of the Processes of Manufacture and Uses of Printing, Gas-Light, Pottery, Glass and Iron, with Numerous Illustrations. —New York: John Bradburn, Publisher, 1864.*

farmers, they were expected to be able to read almanacs; as voters in a republic, they were expected to be able to read ballots, tax bills, and newspapers. Specialists continue to debate whether people learned to read because there was valuable information in almanacs, newspapers, and books, or whether such publications were produced to satisfy a preexisting demand. For whatever reasons, Americans certainly did read, as evidenced by the strength of the home-grown publishing trades.

A third kind of change that would favor the growth of popular newspapers was *social*. In the 1830s, enough people were living in cities, and enough people had incomes of sufficient size, that it could be said that the United States had the beginnings of an urban middle class. At least, there were more people of middling ranks living in cities than at any time before the 1830s. This was important, because in order for a newspaper to achieve a mass circulation, it had to be based in a big city. Only there would the density of the population make it possible to gather, write, and disseminate information all in one day. Without telephones or computers, newspapers depended on that vital proximity to both their sources and their customers.

The "capital" of American publishing and other media ventures has tended to follow the patterns of population and commercial growth. Thus, the first center of American publishing and journalism was Boston, which was the early leader among the ports of the English colonies. Later the lead shifted to Philadelphia.

By the time of the first national census in 1790, the largest city in the new United States was New York, which has kept the title ever since. Because of its population density, its supply of financing, and its critical mass of other resources, New York City rapidly emerged in the nineteenth century as the unofficial center of American book, newspaper, and magazine publishing.[6]

Thus the stage was set. These changes in technology, culture, and society were in place. They were all necessary conditions for a successful mass-circulation daily newspaper to get started, but they were not sufficient. For that to happen, somebody had to *do* something. Some individual had to take advantage of those conditions and try his luck.

* * *

ON SEPTEMBER 3, 1833, BENJAMIN DAY began a revolution in journalism when he started publishing his new newspaper, the *Sun,* in New York City. There had been attempts to bring out cheap daily papers before his,[7] but none had the staying power or impact of the *Sun,* which became the pioneer of the "penny press." Declaring, "It shines for all," the *Sun* announced itself to readers that day by explaining its governing philosophy: "The object of this paper is to lay before the public, at a price within the means of every one, ALL THE NEWS OF THE DAY, and at the same time afford an advantageous medium for advertising."

Soon, Day literally could not print copies fast enough. One of the keys to his success lay in a series of decisions he made on the business side of the paper—above all, the decision to price the paper at a penny a copy, at a time when most newspapers in New York City cost six cents. At a penny, the *Sun* was within the price range of the growing legions of clerks, laborers, and practitioners of every craft in the city—from coopers to brewers to farriers. Moreover, Day decided to encourage sales of the *Sun* one day at time rather than by annual subscription, which was the usual way of selling newspapers. Taken together, these changes in business practices had fateful consequences for journalism in America. They meant that the market for the *Sun* was almost unlimited—potentially including every literate adult within the physical reach of the paper. They also meant that there would always be considerable pressure on the newspaper to recapture those readers day in and day out. Each day's news offerings—and later, each day's headlines—had to shout, amaze, and reward if the newspaper was going to be worth the pennies of a new day's customers.

In that setting, Day also offered readers a novel interpretation of just what kind of material belonged in a daily paper. Putting his definition—"all the news of the day"—into practice, Day immediately began to broaden the scope beyond the familiar bounds of business and politics. He decided to mine what would turn out to be one of the mother lodes of journalism: the world of crime.[8] To a far greater extent than the editors who had preceded him at the partisan or commercial papers, Day actively searched out news of gore, pathos, and the occasional uplifting tale in New York's police stations and courthouses. In the very first edition he included the following account:

> MELANCHOLY SUICIDE.—a Mr. Fred A. Hall, a young gentleman from Boston, who had been a boarder at Webb's Congress Hall, for a week or ten days previous, put an end to his life on Sunday last by taking laudanum [an alcoholic extract of opium]. Late in the afternoon Mr. Webb having occasion to go into his room, found the door locked on the inside; but hearing a noise as of a person in distress, and after knocking and calling several times without any answer, he burst open the door, and found him apparently dying. Physicians were immediately called and the stomach pump applied, but without success.

As the story went on to reveal, young Mr. Hall was about to be packed off to Sumatra by his father, a wealthy merchant back in Boston, apparently to break up a budding romance. The suicide was brought on by "an affair of the heart in which his happiness was deeply involved."

Under a column headed "POLICE OFFICE," the *Sun* offered more reporting in the same vein, exploring the cases of various miscreants who were brought up before the bench of justice, where they might be sentenced to time in the "bridewell," or local jail, as in this item: "John McMan, brought up for whipping Juda McMan, his darling wife—his excuse was, that his head was rather thick, in consequence of taking a wee drap of whiskey. Not being able to find bail he was accommodated with a room in bridewell." Readers could also learn of the unceremonious betrothal of William Scott and his cohabiting girlfriend, Charlotte Gray:

> Wm. Scott from Centre Market, brought up for assaulting Charlotte Gray, a young woman with whom he lived. The magistrate, learning that they never were married, offered the prisoner a discharge on condition that he would marry the injured girl, who was very willing to withdraw the complaint on such terms. Mr. Scott cast a sheep's eye towards the girl, and then looking out of the window, gave the bridewell a melancholy survey; he then gave the girl another look, and was hesitating as to which he should choose—a wife or a prison. The Justice insisted on an immediate answer. At length he concluded that he "might as well marry the critter," and they left the office apparently satisfied.

There, already in full-blown form, is a classic example of the brief "human interest" piece, or "kicker," as it is sometimes called. Day seems to have had the journalistic equivalent of perfect pitch. On his very first try, he wrote a story that could have appeared in any general-interest newspaper (or local news broadcast) ever since. With a brutal compression of background and nuance, Day introduces two people who are strangers to the audience of readers; they are presented in an awkward situation; and Day delivers the humorous (if male chauvinistic) resolution, complete with a verbatim quip!

Readers loved it, and indeed it was the readers who deserve the ultimate credit for shaping the news. When news is a product for sale, the customers give powerful signals to the producers about what they like and don't like, about what they believe and don't believe. If readers don't buy, then even the most admirable or worthwhile experiments fizzle; if readers don't buy, older species go extinct and new mutations disappear. Readers provide the feedback that lets editors know what they consider worth paying for. At the *Sun,* circulation shot up, proving that there was a market for that brand of news, at that price. The key ingredients were simple: the news that Day was offering was *local.* It allowed New Yorkers to learn something about their neighbors, a subject that New Yorkers were becoming fascinated by. The first issue of the *Sun* made passing reference to this fact when it observed that New York City was "nearly full of strangers from all parts of this country and Europe." People like Fred Hall and Charlotte Gray were not important people, and they were certainly not public figures. What Day had stumbled upon was the fact that big cities are full of people who don't know one another but would like to know a bit more—from the safe distance of a mediating vehicle like a newspaper. Suddenly, all manner of private life was opened to public scrutiny and comment. In the *Sun,* the news was offered not for the purpose of putting one political party or the other into power in Albany or Washington, but always with the primary goal of grabbing the attention of readers and holding it so they would want to buy another copy the next day.

And buy they did. New Yorkers snapped up copies of the *Sun,* with its breezy local news about ordinary people. Day plunged into police stories and shunned political news. In the same week the paper was founded, Day expanded on his view of what constitutes news, providing one of the earliest formulas for sensationalism: "We newspaper people thrive best on the calamities of others. Give us one of your real Moscow fires, or your Waterloo battlefields; let a Napoleon be dashing with his legions throughout the world, overturning the thrones of a thousand years and deluging the world with blood and tears; and then we of the types are in our glory."[9] Circulation soared as the *Sun* met the only test that mattered to Day: the test of the marketplace. Within four months it reached a circulation of five thousand and within a year ten thousand. In two years it hit nineteen thousand copies a day and thus became the best-selling newspaper in the world, eclipsing even the *Times* of London.[10]

Soon, Day found that he could not sustain the effort required to report the news, print it, and sell it all by himself. One of his first moves was to hire somebody to focus on the new enterprise of actively gathering information. He found "a young printer out of work" named George W. Wisner, who may well have been the first full-time news reporter in U.S. history. Day promised Wisner four dollars a week in wages; in return, the young man had to get up mighty early: Day wanted him to cover police court, which began its sessions at 4 a.m.[11] It is worth noting that Day was hiring Wisner not as a journeyman printer but instead as a new category of worker. Unlike the journeyman, the reporter was not expected to rise to a position anything like that of a master printer. The terms were strictly wages—take it or leave it. A little while later, Day achieved another first: he hired the first newsboy. Previously, newspapers had been sold strictly by subscription, and the subscribers either came to the print shop to pick up their copies or had them delivered to their home. Day's newsboy was going to go out into the streets of Manhattan, shout like a peddler, and sell the paper to anybody passing by with a spare penny.

At the historical moment when Day brought out his paper, there was no censor whose imprimatur he needed. There was no board of his peers or professional licensing body. It didn't matter what the authorities or the party bosses thought. No church, no government agency, no craft or professional guild stood in his way, as long as the people voted for him with their pennies. In that sense, the *Sun* won an election every day. Soon, Day was making so much money that he could put politicians on notice: there was a new relationship between his newspaper and the political parties. No longer would the newspaper (or at least his newspaper) be dependent on officeholders for subsidies, printing contracts, or other spoils of political victory. Instead the *Sun* would be independent, handing out praise and criticism to politicians of any party according to merit. In his declaration of editorial independence on March 31, 1834, Day pulled no punches: "Whenever the villainous conduct of a man . . . may deserve exposure . . . as sure as we hold within our hands the whip, so sure will we 'Lash the rascals naked through the world.'" Here indeed was a new relationship between the press and the parties. According to Day, the newspaper would now have the whip hand and lash those rascals.

In this way, Day was also expanding the universe of potential readers. The size of the party papers' readership was always constrained—not only by the popularity of their party but also by the practical limits of distribution. Except for papers sent by mail, circulation was usually restricted to the number of readers who could pick up the paper at the printer's office. To make matters worse, most party papers were sold by annual subscription, so they were too expensive for anyone in the poor or middling ranks. And most party papers did not make much of an effort to appeal to women, and even less to blacks, neither of whom could vote. In short, they were operating on a business model that placed inherent limits on their size; they were aimed at well-to-do white men, period. Day's ambition, by contrast, was to sell his paper to everyone. If he appealed to one party, he might lose readers from the other. If he priced his paper any higher, he would lose poorer readers. If his *Sun* was going to shine on all, it would have to offer something to everyone, at a price anyone could afford. With that approach, there was no longer any limit to the circulation of a daily paper; it could grow as large as the population of the city it called home. In this sense the penny press can be seen as the forerunner of the mass media that followed. Profit-maximizing private enterprises, most of them, they follow the simple but ruthless logic of the seller: some is good, more is better, and all is best.

The ultimate proof of Day's success came in the form of imitators. One of the first and most serious competitors was a sour, furious man named James Gordon Bennett. As a boy in Scotland, Bennett had attended public schools and went to college for four years, reading Hume and Adam Smith. Bennett also read Franklin's *Autobiography,* which inspired him to set sail for America. He landed in Boston in 1819, at age twenty-four, and clerked in a bookstore before moving on to New York and then Charleston, where he worked for the *Courier* and made his acquaintance with slavery and slaveholders. He next went to work for a New York newspaper, the *Enquirer,* serving as the paper's Washington correspondent. (Since this appears not to have been a full-time position, Wisner edges him out as the first full-time news reporter.) After a merger, the *Courier and Enquirer* became the most popular paper in America, selling four thousand copies a day, or more than all other New York morning papers combined.[12] In those years Bennett was discovering the techniques associated with news *reporting*—covering the action in Congress, attending murder trials, witnessing all sorts of occurrences firsthand and describing them in the paper. He was also discovering that he was not suited to work for someone else. He quit the *Courier and Enquirer* in a dispute over chartering a national bank, then bounced around in a series of jobs at other papers, always looking for a chance to run his own.

Seeing the success of the *Sun,* Bennett scraped together $500 and commenced to take on the *Sun* all alone, operating out of a basement office and using some planks stretched across packing crates as a desk. On May 6, 1835, the first edition of his *New York Herald* appeared—priced, like the *Sun,* at a penny a copy—carrying Bennett's journalistic credo:

> We shall support no party—be the organ of no faction or *coterie,* and care nothing for any election or candidate from president on down to constable. We shall endeavor to record facts, on every public and proper subject, stripped of verbiage and coloring, with comments when suitable, just, independent, fearless, and good-tempered.

Bennett was definitely independent and fearless, but nobody ever accused him of being "just" and certainly not "good-tempered." Significantly, he declared that he would not be working to support any political party, although he was not turning his back on coverage of politics. He went on to identify the target audience he had in mind for the new *Herald:* "It is especially intended for the great masses of the community—the merchant, mechanic, working people—the private family as well as the public hotel—the journeyman and his employer—the clerk and his principal." In this way, Bennett was stating his ambition to go beyond even the *Sun* in appealing to all classes of New Yorkers. He did this by beefing up

3.2 **THE "GREAT MOON HOAX"** was one of the weird fruits of the new, more popular style of newspapers known as the penny press. This illustration of a batlike creature on the moon ran in 1835 in the *Sun*, which was founded by Benjamin Day in New York City in 1833. By filling his newspaper with interesting news items about ordinary people, Day helped pioneer the mass-circulation big-city daily paper. —*Wikimedia Commons.*

the paper's coverage of trading on Wall Street and adding a column of his own titled "Money Matters" while working frenetically to outdo the *Sun* in coverage of crime, local politics, and the latest news to arrive in New York Harbor by ship. According to one historian, "Here was something for everyone: short, concise news summaries written with zest; local news emphasizing the humorous and the tragic, especially in the police courts; entertaining and edifying features; and economic news."[13] To judge by sales, Bennett was onto something. Within months his circulation was soaring, and he began to run stories highlighting his own success. Between the *Sun* and the *Herald,* the penny papers were proving that there was a vast untapped market of readers (fig. 3.2).

By separating themselves from the party papers, the penny papers began laying the groundwork for the claim that would become the hallmark of the American mass media, the principle that eventually came to be known as "objectivity." Although that term was not in use in the 1830s, the ideas associated with it were beginning to appear. For the time being, the bedrock concept was that of nonpartisanship. Previously it had been assumed that most newspapers belonged to one party or another and thus saw things—especially political matters—from that perspective. Was a national bank a sensible remedy for real problems or a corrupt conspiracy? Was slavery a matter of states' rights, or was it a moral horror? Most partisan editors were frank about their loyalties, and readers understood what they were buying. Beginning with Day and Bennett, however, editors began to take a different stance. It's not that they weren't interested in politics; far from it. The difference was that they claimed to be *independent* in politics, to be able to tell the parties what to do. The information in their papers was not presented to advance any partisan cause. Nor was it presented to appeal to partisan readers. These papers aimed for a universal appeal ("It shines for all"), and they presented themselves as free of the distorting lens of party loyalty.[14]

Eager to bring in enough money to make good on his promise of independence, Bennett devoted his attention to advertising. He put his accounts on a cash-only basis and inaugurated the practice of requiring advertisers to change their copy. Previously, merchants had placed ads that ran unaltered for months or even years. Bennett wanted everything in his paper to be *new,* and he eventually made it a rule that ads had to change every day.[15] Otherwise, Bennett had little compunction about the content of advertising copy, filling his pages with ads for patent medicines. When a reader complained in June 1836 about ads (and "stories") touting Dr. Brandreth's wonder pills, Bennett fired off an angry reply: "Send us more advertisements than Dr. Brandreth does—give us higher prices— we'll cut Dr. Brandreth dead—or at least curtail his space. Business is business— money is money. . . . We permit no blockhead to interfere with our business."[16]

In 1836, Bennett and Day both had a field day covering a sensational crime story that seemed tailor-made for the penny papers.[17] On April 9 a young prostitute named Helen Jewett was found dead, battered by an ax in her bedroom in a bordello in downtown New York. Soon a young man of good background, a clerk named Richard P. Robinson, was arrested and charged with the heinous crime. The murder, the arrest, and the trial all offered up the perfect ingredients for the new kind of newspaper: the case had sex, blood, beauty, and gore. Alone, either the *Sun* or the *Herald* could have been counted on to "play it up" and extract every ounce of interest, but in competition with each other they would spare no effort. Bennett claimed one of the greatest "scoops" for himself when he described his own visit to the scene of the crime, including the bedroom itself—while the body was still lying there. Enamored of his own exclusive story, Bennett wrote a breathless first-person account:

> Slowly I began to discover the lineaments of the corpse as one would
> the beauties of a statue of marble. "My God," exclaimed I, "how like a
> statue! I can scarce conceive that form to be a corpse!" Not a vein was
> to be seen. The body looked as white, as full, as polished as the purest
> Parian marble. The perfect figure—the exquisite limbs—the fine face—
> the full arms—the beautiful bust—all—all surpassed in every respect
> the Venus de Medici.[18]

In this pioneering use of sex and violence, the penny papers worked out most of the strategies that would be duplicated by later generations of journalists working in the style known as "sensationalism" or "tabloid journalism." The only concession to conventional taste and morality was that some of the penny press editors claimed that their motives in the Jewett case went beyond mere titillation. In Bennett's view, the newspaper was serving two worthy public functions: it was offering an instructive moral tale that could prevent others from falling into a life of depravity, while at the same time opening up the criminal justice system to public scrutiny.

Despite such self-serving rationalizations, the penny papers came under attack from the old-line six-cent papers. Bennett in particular became the focus of an 1840 campaign known as "the moral war." The editors of the established commercial and party papers loathed Bennett—and no doubt feared his success. Bennett was also a genius at provoking people (he was the subject of no fewer than three public beatings) by editorially attacking their politics, their business acumen, or their religion. In 1840 a group of editors tried to ruin him by organizing a boycott of the *Herald* by all the city's respectable readers and advertisers.[19] Bennett was personally accused of "indecency, blasphemy, black-mail, lying and libel."[20] For his part, Bennett never flinched. He returned fire, both in editorials and in news stories that boasted of his continued gains in circulation. As a case of attempted reform through economic coercion, the moral war—a rearguard action by an embattled elite—was a campaign that failed.

Bennett came back stronger than ever. On May 7, 1842, during the coverage of another sensational murder case—one in which the victim was found naked and stuffed into a wooden shipping crate in the hold of a freighter bound for New Orleans—Bennett once again attempted to justify his ways to his readers: "There is nothing like going the whole figure in a thing, even in that which startles and terrifies—men who have killed their wives, and committed other such every-day matters, have been condemned, executed, and are forgotten—but it takes a deed that has some of the sublime horror about it to attract attention, rally eloquence and energy, and set people crazy, in addition, to see the lion that perpetrated it." In other words, he viewed himself as the servant of that great public hunger. More than anyone else, Bennett helped establish the idea once and for all that the material in a newspaper should be *timely*. No more travelers' letters about events of months ago; no more clippings of stale items from other newspapers. After Bennett, news was defined as any astounding thing that had just happened—ideally, any astounding thing that the other papers *didn't have*.

*   *   *

ON AUGUST 17, 1831, A YOUNG MAN from New England arrived in New York, alone and unheralded, to seek his fortune. With just ten dollars in his pocket, Horace Greeley had more ambition than resources when he came from the countryside looking for a position in the printing trade in the city that had become the largest in the United States. But—like Ben Franklin, who had arrived in Philadelphia a century earlier with just a roll of bread under his arm—Greeley was not about to let a lack of funds stop him. After all, Greeley had grown up reading Franklin's *Autobiography,* so he had both a hero and a life plan. He intended to set type carefully, to educate himself by reading widely, and to engage his considerable energies in the great public issues of his day. Later, Greeley also developed a reform program he wanted to offer America, covering an array of issues and causes: he would promote a version of socialism in economic affairs and strict temperance in personal affairs; he would support the North during the Civil War then run for president on a program of reconciliation; he would urge taxes on imported goods and government spending on the kind of "internal improvements" that would encourage expansion into the vast American West. Along the way, Horace Greeley would build the largest-circulating general-interest newspaper in the country.

Earlier that same year another young man had launched his own publication. Called *The Liberator,* it appeared in Boston on January 1, 1831. This was not just a new paper; it was very nearly a new *kind* of paper, because its founder, William Lloyd Garrison, determined that it would be devoted to a single subject: the immense moral challenge of abolishing slavery. In addressing that cause week in and week out for the next thirty-five years, *The Liberator* was taking up the great item of business left undone by the generation of the Founders. Confronted with the issue of slavery, Jefferson, Adams, Washington, and the rest of the leadership essentially compromised in writing the Constitution and put the matter off. Now, according to the young printer Garrison in his first issue, the time had come for "the IMMEDIATE EMANCIPATION of two million and a half of American SLAVES." From his base in Boston, Garrison eventually emerged as one of the most influential journalists in American history, a homegrown radical, a man who would not rest until the stain of slavery was washed clean. His mission was to change his society, his weapon of choice a newspaper.

Between them, Greeley and Garrison—along with many of their enemies, rivals, and imitators—played indispensable roles in pushing the news business in new directions in the 1830s and 1840s. With his thunderous editorials and his militancy, Garrison proved that the newspaper could be used as a single-issue advocate. What's more, he showed that such a newspaper could do more than survive; it could actually shape the course of history. For his part, Greeley pushed the limits of success for the big-city daily newspaper.

The editor who eventually emerged as the most respected and influential of the era was an odd-looking, self-taught, self-righteous man of many causes. Horace Greeley was born in Amherst, New Hampshire, in 1811, at a time when the rocky soil of rural New England was already causing it to fail as a home to farming. The region's major crops appeared to be stone walls and young people. Especially after the opening of the Erie Canal in 1819, the lands of western New York and Ohio began to lure easterners, who had begun to wear out the best farming areas in the states along the Atlantic seaboard. Within a year of the opening of the canal, which linked the western reaches of New York State with the Hudson River, almost 800,000 former residents of New England were living in the area between Albany and Buffalo, and thousands more were plowing fields in Ohio and Indiana.[21] Clearly, the future lay in the West.

As a boy, Horace helped with the chores on the family farm, keeping busy plowing fields, chopping wood, and making charcoal. The Greeleys raised corn, hops, and apples, but Horace's father was a prodigious drinker and not much of a farmer. Horace's mother doted on her boy, as he recalled many years later in his autobiography: "I learned to read at her knee,—of course, longer ago than I can remember." Horace also attended a one-room school, where he proved to be a good speller and an overall excellent student. The emphasis was on reading and writing. "Geography was scarcely studied at all; while chemistry, geology and other departments of natural science, had never been heard of in rural school houses."[22] Rather sickly, he was a keen reader. As he recalled, the first book he ever owned was *The Columbian Orator,* a widely used collection of speeches intended to teach rhetorical skills while instilling patriotism. (A few years later, a copy of the *Orator* would be the first book ever owned by a young slave in Maryland named Frederick Bailey, who became known after his flight from slavery as Frederick Douglass.) Greeley was such a rapid learner that some of the family's neighbors in New Hampshire offered to sponsor the boy as a student at Exeter Academy, but the Greeleys declined. "They would give their children the best education they could afford, and there stop," Horace remembered years later.[23]

The family struggled, moving four times before settling in 1820, when Horace was ten, in tiny East Poultney, Vermont, near Rutland on the New York border. "We now made the acquaintance of genuine poverty," Greeley wrote. In later years Greeley vividly recalled the hard times in the countryside, which he blamed on an influx of cheap manufactured goods from Britain, which were wiping out the market for homemade crafts. From this experience he drew his lifelong political commitment to high tariffs on imported goods in the name of protecting domestic producers from the predations of foreign competitors. As the family struggled, Horace had to give up his classroom learning at age fourteen, and the following year he signed on as a printer's apprentice at Poultney's newspaper, the *Northern Spectator.* "Having loved and devoured newspapers—indeed, every form of periodical—from childhood, I early resolved to be a printer if I could."[24]

The workday was long and hard, but Horace was adept. With his good spelling and nimble fingers, he quickly succeeded in learning how to set type. A few years later, his family joined the westward migration and settled in Erie, Pennsylvania, where Horace joined the *Erie Gazette.* Conditions were not much better in Erie, so in 1831 he resolved to make something of himself by moving to the great and growing city of New York. He arrived on foot, with his savings reduced to about ten dollars. He carried with him no letters of recommendation, and he knew no one in the big city. He was now a journeyman, which meant that he had learned all the mysteries of the printing trade but lacked the capital to open his own shop. About all he had going for him was his love of reading and his faith in himself. Also, he did not drink alcohol—a fact that set him apart from most of his fellow Americans, and certainly from his fellow journalists.

While Day and Bennett were competing, Horace Greeley was observing the New York newspaper scene with an intense professional interest. Following his arrival in New York in 1831, Greeley had spent a decade doing other people's bidding.[25] For the first fourteen months he set type for a miniature version of the Bible. Eventually he and a friend set up shop as job printers—that is, they were available to all comers to print all sorts of material. Greeley & Co. began to thrive, thanks in part to a contract the company had to print the New York State lottery tickets—which was due in turn to Greeley's growing links to the state's Whig Party establishment. In 1834, Greeley launched a literary and political weekly magazine called *The New-Yorker,* which gave him an outlet for his progressive views on reform and slavery. The magazine won him respect but lost him money.

So he was amenable when he was approached in the late 1830s by Thurlow Weed, the publisher of the *Albany Evening Journal* and an offstage leader of the Whig Party in New York State. Although he had never met Greeley, Weed offered him $1,000 to run a Whig paper for the 1838 election. Being broke, Greeley accepted and began putting out *The Jeffersonian.* Two years later Greeley answered the party's call again and put out another Whig election rag, *The Log Cabin,* in a successful effort to help elect William Henry Harrison president. Greeley had been thinking about launching a general-interest newspaper of his own in New York, despite the challenges, which were formidable. For one thing, there were already more than two dozen newspapers in the city, including the successful *Sun* and *Herald.* Besides, the cost of starting up a newspaper kept rising. Consider just one factor: even though the price of newsprint-quality paper was dropping throughout most of the nineteenth century, a mass-circulation daily needed so much paper that it required more and more capital just to break into the competition. Greeley, however, did have the support of "several Whig friends" because the existing penny papers, while professing independence from political parties, both leaned toward the Democrats. In any event, taking stock of his prospects, he recalled, "I had been ten years in New York, was thirty years old, in full health and vigor, and worth, I presume, about two thousand dollars."[26]

On April 10, 1841, the *New York Tribune*—cost, one penny—made its debut. Because Greeley was its editor, it was naturally in sympathy with the Whig Party and its program of high tariffs to protect U.S. manufacturers and government investments in "internal improvements" that would open up the West. But as Greeley put it in his memoirs, his goal was to guide the party, not to serve it: "My leading idea was the establishment of a journal removed alike from servile partisanship on the one hand and from gagged, mincing neutrality on the other."[27] The goal, in other words, was not to be neutral or disengaged from politics; the goal was to stand on principle and shout from there. He recruited an able young man as his deputy—Henry J. Raymond, who went on to found a newspaper he called the *New-York Daily Times* (the forerunner of today's *New York Times*). Because of his need for more capital and for someone with better business skills, Greeley soon found a business partner, Thomas McElrath, who invested $2,000 to become publisher and co-owner. McElrath was the ideal partner for Greeley; he kept the books and never questioned Greeley's editorial enthusiasms.

At the start, Greeley's *Tribune* had a press run of five thousand, of which only 10 percent went to subscribers; the rest had to be hawked on the street against the lurid offerings of the *Sun* and *Herald.* But Greeley, the reformer and moralist, was not trying to beat the other penny papers at their own game. He was trying to reach a more refined, middle-class audience, and of course he was hoping to embrace the unserved Whig population. After a few months Greeley hit upon a brilliant variation on the penny-paper business model: he brought out a weekly version of his daily *Tribune,* merged his old *New-Yorker* magazine into it, and targeted the resulting weekly to readers in the countryside. Never quite at home in the city himself, Greeley discovered a vast audience eager for his editorials in the farming communities and small towns. Taking advantage of the reduced postal rates that Congress had made available to all newspapers,[28] Greeley quickly found his best and biggest audience. Mainly on the strength of his editorials, Greeley, known as "Uncle Horace," became as familiar in the rural North as Franklin's Poor Richard had been a century earlier. In the coming decades Bennett consistently had the largest circulation of any daily paper, but Greeley's combined city and country circulation was unsurpassed (fig. 3.3).

The views that Greeley was pushing amounted to a grab bag of progressive reforms. While not a particularly deep or systematic thinker, Greeley had a nimble mind and a flair for expressing ideas that were swirling about. One of his major causes before the Civil War was socialism. He had a keen sympathy with the members of society he considered "producers"—that is, people who made things or grew things. People who did not produce—including speculators, investors, landlords, and their ilk, along with the lazy—drew his scorn. Greeley became a follower of Fourierism, a program of political economy that called for the formation of "associations," which were voluntary groupings of families of workers, as many as four or five hundred, who would share some two thousand acres along with communal workshops. The idea of associations was expounded by Greeley and also by Albert Brisbane, who wrote a column in the *Tribune* for two years promoting the idea.[29] Greeley also attempted to put some of his ideas into practice at the *Tribune.*[30] He reorganized the company as the Tribune Association and allowed employees to buy in (much as workers might participate today in an "employee stock ownership plan"). In practice, however, Greeley unaccountably priced shares in the enterprise at $1,000 each, which was out of the reach of most

3.3 **HORACE GREELEY, SHOWN HERE** in a daguerreotype taken in the studio of the photographer Mathew Brady, became the most widely read journalist in the country before the Civil War. Daily and weekly editions of Greeley's *Tribune* were read by approximately half a million people.
—*Library of Congress.*

of his employees, and he did allow some outsiders to buy in.[31] So the *Tribune* never truly embodied the socialist ideal; in fact, it more closely foreshadowed the "public corporation" model of the twentieth century.

In other areas Greeley was equally outspoken. He exposed and denounced the growing misery that he witnessed among the expanding ranks of unskilled or unemployed labor in New York City, which, he lamented, was becoming "the metropolis of beggary."[32] He also endorsed homesteading as a cure for America's problems, and he insisted with growing vehemence that the West should remain a free-soil, free-labor zone, out of the grasp of the Slave Power. He so often touted the popular slogan "Go West, young man!" that he is forever associated with it.[33] He also endorsed feminism, at least in part. Although he seems to have favored a lost son over his surviving daughters, and although he condemned divorce as the road to perdition, Greeley was in the editorial forefront in support of women's rights. One of the ways he showed his commitment was through his decision to hire Margaret Fuller, one of the brightest lights in the constellation of writers and thinkers in the Transcendentalist movement centered near Boston. She was among the first women to work full-time for a big-city newspaper, and the first female foreign correspondent when she went to Italy for Greeley.[34] In all, Greeley had brought a bundle of changes to the news business.

* * *

WILLIAM LLOYD GARRISON GREW UP in Newburyport, a busy seaport about thirty-five miles north of Boston.[35] He was born there in 1805 (six years before Horace
Greeley), as Thomas Jefferson was beginning his second term as president. Garrison's father ran off when Lloyd (as the boy was known) was just a toddler, leaving
Lloyd's destitute mother, Fanny, to raise three children alone. A few years later Fanny Garrison abandoned Lloyd, too. Desperate for money, she left the young boy in
the care of a friend and moved twenty miles away to the shoemaking city of Lynn.
Lloyd stayed behind and attended the local public grammar school in Newburyport, where he read *The Columbian Orator,* John Bunyan's *Pilgrim's Progress,* and
the school's motley collection of other books. When he was almost ten years old, he
was reunited with his mother, but she soon decided to try Baltimore. Abandoned
again, Lloyd was shipped back to Newburyport. During this period the boy served
several trying years as an apprentice to a shoemaker, a cabinetmaker, and a printer.

Eventually Lloyd found his calling when he went to work—at age thirteen—at
the local newspaper, the *Newburyport Herald.* Like Franklin before him, he entered
the field at the bottom, holding the lowly position known as "printer's devil." It was
hard work, and none too pleasant either, but it was Lloyd's last chance to find his
way into a suitable trade in town. Like any apprentice, he tended the fire, swept
the floor, and hauled water. As the newest boy in a print shop, Lloyd drew some
especially unpleasant chores, which included tending a boiling pot of varnish and
blacking that combined in a stew to form the sticky, smelly printer's ink. "Worse
yet," according to his biographer Henry Mayer, "Lloyd had to soften the sheepskin
used for covering the rag-and-wool balls with which the ink was applied to the
press. To become sufficiently pliable ('as soft as a lady's glove' was the measure) the
pelts had to be soaked in urine for a fortnight, but each day the apprentice had to
pull the skins out of the reeking pail, twist them in his hands to wring out some of
the moisture, roll them in old newspapers, and stomp on them with his feet until
they were dry enough for the next night's soaking."[36] If anyone ever epitomized the
role of "the ink-stained wretch," it was the pitiable little Lloyd Garrison.

The editor of the *Herald,* Ephraim Allen, liked the young apprentice and valued
his skill. Garrison moved into the master's house, a happy and relatively prosperous household, in which he had access to books and could read not only the Bible
but also Shakespeare, Milton, Sir Walter Scott, and the passionate new poetry of
Lord Byron. He read avidly, but not widely or systematically, and his scant few
years in the classroom had left him without a grounding in Latin or Greek, mathematics or science. Like his hero Franklin and his contemporary Greeley, Garrison would have to teach himself most of what he would come to know. When he
turned twenty-one, his apprenticeship ended, and the nearly penniless Garrison
found himself with few immediate prospects. He stayed on at the *Herald* as a
journeyman, which meant that he now had to be paid a wage but could no longer
expect room and board.

After a brief spell editing a rival newspaper in Newburyport, he headed to the nearest big city, Boston, which had almost sixty thousand inhabitants in 1826. He moved into a boardinghouse run by a Baptist preacher, the Reverend William Collier, located a few blocks from the house where Ben Franklin had been raised just over a century earlier. (Franklin would have been at a bit of a loss in his old neighborhood, however: many important streets had been renamed after the Revolution in a more republican fashion: Washington, State, Congress, Federal.) In the boardinghouse and in the many churches of Boston, Garrison began to sense the riptide of reform in the swirling currents of social thought. He and some friends devoted themselves to the movement of organized benevolence, and one of Garrison's first commitments was to the cause of temperance. Recruited to edit a pro-temperance newspaper, the *National Philanthropist,* he set out to "raise the moral tone of the country." In his view, a man could be either a teetotaler or a demon; there was no middle ground. In fact, on the paper's masthead, Garrison added a warning against moderation itself: "Moderate Drinking Is the Downhill Road to Intemperance and Drunkenness."[37] There would be no half measures for William Lloyd Garrison!

While battling editorially against strong spirits, Garrison had an encounter at Collier's boardinghouse in March 1828 that changed his life and set him on a course to alter American history. Garrison met Benjamin Lundy, a Quaker who was himself on a mission to abolish slavery as editor of a newspaper he called *Genius of Universal Emancipation.* The gentle Quaker's vigorous denunciation of slavery, Garrison recalled much later, "opened my eyes" and "inflamed my mind" against the evil that still pervaded so much of America. In Massachusetts, slavery had been abolished shortly after the Revolution, but there were approximately 2 million slaves living in those states that still tolerated it, mainly in the South.

Garrison's conversion to the cause was swift and complete. In July 1828 he quit his job editing the temperance newspaper and plunged into antislavery work. "My soul was on fire then,"[38] he wrote, and when he was offered the chance to speak in public about slavery, he took it. The date was the Fourth of July, 1829. The occasion was an annual gathering in Boston's Park Street Church of supporters of the American Colonization Society, a group founded more than a decade earlier that aimed to remedy the problem of slavery by removing slaves from American soil and returning them to Africa to live in a "colony" called Liberia. Just twenty-four years old, Garrison took to the pulpit and declared that because of slavery, "our politics are rotten to the core."[39] Invoking the Declaration of Independence and quoting frequently from the Bible, Garrison reminded his listeners of the self-evident truth that all men are created equal, with the unalienable right to liberty. He called for the gradual emancipation of all slaves by means of prayer and by the moral suasion that could be brought to bear by the nation's churches and newspapers. It was quite a debut, but there was much more to come from William Lloyd Garrison.

Lundy invited Garrison to become editor of his abolitionist newspaper, which meant moving to Baltimore. There Garrison boarded with free blacks and had his first sustained contact with slavery and slave trading.[40] In 1830 he was charged with printing a libel against a slave trader and was forced to serve forty-nine days in a Baltimore jail, an experience that only strengthened his commitment to the cause.

Garrison moved back to Boston and, with help from friends, decided to continue the fight against abolition as editor of a newspaper that would take up that cause and no other. On January 1, 1831, the first issue hit the streets of Boston. In heavy block letters it bore the bold name *The Liberator,* and it carried a motto that Garrison had adapted from Thomas Paine: "Our Country Is the World—Our Countrymen are Mankind." The paper spoke with an even bolder voice, declaring that the time for moderation, compromise, and accommodation was over. In the first issue Garrison addressed his readers directly, in one of the most stirring declarations of editorial principles ever written:

> I am aware, that many object to the severity of my language; but is there not cause for severity? I *will be* as harsh as truth, and as uncompromising as justice. On this subject, I do not wish to think, or speak, or write with moderation. No! No! Tell a man whose house is on fire, to give a moderate alarm; tell him to moderately rescue his wife from the hands of the ravisher; tell the mother to gradually extricate her babe from the fire into which it has fallen; —but urge me not to use moderation in a cause like the present. I am in earnest—I will not equivocate—I will not excuse—I will not retreat a single inch—AND I WILL BE HEARD.[41]

With that trumpet blast, the twenty-five-year-old editor launched a newspaper that became both a crusade and a career. Every week William Lloyd Garrison thundered away. He drew on America's past, combining the careful typesetting of Franklin with the passionate advocacy of Paine as well as the legal philosophy of Jefferson, and yet he had his eye fixed firmly on an American future in which no human being could ever be bought and sold as a piece of property. For Garrison, it was not enough to *describe* the world; for him, the only point in editing a newspaper was to *save* the world.

In renewing the advocacy tradition in American journalism, he certainly brought passion to the cause. A friend later recounted that Garrison slept in the *Liberator*'s office and made it a practice to set his articles directly in type, without the benefit of writing them out first in longhand. Garrison welcomed free blacks to contribute to his paper, and he sought out black subscribers—who actually carried *The Liberator* through its first year in business, accounting for all but fifty of his total circulation in 1832.[42] As one of the most radical white voices in the debate over slavery, Garrison lived in financial peril, but he never seemed to care much. For him, success was not to be measured by revenue, or even by circulation. After all, he never sold more than about three thousand copies of his weekly at any point. Instead, Garrison measured success by the spread of his ideas. Soon he settled on a political program from which he never wavered: immediate abolition of slavery, to be followed not by a new forced exile through colonization in Liberia but by full civil rights for freed blacks in the United States—all to be accomplished without violence. Eventually he came to see his role this way: citing the Apostle Paul, he compared his work in *The Liberator* to "the little leaven" that causes the whole loaf to rise.[43] Once it rose, though, the whole loaf would have to pass through the fires of war.

* * *

IN THE 1840S THE FIELD of communication was shaken by a thunderbolt, a truly stupendous technological innovation, one that ranks with Gutenberg's printing press in the history of communication: the *electromagnetic telegraph machine.* With this new technology, the flow of information speeded up by many orders of magnitude.[44] For all of human history up to then, the pace of communication had almost always been constrained—usually limited to the speed of the messenger, whether it be a person, a horse, or a pigeon. All that changed with the telegraph. For the first time in history, a machine could provide instant, interactive communication that was not dependent on any living thing. Information and verbal expression were liberated from the bonds of mere travel. All the machines that followed were improvements on the telegraph, to be sure, but none of them represented as profound a change as the one wrought by Samuel F. B. Morse.

A painter and inventor, Morse built upon a lengthening chain of developments in the understanding and control of electricity which had begun with Ben Franklin. Morse also built upon a legacy of innovations in communications, including several successful systems in Europe that conveyed messages almost instantly across great distances by means of beacon fires or large coded flags known as semaphores. Such systems were known by the early nineteenth century as *telegraphs* (from the Greek words for "far" and "writing"). Located on a string of hilltops, these optical telegraphs could relay messages quite effectively, under favorable conditions. But most could not operate at night or in foul weather.[45] Morse is generally credited with being the first to apply an electric current as the means to power a mechanical device that could register and record changes in the current. Morse had one other great insight: the code that bears his name. With his system of short dots and long dashes to represent the numbers and letters, along with the wires and receivers, the telegraph had what might be described as both the "hardware" and the "software" needed to make communication by wire possible.

Morse and a young assistant, Alfred Vail, worked out the scientific and technical difficulties but could not find financing. Finally, when a Whig majority briefly materialized, they persuaded Congress to subsidize them (with $30,000 in public funds), and in 1844 they built the first working telegraph line in America, between Washington, D.C., and Baltimore.[46] Its initial test came on May 1, 1844, while the line was still under construction, when Vail sent a message from the Whig political convention in Baltimore announcing the names of the party's nominees. The tele-graph line ran along the railroad track; confirmation arrived more than an hour later by steam-powered locomotive. Three weeks after that, sending the first offi-cial telegraph message, from a transmitter located at the Supreme Court building, Morse transmitted the biblical passage "What hath God wrought." News of the technology's application arrived at the *Baltimore Patriot and Commercial Gazette*, which carried a sidebar story the next day about the wonderful new contraption, calling it "MORSE'S ELECTRO MAGNETIC TELEGRAPH." As an anonymous but poetic writer at the paper put it, "This is indeed the annihilation of space." And in fact the telegraph can lay claim to being one of the essential innovations separating the modern era from all that went before.

The initial steps were halting. It is humbling to recall that the first news story ever conveyed by telegraph concerned a vote in Congress in which the reporter got the tally wrong—proving that while news could travel faster, it was not necessarily any more accurate. Soon enough, Morse started finding customers for his machine. One of the first, naturally, was the press. Newspaper editors could see in the tele-graph the ultimate weapon in the battle already raging to be first to publish the very latest news. With growing ferocity since the founding of the penny papers in 1833, editors had been trying to outdo one another in mobilizing horses, pigeons, steam-boats, and locomotives to move news from place to place. They rapidly began to patronize the company formed by Morse and several other investors. With power in Congress passing back into Democrats' hands, the U.S. government opted not to develop the telegraph as a branch of the Post Office, as many other countries did.[47] Turning to private sources of capital, the telegraph operators got busy meeting the demand for their product and seeking new markets. One important partner was the rapidly expanding rail system: railroads could offer the rights-of-way for plant-ing poles and stringing wires, and the telegraph could enable railroads to coordi-nate the movements of engines and cars. By the end of 1846, there was a telegraph line from Washington to Boston (except that it could not yet cross the Hudson River, so messages had to be ferried across, then transmitted northward). By 1852, more than 23,000 miles of line had been strung; by 1860, there were 50,000 miles. And in 1861, a line stretched across the United States from sea to sea.

The impact of the telegraph on the news business was fairly direct. First and foremost, it greatly accelerated the process of *gathering* news. The telegraph had little impact on *disseminating* news; it was a "point-to-point" technology, capable of transmitting a message from one sender to one recipient, which made it of little use for reaching masses of people at once. But it enabled reporters in the field to relay information back to their newsrooms almost instantaneously, across almost any distance. During the Civil War the telegraph came into its own—both as a military resource and as a journalistic tool—in a vast conflict that extended across more than a thousand miles, with battlefields as far apart as Pennsylvania and Texas. Such speed also strengthened the perception that had been fostered so strenuously by the editors of the penny press: that a newspaper ought to carry *news*. Previously, most of the contents of a newspaper were not very new. With the coming of the telegraph, that old standard would never satisfy. Adopting a new bedrock definition of journalism, readers came to expect that even if the news was slanted, and even if it was irrelevant, at least it was *new*.

In addition to expediting the movement of news, the telegraph clearly contributed to the development of a new style of writing news. Because telegraph tolls were assessed by the word, it became of paramount importance for journalistic writing to be concise. In that sense the telegraph contributed to the rise of what is called a "hard news lead," that is, an opening paragraph that summarizes the major points of the entire story. No longer could a reporter beat around the bush or indulge in meandering or leisurely narratives. When the newspaper is paying by the word, or when a customer has access to the telegraph key for only the allotted fifteen minutes, the reporter had better not waste time or money but instead get right to the point. Editors (and readers) would want to know: Did the legislation pass or fail? Who won the battle? How many died? Did stock prices go up or down?

In the telegraphic style, the journalist usually had to alter, or even obliterate, the natural chronology by which events unfolded or by which the reporter learned of them. Stories could not be written like letters to loved ones at home or like novels or histories. In the telegraphic style of newswriting, less is more. This phenomenon was noted by Bennett's *Herald,* which opined just after the Civil War: "There can be no doubt that the telegraphic communication with Europe will revolutionize the newspaper business on both continents. It tends to produce a condensation of style in newspaper articles. Already we observe, since the telegraph has been established throughout Europe, a terseness in the writings of English journals which forms a strong contrast to the former long-winded style."[48] This point about compression of thought is important and not coincidental; it is embedded in the architecture of the technology. That is one way that the medium shapes the message. According to one historian, Morse's assistant, Alfred Vail, submitted a study to the U.S. postmaster general pointing up the fact that the telegraph could accelerate the flow of information only so long as that information came in small packages. Vail calculated that it would be possible to transmit an entire Old Testament from New York to Boston via the postal express in ten hours but that it would take more than five *days* to transmit the same material by telegraph.[49] Of course, any one *passage*—or (God forbid!) a *summary* of the holy Scriptures—could be telegraphed more rapidly, but not the whole megillah.

By giving force to the values of timeliness and concision, the telegraph exerted a strong and lasting influence on American journalism. But its impact also raised a key question: Who would control such a powerful force? As James Gordon Bennett shrewdly observed, the telegraph brought with it the promise to supply "the whole nation . . . with the same idea at the same time."[50] After a brief period of ownership of the new technology, the U.S. government opted out. Instead, Morse created the Magnetic Telegraph Company and began selling shares, while reserving half the stock for himself and other patent holders. The largest investor was from the newspaper industry, William Swain, owner of the *Philadelphia Public Ledger,* with smaller investments coming from penny press editors such as Greeley and Bennett.[51] At first, telegraph companies proliferated, sometimes competing and sometimes cooperating. Partly on the strength of exclusive contracts with railroads for rights-of-way and partly by acquiring its competitors, one company emerged by 1867 as the undisputed monopoly in the field: Western Union. There were sporadic calls in the following decades for the government to create a public utility alternative to Western Union that would be housed in the Post Office, but the idea was never implemented.[52] Instead, it was left to Western Union to carry the news, or else the news would have to walk, ride, or find a pigeon to carry it.

* * *

ONCE THEY WERE UP AND running, telegraph wires started carrying all sorts of messages, and a growing part of that traffic involved news stories. An immense challenge for the new medium and its newspaper customers came along in short order when the United States provoked a war with Mexico late in 1845. The following year, with the war still raging, a New York City publisher took a step that eventually led to the creation of a new kind of newsgathering operation, The Associated Press (here I follow the news agency's preference by capitalizing the article "The" in the name). The initiative came from Moses Yale Beach, now the publisher of the *New York Sun.* Beach was a brother-in-law of the *Sun*'s founder, Benjamin Day, and he had bought the paper from Day in 1838. Beach was a tough competitor in a competitive market. Under Beach, the *Sun* kept seeking ways to beat Bennett's *Herald* and the other New York papers, taking such steps as hiring express riders and special trains to speed news to the *Sun.* Beach also paid to hire swift boats that could race out into New York Harbor to greet the big ships arriving from Europe and get the latest news from them. When he built a new home for the *Sun* in 1842 (at the corner of Fulton and Nassau streets in lower Manhattan), he installed an elaborate pigeon coop on the roof to accommodate his flock of trained birds, which carried airborne messages to the newspaper's headquarters from Sandy Hook, New Jersey, at the mouth of the harbor, and from as far away as Albany and Washington.[53]

Beach's appetite for the latest news only grew with the outbreak of war. Within a few months he had worked out an arrangement for relaying the news from Mexico to New York (fig. 3.4). Reports first had to arrive by boat in Mobile, Alabama, on the Gulf Coast. Then special express riders carried the dispatches by relays of horses to Montgomery, where they were sent via the U.S. mail service aboard stagecoaches about seven hundred miles to a point in Virginia near Richmond that marked the southern terminus of telegraph service. From there, news could be relayed by wire to New York. Using this improvised, private system, Beach could get news into the *Sun* a whole day ahead of his competitors. In

3.4 **READERS GET THE LATEST NEWS FROM MEXICO** in this 1848 painting, *War News from Mexico*, by Richard Caton Woodville. The painting also suggests that such weighty matters were primarily the concern of white men and not of the disenfranchised black man sitting on the step or the woman in the window.
—*Library of Congress.*

May 1846, Beach decided to invite his rivals to join him in a cooperative venture, sharing costs and sharing news dispatches.[54] Some of these editors were already cooperating in joint ventures that allowed them to cut their growing bills for telegraph usage by sharing a single report from a joint correspondent or a single fast boat to greet the big ships arriving from Europe with the latest news from the Continent.[55] Such arrangements had obvious advantages for those involved: they could cut costs, avoid missing important information, and put their remaining resources into competition over local news and features. Out of this series of ad hoc agreements among a handful of New York newspaper publishers there evolved the organization that became known as the Associated Press.[56]

Although the AP went through many changes after 1846—often in order to adapt to changing technology—some of its essential features remained constant. Though headquartered in New York City near other powerful media institutions, it has never fit the prevailing mode of American journalism because it has never been a private, for-profit company. Instead, it has been a nonprofit cooperative established to meet the needs of its "members," who appoint the AP's top management and set the overall journalistic policies. It has operated, in a sense, as a wholesaler of news stories, which are sold to the general public through the retail outlets of the individual newspapers (and, in later years, the individual broadcast outlets). The AP did not deal directly with the public, and it did not carry any advertising. It was put on an annual operating budget, and it had to live within those means; in that way it operated more like a government agency than a private business. Its only customer was the news industry as a whole.

The AP has always been concerned with the rapid and simultaneous transmission of news to clients on the receiving end. Indeed, the company's use of telegraphic and other wired means of communication was so extensive that the AP and its rivals became known as "wire services," and newspaper editors who wanted to learn the latest news would "check the wires." At the same time, the AP's thousands of correspondents have always had to labor—often in obscurity—on behalf of many masters.

The history of the Associated Press is not well known even in the journalistic community. One of the few historians who have looked at the AP calls its past a "hidden history," in part because the AP operates at one remove from the news-consuming public and in part because the newspapers have never wanted to publicize their reliance on this giant newsgathering utility they all share. The history of the AP should be better known, for it is a significant American institution in its own right, one that continues to exert a strong but subtle influence on the practice of journalism both at home and abroad. In addition, the AP has played an important role from its inception as the nexus between the news business and the telegraph business, eventually becoming part of a "dual monopoly" (along with Western Union) in the distribution of news.[57]

From its start in 1846, membership in the Associated Press conveyed immediate advantages to those newspapers that were part of the news-sharing arrangement. Over the years, membership criteria were changed several times, tending in the direction of opening the ranks to more and more news organizations, eventually including radio and television stations as well as newspapers. But initially, the owners of the founding newspapers, wanting to exploit their advantage, tried to monopolize their asset. For years they used what amounted to a blackball system, which allowed any existing member to veto the addition of any new newspaper in its circulation area, thereby maintaining the value of its AP franchise. A major benefit of AP membership was the exclusive access to the latest news from Europe, which was relayed to New York by a system of boats, horses, and telegraph, arranged by one of the AP's first managers, the intrepid Daniel Craig.

Another very powerful impact of the AP from its inception was its role in the development of a philosophical ideal in American journalism: the notion that a news story should be a collection of facts, arranged in a logical order and free of any political bias or agenda. This idea is widespread today in the thinking of those who call for "objective" reporting. But even before the term "objectivity" was applied to news, the AP was pioneering its techniques. This was an impor-

tant but entirely unintended consequence of the AP's creation: each AP story had
to satisfy the demands of many editors—a half dozen at first but later hundreds
and, eventually, thousands. For the news copy to pass muster, it had to be politically inert. This was certainly a departure from the thinking of the editors of the
partisan press or that of an advocate like Garrison, but it was also different from
the approach taken by the editors of the penny press. Day, Bennett, and Greeley
all made a show of declaring their independence from the political parties, but
this did not mean that those men were without their own political views. Indeed
they had strong views on all the issues of the day, and they did not hesitate to
express those views in the columns of their papers, which were not yet consistently divided into separate "news" and "editorial" sections.

Without any guiding directives or statement of philosophy, the early correspondents for AP quickly figured out that they would do well not to include any
polemics in their accounts. This was the opening wedge in the great division in
American journalism between those practitioners who declare candidly to their
audience that they have a point of view and those who say they do not. There is
no greater example of this divide than the career of Lawrence Gobright, who was
the AP's first Washington correspondent. His assignment was to report on the
doings of Congress and the federal government at a time when that government
and the rest of the country were literally splitting apart. How could he possibly
write stories about slavery, sectionalism, states' rights, or any of the other great
issues of the day without offending at least some of the editors he was working for? The answer that he hit upon came in the form of what might be called
"Gobright's Credo":

> My business is to communicate facts; my instructions do not allow
> me to make any comment upon the facts which I communicate. My
> dispatches are sent to papers of all manner of politics, and the editors
> say they are able to make their own comments upon the facts which
> are sent them. I therefore confine myself to what I consider legitimate
> news. I do not act as a politician belonging to any school, but try to be
> truthful and impartial. My dispatches are merely dry matters of fact
> and detail. Some special correspondents may write to suit the temper
> of their organs. Although I try to write without regard to men or poli-
> tics, I do not always escape censure.[58]

He did not use the term "objectivity," which would not become popular until the
twentieth century, but he was talking about a similar idea. It is also worth noting that final qualifier in Gobright's statement. Try as he might to stick strictly to
facts, it comes as no surprise that even Gobright found that he could not please
every editor all of the time (fig. 3.5).

His boss was Daniel Craig, the "general agent" of the Associated Press. In 1854,

3.5 THE JOURNALIST WHO PIONEERED NEUTRAL POLITICAL NEWS, Lawrence Gobright, was the chief Washington correspondent for the Associated Press during the 1850s and 1860s. In those years of political conflict, Gobright was required to write news stories that would pass muster by editors of Republican and Copperhead newspapers, forcing him to stick to what he called "dry matters of fact and detail."
—*Library of Congress.*

Craig laid out his view of what kind of news the AP was interested in receiving from domestic correspondents—a view that has not changed much since. Above all, he laid down the law on sticking to facts while leaving out subjectivity and extra words:

> We would say that we want *everything that is* IMPORTANT and everything that would be of General Interest in this City, State, or the country at large.
>
> In preparing dispatches for transmission, it is desirable always to bear in mind that we want only the material facts in regard to any matter or event, and those facts in the fewest words possible.
>
> All expressions of opinion upon any matters; all political, religious, and social biases; and especially all *personal feelings* on any subject on the part of the Reporter, must be kept out of his dispatches.[59]

The bundle of organizational, technological, and conceptual changes that took place in the 1830s and 1840s marked a turning point in the history of American journalism. By trial and error, by responding to the cues of the marketplace, newspaper editors pushed the process of gathering, defining, and disseminating news in directions that have largely endured ever since. Through those separate efforts, they created the foundations of the modern media system, in which for-profit private companies sought a mass audience by using instant communications and aggressive reporting to publish the latest items that might interest the greatest number of people, in turn making them available to advertisers. These changes did not spread immediately to every newspaper in every hamlet in the country, but they marked the leading edge of developments that did eventually permeate the field.

At the core of this transformation was a reorganization of the old print shop along new lines. Before the 1830s, most newspapers operated in the traditional way: a master printer taught his apprentice how to set type and run a press while keeping an eye out for suitable material to offer the public. By age twenty-one, the apprentice was ready to journey on to another shop and sign on as a "journey-man." Now he would be paid, and was expected to make a major contribution to the shop's output. Over the course of the next few years the young journey-men would perfect his skills and try to save enough money to buy the equipment he would need to open a shop of his own. In return for his hard work, frugal-ity, and respect for his masters, he could expect to become a master in his own right. Through this system of mutual obligations, individuals re-created a stable, orderly, hierarchical web of social relations in each new generation.

In the America of the 1830s, however, this traditional way of life was under tremendous stress. Editors of the penny papers such as Bennett, Day, and Gree-ley were so successful that they outgrew the old master-apprentice model. They started hiring help to carry out specific tasks in an increasingly elaborate division of labor. Whereas Franklin and the other printer-editors of his era would have written an item *and* set the type *and* run it through the press *and* sold a subscrip-tion to someone who stopped by the shop, now those jobs were done by different people. By 1845, the *Herald* was employing fifteen reporters and editors, including Bennett and his managing editor, Frederic Hudson.[60] By 1850, the *Tribune* had seven reporters and three dozen printers.[61]

As these printers moved out of the old shop, they were also creating a physical separation between home and work. In Franklin's day, most printers' shops were located in the building in which the printer lived with his family and appren-tice. In those circumstances, printers' wives and daughters sometimes pitched in, and a few managed to learn the trade. But in the changing economy of the antebellum years, production moved away from the home and into noisy, grimy, and ever-larger shops that were located in their own neighborhoods or districts. In the New York City of the 1830s, the printing trade was just one of many that were evolving in this direction, as businessmen set up bigger and bigger work-shops, hired more and more of the surplus labor coming into the city from the countryside or from Europe, and often drove down wages in a process known as "sweating."[62] In doing so, they were smashing the older way of life, with its many bonds of mutual obligation between masters and apprentices. It was a dra-matic case of the "creative destruction" of the capitalist system, remaking society in the process. Now, in place of the old print shop came the sweatshop, where skills were reduced to a minimum and labor intensified to a maximum. In this new model, master printers began to act like businessmen concerned with organizing the labor of others, and young printers began to realize that they would probably never rise to the status of master but would instead spend their entire lives working for wages. Newspapers were among the first industries to move from the shop model to something approximating a factory model.

Since they were private businesses to begin with, newspapers were well positioned to take advantage of the commercial possibilities that arose in the 1830s. With the coming of daily publication in a big city with mass circulation, a paper like the *Sun* or the *Herald* became the ideal vehicle for businesses that wanted to reach thousands of customers at once. To reach such a mass audience, these metropolitan papers were sold at a rock-bottom price, and they could be hawked in the street one day at a time. Advertising became an increasingly important source of revenue for these papers, and the combined effects of the mutually reinforcing gains in circulation and advertising pushed the successful penny papers to a new level of size and profitability. Those greater revenues made it possible for editors like Bennett and Greeley to operate without the earlier generation's dependence on political parties and public subsidies. In this new era, editors who prized their independence could stand apart from the political parties and try to shape public policies. They would lash the rascals as they saw fit.

Part of the new division of labor in the penny papers involved the creation of a specialized role for someone who would eventually become known as a *reporter*. These men (and, for nearly a century, they were almost all men) fanned out from the newspaper's headquarters and sought out facts on the docks, in the courts, and at the police stations of the big city. In the process, they hit upon a new working definition of *news:* any recent development that would surprise, shock, amuse, or edify thousands and thousands of people from the lower and middling walks of life. No longer would newspapers focus just on business and politics; now the whole of the human condition, in all its depravity and banality, could be mined by the newspaper as potential material. One perhaps paradoxical result was the publication in the penny papers of a large amount of local news.

These papers changed in another realm as well. They became mechanical powerhouses compared to the hand-operated presses of Franklin's time. With their increasing amounts of working capital, and the efforts of tinkerers in many fields, newspaper editors could take advantage of several technical breakthroughs in the 1830s and 1840s, and for the newspaper business, two developments were key: the advent of steam-powered presses and the invention of the rotary press (which wraps the material to be printed around a cylinder, which can be driven much faster than a flat plate that must be raised and lowered). Together these innovations made it possible to reach a mass audience by printing tens of thousands of copies per day, day in and day out. Outside the newspaper, change was dramatic as well. These two decades saw an explosion of building of roads, canals, and railroads that put people, mail, goods, and ideas into circulation at a faster pace than ever before. The ultimate technical change followed in the late 1840s with the "annihilation of space" by the telegraph.

All told, these changes eventually transformed the news trade. The evidence is unmistakable. In 1830 there were 650 weekly papers operating in the United States and 65 daily papers. The average circulation for the dailies was about 1,200, making for a total daily circulation of about 78,000 copies—each of which was read, on average, by several people. Just ten years later, all those figures had about doubled. There were 1,141 weeklies in 1840, as well as 138 daily papers. Not only were there more dailies, but their average circulation was up as well, for an estimated output of 300,000 papers a day. Here was the start of a truly mass medium. Whether they embodied the idealism of a Garrison or the cynicism of a Bennett, these newspapers were going to have an impact. Indeed, given the global reach of the telegraph and a continent-wide news cooperative like the Associated Press, it now became possible for the news industry, as Bennett had observed, to "impress the whole nation . . . with the same idea at the same time."[63]

CHAPTER 4

Radicals All! 1830–1875

COVERING SLAVERY AND THE CIVIL WAR

Public sentiment is every thing. With it, nothing can fail; against it, nothing can succeed.
Whoever moulds public sentiment, goes deeper than he who enacts statutes, or pronounces
judicial decisions. He makes possible the inforcement of these, else impossible.
—Abraham Lincoln, 1858

THE PROSPECT OF AN American army taking the field to do battle is a dreadful one. Even more terrible to contemplate is the prospect of *two* American armies taking the field, prepared to slaughter each other unceasingly until one can claim ultimate victory. Such was the military face of the Civil War, a conflict of unparalleled moral, political, legal, and social consequence for Americans. At stake, ultimately, was nothing less than the definition of what it meant to be human. In all its fullness, the great conflict, which sundered churches, political parties, the military, and even families, was for Americans the defining act of the nineteenth century, comparable only to the American Revolution itself. It was therefore the greatest news story of the century. In journalistic terms, however, the Revolution and the Civil War took place in very different settings. By 1861 the practice of journalism in the United States was more than a century and a half old, and more than a few American newspapers were prepared to cover a modern war, or at least to attempt it.

The Civil War tested American journalism, as it tested most institutions. This was not, however, a period of great innovation in the news business: there were no breakthroughs comparable to the telegraph, the rotary press, or the big-city daily itself, with its division of labor and its appetite for news. All the essential ways and means of covering the news—the wholesale reporting by the Associated Press, the transmission network of the telegraph companies, the hundreds of privately owned daily and weekly newspapers—were already in place. Instead of innovation, the Civil War brought a period of adaptation and improvisation, along with the usual mix of heroics, hijinks, shortcomings, and screw-ups, as the technology and methods that journalists had so recently adopted were stretched to their limits.

American journalists had very little influence on the conduct or the outcome of the war itself, but as Lincoln foresaw, they did play a major role in the years leading up to the war. American newspapers hastened the coming of the conflict in two ways: they made the issues of sectionalism, union, and slavery impossible to ignore or smooth over, and they gave voice to radicals on both sides who leaned always in the direction of confrontation and away from compromise. Journalists amplified the issues, and—whether in pursuit of higher circulation or some other goal—managed to polarize attitudes among Americans, often working at cross-purposes to the political factions. Whereas leaders of religious denominations, political parties, and all sorts of social movements had once shown an ability to compromise, they no longer did so. Advocacy became more strident, and neutrality became nearly untenable. By 1861, when the first shots were fired, fewer and fewer newspapers—North or South—favored stopping; more and more papers urged their readers to press on and settle the great issue once and for all.

In the decades before the war, the U.S. population was growing and changing. In 1830, according to the U.S. Census, the total population stood at 12.9 million, including 10.5 million people identified as white—meaning that they or their ancestors had come to America from Europe, either free or in some form of temporary servitude. Another 2.3 million were identified as black, meaning that they or their ancestors had come from Africa, almost all of them in bondage. Not all African Americans, however, were slaves in 1830. The census counted a slave population that year of just over 2 million—most but not all of them in the South—as well as a population of more than 300,000 blacks who were free. Those free blacks, constituting almost 14 percent of the black population, lived in both the North and the South, in the city as well as the country. Thirty years later, the 1860 census showed substantial increases. Over the course of one generation, the total U.S. population had risen from under 13 million to more than 31.4 million, including almost 27 million whites and 4.4 million blacks, of whom only 11 percent—or fewer than half a million—were free.[1]

During this period most blacks could not read, for the simple reason that it was a crime in most slave states to teach a slave to read or write. Even the most virulent racists had to acknowledge that blacks had the intellectual capacity required for learning their letters. (Otherwise, why bother to criminalize it?) In fact, the ban on teaching slaves to read was quite practical; it was an essential tool in keeping them from organizing, communicating, and gaining their freedom. This point was not lost on young Frederick Bailey, a slave living in Maryland who later ran away, changed his name to Frederick Douglass, and became one of the most prominent journalists and social activists of his era. Young Frederick was about eight years old when, in 1827, his master sent him to live with and work for Hugh and Sophia Auld in Baltimore. Sophia taught Frederick the alphabet, and she was teaching him to read simple words when her husband discovered them. Douglass recounted the incident in his *Narrative* of his life: "To use his [Auld's] own words, further, he said, ' . . . A nigger should know nothing but to obey his master—to do as he is told to do. Learning would *spoil* the best nigger in the world. Now,' said he, 'if you teach that nigger (speaking of myself) how to read, there would be no keeping him. It would forever unfit him to be a slave. He would at once become unmanageable, and of no value to his master. . . . It would make him discontented and unhappy.' " Looking back on the incident, Douglass declared that this insight into the power of literacy marked the moment when he understood how whites were able to enslave millions of blacks. No less important, it was the moment when he "understood the pathway from slavery to freedom."[2]

In the same period, during the 1820s, free blacks were beginning to form a large enough community to support a newspaper. As it happened, during the very year that Frederick Bailey started learning to read, the first newspaper in America owned by blacks was founded. *Freedom's Journal* began publishing in March 1827 in New York. The editors were the Reverend Samuel Cornish, a minister, and John Russwurm, an alumnus of Bowdoin College, who was the first black person to graduate from an American college. In their first number the editors explained their goal, stating: "We wish to plead our own cause. Too long have others spoken for us." Not surprisingly, the paper was editorially opposed to slavery, and it published the first account of a lynching ever printed in the United States.[3] At the same time, it served its largely black readership by running newsy items of general interest, as well as sermons, poetry, and advertisements.

.*   *   *

JUST A FEW YEARS LATER, black readers also began to support the white abolitionist William Lloyd Garrison and his new weekly, *The Liberator*, which depended heavily at first on black subscribers.[4] Garrison's paper almost did not survive its first year, and Garrison himself almost did not survive the paper's first decade. In August 1831, just eight months after *The Liberator* appeared, a slave named Nat Turner led a brief, bloody rebellion in Virginia. Although there is no reason to believe that even a single copy of *The Liberator* had reached Virginia's Southampton County, and although Garrison explicitly rejected violence (when he heard the news of Turner's uprising, he pronounced himself "horror-struck at the late tidings"),[5] many whites leaped to the conclusion that Garrison was to blame for Turner's insurrection. The publisher was denounced and threatened with death. Across the South, officials took steps to make sure that no copies of *The Liberator* could circulate within their jurisdiction. In Georgia, the legislature offered $5,000 to anyone who could capture Garrison and bring him south to face trial on a charge of seditious libel.[6] Many times in the coming decades, Southern officials would attempt to impose prior restraint on Garrison, with limited success.

None of these efforts at suppression did anything to discourage him; instead, they only added to his growing fame. At first it seemed that just about every one of Garrison's fellow citizens disagreed with him; even among the small number of whites who were coming to oppose slavery, most rejected the fundamentals of Garrisonianism: immediate emancipation and full civil rights for blacks by strictly nonviolent means. Many of those who opposed slavery could not envision a future America in which whites and blacks would live together in equality; most wanted to return the freed slaves to Africa. Thus, from the start of his career as an abolitionist, Garrison was involved in fighting factional political battles inside the antislavery movement, starting with an attack on the idea of colonization, which he denounced as pure racism. Garrison took the position that any person born in the United States is just as much an American as any other, and he never wavered.

As it grew, the abolition movement was wracked by debate over the role of women. Could women belong to a group like the American Anti-Slavery Society? If so, could they speak in public at its meetings—even if that meant they were lecturing their menfolk? Could a woman hold—and state publicly—an opinion different from that of her husband? At the time, these questions were quite urgent. Garrison always favored the most expansive role for women, and the abolition movement became an important training ground for the women (such as Lucretia Mott and Elizabeth Cady Stanton) who would go on to lead the suffrage and women's rights movements. Still later, the focus of movement politics within abolitionism turned to the question of methods. A few radical abolitionists favored violent uprisings like the one John Brown led on the federal arsenal in Harpers Ferry, Virginia, in 1859. Most abolitionists did not endorse violence, and a substantial number believed that abolition would require working within the political system, even if that sometimes meant compromise. Not Garrison. A radical Christian pacifist,[7] Garrison saw all politicians, even Lincoln, as morally compromised, and he would have no truck with them. He never quite managed to explain how abolition was to come about, but he editorialized in favor of moral suasion.

Garrison exhibited a flair for making people angry at him.[8] One reason was his writing style, which was remarkably consistent, right from the launching of *The Liberator* in 1831. Like Paine, whose work he read, Garrison drew heavily from two favorite wellsprings, sources that every American already knew. One was the Declaration of Independence—especially Jefferson's famous passage about all men being created equal, with inalienable rights to life, liberty, and the pursuit of happiness. Garrison saw abolition as the fulfillment of Jefferson's promise and the remedy for the great moral failure of the generation that founded America.[9] Garrison's other great source of inspiration was the Bible, especially the Book of Exodus, for its story of Moses leading the Jews out of slavery in Egypt toward the Promised Land; the Gospels, for their attacks on hypocrites; and the Acts of the

Apostles, for the inspiring power of a small band of true believers to change the world. Above all, Garrison seemed to draw strength from the Hebrew prophets, often quoting Isaiah and Jeremiah. Like them, he warned his people to repent or face some great doom.

Another reason why Garrison became such a focus of criticism and anger was his activism, which was of a piece with his advocacy. He was not content merely to write against slavery; he was also a founder and officer of the New England Anti-Slavery Society and the American Anti-Slavery Society. His activism and his advocacy combined to make him a lightning rod. In the fall of 1835, Garrison came close to losing his life for the cause.[10] The occasion was the first anniversary of the Boston Female Anti-Slavery Society, which was to feature a talk by the radical English abolitionist George Thompson. That news triggered something of an upper-class revolt in Boston, where many of the city's leading merchants had strong business ties to suppliers and customers in the South and therefore had an economic stake in not disrupting slavery. They saw Garrison's calls for abolition as a threat to their livelihoods, and they swung into action. A group of such "patriotic citizens"—including an editor of one of Boston's commercial newspapers—offered a bounty on Thompson, and the merchants paid to print and distribute handbills calling for public action to oppose the "infamous foreign scoundrel."

As it happened, Thompson had already left Boston, but the meeting went ahead anyway on October 21, 1835, inside the headquarters of the ladies' abolitionist group at 45 Washington Street. Drawn by the handbills, men began filling the streets around the site. Their ranks, according to Garrison's biographer Henry Mayer, included "commercial men from the surrounding offices, truckmen and food handlers from nearby Quincy Market, and apprentices and clerks who had slipped out for excitement." Word spread that the English speaker was not there, followed by the rumor that Garrison was on hand instead. At some point in the afternoon, the mob surged toward the building, and Garrison retreated to a small room in the rear. Mayor Theodore Lyman arrived and informed the ladies that he could guarantee their safety only if they left immediately. Arm in arm they made their way out, leaving Garrison to face the mob alone.

Outside, cries went up to give Garrison a lynching, or at least a good tarring. The editor sneaked out a back window and tried to slip away, only to be discovered in the loft of a nearby shop. Members of the mob bound him with a rope and marched him down a ladder to the waiting crowd. At just that moment, two brothers—Daniel and Buff Cooley—stepped forward, hoisted Garrison between them, and swept him away. They made it as far as City Hall, where they deposited Garrison while the crowd, now turning into a lynch mob, thronged outside. The mayor told the editor that the only way he could ensure his safety was to lock him up, so Garrison was ushered out a back door and whisked off to the jail on Leverett Street.[11] When tempers cooled, he was released. In typical fashion, Garrison saw his pursuit by the mob as a reason for renewed devotion. "Give me brickbats in the cause of God," he declared, rather than "wedges of gold in the cause of sin."

Garrison, who was not the only abolitionist editor to face a mob, was lucky to survive. In 1837, just two years after Garrison's escape from the Boston crowd, another met a tragic end.[12] Elijah P. Lovejoy, a native of Maine, was a preacher and the editor of a religious newspaper in St. Louis. He supported the gradual emancipation of slaves, a position that was more moderate than Garrison's but still did not sit well with many of his fellow Missourians. Lovejoy was in an even more vulnerable position than Garrison, since he was living and working near the front lines of the violent struggle over the expansion of slavery to the West. In May 1836, after Lovejoy editorialized against the lynching of a free black man, a white mob attacked his press. Lovejoy moved across the Mississippi River to the town of Alton in the free state of Illinois, but a mob there destroyed his press before he could even unpack it. He vowed to soldier on in the cause of abolition, and his presses were wrecked by mob action twice more. Undeterred, Lovejoy tried in October 1837 to call a meeting to form a Missouri branch of the American Anti-Slavery Society. When told to get out of town, he refused. Sympathizers around the country raised funds for a new printing press. On November 7 the mob returned, only to find Lovejoy and a small group of supporters inside, armed to defend his newest printing press. When Lovejoy came outside to try to prevent a fire on the roof, he was shot five times and killed. Garrison and other abolitionist editors promptly hailed Lovejoy as a martyr to the cause and kept on publishing.[13]

In August 1841, Garrison traveled to the whaling island of Nantucket off the Massachusetts coast for a convention of the Massachusetts Anti-Slavery Society.[14] Late in the day on August 11, a young black man who was not known to Garrison or most of the other abolitionists at the meeting stood up and asked to speak. His name, which he had newly adopted, was Frederick Douglass. At that moment, two men who would prove to be among the most effective and influential editors of the nineteenth century met for the first time. Garrison, thirty-five years old, an austere figure with a soaring forehead and prim spectacles, was already famous, after a decade of journalism, advocacy and controversy. Douglass, thirteen years younger, tall and strong but bearing a scar on his forehead from a beating by a plantation overseer, was a poor and obscure figure. He was only three years removed from slavery himself, having run away from his owner in Maryland. For Douglass to speak in public was not only a personal challenge but also a tremendous risk, since even Massachusetts had its share of slave-catchers who would be only too happy to return a fugitive like Douglass to the horrors of slavery.

For Douglass, the moment he rose to speak was the start of a new chapter. The chapter that was just ending had begun in 1838, when Douglass made his successful escape from slavery with help from his fiancée, Anna Murray. Using travel papers borrowed from a retired black seaman, he fled Baltimore and, relying on the abolitionist network, moved by train and steamboat to Philadelphia and then New York, where he began using the common last name Johnson instead of the identifying slave name Bailey. After he and Anna married, the couple pressed on northward, to New Bedford. Because so many black residents of the town were already named Johnson, Frederick accepted a friend's suggestion and adopted a new last name: Douglass. Thanks to an apprenticeship while still a slave, Douglass was skilled at the caulking trade; but the white caulkers in New Bedford would not tolerate competition, so he was forced to take a job on the docks as an unskilled laborer. While working there, Douglass began to read the abolitionist newspaper published thirty miles away in Boston, Garrison's *Liberator*. "His paper took its place with me next to the bible," Douglass wrote later. "I not only liked—I *loved* this paper, and its editor."[15] He admired Garrison's uncompromising style and his demand for complete emancipation.

Occasionally Douglass would speak during meetings at a black church in New Bedford, and on one of those occasions he was heard by a white abolitionist, William C. Coffin. When the 1841 abolitionist convention was set for Nantucket, just a few miles off the Massachusetts coast from New Bedford, Coffin urged Douglass to attend and to speak. Rising to his feet to address an audience of white listeners, Douglass was so nervous that he could not recall later what he had talked about. According to those who heard him, Douglass gave his first public description to whites of the details of slavery. For many in the audience, abolitionists all, it was a revelation. Garrison was certainly moved. When Douglass finished, Garrison penetrated to the heart of the matter, asking the delegates,

"Have we been listening to a thing, a piece of property, or to a man?"

"A man! A man!" came the reply.

"And should such a man be held as a slave in a republican and Christian land?"

"Never! Never!" shouted the crowd.[16]

With the encouragement of Garrison and others, Douglass was promptly retained as an agent of the Massachusetts Anti-Slavery Society, which supplied him with the means to embark on a new career, traveling around New England to sell subscriptions to *The Liberator* while making regular appearances as a runaway slave who could testify to the shocking, heartrending truth about slavery. Douglass spoke regularly in public about the abuses he had witnessed as a boy, taking pains not to reveal any names or details that would allow his master to track him down and reclaim him. Eventually Douglass tired of the constant retellings and began to chafe. "Give us the facts," one of his abolitionist backers said. "We will take care of the philosophy." But Douglass was not content. "It did not entirely satisfy me to *narrate* wrongs; I felt like *denouncing* them."[17]

So he produced his first great written work, the original version of his autobiography, published in 1845. With encouragement and printing assistance from Garrison, Douglass titled his book *Narrative of the Life of Frederick Douglass, An American Slave*. As if to anticipate the doubters, he added a telling subtitle: *Writ-*

ten by Himself. In a sense, Douglass was using the assertion of authorship to stake a claim for himself as a full human being. The book opened with a preface by Garrison, who assured readers that Douglass had actually written it and that Douglass's experiences were typical of life under slavery. The *Narrative* sold well— thirty thousand copies within five years—and it had the desired effect. Here at last, beyond refutation by Southern apologists, was the bare face of slavery. These were no traveler's tales, no fictional guesswork. Douglass supplied names and dates and details. Seven years before Harriet Beecher Stowe published her novel about slavery, *Uncle Tom's Cabin,* Douglass showed his readers the routine beatings, the gruesome whippings, the sexual predations—the whole sordid spectacle, all from the point of view of an intelligent, sensitive boy growing to manhood.

But for all its success, publication of the *Narrative* presented a fresh peril to Douglass personally by exposing him to the risk of capture. So the fugitive fled once more, this time to England and Ireland, where he was well received. While he was living in England, some supporters even raised the money to purchase Douglass's freedom from his master and owner, Hugh Auld, who—in return for $711.66—declared Douglass "to be henceforth free, manumitted, and discharged from all manner of servitude" as of December 5, 1846. Other friends in England arranged to establish Douglass, upon his return to America as a legally free man, in a business—the same business that Garrison was pursuing. Douglass thought that his friends in the abolition movement would be delighted to welcome him home and into the role of abolitionist editor, but in fact he discovered that they were not. His friends, including Garrison, objected, on the grounds that a new abolitionist newspaper would only undermine *The Liberator* and cut into Douglass's effectiveness as an antislavery speaker. (Some abolitionists had even objected to the purchase of Douglass's freedom on the grounds that it represented acquiescence to the system in which humans could be traded as property. Douglass, understandably, considered the transaction worthwhile.)

Undeterred, Douglass struck out for Rochester, New York, and established his own newspaper, *The North Star,* a four-page weekly. Rochester appealed to Douglass because the city had already supported an antislavery movement for more than a decade and because it could serve as an important relay on the Underground Railroad, helping runaway slaves escape to Canada.[18] In his first edition, on December 3, 1847, Douglass introduced the sweeping motto of *The North Star:* "Right is of no Sex—Truth is of no Color—God is Father of us all, and we are all Brethren." The following year he attended the first women's rights convention, held at Seneca Falls, New York, and took up the second great cause of his life, equal rights for women. For the rest of his career Douglass was a tireless supporter of women's suffrage and other reform causes, as well as a personal friend of Susan B. Anthony and other feminist leaders (fig. 4.1).

At the same time, though, Douglass was losing Garrison as a friend. The two abolitionist editors, now rivals in publishing, fell out over a fundamental issue.

4.1 **FREDERICK DOUGLASS, THE ESCAPED SLAVE** who became a leading abolitionist, spent most of his adult life as a writer and a newspaper editor.
—*Library of Congress.*

Garrison held that the U.S. Constitution was the formal expression of a corrupt bargain made at the founding of the country and that it was designed to protect slavery as a permanent feature of American life. He believed that the Constitution could not be remedied, and he rejected any attempt to work within the system—even to the extent of rejecting the use of the vote to create social change. For Garrison, the only way to achieve reform was to bring about a moral revolution through prayer, agitation, and *The Liberator*. At first, Douglass agreed with Garrison. But after what he called "a careful reconsideration," Douglass came to believe that the Constitution was "in its letter and spirit an anti-slavery instrument" that could be a means of liberation rather than enslavement.[19]

In the pages of *The North Star*, Douglass started to advocate more overtly political tactics in the war against the Slave Power. This was more than Garrison could tolerate, and he withdrew the endorsement of the American Anti-Slavery Society (AAS) from Douglass's paper in 1851. In Garrison's mind, there was not much difference between error and sin; any idea that he judged wrong was also evil. So he gave Douglass the same treatment that he gave most people who disagreed with him: criticism followed by denunciation. That same year Douglass merged his paper with another and began publishing what he called *Frederick Douglass' Paper*. Declaring "All Rights for All!" it challenged *The Liberator* for nearly a decade as the guiding light of the movement. Within two years Douglass and Garrison were engaged in a feud so bitter that Douglass even stopped attending AAS meetings. Although the two editors remained estranged for almost twenty years, their newspapers both succeeded. That is, although neither one ever made much money (in fact, Garrison was almost always nearly broke), they both were effective in advancing the great cause. Both editors criticized the war with Mexico in 1848, denounced the Compromise of 1850, and continued to turn up the heat under the boiling pot of sectional conflict.

By the end of the 1830s it was becoming clear that Garrison and other abolitionist editors were having an impact. The Slave Power struck back with a series of responses, legal and illegal, aimed at silencing the abolitionist press. In addition to mob violence,[20] anti-abolitionists, led by Senator John C. Calhoun and President Andrew Jackson, turned to a set of tactics involving the U.S. Post Office, an institution that had done so much to build the early American press through the free exchange of newspapers.[21] In response to a flood of abolitionist material from Garrison and other Northern opponents of slavery, Virginia passed a law in March 1836 titled "An Act to suppress the circulation of incendiary publications." Aimed at what it called "evil disposed persons," the law made it a crime to incite slave revolts by using the Post Office to distribute "certain incendiary books, pamphlets, or other writings of an inflammatory and mischievous character and tendency." Violators would be punished according to their race: if "a slave or coloured person," they would be whipped; if white, they would be fined. The law also imposed a duty on each Virginia postmaster: if he noticed any abolitionist writings in the mail, he was obligated to have the offending materials "burned in his presence."[22] The First Amendment notwithstanding, the writing and distribution of certain ideas, in certain places, had become a crime.

In addition, the abolitionist press inspired an editorial backlash from Southern and border-state newspapers. The most hot-tempered of the proslavery editors became known as "fire-eaters," and they did their best to live up to the nickname. In general, they argued that blacks were inferior to whites and had no claim to equality, that the Constitution acknowledged slavery, that each state had the power to rule on slavery within its borders, and that "Black Republicans" like Lincoln in league with abolitionist "fanatics" like Garrison were to blame for destroying the Republic. These views were found across the South, in growing uniformity over the years leading up to 1861, as well as in some papers in the North, usually those edited by Democrats like James Gordon Bennett in New York City. With his knack for antagonizing people, Bennett used his *Herald* to blame the entire secession crisis on both the "nigger-drivers" of the South and the "nigger-lovers" of the North.[23]

One incident that drew widespread editorial comment occurred in May 1856, when a member of the U.S. Senate from Massachusetts, Charles Sumner, delivered a blistering rhetorical attack on slavery and its defenders. A member of the House from South Carolina, Preston Brooks, grew so incensed at Sumner's remarks that he entered the Senate Chamber, waited until the ladies had left the gallery, then came up behind Sumner's seat and beat him about the head with a cane. In nearby Richmond, the *Enquirer,* one of the most widely read Southern papers, placed the blame for the assault on the fanaticism of the abolitionists, editorializing: "A community of Abolitionists could only be governed by a penitentiary system. They are as unfit for liberty as maniacs, criminals or wild beasts."[24] While Sumner was still recuperating from his wounds, another Richmond paper, the *Whig,* piled on, insinuating that Sumner had not really been injured at all but was playing possum and staying away from the Senate "to keep alive and diffuse and strengthen the sympathy awakened for him among his confederates in the North, Nigger-worshipping fanatics of the male gender, and weak-minded women and silly children who are horribly affected at the thought of blood oozing from a pin-scratch."[25]

Another prominent "fire-eater" was Robert Barnwell Rhett Jr. of South Carolina, editor of the *Charleston Mercury* and a passionate advocate for states' rights, secession, and racial superiority. Even after war broke out, Rhett kept up his criticisms, only changing the target to Jefferson Davis, the president of the Confederate States. Under many of the same pressures as President Lincoln, Davis tried to expand the powers of his office at the expense of states' prerogatives. Rhett opposed him at every step. The ultimate crisis came late in the war, when Davis proposed using slaves in the Confederate war effort—first as laborers and then, in a desperate last-ditch effort, as soldiers. Warning that if the South asked slaves to fight for their masters, those slaves could be expected to demand their freedom in return, Rhett finally spat out a backhanded compliment to the enslaved population: "To expect the negroes to fight on our side for less is simply absurd. He may not be a creature particularly given to logic or to metaphysical reasoning; but he is not altogether a monkey."[26]

*   *   *

PROBABLY THE MOST INFLUENTIAL NEWSPAPERMAN of the era was Horace Greeley, the printer-editor at the helm of the *New York Tribune,* a tireless advocate for reform who operated as a party of one. Promoting his program of temperance, women's rights, free labor, and western expansion, Greeley came to focus more and more of his attention on the vexed issue of slavery. During the 1850s, owing in part to the efforts of Garrison and Douglass, slavery became the predominant issue, in journalism as well as in politics.

Unlike some of his rivals in New York City, such as Bennett, Greeley was never much of a reporter. He was a first-rate printer, however, and a champion at spotting talent in others. Among the writers who toiled for Greeley were a young German correspondent named Karl Marx (who contributed about 350 articles over a dozen years),[27] the brilliant proto-feminist Margaret Fuller, and a young Missourian named Samuel Clemens, who wrote under the name Mark Twain. Greeley also had the good sense to hire Charles A. Dana, his accomplished (and far better organized) managing editor. And he relied on his publisher to handle all business matters for the *Tribune.*

Under those arrangements, Greeley and his paper flourished. By the end of the 1850s, Greeley's daily *Tribune* was selling 55,000 copies a day in New York City, putting him in third place among penny press editors behind Bennett at the *Herald* (77,000) and Benjamin Day of the *Sun* (60,000). But since Greeley compiled articles from the daily *Tribune* into a weekly edition delivered by mail that sold a mammoth 200,000 copies a week, "Uncle Horace," as he was known to his many loyal subscribers in the countryside, was read by probably half a million people every week—this at a time when the total population in the North was only about 13 million and the literate adult population less than half that. In other words, among roughly 6 million literate adults, Greeley was read by at least one out of every dozen people.[28]

In New York State and on the national stage, Greeley was an important political figure in his own right. Like many other editors in the first half of the nineteenth century, he was deeply involved in partisan causes—first with the Whig Party, then with the Republicans. He served part of a brief (and undistinguished) term in Congress, and several times sought the governor's post in Albany. Behind the scenes he was perennially active as a kingmaker at the Whig and Republican national conventions, and he even ran for president in 1872 in the hope of unseating the hard-drinking, cigar-smoking war hero Ulysses S. Grant. In their wisdom, the voters rejected Greeley by a wide margin.

Horace Greeley's real genius was for editorializing. In their day, those editorials made Greeley one of the best-known and certainly one of the most influential men of his era. Far more than whatever business or political success he found, his impact as an editorialist was a towering achievement. With that influence he sought uplift, reform, and improvement. He was seriously committed to finding progressive answers to social problems like poverty and "idleness." He wanted to make all of America what he would consider a better place—by which he meant a morally decent and prosperous place. He tried to sustain and renew the American facility for compromise, although he ultimately lost out to journalistic radicals like Garrison and political radicals like Calhoun. On the great issue of his day—slavery and the threat it posed to America's precious liberty and union—Greeley moved steadily toward the view that slavery was wrong and must be stopped. Although an ardent polemicist, Greeley was never a radical abolitionist; he did not demand, as Garrison did, the immediate emancipation of the slaves. Until the Civil War broke out, Greeley was content to let the South keep its slavery and even depart the Union. In the 1850s one of the major themes of Greeley's editorials was the need to stop the expansion of slavery into the new states of the West. There he demanded free labor on free soil. In his role as editorialist, Greeley had an instinct for carving out stances that would challenge public opinion without getting too far in front of it.

Although not a radical agitator in a class with Garrison, Greeley still came in for his share of criticism. Southern newspapers blasted him, and one Southern politician, Congressman Albert Rust of Arkansas, was moved to give Greeley a beating when they met on the streets of Washington in 1856. While still in Washington nursing his wounds, Greeley fought back, declaring in the *Tribune,* "My business here is to unmask hypocrisy, defeat treachery and rebuke meanness."[29] More often, Greeley was attacked with words. His chief antagonist, Bennett of the *New York Herald,* rarely missed a chance to abuse him. In 1857, when the *Tribune* was suffering financial losses in the general economic panic, Bennett chortled at the thought that the *Tribune* might fold, exulting, "Nigger worship is nearly at its close . . . anti-slavery agitation is going down, and . . . whenever it becomes defunct, the *Tribune's* nigger circulation will collapse."[30]

The activism of Garrison, Douglass, and Greeley culminated in the election of 1860. Greeley attended the Republican Party convention in Chicago that year and, by working to block the nomination of his fellow New Yorker William Seward, helped swing the nomination to Abraham Lincoln. Like Greeley, Lincoln was opposed to the expansion of slavery; unlike Greeley, Lincoln would not tolerate secession by any of the slave states. When Lincoln won the election, the outcome provided an occasion for every newspaper in the country to interpret the fateful step. Most of the "fire-eaters" across the South saw Lincoln as a "fanatic" Black Republican who threatened their region with immediate emancipation (although he did not).

Someone who really did seek immediate emancipation was Garrison, still publishing his abolitionist weekly up in Boston. In the pages of *The Liberator,* Garrison expressed some disappointment that Lincoln was not more of a radical, and he went on to observe that Southern slaveholders were being driven mad by their own wickedness and by their mistaken perception that Lincoln was an abolitionist: "They are insane from their fears, their guilty forebodings, their lust for power and rule, their hatred of free institutions, their consciousness of merited judgments; so that they may be properly classed with the inmates of a lunatic asylum."[31]

In the pages of the *Tribune,* Greeley responded to Lincoln's election by straining to articulate a reason for his readers to hold fast to the shrinking parcel of political common ground that remained. He praised Lincoln's victory but wrestled with the options it presented to the divided nation. Lincoln could continue trying to compromise with slavery; he could let the slave states secede; or he could wage war to stop them. With Northern opinion tilting against slavery, Greeley found compromise no longer an option. At the same time, he also rejected war, which he called "a hideous necessity at best."[32] In the end, he argued that the least bad choice was to call the South's bluff and let slave states secede rather than coerce them with violence.

Almost no one foresaw what actually happened. No prominent newspaper predicted—and certainly none endorsed—a war to preserve the Union that would last four years, cost more than 600,000 lives, and end up freeing the slaves. That was one outcome, and perhaps the only one, that had no prominent advocate on the eve of the Civil War.

*   *   *

IN THE WINTER OF 1860–61, Abraham Lincoln found himself in a nearly impossible situation as he tried to prevent war. Elected in November 1860 with less than a majority of the vote, he was forced to watch the Union come apart before he could even take office on March 4. Among his many tribulations were the nation's newspapers. By the time of Lincoln's election, most of the successful large-circulation daily newspapers were prosperous enough to be independent of the political parties. Using the business model pioneered by Benjamin Day, editors now made money by selling papers to a mass audience and selling that audience to advertisers. No longer dependent on the government for subsidies, they not only stood apart from the political parties but also tried to dictate to them. So even when the parties attempted, as they did, to compromise or find nonviolent remedies, the editors of the mass-circulation dailies—North and South—were free to push their own views and urge rejection of compromise. From the start, political factions and parties had used compromise to govern America, beginning with the adoption of the Constitution itself. Again in 1820, leaders of the major political parties were able to compromise, this time over slavery in Missouri. But by the 1850s, the politicians were finding it harder to reach compromises—and to make them stick. Among the reasons must be counted the growing influence of these newspapers, whose editors had a stake in expanding circulation, not in winning elections or preserving national unity. Their paramount goal was to sell more papers, in war as well as in peace.

While Lincoln was still preparing to take office, South Carolina became the first state to secede, on December 20, 1860 (fig. 4.2). As he brought his state out of the Union, the governor offered a public statement of his views, relying in part on the arguments made by none other than the Yankee editor Horace Greeley. But there was no true meeting of the minds. In fact, the reality of secession, after so many years of discussion, debates, and threats, had a galvanizing effect on attitudes in both the North and the South. Confronting that reality, Greeley now thundered against the new Confederacy and demanded something he had not suggested previously: a final showdown between "the Slave Power" and "the Union."

With the bombing of Fort Sumter in Charleston Harbor on April 12, 1861,[33] attitudes rapidly hardened. The *Tribune,* suddenly dropping its opposition to war, declared: "Fort Sumter is lost, but Freedom is saved. . . . We are at war. Let us stop mere fending off and strike home."[34] Across the North and the South, newspapers fell into a familiar pattern: once the shooting started, most debate stopped. Newspapers dropped their calls for moderation and now tried to outdo one another in showing their loyalty and declaring their belligerence. According to one study of newspaper coverage of the secession crisis, "the attack on Fort Sumter, and

the way in which newspapers presented the story and explained its implications, hardened opposition to compromise, reinforcing the fear and hostility of the people in one region toward those in the other."[35] Even Bennett, who had long supported the South and routinely denounced "niggers" and their supporters, suddenly ordered the Stars and Stripes hoisted above the *Herald*'s office and came out in favor of preserving the Union. Whatever their level of enthusiasm, most newspapers mustered into a regional consensus, demanding loyalty to the new cause and denouncing the other side.

In this new climate of militancy, Greeley suddenly began calling on Lincoln to act more swiftly and decisively to crush the rebellion. Repeatedly the *Tribune* promoted its new slogan "Forward to Richmond!" in an editorial campaign urging an immediate federal assault on the Confederate capital, less than a hundred miles south of Washington. Pressured by the demands of Greeley and other editors, Lincoln agreed to the decision to attack at Bull Run in June 1861, before federal troops (or most members of the press corps) were ready. Because the battlefield was so near the federal capital, reporters turned out in great numbers, along with dignitaries and other curious onlookers. At first the Union troops had the advantage, and reporters raced one another to describe the great victory. Later, however, when the tide of battle turned, most newspapers failed to get the late word. As a result, when readers in Northern cities finally received something like a straight story several days later, the news was not just bad; it was late. When the loss sank in, Greeley for one was apoplectic with guilt and regret, at least for the moment.

Part of the confusion in the early reporting about Bull Run can be laid to the press corps and its lack of experience. Only a few old hands had been through the war with Mexico thirteen years earlier, and almost no American correspondents had ventured to the scene of the most recent major war, in the Crimea. As a result, the average reporter was as raw as the average recruit, uneasy in the smoke and danger of battle and unable to tell a flanking movement from a retreat. Correspondents also tended to overheat their prose with heroic adjectives, something most of them soon outgrew.

There was another reason for the confusion surrounding Bull Run: censorship. For the first time, an American president was attempting to impose a systematic regime of censorship as a matter of government-wide policy. In previous wars, beginning with the Revolution and continuing through the War of 1812 and the Mexican War, individual commanders had barred journalists, or sometimes detained them physically, in order to protect a military advantage. But such efforts were usually piecemeal and not very effective. Besides, in those earlier wars it usually took correspondents so long to relay their stories home and get them printed that the information no longer had any military significance. By 1861, however, war was unfolding in a new setting. This war, fought on home soil, is often called the first modern war because of several critical new technolo-

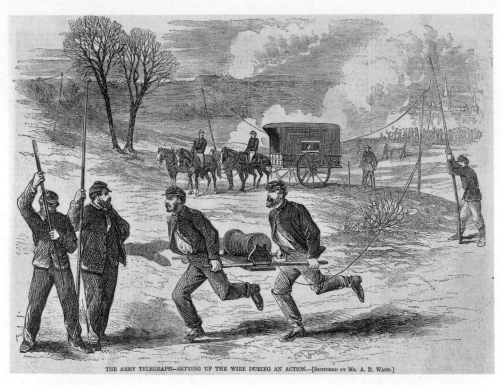

THE ARMY TELEGRAPH—SETTING UP THE WIRE DURING AN ACTION.—[Sketched by Mr. A. R. Waud.]

4.3 **SOLDIERS RUSH TO STRING TELEGRAPH WIRE** during "an action" in the Civil War. Sketch artist Alfred Waud drew this image for *Harper's Weekly* in 1863 to illustrate the importance of the telegraph in speeding up communications—which was critical to journalists as well as soldiers. —*Harper's Weekly.*

gies. With steam engines, thousands of troops could cover distances in days that once took months, and steel-clad steamships could lay waste a traditional navy of wood and sail. With the telegraph, commanders could send orders—and reporters could send stories—in minutes rather than days (fig. 4.3). Everything about the Civil War occurred on a scale without precedent in the experience of Americans, including censorship.

The Lincoln administration began imposing censorship within days of the Confederate attack on Fort Sumter. Thanks to the telegraph, it was a fairly straightforward task. Almost all the lines connecting the South to Northern cities such as Philadelphia, New York, and Boston passed through Washington, so the physical means of stopping transmissions was readily at hand. About a month after the attack on Sumter, top officials of the American Telegraph Company met in Washington and decided to split into separate Northern and Southern companies. Then federal officials seized telegraph offices in Louisville that had been handling most of the rest of the North-South telegraph traffic. Those moves effectively sealed off the two regions from each other.

But what about correspondents working within territory held by the North? The Lincoln administration had two means of censoring the news. In some cases, reporters were not allowed to leave a battle zone without first submitting drafts of their stories to a military official on the scene. Alternatively, dispatches were stopped in Washington and read by a military censor stationed in the telegraph office.[36] It was a matter of dispute whether such measures violated the First Amendment, but it was a matter of fact that press censorship was one of several areas (suspension of the right to habeas corpus being the most prominent) in which Lincoln's wartime government pushed the Constitution to the breaking point in the name of national survival. At Bull Run, censorship compounded the confusion over the outcome. Reporters who returned to Washington and filed their stories early were allowed to transmit the impression of Union success. When their colleagues limped in later with news of a Union defeat, military censors would not allow their copy to be transmitted until the following day.

Civil War censorship did not make anyone completely happy. The Lincoln administration learned that it is one thing to announce a policy and another to enforce it. In practice, the enforcement of censorship was hit or miss, for several reasons. For one, since the war was being fought on native ground, correspondents found ways and means of evading censors—for example, by sending news accounts via mail rather than telegraph, by hopping on a train and traveling back to the home office to write the story there, or by resorting to all sorts of subterfuges, like smuggling news copy past guards or bribing officials with whisky or cash. In extreme cases, some correspondents fell back on older methods like carrier pigeons to evade telegraphic censorship. In addition, Northern generals interpreted policy to suit themselves. Some enjoyed seeing their names in print and—perhaps with an eye to running for office someday—cultivated correspondents. Others were notorious for hating the press and went beyond measures that were strictly necessary. General William Tecumseh Sherman, for example, developed a loathing for reporters (which may be traceable to a rash of stories early in the war that called him "insane") and constantly threatened to treat them as spies, which could have meant death by hanging. Another Union general, Joseph "Fighting Joe" Hooker, hit upon a different device for controlling correspondents: he ordered them to begin their stories with bylines, which had been rather rare in newspapers up to that point, as a way of holding individual reporters accountable.[37] Little did he know that he was nurturing a trend that would one day make some journalists better known than most generals.

The press had other problems with the Lincoln administration. In the North, a sizable minority of newspapers remained opposed to the war for the duration. While most newspaper editors decided to support both the war and the commander in chief once the shooting began, some did not. The most virulent, usually associated with the "Copperhead" movement of Democrats whose top priority was peace, editorialized in favor of stopping the war at any cost. Some even advised young men to evade the draft or urged soldiers to desert. Lincoln was often pounded in the press, even by editors who generally approved of the war.

Not only were his policies attacked and his judgment questioned, but also Lincoln was personally vilified: he was routinely depicted as an ape, often cartooned in the arms of a black harlot; he was also branded a butcher, called the "widow-maker," or condemned as a "nigger-lover." This much he put up with. What he could not tolerate was outright support for the Confederacy or its corollary, editorial encouragement of Northern men to desert from the Union Army. Lincoln saw some of these editorials, as presidents are inclined to do, as acts of treason. At one point, in a letter to a prominent New York Democrat, Lincoln asked: "Must I shoot a simple-minded soldier boy who deserts, while I must not touch a hair of the wily agitator who induces him to desert?"[38] On several occasions, Union commanders seized or suppressed newspapers that they felt were willfully undermining the war effort.[39]

As it became clear that the war would not end quickly, newspapers adjusted. During the war years, the news business actually enjoyed something of a boom, at least in the North. Profits rose, advertising rose, circulation rose, and prices followed, reaching five cents a copy at most Northern papers by 1865.[40] With the surge in demand for war information, many publishers overcame their reluctance to do business on the Christian Sabbath and started offering Sunday editions. In the pages of the typical newspaper, the war brought change as well. Stories about battles and lists of casualties moved to the front page, displacing the ads for quack remedies. The War Department did not consider it the government's duty to inform families about the fate of their loved ones, so newspapers stepped in and supplied what was often the only information available about the dead and wounded.[41] More and better maps and portraits began to appear in newspapers, along with etchings and line drawings. The technology of printing still did not allow photographs to appear on a page alongside text, so it was impossible for newspapers to display the fruits of the emerging field of photojournalism. Instead, they relied on sketch artists, including the young Winslow Homer and Thomas Nast, to provide drawings suitable for the printing process (fig. 4.4). All of this cost money. Newspapers were earning and spending money as never before. One historian has found that the cost of keeping a correspondent in the field for a year ranged from at least $1,000 to as much as $5,000 (depending largely on how many horses the man wore out or had shot out from under him and needed to replace). No newspaper outdid or outspent Bennett's *Herald*, which employed a roster of sixty-three different correspondents over the course of the war and spent as much as $750,000 on telegraph charges alone.[42]

As the newspapers adapted, so did the government. By late 1861 the Lincoln administration was actively managing war news in ways that went beyond censorship. Secretary of War Edwin M. Stanton and other top officials granted exclusive access to Associated Press reporters such as Lawrence Gobright; in return, the AP reporters filed dispatches that tended to portray all developments from

4.4 **WINSLOW HOMER DREW THIS SKETCH** of a sharpshooter during the Civil War. Because it was not technically feasible to print photographs and text on the same page, newspapers sent artists to the battlefields to make quick sketches that could be turned into engravings, which could be printed alongside text.
—*National Gallery of Art.*

the administration's point of view. "The wire service was an authoritative source for news throughout the military conflict," one historian has written. "The government supplied it exclusively with its bulletins and official announcements, and the AP assumed the position of a semi-official medium for the distribution of information emanating from sources in the administration."[43] For its part, the AP rarely broke news and stuck mainly to Washington, while the newspapers flooded the theaters of war with their special correspondents—or "specials," as they were known. Lincoln also broke with tradition by not establishing or designating any particular newspaper to serve as his official organ. This decision may have been based in part on the creation in 1860 of the Government Printing Office, leaving the president without valuable printing contracts that he could use to subsidize such a paper.[44]

While his administration handled the AP, Lincoln himself cultivated certain editors—Horace Greeley above all. Lincoln even reserved a pigeonhole above his desk just for correspondence from the *Tribune* editor.[45] By late 1861, Lincoln had mastered the technique of favoring Greeley with certain tidbits in order to gauge public reaction. "The arrangement suited both their purposes," historian Richard Kluger has noted, because it allowed Lincoln to float "trial balloons" in the *Tribune,* while the exclusive access kept Greeley happy. "Having him firmly behind me," Lincoln wrote of Greeley, "will be as helpful as an army of 100,000 men."[46]

He would need that support. In the summer of 1863 came the titanic struggle of Gettysburg, perhaps the greatest news story in the greatest conflict of the nineteenth century. The massed strength of the Union and Confederate armies more or less collided at Gettysburg in early July 1863. Confederate general Robert E. Lee invaded Pennsylvania with a force of more than seventy thousand men. He met the Union Army under General George Meade (Ulysses S. Grant had not yet been promoted to overall command of the army) with a force of about ninety thousand. For three days they fought ferociously, often hand to hand, on the fields and hillsides of the small town. Amid the smoke and confusion, the gunfire and death, a squadron of journalists was on hand to attempt to record the action. To do that, they would need all the skill and experience they had gained during the first two years of the war, since at most points during the battle, even the commanders could not say with any precision what was happening.

Some correspondents were tested to the extreme. Consider Sam Wilkeson, who had left the *Tribune* to work for the *New-York Times,* which had become a success since its founding as a Republican paper in 1851. Wilkeson was among the reporters at Gettysburg, and in the early going he learned that his own son, Lieutenant Bayard Wilkeson of the Fourth U.S. Artillery, had been wounded in the leg in the initial skirmishing. In fact, his son met a gruesome death. Lieutenant Wilkeson was indeed wounded in the leg, which landed him in an army field hospital, set up in a barn. While he was undergoing an operation (probably an amputation, almost certainly without benefit of anesthesia or antibiotics), some Confederate forces drew near the barn. The army doctors left the young Wilkeson to die, and that is where his father found him. Sam Wilkeson buried his son, and then, in a burst of professional zeal, went on to file his news story. He wrote:

> Headquarters, Army of the Potomac, Saturday Night, July 4:
> Who can write the history of a battle whose eyes are immovably fastened upon a central figure of transcendingly absorbing interest—the dead body of an eldest born, crushed by a shell in a position where a battery should never have been sent, and abandoned to death in a building where surgeons dared not to stay?

A bit further along in his dispatch, Wilkeson allowed himself this observation:

> My pen is heavy. . . . O, you dead, who died at Gettysburg have baptized with your blood the second birth of freedom in America, how you are to be envied. I rise from a grave of wet clay I have passionately kissed, and I look up to see Christ spanning this battlefield.[47]

He then resumed his account of the fighting, including a list of the names and regiments of dozens of the dead and wounded (fig. 4.5).

Shortly after the Union success at Gettysburg, General Grant added a victory at Vicksburg, giving many Northerners reason to hope that the tide had swung toward ultimate triumph. But those victories had come at tremendous cost in soldiers killed and wounded. With an insatiable need for more troops, the Lincoln administration issued a call for a draft. Under the terms of the conscription act passed a few months earlier, all men aged eighteen to forty-five had to register for duty (if married, only up to age thirty). But men could avoid service by paying $300 instead—a provision that was bitterly denounced as further evidence that

4,5 **CIVIL WAR DEAD.** The state of the art of photography during the Civil War prevented cameras from taking photos fast enough to stop action. As a result, to avoid blurred images, all subjects had to be either posed or dead. (In some cases, they were both posed and dead, if photographers moved corpses to make a better composition.) These are bodies gathered for burial at Gettysburg, photographed by Alexander Gardner. —*Library of Congress.*

the North was waging "a rich man's war but a poor man's fight." Many of the poorest and most resentful of draft-age men lived in New York City. Among the city's large and growing working class, especially among the Irish immigrants, many people opposed the war and the Lincoln administration. New immigrants felt little commitment to the Northern cause, since they had not enslaved anyone, and they questioned why they should fight to liberate millions of people who, when freed, would just become their competitors for jobs. Several New York newspapers, including Bennett's *Herald,* encouraged resistance to the draft.

Officials began drawing names out of a big drum at the local draft board on Saturday, July 11. Two days later, when the drawing resumed, violence broke out. A team of firefighters, who had thought they were exempt from military service, showed up and burned down the government office. Suddenly, mobs swept into the city's streets, including many Irish. Shouting, "Down with the rich!" they beat a police superintendent, then rushed to the Colored Orphan Asylum at Fifth Avenue and Forty-fourth Street and torched the building. "People of all walks of life were suddenly threatened by a war within a war at their doorsteps," one historian wrote, noting that the three days of violence, which killed an estimated 119 people, were the worst domestic disturbance in U.S. history.[48]

In Printing House Square, near New York's City Hall, editors of the city's prowar Republican newspapers braced for the worst. Henry Raymond, editor of the *Times,* had used his contacts in the administration to secure three Gatling guns from the army; two were positioned in upper windows, the third on the roof. At the *Tribune,* Greeley (an instinctive pacifist who had reluctantly become a supporter of the war and the draft that maintained it) refused to take defensive measures, reportedly declaring: "Do not bring a musket into the building. Let them strike the first blow. All my life I have worked for the workingmen; if they would now burn my office and hang me, why, let them do it."[49] They nearly did just that. A mob quickly formed outside the *Tribune* building, where one leader denounced Greeley as "a goddamned scoundrel and a damned abolitionist" and promised to cut the editor's heart out.[50] That evening, rioters burst in and started a fire. Just then, police arrived in force, and *Tribune* staffers managed to put the fire out. In solidarity, Raymond sent over sixteen *Times* employees armed with rifles. Greeley, meanwhile, was safely out to dinner with friends, who wanted to make sure he was far from the expected attack. During the night of violence, all but three *Tribune* staffers fled. Even so, the newspaper appeared on schedule the next day, with a front page full of riot news. After three days, the riots were suppressed by several regiments of regular army troops, and the draft resumed in August.

As the war ground on, many people began to see a Northern victory as inevitable, the only question being when the end would come. In March 1865, Union forces retook the prize of Charleston, South Carolina. When the news reached Boston, William Lloyd Garrison—still publishing his *Liberator* every week, as he had for thirty-four years—spoke to a cheering crowd in Boston's Music Hall. During his speech, Garrison stood on an auction block that had once been a fixture in the Charleston slave market. Under his feet was a Confederate flag.[51] A few weeks later, Secretary of War Edwin Stanton invited Garrison to join the dignitaries at Fort Sumter for the ceremony to raise the U.S. flag—the same one that had come down in April 1861—above Charleston Harbor. While Garrison was there, news came of Lee's surrender to Grant at Appomattox on April 9, touching off celebrations among the visitors and among Charleston's population of newly freed former slaves.[52]

Less than a week later, President Lincoln allowed himself the treat of seeing a play. He left the Executive Mansion with Mrs. Lincoln and proceeded to his box at Ford's Theatre. Not far away, Lawrence Gobright, the chief Washington correspondent for the Associated Press, was on duty. "I was sitting in my office alone, everything quiet," Gobright recounted in his memoir. "A hasty step was heard at the entrance of the door, and a gentleman addressed me, in a hurried and excited manner, informing me that the President had been assassinated, and telling me to come with him! I at first could scarcely believe the intelligence."[53] Before heading to the theater to report firsthand, Gobright swung by the telegraph office and filed a bulletin that stands as a model of the factual, summarizing "news lead"—a form of compressed communication almost unknown before the war. In haste, while the president still lingered between life and death, Gobright wrote the following twelve-word sentence: "The president was shot in a theatre tonight and perhaps mortally wounded."[54]

*   *   *

HOW WELL DID AMERICAN JOURNALISTS cover the Civil War? How did they meet the tests presented by modern battle and by government censorship? One assessment comes from Phillip Knightley in his magisterial survey of war reporting, *The First Casualty.* His judgment is severe: "The majority of Northern correspondents were ignorant, dishonest, and unethical . . . the dispatches they wrote were frequently inaccurate, often invented, partisan and inflammatory."[55] There is certainly ample evidence to support the charge: from Fort Sumter to the siege of Richmond, in the reporting on nearly every battle, errors can be found. Some were trivial, others not. Some were the result of innocent mistakes, others not. Still, the record of Civil War reporting is so vast that it is not a simple matter to come to an overall assessment.

First, consider some of the handicaps borne by the several hundred "special correspondents" who did the bulk of the war reporting:

- Correspondents lacked experience in covering war, certainly at the outset. Many correspondents were in their twenties, and some were still teenagers.

- Pay was low, usually no more than $25 a week and sometimes as little as $10.

- Editors were demanding, always harassing their correspondents for the latest news and casualty lists. In an extreme example, Wilbur Storey of the *Chicago Times* sent this infamous order to his correspondents in the field: "Telegraph fully all news you can get and when there is no news send rumors."[56]

- Many of the field commanders hated correspondents and threatened to treat them as spies. Sherman, in particular, did such a thorough job of chasing away the "buzzards" of the press that when he made his march to the sea through the South, few reporters dared take note.[57] Thus, while Sherman was busy inventing the modern approach to "total war" by attacking the South's industry and infrastructure, readers were left in the dark.

In routine circumstances the life of a "special" was a difficult one of constant danger, accompanied by relentless heat, dust, and thirst.[58]

Even so, the journalists of the Civil War era could point to several innovations, some of them quite significant:

- Under the pressure of time and space constraints, and spurred by the need to pay telegraph fees by the word, correspondents developed a new style, the "hard news lead," which opened their stories with a paragraph that briskly summarized the major points.[59] Those correspondents also had an unlikely writing coach in the person of Secretary of War Stanton. During the war, Stanton issued nearly daily bulletins that were relayed verbatim by the AP and printed widely, usually on front pages. They were models of brevity and clarity.[60]

- Another major change was the emergence of the correspondent as an important figure in his own right. This can be seen in the spread of the use of bylines, which were virtually unheard of before the war.

- In terms of design, wartime newspapers began adding rows, or "decks," to their headlines so as to provide more information more quickly. Newspapers also made increased use of graphics, especially maps depicting major battles.

- Another great wartime achievement was the record of photojournalism assembled by Mathew Brady and his assistants. They took thousands of photographs, many of which are now part of our national memory. Although the technology did not yet exist to print the photos in newspapers, they were often used by newspapers' sketch artists to make the woodcuts and lithographs that illustrated the papers during the war (fig. 4.6).

Overall, then, the record of Civil War journalism is a mixture of failures and successes. Across the South, many newspapers simply collapsed. Across the North, though, most of the essential features of the modern newspaper industry had survived the war, often strengthened. The new business model, pioneered in the 1830s, proved its resilience. There was no turning back to the older master-journeyman-apprentice model of the colonial print shop, with its hand-powered presses and its web of mutual obligations. The new model had called for a complete overhaul of operations, which now involved many more employees, in specialized roles. There was a publisher in the business office; there were editors and reporters in the newsroom and printers and compositors in the press room—nearly every one of them a hired hand. Sales of ads brought in a significant share of revenues, which were now high enough to allow the papers not simply to operate independently of political parties or the government but to try to influence their actions. Increased amounts of capital and new technology allowed steam-powered printing, which could produce enough copies fast enough to reach audiences of unprecedented scale. As a result, sales were now measured in the tens of thousands. The newspaper had become, in sum, a factory.

For all its faults, American journalism emerged from the war with a set of practices that made it faster, more visual, and more aggressive than ever before. The next generation would push all those trends even further.

4.6 MATHEW BRADY used this wagon to bring glass plates and other gear into the field under a government contract to document the Civil War. Many photographs made by Brady or his assistants provided the basis for engravings that were used to illustrate news of the war. —*Library of Congress.*

Horace Greeley stumbled several times late in his career. In 1864 he made a clumsy attempt to open peace talks with Confederate agents; in 1867 he was one of three signers of a bond that bailed Jefferson Davis out of jail. For both actions he was severely criticized. Nevertheless, he topped off his career in 1872 by being nominated by the Democratic Party for the presidency. He lost the election to Ulysses S. Grant just days after losing his wife. Within a few weeks Greeley lost his mind, then his life. He died on November 29, 1872.

After seeing his last Liberator to press on January 1, 1866, exactly thirty-five years after the first issue, William Lloyd Garrison retired, in a fashion. He remained active politically, supporting equal rights for blacks, women, immigrants, and Native Americans, while also traveling. Late in life he had a glimpse of two new inventions: the telephone and the typewriter. When he died in 1879, one of his eulogies was delivered by his former protégé, Frederick Douglass.

For his part, Douglass moved to Washington, took over a publication he called The New National Era, *campaigned for women's rights and against the rise of Jim Crow in the South, and, after his wife, Anna's, death, married a white woman. He was appointed to a number of government posts, including U.S. minister to Haiti, and he helped a young journalist, Ida B. Wells, lead a campaign against lynching. He died in 1895.*

Crusaders and Conservatives, 1875–1912

JOURNALISM IN YELLOW AND GRAY

It will be my earnest aim that the New York Times *give the news, all the news, . . . impartially,*
without fear or favor, regardless of any party, sect or interest involved.
—Adolph Ochs, 1896

We muck-raked not because we hated our world but because we loved it.
—Ray Stannard Baker, 1945

AFTER THE GREAT BATTLEFIELD triumphs by Northern armies at Gettysburg and Vicksburg in the summer of 1863, the Union's ultimate victory was
practically assured. President Lincoln, however, still faced a pressing problem:
his army had suffered so many casualties that summer that he would need many,
many more men to fill up its battered ranks. But where would he find them? The
draft riots in the summer of 1863 proved that it would be difficult. So the Lincoln
administration sent recruiting agents far and wide, and they were none too particular about the kind of men they signed up. In addition, American towns that
could not meet their quotas for recruits were vying to find young men anywhere
they could. It was becoming a soldier's market.

Thousands of miles away, in the city of Mako in what is now Hungary, a young
man named Joseph Pulitzer had a very different problem: he despised his stepfa-
ther and couldn't get away from him fast enough. At age seventeen the scrawny,
nearsighted boy tried to enlist in the Austrian army. He was rejected. Then he
heard about a U.S. recruiter in Hamburg who was offering to pay travel expenses
to America for new soldiers, plus a bounty of $100. A recruit didn't even have
to speak English (which was good, because Pulitzer couldn't). Soon, it was on
to Antwerp to board the ship that would take him across the Atlantic. When
he arrived in Boston, though, Pulitzer decided that he could improve on the
recruiter's promises. He sneaked off and made his way to New York City, where

he presented himself for duty and pocketed close to $200. Although not much of a physical specimen, Pulitzer was already exhibiting those qualities—daring, will-power, and a head for making money—that would turn this desperate teenager into the publisher of America's biggest newspaper in little more than twenty years from the day he landed on the shores of a country where he had no friends, no family, and almost no money.[1]

After the Civil War, a new generation that included Joseph Pulitzer brought dramatic and lasting change to American journalism. Unlike previous generations, most of these new leaders did not come from New England or from Great Britain (as had Franklin, Paine, and Greeley). Many of the most prominent new figures came out of the West: Mark Twain from the river towns of Missouri, the silver-mining camps of Nevada, and the boomtowns of California; Joseph Pulitzer from his adopted home in St. Louis; William Randolph Hearst, blessed with his father's silver-mining fortune, from San Francisco; and Adolph Ochs, the future owner of the *New York Times,* out of Tennessee. To make their mark, they all felt they had to come east, to the city that was by now clearly established as the media capital of America—New York, which by 1890 was home not only to the nation's biggest newspapers but also to its leading magazines and its major telegraph and telephone companies. Once they arrived in New York, these men made their way to one city block in particular—to Park Row in lower Manhattan, just a stone's throw from City Hall, where the publishers of the great dailies strove to outdo one another by putting up ever higher and finer skyscrapers.[2] By expanding on the innovations of the penny press, they were able to create a new kind of journalism; indeed, it was called "the new journalism" until the nickname "yellow journalism" came along. They completed the commercialization of the news and turned the big-city daily paper into a powerhouse of immense profit, personal fame, and political influence.

For many Americans, the decades after the Civil War began as a time of disappointment and disillusionment. The struggle over Reconstruction in the South pleased almost no one. In the end, a cynical compromise between the major parties in 1877 left freed blacks in the South little better off than they had been under slavery. In Washington, the administration of Ulysses S. Grant proved to be one of the most corrupt in history. In New York City, the local government was even more corrupt, if that was possible. Under Henry Raymond's successor, George Jones, the *New York Times* conducted one of the first successful exposés of municipal corruption during the early 1870s. The target was the notorious political boss William M. Tweed, leader of New York City's Democratic Party, headquartered at Tammany Hall. The *Times* obtained and published documentary evidence that "Boss" Tweed and his gang were milking the taxpayers. In this crusade the paper found an ally in *Harper's Weekly,* where cartoonist Thomas Nast depicted the Tammany gang as a rampaging tiger.[3] In the end, the newspapers drove Tweed

5.1 **CARTOONIST THOMAS NAST** elevated the practice of editorial cartooning and put it in the service of political reform. After sketching scenes of the Civil War, Nast became one of the most celebrated cartoonists of the late nineteenth century, creating lasting images of Santa Claus and the mascots of the major political parties. Nast's greatest target was the corrupt Tammany Hall politician known as "Boss Tweed."

—*Library of Congress.*

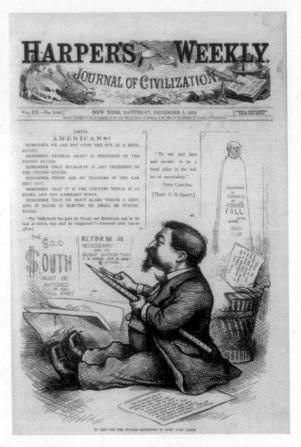

from power. It would have been premature to say they stamped out corruption in New York City, but they did show what was possible for a crusading form of journalism to accomplish (fig. 5.1).

* * *

THE NEXT BURST OF INNOVATION in American journalism emerged in the 1880s, and it came primarily from Joseph Pulitzer. After his service in the Union Army (spent with an all-German-speaking cavalry unit, riding up and down the Shenandoah Valley), Pulitzer mustered out and ended up in St. Louis, a growing city with a substantial German-speaking population. While working at odd jobs, he studied law and passed the bar exam. In 1867 he became a U.S. citizen. He fell into a job at a German newspaper in St. Louis, the *Westliche Post*, where he proved to be a tireless reporter. The paper's owner, Carl Schurz, gave Pulitzer an ownership interest in the paper, only to change his mind and buy back Pulitzer's share, allowing the once penniless immigrant to pocket $30,000. Disgusted by the reports he read of the corruption around President Grant, Pulitzer abandoned the Republican Party, and began his commitment to the Democrats. In 1877, Pulitzer moved to Washington, where he renewed his acquaintance with a twenty-three-year-old friend, Kate Davis. That June they were married in an Episcopal church in Washington; they did not tell her parents about Pulitzer's Jewish ancestors in Hungary. Pulitzer himself was "an agnostic with no religious affiliation or prejudices," according to a biographer, but that did not stop those who were deranged by anti-Semitism from periodically attacking Pulitzer for his supposed Jewishness.[4]

The next year marked the beginning of Pulitzer's career as a newspaper publisher. In December 1878 he bought the English-language *St. Louis Dispatch* at auction for the rock-bottom price of $2,500. He soon merged it with the *St. Louis Post* and furiously plunged into running the newspaper, often doing every job in the place himself. The following year he moved his *St. Louis Post-Dispatch* into a new building, outfitted with a new four-cylinder Hoe printing press to meet the growing demand. He used his newspaper to crusade against gambling, prostitution, and local political corruption. In fact, Pulitzer ran so many exposés that he felt the need to start carrying a gun for self-defense. He took another significant step in 1880 when he hired John Cockerill as his managing editor. Already Pulitzer was showing signs—a persistent cough and constant headaches—of the infirmities that would plague his adult years. For decades Cockerill proved to be Pulitzer's indispensable journalistic partner, executing many of the ideas that Pulitzer was too busy or too sick to implement himself.

Pulitzer's brother Albert, meanwhile, was also in the news business. In 1882 he launched a newspaper in New York City called the *Journal*. It was a penny sheet with no great ambitions; with its heavy doses of sex, scandal, and society news, it became known as "the chambermaid's delight." Joseph Pulitzer, by contrast, had no intention of entering the New York City newspaper market, but on a visit to Manhattan in 1883, he heard that the *World* was for sale. At the time it belonged to the notorious "robber baron" Jay Gould, who was said to be losing $40,000 a year on it and looking for a way to unload it. Pulitzer knew that negotiating with Gould would not be easy. For one thing, Gould's railroad interests extended to St. Louis; of the two lawyers who represented Gould there, Pulitzer's managing editor, Cockerill, had called one a liar and had shot the other man dead. Not only that, but Pulitzer had denounced Gould personally in an editorial as "one of the most sinister figures that ever flitted bat-like across the vision of the American people."[5] To make matters worse, Gould was asking an outrageous $500,000 for the money-losing paper.

Even so, Pulitzer was interested. For one thing, his wife favored the deal, hoping it would be good for Joseph's health. (It turned out not to be.) Perhaps more important, Pulitzer believed that he was the kind of Democrat who could bring a much-needed voice to the New York editorial establishment, which was strongly Republican. He countered Gould's price with an offer of $346,000, and on May 10, 1883, Joseph Pulitzer became owner of the *World*.[6] He made several key decisions right away. He would keep his *St. Louis Post-Dispatch* and publish two large daily newspapers all at once, but he summoned Cockerill from St. Louis to run the *World.* Pulitzer also decided to make his principal home in New York and focus most of his energies on the greatest newspaper market in the United States. Located at 32 Park Row, the *World* faced a street full of competitors: the *Sun,* the *Herald,* the *Times,* the *Tribune,* his brother's *Journal,* and a handful of others. Setting the price at two cents a copy, Pulitzer wanted to make sure that his would be the paper of choice among the city's surging population of wage earners, laborers, and immigrants. In his inaugural issue, Pulitzer promised to "expose all fraud and sham," to "fight all public evils" and to "battle for the people with earnest sincerity."[7] With a circulation of less than 23,000, he was starting in the back of the pack.

Soon, however, he began surging to the front. Within a month he put together a series of articles on the opening of the Brooklyn Bridge that featured an engraving spanning four columns, the first illustration ever used in the *World.* When the crowds at the opening of the bridge panicked and stampeded, Pulitzer followed up with a huge front-page headline screaming "BAPTIZED IN BLOOD." And he kept it up. He covered the executions of murderers. He used the Sunday edition to experiment with new features and approaches.[8] He created the first separate sports department, focusing on popular diversions of the day such as boxing, horse racing, baseball, and yachting. He also launched the first of his many editorial crusades. At the time, New York City was plagued by sales of tainted and watered-down milk, a problem serious enough to cause many infant deaths. Pulitzer took up the cause, employing both the news and opinion columns of the *World* to expose the scandal and demand reform. In the process, he made an important discovery: he could use his newspaper to attack evil on behalf of the poor and the working class, bring malefactors to justice, and gain circulation at every step of the way. This became the model for dozens of Pulitzer crusades in the decades to follow.

Part of Pulitzer's remarkable success was due to the luck of his timing. He happened to arrive on the New York scene at a propitious moment, when conditions were ripe for the kinds of experiments he was carrying out. During the 1870s and 1880s, inventors were bringing changes to the technology of newspaper production on a scale comparable to that of the 1830s and 1840s. Some of these innovations affected the newsroom, including the telephone and the typewriter, which made it easier and faster for reporters and editors at a big-city newspaper to handle the growing flow of words. The arrival of the telephone changed the way news was gathered. As soon as telephones became commonplace, reporters used them to call headquarters and dictate their notes to the rewrite desk in the newsroom, where someone else would write the news story. As a result, many reporters—especially cub reporters sent to stake out remote locations—became known as "legmen," meaning that they no longer wrote about the events they went out to cover. Instead a "rewrite man" working at a desk in the newsroom turned the details into story form. This system persisted at many papers for decades (and is still used in emergencies, though most journalists today write the stories they report).

In this period another set of technical innovations affected the pressroom. One was a method known as the "halftone" process, which finally allowed newspapers to reproduce photographs through a system using dots of ink to represent areas of shading. Although the first such photo appeared in the *New York Daily Graphic* in 1880, most big newspapers did not adopt the halftone until about 1897.[9] This invention gave newspapers and magazines a powerful technique for conveying information, and it gave rise to a new subgenre, the picture paper, which was nearly all photos. Eventually this development would make possible the whole field of photojournalism. Other inventors were dramatically reducing the cost of newsprint paper and increasing the speed of printing presses and folding machines. Around the same time, the composing room got a jolt when a man named Ottmar Mergenthaler, a German immigrant to America, transformed the ancient process by which printers set type. For centuries printers had had to select each letter from its case, one by one, and place it in position on the line of type. Mergenthaler's machine automated the whole procedure, making it possible for an operator using a special keyboard to set an entire line of type at once. His invention, which he patented in 1884, was called the linotype, and it greatly speeded up the printing process while slashing the cost of composition.[10] All together, these mechanical innovations made it possible to create forms of journalism that were faster, fresher, cheaper to produce, and more visually attractive than ever before. Still, someone would have to plunge in and make those changes happen.

The news business was also facing a series of changes in American society in the late nineteenth century. Foremost among them was a fresh burst of immigration that saw the arrival of millions of new Americans. By 1900 the United States had 26 million residents whose parents were immigrants, plus another 10 million who were immigrants themselves; combined, they made up 26 percent of the population (fig. 5.2). Streams of immigrants kept coming to America from the traditional sources—Ireland and Germany—but they were being joined now by multitudes of newcomers from eastern and southern Europe, especially Italy, Poland, and Russia. Millions entered by sailing into New York Harbor, and many of these immigrants stayed on in New York, ensuring its status as the nation's largest and most cosmopolitan city. Others passed through and added to the populations of other great cities, from Pittsburgh to Chicago and St. Louis, all the way to San Francisco. Once settled, these immigrants became a potentially vast new market for newspapers—at least for those publishers and editors willing to cater to the newcomers.

At the same time, other social changes were expanding the market for newspapers. Native-born Americans were leaving their farms and small towns and heading to the cities, swelling their populations and prompting a further series of changes in urban life. One was the growing separation of home and work, a trend that gave rise to the growing ranks of daily commuters riding horse-drawn buses and, eventually, subways. During those daily trips back and forth, many of the passengers developed the habit of reading the newspaper. At the same time,

5.2 JACOB RIIS USED PHOTOS TO URGE REFORM. An immigrant from Denmark, Riis documented the misery of tenement life in New York City, including this "Italian rag-picker." His 1890 book, *How the Other Half Lives*, helped build public support for the political movement to outlaw many of the worst features of New York's slums.

—*Museum of the City of New York*.

American women were taking on new roles and identities. In increasing numbers they were entering the paid labor force. In the domestic sphere, especially among the middle class, women began to shop for products that were once made at home—fabrics, soap, furniture, even food—and abandoned traditional female roles such as spinning and weaving. If they were to buy things, they would need information about what was for sale and where to find it; answers would come in the form of newspaper advertising. In turn, companies selling detergent, clothing, and all the wonders of the modern age needed to reach consumers. This was especially true for the owners of the giant department stores like Macy's and Gimbels and the owners of companies that were trying to establish the first national brands, such as Ivory soap and Edison phonographs. Advertisers became eager partners in the big-city newspaper business.[11] In this way, mass production, mass marketing, and mass communication joined forces in a new dynamic.

In economic terms, American capitalism, with its origins in small-scale private enterprise, was becoming fully industrial in this period. Traditional ways of making things, based on the master-apprentice model, were giving way to the factory method, in which machines (or "capital," in economic terminology) were increasingly important and skilled human beings less so. The organizers of the vast new enterprises in steel making, textiles, mining, railroads, and the like were not content to increase the scale of production by old methods; instead they were smashing the old ways of doing things altogether and staking their futures on machines to improve productivity and profit, no matter what the cost to others. And in this trend the big-city daily papers were at the forefront. By 1890, Pulitzer himself had 1,200 employees, and he was on his way to producing a million copies a day.

As a result of the increasing role of machinery, it became more and more expensive to start a newspaper, especially in the urban markets. The newspaper business saw a dramatic rise in what economists call "barriers to entry," the costs of entering a field of economic activity. In 1835, for example, James Gordon Bennett had started the *Herald* with just $500. A few years later Horace Greeley needed to ante up four times that amount to launch the *Tribune*. And in 1851 Henry Raymond needed $100,000 to start his *New-York Daily Times*.[12] After the Civil War, the trend continued. Charles A. Dana paid $175,000 for the *Sun* in 1868.[13] Four years later, after Greeley's death, Whitelaw Reid paid $510,000 for the *Tribune*.[14] In 1883, when Pulitzer bought the *World*, it was relatively cheap at $346,000.[15] In 1895, William Randolph Hearst paid $150,000 for the *Journal*, but he needed at least another $250,000 from his mother for immediate investment in the paper.[16] The following year, Adolph Ochs needed only $75,000 in cash to buy the *Times*, but he had to raise another $500,000 in bonds.[17] Thus, by the turn of the century, it would be safe to say that the cost of entering the news business, at least in New York, was approaching $1 million. An issue of growing importance in the sale price of newspapers during these decades was the Associated Press franchise. Under company rules that were in effect from the 1850s to 1945, any existing member of the AP could veto the addition of any proposed new member. Thus, outside New York City, most AP-affiliated papers had a monopoly over telegraphic news within their own circulation areas, and the value of that exclusive franchise was reflected in the newspaper's value as a business.[18]

The new business model had other consequences as well, some of them profound. Ever since the advent of the factory-style approach to newspapering, the day-to-day practice of most daily journalism in the United States has been beyond the effective reach of the First Amendment. The reason is that while the First Amendment protects journalists from the *government*, it does nothing to protect them from their *employers*. Journalists are hired hands who can be told which subjects to write about, which ones *not* to write about, and how to approach the approved topics. Employees who defy their bosses are punished or fired, with no recourse under the First Amendment. They may enjoy the protection of a union or an individual contract, which they can use to prevent arbitrary dismissal. But for most journalists, most of the time, the First Amendment is effectively repealed as soon as they accept a paycheck. The journalistic ideal enshrined in the Constitution—that of a small-scale, independent voice offering one point of view among many—was passing, in the late nineteenth century, into the realm of the horse and carriage. In fact, the reality of working for a boss who has the power to censor has been the routine experience for most journalists since at least 1833— except for those few who actually own a press (or those who, like most bloggers, have no boss at all).[19]

When journalists work as employees, they take on a new set of relationships. In legal terms, they produce what is known as "work for hire"—that is, the information they gather, the photos they take, or the stories they write belong not to themselves but to their employer. Even the copyright to the unique arrangement of words they write is not their own; it immediately upon creation becomes the property of their employer. These conditions do not apply to the self-employed, who made up the bulk of journalists at the time they were brought under the protection of the First Amendment in the late eighteenth century. Under the reorganization of the business by Pulitzer and his rivals in the late nineteenth century, however, the practice of journalism completed the transition from a stand-alone shop to a giant industrial enterprise. Since then, the principle of press freedom has extended largely to the corporations that sponsor journalism and employ the rank and file of reporters and editors.

Through a series of experiments, Pulitzer created a newspaper so perfectly adapted to the particular business environment he faced that it flourished and grew into the nation's largest. He was a whirlwind with ultimate authority over both the *World*'s news coverage and its business operations. Notwithstanding his many health problems, Pulitzer was a hands-on manager. Even during the years when his "nerves" made it impossible for him to be in the newsroom, he still controlled many of the operations of his newspaper through an endless series of memos he dictated to a rotating staff of personal assistants. Although the scale of his operations was expanding far beyond the size of even the most successful penny press papers, Pulitzer was still able to put his personal stamp on the *World*.

Almost immediately on taking ownership, Pulitzer started making changes. On the business side, he decided to price the *World* at two cents. Over the years since the founding of the penny press in 1833, the cost of a New York City newspaper had crept up into the range of three to as much as six cents a copy. By selling the *World* at two cents, Pulitzer seized two great advantages: he put his paper within the budget of the working-class and immigrant readers he was seeking, and he put his rivals into an economic vise. Many of the other dailies were barely making money even at their higher prices; at two cents a copy, they would certainly go broke unless they could sell a tremendous number of papers every day.

Pulitzer also brought change to the advertising department. He established a policy of setting ad rates strictly on the basis of circulation. As his *World* reached more readers than the competition, he argued, each ad could influence more potential customers and therefore ought to cost more. Whereas circulation figures were once handled almost like trade secrets, Pulitzer set out to make the size of his circulation an element in his business success and, eventually, a point of public boasting on his own front page. He also promoted the *World* by advertising it in other locations and by proudly letting readers know whenever he had a story that could be called "Exclusive!" Pulitzer also dropped the publishers' traditional hostility to advertisers who wanted to break up columns by running ads that spread out sideways across the page. Instead, he ordered his staff to cooperate with advertisers in designing larger and more attractive ads. Before this, most ads were small, print-only notices, usually set in tiny type, resembling today's classified ads or stock tables. James Gordon Bennett had introduced the idea that the ads in his *Herald* should be as interesting as the news, and he was the first to impose a requirement that all ads be regularly updated. Pulitzer pushed this policy to new heights.

Previously, most advertising was handled locally and personally. If a business wanted to advertise, someone from the company would contact the newspaper directly and negotiate the arrangement. With the growth in demand for advertising by department stores, name-brand manufacturers, and other retailers, these transactions were becoming cumbersome for both parties. In the late nineteenth century, this problem was solved by the rise of advertising agencies, especially in the nation's business and publishing capital, New York City. The first modern advertising agency was N. W. Ayer and Son, founded in 1875.[20] Others soon followed, operating as middlemen who served to bring a degree of efficiency and rationality to advertising practices. The agencies spared their clients the time and bother of actually placing advertising; they also began designing the layout and slogans used in ads. As a result, most newspapers became more dependent than ever on advertising as a core source of revenue. The allocation of space in newspapers changed significantly. At a newspaper, the overall space is divided between ads and editorial matter—all the words, photos, and headlines that all the writers, photographers, and their editors create. The space devoted to editorial content is known as the "news hole" (because it must be filled up every day). The ratio of news hole to ads changed from an average of 70 percent news and 30 percent advertising to about 50–50 during the 1880s, and the money followed suit. Whereas revenue from advertising accounted for about 44 percent of total newspaper income in 1880, by 1900 it was up to 55 percent.[21]

Taken together, these two great rivers of revenue—circulation and advertising—created a bonanza of opportunities, which Pulitzer and his imitators seized. One of the uses they found for all the money was to elevate the practice of reporting, taking it to heights of derring-do that surpassed even the frenetic Bennett and the rest of the penny press gang. In the late nineteenth century, Pulitzer and other publishers financed reporters like Nellie Bly, who became the most famous correspondent in America by dashing around the world just to say she had done it, and Richard Harding Davis, who succeeded her as the country's best-known correspondent by racing off across the globe to report on wars. Reporting, in the sense of collecting new information from distant points, became a point of pride and competition among the newspapers that were profitable enough to take part in the great game.

Drawing on his experience in St. Louis, Pulitzer also set out to overhaul the *World*'s news and opinion pages. Few of the changes that Pulitzer introduced were completely original. What set him apart was that he brought more change, more rapidly, and more systematically to his newspaper than any other publisher or editor. The resulting style is often called "sensationalism," usually with a dismissive or negative connotation. In fact, Pulitzer's sensational style was woven from several strands, and it has a more complicated texture than many give it credit for.

In one respect, sensationalism was literal: that is, in the news columns of the *World,* Pulitzer urged his writers and editors to present vivid word-pictures that appealed to the senses. He wanted his readers to see how things looked, hear how they sounded, even to smell them. (In 1898 the *World* took this literal meaning to an extreme by publishing a Sunday supplement that was perfumed.) That kind of writing calls for precise observation by reporters and for colorful prose from writers. At a time when many newspapers labored under Victorian codes of propriety, Pulitzer waded into the sordid, the squalid, and the shocking. Murder became a staple item, especially if it featured a sexual scandal, multiple victims, or some novel weapon or method. In the *World,* another common type of story involved disasters, especially those terrifying mishaps that took place on steamboats or railroads.

Yet another feature of Pulitzer's approach to news was the "crusade." In this form of journalistic effort, news coverage and opinion pages are coordinated to provoke some outcome of the newspaper owner's choosing. A classic example involved Pulitzer's handling of the Statue of Liberty, which had been commissioned by the government of France to commemorate the centennial of American independence in 1876. The sculptor, Auguste Bartholdi, completed his assignment, but the sections of the finished piece languished in packing crates for lack of a place to mount the statue in the United States. On several occasions Congress balked at the cost. Joseph Pulitzer seized the day. He challenged the people of New York to rise to the occasion through their own voluntary donations. "Take this appeal to yourself personally," he editorialized. "Give something, however little." To set a good example, Pulitzer announced that he was giving $250. Soon, contributions began flowing in—not to the government but to the Park Row offices of the *World,* which served as both banker and cheerleader for installing the statue in New York. In the news columns, the *World* documented the flow of funds and featured the newspaper's benevolent role. The news stories also dramatized the effort by reprinting excerpts from notes the *World* received, such as these heart-tugging examples: "Inclosed please find five cents as a poor office boy's mite toward the Pedestal Fund. As being loyal to the Stars and Stripes, I thought even five cents would be acceptable," or "I am a wee bit of a girl, yet I am ever so glad I was born in time to contribute my mite ($1) to the Pedestal." At the end of the five-month campaign, Pulitzer could report that the *World* had collected enough nickels and dollars to pay for the monumental pedestal. When the dedication ceremonies were held on October 28, 1886, Pulitzer was among the dignitaries invited, although he chose to observe the festivities from a nearby ship.[22]

A similar form of journalistic crusade employed by Pulitzer was the "exposé." The typical exposé shares some features with the crusade, but the two types of stories are distinct in at least one important way: the true exposé is aimed at revealing some wrongdoing. Under Pulitzer, the *World* directed its reporting energies toward exposing the misdeeds of those in power, either crooked politicians or the malefactors of wealth who ran the big corporations, or the many business trusts that then dominated the economy. A classic example of the exposé was carried out by a remarkable young woman who talked her way into a job on the *World* in 1887. In just a few years her byline would be the most recognized in the world—Nellie Bly—but she first had to win a terrifying dare.[23] When Bly, a poor twenty-three-year-old reporter from Pittsburgh, tried to land a job at the *World,* Pulitzer's managing editor, John Cockerill, was skeptical. Journalism was very much a man's world, after all, and Nellie Bly was an unknown with little experience. But Cockerill made her an offer: if she could get herself committed to a mental asylum and write a story about it, she could have a job at Joseph Pulitzer's newspaper. Seeing no alternative, Bly took the challenge. She checked into a boarding house for working women, then pretended to be mentally ill. Soon enough, the police were called, and Bly found herself before a judge; saying he was sure she was "somebody's darling," he sent her to Bellevue for examination.[24]

Nellie then reached her goal: the insane asylum for women on Blackwell's Island (since renamed Roosevelt Island) in the East River. There she entered a house of horrors, complete with wretched food, cold baths, and abusive attendants. As she described it, the asylum was a place where mental illness was induced rather than cured. When ten days had passed, Pulitzer sent an attorney to spring Bly, and she went to work writing up her experiences. A two-part series ran in October 1887, and it was picked up by newspapers outside New York, setting off an outcry near and far. Her undercover reporting resulted in a first-person account that was irrefutable. The officials responsible for running the asylum could not deny or explain away her findings, although they certainly tried. Within weeks, New York officials approved an appropriation of an extra $1 million to improve conditions. And Nellie Bly got a job.

A fourth weapon in Pulitzer's arsenal was the "scandal" story. Sometimes these stories also overlapped with the exposé, but the scandal story was coming into its own. One excellent definition came from Cockerill himself, who said that a scandal is "any hitherto unprinted occurrence which involves the violation of any one of the Ten Commandments." He went on to clarify that some news is "better" than other news, especially if it has the added factor of celebrity, and "if it involves a fracture of the Vth, VIth, VIIth, VIIIth or IXth Commandments and by those people whose names people have heard and in whose doings they are specifically interested by knowledge of their official or social position, then it is great news."[25] Thus a divorce involving a prominent person would qualify as news, and soon the *World* and other papers began carrying more and more such stories. Pulitzer also liked to treat his readers to a variant of the scandal story, the society story. He sent reporters to the mansions and clubs of the glittering stars of the Gilded

Age, then printed leering accounts of the clothes, homes, dining, and dancing of New York City's upper class.

Sometimes stories appeared for no other reason than sheer "celebrity."[26] Pulitzer was part of a broader trend in news coverage during this period that elevated certain people to a pedestal of prominence, giving millions of strangers a (false) sense of intimacy with them. The decades after the Civil War were the formative years for the celebrity, a figure like the boxer John L. Sullivan or the "professional beauty" Lillie Langtry, public characters whose every doing became grist for newspaper coverage. What these celebrities offered the newspapers was "good copy"—that is, a regular supply of titillating, amazing, or pathetic stories. What the newspapers offered in return was the oxygen of publicity. For the readers, especially those urban readers who found themselves living among crowds of strangers, news about such celebrities offered a common topic of conversation, a way of appearing to be in the know. Up until then, people had gossiped about their actual neighbors; now, when they came together in taverns, or on the factory floor, or in the trolley car, they could participate confidently in discussions about the personal foibles and heroic qualities of people they had never met but only read about in the papers.

Pulitzer also used another journalistic technique, one that he made famous: the "stunt." In Joseph Pulitzer's approach to running a newspaper, there was no such thing as a slow news day. When news did not do him the favor of breaking out, he was determined to provide his readers with their daily dose of amazing reports anyway. So he was not above staging pseudo-events that would make for lively news copy. Again, Nellie Bly provides a classic example. In 1873 the French author Jules Verne had published his popular novel *Around the World in 80 Days*, in which the protagonist, Phileas Fogg, marveling at all the recent inventions speeding up transportation, sets out to circumnavigate the Earth in eighty days. In 1889, Nellie Bly decided to take up the challenge for real. Pulitzer agreed that his daredevil young reporter was perfect for the job, and—in a further stroke of promotional genius—launched a contest to see who could guess how long the journey would actually take her. (The contest brought in almost a million submissions.)[27]

Gamely, Bly took off with a small valise aboard steamships, trains, ferries, and every other form of transport, dodging bandits, monsoons, and suitors along the way (fig. 5.3). Whenever possible, she filed dispatches back to the *World* so that enthralled readers could track her progress. After getting most of the way around the world, she and her pet monkey landed in San Francisco, where Pulitzer had a special train waiting for her. With flags flying, the train dashed across the United States, delivering Nellie Bly to a ten-gun salute in Jersey City after a 24,899-mile race. On the front page Pulitzer hailed her accomplishment with deck after deck of headlines, and the newspaper proudly noted her time: seventy-two days, six hours, eleven minutes, fourteen seconds. In the newspapers' trade magazine of the day, *The Journalist,* an observer sniffed at the stunt, saying that the whole

5.3 REPORTER NELLIE BLY WAVES GOODBYE as she sets off to another destination on her trip around the globe for Joseph Pulitzer's *New York World*, 1889–90. Such adventures made Bly (who completed her trip in seventy-two days and sent regular dispatches on her progress) one of the most famous journalists of her era.—*Library of Congress*.

affair had been "a great advertisement for the *New York World* and Miss Nellie Bly"—which was, of course, the point.[28]

Finally, Pulitzer pioneered one more technique that became a standby in the pages of the *World:* the "sob story." This was the nickname for a type of feature story that drew the reader's attention to the plight of some poor, miserable individual on the urban scene—ideally an immigrant, an orphan, or a widow. These were stories that Nellie Bly could certainly handle, and she wrote her share of them. But she was not alone. Pulitzer hired more and more women reporters, and many of them were assigned to these tear-jerking tales. Eventually they became known as "sob sisters" for their mastery of the literary form. Their stories usually focused on an individual or a family facing some calamity or other. None of these articles qualified as "news" in the strict sense, but that hardly seemed to matter. As long as the people wanted to read them, the publisher wanted to provide them.

Taken together, these changes in the approach went a long way toward defining what was being called the "new journalism." The techniques of sensation, crusade, exposé, scandal, stunt, and the sob story combined to give Pulitzer's pages an energy and drama that other papers lacked. Readers noticed the difference, and they pushed the circulation of the *World* from 15,000 in 1883 to about 250,000 just three years later. By 1888, Pulitzer was so successful that he had the cash to pay $630,000 to buy the old French's Hotel (an establishment he had been kicked out of twenty-three years earlier because he looked so scruffy). Not only that, but Pulitzer tore down the hotel and used the empty lot to put up the tallest building in New York as the home for his *World.* It was capped by a giant dome he designed himself, the physical embodiment of his success when it opened in 1889. Even better, his building was so tall that it literally plunged the *Sun* into the shade.[29] And it was all due to those hundreds of thousands of readers.

To be sure, Pulitzer had his detractors too, especially among editors of the more sedate New York newspapers. He was criticized (as Bennett had been a generation earlier) for pounding away at stories of lurid or depraved behavior. In reply Pulitzer wrote: "The complaint of the 'low moral tone of the press' is common but very unjust. A newspaper relates the events of the day. It does not manufacture its record of corruptions and crimes, but tells of them as they occur. If it failed to do so it would be an unfaithful chronicler. The daily journal is like the mirror—it reflects that which is before it. Let those who are startled by it blame the people who are before the mirror, and not the mirror, which only reflects their features and actions."[30] It is hard to determine if Pulitzer actually believed in the literal truth of these statements, with all their implications. In part, his reply was a renewal of Franklin's plea to critics not to shoot the messenger when they read stories they didn't like. But Pulitzer went a step further in arguing that a newspaper is a mere "mirror" of the world's doings. Could Pulitzer really have believed that the editorial process involves no selection, no emphasis, no interpretation? His *World* may have been a mirror, but it was one marred by cracks, distortions, and fog.

Eventually Pulitzer made further refinements to his journalistic style. During the 1890s, when he faced competition from editors who were trying to beat him at his own game, Pulitzer pushed for a bolder approach to graphics. Headlines in the *World* became larger and larger, routinely spreading across several columns and ultimately across the entire front page. As soon as it became possible to do so, Pulitzer introduced photographs and made lavish use of them. He also inaugurated a separate section devoted to sports and followed that with other special-interest departments. Many of his experiments were carried out in the Sunday edition, which served as his journalistic laboratory. If an idea proved popular on Sunday, then it would become a regular feature during the week.

One of his most successful experiments involved a cartoon. Pulitzer, who was the first publisher to offer comics in color,[31] hired a young illustrator named R. F. Outcault in 1896, soon after Outcault brought Pulitzer some drawings depicting life in a street of crowded tenements. The series was soon titled "Hogan's Alley." One of the regular characters was a daffy-looking toddler who wore a long night-shirt. Another *World* employee experimented with using bright yellow ink for the shirt, and the figure quickly became known as "The Yellow Kid." The urchin was so popular that Pulitzer's eventual rival, William Randolph Hearst, lured Outcault away with higher pay. Pulitzer responded by finding another artist to continue drawing "Hogan's Alley." Now both newspapers had their splash of yellow, and the new style of journalism with which both of the papers were associated became known as "yellow journalism."[32] In a poignant twist of fate, however, Pulitzer never saw most of the visual changes he brought to the *World*. By 1888 he was almost completely blind and depended on assistants to read to him.

Pulitzer brought a bundle of innovations to the newspaper business, but there was one other area where he also stood out. In the political opinions expressed in his newspapers, Joseph Pulitzer spoke loudly, clearly, and forcefully. From his earliest days in St. Louis, Pulitzer stood in solidarity with the poor, the immigrant, and the laboring masses, and he never wavered.[33] Pulitzer himself had been poor, of course, and he had been an immigrant. And he had worked hard. But unlike many people who amass great fortunes, he remained loyal to his roots. He expressed a lifelong hostility to the corrupting influence of wealthy individuals and corporations, and he kept a close eye on government as well, on the theory that it could turn into a plutocracy if not vigorously watched. By nature a democrat, he was also a staunch supporter of the Democratic Party, but he was ready to criticize the Democrats when he thought they were wrong. As Pulitzer himself once put it: "Always fight for progress and reform; never tolerate injustice or corruption; always fight demagogues of all parties; never belong to any party; always oppose privileged classes and public plunder; never lack sympathy for the poor; always remain devoted to the public welfare; never be satisfied with merely printing the news; always be drastically independent; never be afraid to attack wrong, whether by predatory plutocracy or predatory poverty."[34]

Time and again he coordinated his news coverage and his editorials in the cause of reform. In St. Louis he once hid a reporter behind a locked door to expose details about a local gambling scandal. In Pulitzer's view, exposure was the best way not only to punish wrongdoing but to prevent it as well. "The press may be licentious," Pulitzer once wrote, "but it is the most magnificently representative moral agent in the world today. More crime, immorality and rascality is prevented by the fear of exposure in the newspapers than by all the laws, moral and statute, ever devised."[35] Pulitzer was never a radical, and he never questioned the role of private property in the industrial economy. But he was among those at the forefront of progressive reform thinking. As much as any of his contemporaries, Pulitzer embodied the wisdom of the fictional observer Mr. Dooley, who remarked in 1902, "The job of a newspaper is to comfort the afflicted and afflict the comfortable."[36]

Ultimately, though, it was the public who made Joseph Pulitzer a success. Through the decisions they made day after day, the readers expressed their approval; after all, they did not *have* to buy his newspaper, or any newspaper at all. As they hustled along the streets, listening to the "newsies" hawking the day's headlines, busy commuters had their pick of diversions (fig. 5.4). By giving their pennies to Pulitzer, they were, in a sense, voting for him on a daily basis. In so doing, they deserve a large measure of the credit and bear a large measure of responsibility for shaping American journalism. Many of Pulitzer's readers had switched over from the old *Sun,* the original working-class penny paper. Under Charles A. Dana, the *Sun* had been the largest-selling newspaper in the nation's largest city for more than a decade after the Civil War. But in the election of 1884 Dana defected from the Democrats, while Pulitzer backed the Democratic nominee, Grover Cleveland.[37] As a result, Pulitzer captured thousands of former *Sun* readers.[38] Even as Pulitzer grew wealthy and influential, even as he lost his eyesight and spent more and more of his time roaming the seas aboard his insulated yacht *Liberty,* he managed to exhibit a rare sympathy for the growing ranks of wage workers in the new industrial economy. There is no evidence that Pulitzer's sympathy was anything less than genuine. At the same time, it is a matter of fact that from a publisher's point of view the laboring masses have one great virtue that makes them very attractive: there are *lots of them.*

*   *   *

ONE OF PULITZER'S CLOSEST READERS was a young man named William Randolph Hearst.[39] When he first started reading the *World,* Hearst was a feckless youth attending Harvard College who liked to slip away from his studies in Cambridge and take the train to New York City, where he could enjoy the theatrical delights and feminine offerings available on Broadway. While visiting New York, he naturally read the city's many newspapers, and one in particular caught his eye. Within a year or two of Pulitzer's takeover of the *World,* Hearst could see that this

5.4 **"NEWSIES" SOLD THE GREAT DAILY PAPERS** in the streets of the big U.S. cities in the late nineteenth century. Photographer Lewis Hine captured this image of three young "newsies" smoking as they made their rounds. —*Library of Congress.*

was a great new kind of newspaper—just the kind of newspaper he would edit if he owned one. Within a decade Hearst would own not just one but—like Pulitzer—two newspapers, and he would be locked in a ferocious competition with none other than Joseph Pulitzer himself. Hearst thrived on the competition and became the first of the press lords to branch out into all the existing media of his day. By the end of his long life Hearst would accumulate a lengthy list of critics, who saw him as a threat not just to responsible journalism but to democracy itself. A man of immense drive, ambition, and wealth, he was also a man of deep contradictions: a war hawk who opposed U.S. intervention in two world wars, a rich man who sought to speak for the common man, a creative businessman who stole most of his ideas and personnel from others.

For Hearst, success in business was a tale of riches to riches. He began life in April 1863 in a world of immense new wealth, power, and privilege. His father, George Hearst, an early migrant to California, had roamed the West widely in search of minerals; he'd made his first fortune by staking one of the early claims to the fabulous Comstock Lode of gold and silver in Virginia City, Nevada. In June 1862, George married a woman twenty years his junior, Phoebe Apperson, a schoolteacher from Missouri. George Hearst added to his fortune by buying vast tracts of land in Mexico and California, including forty thousand acres near San Simeon Bay, then continued to make more mining strikes across the West. He was in a mining camp when his only child, Willie, was born. George's absences continued, as he kept on staking and defending his mining claims, leaving Phoebe to raise their son by herself. Despite some financial reverses, Phoebe set out to spoil young Willie. When he was just ten, she took him out of school for a year on a Grand Tour of Europe.

In the 1870s George Hearst really struck it big. A partner in a series of silver mines in Nevada and Utah that made fortunes, he went on to enjoy major shares in the Homestake gold mine in South Dakota and the Anaconda copper mine in Montana. With the new fortune, the Hearsts were wealthy almost beyond measure. Phoebe could now execute her most ambitious plans for Willie. She sent him to the elite St. Paul's School in Concord, New Hampshire, to prepare him for Harvard. In 1880, George Hearst acquired another asset, one that could be helpful in the political career he now aspired to: he bought a newspaper in his home state, the money-losing *San Francisco Examiner*. Six years later a Democratic majority in the legislature in Sacramento named George Hearst the new United States Senator from California. To his vast fortune he now added political power.

So when Willie Hearst entered Harvard in the fall of 1882, while he may have lacked the social polish of the eastern establishment boys whose families had been going to Harvard for generations, he was not lacking for anything else. He got himself admitted to one of Harvard's best social clubs, partly on the strength of his prodigious allowance, which one biographer reckons to have been worth the equivalent of more than $2,500 a month (that was just spending money; his room and board were paid separately). Hearst also found a use for his money that tested his talents for running a publication; he became business manager of the *Harvard Lampoon,* the undergraduate humor magazine. Under his direction the magazine's circulation and advertising revenue shot up, and he actually showed a year-end profit. Hearst also marked another accomplishment during his Harvard years. After devoting his first few semesters to the prodigious drinking that was so commonplace among the college's young scholars, Hearst reformed and adopted a lifelong practice of hosting parties where he served booze freely but personally abstained, giving himself a frequent advantage over others.[40]

Willie Hearst had no real life plan. He loved the theater, and he was deeply interested in politics, but the thing he kept coming back to was his father's newspaper, the *Examiner.* Indeed, while he was still an undergraduate Willie began to correspond with his father about the paper, and he was soon offering suggestions on how to improve it. In 1885 he wrote a rather impertinent letter to his father, sketching out some of his ideas. "I have begun to have a strange fondness for our little paper—a tenderness like unto that which a mother feels for a puny or deformed offspring," he declared, going on to assure his father that he felt confident in his own ability to run a successful newspaper. He then offered three specific suggestions. He recommended that the *Examiner* reduce the number of columns per page from nine to seven, leaving more white space and thus presenting a "much cleaner and neater appearance." The paper should also rely on original reporting by its own correspondents and eliminate "clippings" from other papers, and he wanted the *Examiner* to advertise itself, from Oregon to New Mexico.[41] All the while, the young Hearst was proving to be not much of a student. He was chronically on academic probation at Harvard, usually because the time he devoted to theater, politics, and parties cut into his studying. Hearst certainly did not endear himself to the Harvard faculty when he had a set of chamber pots made up for his professors, customized so that each professor's name was right in the bull's-eye.[42] Even so, Harvard continued to give him second chances before finally running out of patience and rejecting his request to make up his exams with the help of a tutor.

Unlike many other college dropouts, Hearst had a family business to step into. On March 4, 1887, the same day his father was sworn in as a senator, the *San Francisco Examiner* carried an updated masthead, which included the name "W. R. Hearst, Proprietor." Just twenty-four, Willie found himself in what was for him an unusual position. The *Examiner* was the third-ranking paper in San Francisco, so Hearst was now the underdog, scrapping for notice. He made sure his paper got that notice. Like Pulitzer, Hearst assigned himself the job of editor as well as publisher, and he stayed at the paper most nights, pushing his staff to create stories and illustrations that would expand circulation, which he could use as leverage with advertisers. He began pounding away at the same themes that Pulitzer was using in New York: sex, crime, and scandal. Ideally a story included a role for the newspaper itself. As biographer David Nasaw notes: "Hearst not only inserted his reporters into his crime and scandal stories, but also made them heroes and heroines of a morality play within a play. *Examiner* crime stories uncovered two layers of crime at once. They exposed the original crimes in all their bestiality and then analyzed at great length the blundering, sometimes criminal, incompetence of the officials investigating and prosecuting the case. Because the police and prosecutors were not doing their job, the *Examiner* reporters were forced to do it for them."[43] Hearst also determined that he would, in journalistic terms, repeal the law of gravity and eliminate the dreaded "slow news day." When he took over the *Examiner*, according to an earlier biographer, W. A. Swanberg, Hearst "was confronted by a journalistic fact known to all circulation-conscious editors—namely, that stupefying things do not happen every day. He solved this by creating them."[44] On one occasion Hearst dreamed up an assignment to ensure that his paper would always have something exciting to report: he dispatched a reporter to find the last living grizzly bear in California. Not only that, but the reporter was instructed to capture the beast and return with it to San Francisco, where the *Examiner* could proudly display it. At each stage of the perilous quest, the reporter was to write up his latest adventures. It wasn't news, exactly, but it sold papers. The *Examiner*'s circulation doubled in Hearst's first year, and, by 1890, it pulled even with the *Chronicle*.[45]

After his father died, Hearst began to act on his boundless ambition and went shopping for a newspaper to buy in New York City. In 1895 there were three papers for sale: the *Recorder,* founded just a few years earlier by the tobacco millionaire James B. Duke; the faltering but overpriced *New York Times;* and the *Morning Journal,* the paper that had been founded by Albert Pulitzer.[46] Hearst was in a somewhat awkward position, because his father had left almost all of his considerable estate to his wife, Phoebe, and almost nothing to his son. At this point, in his early thirties, Hearst had comparatively little money of his own, and his mother rarely doled out more than he could wheedle from her. Nevertheless, he came up with $150,000 to buy the *Morning Journal* and got a German-language version in the bargain. But he needed another $250,000 for immediate improvements to start making the paper competitive.[47]

One of his tactics was to open his checkbook and raid the staff that Joseph Pulitzer had assembled at the *World.* Singly and in groups, Pulitzer's reporters, writers, and editors (as well as "Yellow Kid" cartoonist Outcault) defected to the higher-paying Hearst.[48] Hearst also let fly with every means he could think of to draw readers' attention. In this ferocious competition, Pulitzer was literally handicapped by his physical and mental ailments. Now virtually blind, he was also plagued by most noises. When he traveled, his aides were ordered to book not only a suite for Mr. Pulitzer but also the rooms on either side, above it, and below it as well, to insulate him from any sound. More and more often, Pulitzer fled New York altogether and wandered aboard his yacht from resort to resort. Pulitzer never relinquished control, though. Instead he kept two assistants busy taking dictation with orders to his top editors instructing them how to run the *World.*[49] Nothing he did, however, could stop Hearst, who was able to boast on election day in 1896 that the combined circulation of the morning, evening, and German-language editions of the *Journal* had reached 1.5 million, a figure not even Pulitzer could claim.[50]

*   *   *

THE MOST NOTORIOUS EPISODE IN the Hearst-Pulitzer competition came within two years, in the events leading up to the U.S. war with Spain in 1898.[51] Both men have been accused of using their newspapers to whip up war fever for no other reason than a cynical ploy to increase circulation (fig. 5.5). While both Pulitzer and Hearst were certainly cynical, and both certainly sought higher circulation, it is an overstatement to say they "caused" the war. It was not within the power of even their combined efforts to create a war out of whole cloth. In the late 1890s they had plenty of allies; there were many high-ranking members of the U.S. military, industrial, and political establishment who were also spoiling for war. In their view, the tremendous output of American farms and factories needed global markets, which some believed could be secured only by a global navy. In addition, they felt that it was time for the U.S. to show the world that it had recovered from the Civil

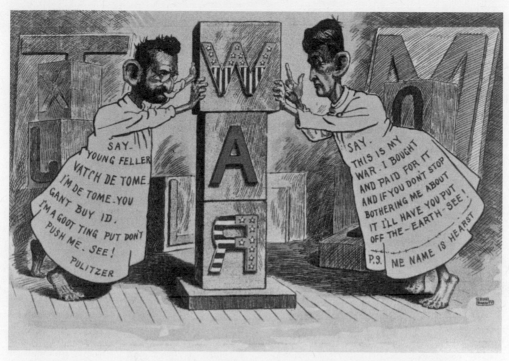

5.5 JOSEPH PULITZER AND WILLIAM RANDOLPH HEARST, rivals in "yellow journalism," are mocked in this caustic cartoon, which appeared in *Vim* magazine in 1898. The two publishers, who used their papers to push for war with Spain, are depicted as spoiled children playing at war. —*Library of Congress.*

War and was now ready to declare itself a world power.[52] Ambitious young men like Theodore Roosevelt were just as eager as Hearst or Pulitzer for war—especially for a "splendid little war" (as T.R. later called it) that would result in a U.S. victory—and they probably mattered more in the end than two New York publishers. It is nevertheless true that Hearst and Pulitzer contributed to a climate of public opinion that encouraged the move toward war.[53]

Pulitzer, according to his assistant Don Carlos Seitz, admitted as much. "He once confessed that he had rather liked the idea of a war—not a big one—but one that would arouse interest and give him a chance to gauge the reflex in his circulation figures."[54] To his credit, after the conflict ended, Pulitzer had the decency to regret his own war fever and vowed to be more responsible.[55] Hearst, by all accounts, relished the war and never questioned its rightness. He plunged in with gusto. When war with Spain was declared on April 25, 1898, Hearst had rockets fired from the roof of the *Journal* building in New York to celebrate, and a few weeks later, on May 8, he posed this boastful question on his front page: "HOW DO YOU LIKE THE JOURNAL'S WAR?"

The coverage of the war began well before the actual shooting. Since the mid-1890s, an independence movement had been growing in Cuba and other colonies held by Spain. To meet this threat, Spain sent 150,000 troops to Cuba under the command of General Valeriano Weyler (branded "the Butcher"), who launched a campaign to "concentrate" the Cuban population into camps, the better to control them. Immediately and unequivocally, Hearst and Pulitzer both sided with the rebels, portraying them as victims of a corrupt and greedy foreign power. Well before the United States became involved, Hearst hired one of the most dashing war correspondents of the era, Richard Harding Davis. Perfectly groomed and equipped with a pair of pistols, Davis cut quite a figure as he played up the guts, glory, and honor of war.[56] In an early dispatch he described the execution of a Cuban rebel by a Spanish firing squad, complete with "the blood from his breast sinking into the soil he had tried to free."[57]

Hearst also hired the prominent artist Frederick Remington to go to Cuba to illustrate articles, and he sent one of his top reporters as well, James Creelman. The two were hanging around in Havana and finding precious little action to describe. Remington sent a telegram to the boss stating: "Everything is quiet. There is no trouble here. There will be no war." Hearst's reply has become the stuff of journalistic legend. According to Creelman, Hearst telegraphed back: "Please remain. You furnish the pictures, and I'll furnish the war." It is important to note that there is no physical evidence to support this oft-repeated anecdote. The only source is Creelman's memoir, written in 1901.[58] It is also worth noting that Hearst denied sending such a message. Nevertheless, even if it was never sent, the notorious "telegram" has passed into the realm of legend, probably because it so neatly encapsulates a certain truth about Hearst. The putative telegram evokes the perception that Hearst saw himself as a cause of news as well as a recorder of it, along with the perception that he would stop at nothing to sell more newspapers.[59]

As tensions rose between the Cuban rebels and the Spanish occupiers, there came an opportunity both to make news and to sell papers, and Hearst jumped at it. In the summer of 1897 a young woman named Evangelina Cisneros (always described with the epithet "raven-haired"), the daughter of a jailed Cuban rebel, was thrown into prison herself in Havana. Her crime? She had dared to defend her honor against a rapacious Spanish colonel. Here was an answer to Hearst's prayers: an innocent (and attractive) victim of a corrupt, brutal regime. The *Journal* thundered for her release—in headlines, news stories, line drawings, and editorials. Hearst personally led a campaign for her freedom, ordering his correspondents across the country to call on prominent women to sign a petition to be sent to the Queen Regent of Spain. Hearst himself went to work on Mrs. McKinley, pleading with the first lady to help "a child, sick, defenseless, and in prison." Then the story got even better (from Hearst's point of view). When the Spanish refused to release the young woman, the editor dispatched a reporter named Karl Decker to Cuba, equipped with bribe money. Decker managed to help the damsel escape and brought her to New York, where she could be fêted and displayed. That allowed the *Journal* to crow, in decks of headlines arrayed in an inverted pyramid:

MISS EVANGELINA CISNEROS RESCUED BY THE JOURNAL.
An American Newspaper Accomplishes at a Single
Stroke What the Best Efforts of Diplomacy
Failed Utterly to Bring About in
Many Months.[60]

At every step Hearst emphasized the plight of the innocent (and attractive) victim, the barbarity of her captors, and the gallant role played by his own newspaper. This episode nicely illustrates one of the core features of yellow journalism. Hearst and Pulitzer were urging the government to wage war not on the basis of such modern considerations as economics, diplomacy, statecraft, or even religion. Instead they were pushing a more old-fashioned view—that the fate of a single person (a beauty, to be sure, like Helen of Troy or Guinevere) should be enough to launch armies and navies into battle.

The following January, rioting broke out in Havana against the Spanish government. As a precaution, President McKinley ordered a warship, the USS *Maine*, to Cuba. On the evening of February 15, 1898, an explosion rocked the ship while it lay at anchor in Havana Harbor, killing more than 250 U.S. sailors, marines, and officers. Never mind that the cause of the blast has never been explained. Never mind that Spanish officials rushed to deny any role and to express sympathy. Never mind that the captain of the *Maine*, Charles Sigsbee, who somehow escaped injury, pleaded for Americans to withhold judgment.[61] Hearst and Pulitzer both leaped to the conclusion that the ship and its American crew had been destroyed by a Spanish mine. The clamor for war reached a peak.

To his credit, Pulitzer actually ran a second-day front page with a headline that ended in a question mark, suggesting that the cause of the *Maine*'s sinking was still uncertain. In the meantime, he announced that the *World* was sending a special ship to investigate. (It never arrived.) By the next day, though, he could not restrain himself any longer. On that day both Pulitzer and Hearst published details from a "secret" cable sent by Captain Sigsbee to the secretary of the navy hinting darkly that the sinking was not an accident. The "cable" turned out to be a fake,[62] but both editors were now in full cry. Newspaper sales passed a million a day, and Hearst wanted more. Both papers offered "illustrations" of the *Maine* at the moment of the explosion—an image that was, of course, wholly imaginary, since none of the artists had actually seen it blow up (fig. 5.6). In the face of such pressure, combined with calls for war from members of Congress and from within his own administration (including Assistant Navy Secretary Theodore Roosevelt), McKinley jumped on the bandwagon. On April 25, 1898, the United States declared war against Spain.

Now it was off to the races for both newspapers. Pulitzer did his best to compete, sending the author Stephen Crane and a large supporting cast, but it was impossible to match Hearst's money and devotion to the cause. With a battalion

5.6 WILLIAM RANDOLPH HEARST CLAMORED FOR WAR after the USS *Maine* sank in Havana Harbor under mysterious circumstances. Despite pleas from the captain not to jump to conclusions, Hearst swept aside all doubts and demanded retaliation against Spain, even offering his own personal reward money. —*New York Journal.*

of reporters and a taskforce of private ships, Hearst threw all his resources into the coverage. Not only that, but he also topped Pulitzer by going to Cuba himself to take part in the reporting. He quickly got into the thick of things. First, he arranged transportation, on board a leased ship called the *Sylvia,* which he outfitted with "printing presses, dark rooms, medical supplies, food fit for a king, and enough ice to resupply the American military hospital in Cuba when it ran out."[63] He brought with him more than a dozen crew and *Journal* staffers, as well as the beguiling Willson sisters, two chorus girls he had grown fond of.

Then, accompanied by his intrepid reporter James Creelman, Hearst himself pushed on to the front lines. Moving with American forces, they were approaching the town of El Caney, site of a Spanish fortification. By his own account, Creelman was in the forefront of a successful bayonet charge on the Spanish position but was wounded shortly thereafter and laid in a grassy area with other casualties. In his memoir, he recalled:

> Some one knelt in the grass beside me and put his hand on my fevered head. Opening my eyes, I saw Mr. Hearst, the proprietor of the *New York Journal,* a straw hat with a bright ribbon on his head, a revolver at his belt, and a pencil and note-book in his hand. The man who had provoked the war had come to see the result with his own eyes and, finding one of his correspondents prostrate, was doing the work himself. Slowly he took down my story of the fight. Again and again the ting-ing of Mauser bullets interrupted. But he seemed unmoved. The battle had to be reported somehow.
>
> "I'm sorry you're hurt, but"—and his face was radiant with enthusiasm—"wasn't it a splendid fight? We must beat every paper in the world."
>
> After doing what he could to make me comfortable, Mr. Hearst mounted his horse and dashed away for the seacoast, where a fast steamer was waiting to carry him across the sea to a cable station.[64]

According to Creelman, Hearst left him to lie where he had fallen for almost two days, without food or medicine. "I had to rise from my litter and stagger seven miles through the hills and the mud without an attendant. . . . I expect no gratitude but I do expect a chance for my life," Creelman wrote to Hearst, in a letter he signed "Faithfully yours."[65] Cruising aboard the *Sylvia,* Hearst stayed in the vicinity for about a month before returning to New York. His exposure to war seemed only to reinforce his enthusiasm for it. Looking farther abroad at U.S. military victories in the Philippines, Hearst editorialized in favor of American ambitions in the Far East as well as the Caribbean. "We'll rule in Asia as we rule at home. We shall establish in Asia a branch agent of the true American movement towards liberty," he boasted in a burst of imperial hubris.[66]

As a military matter, the Spanish-American war ended swiftly and, from the viewpoint of American expansionists, successfully. The United States military decisively defeated Spain and took control of its colonies in Cuba, Puerto Rico, and the Philippines. As a journalistic matter, however, the conflict was more ambiguous. The McKinley administration imposed almost no effective censorship on American reporters, especially in Cuba, which was so close to Florida that ambitious journalists like Hearst could simply show up at the major battlefields on their own—and, in some cases, could do so before U.S. troops arrived, and with better provisions. In addition, since McKinley and other imperialists wanted to use the war to raise the U.S. profile abroad, it would hardly make sense to discourage descriptions of the anticipated victories. For this reason, heroes like Admiral Dewey and Colonel Roosevelt were created almost overnight in a war that lasted only about three months. The war certainly provided good material, which made careers and boosted circulation. But it is unclear whether the increased sales meant more profit for American newspapers. In Hearst's case it almost certainly did not, because he spent so much money on covering the war. Finally, it must be asked what responsibility the press bears for helping to start a war that was clearly not a matter of national survival. Historians differ in their assessment of how instrumental the jingoistic mood of the country was in *causing* the war, but most agree that the coverage of the yellow press certainly *contributed* to an unnecessary conflict.

E. L. Godkin, editor of *The Nation,* was appalled by "the *Journal's* war" and by the *Journal's* publisher. "A blackguard boy with several millions of dollars at his disposal," Godkin observed, "has more influence on the use a great nation may make of its credit, of its army and navy, of its name and traditions than all the statesmen and philosophers and professors in the country."[67]

*   *   *

THE YELLOW JOURNALISM THAT SHOCKED readers and helped launch a military adventure was not the only style of journalism available to American readers in the late nineteenth century. In fact there were at least two competing models of journalism by the 1890s, both of which persist today. One model, developed under Pulitzer and Hearst, focused on the idea of news as primarily a good *story*— the telling of individual human dramas. This was the kind of journalism they and their imitators did, and did well. Think of Nellie Bly. She did not investigate mental institutions in general and draw broad conclusions. She got committed to one herself and told readers what it felt like to eat rancid butter or be forced to take a cold bath. She did not describe innovations in travel; she went around the world herself and sent home a dramatic narrative. The alternative model of journalism, the approach developed under a new generation of editors, focused on news as *information*—the presentation of facts in a reasoned way. In this view, the news consists of information presented according to the rules of logic, not the needs of drama. This was the ideal of a journalism that would be dispassionate, neutral, objective.[68] This ideal was the one espoused and (usually) embodied in a newspaper located just a few steps down Park Row from Hearst's *Journal* and Pulitzer's *World*—at the *New-York Times.*

The *Times* was already almost half a century old.[69] It had been founded in 1851 by Henry Jarvis Raymond, who was Horace Greeley's first assistant before moving on to other newspaper opportunities. Originally called the *New-York Daily Times,* the paper dropped the adjective "Daily" not long afterwards. (The hyphen in "New-York" lived on until 1896.) Raymond set a tone of calm and dignity right at the start. In his opening number in 1851 he pledged, "We do not mean to write as if we were In a passion, unless that shall really be the case; and we shall make it a point to get into a passion as rarely as possible."[70] Circulation climbed, and Raymond appeared headed for success in both journalism and politics, where he was active in Whig and Republican Party affairs. But he died prematurely in 1869, suffering a heart attack while visiting the apartment of his lover, the actress Rose Eytinge.[71] After his death, the paper was taken over by his business partner, a former banker named George Jones. It was under Jones that the *Times* achieved one of its greatest successes, the exposé of Boss Tweed and the ensuing reforms to New York's city government. Nevertheless, the paper languished throughout most of the 1880s and 1890s, running far behind the *Sun,* the *World,* and the *Journal* in the circulation wars. By 1896 the circulation of the *Times* had shrunk to nine thousand, and it was said to be losing $1,000 a day. So it was relatively affordable when a buyer came looking. That buyer was Adolph Ochs.

Born in 1858, Adolph was the son of Julius Ochs, who had emigrated from Bavaria in what is now southern Germany.[72] With fluency in Hebrew and religious training in Judaism, Julius often served as a kind of lay rabbi to tiny congregations in several southern cities where he lived.[73] Eventually he became a drygoods salesman with a knack for failing in business. The family suffered financially, so Adolph took a job at age eleven as a newsboy delivering the *Knoxville Chronicle.* An admirer of Horace Greeley, young Adolph impressed his employer and quickly advanced to the position of printer's devil, then moved on to the status of journeyman printer. At age fourteen Adolph left school to work full-time, bringing his earnings home. A few years later he tried to start up a newspaper in Chattanooga with some friends, but it failed. Nevertheless, he stayed on and published a city directory that was such a success that he was able to get financing to buy the *Chattanooga Times* in 1878. That paper prospered, and in 1883 Ochs was able to make a prestigious marriage with Effie Miriam Wise, the daughter of Isaac Wise, the head of the Reform Jewish movement in the United States. Ten years later, during the economic panic of 1893, Ochs ran into financial difficulties. His solution was not to retrench but to try to increase his revenues by buying a second newspaper.

He looked for one in New York City, equipped with letters of introduction he had secured from fellow publishers. As the publisher of a small country paper, deeply in debt himself, Ochs was a long shot. But he shrewdly kept up a brave front and began assembling the financing he would need to take over the now-bankrupt *New-York Times.* In the end, he managed to put together a new corporation that would sell $500,000 in bonds backed by the assets of the paper itself. In the short run, all he would need to do was earn enough money to pay the interest on the bonds. The company would also issue $1 million worth of stock, and—if he could show a profit for three years running—Ochs would end up owning the majority of it. He needed approval from the newspaper's existing stockholders, and he talked J. P. Morgan and the others into going along. Ochs's personal stake in the paper was limited to $75,000, though it is unclear how he assembled even that amount, since he had less than $1,000 to his name at the time. In any case, on August 17, 1896, the creditors and stockholders approved his plan, and Adolph Ochs became publisher of the *New-York Times*. He now owned a newspaper valued at $1.5 million in the nation's biggest market, and he had done it entirely with other people's money.[74]

Now he had to make some money of his own. It would not be easy, since the *Times,* for all its respectability and its glorious past, was at the bottom of the heap among the major English-language New York City dailies in terms of circulation (see Table 5.1). Ochs set about trying to revive the paper. As so often happens when a new owner takes over a newspaper, he decided to greet his new readers with an opening declaration of his journalistic principles:

> It will be my earnest aim that *The New-York Times* give the news, all the news, in concise and attractive form, in language that is parliamentary in good society, and give it as early, if not earlier, than it can be learned through any other reliable medium; to give the news impartially, without fear or favor, regardless of any party, sect or interest involved; to make the columns of *The New-York Times* a forum for the consideration of all questions of public importance, and to that end to invite intelligent discussion from all shades of opinion.

This famous opening statement is noteworthy for several reasons. Among them is the fact that Ochs was apparently sincere. He was indeed earnest, and he did indeed emphasize the paper's role as a gatherer of facts. It was characteristic that he promised to render those facts in decent terms, not the sort of sex and gore found in the yellow papers. He also promised to operate as a political independent, although he had touted himself to his financial backers as a Democrat. Nevertheless, his famous formulation—"without fear or favor"—became widely accepted as a professional ideal, both at the *Times* and across the news business. Finally, Ochs revived the idea that Benjamin Franklin had expressed a century and a half earlier—that a newspaper should serve as a "forum" for the consideration of matters of great public interest. In this, Ochs foresaw the institution that would become known as the op-ed page, after the *Times* itself introduced one in 1970, which is now a fixture in most American newspapers.[75] In that one dense paragraph, Ochs was setting an ambitious course; he was promising nothing less than a newspaper that would be factual, fair, fast, and free of partisan loyalties. It was an imposing agenda. Two months after he bought the paper, Ochs settled upon a motto (one he had thought up himself) and put it on display every day in one of the newspaper's two "ears" atop the front page. From then on, the *Times* claimed to offer "All the News That's Fit to Print."

TABLE 5.1

Circulation figures for major New York City daily newspapers, circa 1896

PAPER	COPIES SOLD PER DAY
World (Pulitzer; a.m. and p.m.)	600,000
Journal (Hearst)	430,000
Herald	140,000
Sun	130,000
Evening Post	19,000
Tribune	16,000
Times (Ochs)	9,000
TOTAL	**1,344,000**

Unlike his rivals at the mass-circulation dailies, Hearst and Pulitzer, Ochs did not set out to be the lord of the newsroom. Instead he focused on the modern role of the newspaper publisher: someone who has a large financial stake in the operation and who sets a general editorial direction but focuses on the business side and gives most of his attention to advertising, circulation, production, and the like. As newspapers grew in scale, the people trying to run them came up with a division of labor that was very similar to that employed in other large capitalistic enterprises of the era. Naturally, change came to different newspapers at different rates, but the big-city dailies were among the earliest businesses to industrialize fully. In a very real sense, a newspaper is a *manufacturing* operation, as well as a vehicle for disseminating information, opinions, and culture. Each day, thousands or millions of products must be mass-produced and shipped. Even a short visit to a pressroom makes this clear; it is a noisy, dirty, sometimes dangerous place where blue-collar workers are busy handling tons of paper, ink, and machinery. In the era of "hot type," the composing room was full of linotype machines, which made a tremendous racket, and the press room was filled with roaring presses printing miles of newsprint every day. Upstairs in the newsroom, a mistake could lead to a correction or a demotion; down in the pressroom, a mistake could lead to a mangled limb.

On the business side, in the typical big-city newspaper, an owner-publisher had several top executives, each taking responsibility for the paper's vital operations: advertising, circulation, production, and editorial. On the editorial side, there was usually a strict hierarchy, topped by an editor in chief, or simply The Editor. Such an eminence usually held complete sway over all the news pages, the opinion columns, and the illustrations. On the news side, most papers used a managing editor to oversee the newsgathering, who might be assisted by deputies with specific areas of responsibility such as coverage of the home city, the state capital, business, sports, and the like. Under each of those assistant editors were still more layers of editors: some handed out assignments and told reporters what to do; others read the finished stories and actually edited them. In many cases, as was mentioned, news was gathered first by "legmen," who went to the trials, fires, strikes, and other incidents, then telephoned their notes to the waiting "desk men," who wove the notes into stories. The stories were then passed on to an editor sitting along the rim of a big array of desks, who would scrutinize it for errors and write a headline.[76]

In his role as publisher of the *Times*, Ochs became a distinct success. After a modest increase in circulation during his first two years, he decided to try one of the oldest ploys in the book: he slashed his price from three cents a copy down to a penny. The impact was dramatic. Circulation shot up from 25,000 to 75,000 a day. Each paper brought in just a third of what it had previously, but there were now three times as many being sold. On the basis of circulation alone, the *Times*' revenue was unchanged. But Ochs could now argue to his advertisers that their displays were being seen by many more people, so he was able to increase his ad rates.

On the editorial side, Ochs set the course. He hired strong editors and generally stayed out of their way. The most important of these was Carr Van Anda, who came to the *Times* in 1904 from the *Sun* and ruled over the newsroom for the next three decades. Ochs insisted that the paper improve its appearance, and he established a tone of seriousness, decency, and decorum in the news columns. Ochs also determined that the *Times* would shun the new practice of running photographs to illustrate news stories, and for decades the paper ran very few of them, eventually earning the nickname "The Great Gray Lady." Of course, he forbade comic strips altogether. In all these ways, Ochs was a newspaper conservative where Hearst and Pulitzer were radical experimenters. Ochs also beefed up the paper's business coverage, thereby helping to lock in a readership that was affluent and desirable to advertisers out of all proportion to their numbers. In these various ways Ochs was inventing a strategy for succeeding in the New York market without having to outdo the yellow papers at their own game. He was trying to play by a different set of rules, as he indicated when he advertised the *Times* by asserting, "It does not soil the breakfast cloth."[77]

Gradually, the *Times* began to evolve into the bastion of journalistic respectability that Ochs envisioned. The paper also benefited from the hard work and high standards of its editors and reporters. But if there was one key to its success, it can be attributed to the publisher himself: Ochs made money, and he used that money to improve the paper. Rather than building castles for himself or trying to buy his way into high elective office, Adolph Ochs established a policy, still followed by his great-grandson today, of leading a comparatively modest life in order to reinvest a substantial proportion of the profits back into operations. As a result, the *Times* could afford to open more bureaus, to hire more foreign correspondents, to buy new presses, trucks, and buildings—to do the practical, costly things that make great journalism possible. Readers noticed and (to their credit) started flocking to the *Times*. Circulation hit 82,000 in 1900, 192,000 in 1910, and shot up to 340,000 by 1920. Along the way, the *Times* made one more decision that helped secure its place. In 1913 the paper began publishing an annual index to the vast number of topics covered in its pages, a step that made the *Times* the favorite resource of librarians and researchers and established its reputation as "the newspaper of record."

* * *

IN THE EARLY 1890S, LATE in his long life, Frederick Douglass formed a friendship with a young, crusading black journalist. Her name was Ida B. Wells, and she was just beginning a career as one of the most prominent reform-minded journalists of the era. Wells had been born into slavery in Mississippi and emancipated as a toddler. After losing her parents to yellow fever, she moved as a young woman to Memphis and went to work as a teacher in the nearby town of Woodstock, Tennessee. The era of Reconstruction was over, and black Southerners, though constitutionally freed from slavery, were facing a widespread assault on their civil rights in the white backlash known as Jim Crow. While traveling to work one day in 1883 aboard a train, Wells was ordered to leave the "ladies car" and head back to the smoking car, where all black passengers were expected to sit. She not only refused but actually bit the conductor. Wells went on to file a lawsuit against the railroad (which she lost on appeal), and she described her case in a local black newspaper. With that introduction to journalism, she continued teaching and writing. A few years later she became part owner and editor of a black newspaper, the *Memphis Free Speech and Headlight,* and she became secretary of the black-run National Press Association in 1887.[78]

Five years later, Wells found the great calling of her life when three young men who were friends of hers were lynched in Memphis. Taking up their cause, she turned to a general campaign against lynching. After angry whites attacked the *Free Speech* office in Memphis, she moved to New York and joined the *New York Age.* Continuing the campaign to expose and denounce lynching, she produced a pamphlet titled *Southern Horrors: Lynch Law in All Its Phases,* which was widely distributed in the hopes of ending the practice (fig. 5.7). In *Southern Horrors,* Wells not only documented recent cases of lynching but also went on to argue that much of the rationale for lynching was based on "the old thread bare lie that Negro men rape white women."[79] In fact, she continued, most of the sex that occurred between black men and white women (as well as between white men and black women) was actually consensual—a truth that many whites had trouble accepting. Furthermore, she proposed several steps for blacks to take to protect themselves, which included waging a kind of general strike against white employers and moving out of the South altogether. She went on to urge a more radical solution: armed self-defense. Pointing out that the only cases in which threatened lynching did not materialize involved situations in which blacks were armed, she wrote, "A Winchester rifle should have a place of honor in every black home, and it should be used for that protection which the law refuses to give."[80] In 1893 she attended the World's Columbian Exposition in Chicago and joined

5.7 JOURNALIST IDA B. WELLS FOUGHT AGAINST LYNCHING through her reporting and writing, from the 1880s through the 1920s. She is shown here on the cover of her 1892 book *Southern Horrors*.

—*Wikimedia Commons.*

with Douglass and a Chicago lawyer named Ferdinand L. Barnett (who was also editor of a black newspaper) to agitate against lynching. Wells married Barnett in 1895 and took on the editor's role at Barnett's newspaper, the *Chicago Conservator*. Under the byline Ida Wells-Barnett, she continued to press for racial justice.

In her campaign against lynching, Wells-Barnett was carrying on a tradition in American journalism that traced back at least several decades. Earlier journalists had used the techniques of exposure and denunciation to address such problems as swill milk, corruption among New York's Tammany Hall political gang, the treatment of mental patients at Blackwell Island, and others. Just a few years earlier, the Danish immigrant Jacob Riis had published his exposé of slum conditions in New York, titled *How the Other Half Lives*, using photographs as well as words to document the human misery. Each campaign, however, was isolated and sporadic, never gaining much momentum beyond the immediate local problem. That began to change dramatically just after 1900 with the blossoming of a journalistic movement that has become known as "muckraking."

As a coherent national movement, muckraking can be traced to the year 1902. The setting was a monthly magazine called *McClure's,* which had been founded by S. S. McClure, an Irish-born journalist, in 1893 in New York City. Sam McClure was a pioneer in a new kind of publication then sweeping the country. Although magazines had been published in America for more than a century, they generally steered clear of journalism and focused instead on literature, fiction, ladies' fashion, or housekeeping hints. Traditional magazines like the *Atlantic Monthly, Scribner's,* or *Harper's* were also typically quite expensive in price and conservative in outlook. But starting in the 1880s, a new kind of magazine appeared. Thanks to dramatic drops in the cost of paper, magazines could now be priced to reach middle- and working-class audiences. And thanks to the halftone engraving process, they could print extensive displays of photographs. It is also important to note that, unlike even the biggest daily newspapers, which were rarely distributed far beyond their home base, these magazines circulated around the country. The emergence of cheap, well-illustrated monthly magazines created the possibility, for the first time, of a mass national audience focused on news and public affairs. Until the advent of radio networks in the 1920s, such magazines were the only truly *national* outlet for journalism.[81]

Still, it took some initiative to capitalize on this new possibility and to turn it in a politically progressive direction. That was precisely where Sam McClure, after making a fortune in syndication, led the way. One of McClure's first hires for his magazine was a young woman named Ida Tarbell, who spent most of the 1890s working on lengthy serialized biographical sketches—first of Napoleon, then of Lincoln. Two other key additions were a contributing editor, veteran Chicago reporter Ray Stannard Baker, and a managing editor, Lincoln Steffens, hired in 1900. In January 1903, *McClure's Magazine* assembled an issue that has been called the most famous in American magazine history.[82] It contained three articles that became recognized as classics of modern muckraking: part three of Tarbell's history of John D. Rockefeller's Standard Oil trust, Steffens's exposé of municipal corruption in Minneapolis, and an article by Baker on a brutal coal-mining strike in Pennsylvania—all accompanied by an editorial written by McClure that attempted to frame the entire issue as one that raised serious questions about American society. "Capitalists, workingmen, politicians, citizens—all breaking the law, or letting it be broken. Who is left to uphold it?" he asked. "There is no one left; none but all of us."[83]

Tarbell's nineteen-part series on Standard Oil became a sensation and set the standard for the techniques of exposé. Tarbell, who had grown up in the oil fields of western Pennsylvania, where Rockefeller built his business, was a scrupulous researcher, and she relied heavily on official government documents and court records to build the case against him. Rockefeller's companies had been sued and investigated for many years, and there was an extensive paper record dispersed across dozens of courthouses and state agencies, but no one had committed the time and expense (McClure sank an astonishing $50,000 into the project) to pull it all together in a dramatic narrative for a national audience. Tarbell's account was quickly published in book form, and two years later, the administration of Theodore Roosevelt filed a federal antitrust suit against Rockefeller's Standard Oil. For *McClure's Magazine,* the impact was also great. From a circulation of about 370,000 in 1900, the magazine shot past half a million after it began running exposés.

Soon, others joined in.[84] Journalists began looking into child labor, race relations, lynching, prostitution, and an array of other social ills. They produced a floodtide of "literature of exposure"—both in traditional journalistic forms and in novels as well. One of the most famous was written by the young socialist writer Upton Sinclair. His investigation into the meatpacking industry in Chicago began with support from Julius Wayland, the head of the largest-circulation socialist newspaper in American history, the *Appeal to Reason,* based in tiny Girard, Kansas. Wayland gave Sinclair an advance of $500 to live on while he explored the rotten underside of Packingtown, then published his work serially in the *Appeal to Reason* before it was published as a novel.[85] Sinclair created a thin plotline to weave together his graphic descriptions of brutal working conditions:

> There would be meat that had tumbled out on the floor, in the dirt and sawdust, where the workers had tramped and spit uncounted billions of consumption germs. There would be meat stored in great piles in rooms; and the water from leaky roofs would drip over it, and thousands of rats would race about on it. It was too dark in these storage places to see well, but a man could run his hand over these piles of meat and sweep off handfuls of the dried dung of rats. These rats were nuisances, and the packers would put poisoned bread out for them; they would die, and then rats, bread and meat would go into the hoppers together.[86]

Publication of *The Jungle* had an immediate impact. Among readers, it touched off a vogue for vegetarianism. In politics, it prompted swift reaction. Roosevelt invited Sinclair to the White House, and within months the president signed the Pure Food and Drug Act, which set up government agencies to prevent the revolting and dangerous practices that Sinclair had described. As for Sinclair, he was disappointed. He had hoped that the workers' plight in *The Jungle* would encourage more Americans to see that the real problem was capitalism and therefore turn to socialism. "I aimed at the public's heart," he wrote later, "and by accident I hit it in the stomach."[87]

These articles and many others contributed directly to an impressive record of reform—from food inspections to civil service rules to the outlawing of child labor. That legacy is based on several factors. One reason why such an assault on corruption worked was that America was in fact a highly corrupt society at the time. Industrial capitalism was in a particularly brutal phase, race relations were at a low point, and government at all levels was wide open to bossism. At the same time, though, it must be said that America was not *utterly* corrupt. Journalists who published indictments of powerful people and institutions were not charged with sedition, censored, or killed, as they are in societies where power is unchecked. American institutions retained the possibility of revival, especially through electoral politics. Muckraking journalism found important allies among Progressive politicians, and each side in the partnership strengthened the other.

A key figure is Teddy Roosevelt. Boosted by his exploits in Cuba (as dramatized by the yellow press), T.R. was the vice president on the Republican ticket when McKinley ran for reelection in 1900. After the president was assassinated in 1901 (by an assailant immersed in anti-McKinley vitriol, much of it printed by Hearst),[88] Roosevelt became president. He added to his reputation as a reformer by acting swiftly in response to exposés about the oil trust and the meatpacking industry. But even though he benefited politically from leading such reforms, Roosevelt was also quite defensive about the growing movement of exposure and reform. In 1906, while laying a cornerstone for the new House Office Building in Washington, Roosevelt uttered the warning that gave the movement its name. Invoking the allegorical *Pilgrim's Progress* by John Bunyan, he referred to Bunyan's "Man with the Muck-rake," a character who is always looking down into the mud and filth. "There is filth on the floor, and it must be scraped up with the muck-rake," Roosevelt acknowledged. "But the man who never does anything else, who never thinks or speaks or writes, save of his feats with the muck-rake, becomes, not a help to society, not an incitement to good, but one of the most potent forces for evil."[89] If Roosevelt hoped to discourage the practice of muckraking, he certainly failed. In the century since then, journalists have taken the phrase to heart as a badge of honor, and most journalists see the period at the start of the twentieth century as a golden era of dramatic investigations and effective reforms.

Even so, the classical era of muckraking eventually ran out of steam after about a decade, for several reasons. In some cases, individual journalists simply moved on professionally to new topics and styles. At the same time, some of the muckraking magazines found themselves under financial pressure from advertisers or bankers who did not appreciate their assaults on the titans of American industry. For a while, such retaliation from big business could be offset by gains in circulation, but there was ultimately a price to be paid.[90] It has also been argued that the muckrakers' impact was limited because they attacked symptoms rather than root causes and never developed a coherent critique of American political economy. This is a charge to which most muckrakers would likely plead guilty;

after all, they were not a political party (although they often made common cause with Progressive politicians) but a spontaneous collection of individuals. Some, like Sinclair, were Socialists; others were reform-minded liberals trying to perfect America rather than change anything fundamental about it. They specialized in attacking dishonesty, inefficiency, cruelty, venality—especially in individuals like Rockefeller or in corrupt political bosses. As the journalist Ray Stannard Baker summed it up: "We muckraked not because we hated our world but because we loved it. We were not hopeless, we were not cynical, we were not bitter."[91]

More important reasons for the demise of muckraking go beyond the journalists themselves. Much of the credit for the success and impact of the practice must go to its readers. They are the ones who bought the magazines, and they are the ones who voted for the politicians and policies that brought change. Over time, however, readers naturally turned to other interests, or they developed what is known as "compassion fatigue." It is impossible, after all, to expect people to remain agitated as a permanent condition. By definition, outrage is temporary— as all editors know. Furthermore, there is a final paradox: the muckrakers and their Progressive allies were so effective that they largely put themselves out of business. In approximately a decade, between 1904 and 1914, they brought about so much deep and lasting reform that they had, by and large, satiated the public demand for change. Their investigations led not only to the direct election of U.S. senators (taking the matter out of the hands of corrupt state legislatures) and to a court order breaking up Standard Oil but also to the creation of government agencies that (in theory, at least) were supposed to take over the watchdog function from the magazines and to make investigations a routine part of government operations. With government inspectors on hand at the slaughterhouses, mines, and factories, the muckraking journalists were no longer needed as much as they had been just a few years earlier.

In addition to the reforms, the muckrakers left another legacy, this one quite unintended: the creation of the field of public relations. In a backhanded compliment to the power of muckraking, corporations began to see that they needed to wage their own campaigns to influence public opinion. The practice of seeking favorable publicity was not invented from scratch, of course. Beginning in the early nineteenth century, press agents had offered newspapers information and suggestions for stories. A few geniuses of promotion such as P. T. Barnum built whole careers on dazzling the press corps and bamboozling the public. But at the start of the twentieth century, the practice became an industry in itself, available for hire. One of the most visible pioneers was a former reporter named Ivy Lee, who opened a business in New York City in 1905 representing railroads and other corporations. The figure generally recognized as the first major client of modern public relations was none other than John D. Rockefeller, whose image as a cutthroat had been fixed in the public mind by Ida Tarbell. Rockefeller's reputation only worsened in 1914 when a company he owned waged a brutal battle against coal miners in Ludlow, Colorado. Company thugs opened fire on the strikers, killing twenty-four people, including a dozen children. As blame settled on Rockefeller, his son, John D. Rockefeller Jr., retained Lee to try to undo the damage. Lee was criticized (by Upton Sinclair, who nicknamed him "Poison Ivy," and by Carl Sandburg, who called him "a paid liar," among others), but Lee's long-range campaign of releasing selected bits of factual information to the press eventually paid off for his clients. And, of course, it paid him quite handsomely as well.[92]

At the start of the twentieth century, newspapers and magazines were more powerful and more profitable than ever before. Still, they had plenty of shortcomings. Unlike Joseph Pulitzer, most newspaper publishers were not friends of the workers, immigrants, or anyone else outside their local commercial establishment. It was also almost impossible to find any real news about black Americans in the pages of most American newspapers. In the big cities, where newspaper competition was at its fiercest, reporters and editors were under constant pressure to hurry, to exaggerate, even to invent. To be sure, newspapers *looked* better after Pulitzer got through reinventing the front page, the comics page, and the Sunday edition. And when they put their minds to it, crusading editors of daily newspapers and muckraking editors of national magazines could provide valuable documentary evidence of corruption in business and government. When they worked at it, they were capable of living up to the goal set by Mr. Dooley—to comfort the afflicted and to afflict the comfortable.

Pulitzer and Hearst stand out in their era because they were innovators. Seeking a mass audience, the new publishers built enormous word factories with industrial-scale machinery and workforces. The daily newspaper became a profitable powerhouse, able to sell ideas and candidates as well as soap and corsets. But for all the change they initiated, Pulitzer and Hearst left one fundamental part of the newspaper business unchanged. They did nothing to alter the basic ownership structure. Pulitzer and Hearst, as well as Adolph Ochs and nearly every one of their contemporaries, were either the sole owners or the major owners of private companies. In essence, most publishers were completely unaccountable most of the time. They could decide, as Ochs did, to reinvest their profits in the paper; they could decide, as Pulitzer did, to spend much of his money on expensive travel, then give most of the rest away; or they could decide, as Hearst did, to build a media empire, to buy the castles and art treasures of Europe, and even to try to buy the White House. Thanks to their readers, these publishers had realized the goal of independence; that is, they were independent of just about everyone, except their advertisers.

Hearst and Pulitzer are often lumped together in histories of their times, like mischievous siblings or co-defendants. But that's not quite fair, especially to Pulitzer. From a journalistic point of view, Pulitzer is clearly the more seminal figure. Almost all of the techniques and features, and even many of the people, that Hearst employed in his *Journal* were taken from Pulitzer's *World*. In editorial terms, Pulitzer is easily distinguished from Hearst by his greater commitment to principles, his unwavering support for working-class and immigrant interests, and his determination to use his newspaper as an instrument of reform. Except for promoting the war with Spain, which he regretted as soon as it was over, Pulitzer usually resisted jingoism, stood apart from U.S. government policy, and freely criticized the corporate and political establishment. Hearst was always more cynical than Pulitzer (not to mention more racist), and he became much more conservative over the course of his much longer life. By the end, Hearst was a despised figure among many American progressives, associated with a frightening brand of domestic fascism.

In the end, though, the more important competition was not the one between Pulitzer and Hearst but the one between two philosophies: sensationalism and professionalism. That dynamic would shape much of the debate in journalism for the coming century.

When he died in 1911, Joseph Pulitzer left $2 million to Columbia University to endow a school of journalism and to pay for the annual journalism prizes that still bear his name.[93]

His death also triggered an outpouring of testimonials and tributes. One of the best came from a reporter on the World, *who recalled that he had once covered a religious revival meeting, during which the preacher invited the man to come forward and join the converts sitting up front. Explaining that he was a reporter and was there on business, he declined.*

The preacher insisted, saying, "There's no business as momentous as the Lord's business."

"Maybe not," the reporter replied, "but you don't know Mr. Pulitzer!"

CHAPTER 6

Professionalizing the News in Peace and War, 1900–1920

There are reporters by the thousand who could not pass the entrance examination for
Harvard or Tuskegee, or even Yale. It is this vast and militant ignorance, this wide-spread and
fathomless prejudice against intelligence, that makes American journalism so pathetically
feeble and vulgar, and so generally disreputable.
— H. L. Mencken, 1941

CAN JOURNALISM BE TAUGHT?

By the time H. L. Mencken pondered that question in his memoir of his early days in the newspaper business, a campaign had long been under way to try to elevate the practice of journalism in America, largely by improving the training of each new crop of reporters. Some even hoped to—someday, somehow—make journalism into something approaching an exact science. If they could not accomplish that lofty goal, at least they might be able to address practices like reporters' faking the news, drinking on the job, and taking payoffs from people being covered. Maybe they could *begin*, at least, to turn journalism into a real profession, like teaching or the ministry, or like law or medicine. By the late nineteenth century, those last two fields were well on their way to full professional status, with well-defined bodies of knowledge and systems of licensure that legally defined who could practice in those areas—and who could not.[1]

The earliest efforts to professionalize American journalism can be traced back at least as far as 1869—and to a perhaps unlikely source. That year marks the date when classes for journalists were first offered at a school in Virginia called Washington College. Now known as Washington & Lee University, the college was the first place of employment after the Civil War for the defeated Confederate general Robert E. Lee. According to one account, Lee "shocked his colleagues and the editors of his day" when he proposed offering instruction in the techniques of "printing or journalism." Before he could execute his plans, though, Lee fell ill and died in 1870. Within a decade the journalism program fizzled, but it marked a starting point in the instruction of journalists in American higher education.[2]

In proposing to teach journalism, advocates of instruction first had to overcome a deep skepticism within the field. From the very beginning, journalists had had a tradition of learning by doing. A few editors in the late nineteenth century held the view that there would be no harm (and potentially some benefit) in a young man's attending college for a general course of studies, provided that he was willing, after graduation, to start at the bottom in the newsroom.[3] But practical training, on the job, under the eye of an editor was widely considered the gold standard. Frederic Hudson, an editor at the *New York Herald* in the mid-nineteenth century (and one of the first modern historians of journalism), typified the old school of thought when he wrote that the newsroom is "the true college for newspaper students." At the time he wrote that, in 1873, this was indeed the prevailing wisdom. "Professor James Gordon Bennett or Professor Horace Greeley would turn out more real journalists," Hudson wrote, "than the Harvards, the Yales, and the Dartmouths could produce in a generation."[4] Such skepticism remained the dominant view until early in the twentieth century.[5]

A classic statement in favor of on-the-job-training came from Horace White, an editor of the *Chicago Tribune*. In an article in the *North American Review* in 1904, White vigorously stated the case against academic journalism education. "I maintain . . . that the university has nothing to teach journalists in the special sense that it has to teach lawyers, physicians, architects and engineers." All universities teach English composition, he observed. After that, what does a journalist really need? The main requirement for journalistic success was "a nose for news," according to White, by which he meant the ability to recognize and rank the importance of events. Citing himself as a case in point, White noted that he had attended college before entering the newspaper business in 1854 and had never taken a single course in journalism. His insinuation was clear: if such an approach was good enough for him, it should be good enough for succeeding generations of reporters.[6]

The editors of the *North American Review* then invited Pulitzer to reply. In the May 1904 edition Pulitzer began by noting that he had given the question of journalism education considerable thought. "I am more firmly convinced than ever of the ultimate success of the idea. Before the century closes schools of journalism will be generally accepted as a feature of specialized higher education, like schools of law or of medicine."[7] He then addressed the belief that the only true journalist is a "born journalist" by arguing that even people with obvious native talent, such as Shakespeare, must work hard to improve on their innate abilities. Pulitzer was willing to grant White's point that the "news instinct" cannot be taught. "I admit it," he wrote. "No college can give imagination, initiative, impulses, enthusiasm, a sense of humor or irony. These must be inborn." But, he argued, while such innate qualities might be necessary, they were not sufficient, and they could certainly be strengthened in the classroom. Next Pulitzer took on the folk wisdom in the news trade which holds that journalism must be taught in the newsroom, not in the classroom. "Nobody in a newspaper office has the time or the inclination to teach a raw reporter the things he ought to know before taking up even the humblest work of the journalist," Pulitzer wrote. Citing himself as a case in point, Pulitzer noted that when he get his start in a newsroom, no one bothered to teach him anything.

Stepping back, Pulitzer then posed the fundamental question. "What is a journalist?" he asked, offering this answer: "A journalist is the lookout on the bridge of the ship of state. He notes the passing sail, the little things of interest that dot the horizon in fine weather. He reports the drifting castaway whom the ship can save. He peers through fog and storm to give warnings of dangers ahead. He is not thinking of his wages, or of the profits of his owners. He is there to watch over the safety and the welfare of the people who trust him." Above all, then, the journalist is someone with a vital role to play in society by serving the readers. Pulitzer went on to state, rather pointedly, that although journalists operate in a commercial setting, they are *not* businessmen. He then provided one of the most eloquent statements of the belief that there should be a kind of "separation of church and state" at a newspaper to insulate the newsroom from the pressures of the business side of the operation: "Commercialism has a legitimate place in a newspaper, namely, in the business office. The more successful a newspaper is commercially, the better for its moral side. The more prosperous it is, the more independent it can afford to be, the higher salaries it can pay to editors and reporters, the less subject it will be to temptation, the better it can stand losses for the sake of principle and conviction." Finally, Pulitzer turned to the question of what should be taught in a school of journalism. First off, everyone should master clear, concise English prose. Then he listed a number of other subjects, including law, ethics, research skills, history (including the history of journalism), economics, statistics, modern languages, and science (a list of desirable areas of knowledge not very different from the one proposed by Ben Franklin in 1729). Ultimately, he wrote, journalism students would need the kind of training they could get only by putting out a newspaper of their own, perhaps once a week, under the supervision of their editor-professors. All this, he concluded, would strengthen the ranks of new journalists, which would strengthen the institution of the press, which would in turn serve the greater goal of strengthening the American experiment in self-government. According to Pulitzer, "Our Republic and its press will rise or fall together."

Given his vast fortune and his determination, it is perhaps no surprise that Pulitzer was eventually able to make his view a reality. Before he did so, though, another program beat him to the punch. The first college to found a school of journalism in America, and likely the first in the world, was a land-grant school, the University of Missouri, in 1908. Its dean was Walter Williams, who had been the editor of a weekly newspaper in the university's hometown, Columbia. He also devised the school's first journalism curriculum, designed to train under-graduates in newspaper work through a combination of traditional academic pursuits such as history and economics, along with a stiff dose of practical train-ing. Hands-on learning was acquired through the publication of a student daily newspaper. The paper provided the laboratory for the first batch of would-be journalists (fifty-eight men and six women) to enter the field by a route other than the old apprentice method. "Our school seeks to do for journalism what schools of law, medicine and agriculture have done for those vocations," Williams told a press association.[8]

Williams also wrote "The Journalist's Creed," a declaration of principles that came to guide the Missouri program. "I believe in the profession of journalism. I believe that the public journal is a public trust; that all connected with it are, to the full measure of their responsibility, trustees for the public; that acceptance of a lesser service than the public service is betrayal of this trust," he declared, making the point that a newspaper is more than a mere business and adding that it must be "stoutly independent."[9] Above all, Williams emphasized this last point, that the journalist should answer to no one and nothing but the truth and should be absolutely *independent*—independent from the government, independent from partisan loyalties, independent from the advertisers and even the paper's own business office.

Pulitzer's project did not lag far behind. Under its new president Nicholas Mur-ray Butler, Columbia University in New York City came to terms with Pulitzer in 1904. In essence, Pulitzer promised to give Columbia $2 million (the equivalent of at least $35 million in today's dollars) to endow a school of journalism, to con-struct a new building to house it, and to support the journalism prizes that bear his name.[10] The major hitch: the university would not get the money until after Pulit-zer died. On October 29, 1911, Joseph Pulitzer succumbed to his many ailments, prompting an outpouring of obituaries and testimonials from around the globe. At Columbia University, officials moved swiftly to tap his bequest and start setting up the new school for news. In the meantime, however, that provision had allowed Missouri to slip in ahead and claim the title of America's first journalism school.

Soon afterward, other universities joined in. Since no one in America already held a degree in journalism, faculty had to be recruited from other fields. Some came from English departments, but most were editors who came straight from the nation's newsrooms, and for a long time, they were almost all white men. During the first dozen years after 1912, growth was dramatic, especially among the less academic, more practical-minded public universities. By 1924 there were about sixty journalism schools and programs nationwide.[11] Eventually the public colleges and universities became predominant in the field of journalism education. Today they make up the bulk of the 109 accredited programs in the United States.[12]

During this same period, from about 1880 to 1920, American publishers and editors were taking other steps to professionalize the field of journalism. Those decades saw a proliferation of local, regional, and national associations, many of which were devoted to raising standards, ethics, and working conditions. In 1884 the first trade journal in the field of newspapering got started. Known as *The Journalist,* published in New York, and shaped by a succession of editors, the weekly paper offered glowing portraits of successful publishers and prominent editors, and it included a roundup of news about newspapering from across the United States and Canada. Editorially, *The Journalist* waged a few crusades intended to elevate the practice of journalism. One target was excessive drinking by reporters. In the very first issue, editor C. A. Byrne mentioned a recent boat trip by a group of reporters to cover the arrival of a circus elephant; in pursuit of the story, several reporters apparently succumbed to their great thirst. "I object to seeing newspaper men get drunk upon these occasions," Byrne complained (as if chasing after elephants required a higher level of decorum). "It lowers the standing of the profession and conveys the inference that all a man has to do to get a writer's services is to make him intoxicated."[13]

The importance of the newspaper's independence was a theme that would be echoed repeatedly in the pages of *The Journalist* in the coming years. In 1893, for example, the paper reprinted a speech by C. V. Barton, city editor of the *Denver Times,* who argued, "The political organ is the bane of the real newspaper man who follows his profession because he loves it, and who hopes to elevate the standard for both himself and his profession."[14] The answer was independence: "The prostitution of the newspaper to the ambition of any politician, set of politicians or political party, is a thing to be condemned; and by none is it more surely condemned than by the genuine newspaper man who has no 'axes to grind.'" This thinking was at its most consistent when proponents were defending journalistic *institutions* against interference from politicians or advertisers. But the advocates of independence never quite resolved the problem of journalists as *individuals* who wish to be independent of their own editors or publishers. They remained condemned, in practice, to having to go along to get along.

Printers, editors, and other journalists had long formed local and regional associations, but they were mostly devoted either to practical business matters or to eating and (of course) drinking. After the founding of *The Journalist* in 1884, however, there followed a flurry of professional organizing among journalists, first on a regional basis, then along national lines.[15] These associations were organized according to specialty, representing publishers, editors, reporters, and photographers. In 1933, newspaper reporters formed their first successful trade union, the American Newspaper Guild (now called The Newspaper Guild and affiliated with the Communications Workers of America, AFL-CIO). Today the guild represents about 34,000 reporters, editors, and other newsroom employees in collective bargaining with their bosses.

In the space of two decades, give or take, the basic apparatus of a professional organization sprang into place. In their early years, these groups often had high aims; almost always, one of their stated goals was to improve the standards of journalism. That effort took many forms: conventions, conferences, prizes intended to reward superior work, formal (but voluntary) codes of ethics. Along with the growing ranks of journalism professors in the colleges and universities, they shared a perspective on the field that was national, high-minded, and ambitious. Many of them also shared another goal: to turn journalism into a true profession, with its own standards, oversight, and even—in the view of a minority—licensure. That last goal, never a universal ideal, proved the most elusive. Every attempt to reorganize American journalism along the lines of law and medicine, with their legal enforcement of admission and standards, has run aground on the same fundamental fact: the First Amendment forbids any government role in running the news business.[16]

A sense of professionalism took hold among reporters and editors of the era, based on the bedrock belief that the best journalism was the most independent. Independence—more than objectivity, more than advocacy, more than profitability, more than raising circulation—emerged in the early twentieth century as the goal that enjoyed the widest support among working journalists. This was the very value that would soon be most severely tested when the United States plunged into war in Europe. How would the newly articulated professional value of independence hold up? (fig. 6.1)

*   *   *

WHILE THE MOVEMENT TOWARD PROFESSIONALIZING journalism was still gathering steam in an industry that was scaling new heights of profit, reach, and influence, the news business came under fire from another powerful institution: the federal government. The occasion was the Great War. Although the nation was involved only during 1917–18, the conflict nevertheless put American journalism to its greatest test yet. When the United States finally entered the war, the federal government, especially the executive branch under President Woodrow Wilson, took several important steps to expand its powers over ordinary Americans—in its power to tax them, draft them, and control what they could read. In many ways, Wilson's approach was aimed at getting Americans to volunteer to help the cause (by going meatless on Mondays, for example, or by buying war bonds). Thus, to a great extent, the federal government relied on regulating thought and culture in order to influence behavior. As so often happens in wartime, one of the sharpest conflicts arose over redefining the relations between the press and the government. The emerging professional doctrine of journalistic independence would be challenged by political and legal demands for conformity and patriotism. Individual newspapers and magazines, especially those serving unpopular or minority audiences

6.1 **TIMES SQUARE IN NEW YORK CITY** was named for the *New York Times,* which moved into this elegant building commissioned by publisher Adolph Ochs in 1904. Ochs, the patriarch of the family that still owns the *New York Times,* soon had to move his growing newspaper to a larger building nearby, but the tower remained and serves as the site of the annual "ball drop" on New Year's Eve.

—*Library of Congress.*

such as socialists or German-speakers, were pressed hard and sometimes crushed entirely by government harassment and criminal prosecution. The federal government went so far as to revive the old legal doctrine of sedition in a campaign to coerce and intimidate American news institutions into closing ranks and supporting a war on foreign soil. In doing so, Wilson pioneered many of the techniques that later presidents would use to pressure, intimidate, and propagandize journalists in the numerous armed conflicts that followed.

When Archduke Franz Ferdinand of Austria was shot in Sarajevo in 1914, it was by no means obvious that his assassination would lead to the dispatching of U.S. troops to fight in Europe. In fact, many Americans had their own, strongly felt reasons for wanting to stay out of the conflict, on the grounds of ethnic loyalties if nothing else, particularly as the war emerged as a contest primarily between forces led by England on one side and Germany on the other. America's large population of immigrants from Germany and their descendants certainly did not relish the thought of American troops going off to fight against their homeland. And many of the country's large Irish American population felt no sympathy for the British, as a result of centuries of English oppression of Ireland. These and other ethnic groups supported hundreds of foreign-language newspapers, usually published weekly; in the biggest cities, there were even a few foreign-language daily papers. Most of those ethnic papers opposed American involvement.

Many voices in the black press were equally skeptical, especially before the United States entered the war. By 1914, African Americans were being served by a growing number of successful publications. After the founding of *Freedom's Journal* in New York City in 1827, the fortunes of black-owned newspapers and magazines remained hazardous throughout the nineteenth century. Most were undercapitalized and lacked advertising support. But that began to change around the turn of the twentieth century, as ever larger numbers of literate blacks moved into big cities. In the space of a few years, four nationally prominent newspapers were founded: the *Baltimore Afro-American* (1892), the *Chicago Defender* (1905), the *Pittsburgh Courier* (1907), and New York City's *Amsterdam News* (1909). In 1910, with support from the NAACP, the magazine *The Crisis* was launched under the editorship of W. E. B. Du Bois. Seven years later, labor leader A. Philip Randolph launched the *Messenger,* with a pacifist and socialist agenda. These publications all circulated widely and played important roles in community-building among blacks nationwide.[17]

Of these, the *Chicago Defender* grew most rapidly. It was founded by Robert Sengstacke Abbott, a son of former slaves who attended Hampton Institute in Virginia, where he learned the printing trade and heard both Frederick Douglass and Ida B. Wells speak. During World War I, the *Defender* launched an editorial crusade to urge blacks living in the rural South to migrate northward, especially to Chicago.[18] Abbott's campaign was so successful that the *Defender* was banned in some cities in the Deep South and had to be smuggled in by Pullman porters aboard trains heading south from Chicago. By the time of the war, the *Defender* was a lively mix of general-interest news, social notes, celebrations of black achievements, obsessive coverage of the boxer Jack Johnson (two or three front-page stories per issue), advice columns, and ads.

When fighting broke out in Europe, the *Defender* reacted with general condemnation. But Abbott believed that there could be a silver lining. In August 1914 the *Defender* ran a long article noting that the war was likely to choke off the flow of immigrants from Europe, who competed in America with blacks for jobs. Not only that, but also many of the European combatants would now want to summon home their young men living abroad, thus further eliminating competition for blacks in the labor force. "It may now dawn upon the American manufacturer, the American captains of industry, and the American controller of commerce that the Afro-American is the most dependable laborer," the paper observed. "He, at least, is not subject to be called across the seas to bear arms when some monarch of the old world would extend his power."[19]

Once the United States entered the war, however, the *Defender* turned to patriotic themes and generally backed the effort. The paper's editorial voice turned away from objecting to war and toward objecting to fighting the war without black troops. The *Defender* called again and again for integration of the armed forces, including demands for the appointment of black officers and for admitting African Americans into the U.S. Navy, which remained all-white. Black Americans, the paper said, did not want to just peel potatoes or haul loads. "They want to fight. They want to be in the front, where they can watch the Germans fall."[20] The position expressed throughout the war was that black Americans deserved a chance to prove themselves in combat and thereby win the lasting respect of whites. A paramount goal was to prove that blacks deserved full citizenship. In a famous essay titled "Close Ranks," Du Bois picked up the theme and argued that in a showdown between America and Germany, there was, for black Americans, a clear choice:

> We of the colored race have no ordinary interest in the outcome. That which the German power represents spells death to the aspirations of Negroes and all dark races for equality, freedom, and democracy. Let us not hesitate. Let us, while this war lasts, forget our special grievances and close ranks shoulder to shoulder with our own white fellow-citizens. . . . We make no ordinary sacrifice, but we make it gladly and willingly with our eyes lifted to the hills (fig. 6.2).[21]

In addition to the black and ethnic papers, there was a vigorous socialist press in America in the years leading up to the Great War which also opposed the war in Europe. Some of the socialist papers were local, some regional; but they all

6.2 **W. E. B. DU BOIS**, shown here in 1907, was a prominent intellectual, scholar, teacher, and writer who also edited the monthly magazine *The Crisis* beginning at its founding in 1910. After editorializing against U.S. involvement in the war in Europe, Du Bois wrote a famous essay, "Close Ranks," urging black readers to suspend their grievances and to earn greater respect by helping to win the war.
—*Department of Special Collections and University Archives, W. E. B. Du Bois Library, University of Massachusetts Amherst.*

revived and intensified the advocacy tradition in American journalism during the 1890s and early 1900s. The most successful of the early socialist papers was the *Appeal to Reason,* published by Julius Wayland, a former "printer's devil," in the small town of Girard, Kansas. From the center of the heartland, his newspaper reached far and wide, with the help of the U.S. Post Office. Wayland had a staff of more than one hundred, including Eugene V. Debs, who became the leader of the Socialist Party of America and a candidate in the 1912 U.S. presidential race, in which he won nearly a million votes. *Appeal to Reason* provided a sharp alternative to most of the big-city press, supplying coverage of labor issues from the worker's point of view. *Appeal to Reason* also did its share of muckraking; it was Wayland who had sponsored Upton Sinclair's investigation of the meatpacking industry and published Sinclair's work as a series before it appeared in book form as *The Jungle.*[22] Between 1908 and 1912, *Appeal to Reason* was reaching more than half a million subscribers a week, from coast to coast.

Appeal to Reason flatly opposed the war in Europe and any U.S. involvement in it, seeing the war as a contest among capitalist powers, monarchies, and other ruling-class exploiters which promised no good outcome to the workers of the world. In 1915 the paper printed Debs's view:

> I have no country to fight for; my country is the earth; I am a citizen
> of the world. I would not violate my principles for God, much less for
> a crazy kaiser, a savage czar, a degenerate king, or a gang·of pot-bellied
> parasites.
>
> I am opposed to every war but one; I am for that war with heart and
> soul, and that is the worldwide war of social revolution. In that war,
> I am prepared to fight in any way the ruling class may make neces-
> sary, even to the barricades. . . . I stand for the overthrow of the entire
> system.[23]

As socialists looked at the war, there was simply no side worth joining—not for the working people of Europe and certainly not for the workers of America.

The opposition to the war expressed by ethnic and socialist papers only added force to another strand of thinking that bolstered American opposition to foreign wars—the viewpoint known as isolationism. In essence, isolationism held that America should take advantage of its natural physical isolation from the rest of the world and stay out of the endless squabbles abroad, especially those of Europe. The United States, according to the isolationists, should maintain cordial relations with Canada and Mexico and let the oceans provide protection from other nations. It was a well-established theme in American thinking about foreign policy, one that can be traced back at least as far as Paine, Jefferson, and Washington. Isolationism was a popular editorial stance among American newspapers, too, especially in the growing number of large cities far away from the coasts. Editors in Chicago, St. Louis, and elsewhere embraced the view that the United States should avoid entanglements with other countries, particularly if those involvements threatened to drag the country into war. But isolationism was not limited to the heartland.

One of the boldest—and certainly the loudest—champions of isolationism was William Randolph Hearst. No longer the brash young progressive, Hearst was by 1917 lord of the largest media empire in the world. From his base in newspapers and magazines, he kept branching out. In the years just before the Great War, Hearst had devised a syndication plan for sharing material among his newspapers and selling it to outsiders who did not compete with him, calling it the International News Service, or INS. Hearst also founded a division to make and distribute weekly newsreels, showing moving-picture footage of recent world events to theatergoers. And he was just getting started producing feature films. Far more so than his late rival Pulitzer, Hearst became the greatest of the "press barons," creating a coast-to-coast, multimedia communications empire. He used profits from one area of his empire to launch another, and he used each of them to publicize his holdings in all the others. When the war in Europe began, he had a combined audience that was approaching 10 million for his Sunday newspapers alone and uncounted millions more in magazines, newsreels, and movies.[24]

In the years since the Spanish-American War of 1898, Hearst had changed his view on U.S. military engagement abroad. He now believed, with all the stubbornness and bombast that he brought to most major issues, that the United States should stay out of Europe's perpetual conflicts. When fighting broke out in Europe in 1914, Hearst immediately denounced it. "This is a war of kings," he declared in a signed editorial that ran on the front page of all his newspapers; those who were responsible for the war "will not be described as heroes, but as homicidal maniacs."[25] Not content with editorializing, Hearst organized antiwar rallies in San Francisco and Manhattan, complete with marching bands and choruses. At the time, Hearst's loudest call was for the United States to remain neutral, a position that aligned him precisely with Woodrow Wilson (for the time being) as well as with many of the immigrants who bought Hearst's newspapers. By denouncing England along with Germany, Hearst managed to enjoy the support of Irish Americans as well as German Americans.

Despite his misgivings about Wilson, Hearst gave the Democrat a mild endorsement for reelection in 1916. After the election, Hearst continued to insist on U.S. neutrality. On February 9, 1917, his newspapers carried an editorial headlined "Let Us Firmly Resolve That under No Circumstances Will We Waste Our Wealth and Slaughter Our Youth in the Wars of European Alliances." When the German U-boat campaign in the spring of 1917 began to turn some Americans against Germany, Hearst tried to immunize himself against charges of disloyalty. Initiating a now familiar strategy of flag-waving, he instructed the manager of his newspapers literally to wrap the Hearst press in the flag—ordering up "little American flags to right and left of date lines on inside pages"—and to print the words to "The Star-Spangled Banner" above the editorial pages. When war finally came, in April 1917, Hearst insisted on a policy of "America first!" By that he meant that the United States should now hoard all its military supplies (and not give them to our allies) and should set about protecting the homeland against possible invasion (rather than dispatching U.S. troops to foreign soil).

Such hard-line support for isolation left Hearst himself increasingly isolated. As soon as Congress commenced hostilities against Germany, most American newspapers that had espoused isolationism dropped the idea in favor of support for the war cause. That left Hearst one of the few newspaper publishers—and certainly the most prominent—to persist in opposing the sending of U.S. troops to Europe. His fellow publishers denounced Hearst as pro-German, he was burned in effigy in several cities, and he became the target of an extensive federal investigation. Even so, Hearst never backed down. Popular with his millions of readers, dead-set in his views, and answerable to no stockholders, Hearst had no reason to.[26]

The isolationist viewpoint was also embraced, at least initially, by the president himself, Democrat Woodrow Wilson. From the moment the war in Europe broke out in 1914, Wilson tried to keep the United States out of it, urging Americans to stay "neutral in fact as well as in name." During his campaign for reelection in 1916, one of Wilson's political slogans was "He Kept Us Out of War." But Wilson eventually yielded to the pressure that the neutral nations were feeling from both of the warring alliances in Europe. After Germany decided to engage in unrestricted submarine warfare against all neutral nations, including the United States, Wilson performed an abrupt about-face in early 1917. The deliberate sinking of U.S. ships by Germany was ultimately intolerable, particularly when Wilson learned from Britain about German plans to enlist Mexico as a belligerent against the United States. By the time of his second inauguration, Wilson had asked Congress for a declaration of war. Four days later, on April 16, 1917, Congress voted to declare war on Germany. A month later, Congress imposed a military draft.

The impact of war on the news business was swift and dramatic. As it had been during the Civil War, the news business was tested once again. In its crusade to "make the world safe for democracy," the Wilson administration took immediate steps at home to curtail one of the pillars of democracy—press freedom—by implementing a plan to control, manipulate, and censor all news coverage, on a scale unprecedented in U.S. history. In just a few months, Wilson imposed a sweeping array of controls on what Americans could see, hear, and say during the war. In retrospect, there had been signs that Wilson would not tolerate press freedom in wartime. His counterparts on both sides of the conflict in Europe had already established elaborate bureaus of censorship and propaganda. Ever since the start of fighting in 1914, the German and British governments had been trying to influence public opinion, both in their home countries and in neutral countries such as the United States. In addition, well before the U.S. involvement in the war in Europe, Wilson had expressed the expectation that his fellow Americans would show what he considered "loyalty." Repeatedly in his public statements the president condemned spies and warned Americans that they must set aside any feelings for the lands of their ancestors. When the time came to seek a declaration of war, Wilson drew a line. "If there should be disloyalty," he warned, "it will be dealt with with a firm hand of stern repression."[27]

Immediately upon entering the war, the Wilson administration brought the most modern management techniques to bear in the area of government-press relations. Going well beyond the efforts of the Lincoln administration to control the press, Wilson imposed a systematic program of censorship not just on the battlefield but on all printed materials on the home front, including newspapers, magazines, telegrams, and mail. He initiated one of the earliest uses of government propaganda and waged a campaign of intimidation and outright suppression against those ethnic and socialist papers that continued to oppose the war. Taken together, these wartime measures added up to an unprecedented assault on press freedom.

How would the increasingly profitable and professionally independent American press respond?

6.3 **GOVERNMENT PROPAGANDA IN WORLD WAR I** became pervasive. Uncertain about popular support for a war the he initially opposed himself, President Wilson launched the federal Committee on Public Information, which spread the prowar message through news releases and posters such as this one.
—*Library of Congress.*

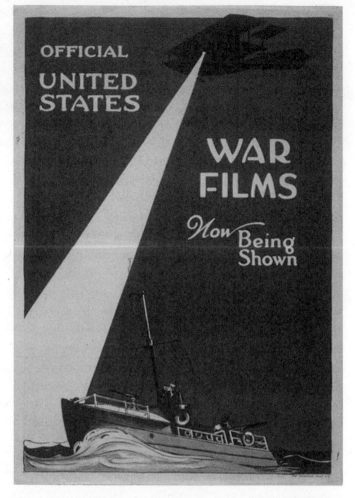

* * *

PRESIDENT WILSON EXPECTED THE PRESS to exhibit complete loyalty, as he defined it. Within a week of securing the declaration of war—even before putting a draft law into place—Wilson issued an executive order, on April 13, 1917, creating a new federal agency that would put the government in the business of actively shaping the content of press coverage in a way that no American president had ever attempted before. That agency was the Committee on Public Information (CPI), which would take on the task of explaining to millions of young men being drafted into military service—and to the millions of other Americans who had so recently supported neutrality—why they should now support war. Presidents and other leaders, of course, had long appreciated the power of public opinion in democratic government. And presidents had long attempted to promulgate stories in the press about their doings, especially favorable stories.[28] But Wilson was striking out into uncharted territory with the Committee on Public Information, which one scholar has called "the nation's first ministry of information" (fig. 6.3).[29]

The new agency was often referred to as the Creel Committee for its chairman, George Creel, who had been a journalist before the war.[30] A political progressive, he was a strong political supporter of Wilson and had helped organize a committee of writers and publicists to back Wilson in the 1916 election, a fact that no doubt endeared him to the president's team of advisers.[31] The president was also presumably hoping to take advantage of Creel's professional standing to ensure that the new agency would be credible to the nation's newspaper editors and publishers. At first, Creel was greeted with some skepticism. The *New York Times,* for one, questioned his ability to win cooperation from the press. Under Wilson's executive order, Creel served as the CPI's civilian chairman. The other members of its board were Secretary of State Robert Lansing, Secretary of War Newton Baker, and Secretary of the Navy Josephus Daniels (who was also the editor of the *Raleigh News and Observer* and several other papers in North Carolina).[32] From the start, the CPI was "a veritable magnet" for political progressives of all stripes—intellectuals, muckrakers, even some socialists—all sharing a sense of the threat to democracy posed by German militarism. Idealistic journalists like S. S. McClure and Ida Tarbell signed on, joining others who shared their belief in Wilson's crusade to make the world safe for democracy.

Starting from scratch, Creel organized the CPI into several functional divisions. At the broadest level, the committee established a Domestic Section to influence public opinion at home and a Foreign Section, which eventually operated in more than thirty countries. In its efforts to reach Americans, the CPI took advantage of a broad range of communications. The Speaking Division recruited some 75,000 specialists in public speaking, who became known as "Four-Minute Men" for their ability to give speeches outlining the administration's war aims in under five minutes. The Film Division produced newsreels intended to rally support by showing images in movie theaters that emphasized the heroism of the Allies and the barbarism of the Germans. The Foreign Language Newspaper Division kept an eye on the considerable number of weekly and daily newspapers published in the United States in languages other than English.

Another division secured free advertising space in American publications to promote campaigns aimed at selling war bonds, recruiting new soldiers, stimulating patriotism, and reinforcing the general message that the nation was involved in a great crusade against a bloodthirsty, antidemocratic enemy. Some of the advertising showed off the work of another CPI unit—the Division of Pictorial Publicity—which was led by a group of volunteer artists and illustrators, including Charles Dana Gibson. The work of these illustrators created some of the most enduring images of this period, including the portrait by James Montgomery Flagg of a vigorous Uncle Sam, goateed and top-hatted, declaring, "I WANT YOU FOR THE U.S. ARMY!" Other ads showed cruel "Huns" with blood dripping from their pointed teeth, hinting that Germans were guilty of bestial attacks on defenseless women and children. "Such a civilization is not fit to live," one ad concluded.[33]

Creel denied charges that his committee's work amounted to propaganda, but he acknowledged that he was engaged in a battle of perceptions. "The war was not fought in France alone," he wrote in 1920, after it was all over. "It was in this recognition of Public Opinion as a major force that the Great War differed most essentially from all previous conflicts." He described the work of the CPI as "a plain publicity proposition, a vast enterprise in salesmanship, the world's greatest adventure in advertising." If its work was done right, Creel thought, the CPI could aid the war effort by fighting ignorance and lies abroad, boosting morale at home, and winning over neutral nations. He specifically rejected the "propaganda" label, which some of his critics pinned on him, because "that word, in German hands, had come to be associated with deceit and corruption." Instead, Creel saw his agency as a source of information that should be trusted. "Our job, therefore, was to present the facts without the slightest trace of color or bias," he declared.[34] Creel may have believed that, but he probably did not convince many newspaper editors.

For most journalists, the bulk of their contact with the CPI was through its News Division, which became a veritable engine of propaganda on a par with similar government operations in Germany and England but of a sort previously unknown in the United States. In the year and a half of its existence, the CPI's News Division set out to shape the coverage of the war in U.S. newspapers and magazines. One technique was to bury the news business in paper, creating and distributing some six thousand press releases—or, on average, handing out more than ten a day (making the practice so commonplace that the word "handout" became synonymous with press release). The whole operation took advantage of a fact of journalistic life: in times of war, readers hunger for news, and newspapers attempt to meet that demand. But at the same time, the government was taking other steps to restrict reporters' access to soldiers, generals, munitions makers, and others involved in the struggle. So, after stimulating the demand for news while artificially restraining the supply, the government stepped into the resulting vacuum and provided a vast number of official stories that looked like news. Most editors found the supply irresistible. These government-written offerings appeared in at least twenty thousand newspaper columns each week, by one estimate, at a cost to taxpayers of only $76,000.[35]

In addition, the CPI issued a set of voluntary "guidelines" for U.S. newspapers, to help those patriotic editors who wanted to support the war effort (with the implication that those editors who did not follow the guidelines were less patriotic than those who did). Written by Creel himself, the guidelines were titled "What the Government Asks of the Press." Many provisions seem rather straightforward and reasonable, at least under the conditions of modern warfare. They called on editors to suppress any details involving classic military secrets such as the timing of troop movements or the embarkation of navy ships. Even so, the guidelines prompted complaints from some papers, at least initially. According to Creel's memoir, "all through the first months it was a steady whine and nag and threat."[36]

The CPI News Division then went a step further. It created a publication titled *Official Bulletin,* which was something new in the American experience: a daily newspaper published by the government itself. This went well beyond the papers of the partisan press days, which were always operated as private businesses, no matter how heavily subsidized they might be, and no matter how favored by the administration in power. The Wilson-era *Official Bulletin* was entirely a governmental publication, sent out each day and posted in every military installation and post office as well as in many other government offices. In some respects it is the closest the United States has come to a paper like the Soviet Union's *Pravda* or China's *People's Daily* and represents the greatest level of involvement by the federal government in the business of disseminating information to a civilian, domestic audience of Americans.

The CPI was, in short, a vast effort in propaganda.[37] The committee built upon the pioneering efforts of p.r. man Ivy Lee and others but pushed the practice to a greater extent than had ever been attempted in this country. The CPI hired a sizable fraction of all the Americans who had any experience in this new field, and it trained many more. One of the young recruits was Edward L. Bernays, a nephew of Sigmund Freud and a pioneer in theorizing about human thoughts and emotions. Bernays was in his twenties when the war broke out, but poor eyesight kept him out of the army. Instead, he volunteered for the CPI and threw himself into the work. His outlook—a mixture of idealism about the cause of spreading democracy and cynicism about the methods involved—was typical of many at the agency. "The conscious and intelligent manipulation of the organized habits and opinions of the masses is an important element in democratic society," Bernays wrote a few years after the war. "Propaganda is the executive arm of the invisible government."[38] According to one careful study of the CPI, the agency proved quite effective in using advertising, public relations, and the allied techniques of public persuasion to instill nationalistic feelings in Americans. "Their work heightened patriotic pride and drove the nation to greater levels of unity and achievement. It also assisted the profession of advertising," one historian concluded. "There arose a feeling that with proper advertising . . . one could sell anything."[39]

* * *

WHILE THE WILSON ADMINISTRATION KEPT one foot on the gas, as it were, by generating thousands of press releases, ads, and posters, all intended to guide editors and reporters toward churning out stories with approved themes, at the same time it kept one foot on the brake by constructing a wide mechanism of censorship. As some stories, themes, and images were being promulgated, others were being suppressed. The president and the thousands of federal employees who were ultimately involved in the wartime public relations offensive left little to chance. "It has been said," according to one historian of this period, "that in the United States during 1917–18 nearly every right guaranteed under the Constitution was either abridged or nullified, especially freedom of the press and freedom of speech."[40]

One of the clearest abridgments of press freedom came in the form of outright censorship. Just two weeks after creating the CPI, Wilson issued another executive order—this one directing the navy to take over all undersea cables that connected the United States to the rest of the world and ordering the War Department to seize control of all the telegraph and telephone landlines that did the same (but not the lines that connected Americans to one another entirely within the country). From that point on, the government had the power to monitor and disrupt all communications flowing into or out of the United States. Such censorship "affected directly the freedom of the press," according to a detailed study of Wilson's system, because 75 percent of the incoming cable traffic was intended to be received at the major newspapers and wire services. In addition, the bulk of outgoing traffic consisted of dispatches being sent by foreign correspondents based in New York and other U.S. cities. All these words were now subject to censorship: at best, they would be read by a government agent; at worst, they could be suppressed. The hardest hit, naturally, were stories coming from or going to Germany, but the censors also cracked down on newspapers in countries as far away as Argentina if they expressed support for Germany.[41]

The war years also saw what amounted to a government takeover of the fledgling new communication medium known as radio. Originally called "wireless telegraphy," radio had been under development for several decades, in both Europe and the United States, when the Great War broke out. At the time, a rising tide of engineers, joined by hundreds of hobbyists and tinkerers, filled American garages and workshops with new and improved models of wireless transmitters and receivers. Although the technology was spreading, it was still a long way from development into a consumer product. (See chapters 7 and 8). Nevertheless, the military applications of wireless technology were obvious, because signals could be sent without landlines—to ships at sea, for example, or to army units moving rapidly across the countryside, and even from the ground to airplanes overhead. Once the United States entered the war, Navy Secretary Daniels took command of the wireless field in a series of steps that came close to nationalizing the industry.[42] One step was to exclude foreigners. Shortly after Congress declared war, Daniels seized control of the American Marconi Wireless Company (which had been formed by the Italian radio pioneer Guglielmo Marconi) as well as two high-powered radio stations on the East Coast that had been built by Germans. The navy also bought the Federal Telegraph Company's West Coast wireless operations, as well as Marconi's ship and shore network. In all, these steps gave the navy a monopoly over marine radio, including 229 coastal transmitting and receiving stations and 3,776 shipboard stations.

To meet the challenge of war in Europe, the navy—and the Army Signal Corps—suddenly needed thousands of wireless sets, and they all had to work together.

Daniels and other officials could hardly expect to solve that problem by contracting with thousands of independent inventors working in their garages. Instead, they took steps to make sure that a few large corporations could quickly supply the military with standard-issue equipment. "During the war, to facilitate production of radio equipment by private companies, the Navy had removed all patent restrictions, assumed any liability for patent infringement, and set uniform standards for vacuum tubes and other components," writes historian Paul Starr. "New companies, including Westinghouse and Western Electric, entered the field, and instead of producing radios one at a time, as had been the rule before the war, manufacturers mass-produced thousands of sets with standardized parts."[43] By sweeping aside the patent claims and encouraging mass production, the military all but guaranteed that the postwar radio industry would be dominated by a few giant companies.

Another significant wartime abridgment of press freedom came in the form of a new law, also supported by Wilson: the Espionage Act of 1917, which was enacted just two months after the declaration of war. The original draft of the bill would have made it a crime to publish anything that the president decided "is or might be useful to the enemy." Such a sweeping grant of power to one individual naturally provoked criticism and political resistance from the nation's newspapers. The American Newspaper Publishers' Association objected, on the grounds that the bill was a direct blow to freedom of speech and would deprive the people of the information they needed in order to make wise decisions. "In war, especially," the publishers declared, "the press should be free, vigilant, and unfettered." The editors of the *New York Times* objected, too, calling the grant of power to the president "Prussian" and pointing out that a newspaper that "criticizes or points out defects in policies" should not be treated as "a public enemy." When the issue came up for debate in Congress, supporters argued that it would be better to be safe than sorry when it came to publicizing information in wartime. But opponents howled. Representative Fiorello La Guardia of New York warned of a "vicious precedent," and Senator Hiram Johnson of California pointed out that "we lose our judgment" in times of crisis. Representative Martin Madden of Illinois put the issue starkly: "While we are fighting to establish the democracy of the world, we ought not to do the thing that will establish autocracy in America." Despite a last-minute personal appeal from Wilson, the House rejected the grant of presidential power.[44]

Congress was not finished, though—not by any means. After nine weeks of debate, the Espionage Act of 1917 was passed and signed into law. The opening sections dealt with traditional military spying and outlawed such practices as flying over military bases to collect intelligence for a foreign power. Then came the provisions cracking down on the press. Whenever the United States was at war, the law made it a federal crime to:

- "wilfully make or convey false reports or false statements with intent to interfere with the operation or success of the military or naval forces of the United States or to promote the success of its enemies"

- "wilfully cause or attempt to cause insubordination, disloyalty, mutiny, refusal of duty, in the military or naval forces of the United States," or

- "wilfully obstruct the recruiting or enlistment service of the United States."

Violations could be punished by fines of up to $10,000 or by twenty years in prison. Essentially, then, Congress was making it a crime to use words to oppose the war effort or to encourage young men to resist the draft. There would be no repetition of the Copperhead press that Lincoln had endured during the Civil War. In 1917, the greatest immediate impact of the new Espionage Act fell on the socialist and German-language newspapers, many of which were promptly suppressed. Among the publications denied access to the mail were *The Masses,* the *International Socialist Review,* the *Milwaukee Leader,* the *Gaelic American,* and *The Nation.*[45]

But Wilson wanted to go even further. In October 1917, when Congress passed the Trading with the Enemy Act, the president felt he had the legal authority he needed. Citing the new law, he issued another executive order, this time creating the Censorship Board. Creel, as CPI chairman, also served ex officio on the new board, along with representatives of the postmaster general, the secretaries of war and the navy, and the War Trade Board. A key part of the censorship plan involved the U.S. Post Office, which provided a central chokepoint at which practically every newspaper and magazine could readily be inspected—not to mention every letter and parcel. Every printed word now had to pass muster.

The chairman of the new Censorship Board was Robert L. Maddox, a veteran of the Post Office who was also serving as chief postal censor. He, like a few other members of the board, had some reservations about censorship, but they all ended up bowing to the wishes of the military.[46] The censors worked under a set of guidelines that called on them to eliminate any information, plans, or drawings that might be useful to the enemy. They forbade publication of any photographs depicting dead U.S. soldiers or sailors.[47] They were also expected to make judgments that were more subjective, including the requirement "to stop all postal communications containing any false report or false statements concerning the causes or operations of the war." Several agencies supplied the Censorship Board with names of Americans who were considered suspect, and the board added its own names, gleaned from mail intercepts. By the end of the war (that is, in just about a year and a half), the board came up with a master list containing the names and addresses of more than 250,000 suspects—most of them innocent Americans.[48]

* * *

ON TOP OF THIS ELABORATE apparatus of domestic censorship, there remained one more layer of governmental control, one that was in many ways the most important to journalists: the direct censorship of news accounts and photos coming home from the battlefields of Europe. Here, too, the effort was more systematic and more effective than any previous efforts at battlefield censorship by the U.S. military. American soldiers were heading to distant foreign fields under the command of General John "Black Jack" Pershing, who had little regard for the press. The American troops were to be part of the Allied forces operating in several European countries, and Pershing made sure that his censorship rules were enforced wherever correspondents came into contact with U.S. or Allied forces.

A West Point graduate and hero of the 1916 U.S. invasion of Mexico in search of Pancho Villa, Pershing was the commander in chief of the American Expeditionary Force (AEF). In that role he set the direction for other commanders in their dealings with the press by conducting few press conferences and giving no personal interviews. To help him in this, Pershing recruited one of the few journalists he liked, Frederick Palmer, a veteran war correspondent. Pershing promoted Palmer to the rank of major and put him in charge of press policy in the European theater. The battlefield censorship regimen established in that war set a pattern that would shape official U.S. practices for most of the next century, so it bears some scrutiny.

The process began before a correspondent even left the States. According to historian Phillip Knightley:

> The rules for accreditation of a war correspondent to the American Expeditionary Force have to be read to be believed. First, the correspondent had to appear personally before the Secretary of War or his authorized representative and swear that he would "convey the truth to the people of the United States" but refrain from disclosing facts that might aid the enemy.
>
> Then he or his paper had to . . . post a $10,000 bond to ensure that he would comport himself "as a gentleman of the Press." If he were sent back for any infraction of the rules, the $10,000 would be forfeited and given to charity. . . .
>
> Correspondents wore no uniforms, but were obliged to wear a green armband with a large red "C" (fig. 6.4).[49]

Once they were over there, correspondents had to submit all of the stories they wanted to send to their home newspapers to censors in the army's Military Intelligence Division, located at the AEF headquarters in Neufchâteau in northeastern France. Photographers had to submit their film to the Army Signal Corps, which would develop it and then pass judgment on whether it could be sent home for publication. This policy—similar in many ways to the protocols put into practice in 1914 by British, French, and German commanders—imposed a military filter between correspondents in the field and their editors at home, with the result that

6.4 **THE IDEAL OF THE DASHING FOREIGN CORRESPONDENT** was embodied at the turn of the century by reporter and novelist Richard Harding Davis. According to biographer Arthur Lubow, it was Davis's fate "to be famous virtually all one's adult life and forgotten promptly at death."
—*Corbis.*

editors often did not even know what they were missing. And if editors did not know, their readers were certainly in the dark.

Censorship thus became a bedrock issue in the waging and covering of American wars, and it has remained so ever since.[50]

To give the devil his due, it must be acknowledged, on the one hand, that the military censor does some good. For one thing, censorship can be effective, at least in the sense that it usually does protect military secrets. The classic examples of information that is most often targeted for censorship—the timing of troop movements, the codes for encrypting messages, and the like—are of obvious use to any enemy, and most journalists do not hesitate to protect such secrets without even being asked. Censorship can also be beneficial when it keeps journalists from *inadvertently* revealing information in their stories which has a military relevance that the journalist might not grasp. This type of information can range from the apparently trivial, such as the dryness of our troops' socks, to the apocalyptic, as in the case of developing the first atomic bomb (see chapter 9). Censorship also helps journalists when it keeps them from being treated as spies and facilitates candid communication between military personnel and war correspondents. In addition, censorship can be useful when it allows our government to block harmful lies or coded messages planted in our news media by hostile powers. Finally, censorship can be considered a good thing insofar as it allows journalists to keep faith with their audiences. In wartime, after all, most Americans expect reporters and photographers to "pitch in" and to do their part to aid the nation's war effort.

On the other hand, censorship can do great harm—even in wartime, or perhaps especially in wartime. Censorship is readily abused by military officials, who may try to take advantage of it to mask defeats and make our armed forces appear more effective than they really are. As a rule, the only victims of such censorship are the American people, since any enemy usually has a highly accurate picture of the actual military situation, based on the reports of its own intelligence services rather than on the reporting done by the U.S. news media. Censorship can also do harm when it is used to protect incompetent officers from criticism, a practice that can lengthen wars or even lead to defeat. Censorship that prevents free-ranging, independent reporting can also encourage the growth of rumors, which can be very damaging during wartime. At the same time, censorship always involves, to one degree or another, an effort to bamboozle the public, the very people who ultimately must pay for war with their taxes as well as their sons and daughters to fight it. In that sense, censorship is implicated in the violation of another expectation that the public has for journalists: that they will level with their readers and tell it like it is. If our generals are wrong, if our troops or allies won't fight, if our equipment is shoddy—these are the kinds of vital facts that readers must have in wartime if they are to exercise their power of self-government, and these are often the very facts that military censors are eager to keep from the public.[51]

In the Great War, perhaps the most blatant example of military censorship involved one of the great open secrets of the war—the nearly complete failure to equip the U.S. Expeditionary Force with guns and ammunition. U.S. forces ended the war without forwarding a single warplane to the battle zone; U.S. officials contracted for 4,400 tanks to be built, but only fifteen ever got to France, and they arrived *after* the Armistice; and as late as January 1918, eight months into the U.S. involvement, not a single heavy gun had arrived in Europe from America. The correspondents covering the American troops could see all this for themselves, but they were not allowed to report the facts. Several reporters even appealed to Pershing himself for permission, but the secretary of war would have none of it. Finally, Heywood Broun of the *New York Tribune* decided to return to the States, where he would not be subject to military censorship. There he broke the story wide open under the headline "Supply Blunders Hamper First U.S. Units in France." The War Department retaliated by yanking Broun's credentials and confiscating his $10,000 bond as punishment.[52] As far as can be determined, military authorities would have been quite content to keep the supply screwups a secret to this day.

While U.S. forces were fighting in Europe, pushing back the Germans at Château-Thierry and Belleau Wood in the campaign of 1918, the majority of American newspapers enthusiastically supported the war effort. Most cooperated with Creel's efforts to shape the coverage, and when in doubt, most editors engaged in self-censorship.[53] Even so, the president and the Congress were not taking any chances. Congress made another law abridging freedom of the press, the Sedition Act of 1918. For the first time since the Sedition Act of 1798 was used by the Federalists to punish critics of John Adams, Congress was getting back into the business of making the expression of certain ideas a crime. The result was, according to a legal scholar, "the most repressive legislation in American history."[54]

The Sedition Act of 1918 began as a set of amendments to the Espionage Act of 1917. In addition to the earlier bans on publishing false statements that might hurt U.S. armed forces or aid the enemy and on interfering with the draft, the new law made it a crime to

- "publish any disloyal, profane, scurrilous, or abusive language about the form of government of the United States, or the Constitution of the United States, or the military or naval forces of the United States, or the flag . . . or the uniform of the Army or Navy of the United States"

- publish "any language intended to bring the form of government . . . or the Constitution . . . or the military or naval forces . . . or the flag . . . of the United States into contempt, scorn, contumely, or disrepute," or

- "wilfully display the flag of any foreign enemy, or wilfully . . . urge, incite, or advocate any curtailment of production in this country of any thing or things . . . necessary or essential to the prosecution of the war."[55]

Violations could be punished by fines up to $10,000 or twenty years in prison. The law was approved in the Senate by a vote of 48–26 and in the House by an overwhelming vote of 293–1, then signed by the president on May 16. The plain meaning of the act was clear: *Watch what you say. If you displease the government, you will go to jail* (fig. 6.5).

Even in the space of the six months that remained in the war, federal prosecutors got busy filing charges under the Sedition Act, resulting in a series of famous cases that went all the way to the U.S. Supreme Court but were not decided until after the war ended. One month after the law was signed, for example, it was used to bring criminal charges against the most prominent socialist leader in America, Eugene V. Debs.[56] As the Socialist Party candidate in the 1912 presidential election, which gave Wilson his first term, Debs had won almost a million votes. From his writings in *Appeal to Reason* and his frequent public speeches, Debs had become a visible critic of the war with a substantial following nationwide. On June 16, 1918, he addressed a crowd of more than a thousand in Canton, Ohio, in support of three socialists who had been jailed for opposing the war. In his speech, delivered within shouting distance of the jail, Debs noted the

6.5 THE SEDITION ACT OF 1918 gave the government broad powers to enforce "loyalty" and suppress critical speech and writings. As soon as it passed, calls went out to Uncle Sam to crack down, as he is shown here in rounding up scruffy characters labeled IWW, traitor, and spy, along with the bomb-throwing Irishman labeled Sinn Fein.
—*Library of Congress.*

dark irony of a nation fighting for freedom abroad while suppressing freedom at home:

> I realize that in speaking to you this afternoon, there are certain limitations placed upon the right of free speech. I must be exceedingly careful, prudent, as to what I say, and even more careful and prudent as to how I say it. I may not be able to say all I think; but I am not going to say anything I do not think. . . . They tell us that we live in a great free republic; that our institutions are democratic; that we are a free and self-governing people. That is too much, even for a joke.[57]

As if to prove his point, federal officials arrested Debs and charged him with sedition.

At his trial in federal court in Cleveland, Debs did not dispute the facts; he had given that speech in Canton, and he had no intention of denying it. Instead, he threw himself into a direct appeal to the jury. "Gentlemen," he began, "I do not fear to face you in this hour of accusation." In a way, his predicament was like the one John Peter Zenger faced in 1735 when charged with seditious libel.

Both men acknowledged—at their legal peril—that they were responsible for the words that had so offended the authorities, and both made an appeal to higher principles. Debs argued that his resistance to the war, based on his socialist views, was squarely in the American tradition. "Washington, Paine, Adams—they were the rebels of their day," Debs told the jury. "At first they were opposed by the people and denounced by the press. . . . And if the Revolution had failed, the revolutionary fathers would have been executed as felons." In his survey of American history, Debs moved on to the abolitionists, recalling the editors Elijah Lovejoy and William Lloyd Garrison as men who had fought for principle. "You are teaching your children to revere their memories," Debs said, "while all of their detractors are in oblivion." Finally, Debs invoked the Constitution and urged the jury to weigh the consequences. "I am the smallest part of this trial," he told them. "There is an infinitely greater issue that is being tried in this court, though you may not be conscious of it. American institutions are on trial here before a court of American citizens."[58]

It didn't work. The next day, the jury found Debs guilty. At his sentencing a few days later, Debs offered one final declaration to the court, making his ultimate plea for a common humanity across class lines and national boundaries: "Your Honor, years ago I recognized my kinship with all living beings, and I made up my mind that I was not one bit better than the meanest on earth. While there is a lower class, I am in it. While there is a criminal element, I am of it. While there is a soul in prison, I am not free." Indeed, Debs would not be free much longer. Denouncing Debs as "one of those who would strike the sword from the hand of this nation while she is engaged in defending herself," the judge sentenced the sixty-two-year-old war critic, internationally famous socialist leader, and former presidential candidate to ten years in prison.[59]

*   *   *

ALTHOUGH DEBS WAS THE MOST prominent war critic to be imprisoned for his views, he was hardly the only one. Using the Espionage Act and, later, the Sedition Act, the Wilson administration engaged in an unprecedented assault on the First Amendment. Federal prosecutors (and their state-level counterparts) filed criminal charges against thousands of Americans for things they said or wrote.[60] The trials in those cases went on for months, and the appeals took even longer. Even when the Armistice was signed on November 11, 1918, it was far from a complete end to the conflict. In three rulings handed down in 1919, the U.S. Supreme Court put its stamp on the meaning of free speech in wartime.

The first major case to reach the high court, known as *Schenck v. United States,* was decided in March 1919.[61] Surprisingly, perhaps, this landmark ruling represented the first significant attempt by the nation's highest court to interpret the First Amendment—specifically, to say whether it could be used to shield a defendant from prosecution. The case involved a one-page pamphlet or leaflet circulated by Charles Schenck, a leader in the Socialist Party, that attacked the wartime draft. The leaflet, which was sent to men who were facing military enlistment, argued that the draft was unconstitutional and that it was merely the government's way of coercing the working class to do the bidding of Wall Street. Schenck was charged under the Espionage Act, on the grounds that the leaflet would obstruct the operations of the draft, and he was convicted.

When Schenck's appeal reached the Supreme Court, Justice Oliver Wendell Holmes Jr. wrote the unanimous opinion—an opinion that is among the most frequently quoted in the Court's history. In upholding the conviction, Holmes began by dismissing some relatively minor matters, then established the heart of his argument by imputing a motive to Schenck. Writing that Schenck must have been trying to accomplish *something*, the justice decided that Schenck must have intended to induce his readers to obstruct the draft. That, Holmes believed, was intolerable, especially in wartime. "The character of every act depends upon the circumstances in which it is done," he wrote, setting the stage for one of the most famous phrases in American law: "The most stringent protection of free speech would not protect a man in falsely shouting fire in a theatre and causing a panic." According to Holmes, Schenck was guilty of *inciting* his readers to *action*—an action the government had legitimate reason to suppress or punish. Words, that is to say, have consequences, and depending on the circumstances, they can have an impact comparable to actions. "The question in every case is whether the words used are used in such circumstances and are of such a nature as to create a clear and present danger," Holmes continued, firing off another of the most frequently quoted phrases in law. If the words create a "clear and present danger" of bringing about some criminal or destructive act, then Congress may be able to ban such speech. It all depends on the context. "When a nation is at war many things that might be said in time of peace are such a hindrance to its effort that their utterance will not be long endured so long as men fight."[62] Thus, because Schenck wrote and distributed the wrong idea at the wrong time, his guilty verdict was upheld.

It is important to observe that the ruling in *Schenck*, which made pamphleteering against the draft a crime, was seriously flawed and inflicted great, unnecessary harm on the cause of press freedom. With regard to Schenck's case, it could be argued that the First Amendment is absolute. It tells Congress to "make no law" abridging freedom of the press, and that's that. Until the First Amendment is repealed or modified, it means what it says: Hands off. Many journalists hold to this interpretation, and a few Supreme Court justices have as well.[63] More commonly, the argument is made that the First Amendment must be balanced against other provisions of the Constitution—in Schenck's case, the sections establishing the powers of the president, including the duty to serve as commander in chief of the military and to protect the nation's very survival. In such a balancing act, it is argued, the right to press freedom might have to yield sometimes to the imperatives of national self-preservation.

Under that reading of the Constitution, the question remains: Did Schenck have a First Amendment right that should have immunized him against prosecution? Holmes said no, because he found that Schenck was trying to interfere with the draft in time of war. But in fact Schenck did no such thing. His leaflet (which is not read nearly as often as Holmes's ruling) is well worth reading. Under the headline "Assert Your Rights," Schenck makes an argument, drawing on the Constitution itself. He does not urge his readers to *do* anything. He specifically does *not* tell them to resist the draft. Instead he tells them that, in the view of the Socialist Party, it is unconstitutional for anyone to deny them the right to "assert [their] opposition to the draft." Schenck urges his readers to use peaceful means to *change* the law, not to *break* it.[64] His leaflet was not the equivalent of falsely shouting "Fire!" It was the equivalent of saying, "Write a letter to your congressman!" Schenck did not induce or exhort anyone to do anything illegal; he merely argued for a point of view. The chilling aspect of Holmes's ruling is its implication that once the United States launches a war, there is no room left under the Constitution for debate: the ultimate wisdom of the war, the rightness of its aims, the effectiveness of the tactics—all these are beyond debate. The American people have no choice but to fall in line.

The second major wartime First Amendment case to be decided by the Supreme Court involved Debs's appeal of his conviction in the Ohio case. With Holmes again writing the opinion, the Court unanimously rejected the argument that the socialist leader's speech was protected by the First Amendment and upheld Debs's conviction too. In light of the reasoning in *Schenck,* it is hard to see how Debs could have hoped for any other outcome. Holmes did not say that Debs's speech posed a "clear and present danger" (perhaps because it did not), but the Court found against him anyway. If "one purpose of the speech, whether incidental or not does not matter, was to oppose [the] war, . . . and if, in all the circumstances, that would be its probable effect, it would not be protected," Holmes wrote.[65] Like Schenck, Debs did not urge anyone to do anything illegal. In his Ohio speech Debs had merely praised three socialists who had, in turn, denounced the war and the draft. But that was enough for the justices to uphold his ten-year prison sentence. Still, Debs kept up the fight. He entered the 1920 campaign for president and, running from his prison cell in Atlanta, once again won nearly a million votes (fig. 6.6).

The third major First Amendment case growing out of the Great War, *Abrams v. U.S.,* also involved a political pamphlet. In this case, the pamphlets were distributed in New York City (by literally tossing them from a building near Houston Street) on March 23, 1918.[66] In English and in Yiddish, the pamphlets mocked Wilson and charged that the president had ordered an invasion of Russia not for his stated reason—to open an eastern front against Germany—but to roll back the Bolshevik Revolution. The English-language version of the pamphlet called on American workers to support the Russian Revolution and declared, "There

6.6 **SOCIALIST LEADER EUGENE V. DEBS**, after being jailed for speaking against the war effort, ran for president in 1920 from his cell in a federal penitentiary in Georgia. He is shown here greeting his running mate, Seymour Steadman. They won about 3.4 percent of the vote. —*Indiana State University, Special Collections.*

is only one enemy of the workers of the world and that is CAPITALISM."[67] It also specifically denied any sympathy for Germany and its culture of militarism. The Yiddish pamphlet went further: it claimed that the war bonds bought by American workers were going to be used to buy bullets to kill not only German soldiers but also Russian workers, and it called on American workers to resist Wilson's policies by waging a general strike. Thus both pamphlets were aimed at resisting not the declared war in Germany but the undeclared war in Russia. Investigators working for U.S. military intelligence quickly traced the pamphlets to their sources, rounded up half a dozen Russian immigrant anarchists and socialists (the oldest, Jacob Abrams, was twenty-nine), and charged them with violating the Espionage Act as amended by the Sedition Act of 1918.

Again, the crime was words, not deeds. "There was no evidence that one person was led to stop any kind of war work, or even that the pamphlets reached a single munition worker," First Amendment scholar and civil libertarian Zechariah Chafee has noted. "Before the Espionage Act our criminal law punished men almost entirely for acts which take place in the tangible world and are proved by evidence of our five senses. This Act punishes men for words which cause no injury, but have a supposedly bad tendency to harm the state, and also for intentions which are regarded as evil."[68] Under such circumstances, including an openly hostile federal judge imported from Alabama, it is no surprise that the defendants were quickly convicted. The judge sentenced them to as much as twenty years in prison.

On appeal, *Abrams v. U.S.* went to the Supreme Court, which announced a split decision on November 10, 1919. Citing the Court's reasoning as laid out by Holmes eight months earlier in *Schenck,* the majority upheld the convictions of Abrams and the others, which was hardly surprising. What has proven most notable about *Abrams* is the position on free speech articulated by Holmes, who found himself in dissent this time. After a summer of soul-searching about press freedom, Holmes underwent something of a conversion. By October he was writing to a friend that although he still had doubts about absolute freedom of speech, he now considered it so important that, in his words, "I hope I would die for it."[69] In his dissent in the *Abrams* ruling, joined by Justice Louis Brandeis, Holmes held forth anew on the subject:

> When men have realized that time has upset many fighting faiths, they may come to believe . . . that the ultimate good desired is better reached by free trade in ideas—that the best test of truth is the power of the thought to get itself accepted in the competition of the market, and that truth is the only ground upon which their wishes safely can be carried out. That at any rate is the theory of our Constitution. It is an experiment, as all life is an experiment.[70]

With this view in mind, Holmes said there was no question that the defendants' constitutional rights were being violated. Clearly, Holmes had come around to the view—familiar since the time of Milton, Locke, and Franklin—that the people are best served when truth and error are free to do battle in a wide-open "marketplace of ideas" in which the government plays no role. That was probably cold comfort to Abrams and his fellow pamphleteers, however, as they started serving their prison terms.

When the Armistice was signed on November 11, 1918, millions cheered. But the Great War did not end all at once. Many aftershocks continued to be felt for years.

At home, within a month of the Armistice, Congress ordered George Creel to disband the CPI, stop publishing the *Official Bulletin,* and get out of the propaganda business. Creel objected, but he had no choice. He accompanied Wilson on the U.S. mission to the Paris Peace Conference, then returned home and became a feature writer at *Collier's* magazine. In the 1930s Creel joined the New Deal, then ran for governor of California, losing the primary election to the muckraker Upton Sinclair. At the outbreak of World War II, Creel offered to direct the government's publicity efforts once again, but the Roosevelt administration turned him down. As for the rest of the CPI staff, some of those who had been journalists before the war returned to their newspapers or magazines. Many of the rest headed for careers in what turned into a lucrative peacetime profession: public relations. The skills they had developed in the CPI proved to be in great demand among America's big corporations, which either built staffs of their own or hired outside consultants to buff their images, generate favorable publicity, manage crises, and deflect criticism. A leader in the field was Bernays, who wrote in his memoir: "My wartime experience showed me that press-agentry had broader applications than theater, music or the ballet. . . . And I was determined it would be more than that. . . . I had learned I could suggest to people or organizations a course of action that resulted in favorable publicity. I could create events and circumstances from which favorable publicity would stem."[71] From his offices on Wall Street, Bernays comforted the comfortable.

In Washington, meanwhile, Wilson came home from Paris having won European approval for his plan for a League of Nations but still needing to persuade the Senate to endorse it. But on October 2, 1919, Wilson suffered a stroke from which he never fully recovered. For the remainder of his term he played less and less of a public role. In the 1920 election his party lost the White House to Warren G. Harding, the genial Republican publisher of a small-town Ohio newspaper, the *Marion Star.*

But even in its waning months, the Wilson administration was not quite finished. The Russian Revolution of 1917 inspired intense reactions in the United States. On the left, many took inspiration from it and joined the Socialist Party or formed new pro-Bolshevik groups. On the right, many big-business leaders were eager to end the wartime truce with labor, and conservative groups like the American Protective League saw a potential for trouble in the growing ranks of domestic socialists, communists, and anarchists. Threats and actions escalated.[72] Shipyard workers went on strike in Seattle, police officers struck in Boston, and miners and steelworkers waged nationwide walkouts. On April 30, 1919, postal officials in New York discovered thirty-four bombs in the mail, addressed to prominent individuals such as Justice Holmes, oil magnate John D. Rockefeller, and U.S. Attorney General Mitchell Palmer. The next day, police clashed with rioters at May Day protests. About a month later, bombs exploded in eight U.S. cities, killing two and damaging the home of Attorney General Palmer himself. Groups like the American Legion and the Ku Klux Klan demanded action against domestic radicals.

With the president recovering from his stroke, Palmer stepped into the leadership vacuum and mounted a major campaign against anarchists, immigrants, and subversives. In a series of actions known as the "Palmer raids," the attorney general touched off the Red Scare of 1919–20. Within the Justice Department, he set up the General Intelligence Division, housed within the Bureau of Investigation, and appointed the young J. Edgar Hoover to gather names of dangerous radicals. In November 1919, government agents rounded up about six hundred aliens and soon deported almost half of them. On January 2, 1920, Palmer lowered the boom. In raids in thirty-three cities from coast to coast, federal agents swept up four thousand suspected radicals.

How did the press respond? On the whole, not very admirably. Two days after the big raids, the *Washington Post* applauded the crackdown. "There is no time to waste on hairsplitting over infringement of liberty," the paper declared. Even though the Palmer raids were not aimed at newspapers or magazines, they posed an obvious threat to freedom of thought, association, and speech—if not to the press directly. Nonetheless, most newspapers tolerated the government raids in silence, or cheered them on.

One bright moment did occur that gloomy winter. On December 13, 1920, Congress repealed the Sedition Act of 1918 while leaving intact the older provisions that made up the Espionage Act. That law was left on the books.[73]

What, in the end, became of journalism's professional goal of independence? What impact did the war have on the efforts by Pulitzer and others to put the practice of journalism on a footing that would allow it to withstand the legal, political, and cultural pressures of modern war? In the end, the campaign against the press turned into a rout. The combined power of the president, the military, Congress, and the Supreme Court simply overwhelmed the American press. Publications from ethnic communities whose loyalty was questioned (the Germans and the Irish) were quickly suppressed, usually by being banned from the mails. The socialist press was likewise suppressed, often by use of the wartime laws covering espionage and sedition. With rare exceptions, the big-city daily papers fell into line and saluted. Any doubts about the war were brushed aside; all debate about the war was stifled. Military defeats were covered up, and blunders like the supply failure were overlooked. Many stories that Americans needed to read—about the true conditions under which the war was being fought and about the disastrous terms under which it was ended, not to mention the Russian Revolution, which took place in the midst of it—were simply never written or never published. Wilson got his way: loyalty won out over independence.

It would be more than five decades before the press felt powerful and independent enough to challenge the national government directly.

PART TWO

The Media, 1920–

———— ⋆ ————

7.1 **BIG-CITY NEWSPAPERS HAD A HEYDAY** in the early twentieth century, before news began appearing on radio and in weekly magazines, starting in the 1920s. Pictured here is a scene from the classic film comedy *His Girl Friday*, starring Cary Grant and Rosalind Russell, which depicts the hijinks of reporters and editors in Chicago in the 1920s. —*Sony Pictures Entertainment.*

CHAPTER 7

Jazz Age Journalism, 1920–1929

MAGAZINES AND RADIO CHALLENGE THE NEWSPAPER

Well, all I know is what I read in the papers.
—*Will Rogers, 1923*

I<small>N THE EARLY</small> 1920S, in New York City alone there were seventeen English-language daily newspapers.[1] Philadelphia and Chicago each had six. Most cities, and even a lot of small towns, had several, often with more than one edition. The total number of daily newspapers in the country reached an all-time high of 2,461 in 1916, and the number of weekly papers was still climbing.[2] News couldn't wait until the next morning, so many publishers offered evening editions. They were able to compete with the morning papers by providing a mix of updated news, stock market results, and the latest baseball scores at a time when the game was still played in daylight. Many readers also lived in a market where they could readily find a weekly paper or two, as well as specialized kinds of newspapers—in a foreign language, perhaps, or devoted to covering a specific topic, like organized labor or horse racing. In such a competitive industry, reporters and editors recognized no bounds when it came to hijinks, double-crosses, or sheer enterprise in pursuit of an "EXCLUSIVE!" on a big story (fig. 7.1).

With few exceptions, the newspaper business was roaring. In southern California, General Harrison Gray Otis and his son-in-law Harry Chandler were using the *Los Angeles Times* to build a political and financial empire. In Chicago, Colonel Robert R. McCormick ran the *Tribune* as a bulwark against socialism, communism, liberalism, and any other "-ism" that might come along to threaten the heartland. In Louisville, another colonel, Robert Worth Bingham, took the money he got from marrying the richest widow in the country, Mary Flagler, and bought the *Courier-Journal*, founding another family newspaper dynasty. In California, the McClatchys were busy running the *Bee* in Sacramento and buying other papers. In Rochester, New York, Frank Gannett had bought the two papers that would become the first links in his chain, at one point the biggest of them all. In Ohio, the publisher of the *Dayton Daily News*, James M. Cox, ran for president on the Democratic ticket with the young Franklin Roosevelt against another Ohio publisher, Warren G. Harding of the *Marion Star*. Harding won, and Cox went on to found a newspaper chain that would include the *Journal-Constitution* in Atlanta. Another Ohio-based publisher, E. W. Scripps, built one of the first big newspaper chains with the money he made from papers in Cincinnati and Cleveland. And still another Ohio paper, the *Akron Beacon-Journal*, was the home base for John S. Knight, who added papers in Miami and other cities in building Knight Newspapers. All these enterprises operated under the old business model, which would endure well into the 1960s: they were run by individuals and families, with occasional help from outside investors and banks, and were able to do pretty much as the owners pleased. Most of these papers would eventually become local monopolies, which definitely pleased the owners.

In New York City, the biggest newspaper arena of them all, the great dynasties did battle every morning and afternoon all through the 1920s. Adolph Ochs had earned about $100 million in profit in the twenty-four years that he had been running the *Times*, and he had reinvested most of it in operations. A newcomer on the New York newspaper scene, the *Illustrated Daily News*, was making a name for its founder, Joseph Medill Patterson, by bringing photography to the forefront as a way of not only illustrating stories but sometimes telling them as well (fig. 7.2). At the *World*, Pulitzer's heirs were presiding over a decline, lacking the founder's perfect pitch for drawing an audience. At Greeley's old *Tribune*, Whitelaw Reid was buying Bennett's old *Herald*. At the *New York Post*, the paper founded by Alexander Hamilton, the publisher was Oswald Garrison Villard, a grandson of abolitionist William Lloyd Garrison and a progressive on matters of race, labor, and politics. The publisher of the *American* (the successor to the *Journal*), William Randolph Hearst, was dividing his time among different media, running not only a string of newspapers but also magazines, newsreels, feature films, the King Syndicate, and more.

The decade of the 1920s was, in short, the heyday of the big-city daily newspaper. Cities themselves were growing, the economy was booming, and newspapers surged in size and influence. They had the news field to themselves, and things had never looked better. The president of the United States himself, Warren G. Harding, was a former newspaperman. What could possibly go wrong?

In America the magazine has almost as long a history as the newspaper.[3] The first two generally recognized magazines in the colonies appeared within months of

7.2 THIS SHOCKING PHOTOGRAPH OF AN EXECUTION was made in 1928 by photographer Tom Howard for the *Daily News,* which called itself "New York's Picture Newspaper." Knowing that such photos were forbidden, Howard strapped a camera to his ankle, then ran a cable up his pant leg to a plunger in his pocket. He lifted his pant leg and opened the shutter just as Ruth Snyder was executed in the electric chair inside Sing Sing prison.
—*Getty Images.*

each other in 1741—one put out by Ben Franklin, the other by his Philadelphia rival Andrew Bradford.[4] Neither lasted very long, and they were followed by other fitful experiments until the magazine started to come into its own after the Revolution.[5] In 1800 there were about a dozen magazines in America; twenty-five years later there were almost one hundred. In the decades before the Civil War, many magazines were aimed at women and their perceived concerns, focusing on such hardy perennials as food and fashion. Others were devoted to science, medicine, or agriculture. One of the most prestigious and influential was the *North American Review,* established in 1815, and one of the most popular was *Youth's Companion,* founded in 1827. The magazine that claims the longest record of continuous publication is the journal now known as *Scientific American,* which traces its origins to 1845.[6] In many cases, magazines played an important role in social movements, such as those favoring temperance, transcendentalism, abolition, or women's suffrage, and their editors often helped create or strengthen communities or associations of readers who would otherwise never have found one another on the sprawling continent.

Several notable and lasting magazines were launched just before the Civil War, inspired in part by the political and moral crisis posed by slavery. Most were based in New York City. From Manhattan, the U.S. Post Office carried magazines, at favorable rates, to every corner of the growing country. *Frank Leslie's Illustrated Newspaper,* founded in 1855, became a giant seller, reaching a circulation of 200,000. Leslie was a forerunner of the great press barons, in that he branched out and launched other magazines in addition to the *Illustrated.* His motto: "Never shoot over the heads of the people." With that in mind, Leslie gave the people lots of big, exciting pictures. His newspaper and other publishing ventures began to sag after the Civil War, but they revived in the 1880s when Leslie's second wife, Miriam Squier, took over the business after his death, legally changed her name to Frank Leslie, and made millions as the "Empress of Journalism." Equally successful was the new *Harper's Weekly.* The book-publishing Harper brothers brought out their *Weekly* in 1857 and quickly built it into one of the most widely read magazines in the country.[7] Pro-union, moderately antislavery, the *Weekly* threw itself into covering the Civil War and employed a team of sketch artists (including Winslow Homer), cartoonists (including Thomas Nast), and engravers to provide extensive illustrations of the conflict.

Also in 1857, a group of literary eminences—including Ralph Waldo Emerson and Henry Wadsworth Longfellow—met in Boston to plan a new magazine they called the *Atlantic Monthly.*[8] In 1865 another group of eminences gathered in New York City and launched a magazine they called *The Nation,* promising "to wage war upon the vices of violence, exaggeration, and misrepresentation by which so much of the political writing of the day is marred."[9] Though financially perilous, magazines serving black audiences also appeared. Just before the Civil War, one of the most prominent was the *Anglo-African.*[10]

Among the early magazines catering to women, of which there were about one hundred by the time the Civil War began, one stood above all others: *Godey's Lady's Book* (fig. 7.3). Launched in the 1830s by Louis Godey, the magazine really took off after Godey hired Sarah Hale as editor in 1837. Hale (who wrote "Mary Had a Little Lamb" and who persuaded Lincoln to revive Thanksgiving as a national holiday) built the *Lady's Book* up to a circulation of 150,000 by the 1860s and ran it for forty years. In keeping with its era, the magazine was thoroughly Victorian. Recipes involving chicken or turkey breast, for example, referred instead to the birds' "bosoms." *Godey's* published much fiction, but it also engaged with moral and political issues. Hale endorsed the cause of women's education, while embracing the idea that women naturally occupy a domestic sphere. "Remember that woman must *influence* while man *governs,* and that their duties, though equal in dignity and importance, can never be *identical,*" she wrote in 1848.[11] Hale opposed women's suffrage and barely mentioned the Seneca Falls Convention of 1848 while heaping on articles about fashion, home design, recipes, advice about books, and suggestions on the colleges the readers might want to send their sons to. Other

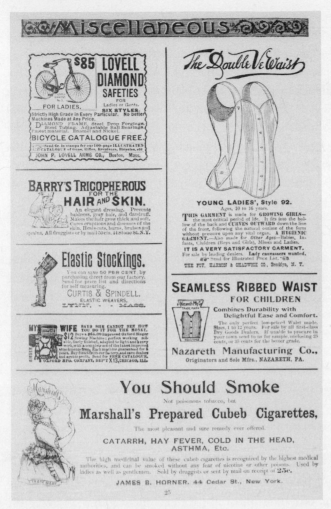

7.3 **MAGAZINES WERE POPULAR** from their start in the late eighteenth century. Most appeared monthly and did not attempt to cover the news. One of the most popular was *Godey's Lady's Book*, which, as this page of advertisements suggests, focused on domestic topics. —*Library of Congress.*

women's magazines, of course, were pro-suffrage, starting with the one edited by Susan B. Anthony and Elizabeth Cady Stanton, which was candidly titled *The Revolution.*

Magazines were the first truly national mass medium, and they attracted ads from businesses that wanted to reach customers from coast to coast. (Kodak cameras, Campbell soups, Ivory soap, and Uneeda biscuits were all early advertisers.) At the same time, advertising agencies began to spring up in New York as go-betweens serving both manufacturers and publishers.[12] The *Saturday Evening Post* was the leading title in the lineup of magazines published by the Curtis Company, which saw its revenues soar from about $500,000 in 1892 to more than $22 million in 1917. The next year it reached 2 million in circulation, a figure that made the *Saturday Evening Post* the largest-selling magazine in America, as it would remain for several decades.

As it turned out, the 1920s were a good time for trying new things. At home, the decade was generally a period of prosperity that built to a dizzying height before the stock market crash of 1929. Before the Great War, only one American home in five had electricity; by the end of the 1920s, two-thirds had it. And Americans were finding plenty of uses for that electricity. In the pages of magazines like the *Saturday Evening Post,* the *Literary Digest,* and *Colliers,* readers were tempted by a host of new electric-powered products: refrigerators, vacuum cleaners, fans, coffee percolators, washing machines, sewing machines, irons, toasters, and radios. Americans were learning how to become consumers of mass production, thanks in part to the growing power and reach of mass communications. In this setting, two very different magazines were founded within two years, just a few New York City blocks apart.

*   *   *

IN THE WINTER OF 1922–23, two young men set up shop in an unimposing office at 9 East Fortieth Street in midtown Manhattan.[13] At the start, their most important piece of equipment was a pair of scissors, which they used to clip news articles out of the *New York Times,* the *Tribune,* and a stack of other newspapers. Then, drawing on bits of French, Latin, and a jazzy lingo that they had picked up at Yale, they set about rewriting the two- and three-day-old news into fresh, bright articles that showed a definite flair for verbal catchiness. Working late into the night, importuning their Yale connections for funds, and dragooning their friends into helping with editorial chores, the two pals put together a new magazine. In the process, they were also inventing a new *kind* of magazine, one that would reshape the landscape of journalism.

In fact, the greatest asset the two men had was one good idea. Harry Luce and Brit Hadden asked themselves this question: What if someone summarized news from around the country and the world, wrought each item into a concise, polished *story* with some history and context, added coverage of the arts and culture, and priced the whole thing at fifteen cents? With such a magazine, people who were too busy to sit down and read three or four newspapers every day could keep up on the important news, or at least *feel* that they were keeping up. With such a magazine, the short bursts of information that people were starting to get over their radios could be put into a larger frame or recurring theme. With such a magazine, the two young Yalies could tell people not only what was happening in the news but also what they should think about those events. After a last-minute name change, they decided to call the new magazine *Time.*

The novel venture was no sure thing. But if anyone could make it work, it was probably Harry Luce and Brit Hadden. They had connections that ran deep into the heart of the American establishment, they had the youthful ability to ignore the high likelihood of failure, and they had very good timing.

Henry Robinson Luce had been born in 1898 to American parents who were then serving as Presbyterian missionaries in Tengchow, China. That particular happenstance would have consequences years later, as it turned out, when Luce became one of the most influential Americans shaping the nation's attitudes and policies toward China. It also sparked in Luce an intense pro-Americanism. His parents had sent him home to Hotchkiss, a boarding school in Connecticut, where he'd had to struggle to keep up with the wealthier, more self-assured boys. He'd also had to battle a stutter that he had had since early childhood. At Hotchkiss, Luce met Briton Hadden, the son of a New York City stockbroker. The two boys competed for the editorship of the student newspaper (Hadden won) and ended up running dueling publications at the school, setting off the rivalry that was always an element in their collaboration.[14]

In 1916 the two friends, known as "Brit" and "Harry," went off to Yale, where they resumed their rivalry by competing for the editorship of the prestigious *Yale Daily News* (Hadden won again). Yale University had changed considerably since its founding in 1701; no longer a training ground for the Protestant clergy, Yale was focusing its efforts on preparing the young men who would wield power—in finance, in government, and in diplomacy. In 1898, the very year Luce and Hadden were born, America had stepped onto the world stage by trouncing Spain in a war engineered by ambitious establishment figures seeking a larger role. Now members of the next generation—or those who went to schools like Hotchkiss and Yale—were preparing to take on that expanded role and see if they could measure up to the likes of Teddy Roosevelt.

When the United States entered the war in Europe in April 1917, Luce and Hadden were thrilled. In the columns of the *Yale Daily News* they wrote editorials in favor of war and patriotism, then reported for duty. In the summer of 1918 they were sent to Camp Jackson in South Carolina, and it was there that they first discussed the idea of publishing a newsmagazine. To their regret, the war ended before they could get into the action, and the two young men headed back to New Haven to resume their studies. As senior year approached, Luce and Hadden were both tapped to join the Order of Skull and Bones—the secretive elite club that by now includes three U.S. presidents as well as Supreme Court justices, cabinet members, diplomats, senators, and business tycoons among its members.

After a trip to Europe and a year spent studying at Oxford, Luce returned home in 1921, broke and unsure what to do next. Briefly he went to work in Chicago for the *Daily News,* where he served as a legman for columnist Ben Hecht.[15] Hadden went off to New York, where he became a cub reporter at the prestigious *World,* then in the hands of Joseph Pulitzer's son Ralph. Luce and Hadden then both went to Baltimore to work briefly for the *News* before deciding to place all their chips on their idea for a newsmagazine. Seeking their fortune, they headed to New York City.

To launch their new venture they would need to find investors willing to give two rookies a lot of money. Still fairly fresh out of Yale, they had plenty of connections; what they lacked was capital. In order to persuade investors, they would

need to be able to explain the idea behind their magazine. In their prospectus
Luce and Hadden made a number of promises:

> There will be no editorial page in *Time*.
>
> No article will be written to prove any special case.
>
> But the editors recognize that complete neutrality on public
> questions and important news is probably as undesirable as it is
> impossible. . . .
>
> But this magazine is not founded to promulgate prejudices, liberal
> or conservative. "To keep men well-informed"—that, first and last, is
> the only axe this magazine has to grind.[16]

They kept their word about having no editorial page, but they immediately
began breaking the promise not to plead any special cases. Almost every article
that ever ran in *Time* made a case—usually the case that Harry Luce wanted the
magazine to make. The prospectus gave little foreshadowing of the many prejudices that the conservative, Christian, internationalist Luce would hold and promote. None of those views would have mattered much, though, were it not for
what happened next.

Equipped with their prospectus, they sought advisers and investors. One stop
was to visit Melville Stone, the former head of the Associated Press, who assured
Hadden and Luce that news entered the public domain very rapidly and did not
legally belong to anybody within days of appearing in a newspaper. (A distinction
is drawn between *information,* which is not subject to copyright, and the unique
expression of that information, which is protected by copyright law.) Others warned
them that it was foolhardy to take on the established *Literary Digest,* including the
advertising executive Bruce Barton, who warned Luce that he and Hadden would
lose every nickel they put into their project. As it happened, Luce and Hadden had
very few nickels to throw into the pot. Luce figured they would need $100,000 to
get *Time* off the ground, and he initially hoped to find ten friends from Yale willing
to kick in $10,000 each. They soon found their investors, beginning with a fellow
Bonesman, Henry P. Davidson Jr., who had followed his father into the House
of Morgan on Wall Street. Other friends led them to Mrs. William L. Harkness,
the wife of a Rockefeller partner. She liked the looks of the two young men and
announced, "You may put me down for $20,000."[17] When they had raised $86,000,
the two twenty-four-year-olds decided they had enough money to plunge in.[18]

The first issue of *Time* was dated March 3, 1923. It was nearly the last. Circulation, which had been projected at 25,000 to start, amounted to just 9,000 copies.
At that rate they could not last long, even though their expenses were minimal.
The original staff consisted of Luce and Hadden, a circulation manager, four staff
writers, and some part-timers, including Stephen Vincent Benét (book reviews)
and Archibald MacLeish (education). Luce himself wrote the Religion section
and a good deal of the Business section as well. The new magazine offered readers

a punchy, concise summary of doings around the world in the space of twenty-eight pages. Slowly at first, business picked up. By the end of the year circulation had reached 20,000 copies a week. On the downside, they had lost $39,454.[19] Over the course of 1924, circulation doubled, from 35,000 to 70,000, and the magazine generated an actual profit: $674.15. They were on their way.

From the start, the head wordsmith was Hadden, who labored over each item, putting his stamp on it. In editing *Time* each week, Hadden confronted a fundamental problem that is familiar to anyone who has ever worked on a rewrite desk: how to make information that is stale or dull sound fresh and important. There are essentially two answers to this question: either do more reporting and advance the story somehow, or polish the prose to make it sound punchy or cute or profound. Lacking a reporting staff at this stage (that would come later), Hadden went to work punching up the copy, giving each article that special *Time* treatment. For this reason, no articles in *Time* carried bylines for decades; instead, everything was written (or rewritten) by Hadden or one of the team of editors he trained. It became pretty easy to become rich working for *Time,* but under the magazine's anonymous word-processing system, it was awfully difficult to become famous.

The way Hadden and his crew wrote became known as "Timespeak" or "Timestyle." Unmistakable it was. Part of the reason was compression; Hadden was determined to pack as much news as possible into as small a space as possible. So *Time* often read in the early years as if it consisted of a batch of telegrams. But there were other Hadden inventions that have no apparent explanation, at least none grounded in the traditional principles of English composition. One favorite was inverted syntax. Instead of the usual sentence structure, Hadden flipped things around: "Forth from the White House followed by innumerable attendants, Mr. and Mrs. Warren G. Harding set out . . . " Another favorite device of Hadden's was to invent adjectives that suggested Homeric epithets. Thus the football running back Red Grange was "eel-hipped," while the Indian leader was the "nut-brown Mahatma Gandhi." Hadden also ransacked his thesaurus and his foreign-language dictionaries. From ancient Greek he introduced the word "kudos" to refer to honors, from Hindi he grabbed the term "pundit," and from Japanese he imported the term "tycoon." When those sources let him down, he simply made up words and coined phrases. A favorite device was to fuse two existing words into a new one, especially if the final sound of the first word approximated the initial sound of the caboose. Thus, a woman who appeared in the movies would be a "cinemactress," and the people who worked at the magazine were called "Timeployees." And for no apparent reason, *Time* usually insisted on publishing the middle names of the high and mighty, no matter how embarrassing. All of these verbal hijinks gave *Time* a distinctive voice. Punch sought Hadden, and punch got he.

Something must have been working. After five years, circulation was headed for 300,000, annual revenue had topped $1 million, and *Time* now needed sixty-eight pages to summarize the week's doings. The staff was expanding, salaries were rising, and people were starting to notice.[20]

Then, tragedy. Hardworking, hard-drinking Hadden developed a *Streptococcus viridans* infection, which traveled through his bloodstream and into his heart.[21] He died on February 27, 1929, at age thirty-one. Despite the rivalry between Luce and Hadden, Luce was devastated. But an urgent question arose: What about the future of the magazine and Hadden's ownership stake? In his will, Hadden had put a family member in charge of his estate, which consisted mainly of his 3,361 shares of stock in Time Inc. Luce was eager to buy as many shares as possible, and he prevailed on the Hadden family to sell to him. The estate decided to sell off 2,828.5 shares, at $360 per share. Using his existing stock as collateral, Luce borrowed enough to buy 625 of Hadden's shares. Most of the rest were sold to other *Time* employees or members of the Time Inc. board of directors. As a result, Luce became the largest single stockholder, with 40 percent of the shares, acquiring effective control over the company. In those days, shares of Time Inc. stock were rarely sold, but within two years, the value of a single share had reached $1,000 (just before a 20-to-1 split), making Luce a young multimillionaire.[22]

With the passing of Hadden, who was something of an iconoclast, *Time* became more than ever a reflection of Harry Luce. One unmistakable difference involved Luce's approach to politics. Whereas Hadden had held few fixed political positions, Luce had plenty, and they started to pervade the magazine. Often they took the form of hero worship. If Harry Luce decided that he admired the cut of a man, then *Time* readers would certainly find out about it. Luce operated on the premise that the great events of history were the accomplishments of Great Men, and he devoted *Time* to discovering and celebrating the Great Men of his own day. Among his favorite kinds of Great Men were business executives. Having discovered the word "tycoon," *Time* practically wore it out. All through the 1920s, and well past the stock market crash, *Time* lavished praise on U.S. business executives, fawning over their profits and flattering them with cover portraits. Luce himself, as the partner most concerned with the magazine's finances, identified with the titans of finance and industry. In 1929 alone, *Time* ran a record sixteen covers featuring business tycoons, including such titans as J. P. Morgan and a comer from a new field—David Sarnoff of RCA.

As *Time* began to prosper, Luce began to flex his muscles, seeking greater and greater influence in affairs of state. As he did so, the valentines to businessmen gave way to portraits of prime ministers, generals, diplomats, and dictators. Among them, Luce gravitated to a type of man he considered particularly great. To begin with, Luce was an instinctive and inveterate anticommunist. As a capitalist and a Christian, he loathed the godlessness and forced collectivization of Stalin's Soviet Union. But Luce was an anticommunist of a particular stripe, which showed in his open and persistent admiration for strong leaders and heads of fascist governments. During the 1930s, *Time* praised men such as Italy's Benito Mussolini ("all-powerful . . . virile, vigorous") and Spain's Francisco Franco— each of whom appeared on *Time*'s cover eight times.[23]

There was one case of hero worship, however, that lasted longer than any other and had more serious consequences. That was Luce's absolute devotion to Chiang Kai-shek, the leader of China's Nationalist movement. As early as 1928, *Time* was already gushing: "The Conqueror of China, Marshal Chiang Kai-shek, who was chosen President last fortnight, assembled last week an all star Cabinet in which every name is packed with potency. . . . Austere President Chiang, though modest and democratic, is above all prudent."[24] From there, it only got worse. Throughout the 1930s, *Time* consistently portrayed Chiang as the indispensable hero of the Chinese people, the only man capable of turning aside the Japanese invasion and preventing the rise of communism in Luce's beloved China. American readers of *Time* had every reason to think that the Generalissimo would prevail and no reason to think that Chiang would ever have to flee to the island refuge of Taiwan in the face of a successful communist uprising. So sure was Luce about Chiang that he regularly rejected and rewrote the dispatches sent to him by two young *Time* correspondents who would soon distinguish themselves as among the greatest reporters of their generation, John Hersey and Theodore H. White. They sent long files to New York that gave a pretty accurate picture of the true situation in China, but Luce stuck with Chiang to the bitter end.

Another feature of Timestyle was the magazine's absolute certainty about all things, great and small. *Time* was judgmental from front to back. Neither Hadden nor Luce apparently felt the need to conform to any of the standard journalistic conventions such as getting "both sides" of a story, or citing people or documents as sources for reporting. In *Time*, the same assured judgment extended to politics as it did to opera. After Hadden's death, for instance, Luce launched a series of articles on the Soviet Union, including a campaign aimed at getting U.S. businesses to boycott the communists. In the article headlined "All Against Russia," *Time* told readers about "nameless and disgusting Bolshevik atrocities," referred to the Soviet government as "perhaps the most criminal in the world," and finally just fired away at Bolsheviks in general, quoting a British baron calling them "unattractive animals which, like boa-constrictors and alligators, accept food, only to show their gratitude by swallowing their keepers."[25] All of those things might have been true, but what was remarkable about *Time* was its willingness to make its own pronouncements in its own voice and on its own authority. Luce once told a friend: "Listen, I don't pretend that this is an objective magazine. It's an editorial magazine from the first page to the last, and whatever comes out has to reflect my view, and that's the way it is."[26] Or as he famously put it, "Show me a man who thinks he's objective, and I'll show you a man who's deceiving himself."[27] Clearly, Luce was offering readers more than facts; he was selling his judgment.

As publisher, Luce became quite the tycoon himself. In 1929 he started making plans to branch out with a magazine devoted to business. The new magazine, originally titled *Power,* was in the planning stages before Hadden's death that year. In a proposal he submitted to the directors of Time Inc., Luce sketched out his vision. "We conceive that the failure of business magazines to realize the dignity and the beauty, the smartness and excitement of modern industry, leaves a unique publishing opportunity," he wrote, adding that the new magazine—now called *Fortune*—would be "beautiful" . . . "authoritative" . . . "brilliantly written." . . . "It will have *Time's* bursting-with-fact, economical, objective merits, but the language will be smoother, more sophisticated."[28] To carry out his plans, Luce hired a glittering young staff, most of whom had no particular background in business, including Dwight Macdonald, Archibald MacLeish (who later became the curator of the Nieman Fellowship and, still later, Librarian of Congress), and a twenty-four-year-old photographer named Margaret Bourke-White. Against long odds, this expensive new magazine devoted to celebrating the Swifts and Rothschilds and all their works was making its debut just as the economy was collapsing but still turned out to be another success. *Fortune* offered readers a shining vision of capitalism's ultimate promise—with never a discouraging word—and readers responded (fig. 7.4).

But the move that really made Luce was still to come. In 1936 he started planning yet another magazine. Even before settling on a name, he described his goal for the new visual showcase:

> To see life; to see the world; to eyewitness great events; to watch the faces of the poor and the gestures of the proud; to see strange things— machines, armies, multitudes, shadows in the jungle and on the moon; to see man's work—his paintings, towers and discoveries; to see things thousands of miles away, things hidden behind walls and within rooms, things dangerous to come to; the women that men love and many children; to see and to take pleasure in seeing; to see and be amazed; to see and be instructed.[29]

The world's existing newspapers and magazines printed plenty of good photos, Luce argued, but no one publication brought together in one place "the cream of all the world's pictures," edited to present a coherent story and printed on quality stock. The idea became known as *Life.* The first edition appeared in November 1936, featuring a cover photo by Bourke-White of the Fort Peck Dam, and it was an instant success. His Chicago printers, Donnelly & Sons, using untested new paper and inks, literally could not print *Life* fast enough to meet the demand for the new weekly. *Life* had two major impacts. One was to develop the practice of photojournalism to a high art, bringing the photo-essay to a mass audience and showing people in a pre-television world what the news looked like as well as what ordinary life looked like.[30] *Life* also became an enormous profit center for the collection of publications that would be known as "the Luce press," ultimately making Harry Luce much wealthier and much more powerful.[31]

7.4 *FORTUNE* MAGAZINE made its debut with this cover in 1930, funded by the profits that publisher Henry Luce was earning from *Time* magazine. Despite the hard times and its high price, *Fortune* was another triumph for Luce and his growing media empire.
—*Fortune*.

It can be difficult now to grasp the reach and power of Luce's magazines, but it helps to remember that in their day, there were no national newspapers, no CNN, no TV networks, and certainly no Internet. Collectively, the Luce press became the successor to the Hearst press in terms of reach and in terms of the boss's eagerness to shape politics. Just as politicians in a democracy derive power from voters, publishers derive power from readers. As the combined circulation of *Time, Fortune,* and *Life* rose, so did Luce's influence. That large and growing audience was the real base of his power, just as it had been for Horace Greeley and Joseph Pulitzer before him. It was the reason why presidents from Roosevelt to Johnson feared Luce and courted him. (FDR loathed Luce and even composed hate mail but, thanks to his staff, never sent it.) What Luce chose to do with that power was what he had always done: advance his faith in God, the Republican Party, and the capitalist system. The blessings of all those causes, he believed, should not belong just to Americans but should flow to all the peoples of the world, from the most benighted peasant in China to the most radical trade unionist in France. In this he broke ranks with many of his fellow U.S. conservatives. At a time when most of them—and a lot of other Americans—were staunchly isolationist or intent on putting "America First," Luce was just as determined to get them to look farther afield, to take up the burden of a great power, and (as his missionary father had done) to spread the word.

*   *   *

ANOTHER GREAT MAGAZINE WAS LAUNCHED in Manhattan during the 1920s: the *New Yorker.* It could hardly have been more different from *Time,* perhaps because it was the brainchild of someone quite different from Harry Luce. That was Harold Ross, the rumpled dropout from the far West, the editor with the surest eye for talent, the young man with enormous curiosity who ended up creating the finest, most interesting, most original magazine in America. Literate in tone, far-reaching in scope, and witty to its bones, the *New Yorker* brought to American journalism a new sophistication. The magazine was unapologetically urban and determined not to pander to popular taste. Although the *New Yorker* never achieved the enormous circulation of *Time,* it has left an unmistakable mark on American letters, humor, criticism, fiction, poetry, and journalism.

The *New Yorker* was almost single-handedly the creation of its founder. In a business full of oddballs, Harold Ross fit right in. Spectacularly homely (with a gap-tooth smile and bristle-brush hair), he never graduated from high school. Frequently divorced, plagued by ulcers, he devoted his adult life to one cause: the *New Yorker* magazine.

Born in 1892 in Aspen, Colorado, the son of an Irish immigrant miner, Ross knocked about the West as a young man.[32] He worked as a reporter while still a teenager and ended up covering the waterfront for a San Francisco newspaper. When the United States entered the war in Europe, Ross enlisted. He was sent in 1917 to France, where he quickly deserted from his Army Engineers regiment. AWOL in France, he made his way to Paris, carrying his portable Corona typewriter. His goal was to join up with the brand-new soldiers' newspaper, the *Stars and Stripes,* which was so desperate for anybody with training that Ross was taken on with no questions asked. This weekly paper was written soldier-to-soldier; the tone was down to earth, and it was very popular with the troops. Even during the brief period of U.S. involvement in the Great War, the circulation of *Stars and Stripes* shot up from essentially zero to 500,000. In Paris, Ross met a number of writers, including Jane Grant, who had been the first woman to work as a reporter in the vast City Room of the *New York Times.* Later she became his first wife (of three). After the Armistice, Ross was promoted to editor of *Stars and Stripes,* but he didn't get to stay long. The army soon decided to put the paper in mothballs, where it remained until 1942.[33]

As for Ross, he headed to New York and never left. In the city he started meeting other writers and joined a circle of critics, dramatists, and wits who gathered at the Round Table in the Algonquin Hotel on West Forty-fourth Street in Manhattan in what has become a legendary episode in American cultural

7.5 THE CULTURAL FLOWERING KNOWN AS THE ROUND TABLE at the Algonquin Hotel was captured by the caricaturist Al Hirschfeld, whose work frequently appeared in the *New York Times* and many other publications. Seated at the table in the foreground, clockwise from the lower left, are Robert Sherwood, Dorothy Parker, Robert Benchley, Alexander Woollcott, Heywood Broun, Marc Connelly, Franklin P. Adams, Edna Ferber, and George S. Kaufman. Many became mainstays at the *New Yorker*.

—© *Al Hirschfeld. Reproduced by arrangement with Hirschfeld's exclusive representative, the Margo Feiden Galleries Ltd., New York.*

history. Over long and liquid lunches, Ross rubbed shoulders and wisecracked with some of the brightest lights in New York's literary chandelier: columnist Franklin P. Adams, who wrote the widely read column "The Conning Tower" for the *Tribune;* Alexander Wollcott of the *Times;* critic Robert Benchley; writer Dorothy Parker (of *Vanity Fair*); journalist and critic Heywood Broun (a writer for the *Tribune* and later the *World* who would launch the Newspaper Guild, the major labor union for newspaper reporters); funnyman Harpo Marx; and a trio of playwrights: George S. Kaufman, Noel Coward, and Charles MacArthur (who co-wrote *The Front Page* with columnist Ben Hecht). The Round Table also spawned a floating poker game that involved Ross and his eventual financial backer Raoul Fleischmann, of the famous yeast-making family (fig. 7.5).

The poker game (known by variations on the name Thanatopsis Literary and Inside Straight Club) figures in the history of American journalism because it led Ross to much of his initial capital when he decided to launch a weekly metropolitan magazine. First, though, Ross had to come up with a business plan. He could see that the magazine business was booming, but he had no intention of copying anything that already existed. A few publications came close to what he had in mind. In Ross's view, though, there was none that spoke directly to him and his friends—young city dwellers home from Paris and bored by the platitudes and predictable features found in most magazines. He wanted to edit a magazine that would engage himself and his circle; if anyone else wanted to read it, so much the better. Part of what made such a magazine even possible was the economic fact of life that New York–based retailers wanted to reach people like Ross. If those retailers bought ads in the *Literary Digest* or the *Saturday Evening Post,* they were wasting a lot of money on people who lived far from Manhattan and would therefore never patronize their stores. Even if those swank Manhattan retailers advertised in the New York newspapers, they were paying to reach people who couldn't afford their products. For those retailers, a substantial base, the perfect vehicle would be one that could deliver the right audience.[34] On that basis, Ross's poker partner Fleischmann was willing to stake him $25,000 to start.

In the fall of 1924, using an office owned by Fleischmann's family at 25 West Forty-fifth Street, (which happened to be the very building where Luce and Hadden were then struggling to keep *Time* going through its second year), Ross got to work on the prospectus for his magazine. The resulting document has become the most famous of its genre:

> *The New Yorker* will be a reflection in word and picture of metropolitan life. It will be human. Its general tenor will be one of gaiety, wit and satire, but it will be more than a jester. It will not be what is commonly called radical or highbrow. It will be what is commonly called sophisticated, in that it will assume a reasonable degree of enlightenment on the part of its readers. It will hate bunk.
>
> As compared to the newspaper, *The New Yorker* will be interpretive rather than stenographic. It will print facts that it will have to go behind the scenes to get, but it will not deal in scandal for the sake of scandal nor sensation for the sake of sensation. Its integrity will be above suspicion. It hopes to be so entertaining and informative as to be a necessity for the person who knows his way about or wants to.

Ross went on to promise regular coverage of contemporary events and vowed to present the truth "without fear and without favor," just as Adolph Ochs had proposed thirty years earlier. Ross also pledged to pay attention to the arts, including extensive listings of New York's many amusements, plus book reviews, commentary, verse, and drawings. Then he made a point that is often quoted to characterize him and his magazine: "*The New Yorker* will be the magazine which is not edited for the old lady in Dubuque. It will not be concerned in what she is thinking about. This is not meant in disrespect, but *The New Yorker* is a magazine avowedly published for a metropolitan audience and thereby will escape an influence which hampers most national publications."[35] In other words, this new magazine was going to be about as different as possible from the one being edited by Luce and Hadden, who were not about to shun the old ladies in Dubuque or anywhere else. The *New Yorker* was not going to respond to events, and it was not going to cater to middle America. Ross's only criterion would be whether a story was interesting—at least to him. He was putting all his chips on a long shot—the idea that there were enough people who shared his interests (or could discover that they did) to support a glossy, cheeky, witty weekly.

Like Luce, Ross almost failed. The cover of the first issue of the *New Yorker*, dated February 21, 1925, carried no portraits of potentates or tycoons, no headlines, no come-ons. Instead it featured a watercolor by Ross's friend Rea Irvin of a dandified figure staring intently through a monocle at (of all things!) a butterfly.

Inside, there could be found a salmagundi of jokes, short poems, a profile, reviews of plays and books, lots of gossip, and a few ads. It was not terribly impressive. At first the magazine struggled, and Ross almost lost it entirely in a poker game. But he pulled it out and got Fleischmann to kick in some more money, and soon the *New Yorker* began gaining readers.

A big part of the reason for Ross's success lay in his genius for spotting talent in others and encouraging them to develop their own voices and styles. One of Ross's key early finds was Katharine S. Angell, who became the magazine's first fiction editor and a reliable reservoir of good sense. In 1926, Ross brought on board James Thurber and E. B. White, who performed a variety of chores—writing, cartooning, creating captions for others' drawings, commentary. They even collaborated on a book, titled *Is Sex Necessary?*, about the conflicts between men and women. As the *New Yorker* found its feet, the writers and editors began perfecting some of its trademark features: the deep profile, ideally written about someone who was not strictly in the news but who deserved to be better known; the lengthy "fact" pieces that ran in the middle of the magazine; and, of course, the cartoons and humor sketches. Intensely curious and obsessively correct in matters grammatical, Ross would go to any length to ensure accuracy and pioneered in the development of a "fact-checking" department—essentially another layer of editors who confirmed every factual statement that every reporter wanted to present in print. (In all fairness, though, it was not the first; Luce already had in place a team of young ladies from Vassar, Bryn Mawr, and Wellesley who checked every fact in *Time*.) A singular feature of the *New Yorker* was its refusal to publish retractions, settle lawsuits, or even print letters to the editor. For years, no one ever got anything more out of the magazine than a private note like the following, sent in 1937: "We do not see how the description of you in the story could conceivably hold you up to ridicule and we feel sure that on reconsideration you will agree with us."[36] During the 1930s, while the country suffered through a long economic depression, the *New Yorker* was sometimes faulted for refusing to address the seriousness of the nation's problems. In the pages of the *New Yorker,* life was almost always amusing, attractive, and fun.

Ross, never much of a manager, spent many years looking for a right-hand man. He had one for a while in Ralph Ingersoll, until Luce raided him. Eventually Ross found William Shawn, who became the magazine's second, long-time editor. Another feature of Ross's management style was that he had the nerve to tell Fleischmann, the money man, to buzz off. Ross insisted on an absolute separation of "church and state," such that an advertising executive could never approach a *New Yorker* writer and suggest a story idea or request a favorable "mention" for a potential advertiser.[37] The only contact was between Ross and Fleischmann, and that was none too frequent. Ross also rapped Fleishmann's knuckles when a member of the business staff came down the hall looking for free tickets to a play. Ross reminded him that he was struggling to keep his writers aloof from "the press-agent, bally-hoo, special-favor gang."[38] Inexplicably, Fleischmann put up with it. Unlike Luce, Ross never managed to become personally rich. Fleischmann, however, eventually got his money back—and then some.[39]

During the 1930s Ross and Luce began to feud openly. It all started when Luce hired Ingersoll in 1930 to be the editor of Luce's new magazine, *Fortune*. Under Ingersoll, *Fortune* not only succeeded but also impressed the doubters. There would be no puff pieces, no automatic praise for business leaders. And Ingersoll recruited a first-rate team of talent: James Agee, Dwight Macdonald, Archibald MacLeish, and Margaret Bourke-White, among others. In 1934, Ingersoll wrote a long piece (anonymously) in *Fortune* about his old boss Ross and the *New Yorker*. Two years later Ross retaliated. He ordered up a very tart profile of Luce, written by Wolcott Gibbs in a parody of Timespeak, which has become a minor classic: " 'Great word! Great word!' would crow Hadden, coming across 'snaggle-toothed,' 'pig faced.' Appearing already were such maddening coagulations as 'cinemaddict' and 'radiorator.' Appearing also were first gratuitous invasions of privacy. Always mentioned as William Randolph Hearst's 'great & good friend' was Cinemactress Marion Davies, stressed was the bastardy of Ramsay Macdonald, the 'cozy hospitality' of Mae West. Backward ran sentences until reeled the mind." Introducing the reader to Luce, Gibbs referred to the young publisher (just as *Time* might) as the "ambitious, gimlet-eyed Baby Tycoon." Finally, the piece wrapped up with a memorable tagline: "Where it will all end, knows God!"[40]

Oddly, Ross and Luce met for dinner and drinks just before publication of the Gibbs piece, each man backed by a "second" from his own publication. Luce was squired by Ingersoll; Ross brought along St. Clair McKelway. Late in the evening, according to Ingersoll, Luce gave in to his feelings of exasperation (and relapsed into his old stammer): "Goddamn it, Ross. This whole goddamn piece is ma-ma-*malicious*!"

"You've put your finger on it, Luce," Ross replied. "I believe in malice."[41]

The *New Yorker* really came into its own—both financially and editorially—during World War II. It finally found its voice, one that was curious, searching, and, ultimately, serious. Ross discovered still more writers—such as A. J. Liebling, Mollie Panter-Downes, and John Hersey, who was raided from Luce—and together they produced some of the best writing of the war. Along the way, the *New Yorker* had a profound impact on American journalism. For one thing, Ross created conditions in which distinctive voices could be heard. For another, the *New Yorker* provided encouragement and an outlet for non-academic authority to flourish; it was a place where all those serious amateurs could discourse on the Dead Sea Scrolls or geology or nuclear war with no credentials other than their own ability to observe, think, and write. Finally, Ross must be credited with expanding the scope of journalism far beyond standard categories of crime and courts, politics and sports. In the pages of the *New Yorker,* readers almost never found the same content as in that week's *Time* magazine, which was more or less what everyone was already thinking about because most of it had been in the daily papers or on radio. Instead, readers of the *New Yorker* might find just about anything else.

*   *   *

IN THE DECADES FOLLOWING ITS invention, the telegraph became a fact of life and an indispensable tool in business, in the military, and in journalism. Still, it had some drawbacks: it could carry a message, but the contents had to be sent in code; messages could be sent only from one point to another, and those two points had to be connected by a copper wire. For these reasons among others, the telegraph was not a popular means of communication but remained a special tool used mainly by businesses.[42] In the late nineteenth century, a flurry of scientific and engineering breakthroughs started to overcome those limitations. In 1876 a Boston University professor named Alexander Graham Bell invented a machine, the telephone, which allowed the human voice to be carried over a wire. Nikola Tesla, a Serbian immigrant to America and the inventor of the alternating-current electric motor, contributed the idea that electromagnetic waves could carry messages. Soon it was proven that such waves could pass through walls. They could scale mountains, even cross the ocean. This created the promise of an amazing possibility: a telegraph without wires!

A young Italian, Guglielmo Marconi, became a pioneer in the new field, devoting himself to working on a way to use radio waves to transmit signals carrying Morse code.[43] Marconi had the resources to tinker with the idea; his mother was an heir to the Jameson family Irish whisky fortune. Rebuffed at home, Marconi went to England, where he formed the Wireless Telegraph Signal Company in 1897, to be followed by an American division of British Marconi a few years later. In 1901, Marconi even managed to send a wireless signal across the Atlantic Ocean, but he struggled to find a business model for his invention. The early applications of the new technology were in the military and in the shipping business, where the ability to send messages without wires had an obvious appeal. At first the technology was referred to as wireless telegraphy, or simply "wireless," but a new term—radio—first popularized in the U.S. Navy, soon won out. In 1906 an American inventor named Reginald Fessenden demonstrated that radio signals could transmit more than just long and short pulses. They could carry music and even the human voice. In the end, that discovery proved indispensable for making radio a truly popular medium.

One of the first big tests of radio, one that made a lasting impact on the public imagination, came in 1912, when the world's greatest luxury ocean liner, the state-of-the-art *Titanic,* made its initial voyage from England to New York.[44] As the great ship crossed the North Atlantic on April 14, it struck an iceberg, and the crew immediately used the ship's wireless equipment to call for help. Some of the other ships in the vicinity had wireless equipment that was turned on and monitored at all times; others had turned their sets off for the night. As a result, the closest ship, the *Californian,* which could have saved all of the *Titanic*'s 1,522 passengers, lay at anchor just nineteen miles away and never responded. The *Carpathia,* which was fifty-eight miles away when the *Titanic* started sinking, took two hours to arrive, and by then, many passengers had drowned in the frigid waters of the North Atlantic. Rescue efforts were also hampered by the many amateur radio operators who filled the airwaves that night with rumors, questions, and interference from their overlapping signals.

In the aftermath of the *Titanic* disaster, the U.S. Congress quickly adopted legislation requiring that all American oceangoing ships and all those entering U.S. ports be equipped with radios, and that the radios be kept on and staffed at all times. Congress also required radio operators to get a license from the U.S. Department of Commerce, and it relegated amateur operators to the bottom of the radio spectrum (the shortwave end) while giving priority to the navy and to commercial companies like Marconi's.[45] Significantly, Congress chose not to follow the European model, in which new technologies including telegraph, telephone, and radio were successively grafted onto a government monopoly such as the postal service, resulting in public communication monopolies like the BBC. In the United States, Congress operated on the principle that radio would be a private enterprise—regulated, to be sure, but private nonetheless. In retrospect, this was one of the constitutive moments shaping the eventual architecture of broadcasting in America, combining elements of technology, law, and economics into a new model.[46]

On the night of the *Titanic* disaster, one of the radio operators in New York handling reports of the sinking was a young man named David Sarnoff. (He was not the *only* one, as he often claimed.) A Russian immigrant who never made it past the eighth grade, Sarnoff would become one of the titans of broadcasting in the twentieth century as president of RCA, the Radio Corporation of America.[47] While working for Marconi, Sarnoff demonstrated great foresight. In 1915, when he was just twenty-four years old, Sarnoff wrote a memo to his boss, giving his thoughts on the business. He envisioned a future for radio that went far beyond transmitting coded messages from point to point. "I have in mind," he wrote, "a plan of development which would make radio a 'household utility' in the same sense as the piano or the phonograph. The idea is to bring music into the home by wireless. . . . The same principle can be extended to numerous other fields as, for example, receiving lectures at home which can be made perfectly audible; also, events of national importance can be simultaneously announced and received."[48] Sarnoff projected a market of 15 million American families. The Marconi company did not think much of Sarnoff's scheme, but Sarnoff clung to the idea that radios could be a popular mass commodity, provided they became easier to use. Never much of engineer, Sarnoff was already showing his true talent: marketing. He switched to management.

While Sarnoff and others were pondering the future of radio, most Americans still had never heard a radio broadcast. A few license-holders were beginning to transmit signals through the airwaves (or into "the ether," as it was called), where they could be heard by anyone with a receiving set. But hardly anyone had one yet. A few corporations, such as United Fruit, were using radio to coordinate their shipping fleets. And of course the army and navy remained deeply involved in radio. But before about 1920, radio remained largely in the hands of the amateurs—most of them young men who were inclined to tinker. Those early adapters usually built their own radio sets. They set up friendly competitions to see who could pull in the faintest or most distant signal (which they called "DXing"). They often traded information and parts in a wave of enthusiasm that had nothing to do with patents, profits, or licenses. Participants in the new movement sometimes referred to what they were doing as "citizen radio."[49] An editorial in one of the first radio journals put it this way: "Do you realize that our radio provides about the only way by which an individual can communicate intelligence to another beyond the sound of his own voice without paying tribute to a government or a commercial interest?"[50] Soon others joined in—women as well as men, universities, stores, even the famous Dr. Brinkley of Kansas, who used radio to promote his theory that implanting goat glands would cure "male trouble." Radio was wide open—diverse, local, nonprofit, and utterly unpredictable.

But not for long. World War I transformed radio, as it did so many other institutions. When the United States entered the war in Europe in April 1917, Navy Secretary Josephus Daniels took steps that almost amounted to nationalizing the radio industry.[51] With the declaration of war, the navy took control of the American Marconi company and of two high-powered radio stations on the East Coast that had been built by Germans. The issue was control, especially of foreign-owned companies. Acting without congressional authority, the navy amassed a monopoly over marine radio. With more than 1 million men in arms, the navy—and the Army Signal Corps as well—suddenly needed thousands of wireless sets. To meet the need, the federal government imposed a moratorium on competition among the leading companies in the field, suspended all patent claims, lifted antitrust requirements, and boosted production of standardized models.

After the war, and after Republican gains in the 1918 elections, Congress was in no mood to nationalize the industry. But what was to become of radio? At the urging of high-ranking navy officials (including the assistant secretary, Franklin Delano Roosevelt), the General Electric company decided to buy out Marconi and transform it into a new subsidiary, the Radio Corporation of America, or RCA. One of the board members was David Sarnoff, who was not yet thirty years old. Next, G.E. joined with AT&T and Westinghouse in a cross-licensing deal that allowed them to share more than one thousand radio patents, and they proceeded to carve up the peacetime market. Still, the assumption was that the way to make money in radio was to build receivers; no one could see how to make a profit by creating or distributing anything to listen to on those radios.

During the 1920s, Republicans took over both the White House and Congress, and they initiated a series of decisions that put radio on a path toward greater commercialization in the hands of corporate owners. Those decisions—mostly by Commerce Secretary Herbert Hoover and his allies in Congress—had implications that were not widely understood at the time. Taken together, those measures, both regulatory and legislative, amounted to what has been called "The Constitution of the Air" because they provided the basic framework for all the decisions that followed over the next six decades.[52] The system created in the 1920s was important beyond its impact on radio. It also served as a legal, financial, and regulatory template for other forms of broadcasting. So when television made its public debut after World War II, the system of patents, ownership, capital formation, licensing, and regulation was already in place, guaranteeing that a small number of large corporations would dominate the industry from its inception and robbing television of a period of grassroots experimentation. Because radio and television turned out to be such important media for delivering news, the decisions that shaped those two fields played an important part in the story of American journalism. None of what happened was inevitable or the product of irresistible "forces of history." They were choices made by certain individuals in specific circumstances, and they bear looking at.

One idea that was briefly considered by some people was a complete government monopoly over radio, similar to the U.S. Post Office. Although this approach did become the basis for communication technologies in many countries, it never got far in the United States. Another idea, supported by the radio amateurs, was the "citizen radio" model, in which the government would stand back and let the uses of the ether simply evolve in the hands of the grassroots users. Commercial interests did not like either of these approaches, and they ultimately prevailed on the Republican officials in Washington to write rules that favored them. One of the earliest such commercial broadcasters (though the claim to being first is a matter of dispute) was KDKA in Pittsburgh, which was the broadcasting outlet of the Westinghouse Corporation, a manufacturing company. KDKA went on the air in November 1920 to announce the results of the presidential election as they became available from the nearby *Pittsburgh Post*. The few people who were listening were able to learn, without having to wait for the morning papers, that Republican Warren G. Harding had defeated Democrat James Cox. But radio was still so new and tentative that many stations issued a request that anybody who could hear the broadcast please send a postcard so they could know how far the signal carried.

What changed radio was the advent of *broadcasting*. Up to about 1920, radio was used mainly as an improvement on the telegraph. It was a device to send a signal from one point to another. (When it carried voices, it could be thought of as wireless *telephony*.) In such a system, which was the forerunner of ham radio, one person uses the airwaves to reach another person, one on one. But radio had other potential uses. One possibility was to generate a powerful signal and transmit it in all directions, taking advantage of the fact that it costs no more to transmit a signal to a million receivers than it does to send it to one. Sending a radio signal at a particular frequency allows anyone with a receiver to listen to it. In other words, broadcasting involved sending the same message from one point to many other points—that is, casting it broadly throughout the ether. Of necessity, most of those on the receiving end would be total strangers to the person doing the transmitting, and to one another. They would be, in other words, an *audience,* receiving one-way communication. Many people could simultaneously hear the same thing, which might be an opera or a pitch for goat glands, a ballgame or a lecture, a joke or a political harangue. It might even be the news.

In 1922, Herbert Hoover, who had been both an engineer and a businessman before joining the Harding cabinet as secretary of the Commerce Department, convened the first of what would become a series of annual Radio Conferences. Hoover's goal was to stimulate business by bringing corporate leaders to Washington, discussing their needs, and serving as an advocate for their industry's development. That same year, the number of new licenses granted to radio operators exploded from just twenty-eight the year before to more than five hundred.[53] Then Hoover went a step further. Acting on his own initiative, he decided to reallocate the radio spectrum, reserving a big chunk of desirable frequencies for broadcasting, while assigning the most desirable ones to the military and the least desirable to amateurs. In the wake of that decision (the action would later be found illegal in court, but the deed was done, and it would be ratified in 1927 by Congress), broadcasting took off. Stations soon numbered in the thousands. For the biggest companies in radio, broadcasting seemed like a good idea because it would give the average person a reason to go out and buy a radio set, and selling radio sets was still their main business.

That same year, AT&T took a fateful step: it set up a station in New York (WEAF) to sell time to those who wanted to get into broadcasting but didn't want the bother of establishing their own station and getting their own license. Borrowing on the model of the telephone business, AT&T proposed to charge a toll for the time a customer spent using its equipment. After a few weeks, a customer showed up: a real estate developer who wanted to advertise a new residential project. Thus was born commercial broadcasting. At first, AT&T executives thought the business would run like its telephone service: the customers would do all the talking. In time they figured out that they would need to fill the air time in between their toll-paying customers, so the company ventured into the new business of programming—that is, producing "content" to be transmitted between ads. Through selling enough ads, broadcasting could be profitable in its own right.[54] At first, though, there was resistance. At the 1922 Radio Conference no less a figure than Hoover expressed his scorn, saying it was "inconceivable that we should allow so great a possibility for service, for news, for entertainment, for education, and for vital commercial purposes, to be drowned in advertising chatter."[55] But the horse was out of the barn: unless there was an outright ban, commercial broadcasting would prove too lucrative to ignore.

In 1926, RCA took broadcasting to a new level with the formation of the first *network,* which it called the National Broadcasting Company, or NBC. The idea was simple: unite a group of radio stations around the country, connect them with land-based telephone lines (leased from RCA's partner AT&T), and supply them all with the same programming, produced in New York. That way each station could collect advertising revenue, but without the expense of creating original content. Stations in such a network were called *affiliates.* Some were "O&Os," meaning they were owned and operated directly by NBC; the others were owned locally but linked to NBC through contracts. The new NBC network was an immediate hit—with listeners as well as with businessmen who wanted to form affiliates. In short order, NBC created two networks, called NBC Blue and NBC Red, to supply the growing number of affiliates with a standard repertoire of entertainment programming, plus a smidgen of news, all managed out of NBC's new headquarters on Fifth Avenue in Manhattan. In charge of it all was the chief executive: the still young David Sarnoff. The network he directed became one of the great profit engines of all time. Indeed, RCA was now positioned to rake in money on both sides of the for-profit radio equation. It could make money by selling advertising time or sponsorships on its broadcasting network, and it could make money by selling people the radios they would need to listen to its programs. Soon RCA could barely churn out enough of its Radiola model sets to keep up with demand, and other manufacturers rushed in to sell the bulky wooden boxes, bearing nameplates such as Westinghouse, Zenith, Philco, and Atwater Kent (fig. 7.6).

Meanwhile, though, with the proliferation of stations sending out signals in the mid-1920s, there arose what some people considered a problem. In more and more places, radio signals were interfering with one another, causing static and defeating the whole purpose of broadcasting. To make matters worse, some broadcasters built supertransmitters intended to overwhelm any weaker signal operating at the same frequency. In response, some broadcasters would move their signal to a different frequency, to avoid being "jammed" by a more powerful rival. As a result, listeners would have to search around the dial to find their favorite station. By 1925 there were some ten thousand stations sending out signals, with no sign of any slowdown. The existing law required a license, but it did not allow the government to deny one to anybody. Hoover and many broadcasters saw this "chaos" on the airwaves as a major crisis. The result was a drive for federal legislation.

But first there was an issue to be addressed: What business did Congress have regulating this area in the first place? Specifically, what about the free speech pro-

7.6 **RADIO WAS THE HOT NEW MEDIUM** in the 1920s, and manufacturers struggled to meet demand. Here, women work at long workbenches assembling radio sets for the Atwater Kent company.
—*Library of Congress.*

tections guaranteed by the First Amendment? Didn't the Constitution explicitly state that Congress shall make no law abridging the freedom of speech or of the press? Certainly, it was argued, when the Founders drafted that language, they meant to protect all speech, in all media. In the 1780s, when Jefferson and his contemporaries used the word "press," they were referring to the entire array of mass communication then in existence: books, magazines, and newspapers. Now that a new medium had come along, why shouldn't that technology enjoy the same protections granted the traditional print press, and for the same reasons? Radio could play an equally important role in our constitutional scheme as newspapers or magazines, but only if it was equally free.

By contrast, Hoover and his allies made the case for regulating radio on the basis of what they saw as fundamental differences between the press and radio that placed the two media on different constitutional grounds. First, they said, radio exists as a result of waves that pass through the ether—that is, the electromagnetic spectrum. That spectrum is a unique public resource, and the portion of it that exists above the territory of the United States belongs to the American people. Furthermore, they said, the airwaves were not like the frontier lands of the American past, which were surveyed and sold or given away to settlers. The spectrum could be measured and divided, but it was not for sale.[56] This idea is sometimes referred to as "listener sovereignty," meaning that the listeners have a collective ownership over the spectrum, which gives the public the right to control it. In addition, said the advocates of regulation, the spectrum has another inherent quality that differentiates it from the traditional press: it has only so much bandwidth. As a result, within any geographic area there is a physical limit on the number of radio signals that can be transmitted without interference. This "spectrum scarcity" means that someone must serve as a gatekeeper, allowing some people to use the spectrum and keeping others out. In radio there is a natural saturation point beyond which no one can enter without harming someone else. For that reason, radio was different from the press, since it is possible to have a practically unlimited number of publications circulating in the same area without impinging on one another. With these arguments, the regulators swept aside any constitutional objections and turned to making laws that would abridge the freedom of the airwaves.

The result was the far-reaching Radio Act of 1927. Among its major provisions was one that created a new regulatory agency, the Federal Radio Commission—later renamed the Federal Communications Commission after Congress broadened its scope. The law empowered the new FRC to deny licenses as well as to grant them or renew them, a change which guaranteed that in the future, the number of licenses would be limited, thus making each one more valuable. Each license assigned the holder a particular frequency and a particular signal strength. The license was allocated to the owner or owners of the station—that is, the people responsible for transmitting radio signals through the air—rather than the corporation running the network. Licenses were also temporary, with regular expiration dates, although most of them were renewed as a matter of routine. But no license was needed to operate a network. Thus NBC escaped any direct oversight by the FRC, although the commission could wield great power over the affiliates.

Next the Radio Act ventured into the disputed terrain of placing controls on the content of radio programming. It required that if a station let one candidate for elective office use the airwaves, it would have to allow the candidate's rivals similar access. And the law came out in favor of freedom of speech, up to a point. It declared that "no regulation . . . shall be promulgated or fixed by the commission which shall interfere with the right of free speech." But in the very next sentence the law introduced the practice of routine censorship in peacetime by specifying, "No person within the jurisdiction of the United States shall utter any obscene, indecent, or profane language by means of radio communication"—a vague standard that would keep lawyers busy for decades. Finally, the law included an unprecedented sort of charter or commandment. It said that radio shall operate according to a standard defined as "public convenience, interest or necessity."[57] That phrase, which was nowhere spelled out, had a ring of nobility about it, but what would it mean in practice? Clearly, Congress did not say that radio shall operate to maximize the profits of its corporate owners. Nor did Congress say that radio shall not make any money at all. But what was the "public interest"? And who would decide? That remained to be seen.

One immediate impact of the law was to set radio on a path toward commercialization. Under the law, all old broadcasting licenses were revoked; anyone who wanted a new one would have to apply to the FRC. No longer was broadcasting a right; now it was a privilege. The FRC established criteria that had the ring of technical neutrality but had the effect of pushing radio into the hands of corporations. The agency stated that it would favor applications from license seekers who could deliver the clearest signal (which gave an advantage to companies like Sarnoff's NBC with the deep pockets to buy the best equipment) and operate around the clock (which certainly undercut the amateur out in the garage). Moreover, the whole regulatory apparatus favored applicants who could go to Washington and master the new rules—or hire lawyers to do it for them. Not surprisingly, then, the universe of broadcasters that emerged from regulation was markedly different from the one that had preceded it. In the three years after passage of the Radio Act, the number of college, religious, or other nonprofit stations plunged from more than two hundred to only sixty-five.[58] The frontier was closing.

At just this moment another innovator came along to challenge NBC. He was William Paley, the son of an immigrant cigar maker.[59] (Sam Paley had come from Kiev, not far from Sarnoff's birthplace near Minsk.) Bill Paley was a young man in a young business. Born in 1901 in Chicago, he moved when his father decided to relocate his Congress Cigar company to Philadelphia, where the cigar workers were not unionized. Bill transferred from the University of Chicago to Penn, where he set out to enjoy himself before entering the family business. After graduation his job was to help the company fend off the threat posed by the growing popularity of cigarettes. To do that, he plunged into a campaign to boost sales of the company's La Palina brand by using the new medium of radio. Working closely with advertising agencies in New York, Bill Paley saw firsthand the impact that radio could have on sales. The mass medium soon boosted sales of La Palinas past 1 million a day. In 1926, Sam Paley sold Congress Cigar for $13.75 million. Young Bill's share was $1 million. He was just twenty-five.

Two years later Bill Paley learned that a fledgling radio network, Columbia, was for sale. Tapping his inheritance, he rounded up smaller investments from his father and other relatives, and, on September 28, 1928, bought the Columbia network for about $1 million.[60] Control of the company remained in private hands until 1937, when Paley took Columbia public as a corporation listed on the New York Stock Exchange. After the stock began trading publicly, Paley kept enough shares to ensure his control of CBS. When CBS went public, this meant that the two leaders in radio were in the hands of large, profitable corporations whose first duty was to maximize the return on their stockholders' investments. How that legal obligation would square with operating in the "public interest" was an open question.

Throughout the 1930s, as the economic depression deepened, radio kept growing. The share of American households owning a radio went from less than 25 percent in 1927, to nearly half in 1930, to more than 65 percent in 1934—or from 6.8 million homes to 20.4 million. In some cities, by 1936 as many as 93 percent of all households had a radio.[61] Radio was a craze if there ever was one. Even as economic conditions deteriorated, Americans clung to their radio sets. Many Americans gave up telephone service first or sold off all their other possessions before giving up that old Philco or Atwater Kent. One reason was simple economics: once you had bought a radio, it was essentially free after that to keep using it. Unlike with a newspaper or magazine, you did not have to pay any continuing newsstand price or subscription fee.

Congress, meanwhile, having decided that there was no constitutional bar to legislating in the field of radio, decided to go further, passing the Communication Act of 1934. With Democrats now in control of the White House and Congress, the law could have provided the vehicle for a New Deal makeover of federal policy, perhaps by breaking up NBC or by giving nonprofit broadcasters more clout. But the Democrats were in no mood to pick a fight with Sarnoff or Paley. In fact, Democrats believed that they had gotten a pretty fair shake from radio, especially in contrast to the editorial opposition the New Deal was getting from most newspapers.[62] The new radio law renamed the FRC the Federal Communications Commission, a body with seven members, and expanded its scope to include the power to regulate telephone, television (still in the laboratory), and future electronic media as well. One notable provision went further than ever in the direction of regulating the content of radio programming. That was Section 315, which called for "equal time" for political candidates vying for the same office. Broadcasters hated it and started fighting immediately to repeal it, or at least to exclude newscasts, a campaign that took until 1959. Other provisions said that candidates must be allowed to buy broadcast time at the station's lowest rate; that if a station sells time to one candidate, it must sell time to all; and that stations cannot censor what candidates say. Many of the 1934 rules were written by politicians, for politicians, and were not of direct interest to the general public. Still, the government's regulation of broadcasting was becoming broader and deeper.

On the airwaves, meanwhile, NBC and CBS were battling for talent, for listeners, and for advertisers. The bulk of the programming involved popular entertainment like the *Amos 'n Andy Show* as well some fairly highbrow offerings such as the NBC Symphony Orchestra conducted by Arturo Toscanini. (During the daytime, when the audience was presumed to consist largely of housewives, many serial dramas were sponsored by soap companies; hence the term "soap operas.")

The presentation of news on radio was much slower to get started. At first, during much of the 1920s, it consisted of men with deep voices reading newspaper stories over the air. But nobody was very happy with the results. Broadcast news requires its own style and pacing. Still, there were some key events during the 1920s that hinted at what was possible in radio news. October 5, 1921, marked the first World Series broadcast, featuring the Giants playing the Yankees at New

York's Polo Grounds. In June 1924 radio carried coverage of a national political convention for the first time. The next year, radio was part of the media horde that descended on Dayton, Tennessee, for the Scopes trial over the teaching of evolution. And in 1927 radio scooped newspapers on one of the most dramatic stories of the century—Charles Lindbergh's solo flight across the Atlantic. Shortly after he was spotted over Dingle Bay in the west of Ireland, radio flashed the news.

Part of the reason for the delay in bringing news to the radio airwaves was the resistance put up by the older, traditional medium—the newspapers. As early as 1922 the nation's newspaper publishers tried to strangle radio news in its infancy, launching what became known as the "Press-Radio War" by ordering the Associated Press and its 1,200 member newspapers to stop letting radio announcers read their stories over the air. This was a classic rearguard move by a media establishment, and it proved as futile as most. The denial of AP material to radio meant that radio station owners had to look elsewhere, and they turned to rival news agencies such as United Press or Hearst's INS. In retaliation, newspapers stopped writing "gee-whiz" articles about the hot new medium, and they stopped printing radio schedules in the daily paper. The conflict simmered until election night in 1932, when radio scooped the papers in announcing Roosevelt's presidential victory. Furious, the publishers stepped up pressure on all the news services to deny access to radio. Paley responded by taking steps to build a genuine in-house news division at CBS, but Sarnoff urged him to sue for peace.

In a series of meetings held at the Biltmore Hotel in New York, representatives of the major publishers, news agencies, and broadcasters hammered out a truce known as the Biltmore Agreement in December 1933. Under its terms, CBS agreed to dismantle its news operation, and the radio networks would pay for a new Press-Radio Bureau that would provide a trickle of news to broadcasters. CBS and NBC agreed to just two five-minute newscasts a day, timed so as not to compete with the morning or evening daily newspapers. No single news item on radio could run longer than thirty words, and every news segment on radio had to sign off with the phrase "For further details, consult your local newspaper."[63] It appeared to be a surrender by the new technology to the older one. But it didn't last long. Within about a year, some radio stations just ignored the agreement (which would never have held up in court), and radio news gradually built up its capacity to report and disseminate news. Along the way, broadcasters like Sarnoff and Paley, by putting news on the air, could show the FCC that they were fulfilling their duty to broadcast "in the public interest."

Beginning in the 1920s, the one-two punch of newsmagazines and news radio changed the journalistic landscape. For one thing, it became appropriate—in fact, necessary—to refer to the news *media,* rather than to the news*papers.* That shift in nomenclature reflected the new technology of point-to-mass communication made possible by radio as well as the mushrooming influence of *Time* magazine.

Because of radio, millions of people could stay abreast of the news, virtually as it was occurring. From the beginning, the newspaper had enjoyed a monopoly over the franchise of telling people what had happened. Now that essential task was being usurped by broadcasters. At the same time, the weekly newsmagazine was threatening to rob the newspaper of another franchise: the interpretation of news. The whole point of *Time* magazine was to summarize, synthesize, and—thanks to Luce—instruct. The writers at *Time* cared about the news, of course, but their real passion lay not in telling people what had happened but in explaining what they should *think* about it.

Moreover, radio and the newsweekly magazines brought vast new amounts of profit and capital to the news business. The early radio stations introduced a hodgepodge of business models to the airwaves, including a large number of non-profits. But soon enough the industry narrowed into the dominant form of corporate ownership. By the late 1920s, the emerging radio networks were organized, as was *Time,* as private, for-profit corporations. Some of them, like RCA, were originally organized as manufacturing businesses, and they had long sold stock to the public. Thus the large, modern "public corporation" made its entrance into the news business during this era. For the first time, journalism was going corporate.

By 1932, Adolph Ochs was getting tired. He had spent thirty-six years running the New York Times *and thirty-five years on the board of directors of the Associated Press. He was not known to most Americans, but he was rich and respected, and he occupied a position of immense authority in the field of journalism. Yet all was not well. In the fall of 1932, after he and his wife, Effie, had bought a palatial estate in White Plains, New York, he entered a period of melancholy from which he would not emerge.*

A serious problem remained unresolved: Who would succeed him as publisher of the Times? *His only daughter, Iphigene, had never been seriously considered, since newspapering was viewed as a man's field. She had done her duty and married a suitable man, Arthur Hays Sulzberger, who was now eager to take over.*

In the spring of 1935, Adolph Ochs died. His obituary ran on page one of the Times *on April 9, 1935, inside a black border. The AP silenced its wires around the world for two minutes. The coverage of his death included tributes from President Roosevelt and other world leaders.*

Not included was any mention of the will that Ochs had left, which would govern the ownership of the newspaper down to the present day. Using his 50.1 percent majority ownership of common stock in the Times, *he had created the Ochs Trust, which would thereafter hold the controlling stake in the company that owned the paper. As trustees he named Iphigene and Arthur Sulzberger, and a cousin, Julius Ochs, thus guaranteeing a 2-to-1 vote in favor of Arthur Sulzberger as the next publisher.*

In the story announcing his selection, Sulzberger promised that he would "never depart from the principles of honest and impersonal journalism" laid down by Adolph Ochs.[64]

Hard Times, 1929–1941

THREE GREAT COLUMNISTS, TWO GREAT REPORTERS, ONE HORRIBLE DECADE

News comes from a distance; it comes helter-skelter, in inconceivable confusion; it deals with matters that are not easily understood; it arrives and is assimilated by busy and tired people who must take what is given to them.

—*Walter Lippmann, 1920*

IN THE 1930S AND early 1940s, the news started off bad and just kept getting worse. Two major stories dominated the coverage. At home, the collapse of the U.S. economy caused misery and dislocation on an unprecedented scale. The New Deal and other attempts by the Roosevelt administration to mobilize the federal government to address the economic crisis generated more news from Washington than had ever occurred before in peacetime. Overseas, the rise of fascism in Europe and militarism in Japan generated a steady drumbeat of stories that pointed toward a growing menace and a revived threat of global war. To complicate matters, American newspapers, newsmagazines, and news radio all had to cover these serious, complicated stories at a time when their own resources were pinched by the economic depression (fig. 8.1).

In that setting, a new generation of journalists rose to unprecedented heights of fame and personal fortune. By the end of the 1930s, most Americans would recognize the names of the reporters and commentators who were pushing the boundaries of the field. Walter Lippmann and Dorothy Thompson were competing to analyze and explain affairs of state. Walter Winchell, the king of the gossip columns, was getting the scoop on other kinds of affairs. Edward R. Murrow was beginning to lay down the record of firsthand reporting on the early stages of Hitler's march to domination. And Ernie Pyle was roaming America, sharpening the skills that made him the country's premier feature writer. In their own ways,

8.1 **PHOTOGRAPHER DOROTHEA LANGE** was part of the team hired by the depression-era Farm Security Administration to document the impact of drought in farming areas of the country. She is shown here seated on the roof of a wood-paneled automobile, holding a large box camera, dressed in sneakers. —*Library of Congress.*

all five of these journalists found methods of disseminating their work that made them not only famous but influential as well, admired by their colleagues and sought out by presidents.

Aside from their individual talents, what these journalists shared was access to methods of distributing their work that amplified their voices and thus opened new possibilities for individual journalists. One key was syndication, a simple business arrangement in which a middleman collects work from writers and packages it for distribution and sale to newspapers. Syndicates dated to the nineteenth century, supplying newspapers with packages of ready-to-use material such as serial fiction, sports commentary, cartoons, advice columns, and the like.[1] One of the most successful early organizers of a syndicate was Sam McClure. Before he founded the muckraking magazine that bore his name, McClure had made a substantial fortune in the 1880s with his literary syndicate. Not long afterward, William Randolph Hearst began to share material among the growing number of newspapers he owned. In 1913, Hearst took the next step and incorporated the Newspaper Feature Service, then followed that two years later with the King Features Syndicate, which sold cartoons drawn by artists in the Hearst stable, such as

"The Katzenjammer Kids," "Popeye," and "Krazy Kat," to non-Hearst papers. Over the years, syndicates added more offerings that might entice newspaper publishers but would not go stale the way the news did—things like recipes, advice to the lovelorn and the perplexed, and columns on everything from hunting to sports to politics and world affairs. In effect, the syndicates operated as wholesalers of material for newspapers, supplying readymade, pre-edited, standard-sized packages of material that a newspaper publisher could just drop into a hole or, in many cases, publish as a stand-alone page or section. Especially in the hinterlands, syndication was a godsend for publishers; it meant they could offer their readers the best-known brand names in the newspaper business without having to find people of the same caliber, develop them, and pay their salaries. As the depression persisted, many publishers found it much cheaper to buy a syndicated column than to foster homegrown talent.

In radio, meanwhile, the big networks kept adding affiliates to their rosters. Like syndication, the affiliate system allowed for reducing costs and sharing talent. At NBC, the most successful radio network, the ranks of affiliated stations reached from coast to coast. Under David Sarnoff's management, NBC became so popular that the network offered two arrays of programming (known as the Red Network and the Blue Network), so that NBC could accommodate two affiliates in the same city and allow them both to put NBC material on the air without sounding exactly the same. At CBS, Bill Paley was trying hard during the 1930s to close the gap with NBC by soliciting more affiliates, by seeking the best comedies and dramas, and by beefing up his network's news division. By the late 1930s, the audiences for network radio material were measured in the millions and even tens of millions. When Dorothy Thompson went on NBC on Monday evenings, or when Walter Winchell brought his gossip column to NBC on Sunday evenings, Americans made a point of being near their radios. At CBS, the voice of Ed Murrow cutting through the static from London with an update about Hitler's assault on England could grab listeners' attention at any time of the day or night.

For the journalists who achieved syndication status or who had a network radio program (or both), these business arrangements could also be a godsend. For one thing, the journalists got a lot more money for the same piece of work. Once a writer had gone to the trouble of crafting a good column for the newspaper that he or she called home, why not resell it a day or two later to other papers? The proceeds from syndication made the top columnists rich—far richer than the typical reporter, and sometimes richer than their own publishers. For the first time, syndication made it possible for a newspaper writer to become wealthy without becoming a business owner; it provided a large income without substantial capital.

For columnists, syndication had another powerful attraction: it multiplied the size of their audience and, in the process, magnified their stature and impact. They became literally household names, as their columns spread to millions and then to tens of millions of readers. An audience of that size cannot be ignored, and neither can the person who commands that audience's trust and attention. In the era before network television, syndicated columnists spoke to more Americans than any religious or political figure.[2] Through syndication and network radio, the way was now open for a small number of journalists who were talented enough or popular enough to slip the bonds of working for someone else and become both more independent and more powerful than ever.

Three of the most prominent and influential syndicated columnists in the country's history got their start in the 1920s and rose to unprecedented prominence in the next two decades. Walter Winchell was the king of gossip in both showbiz and politics, the high priest of the gutter. Walter Lippmann was the epitome of the serious, high-minded analyst of national politics and world affairs, a public intellectual, a man of impeccable credentials and unmatched entrée. Dorothy Thompson was the embodiment of the modern woman, operating in several languages and telling her readers and radio listeners what to think about FDR, Hitler, and all the other major issues of the 1930s. Based in New York and syndicated across the country, all three shaped the editorial climate in a crucial time. They were not the only columnists, by any means, and not always the most widely read. Westbrook Pegler, syndicated by Scripps Howard and later by Hearst, attacked Franklin and Eleanor Roosevelt, labor unions, and anyone else to his left. Arthur Brisbane, until his death in 1936, was the leading voice of the Hearst press, reaching an audience estimated at 20 million. At the *New York Times,* two columnists—Arthur Krock in Washington and Anne O'Hare McCormick roving the world—were widely read in the 1930s and during the war years in Washington and in world capitals. Even more popular was another Times syndicate writer, the wise-cracking Will Rogers. But in terms of impact, Winchell, Lippmann, and Thompson stood out.

* * *

WALTER WINCHELL DID NOT INVENT gossip.[3] Winchell's contribution was to make gossip an industry. More than anyone else, Walter Winchell turned gossip into the foundation of what has become the vast celebrity business that today encompasses hordes of agents, paparazzi, publicists, stylists, reporters, photographers, and editors. Moreover, Winchell helped establish the ground rules of modern politics by offering up juicy items about the previously private lives of presidents and other politicians, as well as business tycoons and even the generalissimos of other countries. No prominent person was safe from Winchell and the leveling blows of what might be called Winchellism. "Democracy is where everybody can kick everybody else's ass," he once remarked. "But you can't kick Winchell's."[4]

Born in 1897 into a poor family of Jewish immigrants, Winchell grew up on the bustling streets of New York City, where he attended school for a few years, then ran off at age thirteen to join a vaudeville troupe.[5] For some reason, Winchell took it upon himself to begin writing short bulletins and items of interest for the cast and posting them on a wall backstage. In his early twenties, Winchell married his vaudeville partner, Rita Greene, who gave him a typewriter. He started submitting typed items to *Billboard*, the vaudeville trade paper, and they were published—at first under a pseudonym, "The Busybody." As it happened, that typewriter was his salvation. Winchell turned out to be much better at written forms of entertainment than theatrical ones. "He had a fine ear and a facility for language," his biographer noted of his writing, "and from his years in vaudeville he had learned a breezy patois and a brisk rhythm that allowed him to whittle a wisecrack to its essentials."[6] In the next few years he jumped to bigger and bigger papers until he landed in 1924 at the city's newest tabloid, the *Graphic*. Winchell had no literary pretensions, nor did he have any keen insights into the great issues of the day. What he had was an insider's knowledge of vaudeville, the stage, and the world of actors, agents, hustlers, promoters, press agents, chorus girls, bootleggers, and their pals. So he wrote what he knew.

Within a few years, many of what would become Winchell's trademark techniques were already on display. He'd fill a column of nine hundred to a thousand words with lots of short "items," each followed by an ellipsis, which Winchell called "three dots." Items lurched from topic to topic with no connecting thread other than the dots. As a result, Winchell's columns had a distinctive energy or rhythm, evocative of the rat-a-tat of a tommy gun or the driving beat of hot jazz. He was tossing aside all the formality and good breeding that were the traditional trappings of literary achievement in America, even at newspapers. Instead, he was candidly, even belligerently, lowbrow. To let his audience know where he stood, Winchell piled on the slang and jive of the street and the speakeasy. Aside from his access and his reportorial energy, Winchell had something else that he put into his columns: his ear. The result was what he called "slanguage." Winchell found that the English language he inherited from Shakespeare, Milton, and Lincoln was not adequate to his purposes. So he changed it, adding coinages as fast as he could think them up, mashing familiar phrases together into portmanteau words, and generally jazzing up the lingo—all without bothering to define or explain the new usages.[7] It was as if his columns were his way of giving his readers a knowing poke in the ribs, recognition that they were in the know, up to the minute, hip to the jive.

Soon the biggest media company of the era—Hearst—came calling and offered Winchell an irresistible package: $500 per week, 50 percent of the gross receipts from syndicating his column, plus a signing bonus.[8] Winchell joined Hearst's tabloid venture, the *Mirror*, in June 1929. Unlike most columnists writing today, he signed on to turn out *six* columns a week (later, seven!). Mondays were reserved for gossip; on another day the column was presented as if it had been written by the columnist's secretary; the rest of the week's offerings were a grab bag of jokes, puns, and random jottings. Somehow it worked, and "The Column" became must reading.[9]

In the fall of 1929 the stock market crashed, signaling the end of the party for most Americans. Although drinking soon became legal again, it was now "last call" for the gaudy nightlife of the 1920s, which had been Winchell's world. With the onset of the economic depression, Winchell began to change his focus, starting to pay attention to the bigger, more serious sorts of issues that were the traditional domain of the Noted Columnist; he began caring about—and then writing about—economics, politics, even international affairs.

At the same time, Winchell dramatically expanded his reach by going on the radio. With no training, no consultants, and no voice coach, he just sat down before a microphone and started yakking away. He experimented and came up with several trademark features for his Sunday evening radio show. Just to get himself in the right mood, Winchell wore his fedora in the studio during every broadcast. He settled on an opening line that became part of the language: "Good evening, Mr. and Mrs. North America, from border to border and coast to coast, and all the ships at sea. Let's go to press!" Next, listeners would hear the high-speed tapping of a telegraph machine that Winchell kept by his side as a prop. Then came item after item, all punctuated by the rattle of the telegraph. It was like nothing else on radio. Winchell turned out to be a natural at the hottest new medium. For one thing, he could really talk. In his nasal Noo Yawk accent, he charged into his material at about two hundred words a minute.[10] You had to listen up. If you didn't, you might miss a joke or a gag or a whole item. In between, he was constantly lurching from topic to topic—from an impending elopement by the drummer in the Tommy Dorsey band . . . to the chances of a third term for FDR . . . to the latest FBI triumph over the mob . . . to America's relations with Stalin (always pronounced "Stah-LEEN").

When Winchell's program moved to NBC, his voice could be heard from coast to coast, over fifty stations with a combined audience in the millions. As it turned out, Walter Winchell had some ideas about politics—very definite ideas. Although he was not an observant Jew, he never forgot where he came from, which led him to an early and vigorous hatred of Adolf Hitler and everything he stood for. Indeed, Winchell's hatred for Nazism led him to a general opposition to fascism in all its forms. At the same time, he became an ardent, open, unapologetic admirer of Franklin Roosevelt. For most of the late 1930s, Winchell combined both causes by urging Americans to support Roosevelt and to back a military buildup to prepare for a showdown with Hitler and his allies. Hearst—who was, after all, Winchell's employer at the *Daily Mirror*—was dead set against Roosevelt and against intervention in Europe, too. But it was a mark of the clout that came with Winchell's huge audience that Hearst himself bowed to Winchell's popularity and let the columnist tout his own causes. At a time when most American newspapers were published by businessmen who supported the Republican Party and hated Roosevelt, Winchell (along with a few other progressives like Murrow) was one of the few prominent voices raised in support of fighting fascism (fig. 8.2).

Eventually the political tacticians in the Roosevelt administration decided to reach out to Winchell and work with him. At one of their meetings, the president

8.2 **GOSSIP COLUMNIST WALTER WINCHELL** was at the height of his fame in the 1930s, when he had both a syndicated newspaper column and a weekly radio program. He is shown here wearing his trademark fedora. —*AP Photo.*

even began by slapping Winchell on the knee and promising, "Have I got an item for *you*!"[11]

* * *

WALTER LIPPMANN MAY HAVE BEEN the most influential American of the twentieth century never to have held elective office. While it is difficult to measure such an amorphous quality as influence, there is near-universal agreement that Lippmann had it. His syndicated column, titled "Today and Tomorrow," appeared in hundreds of newspapers with a total readership in the millions, over a span of thirty-five years. He was an editor of the small but influential magazine the *New Republic* as well as an editor of one of the country's leading newspapers, Pulitzer's *World*. He had the ear of several presidents and dozens of foreign ministers and other world leaders. For more than five decades, between 1914 and the late 1960s, he could get just about anyone on the planet to take his telephone calls or to receive him in their offices. His address book had to be one of the most valuable documents in private hands. Although he had rivals, he was a claimant to the title of best-informed, most widely traveled, best-connected American journalist of the twentieth century.[12]

Lippmann was a phenomenon. By the time of his birth in 1889, the age of the heroic, independent American newspaper editor had all but vanished. Most journalism was practiced by reporters who worked for wages (and none too high wages at that) and who lived for scoops. Reporting was essentially a scruffy blue-collar occupation in which many men drank heavily, smoked constantly, and dressed shabbily while making their rounds in saloons, lockups, precinct houses, and morgues, as well as on the docks and at the racetracks. In that setting Lippmann certainly stood out. He came from a wealthy, fairly established family; he had top-drawer credentials; he had connections. He managed to combine several large roles at once: he was first and foremost a solid reporter who dug out his own facts; he was also a public intellectual who engaged serious ideas with a mass audience; and he was a key figure in the U.S. establishment, especially in his role as a formulator and a critic of American foreign policy. A young radical, he eventually became the epitome of centrism, disappointing many on the Left as he became one of the most prominent skeptics about democracy itself (only to turn into one of the earliest critics of the U.S. folly in Vietnam).

Walter Lippmann began life with several advantages. As a descendant of German Jews who had become established in New York, he went to excellent schools, then entered Harvard in 1906. There he plunged into his studies and impressed his professors, including William James and George Santayana. His fellow students in the class of 1910 were quite a group, even by Harvard standards. Besides Lippmann, there was John Reed, the journalist who would soon write the first-hand account of the Russian Revolution, *Ten Days That Shook the World*. There was a young poet named T. S. Eliot. There was another journalist named Heywood Broun, who would later become Lippmann's colleague at the *New York World* and go on to found the first labor union for newspaper reporters. There was Hans von Kaltenborn (better known as H. V. Kaltenborn), who went to work for Bill Paley at CBS Radio and became a well-known commentator of the airwaves. For serious, ambitious students like Lippmann, it was a stimulating place to be. He filled his schedule with classes in philosophy, languages (Latin, French, and Italian), economics, history, and government. He disavowed the last traces of his Judaism and became the founding president of the Socialist Club at Harvard.

Lippmann had a gift for meeting and befriending eminent people, and one of the illustrious writers he had met during college was Lincoln Steffens. Shortly after graduation, Lippmann wrote to the veteran muckraker and asked if he could be of assistance. His timing was, as usual, perfect. At that very moment Steffens was looking for a new project. He had recently joined the staff of *Everybody's* magazine, and he was thinking of launching an exposé of financial corruption. Steffens was also looking for a young subject who would enable him to test one of his pet theories about journalism training. "Give me an intelligent college-educated man for a year,"

Steffens told his editors, "and I'll make a good journalist out of him." So he offered to take the young man on as his research assistant.[13] For most of the next year, Lippmann learned from a master how to get to the bottom of things.

In 1912 a friend asked Lippmann if he would like to write a book. Lippmann published *A Preface to Politics* the next year to favorable reviews, and while living in New York and mingling with the leftist and bohemian crowd around the intellectual and patron Mabel Dodge, he started another book. While he was working on it, Lippmann got an invitation to lunch from Herbert Croly, a prominent Progressive thinker and journalist. Croly, who had been impressed by Lippmann's debut book, had a proposition: How would Lippmann like to join the staff of a new magazine Croly was putting together? The magazine was to be smart, literate, and progressive. He could write and edit and make $60 a week. Lippmann jumped at the offer. It was another stroke of good fortune. The magazine, which still had no name, was eventually called the *New Republic,* and it became one of the most influential journals of opinion and analysis of the twentieth century.[14] Croly's goal was to "be radical without being socialistic"[15] and to advance his view that the small, weak central government envisioned by Jefferson could not possibly deal with the challenges posed by companies like Standard Oil or the big meatpacking firms or the sugar trust. Instead, the country needed new agencies like the Interstate Commerce Commission or the Food and Drug Administration, staffed by a new class of expert public servants who would have the power to police and guide these huge private enterprises. This was just the outlook that Lippmann had been moving toward ever since he left Harvard, one that ultimately drove him away from the socialists and muckrakers of his youth.

When the war came, Lippmann got a position as a special assistant to Secretary of War Newton Baker, helping to draw up plans for the postwar world. Then, in June 1918, Lippmann was recruited to join a new intelligence unit being formed within the army to supplement the civilian propaganda efforts already being carried out by the Creel Committee (see chapter 6). Commissioned as an army captain, Lippmann sailed for Europe, arriving just in time for an Allied conference in London on propaganda. His role in the psychological warfare unit was to write pamphlets that could be dropped behind enemy lines to encourage German soldiers to surrender or desert. One of Lippmann's leaflets became something of a classic in propaganda. Written as if by a German soldier now being held by the Allies, it read: "Do not worry about me. I am out of the war. I am well fed. The American army gives its prisoners the same rations it gives its own soldiers: beef, white bread, potatoes, prunes, coffee, milk, butter." More than 1 million copies of the pamphlet were printed, and it turned out to be the most common piece of propaganda found among deserting Germans.[16] From his brief involvement in the propaganda offensive, Lippmann took a lesson that stayed with him: he had seen firsthand how easy it was to manipulate public opinion, which would forever shape his thinking about journalism and democracy and feed his skepticism about whether either one could withstand the challenges of deliberate manipulation.

Once back home, Lippmann rejoined the *New Republic* and began work on a new book, one of his most important. That book, *Public Opinion* (1922), addresses a fundamental question: In a democracy, where the majority rules, how can there be any degree of confidence that the majority will be knowledgeable, wise, and foresighted? Lippmann begins his inquiry with an observation, drawing on Plato's allegory of the cave, in which bound prisoners can see only shadows on the cave wall rather than the real objects casting those shadows. The famous allegory suggests, at a minimum, that there is a discrepancy between perception and reality. As Lippmann put it, "What each man does is based not on direct and certain knowledge, but on pictures made by himself or given to him."[17]

In the modern world, he asked, where do men (and, although he did not say so, women too) get those pictures in their heads? Increasingly, Lippmann argued, they get them not from direct experience and not from their neighbors, their teachers, or their ministers, but from mass communications—not just from the news but from entertainment and advertising as well. To make matters worse, most people do not make any kind of systematic effort to inform themselves; instead they acquire perceptions willy-nilly, in a blur of sensations, half-truths, isolated details, and unverified impressions. The result is a bundle of stereotypes overlaid on a set of prejudices based on one's race, gender, and class. "On the unseen environment, Mexico, the European war, our grip is slight though our feeling may be intense," he wrote. "These pictures fade and are hard to keep steady; their contours and their pulse fluctuate."[18] With his great confidence in his own perceptions, Lippmann could be quite eloquent on the subject of confusion: "As you go further away from experience, you go higher up into generalization or subtlety. As you go up in the balloon you throw more and more concrete objects overboard, and when you have reached the top with some phrase like the Rights of Humanity or the World Made Safe for Democracy, you see far and wide, but you see very little."[19]

Operating with an intuitive sense of the public's limitations and passions, most leaders engage in manipulating public opinion—which Lippmann labeled "the manufacture of consent"—by appealing to existing prejudices, symbols, and simple ideas. Strengthened by the lessons learned during the war, the masters of the new techniques of propaganda threatened to make people more vulnerable. "Within the life of the generation now in control of public affairs, persuasion has become a self-conscious art and a regular organ of popular government," he wrote.[20] The implications for democracy, he believed, were disquieting. The whole theory of representative democracy, after all, rested on the assumption that the people (or at least the electorate) had enough accurate knowledge of matters of state to actually govern. In Lippmann's view, this idea—while attractive—was just not realistic. In fact, most people are not very well qualified for their public duty, even if that just means voting every so often. In Jefferson's day, he wrote, "only a few men had affairs that took them across state lines. Even fewer had reason to go abroad. Most voters lived their whole lives in one environment, and with nothing but a few feeble newspapers, some pamphlets, political speeches, their religious training, and rumor to go on, they had to conceive that larger environment of commerce and finance, of war and peace."[21] Now that the United States was a continental nation of millions, with huge cities of strangers and endless foreign entanglements, the whole idea of government by democracy seemed a dubious proposition.

Most people are not capable of sustaining interest in "things unseen," and they will not pay to support truly expert journalism. As a result, democracy—beyond the scope of the rural village—was not equal to the task facing it. In making this point, Lippmann showed a shrewd appreciation for the limits of the system bequeathed to Americans by the Founders, but he was not nearly as insightful when it came to solutions. In the end, Lippmann was forced to fall back on the hope that a new cadre of experts and social scientists would emerge who could make sense of distant and complex phenomena, then explain them to journalists, who would in turn inform the general public.[22]

His writings, while earning enthusiastic reviews, provoked alarm among liberal thinkers. The most prominent was the Columbia University philosopher John Dewey, who lavished praise on *Public Opinion* and called it "perhaps the most effective indictment of democracy as currently conceived ever penned." Like other liberals, however, Dewey did not consider democracy doomed, although he did agree that it was threatened; the answer, he believed, was to improve the public schools so that they educated people to play their roles in democracy.[23]

In the same year that he published *Public Opinion*, Lippmann moved into one of the most visible and powerful posts in American journalism. He left the *New Republic* and joined the *New York World*, taking over the editorial page at the very paper that Joseph Pulitzer had used as his crusading vehicle during the heyday of the "yellow press." Now run by Pulitzer's son Ralph, the *World* was reaching higher, abandoning scoops and hijinks for serious reporting and first-rate columns. Lippmann wrote the paper's unsigned editorials in an era when the editorials of big newspapers mattered. Over the next nine years he wrote some 1,200 editorials, including about four hundred on foreign affairs.[24] Writing with flair, power, and ease, Lippmann was nothing if not prolific. He published an estimated 10 million words during his long career. One big chunk was made up of the four thousand or so signed columns titled "Today and Tomorrow" which ran for thirty years in the *Herald Tribune* starting in 1931, after the *World* folded, and which ran in many other papers through syndication.[25] Another large chunk of writing was made up of his books—dozens in all, ranging from reportage to philosophy. On top of that, he wrote thousands of other articles and editorials that appeared in some fifty magazines, as well as an estimated twenty thousand letters.[26]

While at the *World*, Lippmann—still in his thirties—occupied an Olympian spot just below the golden dome on the fourteenth story of the building on Park

Row that Joseph Pulitzer had built. He received a tremendous salary, and he was guaranteed three months off a year to travel and write books. Referred to as "the lord of the tower," Lippmann was an imposing figure—physically fit, handsome, and nattily tailored. He occupied a town house in Manhattan and a country house on Long Island. Lippmann was in great demand as a public speaker and as a dinner party guest. He also became prominent in the new Council on Foreign Relations and set out to meet all the people who mattered whom he did not already know.

Through the 1930s his stock kept rising. When the *World* collapsed in 1931, a number of suitors came calling for Lippmann, including Hearst and Ochs, among others. Instead he went to the conservative *New York Herald Tribune,* the paper that resulted from the 1924 merger of the two dailies founded before the Civil War by James Gordon Bennett and Horace Greeley. The *Herald Tribune*'s publisher, Ogden Reid, was eager to land him and agreed to all of Lippmann's terms, which meant four signed columns a week (soon cut to three) that reflected Lippmann's own views and not the paper's.

In his chosen field—regular, signed political analysis through the column "Today and Tomorrow," combined with the regular production of books developing his public philosophy—Lippmann stood almost alone. Politicians could see this, and they courted him. One who tried, and failed, was Franklin Roosevelt. During the campaign of 1932, Lippmann was sharply critical of Herbert Hoover and the Republican response to the economic depression, but he did not think too highly of the Democratic challenger either. Roosevelt, who had gone through Harvard a few years before Lippmann (and served as president of the *Crimson*), came across as charming but out of his depth. In a "Today and Tomorrow" column in early 1932, Lippmann dismissed Roosevelt in a famous putdown as "a pleasant man who, without any important qualifications for the office, would very much like to be President."[27] But after he saw Roosevelt in action as president, Lippmann was impressed, and he said so. "By the greatest good fortune which has befallen this country in many a day," Lippmann opined in the fateful spring of 1933, "a kindly and intelligent man has the wit to realize that a great crisis is a great opportunity."[28] For the next two years, Lippmann supported the New Deal and accepted the idea that the federal government would henceforth be responsible for managing the economy. But he had growing doubts about FDR, and those doubts turned to bitterness in 1937, when Roosevelt tried to "pack" the Supreme Court.

Lippmann's greatest impact came not from his pronouncements on national politics but from his views in the international arena. And indeed the most important feature of Lippmann's column was not any particular judgment about foreign policy or his assessments of individual world leaders. It was simply his sustained engagement with the rest of the world. After the war in Europe and the collapse of the League of Nations, many Americans grew disillusioned with foreign affairs in the 1920s and returned to their embrace of isolationism. The war and the resulting peace seemed to confirm the belief that other countries were

"Lippman Scares me this morning."

8.3 **THE IMPACT OF COLUMNIST WALTER LIPPMANN** got a back-handed compliment in this *New Yorker* cartoon from April 20, 1935, by James Thurber.
—*The New Yorker.*

doomed to an endless round of squabbling, and Americans who felt that way turned their focus inward. As the situation in Europe worsened, groups like the America First Committee campaigned tirelessly for the United States to stay out. Powerful editors such as Hearst agreed and opened their pages to Hitler and Mussolini; Hearst himself repeated his arguments from 1914–1917 about the supreme importance of keeping America out of Europe's endless conflicts.

Lippmann, however, urged his millions of readers not to turn their backs on the rest of the world. He considered such an attitude unworthy of a great power. But even while he was a fervent *internationalist,* that did not make him an *interventionist.* He did not believe that every problem in the world has an American solution—and certainly not a military one. He thought that the United States should use other instruments of power, such as trade and diplomacy, rather than sending troops to every hotspot in the world. Just as he had supported the League of Nations, he continued to support the building of international institutions that could prevent war, or make it obsolete, and he continued to see the Atlantic trading and shipping orbit as a vital American interest.[29] But well into the 1930s (when his marriage broke up and he moved to Washington), despite the growing threat posed by fascism, Lippmann argued that the United States should remain neutral—well armed, but neutral (fig. 8.3).

* * *

ONE COLUMNIST WHO RIVALED WALTER Lippmann, at least for about a decade or so, was Dorothy Thompson. For a few years, their offices were on the same hallway at the *New York Herald Tribune.*[30] Their columns appeared on alternating days of the week, and they were both syndicated widely to hundreds of other newspapers. Like Lippmann, Thompson focused on affairs of state, both foreign and domestic. Like Lippmann, too, she was fluent in several European languages, she was on a first-name basis with heads of state and other people who mattered in dozens of countries, she traveled widely to buttress her column with her own reporting, and she cut quite a figure in evening wear. But there the resemblances to Lippmann stopped. Thompson was an entirely independent journalist who had strong views that usually differed from Lippmann's. Married three times (including a stretch with the novelist Sinclair Lewis), wealthy from sales of her columns, books, and radio program, she was also the epitome of the emancipated woman (even providing the inspiration for a hit Hollywood movie). During the height of her influence in the 1930s and 1940s, she was judged to be one of the most influential women in America.[31]

Born in 1893 outside Buffalo, she attended Syracuse University (which offered her free tuition as the child of a Methodist minister), then worked for a few years for a women's suffrage organization. In the early 1920s she traveled in Europe, working as a freelance journalist for clients in the United States, including Hearst's International News Service (INS). After living in Vienna and Paris, she became the Berlin correspondent for the *Philadelphia Ledger* and set about becoming an expert on Germany.

Already married once and divorced, she was introduced by friends to the famous novelist Sinclair Lewis at her own birthday party in 1927. He proposed to her that very night and pursued her until she married him in 1928.[32] In 1930 they had a son. (Thompson was a fairly feckless mother, as bad a parent as many of the globetrotting, career-hungry men in positions like hers.) They bought a country house in Barnard, Vermont, called Twin Farms, and Thompson turned it into a rural version of their place in Bronxville—a locale for a whirl of friends, refugees, and distinguished guests who filled her home and kept her informed. After several years of toning down her activities and trying to be something like a traditional wife, Thompson finally had enough and headed back to Europe and journalism.

On assignment from Hearst's *Cosmopolitan* magazine, she went to Germany in November 1930 and landed an interview with Adolf Hitler, which she developed into a book about him and his Nazi movement, *I Saw Hitler!* In a rare misstep, she misread the mustachioed crackpot as badly as Lippmann initially underestimated Roosevelt. Thompson wrote that before the interview, she was convinced that she was meeting the future dictator of Germany, but after less than a minute in his presence, she changed her mind: "It took just that time to measure the startling insignificance of this man who has set the whole world agog. . . . He is inconsequent and voluble, ill-poised, insecure. He is the very prototype of the Little Man."[33] To her credit, though, Thompson soon changed her mind about Hitler and became one of his most vocal American critics. So outspoken was Thompson in her denunciations of Hitler and his anti-Semitic campaign that in 1934 the Nazi government expelled her from the country—"for journalistic activities inimical to Germany." According to one biographer, Thompson "had the expulsion order framed and hung it on her wall as a proud trophy."[34]

Her expulsion earned her front-page coverage in the United States, and Thompson was more in demand than ever. In late 1934 she was approached by

Helen Reid, the co-owner of the *Herald Tribune,* who had been a suffragist and was committed to helping women succeed in the male-dominated world of newspapers. Mrs. Reid offered Thompson her own signed column, to appear in the *Trib* (as the paper was always called) alternately with Lippmann's "Today and Tomorrow" column. Feeling inadequately versed in domestic politics, Thompson went off to Washington to get acquainted with the New Deal and the people running the Roosevelt administration. In early 1936 she was ready, and her column, titled "On the Record," made its debut. At the time, she described herself as someone who could offer a fresh political outlook, which she referred to as a "new liberal conservatism." It would take years for her to flesh out the possible meaning of that apparent paradox. In any case, her column quickly became popular, generating bags of mail. On the anniversary of her debut, the *Trib* crowed about her success: "One reason why: unique among women columnists, men read her as much as do women, men look forward to her tomorrow's comment on today's news—as frequently as women." In what the paper no doubt intended as the ultimate accolade, the ad continued, "Men ask her to address exclusively male meetings."[35] In 1937 her column was being syndicated to more than 130 newspapers, she was becoming a star of radio through a weekly commentary on NBC, and she was asked to write a monthly column for *Ladies' Home Journal,* which she continued for more than twenty years.

In all these forums the conservative meaning of her "liberal conservatism" became apparent first and most clearly in terms of domestic affairs. In the 1936 presidential race she supported Republican Alf Landon over FDR. As her columns piled up, a viewpoint emerged that might be considered conservative in a traditional, almost nostalgic sense: she believed that government works best when it works like the town meetings in the villages of her beloved Vermont. In the huge agencies of the New Deal and the war effort she saw a threat of fascism. One of her most significant columns was titled "The Right to Insecurity," in which Thompson warned against the seductions and the subtle encroachments of the welfare state: "I was brought up to believe that there's only one certainty in life and that is that one eventually dies. Never having had the slightest feeling of security, it's a luxury that I do not miss. I prefer exhilaration to certainty, risk to dullness, danger to boredom, work to a job, and independence to a pension."[36] Many liberals read columns like that and heard yet another voice against the New Deal. Indeed, in 1940 she supported the Republican Wendell Willkie for president almost until Election Day, when she had a last-minute conversion and came out for Roosevelt (fig. 8.4).

In foreign affairs, however, Thompson showed a different side, offering one of the most consistent and most impassioned voices against the growing fascist threat in Europe. In column after column she warned about Hitler and urged America to prepare for war. By one tally, more than 60 percent of the words she wrote between 1938 and 1940 were devoted to attacking Hitler's government and policies.[37] In column after column she took up the cause of Jews who were being

forced to flee from Germany and, later, from Austria, and eventually from all of Europe. Often she used the plight of one person or family to illuminate the bigger trends and crises. In many cases Thompson invited refugees to stay with her in New York or Vermont until they could get situated, and she helped raise money for refugee agencies.

During these years Thompson was a one-woman industry. She wrote her syndicated column three times a week; she spoke on NBC every Monday at 9 p.m.; she wrote a column for *Ladies' Home Journal* every month; she came out with a book every two or three years; and she was in constant demand as a lecturer. In 1938 her earnings passed $100,000, making her one of the highest-paid journalists in the country. She wrote a quarter-million words that year, and she was contracted to write more the next year. Her regimen was one that most journalists would envy. She woke around 10:00 in her Manhattan town house, then wrote in bed in longhand on yellow pads until lunchtime. Three secretaries (all with variations on the name Madeleine) handled the hundreds of letters she got every week, juggled her appointments, and typed her columns after checking the facts. In the early 1940s she had a staff of half a dozen revolving around her in the spacious apartment at 237 East Forty-eighth Street, including a French cook, a chambermaid, a research assistant, and a housekeeper.

The whirlwind came at a price. As a woman, she was subject to a double standard that did not affect her male colleagues: she had to measure up not only as a journalist but also as a wife and mother. (She and Lewis divorced in early 1942. She barely knew her son, Michael, who was packed off to a succession of boarding schools.) And when critics wanted to fault her, they called her column too emotional. Even so, she ranked as the most famous woman journalist in America since Nellie Bly. Comparing her to Eleanor Roosevelt in terms of influence, *Time* magazine marveled in 1939 that Thompson had 7.55 million readers in 196 newspapers, plus 5.5 million radio listeners on NBC. *Time* observed that millions of women considered her a cross between Cassandra and Joan of Arc. "She is read, believed and quoted by millions of women who used to get their political opinions from their husbands, who got them from Walter Lippmann," declared the magazine. "Her opinion is valued by Congressional committees. She has been given the degree of Doctor of Humane Letters by six universities, including Columbia, and has received a dozen medals and special awards for achievement. She is the only woman ever to have addressed the Union League Club, the Harvard Club of New York, the National Association of Manufacturers and the U.S. Chamber of Commerce."[38] Thompson was even the inspiration for a hit Hollywood movie, *Woman of the Year,* which came out in 1942, starring Katharine Hepburn as a brilliant, globetrotting, multilingual newspaper columnist who is a comical failure as a wife. It must have been flattering on some level, but Thompson said she hated it.

By the late 1930s, Thompson, Lippmann, and Winchell were all prominent enough to be written about in the news media of the day, and eventually all three columnists became household names. They were so prominent that at the *New Yorker,* cartoonists built jokes around their reputations. In their very different ways, Winchell, Lippmann, and Thompson expanded the boundaries of American journalism. Through their columns, which became required reading for millions, they show how far an individual journalist could go in the context of their times. Thanks to the power of syndication and radio, all three were able to enjoy the reach, fame, and income of the press lords of an earlier generation, without actually having to manage a large capitalist enterprise. While businessmen like Hearst and Luce were running vast media empires and exerting influence mostly indirectly, from behind the scenes, Winchell, Lippmann, and Thompson could speak directly, and in their own voices, to an audience that included just about everyone, from Main Street to Wall Street to Pennsylvania Avenue.

* * *

ON THE RADIO AIRWAVES, WHILE commentators and analysts like Dorothy Thompson were bringing public affairs to listeners in the 1930s, even the big networks struggled to cover news on radio. A turning point in the growth of radio news came in 1935, when Bill Paley of CBS hired Edward R. Murrow.[39] Paley was thirty-four years old, Murrow just twenty-seven. At the time, neither NBC nor CBS could yet claim much of a news operation. What passed for news on radio consisted mainly of *announcing* developments learned from other news agencies, or *commenting* on those developments in such a way as to seem shrewd and not too partisan. News in the sense of original *reporting* had yet to come to radio. But in Murrow, Paley had discovered one of the pioneers in broadcast journalism—someone who could find out what was happening, who could capture the actual sounds of history as it was unfolding, and who could tell Americans exactly what he thought it all meant. Not only that, but Murrow could deliver the news in language that was simple but nearly poetic and in a voice that was one of a kind—deep, strong, infused with an air of unforced authority. When Murrow spoke, you might think you were listening to a lumberjack tell you which way a tree was about to fall; you'd be certain to pay attention, you'd thank him for the warning, and you'd sure as hell listen closely the next time he spoke.

Murrow, who would one day know kings and presidents, was born in 1908 in a little place called Polecat Creek near Greensboro in the textile-weaving and furniture-making belt of the North Carolina Piedmont.[40] His father, an unsuccessful small farmer, pulled up stakes in 1913 and moved the family to the farthest corner of the country, the lumbering district near Puget Sound in the state of Washington. There young Ed proved to be a superachiever in school (including speech and debate), and he worked summers in the logging camps swinging an axe to raise money for college. He went on to Washington State College, where he took up drilling for ROTC, acting in student dramas, and participating in the student government, which provided his ticket out. He became active in the National Student Federation of America, which brought him to New York and to his first contact with CBS—as the NSFA officer in charge of arranging speakers for the network's *University of the Air* radio program. Murrow spent the next few years working at the Institute of International Education, a Carnegie offshoot devoted to international educational exchanges, which evolved into the Fulbright program. At the IIE Murrow got to travel widely, meet dozens and dozens of influential people, and discuss the great issues of the day. Without having planned it, Murrow was in training to become a foreign correspondent.

In 1935 his contacts at CBS blossomed into a job offer: Murrow was to fill a position known as Director of Talks. His responsibilities included lining up diplomats, politicians, and experts to discuss current affairs. It was all very educational and not very journalistic—and certainly not partisan, in keeping with CBS policies. In a 1937 speech Paley expressed his view of the network's approach to issues, controversy, and partisanship. CBS would be "wholly, honestly and militantly non-partisan," the chairman promised, largely in deference to the policies of the FCC. "We must never have an editorial page. We must never seek to maintain views of our own . . . and discussion must never be one-sided so long as there can be found anyone to take the other side."[41] Under that interpretation of the "public interest" (which had been federal law since 1927), radio should serve as a common carrier that makes the airwaves available for others to express their views, which should be, over some reasonable period of time, roughly balanced. It was a stance that made sense for a government-regulated, profit-seeking company like CBS (or NBC), but it would be tested time and again—by the passions of politics, which were then swirling around the New Deal at home and the rise of fascism in Europe and would later swirl around the toxic issue of domestic communism.

In 1937, Murrow got an offer he was not expecting: European Director for CBS. At the time, CBS lagged behind NBC, especially in forging alliances with the European radio networks, which were often government-run monopolies. Murrow's assignment was essentially a continuation of his old one (arranging talks), only now the speakers would be European. One thing he was specifically *not* supposed to do was speak on the radio himself, no matter how much he might want to. Any description of events in Europe or analysis of their meaning was to come from experts. (In fact, Murrow was so removed from covering news that when he first applied for membership in the foreign correspondents association, he was rejected.) Murrow set to work in CBS's modest office across the street from the BBC's imposing Broadcasting House in central London. One of his first (and best) decisions was to hire William Shirer. Unlike Murrow, Shirer was a bona fide journalist, a foreign correspondent, first for the *Chicago Tribune,* then for Hearst's INS wire service. Shirer had traveled all over Europe, spoke several languages, and knew even more people than Ed Murrow did. When Murrow hired him for CBS, Shirer's job was to help arrange talks from his post in Berlin. No on-air reporting for him, either.[42]

But the pace of events in Europe soon demolished a lot of assumptions, including the expectations about their roles. In March 1938, Shirer was in Vienna when he got word of the impending *Anschluss,* the annexation of Austria by Hitler's government in Germany. Shirer flew to London to break the news, while Murrow took his place in Vienna and waited for Hitler to arrive. The two men were improvising, figuring out on the fly how to work as foreign correspondents in the new medium of radio news. Whatever expectations Paley had for the European operation went out the window. Here were two eyewitnesses to events that could not wait for experts to assess; and besides, NBC was getting way ahead in reporting the news from Europe. With armies on the march and the opportunity for worldwide news exclusives, the journalistic imperatives and the technological possibilities all pointed to one conclusion: Murrow and Shirer and the rest of the CBS team should get as close to the action as they could and describe it as fast as they could. So with no training in journalism, either in school or on the job, Murrow plunged in. Initially his reports (like those of Shirer) were

fairly straightforward: short, simple declarative sentences about invasions, ulti-
matums, and declarations of war. It was all so new. There was no real blueprint
for radio news reporting, especially from overseas and from a continent erupting in conflict.

Murrow worked at a furious pace, dealing with technical problems, teaching himself how to report firsthand, and hiring a growing staff. Shortly after the
Anschluss in early 1938, Murrow arranged the first radio news roundup, a technical tour de force that involved linking CBS correspondents, experts, or newspaper reporters in half a dozen European capitals speaking in turn about the
situation in each country. The signal carrying the report had to be relayed to an
underground bunker beneath BBC headquarters in central London. From there
it was sent by shortwave radio across the Atlantic to the CBS studios in midtown Manhattan, where it was rerouted by land-based telephone lines to CBS's
115 affiliated radio stations. At each station that signal was sent up the radio tower
and broadcast into the ether—provided there was no interference from static,
sunspots, or censors. The final report in the roundup was that of Murrow, who
was filling in for Shirer in Vienna. In his first on-air news report for CBS, Murrow spoke in a voice that was deep, steady, and awfully calm for a young man of
not quite thirty. "This is Edward Murrow speaking from Vienna. It's now nearly
3:30 in the morning, and Herr Hitler has not yet arrived. No one seems to know
just when he *will* get here, but most people expect him sometime after ten o'clock
tomorrow morning."[43] The roundup technique, in which correspondents from
several locations speak in sequence about a single topic, was such a success that it
became a staple in radio coverage (and later on television). CBS began a series of
such roundups, calling them "special reports," which lasted throughout the rest
of the war. What Murrow and Shirer had done was to report on and analyze the
urgent question of whether Hitler could enter Austria unopposed, and they had
done it from multiple perspectives, almost as it was happening. Such an undertaking could be carried out by *Time* magazine or the *New York Times,* perhaps,
but they would need a week to pull it off. Not radio. Radio was now—*right* now.

Murrow returned from Vienna to London, where he spent the bulk of the war.
There he began to emerge into the spotlight. With his suits made on Saville Row,
and with his dark and handsome looks and his chain-smoking, he became the
epitome of the suave, modern foreign correspondent. (In 1944 the correspondents' group that had snubbed him in 1937 would elect him its president.) He
also turned to the task of making sure that CBS had its own staff of reporters who
could cover the impending European war on a breaking-news basis. He started
assembling the team that would become known as "the Murrow Boys." (Although
they were not *all* boys. Among them was Mary Martin Breckenridge, a descendant of a presidential candidate; on the radio she sounded just like the actress
Myrna Loy.)[44] After Shirer, Murrow went on a hiring spree, signing up Eric Sevareid, Larry LeSueur, Charles Collingwood, Richard C. Hottelet, and Howard K.

Smith, among others. Most of them went on to spend their careers at CBS, covering wars in Korea and Vietnam, presidential elections, and the other big stories of the following decades. Within a few years the Murrow Boys became known as "the finest news staff anybody had ever put together in Europe," according to Harrison Salisbury, who as London bureau chief for United Press in 1944 was in a position to know.[45] With the equipment and staff in place, Murrow was now as ready as he could be for the task of telling Americans about the world-changing events about to unfold in Europe.

* * *

ON THE AFTERNOON OF SEPTEMBER 12, 1938, CBS radio interrupted its regular weekday programming. It was 2:15 p.m. on America's East Coast when a voice said, "We take you now to Nuremberg." What followed was a description of the closing ceremonies of the annual Nazi Party rally at the giant Nuremberg Stadium, a showpiece of Nazi design. In Germany it was 8:15 p.m., and the stadium's famous "Cathedral of Light," formed by arrays of searchlights, was visible for miles. As Adolf Hitler stepped forward to speak, there was a roar from the half-million supporters standing in ranks and files: *Sieg, heil! Sieg, heil!*

The CBS coverage was coordinated in New York by news analyst H. V. Kaltenborn. From inside Studio 9, Kaltenborn leaned toward the mic:

"Calling Edward Murrow. Come in, Ed Murrow . . . "

After a static-filled pause came the reply:

"Hello, America. This is London calling. . . ."

The voice was Murrow's. He was on duty in London to oversee the reporting of his growing team of correspondents stationed in Berlin and other hotspots across Europe, and increasingly to contribute his own on-air reporting as well. There was plenty to report: Europe seemed to be falling apart that September. After the Nuremberg rally, Hitler stepped up his demands on Czechoslovakia to yield territory to Germany. Britain's Neville Chamberlain, shuttling from London to Berchtesgaden in a desperate effort to avoid war, tried to broker a deal. Czech patriots vowed to resist. What would happen? Peace? War? Murrow and his team scrambled to keep up.

Finally, Murrow hit a wall. "There aren't any experts on European affairs anymore," he said during one broadcast that month. "Things are moving too fast."[46]

They were about to move even faster.

On November 10, 1938, two months after the Nuremberg rally, the gates of hell opened. Out flew the demons of race hatred that had been deliberately cultivated across Germany by Hitler and his Nazi movement. The pretext was the shooting of a German diplomat, Ernst vom Rath, in Paris a few days earlier by a young Jewish man who was angry over the expulsion of thousands of Jews from Germany the month before. When Rath succumbed to his wounds and died a few days later, word was relayed to Hitler, who was then in Munich celebrating the anniversary of his Beer Hall Putsch, his attempt in 1923 to seize power. His minister of propaganda, Josef Goebbels, informed Hitler that violence against Jews was already breaking out around Germany. What should be done? According to Goebbels's diary, Hitler gave the orders for a collective retaliation. "He decides: demonstrations should be allowed to continue. The police should be withdrawn. For once, the Jews should get the feel of popular anger." Thus began the officially sanctioned assault on the Jews of Germany, known as *Kristallnacht*—or in English, the "Night of Broken Glass."[47]

All through the early morning hours of November 10 and well into the day, Nazis in brown and black shirts, aided by ordinary German civilians, went on a rampage of vandalism, book-burning, violence, and murder, as police stood by or even joined in. Synagogues, the most visible symbol of Jewish community, were singled out. Across Germany, about a thousand synagogues were burned or (where there was a risk of fire spreading to non-Jewish-owned property nearby) smashed and looted. By the thousands, homes and shops belonging to Jews were ransacked. Broken glass lay everywhere. The attacks took place in virtually every city, town, and village in Germany where Jews lived, as well as across most of Austria, which Germany had annexed six months earlier. An estimated ninety-one Jews were killed outright, and dozens committed suicide. Thousands more were arrested, rounded up, and sent to concentration camps such as Dachau, which was already operating in the suburbs of Munich. The wave of attacks was not spontaneous, not an accident; nor was it a crime in the ordinary sense. It was far worse. In retrospect, of course, it was a major turning point, one that ripped the mask off Nazism, exposing it as nothing but evil to the core. But at the time it was an event for which many people had no ready mental category.

One thing it was *not* was a secret. The attacks were conducted in broad daylight, and the culprits did not run away. Almost the only people arrested were victims, not perpetrators. And it all took place in view of the world's press, which was still well represented in Berlin and elsewhere in Germany. The foreign press corps included correspondents for several American papers as well as the Associated Press, other news agencies, and the fledgling European operation of CBS Radio. The next day, the *New York Times* played the story on page one under the headline:

BERLIN RAIDS REPLY TO DEATH OF ENVOY
Nazis Loot Jews' Shops, Burn
City's Biggest Synagogue to
Avenge Paris Embassy Aide

After a lengthy introductory clause, the story finally got to the point: "violent anti-Jewish demonstrations broke out all over Berlin early this morning." Then followed details of attacks across the German capital. Understandably, as a first-day story this account was lacking in any details about events outside Berlin, although items in the following days did supply a roundup of reports from Munich,

Frankfurt, and other German cities. The story did not convey the full extent of the horror. It was a fairly ordinary report, except for one remarkable feature: this was one of the rare occasions when the *Times* identified the Nazis' victims as Jews.[48]

In the *Washington Post,* the Kristallnacht assaults were placed inside the paper, at least at first. The paper's initial report came from the United Press out of Berlin. It emphasized the Nazis' anger and threats and reported that one synagogue had been burned and the French tourism office closed. The next day the *Post* followed up with a page-one story, headlined "Goebbels Tells Jews in America to Keep Quiet." The story, by the Associated Press, had a wider perspective on the violence:

> BERLIN, Nov. 11—Germany's sudden Nation-wide outburst of anti-Semitism developed tonight into a series of secret police raids upon Jews of the upper classes amid reports that the ghetto of the Middle Ages was to be re-established in the modern Nazi Reich.

Like many stories about Nazi Germany, this one takes as a premise that Nazi hatred of Jews is a force, like volcanism or the weather, that flares up from time to time, especially if the victims do anything to provoke it. The article goes on to quote Propaganda Minister Goebbels, who issued a statement expressing his annoyance at those foreigners who attempted to put Germany in a bad light over the events of Kristallnacht. "The German people are an anti-Semitic people, and will not tolerate having their rights curtailed or being provoked by a parasitic Jewish race," Goebbels stated. "The anti-German outside world will do well to leave solution of the Jewish problem to Germans. If the outside world wants the Jews, it can have them." (The article made no attempt to determine how an already marginalized minority making up about 1 percent of the German population was managing to oppress the other 99 percent.) The article contained one ominous paragraph noting that a trainload of eight hundred "Jewish prisoners" had left Vienna that night "for an undisclosed location."[49]

The most detailed account of the events of Kristallnacht to appear in the United States ran in the *Chicago Tribune,* owned by the staunch conservative Colonel Robert R. McCormick. In an article on November 10, correspondent Sigrid Schultz laid out the horror for all to see. Under the headline "Hitler Seizes 20,000 Jews," she sketched a brisk overview:

> BERLIN, Nov. 10—Systematic destruction of Jewish property, looting, arson, and wholesale arrests of Jews without official charges swept Germany today. It is estimated that 20,000 Jews were arrested in Germany and what was Austria.

The story went on to note that "the mobs gloated over the smashed stores of Jews" and that two Jews had been shot to death. It was reported, wrote Schultz, that twenty synagogues in Vienna had been destroyed, and "almost all Jewish temples in Germany were gutted or partly destroyed by fire," giving specific locales.

In villages, homes of Jews were set afire. Terrified Jews fled into the countryside, hiding in the woods. Nazi manhunts for Jews started near Breslau and Nuremburg. In Munich hundreds of Jews were ordered to leave the city within 24 to 48 hours with the alternative of being sent to a concentration camp. Since most of them had no passports many were arrested.

And so the story went on, one paragraph after another, with specific facts, names, details. Schultz, who had been the *Tribune*'s Berlin bureau chief since 1926, proved that an American correspondent—one with enough experience and contacts, combined with the ability to speak the local language—could supply the kind of news the American people needed to read. It was impossible to read her story and not grasp the nature of German anti-Semitism. Regrettably, it was just one story in just one paper.

One of the strongest editorial responses in the American news media came from Dorothy Thompson. In her radio address to some 5 million listeners on November 14, 1938, she used the case of the young French assassin Herschel Grynzspan to raise the broader issue of the fate of the Jewish minority under Hitler: "Who is on trial in this case? I say we are all on trial. . . . The Nazi government has announced that if any Jews, anywhere in the world, protest at anything that is happening, further oppressive measures will be taken. They are holding every Jew in Germany as a hostage. Therefore, we who are not Jews must speak, speak our sorrow and indignation and disgust in so many voices that they will be heard."[50] While she was willing to speak, she remained practically a lone voice in 1938 America.

Looking back at this era, we find that the same questions inevitably arise: How could a mass assault like Kristallnacht happen? How could the peoples of the world have allowed Hitler and his many collaborators to do such terrible things? What was the role of the news media? These questions are at once fair and unfair. They are fair in the sense that anyone with any compassion cannot help but feel moved by the now familiar story of the rise of Hitler and the Nazis, the writing of the anti-Jewish laws, the lawless detention of Jews and other perceived enemies of the Reich (homosexuals, the handicapped, communists, radical Catholics, pacifists, and many more), the maniacal system of concentration camps, and the pure evil of the mass exterminations that made up the Final Solution.

Almost no one saw the future very clearly. Some foresaw parts of it, but few could see very much or very far. Indeed, in the 1930s the very word "holocaust" had not entered the vocabulary as a single term that could denote the organizing principle behind the events that we now perceive as a straight line proceeding directly from the fire in the Reichstag to the fires of Auschwitz. For most Americans, our lens for viewing this period is distorted in another way as well. Given the outcome of the war and the rise of the United States to the status of superpower in the decades *after* the war, it is natural to think of the United States as a superpower *before* the war, which is far from the truth. In 1938 the U.S. Army did not even rank among the world's ten largest.

To most Americans, news about Europe's Jews in the late 1930s was far away. Such news was precisely the kind Walter Lippmann had been talking about as early as 1920 when he wrote that "news comes from a distance; it comes helter-skelter, in inconceivable confusion; it deals with matters that are not easily understood; it arrives and is assimilated by busy and tired people who must take what is given to them."[51] The sporadic reports of Germany's anti-Semitism were arriving in newspapers, magazines, and radio broadcasts that were also carrying an increasing number of reports about terrible things happening to many people all around the world. In 1937, Japanese troops had gone marauding through Manchuria, then pounced on Nanking and engaged in weeks of killing, raping, and looting. Italy had invaded Ethiopia in 1935. A civil war in Spain had brought reports of a terrifying new kind of warfare involving bombs dropped on cities from airplanes. In the Soviet Union, Stalin had ordered mass purges of people he merely suspected of disloyalty. Could all these dreadful reports be true? Many Americans were probably not sure. One reason for doubt was that this was still the aftermath of the Great War in Europe, in which all the combatants had rolled out their newest weapon: propaganda. It is difficult to measure, but the experience of the war, and then the postwar revelations about fake atrocity stories had left many people—including editors, reporters, and readers—wary about claims of cruelty. The new round of atrocity stories in the late 1930s struck many people as simply "beyond belief."[52]

Furthermore, to understand the coverage, it would also be sensible to keep in mind the view from the newsroom. The fact is that reporters are not omniscient. Journalists can find only what they are looking for, and they usually depend on others to tell them where to look. When events are taking place far away, the looking is almost entirely in the hands of a tiny number of foreign correspondents. Ordinarily they work for wire services like the AP, or for the handful of large newspapers and newsmagazines that can afford to maintain overseas bureaus. Those foreign correspondents spend a lot of their time covering big, obvious stories that will interest Americans—stories like the Olympic Games, earthquakes, or visits by American dignitaries. They are therefore unlikely to pursue investigations, in a language they may or may not speak, into events that may or may not be happening to a small minority of people whom most Americans don't know or care that much about.[53]

Moreover, it is a fact of journalistic life that the bulk of reporting is done about the things that *others* do or announce, especially from dependable sources like the stock market or major league baseball. Of those sources, the most important and most constant by far is government. In the late 1930s, American news organizations would have been much more involved in covering the plight of European Jews if the U.S. government had shown an interest in the subject. If Congress had held hearings, reporters would have covered them. If the State Department had issued reports, reporters would have covered them. If the president had made threats or demands, reporters would have covered them. The fact is, the U.S. government did not do those things—certainly not often enough and loudly enough to result in sustained coverage.[54] Instead, President Roosevelt adopted an approach that could be called "rescue through victory."

It is also important to bear in mind that what we now call the Holocaust was not one event, occurring at one place, at one time. It was a long chain of events taking place in scattered locales across Germany and, later, in Poland and elsewhere. From our vantage point it is possible—and useful—to group these events into fairly distinct phases. In the early phase, during the 1930s, reporters in Germany knew (or should have known) that Hitler was an anti-Semite who threatened the liberties and livelihood of Jewish Germans. In this period, events like Kristallnacht took place in the open, in part to maximize the terror they were intended to create. Whatever other plans Hitler may have had were, for the time being, kept secret—hidden from all but his inner circle and certainly concealed from the foreign press. During the later phases of the Holocaust, American reporters did not report much about the Final Solution because they had been expelled from Germany and from all areas conquered or held by German troops. Although it was never complete, there was an effective "news blackout." Reports still reached America from Jewish groups, from advocates for refugees, and from the Jewish Telegraphic Agency, which supplied news to anyone who wanted to subscribe. But during the war years it was nearly impossible for an American journalist to do much firsthand reporting about the Final Solution. Only at the bitter end, during the liberation of the camps by Allied troops in 1945, did American reporters see and describe the true horrors of the Holocaust (see chapter 9).

It is true, too, that not all Americans related to the plight of the Jews from the same vantage point. A small number of Americans, mostly German-Americans, were out-and-out supporters of Hitler and belonged to the pro-Nazi Bund, which denounced FDR and his "Jew Deal." A larger number of Americans, while not pro-Nazi, were themselves anti-Semitic to one degree or another and therefore did not much care what Hitler did to Europe's Jews. Precise numbers are hard to determine, but ever since the 1920s, the Ku Klux Klan and similar groups—including the "radio priest" Father Charles Coughlin as well as the industrialist Henry Ford—had been spreading messages of hatred against Jews and finding audiences among Americans. Some of these attitudes pervaded the government as well, including members of Congress and senior officials in the army, navy, and State Department.

One group of Americans clearly had a special interest in the plight of Europe's Jews: the 4.5 million or so Jews living in America. Many American Jews had first-hand knowledge of Hitler's regime, or they had close relatives living in or near

Germany who told them in letters exactly what they were facing. Through organizations such as the American Jewish Congress, Jews who had already made it to America lobbied to loosen immigration restrictions on Jewish refugees seeking to flee Europe. In the 1930s the United States admitted thousands of Jews (including prominent scientists such as Albert Einstein) but never embraced all those seeking asylum. A few American Jews who held positions of power used their influence to aid the cause.

But not all American Jews felt compelled to act. Two of the most notable happened to be among the most prominent journalists in America—Arthur Hays Sulzberger, publisher of the country's most important newspaper, the *New York Times,* and Walter Lippmann, author of the country's most important newspaper column, "Today and Tomorrow." These two men, born two years apart in New York City, deserve special attention because they were uniquely positioned in the late 1930s and throughout the war. Unlike most of their fellow journalists, both men were Jews. Unlike most Jews, they occupied positions at the highest levels of the American establishment. Yet, oddly, Sulzberger and Lippmann were effectively—and voluntarily—mute on the subject of the plight of European Jews throughout the 1930s and 1940s.

Arthur Hays Sulzberger was a scion of one of the most comfortable, established Jewish families in America.[55] His mother's ancestors had arrived in New York in the early 1700s and fought in the American Revolution; later a member of the family had helped found the New York Stock Exchange. His father's family had left Germany in the revolutionary year of 1848 and became successful in business in New York. Thus Arthur Sulzberger was a good match for Iphigene Ochs, the only child of *New York Times* publisher Adolph Ochs; when they married in 1917, it was in part a step intended to provide a male successor to Ochs who could run the paper. A graduate of Columbia University, Arthur Sulzberger was never a very observant Jew. "If Judaism was his faith . . . assimilation was Sulzberger's religion," one critic has written.[56] When Sulzberger became publisher of the *Times* in 1935, his views began to matter very much. He had definite opinions on the subject of Judaism, believing that it was a religion and not a race or nationality. He believed himself to be first and foremost an American, one who happened to have a religious affiliation; in this he believed he was no different from an American who happened to be a Baptist or a Catholic or an atheist. Moreover, he was determined to make sure that the *Times* would not be identified as a "Jewish paper." In Sulzberger's view, that meant no special pleading for Jewish causes in the pages of the newspaper. Under Sulzberger, the *Times* bent so far backwards to avoid any appearance of sympathy to Jews that it usually omitted mentioning the fact that Hitler's victims were mainly Jewish, or buried the information deep inside the paper.[57] Because he was the publisher, his views were, of course, absorbed and reflected throughout the newspaper. As a result, a newspaper that was uniquely positioned to influence the federal government and the leaders of the U.S. news media pulled its punches and largely failed to report salient facts that were well known to the paper's writers and editors.

Like Sulzberger, Walter Lippmann was a highly assimilated Jew who did not wish to be identified with his religion or his coreligionists. Indeed, some Jews considered Lippmann an anti-Semite. During his long writing career Lippmann generally avoided the subject of Judaism, but when he did write about Jewish topics, he tended to demonstrate a blend of unadulterated anti-Semitism and overt snobbery. The principal objection he voiced against American Jews was that they had failed to assimilate as well as he had. Lippmann especially disliked recent Jewish immigrants and working-class Jews. In a notorious episode, he was asked to advise his alma mater, Harvard, in the early 1920s on the question of what (if anything) Harvard should do about the rising number of Jewish men then being admitted under the school's relatively new, comparatively meritocratic admissions policy. President A. Lawrence Lowell was pushing for a quota that would limit Jewish admissions. "I do not regard the Jews as innocent victims," Lippmann wrote to the committee advising Lowell. "They hand on unconsciously and uncritically from one generation to another many distressing personal and social habits, which were selected by a bitter history and intensified by a pharisaical theology." As a result, Lippmann said, as Harvard attempted to compose its student body, it would be hard to expect a fusion of Jew and Gentile. In that case, "my sympathies are with the non-Jew," Lippmann averred. "His personal manners and physical habits are, I believe, distinctly superior to the prevailing manners and habits of Jews."[58]

In his columns Lippmann generally treated the whole subject as taboo. In 1938 he broke a five-year silence with two columns about what he perceived as a problem of "over-population" in Europe. He saw the Continent generating a surplus of about 1 million people a year, and he was sure that the rest of the developed world did not want them. At a time when the Jewish refugee issue was reaching crisis proportions, Lippmann did not refer to Jews specifically; instead he declared that the "extra" Europeans should be resettled outside the existing modern societies. His solution: Africa. For the rest of the war years Lippmann had virtually nothing to say about Europe's Jews. He did not fault Roosevelt for leaving them to their doom, nor did he ever write about the Nazi death camps.[59]

Between them, Sulzberger and Lippmann clearly did not help the Jews, and they almost certainly made things worse. Given the prominence of the two journalists, their silence must have sent a powerful signal to other journalists: If Lippmann and the *Times* didn't care about the Jews, why should anyone else?

* * *

AS THE CONFLICT IN EUROPE turned into a shooting war, the American media—newspapers, magazines, and radio—engaged in a sustained and increasingly fierce debate. At issue was the question: How should America respond to the rising tension and threats around the world? At one pole in the debate were the isolationists, who wanted to keep America out of the wars in Europe and Asia. At the other pole in the debate were the interventionists, an umbrella name for all those who saw the Axis powers threatening not just the democracies of Europe but America as well. Both sides in this high-stakes debate were well represented in the news media, through editorials and—often—through the news coverage itself. One of the leading media opponents of U.S. involvement was Colonel Robert R. McCormick, publisher of the powerful voice of the heartland, the *Chicago Tribune.* Along with his cousin Joseph M. Patterson, publisher of the *New York Daily News,* McCormick was one of the chief financial backers of the America First Committee and a staunch editorial voice for the movement. They were joined in this outlook by William Randolph Hearst, who felt just as he had on the eve of the earlier war in Europe. Hearst combined a mistrust of the European powers with a racist disregard for Japan. In 1938, in a radio address over the NBC radio network, Hearst warned Americans against involvement:

> England needs help; and where should she turn for help except to good old Uncle Sam. . . . Nazis, Communists, Fascists, imperialists are all of the same ilk—all cut from the same cloth—all striving for power and territory—all seeking from time to time a new prize, a new victim. . . . They are all ready to go to war, and all eager to get us to go to war, to add to their imperial conquests. . . . Americans should maintain the traditional policy of our great and independent nation,—great largely because it is independent.[60]

The arguments being advanced by McCormick, Hearst, and their many supporters in Congress reflected the views of millions of Americans and, of course, reinforced those views with each new speech, editorial, or broadcast.

On September 1, 1939, German troops invaded Poland, finally showing Hitler's true agenda: conquest and domination through naked aggression. Hitler's fascist allies, Italy and Japan, were already busy expanding their spheres of influence by invading their own neighbors. In the rising anxiety over Hitler, Congress began to act, passing a burst of wartime legislation that chipped away at the First Amendment. Once again, some Americans saw the threat of war as a reason to limit the rights of other Americans to think, speak, and publish.

In May 1938 the House had voted to create the House Un-American Activities Committee, to be chaired by Texas Democrat Martin Dies. HUAC, which became notorious in later decades for chasing suspected communists, started out as an attempt to rein in domestic Nazis, although the authorizing legislation did not make that point explicit; it said only that the panel should investigate "the extent, character and objects of un-American propaganda activities in the United States." Initially, HUAC focused on the German American Bund and its leader, Fritz Julius Kuhn, a German immigrant to America who favored black leather jackboots. Kuhn built the Bund's membership to some 25,000 by 1938.

The Bund published two German-language newspapers, which often reprinted materials by German Nazis, and ran youth camps to spread the Nazi ideology to young Americans. Despite the threat, Dies quickly steered his committee in a new direction and made it a vehicle for investigating the political Left. In its first report the Dies Committee named hundreds of groups and hundreds of newspapers as "Communistic," including the ACLU and the Boy Scouts. An opponent of the New Deal, Dies believed that the Roosevelt administration was riddled with communists, calling them "purveyors of class hatred" under Stalin's command, and demanded their dismissal. With the aid of newspapers that took his charges at face value and amplified them in lurid headlines, Dies was rehearsing the tactics that Joseph McCarthy would use more than a decade later.[61]

Congress wasn't finished. Fearing that a "Fifth Column" of Nazi sympathizers was plotting to undermine American defenses, Congress revived the Espionage Act of 1917, putting it into effect for the first time in peacetime. A short while later Congress passed the Alien Registration Act of 1940, commonly known as the Smith Act. The law required all aliens to register with the government and made it easier to deport them. It also took a giant step toward criminalizing certain kinds of speech and communication. The Smith Act would punish anyone who "prints, publishes, edits, issues, circulates, sells, distributes, or publicly displays any written or printed matter advocating, advising, or teaching the duty, necessity, desirability, or propriety of overthrowing or destroying any government in the United States by force or violence, or attempts to do so."[62] It was, in effect, a new "sedition act."[63] Once again, expressing certain ideas could send the author to jail. By passing these laws, Congress put the country back on essentially the same footing as it had been in 1798 or 1918. Roosevelt, never much of a stickler about civil liberties or press freedom, allowed it to become law.

Step by step, the war was coming nearer.

In early 1941, Henry Luce decided that the people of America (and, indeed, the world) needed some instruction on just what was at stake. His *Time-Life-Fortune* publishing empire was flourishing, but Roosevelt's reelection in 1940 had made it clear to Luce that the grand prize of the presidency would never be his. If he could not be president, he could still impart to the world what might be called the Luce doctrine. He decided to write a lengthy essay, which he published in *Life* (because *Time* had no editorial page) in February 1941. Under the grandiose title "The American Century," the essay crystallized Luce's thinking about America's role in the world, from an internationalist-Republican point of view, and in the process provided a kind of blueprint for much of the American establishment's thinking about not just the war against Hitler but also the long cold war against communism that followed.

According to Luce, "Americans are unhappy. . . . [W]e don't know why we are preparing to fight, whether it is for democracy or for world power." He declared that America had become "the most powerful and vital nation in the world" but had not faced up to the responsibilities such power brings with it. "And the cure is this: to accept wholeheartedly our duty and our opportunity as the most powerful and vital nation in the world and in consequence to exert upon the world the full impact of our influence, for such purposes as we see fit and by such means as we see fit." In making these sweeping pronouncements, Luce was trying to slip one past his readers: the United States in 1941 was not "the most powerful . . . nation in the world"—far from it. That would be a plausible statement to make *after* the war but hardly before it. Such empirical problems did not trouble the thinking of the great man. Onward pressed Luce.[64]

In a burst of pure bravado, he declared that if the twentieth century was to achieve "any nobility of health and vigor," it must be an American century. In fact, according to Luce, America was already having a huge impact, "from Zanzibar to Hamburg," through the export of American jazz, slang, movies, machines, and products.[65] He called for Americans to be bolder and more explicit about the flow of influence, to export our ideals about freedom, independence, and equality of opportunity.

To Luce's chagrin, most of the reaction was negative. Conservatives failed to rally to the cause, because many of them heard a call to fall in with Roosevelt's international goals, and they were hardly about to support That Man (whose name conservatives could no longer even bring themselves to speak). Liberals shunned the proposed doctrine for what they considered its throwback to gunboat diplomacy and imperialism. The leftist vice president, Henry Wallace, wrote a rebuttal to Luce in which he tried to cast the century as one belonging to "the common man."[66] Socialist leader Norman Thomas denounced Luce's imperial ambitions, comparing Luce to "that British Nazi poet, Rudyard Kipling" for his view that the United States had a duty to elevate the rest of the world.[67] In the end, though, Luce enjoyed a considerable measure of vindication, since his views eventually pervaded the thinking of many American policymakers, from both parties, during the 1950s and 1960s.

As Luce and others tried to rouse the American people, there was a long way yet to go. Even as late as 1941 the United States was far from the industrial colossus that would emerge victorious from the war. On a per capita basis, the economies of Germany and the United States were comparable.[68] But despite Roosevelt's best efforts to arm the country, it still had a relatively small and backward military. The U.S. Army in late 1939 numbered about 200,000 men, at a time when Germany, with about half the population of the United States, had an army four times the size.[69] The U.S. Army was so small that most of the officers knew one another on a first-name basis, and it was so underequipped that for lack of rifles, new recruits trained with broom handles. In 1941 America's military had more horses and mules than airplanes.

Similarly, the American news media were not prepared for what was coming.

Few of the correspondents who would end up doing the bulk of the wartime reporting had any experience with combat. A relatively small number of American journalists had been to Europe for the Great War, but most of them were now retired, dead, or working as editors (like Harold Ross). A handful, like Ernest Hemingway, had covered the Spanish Civil War, but there were not many of them to begin with, and a number of them had never come home. Most of the major newspapers were still feeling the impact of the economic depression of the 1930s, and they were not in any mood to open foreign bureaus to cover a war that the United States still might avoid. As a result, the coverage of the important events of 1936–1939 and the first two years of fighting in Europe and the Pacific was spotty, amateurish, sometimes wrong, and often simply nonexistent. Like the country's armed forces, the American press corps had a lot of catching up to do.

*   *   *

AS THE WAR DREW CLOSER, more and more Americans began facing up to it and thinking about their places in it. One of them was a newspaper columnist in his late thirties named Ernie Pyle. The son of farmers, Pyle left his small town in Indiana and, in the space of a few years, became the best-known and most beloved journalist of his generation.[70]

Young Ernie escaped from his hometown of Dana by going to Indiana University in Bloomington, where he studied economics and journalism and came within months of earning a degree. Before that could happen, though, he took a job on a newspaper. Thanks to a recommendation from a friend, Nelson Poynter, Ernie hooked up with the powerful Scripps Howard company. He was offered $30 a week to work for a tabloid that the newspaper chain had recently bought in the nation's capital.[71] In 1925 he married a free-spirited woman named Geraldine Siebolds, who was known as Jerry. Soon after, Ernie and Jerry lit out for the territories. In the spring of 1926 they quit their jobs, sold all they had, bought a Model T, and headed west. They lived out of the car, cooking over an open fire and sleeping on the ground as they treated themselves to a long look at the country. Of all the places they visited, the one they liked best was the high, dry Southwest. A friend described them at the time as "young, wild, unconventional and neurotic," adding that "they were tearing across the country as if someone was after them."[72]

Broke, they landed in New York, and Ernie went back to work, as a copy editor at the *Post*. He didn't like New York, so when he got a letter from Lee Miller, an editor at his old paper in Washington, he jumped at the chance. Miller, who was on the rise in the Scripps Howard operation, offered him a spot on the desk at the *Washington Daily News*. There, just months after Lindbergh's historic crossing of the Atlantic, Ernie launched the first regular column in the country devoted to the field of aviation. He spent most days at his desk job, then spent most evenings hanging around the airfields near Washington and writing his column. While he was busy, Jerry began drinking. At one point Ernie and Jerry took another long trip across the country. When they got back, his newspaper was facing a problem: the syndicated columnist the newspaper usually carried, Heywood Broun, had gone on vacation and suspended his column. To fill the space, Pyle pitched in and wrote eleven pieces about his recent trip. Those columns caught the eye of the top editors at Scripps Howard, and Ernie was rewarded by having one of his life's wishes fulfilled: he was given his own column, to be filled by whatever material he could find by traveling the USA.

From 1935 to 1942, Ernie roamed the country, through the depths of the depression, "a tramp with an expense account," and he made his way to all forty-eight states, as well as Alaska, Hawaii, Canada, and Latin America. He met all sorts of people, from all walks of life. He was not seeking news, he was looking for life—and he found it. Along the way, according to his biographer, the character the world would get to know through the byline "Ernie Pyle" emerged: "a figure of warmth and reassurance, a sensitive, self-deprecating, self-revealing, compassionate friend who shared his sadnesses and exhilarations, his daydreams and funny stories, his ornery moods and nonsensical musings, his settled prejudices and deepest meditations."[73]

His column started off modestly, running in most of the twenty-four Scripps Howard newspapers, although some of the editors shunned him. While columnists like Winchell and Lippmann were reaching millions, Ernie was slowly building an audience in the small towns where Scripps Howard papers circulated. "I have no home," Ernie wrote. "My home is where my extra luggage is, and where the car is stored, and where I happen to be getting mail this time. My home is America." Like a journalistic Woody Guthrie, he went just about everywhere and talked to just about everyone, celebrating the common people he met. His assignment may have sounded like fun, but it was also hard work to churn out a thousand-word column every day, week after week. "One story a day sounds as easy as falling off a log," he once wrote. "Try it sometime."[74] Over the years, his columns became more personal, more colloquial, more conversational. An Indiana junk dealer once explained Pyle's appeal this way: "He comes as near writing like a man talking as anybody I've ever read."[75]

The man who could write as if he were talking was a jumpy bundle of moods, habits, and gifts. He was a scrawny fellow who managed to endure terrible hardships. He had a loveless, childless marriage to a woman he was apparently quite devoted to. He was a hypochondriac who was actually sick a lot. A heavy drinker, he managed to find a wife who drank far more. He was also curious, sympathetic, and gracious. He could walk up to just about anyone or any group of people and strike up a conversation. He wasn't interviewing, exactly; he just seemed to be *talking*, and later on he would figure out what to use in his columns. He had the reporter's eye for detail, and a good ear. He was also a self-taught master of simple, direct English prose.

The work on his column was relentless. He was on the hook for a thousand words a day, which may not sound like much but is a pace that is difficult to sustain. It adds up to about twenty-four pages of double-spaced copy a week, or 1,200 pages a year. But that was just the part that showed. To produce it, he usually followed a grinding regimen:

> Go somewhere, find something new, interesting, and original to write about.
> Talk to some people, usually total strangers. Find a quiet place to write. Bang out four pages of copy.
> Find a way to transmit it to the home office.
> Deal with editing changes. Deal with business matters—fan mail, hate mail, expense accounts.
> Check into a motel. Find something to eat.
> Tomorrow, do it all over again.

In 1938, Pyle's career took a big step when his column went into syndication. This was a business decision that meant more than just business. The Scripps Howard company owned its own syndicate, known as the United Feature Syndicate. It operated like any other: the company acted as a broker, buying material from writers and selling it to newspapers. Usually this was done through long-term contracts on both ends of the deal. That is, the writer would be obligated to write on a fixed schedule (whether he or she felt like it or not), and the syndicate would distribute the material on a schedule. At the receiving end, the newspaper customers could use the material or not, and they could display it prominently or not. For all writers who work this way, there are three measures of success: the number of customers who contract with the syndicate to buy their work, the amount of money that contract brings in, and the display (or "play") their work gets in the pages of those newspapers. A column about chess or sewing might bring in a modest income and receive modest play in a regular corner of an inside page. But a controversial or "hot" column like Winchell's might land a guy on page one and might even make him rich.

For Scripps Howard, syndication meant that Ernie's column would now be for sale to newspapers outside the chain, which might dilute its value to Scripps Howard editors, but it would also mean that the company could make a lot more money from the words it was already paying Ernie to write anyway. Eventually they ironed out the terms, and Ernie's column became available to many, many more readers. In late 1939, Pyle embarked on a long trip, from Seattle to California (where he found a bed-making contest in San Francisco to write about, as well as a chinchilla farm), then to New Orleans and on to Central America. That put him in the vicinity of the Panama Canal, which was emerging as a strategic military chokepoint in the growing world conflict. Ernie wrote about it reluctantly. "I hope the office won't even suggest that I do any military columns down there," he wrote a friend. "If there's one thing in this world I hate and detest, it is writing about the Army."[76]

In the battle for American popular opinion, 1940 was the year when the ground shifted. The interventionists, led by Roosevelt and supported by sympathetic journalists like Luce, Murrow, and Pyle, were gaining support, and the isolationists like Lindbergh and McCormick were losing. The Gallup Poll revealed the shift. Three times that year pollsters asked Americans, "Do you think the United States should keep out of war or do everything possible to help England even at the risk of getting into war ourselves?" The answers changed decisively in a short seven-month stretch of 1940:

> May: 64–36 percent in favor of "stay out"
> November: 50–50 percent
> December: 60–40 percent in favor of "help England."[77]

Part of the reason for that shift in American public opinion was the work of one American journalist who was already compiling a record of firsthand war coverage: Ed Murrow of CBS. He did not have to go looking for the war; as he remained at his post in London, war came to him. In 1940, having defeated Poland and France, Hitler turned his sights on the next phase of conquest—England. His strategy was to use the German Luftwaffe to drive the Royal Air Force out of the skies, then train Germany's air power on the British fleet to eliminate it as a defender of England's homeland. With the skies cleared and the seas open, Hitler could invade England and seize the great prize. Everything depended on the air war. At first, German Messerschmitts attacked British airbases, hoping to cripple the RAF on the ground. But British pilots managed to keep flying. Next, starting in early September 1940, Hitler ordered the Luftwaffe to bomb London itself, a city of limited military value, using "incendiary" bombs designed to start and spread fires. In doing so, Hitler dramatically expanded the use of bombing as a tactic against a civilian population. This campaign, known as the Blitz, was not only a crucial military development but also a moral outrage, a turning point in modern warfare. Murrow now had the world's biggest story unfolding right outside his cramped studio.[78]

Naturally, Murrow wanted to tell Americans all about it, but there was a problem. Murrow was a citizen of a neutral country reporting from a nation at war. British authorities had already imposed a systematic censorship regime on all communications going into and out of their country. In the view of many top British leaders, especially in the war ministries, the last thing they wanted was to have an independent newsman from a foreign country reporting—*live,* as it was happening—about attacks that were still under way. From a military point of view, such reports were a threat because they could be monitored by German spies and used to help German commanders determine how accurate their own bombing was.

Murrow tried to make his case. He enlisted help from sympathetic colleagues at the BBC, but to no avail. A key ally was Roger Eckersley, an Englishman who worked in a division of the BBC known as the American Liaison. Once the war began, the liaison office turned from being helpful minders of Americans to de facto censors. The BBC, as a government agency, was charged not only with obeying the British censorship rules but also with enforcing them on others. Even so, Eckersley fought to change the rules. He agreed with Murrow that the news of Germany's assault on England could help sway American public opinion away from neutrality toward support for the country's old ally. In May 1940, Eckerseley wrote a memo to his superiors about lifting restrictions on Murrow's reports for CBS, casting the issue in terms of opening a front in the propaganda wars: "These relays are listened to by a mass of sentimental, friendly people eager for news, and subconsciously at all events, glad of Allied success and anxious for them to win the war," he wrote. "I am convinced . . . that this . . . is a sure way of enlisting American sympathy and support."[79] The War Office continued to drag its feet, but in late September, after a series of trial runs to prove that he would not spew military secrets all over the airwaves, Murrow finally got from the Ministry of Information what he had been waiting for: permission to broadcast live from London.

On September 20, 1940, Murrow took up a strategic position in the center of the city and made the first in a series of reports from the rooftops of London. Night after night, Americans could hear his deep baritone begin the report with his signature greeting, "This . . . is London." In a typical report on the Blitz, he would go on to paint a word picture, saying that a curtain blowing in an open window looked like a ghost, or describing his office after a bomb fell nearby as looking as if a giant had taken an eggbeater to it. He also began to integrate ambient sounds into his reports, exposing American listeners to the whine of air raid warnings and the "duh-*doom*" concussions of bombs falling near him. Although he had been on the air for only two years and had no prior background in journalism, Murrow already had a mature style: never afraid of using the first-person stance, he told listeners what he was doing, seeing, and thinking. He brought them as close to the action as possible, yet he never shouted or sounded out of breath. His prose was correct and often elegant. He also began using a phrase then popular in London as a signature sign-off: "So long, and good luck."[80]

Although his role did not extend to commenting on the news, Murrow made plain where he stood. His views generally coincided with those of American progressives like FDR, who wanted America to do more to resist the fascist dictatorships. Without ever explicitly editorializing, Murrow's reports from London left listeners with several clear messages: Germany was the aggressor in Europe, the big democracies like France and England might actually lose, and the war was almost certain eventually to engulf neutrals like the United States. These views, given an emotional punch by Murrow's obvious admiration for the plucky English, helped build support among Americans for Roosevelt's policies, including aid to England, the prewar draft, and a move toward military preparedness.

While Murrow continued his broadcasts, other American journalists started trickling into Great Britain. One of them was Ernie Pyle. After listening to Murrow's broadcasts, Pyle had undergone a change of heart and set aside his misgivings about covering the military. On December 9, 1940, Pyle arrived in England and was immediately smitten by the country and its "lovely, courteous people." His goal was not to analyze the master strategies that absorbed a columnist like Lippmann. Instead, as Pyle wrote to his editor, he wanted to be "making people at home see what I see."[81]

He made his way to London and roamed around the city's landmarks and backstreets. On the night of December 29, Pyle could hear German bombers approaching the skies over his room in the Savoy. His hotel had a bomb shelter in the basement, but Pyle headed for a high balcony so he could watch the attack. Under the pounding of 130 bombers loaded with incendiaries, London began to burn. His column, scheduled for release to the papers in the syndicate just before New Year's Day, allowed people at home to see just what he had seen:

> On that night this old, old city—even though I must bite my tongue in shame for saying it—was the most beautiful sight I have ever seen. . . . I shall always remember . . . the monstrous loveliness of that one single view of London on a holiday night—London stabbed with great fires, shaken by explosions, its dark regions along the Thames sparkling with the pin points of white-hot bombs, all of it roofed over with a ceiling of pink that held bursting shells, balloons, flares. . . .
>
> Pinkish-white smoke ballooned upward in a great cloud, and out of this cloud there gradually took shape—so faintly at first that we weren't sure we saw correctly—the gigantic dome of St. Paul's Cathedral.
>
> St. Paul's was surrounded by fire, but it came through. It stood there in its enormous proportions—growing slowly clearer and clearer, the way objects take shape at dawn.[82]

American readers noticed. His column got better and better "play" in the papers that subscribed to the syndicate, and *Time* magazine took note, reprinting his cathedral dome column and describing it as "one of the most vivid, sorrowful dispatches of the war."[83] His bosses were ecstatic, cabling praise and saying that Pyle's London columns were the "TALK OF NEW YORK."[84] The description of the bombing around Saint Paul's won Pyle notice from Eleanor Roosevelt, who praised him in her newspaper column "My Day." Pyle's work also came to the attention of Ed Murrow, who invited him to do a weekly broadcast over CBS Radio. Pyle was flattered, but he declined. He would stick with what he knew best.[85]

Murrow, too, was discovering his own calling at CBS. Although NBC and the much smaller Mutual network also had correspondents in London, none of them matched Murrow. His series *London after Dark* became a fixture in many American households. Soon, Murrow himself was becoming something of a hero. He became a subject for journalists passing through London to write home about, complete with photos of the handsome, well-dressed radio correspondent. Often his broadcasts were transcribed and printed in American newspapers.[86] In late 1941, when he came back to the States for a break, many people already knew who he was. On December 2, CBS threw a glittering reception for Murrow at the Waldorf-Astoria Hotel ballroom, attended by more than a thousand of the biggest names in broadcasting, journalism, and government—all guests of Bill Paley. Among the testimonials to Murrow was one by the poet Archibald MacLeish, who was then serving as the librarian of Congress and head of the federal agency that evolved into the U.S. propaganda arm during the war. "You burned the city of London in our houses," said MacLeish, "and we felt the flames that burned it. You laid the dead of London at our doors, and we knew that the dead were our dead."[87]

Murrow's success proved that radio could work as a medium for delivering news, and it was still expanding dramatically—from 65 percent of all U.S. households in 1934 to 81 percent in 1940.[88] Americans were also listening to radio in a new location: inside their automobiles. Starting in the early 1930s (with the Motorola), radio became standard equipment in new cars and trucks, adding immensely to the total audience. Murrow proved that radio news could be accurate, responsible, even soulful. And it could run rings around newspapers and magazines.

Five days after the event at the Waldorf, Murrow was in Washington. Plans called for him to spend Sunday golfing, then attend dinner at the White House, followed by a private briefing for the president. That afternoon came the news from Pearl Harbor. Murrow sped to the CBS office in the capital, while his wife, Janet, phoned the White House and learned that the Murrows were still expected. They ate scrambled eggs with Mrs. Roosevelt while the top officials in the U.S. government tried to decide how to respond to the attack. Murrow was asked to stand by, and he did, sitting on a bench in a White House hallway, chain-smoking Camel cigarettes and watching the secretaries of the army and navy, the secretary of state, and other top officials shuttle in and out of the Oval Office. Shortly after midnight, Murrow was ushered in. Over beer and sandwiches, FDR asked Murrow about the morale in England. Then the president went on to spell out, in detail, the shocking extent of the U.S. losses at Pearl Harbor, which were still being kept secret from most Americans by navy censorship. At one point Colonel William "Wild Bill" Donovan, who was already setting up a new U.S. intelligence operation, came in. As the three men chatted, by some accounts it became clear that Roosevelt was not altogether upset by the Japanese attack, because it would now tilt U.S. opinion in favor of involvement. What seemed to bother the president most was the fact that the navy had been taken unawares at Pearl Harbor so that American air forces had been destroyed before they could even take off.

"On the ground," Roosevelt moaned. "By God, *on the ground!*"[89]

Afterward, Murrow wrestled with the question of what—if anything—to report about his meeting with the president. FDR had set no ground rules, so it was up to Murrow. In a decision that would be repeated many times in the coming years by Murrow and his colleagues in the U.S. news media, he decided to do what he thought the president would want him to do. So he said nothing.

William Randolph Hearst loomed large over the first half of the twentieth century. As a publisher and politician, he sought to win the support of masses of people. He did that, and he stirred bitter opposition as well.

Perhaps his greatest critic was the young broadcasting genius Orson Welles. In 1941, Welles released his cinematic masterpiece Citizen Kane, *which tells the life story of a media giant, complete with a mistress and a castle. It was a devastating, thinly veiled portrait of Hearst as a homegrown fascist.*

Hearst decided not to sue for libel; instead he used his media empire to try to suppress the film and crush Welles. Hearst employees threatened film distributors to keep them from booking Citizen Kane *into theaters. Hearst magazines investigated Welles and branded him a "red." The entire Hearst empire would refuse any future ads from RKO, the studio that produced the film. In 1942, after losing $150,000, RKO withdrew* Citizen Kane *from distribution. Hearst had won the battle, but he lost the war. Over the following decades,* Citizen Kane *emerged as an American film classic, and it continues to shape the way people perceive William Randolph Hearst.*

After Hearst's death in 1951, his company continued to operate a media empire, and it remained a private corporation. In recent years the Hearst Corporation managed one of the most successful magazine launches in history with Oprah Winfrey's O.

Walter Lippmann remained an influential columnist until his retirement in 1967 (see chapters 9, 10, and 11), but Walter Winchell fell hard. So did Dorothy Thompson. Both of Lippmann's contemporaries found their columns and radio programs much less popular after World War II. That may have been because they both turned rightward after the war and alienated many of the readers and listeners who had made them popular.

In political terms, Thompson became isolated. Before and during the war she was a staunch advocate for Jewish refugees, and she endorsed the Zionist cause as a way to provide a safe haven for Jews fleeing Europe. After the war she became equally committed to supporting the Arabs who were being asked to make room for the new state of Israel. In 1951 she agreed to head the American Friends of the Middle East. These moves horrified many of her former supporters.

In journalistic terms she became isolated as well. After she endorsed FDR for a third term in 1940, the Republican owners of the Trib *could not tolerate her any longer and refused to renew her contract. She quickly found a new home base at the* New York Post, *which was then the liberal voice of the city's Jewish working class. But when she began to support Arab causes, the* Post *dropped her column too. On August 22, 1958, after twenty-one years, she wrote her last "On the Record" column. Along with that final column, her editors at Bell Syndicate attached a note to the editors at the newspapers that still carried her. In part, it read: "No journalist of modern time has been so much written about* as Dorothy Thompson. For a time she reached more readers than any commentator on serious political affairs in the United States. . . . Miss Thompson has, at all times, been highly controversial. Sometimes her enemies have seemed to outnumber her friends."[90]

She began work on an autobiography but did not finish it before she died of a heart attack on January 30, 1961.

Well into the 1950s, Winchell remained wildly popular. Then, suddenly, it was all gone. When Winchell died, his front-page obituary in the Times called him "the country's best-known and most widely read journalist."[91] Today he is almost unknown.

According to Neal Gabler, who wrote a masterly biography of Winchell, "he had gone from the people's champion of the thirties and forties, fighting for Roosevelt and courageously against the Nazis, to the cruel, spiteful rumormonger of the fifties, glorifying McCarthy. . . . If Walter Winchell was responsible for having enlivened journalism, he was also responsible in the eyes of many for having debased it."[92]

Now that gossip and the "gotcha" style of reporting pervade our culture and our politics, perhaps W.W. should be better known. The reasons for Winchell's obscurity are many. A liberal in the decades before World War II, Winchell grew increasingly conservative after the war, embracing General Douglas MacArthur and Senator Joseph McCarthy, which left many fans disappointed and bitter. He got rich and discovered that he did not like paying taxes. He made a lot of enemies, and some of them decided to fight back. His work was scrutinized in a withering series in the New Yorker, which seriously undermined his reputation as a reporter. He was attacked by the New York Post in an enormous twenty-four-part series in 1952, which began by observing that W.W. "spends much of his time justifying the existence of gossip columns and trying to prove he is a heavier thinker than Walter Lippmann."[93]

Winchell was also attacked by his rival Broadway columnist Ed Sullivan. Then came a devastating blow: the depiction of W.W. as the fictional columnist J. J. Hunsecker in the 1957 movie The Sweet Smell of Success. In the film, the columnist is an unscrupulous bully.

Things got even worse for Winchell in the 1960s. Television and the suburbs were killing off his natural environment—Broadway and the nightclubs of Manhattan—so W.W. spent more and more time in California. He tried, but he never really navigated the transition from radio to the new medium of television. After several TV shows flopped, he ended up using his inimitable voice as the narrator for the TV series The Untouchables. His wife left him, and his son, Walt, committed suicide. The 1963 newspaper printers' strike in New York resulted in the death of his home base, the Mirror. Although the brass at the Hearst Corporation found him a new home, things were never the same, and in 1967 they actually canceled The Column, after thirty-eight years. He busied himself by working on a savagely bitter, nearly incomprehensible autobiography. It wasn't published until after his death.

In 1970, Winchell was diagnosed with cancer. On February 20, 1972, he died at the UCLA Medical Center. He was seventy-four. The funeral was arranged by his only surviving close relative, his daughter, Walda, who lived in Arizona. She had him buried the next day at a cemetery near Phoenix. No one came.

The "Good War," 1941–1945

A salute to the infantry—the God-damned infantry, as they like to call themselves.
—Ernie Pyle, 1943

I N 1941 THE AXIS powers made two key mistakes. In June, Hitler shredded his treaty with Stalin and invaded the Soviet Union, an act of arrogance that essentially doomed the Third Reich. Six months later, Japan attacked the United States Navy. On the morning of December 7, 1941, Japanese warplanes staged a successful surprise attack on the American fleet as it lay at anchor at Pearl Harbor. In the space of several hours, fourteen warships were sunk or crippled, about two hundred planes were destroyed (most, as FDR lamented to Murrow, without ever taking off), and some 2,344 American sailors and soldiers were killed. This was one of the most fateful acts of the twentieth century, for it was this attack that finally roused the United States to action, forced Congress to declare war, and changed the course of millions of lives. In a stroke, the debate in the American press over isolationism essentially ceased.

Even before the United States entered the war, the Roosevelt administration had been giving thought to managing news coverage of any military action. As it turned out, the entire program that FDR eventually settled on was an updated version of the approach first used by President Wilson in 1917–18. Almost no policy or procedure used in the Second World War had not been used in the earlier one, except for a few special rules to cover radio. More than a month before Pearl Harbor, Navy Secretary Frank Knox had announced that the navy was training censors to handle all "outgoing communications" from the United States in order to "prevent the leakage of military, naval or economic information to enemy or unfriendly powers." Knox denied that the government was imposing a program of censorship on domestic newspapers and broadcasts, but he went on to voice his "gratification over the excellent cooperation demonstrated by public services in voluntarily avoiding publicity on certain restricted matters."[1] In November the Commerce Department curbed distribution of transatlantic weather reports on the grounds that the information could be helpful to hostile nations.

Even so, when the Japanese attacked at Pearl Harbor, very little institutional apparatus was in place for handling war news, so the navy began improvising. Because Hawaii was a U.S. territory (and not yet a state), there were few legal obstacles to imposing martial law. As quickly as possible, naval officials declared a news blackout. The first news report to come directly from Hawaii was sent out by the United Press, just before the censors blocked communication. The bulletin read:

> HONOLULU, Dec. 7 (UP)—War broke with lightning suddenness in the
> Pacific today, when waves of Japanese bombers assailed Hawaii and
> the United States Fleet struck back with a thunder of big naval rifles.[2]

The story was remarkably balanced. In fact it was overly generous to the navy, whose fleet was too busy putting out fires and rescuing sailors to do much striking back at the attackers. Within hours, and without any legal authority, the navy seized all means of communication between the Hawaiian islands and the mainland United States: telephone, telegraph, and mail. Due to the pervasive censorship, most of the news that day came not from Hawaii but from Washington. It was announced by the White House, which allowed FDR to control just how much Americans learned about the extent of the disaster. Officials released enough information to make Americans mad at Japan but not enough to make them mad at the navy brass, which had left the fleet so vulnerable. The full story trickled out years later, over the course of more than half a dozen investigations.

For the moment, the Roosevelt administration was willing to acknowledge the surprise attack but would admit only that a single battleship (and an "old" one at that) had been sunk, while claiming that U.S. forces had inflicted heavy casualties on the Japanese. The first claim was so selective as to be deliberately misleading, and the second one was pure invention. The goal could not have been to fool the Japanese, since the attackers had their own spotters and intelligence officers who could supply commanders in Tokyo with an exact accounting of the damage. The people most likely to be influenced by the censored version of news about Pearl Harbor were, inevitably, the American people.

The situation would get worse. At about the same time, sources of news were drying up around the globe. In a flurry of declarations over the following days, the United States entered the war against Germany, Japan, and Italy, and those nations all declared war on the United States. As a consequence, American reporters, who were no longer journalists from a neutral nation, were summarily kicked out of all areas under Axis control. Vast expanses of the globe were suddenly off-limits, including most of the areas where the Nazis were stepping up their extermination factories. From now on, information was a weapon.

*   *   *

THE WAR AFFECTED EVERYTHING—FROM WORK habits and marriage plans to living standards and life expectancy. Like other Americans, those in the news business were now scrambling to do their part. Many reporters were young men, and a large number of them headed straight to their local draft boards or enlistment stations. Those who did not put on a uniform (and as it turned out, there were a lot of bad backs, flat feet, and weak eyes among the press corps) could still do their part: they would use their typewriters, notebooks, microphones, and cameras not only to record the great struggle but also to do whatever they could to tip the balance in favor of the United States. In all, the U.S. armed forces accredited more than 1,600 war correspondents, and as many as five hundred full-time American reporters were working overseas at any given time.[3] The biggest delegations belonged to the wire services (the AP, UP, INS) and the major radio networks (NBC, CBS, Mutual), as well as the big daily papers and the weekly magazines such as *Time, Life,* and *Newsweek.*

At the very time when they were losing a sizable chunk of their workforce, newspapers were facing an upsurge in demand; everyone wanted all the latest news about the war now that America was involved. Like many employers, editors found that they had only one place to turn for new recruits: to women. In the wartime newsrooms of newspapers, magazines, and radio stations, doors began to open. A few women—notably Marguerite Higgins, Martha Gellhorn, and Margaret Bourke-White—even made it to the war zones and became frontline combat reporters and photographers. Of the 1,600 accredited correspondents, almost one hundred were women.[4] A much smaller number were black men.

The new generation of war reporters included a few who already had some experience—Ernie Pyle, for one. In 1942, now in his forties, he tried to enlist in the navy but was told he was too small; then somehow he passed the army physical. At the last minute, though, he changed his mind and decided to keep writing his column. Pyle headed back to Britain to cover the American troops who were now gathering there on their way to Africa. Murrow stayed at his post in London and kept adding staff. Soon those beachheads opened the way to a journalistic invasion. A mustached young reporter for United Press named Walter Cronkite left for Europe as well. So did cartoonist Bill Mauldin, reporter Homer Bigart, and photographer Joe Rosenthal, along with hundreds of others. A few on the trailing edge of that generation who would become prominent journalists had not yet started their careers, while others spent the war in uniform. Ben Bradlee, who later became editor of the *Washington Post,* was in the navy; Punch Sulzberger, who was destined to take over the *Times* one day from his father, joined the marines.

Now it was up to them—the young correspondents and photographers, the new generation. Certainly they lacked experience. But in a sense that didn't matter much, because nothing about the trench warfare fought during the horse-and-rifle days of 1914–1918 would have prepared anyone for what was to come in the Second World War. Soon the newspapers and magazines faced another problem. They had more news to report than ever, and with the economy revving into high gear, more ads than ever as well. Trouble was, there was literally not enough paper to print them all on. The war brought shortages of everything, from rubber to butter. In the newspaper and magazine field, the war meant shortages of ink, paper, pencils, trucks, and film. As part of the vast mobilization effort, an organization called the Publishers Newsprint Committee sprang into action and issued a rationing plan intended to allocate newsprint to publishers on a fair basis, whether they owned their own paper mills or not. But everyone had to make do with less. For publishers, the issue was tricky. Should they produce a newspaper of the usual size and sell it to fewer subscribers? Reduce the size of the daily paper and preserve circulation even if it meant rejecting or shrinking the size of ads? Keep the ads and shrink the news? While publishers wrestled with these questions, some magazines like *Time* and the *New Yorker* produced special pocket-size editions to be sent to the troops, a move that won them lifelong readers.

The government's dramatically expanded command role in the economy, combined with the rationing of key materials, had other impacts on the media. In the nascent field of television, the war brought a complete halt for the duration to any further development. For radio, however, the Second World War created a boom. People who owned a radio could listen as much as they liked; there was no rationing on broadcasting, and there was a huge appetite for the latest news. So the size of the audience soared. By 1942, radio had penetrated into more than 80 percent of all American households, and popular commentators like Walter Winchell counted their audiences in the tens of millions.[5] Advertisers were more eager than ever to reach radio's vast audience. Often, however, manufacturers were so involved in war production that they had little to offer consumers. Nevertheless, they kept advertising, if only to remind listeners that they were doing their part in the war effort and to entice them with the promise of new models and products that would be available once the shooting stopped. General Motors, for example, had no cars to sell, but the company decided to sponsor the NBC Symphony Orchestra under maestro Arturo Toscanini. The radio trade magazine *Broadcasting* observed, "To put it bluntly, business is wonderful."[6]

The war years brought one other major change to radio: the breakup of the biggest network, NBC. As far back as 1938, the Federal Communications Commission had begun an investigation into "chain broadcasting"—essentially, the rise of the NBC and CBS networks. The report filed in 1941 called for breaking up NBC, which was so successful that it had already divided itself into a Red Network and a Blue Network, all under one corporate structure. CBS trailed NBC in terms of affiliates and profit, and the Mutual Broadcasting System, formed in 1934, was a distant third. When the FCC, seeking more diversity and competition in radio ownership, attempted to break up NBC, the company filed suit. In May 1943 the Supreme Court upheld the FCC, leaving NBC no choice: the Blue Network was put up for sale for $8 million. The buyer was Edward J. Noble, who had made a fortune selling a candy called Life Savers. The new company would be known as the American Broadcasting Company.[7] ABC immediately set about playing catch-up to NBC and CBS.

*   *   *

IN MOBILIZING FOR WAR, THE Roosevelt administration began placing orders for all the military equipment American factories could make, but officials did not overlook the power of words and images. Just as Woodrow Wilson had done, now Franklin Roosevelt decided to engage in the battle for public opinion, not just at home but among America's armed forces, its allies, and its enemies. That would mean telling the world what we were fighting for, how it was going, how everyone could pitch in, and why the war effort was worth supporting. To do this, the administration had to assemble an army of communicators, eventually including writers, poets, admen, photographers, filmmakers, singers, radio announcers, actors, translators—and some means to coordinate all their efforts. This was a battle that most of the nations already at war had been waging for years, led by the German Ministry of Propaganda under Josef Goebbels, who was refining the techniques pioneered by the Allies in the war of 1914–1918. In the current war, it was obvious that the United States would need to mobilize the entire American people—not only the soldiers, sailors, and airmen in uniform, but also all their families back home, who would be asked to pay for the war through War Bond drives, to enlist in the military, and to keep the factories humming day and night to supply the military with everything from guns to socks and from fighter planes to canned beans.

Even before the United States entered the war, several federal agencies were busy pumping out stories, data, and images for public consumption, using techniques adopted from Madison Avenue. One was a civilian agency, the Office of Facts and Figures, headed by the poet Archibald MacLeish, who had been serving as librarian of Congress. MacLeish, a Roosevelt supporter (and former *Time* rewrite man), recruited other writers, many of whom were liberals and idealists who wanted to cast the coming war as a battle against fascism. At the same time, Roosevelt had approved an agency aimed at overseas audiences—the Office of the Coordinator of Information, headed by William "Wild Bill" Donovan, who went on to head the Office of Strategic Services (OSS). Donovan's first hire at OCI was Roosevelt's speechwriter, the playwright Robert E. Sherwood, who launched the Voice of America radio operation to try to counter Nazi propaganda on the airwaves. By April 1942, VOA was broadcasting to audiences outside the United States around the clock and in several languages.[8] In an effort to bring more coherence to these efforts, FDR signed an executive order in June 1942 creating the Office of War Information.

To head the OWI the president appointed Elmer Davis, a prominent news analyst at CBS Radio. His agency's mandate was to "coordinate the dissemination of war information by all federal agencies and to formulate and carry out, by means of the press, radio and motion pictures, programs designed to facilitate an understanding in the United States and abroad of the progress of the war effort and of the policies, activities, and aims of the Government."[9] Out of the hodgepodge of agencies, the OWI emerged as the most powerful and the most similar to the Creel Committee of World War I. But it was never as effective as some hoped and others feared. Elmer Davis never had anything like the power of Goebbels, who was among Hitler's inner circle. The OWI was essentially involved in putting out messages that were determined by others.[10] And it never had legal power in the domestic sphere to do more than urge, recommend, and encourage.

One of the OWI's great successes was in enlisting the help of Hollywood to articulate the nation's war aims. By 1942, Hollywood movies had a paying audience of some 85 million Americans a week, and there were millions more in captive audiences who could be shown films of the government's choosing in recruiting centers, boot camps, and military bases.[11] Many of Hollywood's top directors enlisted in the OWI filmmaking effort, in some cases switching from comedy or drama to documentary. John Ford made *The Battle of Midway,* John Huston made *The Battle of San Pietro,* and William Wyler made *The Memphis Belle.* But the most deeply involved was Frank Capra, the prizewinning director of such prewar classics as *It Happened One Night* and *Mr. Smith Goes to Washington.* Capra, who had immigrated to America from Sicily with his family when he was a boy, was recruited by army chief of staff George Marshall, and he enthusiastically agreed to help. Drawing on some of Hollywood's top talents, Capra made seven films in all, under the series title "Why We Fight." (The first, titled *Prelude to War,* won an Academy Award for 1942.)[12] Originally intended for viewing just by soldiers, the films were quickly released to the general public. They stuck close to government policy. In *The Battle of Russia,* for example, Capra tried to convince Americans that the Russians, who had been denounced by the government since 1917 but were now U.S. allies, were a courageous and resourceful people who could stand up to the Nazis. Over the course of the two-hour film, Capra's script stayed far away from the words "Soviet" and "communist" (fig. 9.1).

To be fair, it must be noted that World War II propaganda did produce some good results. It kept American morale high, and it helped Americans see the war as more than a retaliation for the attack at Pearl Harbor. It was probably also helpful in encouraging men (and women, too) to enlist and in persuading others to

9.1 **IN THIS PROPAGANDA FILM BY FRANK CAPRA**, America's ally Russia is menaced by the threat of Nazi aggression. Capra, director of such beloved classics as *It's a Wonderful Life*, was one of many Hollywood stars who lent their talents to the Office of War Information to make seven "information films" called *Why We Fight*. —*U.S. War Department.*

buy war bonds. The OWI and the other U.S. propaganda agencies were quite effective in drawing attention to atrocity stories involving enemy countries. Americans were infuriated, for example, by the true accounts of the "Death March" on Bataan. Military propaganda efforts were successful in encouraging some German soldiers to surrender (by promising them safety, warmth, and food). And U.S. propaganda discouraged some residents of Nazi-occupied Europe from participating in the destruction of the Jews. The tactical dissemination of true, if selective, information could and did have an impact.

Still, the OWI was never very popular. Journalists are, by temperament, allergic to propaganda, and they never embraced the OWI. In addition, the Roosevelt administration failed to solve a basic contradiction at the heart of the OWI. It was one thing to say that an agency should articulate the war aims of the government. But how could that be separated from the role of boosting the image of the particular administration then managing the government? In other words, how to sell the country but not the president? In a dictatorship like Germany this was not an issue, because the Führer was identified so closely with not only the German state but also the German *Volk*. Unlike Hitler, however, Roosevelt had domestic opposition, and his opponents never liked the OWI. They believed that in trying to justify the actions of the government, it was actually polishing FDR's image. After the midterm elections of 1942, a coalition of Republicans and conservative Southern Democrats slashed the budget for the OWI by practically eliminating its domestic operations.[13]

Another form of expression that was encouraged by the government was the soldiers' own press and radio. In the print field, the military revived the defunct newspaper *Stars and Stripes,* which had been mothballed since the Armistice in 1918. In its pages appeared one of the great cartoonists of the era, Bill Mauldin, creator of the inimitable, archetypal foot soldiers "Willy and Joe." In issue after issue, these two lowly GIs slogged through rain, mud, and bullets. Unwashed and unshaven, they epitomized the average dogface, trying to survive the hazards of terror, boredom, MPs, and the brass. In 1945, Mauldin won the Pulitzer Prize for editorial cartooning. The military also published a weekly magazine called *Yank,* which was launched in the summer of 1942 and quickly expanded to reach an estimated 2.5 million readers, almost all of them enlisted men. Among the contributors were Irwin Shaw and Walter Bernstein, both screenwriters who were later victims of the Hollywood blacklist; the novelist and biographer Merle Miller; and short story writer and playwright William Saroyan. *Yank*'s main office, in New York City, was staffed with enlisted men (no officers allowed), many of whom had experience as reporters, photographers, and editors. It was printed at ten locations worldwide and distributed from Anzio to Alaska. As a soldier-to-soldier magazine, *Yank* could be blunt. In a lengthy account of the brutal fighting during the Battle of the Bulge, for example, *Yank* described the plight of a soldier whose rifle had frozen:

> During the fighting at Petit Langlier, Pvt. Joseph Hampton found him-
> self in a spot where he had no time. Just as his outfit started into action,
> Hampton found that ice had formed in the chamber of his M1. With
> no time to waste, Hampton thought and acted fast. He urinated into
> the chamber, providing sufficient heat to thaw it out. Not five minutes
> later, he killed a German with his now well-functioning rifle.[14]

In addition, the military set up the Armed Forces Radio Service, which was also popular in the ranks. Soldiers and sailors taxed their ingenuity to rig up receivers to pull in the signal so they could listen to Crosby and Hope, the Andrews Sisters, and Sinatra.[15]

*   *   *

As Murrow and Pyle and hundreds of other journalists fanned out across the globe to try to cover the war, officials in Washington were giving thought not only to what those reporters should say but also to what they should *not*. Again following the example of the Wilson administration, the Roosevelt team set up a formal system of censorship, both at home and in the theaters of war. Immediately after Pearl Harbor, the censors got out their scissors (fig. 9.2).

The World War II censorship regime had two basic features. One was that it operated on the home front. For the most part, domestic censorship efforts were applied after the fact. Once a newspaper or magazine was printed, it would be examined; after a radio show or movie was produced, it would be checked. If anything seemed too revealing or likely to aid the enemy, the censors would step in and confiscate the material or cancel the show. The other essential feature of domestic censorship was that it was voluntary. Rather than confront the First Amendment head-on, the Roosevelt administration decided to take two approaches: the government would appeal to feelings of patriotism among all those in the news media and urge them to shun certain topics in advance; if that

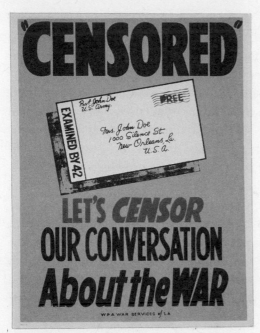

9.2 CENSORSHIP WAS PERVASIVE DURING WORLD WAR II, as U.S. government censors opened millions of pieces of mail to ensure that no private communications aided the enemy.
—*Library of Congress.*

failed and sensitive material got out, censors could reveal the names of violators and hope that public disapproval would force them back into line.

To make all this work, straightaway after Pearl Harbor the government established a new agency. Only two days after the Japanese attack, Roosevelt held a news conference at which he put the nation's reporters, photographers, and editors on notice. He told them that all wartime reporting must meet two criteria: it must be accurate (which should not have been *too* much of an imposition), and it must not help the enemy. Within weeks Roosevelt created a new civilian agency, the Office of Censorship. To run it, Roosevelt appointed Byron Price, a veteran reporter and columnist who had risen to the top news editing position at the Associated Press, giving him instant credibility throughout the journalism world. By January 15, 1942, the Office of Censorship had promulgated the first of a series of guidelines for reporters and editors. The Code of Wartime Practices was intended to let journalists know what was expected of them, and it was predicated on the assumption that journalists wanted to pitch in and help the war effort.

The code spelled out the traditional areas of wartime censorship (such as troop movements and embarkations) and went on to caution against giving out too much information about the performance of the U.S. economy and to restrict reports about the weather. The code also stated that journalists could publish any story that was released by an "appropriate authority," even if it might not square with the rest of the code. The "appropriate authority" rule cut both ways. On the one hand, it caused serious headaches for investigative journalists like the Washington-based columnist Drew Pearson, since journalists had to have an on-the-record source for every story about the war effort, even for things they could see with their own eyes.[16] (Meanwhile, a gossip columnist like Walter Winchell, who often left sources out of his stories altogether, could go right ahead with unsourced speculations about celebrity canoodlings and "Reno-vations.") On the other hand, once a journalist had confirmed an item with an "appropriate authority," it was almost impossible to prevent that item from making its way into print or onto the air. The Office of Censorship issued frequent updates and refinements of the code throughout the war. The result was "an amazing record of compliance," according to a recent study of Price's agency. "No print journalist and only one broadcast journalist ever deliberately defied the code, after having been told the reasons for its provisions."[17]

Even so, President Roosevelt was not always happy with the wartime press, and he would urge his cabinet members to go after those he referred to as "the isolationists" and "the seditionists." In practice, FDR's subordinates tended to drag their feet in such cases, and few were ever pushed to conclusion. One that did come to a head involved Father Charles Coughlin, the vitriolic "radio priest" from Royal Oak, Michigan. Initially a supporter of Roosevelt and the New Deal, the Catholic cleric veered hard to the right during the mid-1930s. But the target in 1942 was Coughlin's magazine *Social Justice,* which accused Jews of both fomenting the communist revolution in Russia and simultaneously running the global capitalist system. In the end, a Roosevelt aide prevailed upon the Roman Catholic bishop of Detroit to silence Coughlin for the duration, and the magazine ceased publication.[18] A handful of other publications—including the *Militant,* published by the Socialist Workers Party, and the *Galilean,* published by the vicious anti-Semite William Dudley Pelley—were also either investigated or suppressed, but most were eventually reinstated.

A special concern of the Office of Censorship involved radio. Some brief consideration was given to ordering a public takeover of all commercial radio during the war, but it was never pursued. Instead the administration tried to bring radio under the same regime as the print media. By early 1942 radio was already a big business. There were more than 900 commercial radio stations, including 510 that were affiliated with the big networks. Under the Code of Wartime Practices, all stations were requested to curtail drastically the information they broadcast about the weather, on the grounds that it might aid the enemy. The restrictions even extended to live broadcasts of baseball games when rain forced a delay or cancellation; announcers were supposed to find a way around divulging the real reasons. Also banned were most forms of ad-libbing and shows that allowed the public to speak directly over the airwaves. Spies were presumed to be everywhere.[19]

Another major focus of government pressure involved the black press. Attitudes among black Americans, of course, varied. Most black newspapers tended to be pro-Roosevelt and generally supported the war, although many were impatient at the pace of integration in the armed forces and demanded that blacks be treated equally and allowed to serve in combat roles and not just as cooks, servants, and laborers. Black papers were regular targets of investigation by FBI director J. Edgar Hoover and by the Post Office, but no black publishers were ever charged with sedition. *The Crisis,* which had been founded by W. E. B. Du Bois, and the *Courier,* which was based in Pittsburgh but had the largest national circulation of any black-owned paper, were two early war critics. They objected to the continuing discrimination both at home and in the military. For many blacks, the issue posed by the war was an old one: Despite their substantial grievances, should blacks support (and fight in) the war in the hope that doing so would lead to the gratitude of whites and meaningful improvement later on? Some black journalists thought so, while others insisted that the war presented an opportunity to press a more militant agenda. One such effort was the "Double V" campaign, launched in 1942 by the *Courier,* which tried to widen the war aims beyond victory over the Axis to include a victory over discrimination at home. NAACP chairman Walter White weighed in on the side of caution, warning that continued editorializing against discrimination in the military might cause a backlash.

In that setting a crucial role was played by John Sengstacke, who had recently succeeded his uncle, Robert Abbott, as publisher of the *Chicago Defender.* In 1941, Sengstacke helped organize the new National Negro Publishers Association (NNPA), and the next year he opened a Washington office for the *Defender* with a part-time correspondent, Harry S. McAlpin. Later in 1942, Sengstacke met with Attorney General Francis Biddle to discuss war coverage, and he offered a proposal: black papers would tone down their rhetoric if the administration would open up to black reporters. "Nobody will talk to us," Sengstacke argued, "so what do you expect us to publish?" The attorney general said that he would try to get the other cabinet members to do better, and he promised not to seek any indictments. He also promised to ask the president to admit a black reporter to his press conferences. It took more than a year, but eventually Harry McAlpin was accredited. In February 1944, Roosevelt invited thirteen NNPA leaders to the White House, and three days later McAlpin made his debut at an Oval Office press conference alongside white reporters. "I'm glad to see you, McAlpin," Roosevelt said, shaking his hand, "and very happy to have you here."[20] Black reporters faced many more challenges during the war and after, but some tangible progress was being made.

*   *   *

ANOTHER KEY ISSUE WAS THE censorship of dispatches from correspondents covering the war itself. During World War II, the war zone censorship procedures were, once again, similar to those used during the earlier world war. Correspondents had to be accredited by the War Department, and they had to agree to submit all stories, scripts, film, and photos to a military intelligence officer before they could be relayed to the home office for publication or broadcast. Correspondents were given uniforms but no insignia other than an armband displaying a "C" for correspondent or "P" for photographer. In practice, reporters wore a grab bag of mismatched uniforms, hats, boots, and whatever else they could scrounge. Few carried weapons, and almost no correspondent ever fired one. For bureaucratic purposes (and in case they were captured), correspondents were assigned the rank of captain. They were instructed to report to a public relations officer, who was supposed to mind them, but once in the field, most correspondents were free to roam. They were not "embedded" with a particular unit, and in most theaters they could go anywhere a jeep could take them.

Naturally there were points of friction between the press corps and the military censors. After all, the censors were army and navy officers whose careers depended on their not releasing information too soon, or in some cases at all. Their working principle seemed to be "When in doubt, cut it out." Correspondents sometimes groused, especially about delays, because the loss of an hour or so in sending a censored story back to the States could mean the difference between beating the competition and ending up with a report that was no longer news. When it came to the substance of the censors' decisions, correspondents could appeal up the chain of command, and sometimes they won. But for the most part, reporters accepted the censors as one more obstacle in their way. In the judgment of Drew Middleton, an AP correspondent who later became the top military specialist for the *New York Times,* the censorship system during World War II actually helped correspondents become informed, because "as long as all copy was submitted to censors before transmission, people in the field, from generals down, felt free to discuss top-secret material with reporters."[21]

One of the most crucial censorship cases involved an attempt on the part of the navy to withhold information about a U.S. victory, not a defeat. The case involved a reporter for the *Chicago Tribune* named Stanley Johnston, who was heading back to the United States aboard a navy ship after witnessing the Battle of the Coral Sea in May 1942. During the long voyage, the reporter chatted with an officer, who divulged that the navy knew the makeup of the Japanese fleet that was then steaming toward Midway Island. The navy had recently broken the Japanese military code, so American officials were able to tell from intercepting radio transmissions what the Japanese planned to do next. For obvious reasons, this was a great advantage, and U.S. officials wanted to exploit this edge for as long as possible. From his position on board a navy transport, Johnston was incommunicado and could make no use of the information anyway. Eventually, though, he made his way home to the *Tribune* newsroom in Chicago. There he saw the news bulletins about the amazing U.S. naval victory in the Battle of Midway in the early days of June. He put two and two together and wrote a sidebar under the headline "Navy Had Word of Jap Plan to Strike at Sea." The story did not explicitly state that the United States had broken the Japanese code, but there were plenty of hints. It said that the makeup of the Japanese task force at Midway "was well known in American circles several days before the battle began." The navy brass were furious, and Roosevelt considered sending the marines to occupy the *Tribune* newsroom and even thought about filing charges of treason against his old nemesis, *Tribune* publisher Robert McCormick. Federal officials demanded to know how the leak had happened. As it turned out, the story simply slipped through the cracks. Because Johnston had returned from the war zone and written the story on U.S. soil, it was not subject to pre-publication military censorship. But it was not covered by the Code of Wartime Practices, either, because the code did not say anything about reporting on *enemy* ships in *enemy* waters. Nevertheless, Roosevelt wanted Biddle to prosecute under the Espionage Act. Biddle went ahead and launched a grand jury investigation, but the case was dropped when navy officials declined to proceed, on the grounds that an espionage indictment would lead to trial in open court, where the code-breaking secret would surely spill out. As it happened, the Japanese apparently did not notice the revelation, and U.S. Navy officers were able to keep exploiting their advantage.[22]

Another special case involved war zone photography. Initially, U.S. military and civilian censors banned the publication of photos showing dead American soldiers or sailors. It was assumed that such images would be bad for civilian morale, and they would probably not bring the troops much cheer either. For twenty months after Pearl Harbor, not a single photo depicting a dead U.S. service member appeared in the news media. Much of the initiative for change came from the editors of *Life* magazine, which, with a circulation of more than 2.5 million a week,[23] had emerged since its founding in 1936 as the nation's premier showcase for photojournalism. Among its wartime staff were Margaret Bourke-White, Carl Mydans, and Robert Capa. With its large format and glossy paper, *Life* gave photos their greatest possible impact. In a 1942 advertisement for itself, *Life* expressed its philosophy: "Never has LIFE glossed over the horrors that stalk in the wake of the Axis aggression, but has shown war as it really is . . . stark, brutal, and devastating."[24] Even so, the censorship guidelines prevented showing dead GIs, so editors at *Life* and elsewhere pressed their case for greater candor. In mid-1943 the Roosevelt administration reversed its earlier policy, and in September officials began releasing the first of the somber photos. The most famous was the one printed in *Life* showing three dead soldiers lying where they had been shot on a beach in New Guinea. The photo, by George Strock, was a masterpiece of composition and understatement. The dead men's faces were not visible, and their wounds were hidden as well. The editors and the military brass all worried about the public reaction, but they need not have: most letters to *Life* supported the decision, and there was no measurable drop-off in American support for the war. Ever since, readers on the home front have been given a closer and more realistic look at war (fig. 9.3).[25]

Overall, the Roosevelt administration was executing the same plays that the Wilson administration had first put into the executive playbook. The Office of War Information was working hard to get the media to pursue certain stories

9.3 **THE FIRST PHOTOS OF DEAD U.S. SOLDIERS** to reach American audiences during World War II did not pass the censors until 1943. Then, the editors of *Life* magazine got permission to publish this photo by George Strock showing three unidentified soldiers on a beach at Papua New Guinea.
—*Getty Images.*

and share certain images. The Office of Censorship was working even harder to suppress or delay certain other facts, themes, and photos. In 1942 the Washington bureau chief of the *New York Times*, Arthur Krock, got the leaders of the censorship effort and the propaganda campaign, Byron Price and Elmer Davis, to talk about their work. "Mr. Price says: 'We tell them what they *cannot* print.' Mr. Davis says: 'We give them stuff we hope they *will* print,'" reported the *Times*.[26] It was a bit more complicated, but that was certainly the general idea.

The most effective form of censorship is the self-imposed kind, which turned out to be pervasive during World War II. One obvious and significant case involved the handling by the press corps of Franklin Roosevelt's health, beginning in the decades before the war. As an adult Roosevelt had been stricken with polio and nearly died. He recovered, but he could never walk again without heavy braces or crutches. He frequently stumbled and sometimes fell. Understandably, he did not want the voters to know about his infirmity. Less understandably, the reporters and photographers who covered Roosevelt went along with his wishes. FDR was always depicted seated at a desk, in position behind a podium, or in his trademark open-top automobile. He was never shown in a wheelchair or in any other way that would raise questions about his overall fitness. Over the course of four presidential elections, this gentlemen's agreement held, as it did even while Roosevelt's health was obviously deteriorating as the fateful spring of 1945 approached.

There are several reasons that likely contributed to the broad immunity granted to FDR and America's top leaders in general, which persisted up until Watergate. One was the growing professional ideal in journalism, which held such keyhole scandals to be beneath the level of dignity to which journalists increasingly aspired. Another was the reporter's perpetual pragmatic concern over access: if you break the gentlemen's agreement about what can and cannot be reported, you will be shut out of those cozy press conferences around the president's desk. Still another was the sense, particularly in the struggles against fascism and communism, that the health of the U.S. president has a direct bearing on the perceived strength of the nation as a whole by the worldwide audience.

The same kind of self-censorship became a hallmark of coverage of the war. As many reporters admitted, they felt that they were part of the team, comrades with the men-at-arms. This feeling seems to have gone beyond the fact that battle zone correspondents wore uniforms or that they marched, rode, ate, and billeted with the troops. The fact was that, down deep, the reporters and photographers covering the war shared a core belief with most of the soldiers, and with most Americans on the home front. Almost unanimously, Americans supported the war effort, and they did so wholeheartedly. There was nearly universal agreement about the nature of U.S. war aims and their validity. The nation was locked in a death struggle with large, powerful enemies who directly threatened American lives. Not only that, but the U.S. armed forces and their allies were fighting for a cause that had a claim to nobility. Hitler and his gang wanted to kill, enslave, annihilate; America and its allies wanted to protect, rescue, and liberate. In that setting, journalists felt a sense of solidarity with the troops to an extent that had never been seen before (and would not last long, either).

Perhaps the most dramatic example of this solidarity between the press and the military involved General George S. Patton.[27] A hero of the North Africa campaign, Patton was the overall U.S. commander of the Allied invasion of Sicily. In August 1943, with the island secured, Patton went on a tour of an army field hospital. Trailed by a group of aides and reporters, Patton greeted the recovering soldiers. Then he came across a patient with no visible wounds, who was being treated for battle fatigue. Patton leaped to the conclusion that the man was faking. He called him a coward and slapped him across the face. Five days later Patton encountered another soldier in a field hospital, again with no obvious wounds. This time Patton called the man "a yellow bastard," slapped him with his gloves, and—for good measure—kicked him in the backside. According to one correspondent who was present, Patton then began to sob and declared that there was no such thing as shell shock—it was just "an invention of the Jews." Under normal circumstances, any reporter would see this as terrific material and would be looking for the nearest transmitter.

But in the setting of 1943, the press corps did not see things that way. Instead, the twenty or so correspondents who had witnessed the incident huddled at the press camp about how to respond. Rather than tell the world about the incident (and likely derail the career of the Allies' most aggressive field commander), they decided to work through the military chain of command. They sent a petition to Patton's superior, General Dwight D. Eisenhower, asking him to step in and make Patton apologize. Agreeing with the correspondents, Ike ordered Patton to apologize to the men he had slapped and to all witnesses to the affair. Patton complied, and that might have been the end of it. But Edward Kennedy, a senior AP correspondent covering the European war, went to see Eisenhower. He argued that since the story would eventually leak out anyway, it should be written right away, and by a correspondent who had been an eyewitness, like himself. Eisenhower admitted that he could not stop the journalists from reporting the incident, but he pointed out that any story about Patton's mistreatment of soldiers would be bad for morale and would hand the enemy a propaganda bonanza. On those grounds he requested that there be no coverage. Kennedy and the other correspondents complied with Eisenhower's wishes and sat on the story.

Months later, as the soldiers from Sicily began to rotate stateside, word of the incident reached Drew Pearson, the Washington columnist, who pounced on it. Since Pearson was not in a war zone, he was not subject to military censorship, but he did submit his column to the civilians in the Office of Censorship. They could not find a reason to suppress it, so the story finally came out. Pearson's revelation appeared to have absolutely no bearing on the course of the war.

* * *

IN THE COVERAGE OF THE battle zones, the performance of the American news media during World War II was uneven. Many of the triumphs of wartime reporting on events such as D-Day or Iwo Jima are deservedly familiar to Americans. Much less well known are the lapses in the coverage. No lapse was more nearly complete, and none had greater consequences, than the failure to tell the story of the Eastern Front. The fighting that took place on Germany's east, extending all the way to the gates of Stalingrad, was a vast battle zone in which the front extended over 1,600 miles—from Murmansk on the arctic Barents Sea to Odessa on the Black Sea in the Caucasus. By almost any measure—the number of men, the number of arms, the number of prisoners taken or killed, the number of casualties, the number of atrocities, the number of civilian deaths, the overall strategic importance to the ultimate outcome of the war—the fighting on the Eastern Front was one of the most important military episodes in all of human history. Like the journalists of the rest of the world, the Americans simply missed it. That failure ended up shaping perceptions that worsened the misunderstanding between the United States and the Soviet Union throughout the Cold War.

The fighting on the Eastern Front began in June 1941, when Hitler double-crossed Stalin and revealed his most ambitious plan of all, launched with a sneak attack code-named "Barbarossa." The idea was to conquer and occupy all the nations of eastern Europe, making room for German expansion, and then snatch the grand prize: Russia. When the invasion began, German forces numbering more than 3 million and supported by heavy mechanized divisions rolled forward, and in their wake, special SS units began systematically murdering the Jewish population in the conquered territory. Within a month, the German assault forces had advanced four hundred miles. (In terms of U.S. geography, it was as if Hitler's armies had conquered every city on the East Coast and headed for Chicago, St. Louis, and the oilfields of Texas.) As the German supply lines lengthened and Soviet resistance stiffened, the huge offensive began to lose momentum that fall along the length of a waving line that stopped just short of Leningrad, Moscow, and Stalingrad. Then came the Russian winter. In the grip of bitter cold, the Germans dug in. For most of 1942 the battle raged, this time back and forth over much shorter distances, deep inside Soviet territory. While Germany was busy occupying western Europe and battling the British in North Africa, the bulk of German forces were engaged in Russia, fighting in desperate close combat. Then winter came again. This time, the Germans succumbed and never regained their momentum. In early 1943, German troops started withdrawing from the Caucasus. The huge German force laying siege to Stalingrad was reduced to eating its horses and finally surrendered to the Soviets on February 2.

Even then the Germans were not finished. As their remaining troops fell back westward, they began to mass around the Kursk salient in July 1943. There, over the course of several days, the Germans and the Russians mounted the largest tank battle in history, and perhaps the largest battle of any kind ever fought on land. When it was all over, the pride of the German army was spent. After Kursk, German forces were never again capable of launching a major offensive. But at this crucial turning point, not a single American correspondent was anywhere nearby. There were no Western reporters present, and hardly any Russian reporters either. The Russian correspondent Vasily Grossman was one of the few.[28]

Much of the blame for the lack of coverage lies with the Soviet dictator Joseph Stalin. He led a regime that was so paranoid and so hostile to a free press that it imposed some of the tightest restrictions ever known on journalists, including those from countries that were ostensibly Stalin's allies. Few Western correspondents were even allowed into the Soviet Union, and those who were admitted were trapped most of the time in Moscow, kept under close scrutiny by spies and fed scraps of information that conformed strictly to the current Soviet line. *New York Times* correspondent William Lawrence complained in a note to his editor about life at the hotel that served as the home base for correspondents in Moscow. "We call the Metropole the 'Correspondents Concentration Camp,'" he wrote, "and I think in many ways a real concentration camp might be preferable because then one wouldn't indulge in idle dreams of trying to reason with your jailers."[29] It made little difference that the Soviets were supposed to be fighting for democracy and against fascism. Stalin dictated conditions, and that was that.

The result was a profound gap in what most Americans knew about the war, a gap whose impact was subtle but far-reaching. Naturally Americans followed their own army and navy most closely, and the fact was that there were no U.S. troops on the Eastern Front. Americans accordingly tend to celebrate the contributions of their own forces to the overall Allied triumph, which is why the United States commemorates such great victories as Midway and D-Day. By the end of the war, however, the Soviets felt, with ample justification, that they had taken Hitler's worst punch—at a cost of millions of lives—and that they deserved the spoils of victory. American newspaper readers found this unbelievable and, as a result, never accepted Stalin's demands for territory in eastern Europe to protect his homeland from future invasions. Throughout the Cold War, the people and the leaders of the two countries were operating on different premises, in part because wartime journalism had yielded two widely divergent sets of facts about the past.

* * *

AMONG AMERICANS, THE MOST FAMOUS World War II correspondent by far was Ernie Pyle. After reporting from London, Pyle decided to tag along with the U.S. troops gathering in England for the assault on German forces in North Africa. "I love the infantry," he wrote, "because they are the underdogs. They are the mud-rain-frost-and-wind boys. They have no comforts, and they even learn to live without the necessities. And in the end they are the guys that wars can't be won without."[30] Among the common foot soldiers—the "dogfaces," as they were known—Pyle found his true calling, and he went the distance with them, starting in the Africa campaign of 1942, then on to Sicily and the Italian campaign, then to France just after D-Day for the horrors of the hedgerow fighting in Normandy. A poet of the foxhole, Pyle became so popular that his syndicated column eventually appeared in three hundred daily newspapers and many more hundreds of weeklies.[31] He avoided writing about what he called "the Big Picture." Instead, he wrote intimate portraits of fighting men trying to cope, personal and poignant stories based on close observation of details. Sometimes his copy read like a Murrow transcript—simple, direct, even poetic (fig. 9.4).

Pyle was not only popular with soldiers and their families but also quite useful to the war effort. The "dogfaces" he wrote about were not superheroes, and they did not love war, but they consistently appeared in his column as plucky, resourceful, and a hell of a lot tougher than you might have guessed if you had met them a few years earlier, back home. In his columns about the Africa campaign, for example, Pyle was often writing about green young American troops

9.4 **ERNIE PYLE** was the most popular American columnist of World War II, filling his columns with detailed accounts of the wartime experiences of ordinary foot soldiers. Pyle is shown here working at his portable Underwood typewriter somewhere in Europe in 1944. —*Corbis.*

coming under fire for the first time as they faced up to the vaunted German military machine. "The reactions of the American soldiers to their first bad bombings were exactly what you would expect of them. They took it in a way to make you proud," Pyle told his readers back home.[32]

He observed that there were about seventy-five correspondents in North Africa during the campaign, including U.S. and British reporters and photographers. Most stayed in the rear; some rotated through the front. A handful just lived at the front, including Pyle. He wrote:

> The outstanding thing about life at the front was its magnificent simplicity. It was a life consisting only of the essentials—food, sleep, transportation, and what little warmth and safety a man could manage to wangle out of it by personal ingenuity. . . .
>
> At the front the usual responsibilities and obligations were gone. There were no appointments to keep, nobody cared how anybody looked, red tape was at a minimum. There were no desks, no designated hours, no washing of hands before eating, or afterward either. It would have been heaven for small boys with dirty ears. . . .
>
> Last and most important of all, was the feeling of vitality, of being in the heart of everything, of being part of it—no mere onlooker, but a member of the team. . . . The army accepted us correspondents as a part of the family.[33]

Unless he was criticizing someone, which was rare, Pyle always mentioned soldiers by name and supplied readers with the soldier's hometown and even his street address. As it turned out, Pyle's experience roaming the United States for

Scripps Howard before the war came in handy now. Whenever Pyle talked to a sailor or soldier, he would ask the man about his hometown; almost invariably, Pyle had been there, or nearby. Sometimes, he would discover that he knew the man's relatives or friends, and soon they would be deep in conversation. In his columns Pyle showed a determination to redeem the individual particularity of each GI, even as all of them were threatened with being swallowed up in the anonymous mass of the largest uniformed force ever fielded. Pyle did not see armies; he saw guys. Where most journalists (and almost all historians) see divisions and nations clashing, Pyle saw individuals. As he slogged on, he kept meeting guys, one at a time, guys who each had a name, a hometown, and something to try to live for. Pyle recoiled against the dissolution of individuality into the anonymity of the mass, the regimented ranks of modern armies.

One of Pyle's finest pieces is a tribute to an individual, titled "This One Is Captain Waskow." Dated January 10, 1944, during the Italian campaign, it tells the story of the evacuation of the body of the dead captain on a moonlit night:

> Dead men had been coming down the mountain all evening, lashed onto the backs of mules. They came lying belly down across the wooden packsaddle. . . .
>
> The first one came early in the morning. They slid him down from the mule. . . .
>
> Then a soldier came into the cowshed and said there were some more bodies outside. We went out into the road. Four mules stood there in the moonlight, in the road where the trail came down off the mountain. The soldiers who led them were waiting.
>
> "This one is Captain Waskow," one of them said quickly. . . .
>
> The uncertain mules moved off to their olive grove. The men in the road seemed reluctant to leave. They stood around, and gradually I could sense them moving, one by one, close to Captain Waskow's body. Not so much to look, I think, as to say something in finality to him and to themselves. I stood close by and I could hear.
>
> One soldier came and looked down, and he said out loud:
>
> "God damn it!"
>
> Another one came, and he said, "God damn it to hell anyway!" He looked down for a few last moments and then turned and left. . . .
>
> Then the first man squatted down, and he reached down and took the captain's hand, and he sat there for a full five minutes holding the dead hand in his own and looking intently into the dead face. And he never uttered a sound all the time he sat there.
>
> Finally he put the hand down. He reached up and gently straightened the points of the captain's shirt collar, and then he sort of rearranged the tattered edges of his uniform around the wound, and then he got up and walked away down the road in the moonlight, all alone.[34]

At his best, Pyle was capable of masterpieces of restraint. And his fondness for the infantry was reciprocated. After reading columns like that one, many soldiers stopped writing letters home, telling their families that if they really wanted to know what it was like on the front lines, they should read Ernie Pyle.

Pyle was the most popular correspondent, but he was far from alone. Hundreds of American journalists flocked to the Western Front, and American methods of news management eventually came to the fore. General Eisenhower, the Supreme Allied Commander, knew what was at stake. As he told a meeting of American newspaper editors, "Public opinion wins war." He went on to say that he considered correspondents assigned to his headquarters to be "quasi-staff."[35] As he did with everything, Eisenhower overwhelmed the problem of public opinion with resources. By late 1944 the Allied public relations headquarters in Paris was processing (which is to say censoring) 3 million words a week from almost one thousand correspondents, plus 35,000 photos and 100,000 feet of newsreel film. Generally speaking, Allied correspondents did an excellent job witnessing and recording the dramas, great and small, of the Western Front.

In covering the war in the Pacific, however, journalists were usually at the mercy of the navy. At the very least, reporters and photographers depended on the navy for transportation over the vast distances they had to cross to get near the action. Then they depended on the navy to transmit their words and pictures back home. The army operated in the Pacific theater too, of course, under the overall command of publicity-conscious General Douglas MacArthur. But after the army's retreat from the Philippines, most of the fighting was done by the navy or its amphibious division, the marines. So it was officials like Navy Secretary Frank Knox, Chief of Naval Operations Ernest King, and Pacific Fleet Commander Chester Nimitz who made the key decisions about not only how the navy would fight but also how that fighting would be covered. Stretching over eleven thousand miles from Panama to Malaysia, the Pacific Ocean would prove a tremendous challenge for all involved.

Advances in military technology meant that the war in the Pacific would be different from all previous naval conflicts. No longer would the outcome be determined by steel-hulled battleships cruising in formation, blasting away at the enemy's ships. In World War II, the signature ship in the Pacific was the aircraft carrier. From those floating airports, bombers and fighter planes could take off and then range over hundreds of miles. Once airborne, military aircraft could bomb islands in support of assaults, find and attack the enemy's fleets, or engage the enemy's air forces. Attacking aircraft usually operated out of sight from their home fleet, literally over the horizon. Starting with the Battle of the Coral Sea in May 1942, most of the major naval engagements of World War II were fought by ships whose commanders never actually saw the enemy's ships. This often meant that reporters could not observe the action either. The other military signature of the war in the Pacific was the Allied "island-hopping campaign." Using coordinated naval, air, and amphibious assaults, the Allies picked islands that would

bring them closer and closer to mainland Japan, preparing the way for the ultimate challenge: the anticipated invasion of the Japanese homeland. All told, it was
a huge, sprawling, and absolutely crucial story.

In the immediate aftermath of Pearl Harbor, one problem confronting many
American journalists was the fundamental, undeniable fact that U.S. and Allied
forces were getting whipped by the Japanese. Within a day of the attack in Hawaii,
Japanese forces destroyed another one hundred U.S. aircraft on the ground in
the Philippines. In short order, Japanese forces assaulted Luzon in the Philippines, then snatched Hong Kong, Thailand, Singapore, and northern Malaya,
forcing the Allies again and again to retreat or face capture. The only good news
for the American public was the militarily insignificant Doolittle raid on Tokyo
in April 1942, which had the intended effect of lifting U.S. morale. The good news
being kept from the American public was the breaking of the Japanese military
code. But even the fruits of the code-breaking were ominous: in April 1942 navy
officials learned that the Japanese were preparing to take Port Moresby in New
Guinea, which would have severed the sea route to a key Pacific ally, Australia.
Amid such gloom, correspondents often clutched at straws, and their editors at
home amplified any promising news with big bold headlines.

In a column written in February 1942 the stateside essayist E. B. White commented on his suspicions about the quality of the war news. In an article in
Harper's magazine, White archly described a typical recent story from UP reporting events in the Dutch East Indies. He pointed out that the "lead" focused on
the Allied sinking of a Japanese cruiser while subordinating the news that "the
greater part of Amboina Island . . . was now practically in Japanese hands." The
headline, White noted, read "ALLIES SINK JAP CRUISER," which was true, as far
as it went, but it was misleading. "You certainly wouldn't know, from looking
over your neighbor's shoulder in the subway, that the second largest naval and air
force base in the Indies had been taken by Japan. You would simply know that
everything was going fine and that the Japanese navy was a goner." He went on to
observe that the *New York Telegram* had a standing headline called "GOOD NEWS,"
under which "it collects each afternoon a few nosegays, favorable to us, ruinous
to the enemy."[36]

Eventually, though, there was some bona fide good news for Americans in the
Pacific. U.S. naval victories in the Battle of the Coral Sea and the Battle of Midway,
followed by the marine invasion of Guadalcanal, began to give a genuine sense of
momentum by the fall of 1942. Still, some correspondents were concerned about
the sugarcoating of news accounts of the Pacific war. Robert Sherrod, a correspondent for *Time* and *Life*, covered the fighting in Tarawa in November 1943.
In a book he published the following year, he charged that too many Americans
were guilty of wishful thinking, lulled into believing that machines could take the
place of soldiers. The official communiqués, he said, were often embellished for
the folks at home by reporters and headline writers:

> The stories almost invariably come out liberally sprinkled with "smash" and "pound" and other "vivid" verbs. These "vivid" verbs impressed the headline writers back in the home office. They impressed the reading public which saw them in tall type. But they sometimes did not impress the miserable, bloody soldiers in the front lines where the action had taken place. . . .
>
> Said a bomber pilot, after returning from the Pacific: "When I told my mother what the war was really like, and how long it was going to take, she sat down and cried. She didn't know we were just beginning to fight the Japs."[37]

The island-hopping campaign wound on through 1943 and 1944. At the same time, the navy was increasingly successful in cutting off shipments of oil to the mainland of Japan, whose industries would lurch to a halt without it. Some began to say that Japan's defeat was now a matter of time. It was time that mattered very much to those who had to do the remaining fighting.

One huge late push came at Iwo Jima, a small island of volcanic ash a fraction the size of Manhattan, dominated by a defunct volcano, Mount Suribachi. Iwo Jima was chosen by U.S. military leaders for its strategic value: from there, huge U.S. bombers could easily reach the Japanese mainland. The Japanese, too, understood this, and they turned Iwo Jima into the most heavily fortified place on the planet, filled with concrete bunkers, mines, and miles of tunnels. In a huge assault beginning in February 1945, about seventy thousand marines approached the island in a naval convoy that stretched over more than seventy miles. The marines waded ashore and commenced a horrendous assault on the heavily fortified Japanese positions. Japanese troops had orders not to surrender, so the marines would have to go over the island inch by inch, under constant fire, eliminating one bunker at a time, usually by means of flame-throwers or hand grenades.

Three days into the battle, a small detachment of marines was sent to the summit of Mount Suribachi, the highest point on the island. The commanding officer told them to take a flag with them and *if* they made it to the top, to raise the flag. Strangely, there was not much resistance near the summit. The platoon got there, found a length of pipe, and raised a U.S. flag. An official marine photographer, Louis Lowery, recorded the moment. From marines all over the island and on ships offshore, a great cry went up.

At that moment Secretary of the Navy James Forrestal was coming ashore on Iwo Jima even while fierce fighting continued at the other end of the island, and he wanted that flag as a memento. When the order came down from Forrestal, the marine commander decided that *he* wanted the flag for the battalion that had taken the summit, so he gave orders for a second detachment of men to go up to the top of the mountain, take down the first flag, hide it, and replace it with another one—this time, a bigger one. Just then, Associated Press photographer Joe Rosenthal was climbing up the mountain with a detachment of marines.

When they got to the top, a group of six marines bent to the task of raising the larger flag. At that very instant, Rosenthal raised his 35-mm Speed Graphic and snapped off what would become the most famous photo of the war. It was the iconic image of faceless regular troops joining forces in a victorious team effort. He sent his film off to Guam for processing and censoring. As soon as the film was developed, the AP photo editor on Guam realized that it was an image for the ages. It was transmitted around the world and published on many front pages, along with news of the marines' success on Iwo Jima. The picture won the 1945 Pulitzer Prize for photography and was later used as the basis for the giant Marine Corps memorial near Washington, D.C.[38]

Rosenthal's famous photo has long been a focus of controversy. The problem arose from a misunderstanding. When he took the flag-raising shot, Rosenthal wasn't sure what he had in his camera, so he encouraged the several dozen marines on the mountaintop to gather together for a typical thumbs-up victory photo (commonly called the "gung-ho" shot). That way he would at least be sure of coming away with something. Later, the AP photo editor told Rosenthal that he had gotten quite a picture at Iwo Jima and asked the photographer if he had staged it. Thinking he was being asked about the "gung-ho" shot, Rosenthal said yes. In fact, the famous flag-raising shot was spontaneous, which is why it retains its proud place in photojournalism.

*   *   *

STALIN HAD BEEN URGING THE Americans and the British for two years to open a Western Front so as to draw off some of the German Wehrmacht from its murderous assault on the Soviet Union. In the spring of 1944 the Americans and the Brits were finally ready. They began massing men and supplies in southern England to prepare for an invasion of occupied France, and reporters started heading that way too. Ed Murrow, of course, was already there, having remained in London for the duration. Ernie Pyle pulled out of Italy and arrived in London in April 1944, in time to learn that his column had won the Pulitzer Prize for the previous year. Walter Cronkite was also in London, to write the overview story of the invasion for United Press. Joe Liebling was there for the *New Yorker*. On assignment for *Colliers,* Martha Gellhorn was nearby, aboard a hospital ship, along with her husband at the time and fellow correspondent Ernest Hemingway. In all, there were more than two hundred American correspondents on hand, along with more than two dozen photographers.[39] All had a sense that something big was in the offing, but nobody knew exactly when or where. Press officers from the Supreme Headquarters, Allied Expeditionary Forces (SHAEF), told them all to write their own obituaries—just in case.

When the big day came on June 6, one of those in the first wave ashore was the Hungarian-born photographer Robert Capa, working for *Life*. He went aboard a landing craft full of soldiers. "We started for the beach," he recalled later in a story for *Life*. "It was rough and some of the boys were politely puking into paper bags.

... We got out of the boat and started wading and then I saw men falling and had to push past their bodies. I said to myself, 'This is not so good.'" He pressed on and made it to Omaha Beach. "It was very unpleasant there and having nothing else to do I started shooting pictures."[40] He got his film into the hands of an army public relations officer and hoped for the best. The film was then rushed aboard a plane to New York, where *Life* darkroom crews were waiting. While the developed photos were being dried, someone forgot to turn on a fan, and the heat in the dryer kept rising. Out of more than one hundred of Capa's D-Day shots, only about a dozen were salvageable. They were enough. Those pictures were among the finest of the war. From a low angle, they captured the chaos, smoke, and fog of the Normandy invasion.[41]

In military terms, the tide had definitely turned. By D-Day, if not earlier, the fate of the Axis powers was sealed. But they were not about to surrender, and a lot of hard fighting remained. As Allied forces secured their beachheads and moved inland, correspondents streamed into Normandy just behind the front lines. By the spring of 1945 there was so much news that reporters could hardly keep up with the flow of major events. The Americans and British were driving toward Germany from the west, and the Red Army was advancing from the east. On April 11, 1945, U.S. and British troops made contact with the Soviets at the Elbe River, forty miles west of Berlin. The following day brought stunning news: President Roosevelt was dead. While visiting Warm Springs, Georgia, the president had suffered a cerebral aneurysm and died swiftly. Thanks to years of suppression of news about his medical condition, the bulletins of his death came as a thunderclap to Americans at home and in the battle zones. Suddenly the whole gigantic machinery of the U.S. government and the armed forces was in the hands of someone hardly anybody knew: Harry Truman.

Events would not wait for the new president to settle in. During April, as the Allies occupied larger and larger sections of western Germany, they came across the concentration camps. In the east, the Red Army was going through the same process, but little information was forthcoming. Because of Soviet paranoia, there were almost no correspondents on hand, and a lot of the evidence of German atrocities seized by the Soviets was promptly hidden or destroyed. In the west, however, the liberation of the concentration camps was witnessed by experienced reporters, who began to lay down the record of Nazi crimes against humanity. One of the first reports came from Ed Murrow, who was racing along with U.S. forces through Germany, covering more than one hundred miles in a week. In a report broadcast on CBS on April 15, Murrow struggled to describe conditions at the notorious Buchenwald camp. He told of the emaciated men, more than a thousand jammed into a building that once stabled eighty horses. "As I walked to the end of the barracks, there was applause from the men too weak to get out of bed. It sounded like the hand clapping of babies; they were so weak." For the first time, many Americans learned the gruesome details: the brutality, the mass murder, the tattooed numbers. "Men kept coming up to speak to me and to touch me, professors from Poland, doctors from Vienna, men from all Europe. Men from the countries that made America." A Czech doctor who had been a prisoner offered to show Murrow the crematorium. He explained that the Germans had recently run out of coke to operate the ovens, so dead bodies were piling up. Murrow described the scene:

> We entered. It was floored with concrete. There were two rows of bodies stacked up like cordwood. They were thin and very white. Some of the bodies were terribly bruised, though there seemed to be little flesh to bruise. Some had been shot through the head, but they bled but little. All except two were naked. I tried to count them as best I could and arrived at the conclusion that all that was mortal of more than 500 men and boys lay there in two neat piles. . . .
>
> If I've offended you by this rather mild account of Buchenwald, I'm not in the least sorry.[42]

Murrow's words were soon repeated to larger and larger audiences. His description was broadcast several times on CBS, and transcripts were printed in newspapers and replayed on the BBC across Britain. In the parts of Germany under Allied control, Murrow's account of Buchenwald was translated into German and played on the radio half a dozen times a day.[43]

Meanwhile, during that same busy spring, one of the deepest secrets of the war was about to be revealed.[44] It began in April 1945, when General Leslie Groves of the U.S. Army approached the managing editor of the *New York Times*. The general wanted to borrow the *Times'* science writer, William Laurence, for the remainder of the war. Without many more preliminaries, Laurence headed off to his new assignment in Oak Ridge, Tennessee. There, Groves pulled back the shroud protecting the nation's biggest wartime gamble and introduced Laurence to the Manhattan Project, the top-secret effort to build the world's first atom bomb. The army wanted a civilian on board who could help with drafting press releases, writing news stories, and simply explaining the vast and complex undertaking to the general public. Laurence was a good choice. A native of Lithuania, Laurence had immigrated to the United States as a teenager and attended Harvard and Boston University. At the *Times* he had pioneered in covering science for a general newspaper and had won the Pulitzer Prize in 1936.

Once attached to the Manhattan Project, Laurence had virtual carte blanche to travel to the various bomb-making sites around the country, interviewing the top scientists and engineers, and he soon knew more about the project than all but a handful of the thousands of people working on it. Groves had instituted a system of information control throughout the Manhattan Project so that workers got assignments and information on a "need to know" basis. Most people were not told how their particular task fit into the overall program, or indeed that they were even working on an atom bomb. Laurence was one of the very few who could see the big picture. In return for his access, Laurence had agreed with the army to sit on the story until the military gave him the go-ahead. In July he went to a site near Alamagordo in the New Mexico desert to witness the first test explosion, code named "Trinity." It was Laurence who wrote the (false) press release that the army used to concoct a cover story. The few civilians in the surrounding areas who saw the great flash on July 15 were assured that there was nothing to worry about, just an old ammo dump that had blown up.

In gratitude for Laurence's services, the army tipped the top management of the *Times* on August 2 about the impending use of the bomb, so the paper could prepare. On August 6, 1945, the world first learned about the atomic bomb when the United States dropped it on the Japanese city of Hiroshima. Three days later the army struck again, this time at Nagasaki. On board one of the aircraft that day was William Laurence. As the official journalist witness to the Manhattan Project, he was now the first American civilian to observe the use of the terrible new weapon in war. His detailed, poetic narrative (which appeared in the *Times* a month later) began simply: "We are on our way to bomb the mainland of Japan." Using the "we" approach that was so typical of World War II journalism, Laurence fully identified with the men and the mission, calling the bomb "a thing of beauty" once it was fully assembled and armed. As the hours ticked by toward achieving the target, Laurence mused in print about the morality of setting out to wipe an entire city off the map. He asked himself if he felt any pity for the "poor devils" who would be obliterated by the bomb. "Not when one thinks of Pearl Harbor and of the Death March on Bataan." In other words, he figured (as did many Americans) that the "Japs" had it coming. Then, over Nagasaki, Laurence and the crew beheld the existential chaos unleashed by splitting the atom:

> Awe-struck, we watched it shoot upward like a meteor coming from the earth instead of from outer space, becoming ever more alive as it climbed skyward through the white clouds. It was no longer smoke, or dust, or even a cloud of fire. It was a living thing, a new species of being, born right before our incredulous eyes.
>
> At one stage of its evolution, covering millions of years in terms of seconds, the entity assumed the form of a giant square totem pole, with its base about three miles long, tapering off to about a mile at the top. Its bottom was brown, its center was amber, its top white. But it was a living totem pole, carved with many grotesque masks grimacing at the earth.
>
> Then, just when it appeared as though the thing had settled down into a state of permanence, there came shooting out of the top a giant mushroom that increased the height of the pillar to a total of about 45,000 feet. The mushroom top was even more alive than the pillar, seething

and boiling in a white fury of creamy foam, sizzling upward and then descending earthward, a thousand Old Faithful geysers rolled into one.

It kept struggling in an elemental fury, like a creature in the act of breaking the bonds that held it down. In a few seconds it had freed itself from its gigantic stem and floated upward with tremendous speed, its momentum carrying into the stratosphere to a height of about 60,000 feet.

But no sooner did this happen when another mushroom, smaller in size than the first one, began emerging out of the pillar. It was as though the decapitated monster was growing a new head.

As the mushroom floated off into the blue it changed its shape into a flowerlike form, its giant petal curving downward, creamy white outside, rose-colored inside. It still retained that shape when we last gazed at it from a distance of about 200 miles.[45]

Laurence struck a note of awe at the dawn of the atomic age. In the coming weeks, he elaborated on the theme in a series of Pulitzer Prize–winning articles explaining for a lay audience the basic principles of atomic energy. But for all the poetic power of his Nagasaki piece, it should be noted that there were limits to Laurence's perspective; he was seeing the experience from the point of view of the attackers. Through no fault of his own, he was peering outward and downward at an object, not observing the individual human agonies unfolding on the ground. There were, of course, no Allied journalists on the ground in Japan at the time, although an advance unit streamed into the country as soon as peace was declared and the occupation began.

Among the first into Japan was Homer Bigart of the *New York Herald Tribune,* who went with a group of journalists to Hiroshima in early September, less than a month after the first bombing. His article attempted to reckon the loss of lives—which he put, fairly accurately, at 53,000 dead and 30,000 missing and presumed dead—then went on to describe the ruins. Starting about three miles from the center of the blast, Bigart reported seeing signs of destruction, typical of the scene in a bombed city in Europe. "But across the river there was only flat, appalling desolation, the starkness accentuated by bare, blackened tree trunks and the occasional shell of a reinforced concrete building."[46] He reported that residents were still dying, at the rate of about one hundred a day, mostly from burns and infection, and he hinted at some of the problems eventually recognized as radiation sickness.

Later the reporter and author John Hersey visited Hiroshima for the *New Yorker* magazine. He stayed longer than Bigart had been allowed to, and he created one of the masterpieces of war correspondence. Through meticulous reporting, Hersey followed the experiences of six individuals who had been in Hiroshima on the morning the bomb exploded. Moment by moment, scene by scene, he re-created the thoughts and actions of each of those survivors, from

9.5 **THE WRITER JOHN HERSEY** covered World War II. In 1945, on assignment for the *New Yorker*, the prize-winning novelist and reporter went to Hiroshima and created a classic work of journalism in his detailed reconstruction of the experiences of a small number of survivors of the atomic bombing.
—*AP Photo.*

the minutes before the blast through the first few days and weeks that followed. His reporting was finished in August 1946. When his editor at the *New Yorker*, Harold Ross, got a look at the material, he decided to dispense with all the rest of the contents scheduled to run and devoted the August 31 issue to Hersey's account.[47] Hersey's story is a key document of twentieth-century history as well as a touchstone for the human imagination in the nuclear age. His hyperfactual tale of immense suffering has become part of the worldview of most people on the planet. He said almost nothing in his own voice—no pontificating, no summarizing. Instead, he brought particular people to life by setting them in action and thereby showing the reader what had happened. The account of the bombing was quickly published as a book, titled simply *Hiroshima*, which became a bestseller and has remained in print ever since. Many consider it the greatest work of journalism by an American (fig. 9.5).[48]

*   *   *

How does one assess the performance of so many people covering such a vast story?

It is a commonplace in journalism history to observe that American journalists covering World War II were "on the team" along with the U.S. military. Observers tend to praise or condemn the news media on that basis, depending on whether they think it is a good thing or a bad thing for journalism to line up and salute when the country goes off to war. But that is too simple a way of looking at it. During the war years, thousands of correspondents, photographers, and editors were involved, and the fact is that their performances ranged from terrible to sublime. We should consider them in different categories rather than as a mass.

One category—a special one—consists of those who died: an estimated sixty-nine journalists from Allied countries, including thirty-nine Americans.[49] In addition, among U.S. news organizations, some 112 correspondents were wounded, and fifty were taken prisoner. Overall, the casualty rate among correspondents was higher than it was among soldiers.[50]

As an institution, the news media displayed some serious shortcomings during the war. There were gaps in the coverage. There were occasional security breaches, although almost no serious ones. There was probably too much censorship, and certainly too much self-censorship. Some of the reporting was far too gung-ho. It is fair to say that before the war, the American news media—that is, the big daily papers, the wire services, the weekly newsmagazines, and the major radio networks—largely fell short of their enormous responsibility. They did not tell Americans soon enough about the true nature of the situations in Germany, Japan, Russia, China, and a dozen other key places.

But like the American military, the major news institutions improved under fire. On the whole, the record suggests a trend toward more aggressive reporting and more clear-eyed writing. By the end, the quality of the coverage surpassed that of the bulk of the reporting done by Americans about the Civil War, the Spanish-American War, or World War I. Ultimately, the record of World War II journalism—by turns horrifying, pitiless, wisecracking, gorgeous, and (it must be said) thrilling—speaks for itself.

Another question is what impact the war had on the continuing practice of journalism in America. The answer is that in the process of defeating the Axis, the war had many unintended consequences whose effects were far-reaching and long-lasting (fig. 9.6).

At war's end, the government dismantled most (but not all) of the apparatus of information control built up during the fighting. The OWI was quickly dissolved. The Voice of America remained in operation, under the direction of the U.S. State Department, which also organized an Office of International Information and Cultural Affairs. These became the leading agencies in the nation's Cold War effort to win the hearts and minds of the world's peoples; they were formalized in

9.6 MARGUERITE HIGGINS talked her way into an assignment covering the fighting in Europe for the *New York Herald Tribune*. In April 1945, she was among the first eyewitnesses to the horrors of the Dachau concentration camp near Munich. (Shown here covering her second war, in Korea.)
—*Getty Images.*

the Smith-Mundt Act of 1948 and became part of what has been called "the first peacetime propaganda program in American history."[51] The Office of Censorship passed unlamented into oblivion on November 15, 1945. Not long afterward, rationing was lifted, and the news business was back in business.

In addition, the war planted the seeds of what has become known as the "imperial presidency." The fact is that the American government, military and civilian both, never fully demobilized after World War II. Finally, the war changed the landscape in an enduring way by vastly expanding the amount of information deemed secret. With a tremendous push from the new cult of secrecy surrounding the development of atomic power, the government launched a system of classifying information that has bedeviled journalists ever since. Starting in 1945, more and more of our national experience was simply off-limits to reporters.

For many decades to come, American journalists would continue grappling with the fallout from the war.

In 1944, after covering the Allied landings at Normandy and the drive toward Germany, Ernie Pyle was exhausted. He decided to head home for a much-needed break. "My spirit is wobbly and my mind is confused," he wrote. "The hurt has finally become too great."[52] On his return, he was greeted like a hero—asked to give interviews and pose for photo shoots for magazine covers. There were honorary degrees and mountains of mail. Hollywood was even making a movie about him.

Then in October, while he was visiting his wife, Jerry, in Albuquerque, Jerry plunged a foot-long pair of scissors into her neck, again and again, and slit her wrist. After all the gore he had seen, Ernie knew that the wounds were not fatal, and he had her admitted to a sanatorium.

Two months later he went ahead with his plans to return to covering the war, this time in the Pacific. He was exchanging Europe for the tropics and the army for the navy. In January 1945 he left Hawaii on board an aircraft carrier in a convoy ferrying the planes that were to bomb Japan.

In April, Pyle was with the marines as they took the tiny island of Ie Shima, part of the assault on nearby Okinawa. Ernie went ashore in the second wave. Next morning he hitched a ride in a jeep with a colonel scouting sites for a new command post. Suddenly, machine gun fire. The men in the jeep dove into a ditch. Ernie raised his head to look around, and the Japanese gunner fired again. A bullet hit him in the left temple. He died instantly.

In his belongings was the draft of a column he was preparing for the impending day of victory in Europe. It began: "And so it is over. . . . "

Creating Big Media, 1945–1963

This instrument can teach, it can illuminate; yes, and it can even inspire. But it can do so only to the extent that humans are determined to use it to those ends. Otherwise it is merely wires and lights in a box.

—Edward R. Murrow, 1958

From the start, Ed Murrow was skeptical about television news. By the end of World War II, Murrow was the king of news on the radio, and radio was riding high. Over the previous twenty years, radio news had arrived. It now had stature, it had immediacy, and it had sponsors. Radio had become powerful and profitable. So why would a serious newsman like Murrow want to get involved with television, which seemed like a novelty? Television threatened to undermine serious journalism by elevating images over substance, pictures over facts. Television looked promising as a medium for dramas and variety shows, and it could certainly demonstrate products; it had obvious commercial potential. But did television really make sense as a medium for conveying important information and ideas? What about stories that couldn't be illustrated? How would television handle those? And it was not just Murrow. The whole team of Murrow Boys had their doubts. "We felt it was kind of unmanly to go on TV and perform, just as it was in an earlier era somehow unmanly for newspapermen to go on radio," recalled Howard K. Smith.[1] Even Bill Paley, who would become best known for his mastery of television as the head of CBS, had doubts. But his great broadcasting rival, David Sarnoff, kept pushing television, and no one wanted to risk getting left behind, so Colonel Paley of CBS maintained tight surveillance on General Sarnoff of NBC and plotted his attack.[2]

News on television was never an easy fit. The attempt to combine journalism with television, while sometimes brilliant and powerful, could also be awkward and difficult. One issue was the dominance of the filmed image over information and analysis. "The notion that a picture was worth a thousand words meant, in practice, that footage of Atlantic City beauty winners, shot at some expense, was considered more valuable than a thousand words from Eric Sevareid on the mounting tensions in Southeast Asia," according to broadcasting historian Erik Barnouw.[3] The need for pictures also gave a new power to those who package events and stage photo opportunities—usually with the goal of selling something. In addition, there was a chronic misfit between the kind of journalism envisioned by Murrow and the like-minded serious journalists coming into TV from radio and newspapers, on the one hand, and the astronomical profits envisioned by Sarnoff and Paley and their many shareholders, on the other. At the end of the war, as the wartime rationing of key materials began to be lifted and television edged closer to becoming a household utility, many questions about TV news remained.

Like most successes, television had many fathers. Television was invented over a period of several decades by several people, including the American prodigy Philo Farnsworth (working for himself as an independent inventor), Peter Goldmark (working for Paley at CBS), and the Russian immigrant Vladimir Zworykin (working for Sarnoff at RCA). An early dramatic demonstration of television came at the 1939 World's Fair, in the big RCA pavilion. President Roosevelt could be seen and heard talking to visitors. At the time, there were about ten thousand TV sets in the New York City area and hardly any in the rest of the country. Then came the war, and television was shelved. The big stars all remained in radio: Amos 'n Andy, Jack Benny, Bob Hope, Bing Crosby, Burns and Allen, Red Skelton. In 1945, the FCC authorized twelve channels in the VHF (very high frequency) range of the spectrum for black and white television transmissions, while approving the UHF (ultrahigh frequency) range for experiments in color television. Soon, television started to catch on—at first in the big cities, as an entertainment medium offering drama, music, and comedies. Most of the radio stars made the transition to television, even if that meant putting on blackface.

When television began to spread widely into American homes during the early 1950s, some thirty years after the dawn of radio as a popular medium, most of the big decisions that would shape broadcasting for the next half century had already been made.[4] Once television was liberated from wartime constraints, it flowed smoothly into foreordained channels. The federal regulatory scheme was already in place; the same arguments about "spectrum scarcity" and "listener sovereignty" that had applied earlier to radio were now applied to television, which was captured at birth in a corral of federal rules and regulations. Television never had the kind of wild childhood that radio had had before the Radio Act of 1927. The FCC was already present at the creation of television, asserting public ownership of the airwaves.

The corporate structures were also in place to develop, market, and profit from television. Television had almost no existence outside the world of the big three broadcast networks—NBC, CBS, and ABC. When the mighty rivers of entertainment, advertising, profits—and, yes, news too—began flowing through television, they ran along the three riverbeds already carved out by radio. The major difference was that everything about television was bigger. There were bigger audiences, bigger profits, bigger potential and impact, bigger egos and salaries, bigger problems, scandals, and regrets. Sales of television sets exploded: in 1947 customers bought some 179,000 of the bulky sets, the next year a million. In 1949, RCA brought out a tabletop model, which sold 2 million units that year alone.[5] At the start of the 1950s, only about one out of ten U.S. households had a television set; by the end, only about one in ten did *not*.[6]

TV was the domain of the existing broadcasting companies, and their executives moved quickly to build television networks, based on the earlier radio model of affiliates—some owned and operated directly by the network, others under contract. In the early days during the 1950s, television operated on the basis of commercial sponsorship. Station owners and the networks did not charge viewers to watch, so the broadcasters had to rely for revenues entirely on the money coming in from advertising. In the early years this usually meant that a single corporation sponsored a half hour or an entire hour at a time, making the sponsor the exclusive source of revenue for that time slot. The name of the sponsoring company could even be incorporated into the name of the program, such as the *Kraft Television Theatre* or the *Camel News Caravan*. Inevitably, this arrangement meant that the sponsor had a keen interest in the size of the audience, and it sometimes meant that the sponsor took an interest in the content of the programming as well.[7] Having secured a sponsor for a program, a network would want to keep that sponsor. This arrangement gave certain big corporate advertisers an extraordinary, though unspoken, veto power over radio and television that invariably ended up narrowing the range of acceptable themes and ideas; usually the result of corporate sponsorship was to pressure programming to move in the direction of the cautious, the cornball, and the conservative.

Americans couldn't get enough of it. By the end of 1954 there were 32 million television sets in the country, and CBS doubled its gross advertising billings in that single year, making it the largest advertising medium in the world.[8] Broadcasters were particularly vulnerable to pressure from advertisers because they were so dependent on them. Unlike newspapers or magazines, they had no second stream of revenue coming in directly from the audience. Viewers pulled the television signal out of the public airwaves using set-top antennas, and they paid nothing for access to all that programming. With no income from subscription, television rested on a single source of money: advertising.

At the start, television news differed from print in that it was banned—by federal regulation—from explicitly expressing any editorial points of view. In 1941, in a ruling that established what was known as the Mayflower doctrine, the FCC had banned radio broadcasters from taking sides in controversies. After years of rising tensions over such radio agitators as Father Coughlin, the FCC imposed new ground rules. "A truly free radio cannot be used to advocate the causes of the licensee," the agency warned, adding, "The broadcaster cannot be an advocate."[9] After World War II, the FCC embarked on a different approach, which became known as the "fairness doctrine." Under the new policy, broadcasters (including television stations) could take stands on issues and allow others to do so, provided they gave a "reasonably balanced presentation"[10] of all views. In other words, they were to operate as something like an editorial common carrier, or like the "open press" of the colonial era—allowing television stations to transmit views to the public without holding (or at least without expressing) any views of their own.

Aside from commercial and regulatory issues, Murrow and the other pioneers in television news also faced other challenges imposed by the medium itself. They had to invent new forms of storytelling that were suited to the small screen. Television made other demands as well. In radio, an individual journalist could operate fairly independently. Armed with a microphone and a tape recorder, a radio reporter could go almost anywhere and describe almost anything. Not so with television. For Murrow to get a story on television would require a team: not just himself but a researcher and writer to help with the reporting, a cameraman and a soundman (or several) and a director to choose the shots and angles, an editor to cut and paste the pictures and sound together, and a producer to oversee the whole unit, hire and pay everybody, and generally organize the enterprise. In different places those titles and lines of responsibility might shift, but all those tasks would always need to get done. Murrow did most of his own reporting and almost all of his own writing, for example, but not even Murrow could produce television news all by himself.

One takeoff point for the presentation of news on television was in 1950, while Murrow was still in radio. That year CBS had fourteen full-time staffers in the TV news division; six years later there were 376. The growth had nothing to do with the usual reason, profit. Far from it. The television news divisions at both NBC and CBS lost money for years, all through the 1950s and well into the 1960s. By one estimate, CBS News alone lost about $10 million a year on average for the decade.[11] The networks made plenty of money on comedies, dramas, and variety shows, so the executives at all three television networks were in a financial position to allow the news divisions to run up red ink year after year.

There were two reasons for this unusual behavior on the part of the top executives of these big, profit-seeking companies. One reason was the pressure of FCC regulation, and news programming seemed to fit the requirement to serve the "public interest" quite nicely. TV news was thus a kind of insurance policy protecting the all-important licenses held by the affiliates. The other reason was more subtle, more personal. As time went by, Paley and Sarnoff and other top executives began to realize that covering the news injected their companies into the heady world of public affairs. Wars, elections, the rise and fall of the stock market, even the World Series—all of these demanded coverage, which put the network news divisions right at ringside, as witnesses to history. Not only that, but also this kind of coverage could convey a vicarious sense of gravitas to all those involved. In the bargain, Sarnoff and Paley and lots of other top television executives got to meet presidents and senators, movie stars and generals, artists and batting champs. It was heady stuff.

Such was the new world of television news that Murrow was being asked to enter. In late 1951, Murrow yielded to his bosses' requests and agreed to launch a weekly television program. One key to the operation was the producer, Fred Friendly. A big, energetic man, Friendly was as homely as Murrow was handsome, as boisterous as Murrow was cool. (Friendly was also color-blind, which could be an issue in a visual medium.) They had first teamed up in 1947, when they put together a record album of historic speeches titled *I Can Hear It Now,* narrated by Murrow. The album was a success and led eventually to a weekly radio program called *Hear It Now.* Friendly's entire background in journalism consisted of a few years as a reporter-producer for a radio station in Providence, but it didn't seem to matter; almost no one else had ever done news on television either. Besides, Friendly had reserves of intelligence, energy, and confidence that served him well as a problem-solver par excellence. Perhaps most important, Murrow trusted him. Also on the team was a young man who had not gone to college but who had trained at the Associated Press—the director Don Hewitt. Together with the rest of the crew, the three of them would make television history.

The new program was called *See It Now.* It was not trying to summarize the news of the day, but it was topical and timely, sort of like putting *Life* magazine on the air. Once a week it would deliver a mix of topics; in a sense it was the original television newsmagazine.[12] Making its debut on November 18, 1951, *See It Now* was a logistical challenge and a technical tour de force. Located at 485 Madison Avenue, near Grand Central Station (CBS did not complete work on its sleek headquarters on Sixth Avenue and Fifty-second Street, known as Black Rock, until 1964), the "studio" was simply the control room—hot, crowded, and crammed with the machinery of television. "This is an old team, trying to learn a new trade," Murrow told the viewers, his deadeye gaze penetrating the camera lens through a screen of cigarette smoke. The half-hour broadcast included film from London, Paris, and Korea, but the showstopper was a technical first: on a split screen, viewers could see simultaneously live television pictures from New York Harbor and San Francisco Bay. The debut of *See It Now* was a great hit with the public and with the critics.[13] All the show needed now was a sponsor. As it happened, the Aluminum Company of America had recently lost an antitrust case and needed to shine up its image. So Alcoa decided to stand next to Edward R. Murrow and hope that some of his glow would reflect on the company.

Between the evening news broadcasts and *See It Now,* the CBS television news division was a growing presence, both within the corporation and within the field of journalism. CBS News passed another milestone the following year in its coverage of the 1952 national conventions of the two major political parties. The head of CBS News, Sig Mickelson, was charged with organizing the coverage, and he naturally wanted Murrow to help out. Reluctantly, Murrow agreed to pitch in, but he turned Mickelson down for the major assignment. Eric Sevareid said no, too, and another Murrow Boy, Charles Collingwood, was out of the country. So Mickelson turned to a reporter who had covered World War II for United Press and was now working for the CBS affiliate in Washington, WTOP-TV. The thirty-five-year-old newsman was Walter Cronkite, who had almost become a Murrow Boy during the war but had turned down Murrow's offer of a job in London. Now, working for CBS, Cronkite took on the task of sitting in front of the cameras through the long hours of the 1952 conventions, earning the first application of the term "anchor" while covering what was probably the last pair of political conventions at which there was any risk of real news breaking out.[14] For the first time, more Americans were watching the conventions on TV than were listening on radio. Cronkite proved to be a natural for the anchor job, and he soon became a household name and a familiar on-screen presence.

After the conventions were over, Mickelson took Cronkite aside and raised another new issue in television journalism.

"Well, Walter, you're famous now. And you are going to want a lot more money," Mickelson told him. "You'd better get an agent."[15]

* * *

As the United States and the Soviet Union embarked on the decades-long period of conflict and competition known as the Cold War (a phrase made popular by Walter Lippmann), journalists on both sides reverted to form. In the Soviet Union, with its state-run media, the press and broadcasters did not "cover" the Cold War in any meaningful sense; they strictly followed the party line. (I refer here to the official media, not to the often heroic and always dangerous work of the underground press.) In the United States, the record is considerably more complex. In general, the news media reported on the actions and policies of the U.S. government, which remained steadfast in its opposition to the Soviet Union throughout the 1950s and 1960s. In its editorial expressions, the bulk of American news media supported U.S. government policies throughout the Cold War—with the notable exception of the war in Vietnam—and almost never had a kind word for the Soviet Union (fig. 10.1).

Even before the end of World War II, Congress was in the business of investigating communism. Long before Senator Joseph McCarthy started doing so in the Senate, a conservative Democrat in the House of Representatives, Martin Dies of Texas, was using the House Un-American Activities Committee to hunt for "reds." HUAC had been established by Congress in 1938 as a "special investiga-

10.1 **THE "THOUSAND-YARD STARE."** During the war in Korea, photojournalist David Douglas Duncan made this haunting portrait of marine captain Ike Fenton for *Life* magazine, just as Fenton gets word that his unit is running out of supplies during the battle to secure No-Name Ridge.
—*David Douglas Duncan/Harry Ransom Center, The University of Texas at Austin.*

tion committee" with the ambiguous mandate to look into "the extent, character, and object of un-American propaganda activities in the United States." The committee initially investigated domestic Nazis and made some perfunctory inquiries into the KKK, but Chairman Dies made sure that the panel focused on threats from the Left—communists and New Dealers, two groups in which he sensed a considerable overlap. The press loved it, finding in Dies a steady source of "revelations" about communists, sympathizers, and fellow travelers. In its first month alone, the committee got more than five hundred column inches of coverage in the *New York Times*.[16]

The conservatives had a point: there *were* communists in America. The liberals also had a point: those communists never posed any *real* threat to the United States government, the Constitution, or the capitalist system. In point of fact, there were never very many hard-core communists, that is, actual atheists who wanted to destroy capitalism and overthrow the U.S. government by violent means. In 1929 the Communist Party of the United States claimed all of seven thousand members, many of them immigrants—this in a wealthy, advanced, stable, religious nation of 150 million.[17] In addition, there were, no doubt, several handfuls of genuine Soviet spies (who were and should have remained a law enforcement problem). Then there was a larger group—still a tiny minority to be sure—who were Trotskyites, labor union radicals from the Congress of Industrial Organizations (CIO), anti-Stalin leftists, and socialists, all of whose numbers swelled during the Great Depression, as well as plain old liberal Democrats, and even people who just treasured civil liberties or supported world peace, who all got lumped together in the conservative imagination. The media rarely made very fine distinctions, either. At one time or another they were all called "reds," especially in headlines. (Was there ever such a gift to headline writers as the word "reds"?)

With help from the media, Dies brought the techniques of red-baiting and witch-hunting to the forefront during the late 1930s and throughout the war years. In 1946, Republicans gained enough seats to take control of the House, and Dies was succeeded by a new chairman, Republican J. Parnell Thomas of New Jersey (under whom HUAC would conduct some of the most notorious hearings of the 1950s, including the Hollywood Ten case and the Alger Hiss case). By now HUAC was just a part of a broader network that included the Senate, the FBI, the Justice Department, and the courts, all engaged in rooting out "disloyal" Americans, especially communists, often using techniques pioneered earlier by the Left in search of fascists. Most newspapers (especially the Hearst and McCormick papers), most broadcasters (especially the postwar Winchell radio program), and most of the mass-circulation magazines (particularly the Luce press and *Reader's Digest*) were leading the charge in the hunt for subversives, disloyals, and reds well before McCarthy was even elected to the Senate. The Republicans who came into office in 1946, making common cause with some conservative anti–New Deal Democrats, saw a threat and went after it. The news media saw a story and went after that. Indeed, in the ensuing conservative media frenzy, a figure like McCarthy was not merely possible but probably inevitable. McCarthy was a ravisher, but the media were certainly no virgins.

In 1949 one of the most important stories of the Cold War broke in China, when the communist Mao Tse-tung led his peasant movement to victory over the Nationalist leader Chiang Kai-shek, who was forced along with his remaining supporters to flee into exile on the island of Taiwan. Most Americans were shocked. In large part their shock was the fault of a single journalist: the gimlet-eyed, high-church tycoon Henry Robinson Luce of *Time* magazine. Chiang had been a U.S. ally during World War II, so Americans were disposed to favor him, but Luce did not stop there. He developed hero worship of Generalissimo Chiang into a mania. Luce was the most vocal of the so-called China lobby, which attempted to shore up support for the Nationalist leader with the president and Congress. Secretary of State George C. Marshall had serious reservations about Chiang, given the popular support that Mao and his communist guerrillas were winning among China's masses. The secretary also questioned Chiang's staying power, given the generalissimo's persistent habit of corruption.[18] Marshall must have had good sources, since his assessment was on target.

Luce had good sources, too, but he refused to listen to them. Indeed, he employed two of the best China hands (and two of the best reporters, period) of the era: John Hersey and Theodore White. But when the correspondents filed their extensive notes from China to *Time* headquarters in Manhattan, those notes got the Luce treatment. The finished stories were written by Luce (or his top Cold War–era foreign news editor, Whittaker Chambers), and somehow the published versions always struck an optimistic note about Chiang and an ominous note about Mao. Hersey and White eventually both quit in frustration, and Luce continued his editorial mission and his lobbying. Luce was not America's only source of reporting about China, of course, but the Luce doctrine, amplified and repeated in the pages of both *Time* and *Life* over many years, made him a force to be reckoned with.[19]

And no voice cried out louder than Luce when China "fell" to the communists. This he did by pounding away at the Truman administration, especially Marshall's successor as secretary of state, Dean Acheson, in the pages of *Time* (circulation almost 2 million) and *Life* (circulation more than 5 million). The question to which Luce demanded an answer was "Who lost China?" By framing the issue that way, of course, Luce was presuming that China, an ancient civilization whose population dwarfed that of the United States, had been somehow "ours" to "lose." No matter. Luce posed the question often enough that eventually it began to answer itself: the only way the United States could have lost China was if there were disloyal Americans in the government who made it happen. To many people it appeared that godless communism was ascendant, encompassing the entire Asian landmass and eastern Europe. What Luce and his allies wanted to know was: Who was to blame? Whenever they found someone in government they considered responsible, the remedy was to demand his immediate ouster.[20]

*   *   *

ON FEBRUARY 9, 1950, SENATOR Joe McCarthy, hardly a household name outside Washington and his home state of Wisconsin, gave a speech to the Women's Republican Club in Wheeling, West Virginia. It was about as far from the centers of media and political power as could be, but that speech launched one of the most notorious episodes in American history. That evening, McCarthy presented the first of his series of accusations about "communists" in government. The Republican senator claimed that he had a list of 205 people "known to the Secretary of State as being members of the Communist party" who were working in the U.S. State Department under the Democratic administration of Harry Truman.[21] Over the next few weeks McCarthy made similar claims, often with different numbers or different descriptions of the supposed security risks, in more than half a dozen cities from coast to coast. That was the genesis of the period and the tragedy known as "McCarthyism," which lasted for almost five years. In retrospect, the McCarthy era stands out as an interval in the much larger Cold War but one that has proven emblematic of the excesses of the entire period. McCarthy, a little-known freshman senator, stumbled across the power of the news media and rode it for as long as he could. For their part, the news media were divided about McCarthy from the start. Some took the view that McCarthy was right and joined the hunt for reds in government; others thought McCarthy was a loudmouth, but one who generated good copy; a small but growing number saw in McCarthy a threat to democracy itself and tried to stop him.

The period of McCarthy's ascendancy raises troubling questions about the American news media. Riding the crest of the existing hostility to communism and the unpopularity of the Truman administration, McCarthy happened upon a winning formula: he could trade on the prestige and credibility of his status as a member of the U.S. Senate to make charges against two already unpopular targets: communists and the federal bureaucracy. In picking on the State Department, McCarthy found an almost perfect whipping boy, since State has hardly any domestic constituency to stick up for it. Initially at least, the media were mostly willing to play along with McCarthy. And why not? He held high office. He was making serious accusations. And he was making them in a way that was sure to excite the public. For all these reasons, his early charges soon took on a momentum that surprised even McCarthy.

One powerful engine driving McCarthy's dramatic rise was the Associated Press.[22] With its nationwide network of news bureaus and member newspapers, the AP was in a unique position to gather news wherever it occurred and, at the same time, to distribute it to every corner of the country. So no matter where McCarthy spoke, his words could be captured and disseminated by the AP. In addition, as long as the news agency was quoting others and not leveling any charges on its own authority, it could also meet another institutional imperative: the need to please editors of various political stripes.

The AP had one more feature that left it especially open to manipulation by someone like McCarthy. That was the relentless demand for new "leads." As regularly as the tides, the AP report swelled each day according to the rhythm of the two daily news "cycles"—AM and PM. One cycle, running from noon to midnight, supplied the morning newspapers; the other cycle, from midnight to noon, supplied the afternoon papers. (When news broke or developed around the slack tide of midday or midnight, AP would designate the copy "BC," meaning the same story was being made available on an emergency basis to papers of both cycles.) Thus, if McCarthy spoke at an evening banquet and made an accusation, his charges would be duly recorded by an AP reporter and rushed to the wire for the morning papers. Chances were that the target of those charges could not be reached in time to comment, so McCarthy would dominate that news cycle. The AP might follow up the next morning with a call to the target of the story.

If the target provided a vigorous reply, then that would become the basis of the new lead, and the "score" would be roughly tied. But if the target of a McCarthy attack had to check some old records before replying or decided not to dignify the charge with a reply, then McCarthy would "win" that cycle too.[23] Conversely, though, if someone attacked McCarthy, the senator was always reachable and always ready with a dramatic "fresh quote." So in the long run, the reachable, quotable senator always came out ahead.

McCarthy's sudden rise to prominence on the basis of unfounded charges points up a broader weakness in U.S. journalism: the prevalent understanding of the philosophy of "objectivity." In practice, this view holds that journalism is neither the pursuit of ultimate truth nor an outlet for the journalist's own personal expression. Instead, the proper role of journalism is to find out what *other* people are doing and saying. In this framing of the role, the journalist is not obligated to get to the bottom of things. It is enough to gather tidbits. If the topic is controversial, then the journalist has the further duty to be "balanced." In this system, accusation and denial are equal and opposite operations, like the freezing and melting of water. If, for example, a reporter writes that So-and-so has been accused of being a communist and then allows the subject the chance to deny it, the reporter has created a "balanced" story that is fair to "both sides." If the accuser is a member of some other powerful institution, so much the better. Such a system was inevitably wide open to exploitation by a cynical opportunist.

A few papers deserve credit for editorializing against McCarthy almost from the start, notably the *Washington Post,* which was under the direction of its young publisher, Philip Graham, a pro-Eisenhower Republican who had taken over the paper in 1946 at age thirty from his father-in-law, Eugene Meyer.[24] Just five days after McCarthy's speech in Wheeling, the *Post* ran an editorial titled "Sewer Politics," in which the paper charged McCarthy with "foul play" and observed, "Rarely has a man in public life crawled and squirmed so abjectly."[25] Some of the *Post*'s toughest, and most effective, criticism of McCarthy came from the pen of cartoonist Herbert Block. Under the nom de plume Herblock, the cartoonist fixed the public's image of McCarthy as an unscrupulous bully. Herblock is also credited with coining the phrase "McCarthyism," which he used as a label on a barrel of tar in a cartoon that appeared on March 29, 1950.[26] *Post* columnist Drew Pearson also criticized McCarthy, early and often, in his widely syndicated column, "The Washington Merry-Go-Round."

Gradually, other newspapers and magazines joined the ranks of McCarthy critics. A significant shift occurred after the 1952 elections, in which Republicans captured the White House and both houses of Congress. Now, the Republicans were in a position they had not occupied since the 1920s. Thanks to the Republican sweep, McCarthy went from being a junior member of the minority to chairman of a Senate committee, the Permanent Subcommittee on Investigations (often referred to as "the McCarthy committee"), with the power to hire staff, set the agenda, and dominate the proceedings. Another element of the partisan realignment, however, turned out to play an even more important role in McCarthy's rise and fall. Now that a Republican was president, any further criticism of the federal government was a reflection not on the Democrat Truman but on the Republican Eisenhower. From here on out, if McCarthy continued to attack the executive branch, the junior senator would be taking on a senior statesman of national stature, the preeminent hero of the Second World War, and the popular leader of McCarthy's own party. That turned out to be a match the senator could not handle.

As McCarthy commenced attacking the Eisenhower administration in 1953 and then took on the army in 1954, more and more Republican publishers found reasons to criticize the senator. One of the most influential was that pillar of the Republican establishment (and friend of Secretary of State John Foster Dulles), Henry Luce. His change of heart was what allowed *Time* editors to claim later that they had been "against McCarthy."[27] As more and more newspapers and magazines turned against McCarthy, pressure also grew on broadcasters—especially Murrow—to "do something." The fact is, if Murrow had attacked McCarthy in 1951 or 1952 (an election year), it would probably have had a much greater impact, but it would also have involved much greater professional risk. By the time Murrow made his move, McCarthy was already showing signs of tumbling. All through 1951 and 1952, friends and colleagues urged Murrow to use *See It Now* to discredit McCarthy and his methods. Murrow appeared to want to "do something," but still he hesitated.

For Murrow, as a television journalist, it was not going to be easy. The climate within CBS was not conducive to liberal crusading. In 1950, CBS instituted its own company-wide loyalty oath, and Murrow (despite misgivings) had signed it.[28] Part of the reason for the oath was a concern about anti-red pressure emanating not from government but from the private sector. For many in the media, the greatest threat came from a company established in the late 1940s by three former FBI agents to battle communism. They produced a mail-order bulletin, *Counterattack: The Newsletter of Facts on Communism,* which specialized in exposing alleged communists and their sympathizers in the media. In June 1950 the editors released a volume called *Red Channels,* naming 151 people in news and entertainment, who suddenly became unemployable.[29] The idea of a blacklist, which originated in Hollywood, had now reached television and was beginning to haunt New York. Because *Counterattack* was a private business and not part of the government, the accused could not invoke the Fifth Amendment, the First Amendment, or any other legal safeguard. CBS subscribed to *Counterattack* and kept a complete set on file.[30]

Despite the rules at CBS, Murrow wanted a clear shot at McCarthy. The confrontation between Murrow and McCarthy is usually told as a triumphal and reassuring tale about the power of a lone heroic, liberal newsman to take down a snarling, bullying proto-fascist.[31] Not to take anything away from Murrow, but that story is far too simple. Murrow knew the CBS News policy requiring objectivity and nonpartisanship on the air, and like it or not, he understood why it had

10.2 **PRODUCER FRED FRIENDLY** (*left*) **AND CORRESPONDENT EDWARD R. MURROW** teamed up to produce the CBS News program *See It Now* and other projects. They are shown here working on a set of recordings titled "I Can Hear It Now."
—*Getty Images.*

been adopted. He knew that television was a lucrative near-monopoly business that operated under the regulatory eye of the federal government. He knew that political neutrality was probably the only strategy that made sense for television news. And yet he did not believe that television news must always be dispassionate and mathematically balanced. "Some issues aren't balanced," he once declared. "We can't sit here every Tuesday night and give the impression that for every argument on one side there is an equal one on the other side."[32]

But in the end, none of that really mattered. In the end, Murrow's hand was forced (indirectly) by McCarthy himself. Sometime in 1953, Murrow and Friendly started collecting and storing reels of film showing McCarthy in action (fig. 10. 2). They sought the tape of his famous red-baiting debut in Wheeling from 1950 but couldn't find it. Then they learned that McCarthy was gathering material about Murrow, charging him with being "red" because of his work years earlier with the IIE in Moscow. That was apparently the last straw for Murrow. After years of entreaties by his friends to take on McCarthy, Murrow was cornered. If McCarthy struck first, then anything that Murrow did later would look like self-justification or revenge. The time had come: Murrow would have to strike first.

In utter secrecy, the *See It Now* crew began going over those miles of film they had accumulated about McCarthy. They did not tell Paley or any other top CBS executives what they had in mind. And it may be that the top brass didn't want to know. As the day of the broadcast drew near in March 1954, Murrow and Friendly did ask CBS management for funds to advertise the McCarthy show, giving only a general description of what was to come, but they were turned down. So Murrow and Friendly paid the $1,500 out of their own pockets to buy an ad in the *New York Times*. There was no CBS logo in the ad—just a program note, signed by Murrow and Friendly as "co-producers."[33] On the day of the broadcast, CBS chairman Bill Paley called Murrow, as he did from time to time, to wish him luck. "I'll be with you tonight, Ed, and I'll be with you tomorrow as well," Paley said, offering his personal reassurance to his most visible newsman.[34]

At 10:30 p.m. eastern time on March 8, 1954, the red light above the TV camera lens went on.[35] Friendly, crouching just off camera, was so nervous he could not work his stopwatch. Murrow was tense but faced the camera with his usual cool seriousness. On air, Murrow wore one of his tailored pinstripe suits and a conservative tie. His dark hair was as always combed straight back and slicked down. As usual for a *See It Now* broadcast, he was shot in a seated position with the camera tilted down, giving extra prominence to his eyes but tending to make him look shorter than he was. Murrow also had a habit of sitting so that he was angled almost forty-five degrees away from the camera, wreathed in cigarette smoke. As a result, he often looked as if he were an executive or some other important person who had been busy with something else when the camera suddenly showed up. From time to time, he would raise his head and look straight at the camera, a gesture that served him well as a mark of punctuation or emphasis. It was subtle but effective. His entire presentation suggested that he was not trying to be your best friend; he was trying to make a point.

Head cocked, Murrow began by explaining the show's method on this night: "Good evening. Tonight, *See It Now* devotes its entire half hour to a report on Senator Joseph McCarthy, told mainly in his own words and pictures." What followed was a sustained piece of advocacy. That in itself was not unprecedented. American journalists had been advocating positions for two centuries by that point, and Murrow's show about McCarthy fit comfortably in the tradition of Paine, Garrison, Steffens, and many others. What was so startling was that this advocacy was being carried over a television network. That was uncharted territory. Murrow plunged in, but first he made a key point: "If the senator feels that we have done violence to his words or pictures, and desires, so to speak, to answer himself, an opportunity will be afforded him on this program." Then Murrow introduced the film clips of McCarthy, attempting to hang the senator with his own words, gestures, and actions. There was very little else—almost no reporting. Instead, film segments from the previous few years consistently depicted McCarthy as a shameless, mocking bully. McCarthy was hardly photogenic, and the camera made him pay the price. Occasionally Murrow would comment on a point McCarthy had made, or offer a correction. ("The attorney general's list does not and never has listed the ACLU as subversive.")

One segment showed McCarthy denouncing his critics in the press as "extreme left-wing." Murrow countered by reading from a tall stack of newspapers from around the country, starting with the archconservative *Chicago Tribune,* all denouncing McCarthy's tactics. Another segment showed the painful grilling McCarthy had inflicted on Reed Harris, a State Department official, over things that Harris had written twenty years earlier. The episode was so patently unfair that it proved Murrow's point: McCarthy was indeed his own worst enemy.

Staring hard at the camera, Murrow closed the program with what can only be called a speech, in the sense that it is not journalistic by the standards of the mid-twentieth century. (That is, it was not empirical. No amount of reporting could confirm it.) Quoting a line that McCarthy himself had used, Murrow asked, "Upon what meat does this our Caesar feed?" Then he answered his own question. "Had he looked three lines earlier in Shakespeare's *Caesar,* he would have found this line, which is not altogether inappropriate: 'The fault, dear Brutus, is not in our stars, but in ourselves.'" Next, Murrow took McCarthy down a few pegs more by depicting him as a tool of larger forces that the senator barely understood, much less controlled. No longer was McCarthy the mastermind and superpatriot; now he was nothing but a poorly groomed opportunist. Murrow concluded:

> We must not confuse dissent with disloyalty. We must remember always that accusation is not proof, and that conviction depends upon evidence and due process of law. We will not walk in fear, one of another. We will not be driven by fear into an age of unreason, if we dig deep in our history and our doctrine and remember that we are not descended from fearful men. Not from men who feared to write, to speak, to associate, and to defend causes that were for the moment unpopular. . . .
>
> The actions of the junior senator from Wisconsin have caused alarm and dismay amongst our allies abroad and given considerable comfort to our enemies. And whose fault is that? Not really his. He didn't create this situation of fear; he merely exploited it, and rather successfully.
>
> Cassius was right. "The fault, dear Brutus, is not in our stars, but in ourselves."
>
> Good night, and good luck.

Within minutes, the telephone lines at CBS were jammed as viewers started calling. Within hours, CBS headquarters had received more than one thousand telegrams. All the next day, reaction poured in, not just at CBS but also at the affiliated television stations around the country. By a huge margin they supported Murrow. Harry Truman called; Albert Einstein wrote a letter asking to meet Murrow. People in the street stopped to thank Murrow, and taxi drivers shook his hand. Then came the responses and the reviews by professional critics—again, overwhelmingly positive. Jack O'Brian, the television critic at the Hearst flagship paper, the *New York Journal-American,* was predictably snide, referring as usual to Murrow as a "pompous port-sider." And Hearst columnist Westbrook Pegler took a shot at Murrow, calling him by his original given name, Egbert: "How could the great Aluminum Company sponsor the left-wing tirades of Murrow . . . ? It's enough to make Andy Mellon turn over in his grave."[36] But most commentary was favorable, with the *Times* calling the program "crusading journalism of high responsibility and genuine courage."[37] And Alcoa stood by Murrow—at least for the time being.

What happened next, though, was more significant in terms of the direction of television news, and much less well understood. In a series of moves, Paley began steadily reducing Murrow's prominence on the air and his autonomy within CBS News. Ironically, after that now famous broadcast, McCarthy was never the same again, but neither was Murrow. Both men's careers began a downward slide that night—McCarthy's much steeper and rougher, Murrow's longer and gentler, but nearly as bitter.

As for McCarthy, he kept right on investigating. The senator was also contemplating his response to Murrow's attack on him. Eventually McCarthy decided to appear in his own defense. With help from Hearst columnist George Sokolsky, McCarthy wrote a vigorous denunciation of Murrow and taped it at CBS's expense. To McCarthy, of course, a good defense meant a brutal offense. The senator went right at Murrow: "Now, ordinarily—ordinarily—I would not take time out from the important work at hand to answer Murrow. However, in this case, I feel justified in doing so because Murrow is a symbol, a leader, and the cleverest of the jackal pack which is always found at the throat of anyone who dares to expose individual communists and traitors. And I am compelled by the facts to say to you that Mr. Edward R. Murrow, as far back as twenty years ago, was engaged in propaganda for communist causes."[38] He went on to charge the "leader of the jackal pack" with all the usual stuff: consorting with people who were communists or sympathizers, holding views that coincided with communist positions, giving comfort to the nation's enemies. McCarthy closed by warning of the threat posed by the Soviet atomic bomb and promising Americans that he would not be swayed by the likes of Edward R. Murrow.

It was vintage McCarthy, yet by 1954 it did not have the old magic. The majority of the press sided with Murrow, and the next day, at his regular Wednesday news conference, President Eisenhower answered a reporter's question about the confrontation by referring to Murrow as "my friend."[39] McCarthy was clearly losing his power to intimidate. Undeterred, however, the senator embarked on the scheme that ultimately brought him down: his investigation of the U.S. Army. Once again, television would prove his nemesis, this time because his hearings would be televised live to a national audience. The key decision to do so was made not by the industry leader, CBS, nor by its close rival, NBC, but by the laggard, ABC. In 1954, CBS and NBC both had daytime schedules packed with popular and lucrative soap operas. ABC had nothing comparable, so while CBS and NBC dropped the hearings after a week, ABC hung in and ultimately provided the nation with an unblinking view of McCarthy at work.[40] By the end of the year, the Senate was ready to censure McCarthy, and a little over two years later, McCarthy was dead. After years of drinking as much as a quart of whisky a day, Joe McCarthy became his own last victim.[41]

Meanwhile, back at CBS, the chips were still falling. A few weeks after the *See It Now* showdown with McCarthy, producer Friendly was summoned to the office of CBS president Frank Stanton, who showed him the results of a special poll CBS had commissioned to gauge the impact of McCarthy's rebuttal program. The good news was that 59 percent of the adult U.S. population had seen the show or heard about it. The bad news was that one-third of them believed that Murrow was a red. Stanton was, according to Friendly, distressed by the poll results because the television executive "believed that such controversy and widespread doubts were harmful to the company's business relationships."[42] For a big company like CBS, trying to please shareholders, trying to please sponsors, trying to please the affiliates, trying to please the FCC, and trying to please viewers—all at the same time and all the time—controversy was the kiss of death. Paley and others in top management did not see it as their role to get involved in direct confrontations with powerful politicians. Yes, CBS had won this round with McCarthy, but what about the next one? How many more of these brawls was the news division going to drag the company into?

Part of the problem, from Paley's point of view, was the sponsor, Alcoa. According to Friendly, Alcoa was beginning to complain—about the McCarthy program and about other *See It Now* programs.[43] In July 1955 the company pulled out completely. When no new sponsor could be found for *See It Now*, Murrow and Friendly were summoned to Paley's office. According to Friendly:

> The chairman commended us for our fine season just ended, but wondered whether a half-hour wasn't "too confining" for the type of documentaries we were now doing so well. What did we think of changing the format and doing a series of eight or ten one-hour *See It Now* reports? Wouldn't this be a more satisfying way of doing things? We asked what the time periods would be. They would be at night, Paley said, and added that sponsorship could probably be obtained. We asked what the alternative was; could we continue in the half-hour time period? The word "no" was never used.[44]

But it could have been, because Paley was in fact easing them out. His "offer" of an occasional hour-long program was not what it appeared. Effectively, it meant the end of *See It Now*, because it meant that Murrow and Friendly did not own any portion of the weekly schedule. From now on, whenever they wanted to put something on the air, they would have to ask permission. From now on, Murrow and Friendly could not decide on projects; they would have to pitch them. It would never be the same again.

Paley (described by Truman Capote as looking "like a man who has just swallowed an entire human being")[45] had gotten what he wanted. He stripped the journalists who could cause him the biggest headaches of the means to do so, and in the bargain, he had avoided an angry public firing. Ultimately, Murrow was just another employee. Despite his heroics in London during the Blitz, despite his labors to establish the preeminence of CBS News, despite his personal friendship with Paley in London during the war, despite his winning more awards than any other broadcaster alive—in spite of everything, even Murrow was expendable.

By 1958 things had reached a breaking point. One chronic source of friction between the Murrow-Friendly team and the top brass at CBS involved the right to reply to hard-hitting television news programs. Often in the wake of a tough piece on *See It Now,* some aggrieved party would call Paley or Stanton and demand time on the CBS schedule to fire back at Murrow. Sometimes the top executives would acquiesce, which infuriated Murrow, because it meant that rather than backing its most accomplished journalist, the company was agreeing with the outsider that the original program had been unfair. After one such episode Murrow and Friendly went to Paley's office. Murrow told Paley that he wanted to be consulted before CBS gave anyone the right to reply on air to a Murrow show. The chairman balked. What followed, according to Friendly, was a shouting match.

> "Bill," Murrow pleaded at one point, "are you going to destroy all this? Don't you want an instrument like the *See It Now* organization, which you have poured so much into for so long, to continue?"
>
> "Yes," said Paley, "but I don't want this constant stomach ache every time you do a controversial project."
>
> "I'm afraid that's a price you have to be willing to pay. It goes with the job."

Nothing else that was said mattered. After seven years and almost two hundred broadcasts, *See It Now* was dead.[46]

So Murrow was left with occasional documentaries and his fluffy celebrity interview show *Person to Person,* on which Murrow "visited" movie stars and other notables in their homes. Instead of making tough-minded documentaries, he was serving up puffballs to people like Humphrey Bogart and Marilyn Monroe. In the end, Paley would manage to do what McCarthy could not do: drive Ed Murrow out of the news business.

In October 1958, Murrow spoke his mind, as he was wont to do, in a speech that would cement his reputation as a teller of difficult truths, but it would also leave him a pariah in the eyes of CBS management.[47] He chose to deliver it to the annual meeting of the Radio and Television News Directors Association, being held that year in Chicago. The setting guaranteed that everyone who mattered in the world of broadcast news, from all three major commercial networks as well as many other radio and TV operations, would hear Murrow's message. He labored over the speech and sent out advance copies to the media, but he decided not to tell either Stanton or Paley about what he had in mind. Just as the television quiz show scandal was beginning to break, Murrow cast himself in the role of the stern prophet, ripping into television for its superficiality, its devotion to profit, and its obsessive pursuit of the largest possible audience at all possible times.

Television, Murrow declared, offered mainly "decadence, escapism, and insulation from the realities of the world in which we live"—especially during prime time. At root was the misfit between journalism and profit: "One of the basic troubles with radio and television news is that both instruments have grown up as an incompatible combination of show business, advertising, and news. Each of the three is a rather bizarre and demanding profession. And when you get all three under one roof, the dust never settles." And what happened when journalistic goals clashed with corporate goals? The corporate imperatives—ratings and profits—always seemed to win out. What should be done?

Murrow devoted much of his speech to that question. He quickly dismissed the idea that broadcast news should be run as a philanthropy or entrusted to foundations. He was seeking solutions within the existing corporate framework. What he came up with was at best optimistic: he thought the big corporations that advertise on television should take it upon themselves to volunteer to underwrite some serious news programming. He felt sure that sponsors and advertisers would aspire to associate themselves with something more noble than "a pretty girl opening the door of a refrigerator, or a horse that talks." Without much evidence, Murrow insisted that those corporations wanted "something better." He called upon the big advertisers to turn over "a tiny tithe" of their annual budgets to, in effect, subsidize the cost of producing first-rate news. This arrangement was not all that different from what would come a bit later to public broadcasting, but Murrow offered no reason for the advertisers or the commercial TV networks to change their ways. What he was proposing was actually a rather modest reform, but he cloaked it in a jeremiad: "This instrument can teach, it can illuminate; yes, and it can even inspire. But it can do so only to the extent that humans are determined to use it to those ends. Otherwise it is merely wires and lights in a box."

In the next few days Murrow drew praise from many colleagues and critics, but Paley was wounded and furious. "He was talking about things he didn't like, which were under my control," Paley said, years later. "So it was very much of a personal attack. Which I resented very deeply."[48] Things had changed considerably over the previous twenty years. In 1938, Murrow had been the rising young star of CBS Radio, the voice of urgent reporting about the gathering crisis in Europe. By 1958, a year in which CBS saw its advertising billings jump by 50 percent and the company set a new profit record, the two men had grown far apart. Paley was now extraordinarily wealthy. (His 1,000,088 shares of CBS Inc. stock were worth more than $37 million.)[49] And he was an enthusiastic Republican, and a personal friend of President Eisenhower. As chairman of the board, Paley had many constituencies: not just CBS News but the much larger entertainment division, along with board members, stockholders, regulators, critics, affiliates, competitors, lawyers—all the trappings and troubles that come with running any big corporation. In this changed setting, Murrow was now a self-righteous scold and even, perhaps, a threat. Paley never blew up at Murrow, but he stepped up the series of moves that would result in marginalizing Murrow within CBS and eventually driving him out.

Murrow read the signs. In 1959 he took a leave of absence. When he returned, he teamed up sporadically with Friendly on the documentary series *CBS Reports,* including the memorable documentary "Harvest of Shame," about the multiple miseries of American farm workers. In 1961, when the new Kennedy administration offered him the position of head of the United States Information Agency, a job that entailed telling America's story to the rest of the world, Murrow took it. He was out of the news business.

As Murrow was leaving, television news was still maturing. With each passing year during the 1950s, the impact of television became greater, and the consequences spread further across the media landscape. Within a few years, the availability of television news would mean the end of the newsreel industry, putting Pathé and other companies out of the business. Within a few more years, television brought a slow death to magazine photojournalism. *Life* and its major competitors, *Look* and the *Saturday Evening Post,* gradually succumbed to the immediacy of television, especially after color became standard on television screens in the 1960s. Television also transformed radio by grabbing much of its programming, along with the bulk of its talent. Once the comedies and dramas that had filled radio's entertainment schedule made the transition to television early in the 1950s, followed by the news operations, radio reinvented itself as a portable jukebox, devoting most of its programming to music. Television also sped the demise of the big-city afternoon newspaper. By the 1950s, the p.m. papers were already struggling to reach readers in the spreading territory of suburbia. No matter how hard they tried and no matter how long they kept the front page open for late stock prices or baseball results, they could not compete with live television news.

*   *   *

THE PRESS HAS ALWAYS HAD critics.[50] Initially, many of those critics came from outside the field of journalism; more often than not, the earliest critics of journalism were its victims, complaining about their own coverage—from Governor Cosby in colonial New York to Abraham Lincoln to John D. Rockefeller. But the press never had a critic quite like A. J. Liebling. Joe Liebling loved food and the fight game, and he wrote well about both. A veteran of general reporting at the *World,* the stout and begoggled Liebling also proved to be, against long odds, an impressive war correspondent for the *New Yorker.* He was on hand for the D-Day invasion, and he followed closely behind the Allies as they fought through the brutal "hedgerow campaign" in Normandy, en route to Paris. In all these fields, Liebling acquitted himself well and contributed some memorable pieces. But his first love was the newspaper, and after the war, Liebling really came into his own as a press critic.

His method was simplicity itself: he subscribed to all the New York City daily papers and spent several hours every morning reading them under the critical lens of his insider's knowledge of newsrooms and his immense native intelligence. His

10.3 **WRITER AND JOURNALISM CRITIC A. J. LIEBLING**, shown patrolling a bookstore in Manhattan during the 1950s.
—*Getty Images.*

great theme was the venality of newspaper publishers, whom he blamed for ruining journalism, like brewers who water their beer. He was so in love with newspapers that he could never forgive anyone he suspected of cheapening them. His style was the essence of the *New Yorker* at its jauntiest—witty, metaphorical, and bristling with arcana. He had the autodidact's great love of erudition and recondite branches of knowledge. But his pieces were never merely obscure; he was a master of the *New Yorker*'s high-low style, and a reference to a French philosophe might be followed by a jab of boxing slang or the drop of a gangster's nickname. (His breezy style was harder to achieve than it might sound—he once described a piece of his own writing as "laboriously offhand.") By temperament a pal of the underdog, Liebling respected reporters, mocked editors, and loathed publishers (fig. 10.3).

Instead of just spotting errors, as many press critics did, Liebling was interested in the performance of the press as a whole, and his body of criticism returned again and again to the systemic and institutional shortcomings that he saw harming his beloved big-city dailies. In particular, he kept returning to the question of how the business side of the news business affected the news side. What he found was a group of owners whom he considered unworthy of the constitutional, literary, and professional duties they were facing. As a class, publishers were guilty of turning the traditional values of the newsroom on their head: they were afflicting the afflicted while comforting the comfortable. The problem, as Liebling saw it, was that the modern big-city newspaper was, by definition, a large business enterprise. Therefore it should surprise no one that the owners of those big businesses shared the values of owners of other big businesses. It was not a matter of character; it was a question of the owners' position in the news business overall and in the wealthy class. That was why the big publishers were almost unanimous in their support for the Republican Party and in their opposition to the income tax, labor unions, and competition from other papers. Readers of such conservative papers could get at the truth, but only if they constantly made mental corrections; Liebling compared it to "aiming a rifle that you know has a deviation to the right."[51] He observed that publishers often acted as if they were engaged in a great nationwide conspiracy, but he put no stock in that theory himself. "When they appear to take positive action with common accord," he wrote, "it is by instinct, like a school of mackerel chasing sardines, rather than by predetermined plan, like warships attacking an enemy fleet. The common objects of their ire—unions, taxes, public welfare, and the Democratic Party—require no pointing out by scout planes."[52] One possible remedy Liebling hit upon was the idea that newspapers might one day be owned by foundations, organized along the lines of a university. (In this, Liebling was being prescient, anticipating the arrival of arrangements like the Poynter Institute, which publishes the *St. Petersburg Times*.) He thought that such papers might counter the bias of the for-profit, conservative press, particularly if they were sponsored by labor unions or political parties. "These will represent definite, undisguised points of view, and will serve as controls on the large profit-making papers expressing definite, ill-disguised points of view." A good newspaper, according to Liebling, is every bit as educational as a good college, and it should enjoy a generous endowment, rather than having to "stake its survival on attracting advertisers of ball-point pens and tickets to Hollywood peep shows."[53]

The issue of monopoly was the real sticking point for Liebling. He could almost understand the attitudes of most owners, but he could not forgive their lust for monopoly. He treated it as the ultimate evidence of the publishers' venality. It was not enough for the publishers to be big, profitable, and influential. No, they had to go and ruin things by buying up or merging with the competition, which led in turn to what Liebling considered the ultimate disaster: the one-newspaper town. When there is no competition, Liebling noted, the monopoly paper can squeeze advertisers (who have no alternative if they want to sell their mattresses or girdles or Oldsmobiles). "What you have in a one-paper town is a privately owned public utility that is constitutionally exempt from public regulation." The monopoly paper can further cut costs by laying off reporters and editors, because the publisher no longer needs to worry about losing readers to a rival with better coverage. "The only losers," he said, "are the readers."[54]

As Liebling memorably observed, "Freedom of the press belongs only to those who own one."[55]

* * *

THROUGH THE CIVIL RIGHTS MOVEMENT, black Americans won for themselves a fuller measure of life, liberty, and the pursuit of happiness.[56] By their own actions, both individual and collective, they stepped forward, often at great cost, to take a hand in writing their own history. In that history-making struggle, the movement enjoyed help from time to time from other individuals and institutions—from people like the white "freedom riders," from government agencies such as the U.S.

Justice Department, and from a small number of federal judges. One such institution in a supporting role was the mainstream news media, which ended up playing a critical part in the movement's success, almost in spite of themselves.

As a mass movement, the civil rights effort depended on the support of millions. But how could a movement of far-flung, largely poor people tap that support? How was that support imagined, sustained, and mobilized? As John Adams suggested in his reflections on the origins of the American Revolution, great social upheavals do not just break out. They occur when large numbers of people are ready individually to change the way they act. In order for that to happen, they must first change the way they think. Throughout the entire history of the United States, changes on that scale have depended on messages carried through the mass media—newspapers, magazines, radio, and television. The facts, ideas, arguments, and images found in the mass media, along with the interpretations placed on those materials by the audience, are essential features of any mass movement.

It is often said that the civil rights movement "exploded" into action or "burst upon the scene" in 1954 with *Brown v. Board of Education,* the U.S. Supreme Court ruling that banned racial segregation in public schools. But that view reflects, at best, only the views of white Americans, who may have been taken by surprise. For black Americans, however, the thinking, planning, fund-raising, organizing, and other activities that would sustain the movement were already well under way.[57] The strength of the movement flowed from several sources. One was the black churches and their network of ministers, who could provide leadership and institutional resources. Another was the labor movement, especially the integrated CIO unions and the other unions that traditionally organized black workers specifically—above all, the Brotherhood of Sleeping Car Porters, the men who served passengers aboard the Pullman railroad cars and, at the same time, served the movement by disseminating black newspapers around the country.[58] Those newspapers turned out to be another key source of strength for the civil rights movement, circulating both information and ideas. Without the black press, the movement might well have foundered.

From its launch in 1827, the black press had been steeped in advocacy, a "fighting press" that sought to document white abuses while celebrating black achievements and filling the need for general information among African Americans, who were usually treated by the white press with disdain or outright hostility. Among the many black papers, several stood out for their high circulation and broad distribution, in particular the *Chicago Defender,* the *Pittsburgh Courier,* the *Baltimore Afro-American,* and the *Amsterdam News* in New York City. None of the major black papers was based in the Deep South, but many of them were mailed there or carried south by visitors—or by railroad porters. During the World War II years, the pages of the black press were brimming with the froth of a rising tide of activism. Black men were demanding combat roles, and doing at least their share of the fighting; black men and women were demanding real jobs in the booming defense plants, and earning the best wages they had ever seen. Expectations were rising, as seen in the "Double V" campaign of the World War II years, which sought victory over fascism abroad along with victory over Jim Crow at home. By the end of the war, those themes were being expressed in more than two hundred black newspapers across the country, with a combined circulation of nearly 2 million (and a much higher overall readership, since papers were often shared)—in retrospect, a high-water mark for the black press.[59] While the mainstream press continued all but ignoring them, black readers turned to the papers that reflected their concerns.

In the years immediately after World War II, two black newspapers in particular proved crucial: the *Chicago Defender,* which had been the circulation leader before the war, and the *Pittsburgh Courier,* which would soon take the lead. Both were weeklies, and both had nationwide distribution. *Ebony* magazine, founded in 1945 and patterned after *Life,* also connected black readers across the country, selling half a million copies a month by the mid-1950s. The pages of these publications were filled with editorials and stories attacking not only such barbarities as lynching but also the constitutional violations of legal segregation and the social degradation of casual, everyday scorn and abuse. The editors had no intention of putting up with another postwar rollback of rights and dignity comparable to that in the 1920s. At the *Defender,* one of the most prominent writers was Langston Hughes, who was given a column in 1943. Although he was best known as a poet and most closely associated with his beloved adopted home in Harlem, Hughes wrote for the Chicago paper for decades, finding his biggest audience and his steadiest pay. In his *Defender* column, Hughes sketched the everyday occurrences in the life of his character Jesse B. Semple, a comic everyman. But Hughes also contributed reporting and commentary to the *Defender,* as he did in his 1945 account of his own "Adventures in Dining." Based on a recent trip through the South, the article recounted the difficulties he faced trying to order food on board passenger trains. He closed with an appeal to readers:

> I would advise Negro travelers in the South to use the diners more. In fact, I wish we would use the diners in droves—so that whites may get used to seeing us in diners. It has been legally established that Negro passengers have a lawful right to eat while traveling. . . . So, folks, when you go South by train, be sure to eat in the diner. Even if you are not hungry, eat anyhow—to help establish that right. Besides, it will be fun to see how you are received.[60]

Like many other black journalists of the era, Hughes was using his writing in support of the broad campaign to defend any ground already gained and to look ahead to the next goal.

The next goal to be met was the landmark 1954 *Brown v. Board of Education* decision banning segregation in public schools. The ruling, along with the conflict over its implementation, marked the start of a new phase in the movement because it raised the issue of civil rights in a way that not only invoked the Constitution but also reached into almost every school district in the country. That sweep, in turn, finally drew the attention of the mainstream, largely white news media. Suddenly the universe of people paying attention to the lives of black Americans expanded dramatically, to include not just the black press, which had been there all along, but now the white-owned papers of the South, as well as the major white-owned media of the North. The last group included national magazines such as *Time, Life,* and *Newsweek;* influential newspapers with high impact in the nation's capital, like the *New York Times* and the *Washington Post;* and the rapidly expanding news divisions of the nationwide television networks. All the outside media had been late in coming to the story, and they had a long way to go to catch up. Most had no black reporters or editors, and they continued to see African Americans as the "other" living amid a complacent majority.

During this phase of the movement, in the 1950s, civil rights leaders embraced two policies that encouraged favorable press coverage, which in turn greatly increased the movement's momentum and ultimate success. One key policy was nonviolence. By adopting it as a tactic, civil rights activists often provoked violent—and unflattering—reactions from Southern whites. That very violence tended to make the civil rights story more compelling in journalistic terms. The violence gave the story action, drama, and victims. By refusing to fight back themselves, the activists ensured that they were not in a position to be blamed for it and were not reduced to a position of moral equivalence with their attackers. The movement's other key policy was the decision to pursue a strategic goal of full citizenship as guaranteed by the Constitution. The resulting demands— the right to vote, the right to attend public schools, the right to travel and use public accommodations—were so reasonable that, as several leading figures from the national media have acknowledged, they won the sympathies of the reporters, photographers, and editors who covered the civil rights movement.[61]

During this phase, most of the action was in the South, and the national news organizations, most of them based in Manhattan, dispatched reporters, photographers, and television crews, some of whom looked upon the South as practically a foreign country. Almost all of them were white men in their thirties or forties, tough generalists who were veterans of all the usual stops in a journalistic career, from sports to crime to politics. Among those outsiders, many were actually Southerners by birth, such as the influential Claude Sitton of the *New York Times.* Sitton proved to be one of the bravest and most energetic members of the entire press corps, crisscrossing the region from one hotspot to another and wearing out four typewriters between 1958 and 1964.[62]

Unlike the reporters for national news organizations, who were visiting the South to cover the newly emerging "race beat," the members of the white-owned media located in the South were not going anywhere. They were not going to rotate back to New York or ship out to the next news hotspot. To them, the South was not a story but a homeland. On the race question, their views ranged across the spectrum. In the South of the 1950s, there were a small number of publishers, editors, and reporters who were true progressives on race questions, like Hodding Carter Jr. of Greenville, Mississippi, or Harry Ashmore of Little Rock, Arkansas. More commonly, the publisher of a newspaper was someone who shared the values of the local white establishment, which was almost uniformly hostile to black aspirations. As the operator of a good-sized business, the publisher was likely to be a member of the Chamber of Commerce and the Rotary Club, if not the country club. He would, of course, know the local sheriff, mayor, and judges. More likely than not, the publisher agreed with his neighbors on most issues and saw to it that the paper generally marched in step, too. If anyone strayed, local whites were likely to crack down with boycotts, cross-burnings, and outright violence. Then there were also some Southern editors who were themselves out-and-out segregationists and white supremacists. James K. Kilpatrick, editor of the *Richmond News Leader,* thundered against mixing the races and urged a revival of the pre–Civil War theory of state sovereignty in order to counter any federal efforts to end Jim Crow.

One of the greatest potential threats to the national coverage of the South arose in 1960 in Montgomery, Alabama. The means of intimidation was not the usual one—violence or the threat of it—but the legal system itself. At risk was the ability of the news media even to cover the movement in an honest, independent way. The threat first arose in April 1960 as an unintended consequence of a decision by a group of civil rights activists to place a full-page advertisement in the *New York Times* decrying the "unprecedented wave of terror" being imposed on the Reverend Dr. Martin Luther King Jr. and student activists. The ad stated: "Again and again, the Southern violators have answered Dr. King's peaceful protests with intimidation and violence. . . . They have bombed his home almost killing his wife and child. They have assaulted his person." For good measure, the ad charged "grave misconduct" on the part of Montgomery officials as a group.[63] The city's police commissioner, L. B. Sullivan, was incensed and decided to sue the *Times* for libel. (It didn't matter that the offending passages were in the form of an advertisement and not a news story produced by a *Times* journalist; under U.S. law, a publisher is equally responsible for all content. It also didn't matter that Sullivan was not singled out by name in the ad; under U.S. law, if an individual can reasonably be identified, that is enough.) Sullivan sued for $500,000 in an Alabama state court, charging the *Times* with publishing damaging falsehoods about him. The threat was clear: if Sullivan won, no paper could afford to cover the civil rights movement. "Silence, not money, was the goal," as one recent history puts it.[64]

For the *Times'* Southern correspondent, Claude Sitton, the suit meant that he had better hightail it out of Alabama to avoid being subpoenaed, so he headed straight for the Georgia line, leaving Alabama essentially uncovered for the next two and a half years. For the paper's lawyers, however, fleeing to another state was not an option, though they tried. It was difficult even to find a lawyer in Alabama who would agree to represent the *Times*. When one was finally found, the lawyers decided that their only recourse was to argue that the suit did not belong in an Alabama court, since the paper did hardly any business in the state. The jurisdictional argument didn't work. The paper lost in the circuit court in Montgomery (where the judge criticized "racial agitators" and praised "white man's justice"),[65] and Sullivan was awarded the full $500,000—the largest libel judgment in that state's history. The *Times* appealed, only to lose again. Further appeals did not look promising, since the U.S. Supreme Court had held that journalists had no constitutional protections against libel claims. So far, the use of the courts to silence the press was working.

The passage through all those courts took years, but the *Times* did not give up. Whatever the publisher and editors thought about civil rights, they were professionally committed to upholding journalistic principles and prerogatives. The final appeal was argued before the U.S. Supreme Court on January 6, 1964. The stakes were high. "The court would decide nothing less than how free the press really could be," one observer has noted. "If the decision went against the *Times*, would reporters be vulnerable to every libel claim filed by a ticked-off sheriff?" And it wasn't just the *Times* that was at risk. All told, Southern officials had filed some seventeen libel suits against various news media, seeking damages that could total more than $288 million.[66] If they succeeded, the cost of covering race in the South would be so prohibitive that even the wealthiest national news media would have to pack up and go home.

On March 9, 1964, the Court issued its unanimous ruling in the *Sullivan* case—in favor of the *Times*. The ruling, a milestone in expanding press freedom, rewrote many of the rules under which journalism has been practiced ever since. The key finding was that the law of libel had to yield to the First Amendment. The Court held that if the award to Sullivan were allowed to stand, the result would amount to a form of government censorship of the press, tantamount to a de facto Sedition Act, forcing every journalist to prove the truth of every statement, which would in turn lead to self-censorship. Instead, the high court said that "debate on public issues should be uninhibited, robust, and wide-open, and that it may well include vehement, caustic, and sometimes unpleasantly sharp attacks on government and public officials."[67]

To make sure that journalists had the breathing room they need to report on and editorialize about the performance of public officials, the Court determined that libel should not be used to trump press freedom. Public figures like Sullivan, who voluntarily enter the public arena by seeking office, must expect to take some criticism. Henceforth it would not be enough for a public official who wanted to win a libel suit just to prove that the published material was false and defamatory. Plaintiffs would have to meet a higher burden of proof, which the Court defined as "actual malice," a legal term meaning that the material in dispute was published with the knowledge that it was false or with "reckless disregard" for the truth. Either way, public figures would have a much harder time winning such suits. The *Times*—and the rest of the media—were free to go back to Alabama and wherever else the civil rights story took them.

During the period between the *Brown* decision in 1954 and the Voting Rights Act in 1965, the civil rights movement shaped American journalism. In turn, American journalism shaped the movement. It was a dynamic, interactive process in several respects. First and foremost, the movement took the initiative and commanded attention. The media did not *make* anything happen. Some events were planned with coverage in mind, to be sure, but that is not the same thing. The fact is that the movement acted, and the media reacted. In the process, the media (that is, the mainstream white media) were changed, because for the first time in their history, they had to pay sustained attention to black Americans.

At the same time, the news media were shaping the civil rights movement in crucial ways. By carrying the words and images of the movement to a national audience, the news media *amplified* the message many-fold. This helped to push certain leaders, especially King, into prominence and to elevate certain themes. More important, the media also *nationalized* the issues raised by the movement, and in a way that certainly accelerated the profound social change. Before 1954, when blacks in the South had attempted to resist Jim Crow, their actions were considered local matters, and they were routinely suppressed by the white establishment at the local, county, or state level. With the arrival of the national media, however, that pattern was broken. Those media included the television networks (CBS, NBC, and ABC), the national news magazines like *Time* and *Newsweek*, the wire services, and a few key newspapers such as the *New York Times* and the *Washington Post*, which did not have truly national distribution in those days but were able to set the agenda in New York and Washington so that federal policy-makers and national opinion shapers could not ignore race. The power of their national reach made this possible, although nothing made it inevitable. In that setting, individual reporters like Sitton and many others rose to the occasion.

In the face of such coverage, the president, the Congress, and the federal courts all had to address the civil rights movement. It was no longer feasible or tolerable for the rights of black Americans to be suppressed piecemeal. What might have passed for local or state policy simply could not stand as national policy, in large measure because of the presence of national media coverage.

In the course of the civil rights campaign, many of the participants, too, were changed by their experiences, and many developed new and broader goals. After 1965 new leaders emerged, new issues evolved, and new tactics appeared. The next phase of the movement was distinctly different from the earlier one. For one thing, the scope shifted by the mid- to late 1960s from the South to include the

North and the West as well, which meant that covering the civil rights struggle no longer had the air of foreign correspondence. Now the stories were unfolding in the media's backyard, even if that often meant in the nearest ghetto. During this phase, the new tactics the movement adopted included riots and other forms of violence, which often made the struggle far less admirable in the eyes of those who covered it. The violence also cast a new light on the police, who were far more sympathetic figures when trying to stop urban riots than they were when setting their dogs on peaceful marchers. Finally, the movement dramatically expanded its goals, passing well beyond the realm of constitutional rights into issues of economic gains, decent housing, resistance to the war in Vietnam, and Black Power. After the assassination of Martin Luther King Jr. in 1968, the mainstream media never found an equally charismatic and eloquent leader to focus on. For all these reasons, the coverage was never as sympathetic again.

This period also saw the first serious efforts in the mainstream media to integrate the newsroom workforce. Often this was a matter of expediency, not principle. When rioting broke out in Watts, Harlem, and areas of other big cities outside the South, the media naturally flocked there to cover the violence. Suddenly, though, reporters found that they were not always welcome in the ghetto, especially if they arrived in the back seat of a squad car, as they sometimes did. So editors began hiring black reporters and photographers, for the first time in substantial numbers.[68] There were not many black students in journalism schools at the time, so the mainstream newspapers, magazines, and television news divisions recruited from the only talent pool there was: the black press. Ironically, the new hiring wave had the unintended effect of weakening the black press by luring many of the most talented young reporters away with higher pay and promises of greater professional challenges and rewards.[69] More than once, *Chicago Defender* publisher John Sengstacke complained that he was stuck "running a training school" for the big white papers.

* * *

IN THE FALL OF 1960, many Americans were still in the process of getting to know Jack Kennedy. Just forty-three years old, he represented the World War II generation, declaring himself ready to take over from Eisenhower, the very man who had commanded the young troops in wartime. Kennedy was not only young, he was also rich, good-looking, and married to a very photogenic wife. With his distinctive accent, his cool demeanor, and his ironic wit, he was well suited to the new medium that was about to make its mark on American politics in a dramatic way—television. Just in time for the 1960 election, Congress had passed a law repealing the FCC's "equal time" rule, which had required broadcasters to give equal amounts of air time to all candidates for office, including fringe candidates and cranks. In 1960, for example, there were more than a dozen political parties offering candidates for president. It would have been impossible—and perhaps illegal—for a broadcaster to hold a debate that excluded any of them.[70] In a step that went a long way toward perpetuating the dominance of the two major parties, Congress decided to lift that ban for the 1960 campaign and to have the FCC study the issue. When the new law was signed on August 24, 1960, the way was clear for the networks to approach the Democrat Kennedy and the Republican Nixon and offer them an exclusive one-on-one format for the first televised presidential debate in history.

The challenger, Kennedy, promptly agreed.[71] The establishment candidate, Nixon, hesitated. As the sitting vice president, he had more to lose in a debate, and Eisenhower urged him to decline. But Nixon did not want to give the appearance of fear, so he accepted. On September 26, 1960, the candidates met at WBBM, the CBS affiliate in Chicago, for the first of four debates. Key roles went to two members of the old Murrow team at CBS: newsman Howard K. Smith would moderate, and Don Hewitt would direct. Shortly before airtime, Nixon entered the studio from one side, Kennedy from the other. Hewitt stepped in between them and tried to break the ice, saying, "I assume you two gentlemen know each other." Then Hewitt asked Kennedy if he wanted any makeup. The senator, tanned from campaigning in California, said no. Nixon, who was exhausted from a recent illness, felt he had to decline too (though his handlers did get him to apply some "Lazy-Shave," a grooming product that was supposed to reduce the effect of Nixon's five o'clock shadow). In the debate, both men proved to be quite skillful, commanding facts and arguments with ease. But Kennedy came off as the far more appealing candidate—at least to those who watched the performance on TV. Confident, calm, witty, he captured television and never let it go.

Although Jack (and Jackie) famously enjoyed favorable press attention, the general tide of editorial opinion in U.S. newspapers and magazines favored the publishers' preferred cause, the Republican Party. In a preelection critique, Liebling quoted an October 18, 1960, headline:

U.S. DAILY NEWSPAPERS SUPPORT
NIXON 4 TO 1, SURVEY SHOWS[72]

And it was not just newspapers. At CBS, Bill Paley—now fabulously wealthy and heedless of any ethical issues raised by partisanship—was personally involved in the Nixon campaign, to which he donated $25,000, a sizable sum.[73] It has often been said that Kennedy's performance in the televised debates, in which he could speak to (and be seen by) the voters directly, put him over the top. Of course, in a close race—Kennedy won by about 100,000 votes out of some 69 million—everything matters, so it could also be said that Kennedy's claims of a "missile gap" or the suspicious votes he got out of Chicago or any number of other factors proved crucial. But given the closeness of the race, it is likely that without the television debates, he probably would not have made it. In 1960 television had arrived just in time to help put Jack Kennedy in the White House (fig. 10.4).

Of all the ways the news media helped Kennedy, probably none mattered so much as what the media did *not* do. Throughout his presidency and for years

10.4 **CBS NEWS PRODUCER DON HEWITT** gestures before the start of the first televised presidential debate, the 1960 match-up between Democrat John F. Kennedy (*seated at left*) and Republican Richard M. Nixon (*seated at right*). Before the cameras rolled, Hewitt offered Nixon make-up, which he declined.
—*Getty Images.*

afterward, reporters, photographers, and their editors turned a blind eye to some of the most reckless behavior ever engaged in by a sitting president. As Walter Cronkite explained the ethos: "In the sixties, the Washington press, like the media elsewhere, operated on a rule of thumb regarding the morals of our public men. The rule had it that, as long as his outside activities, alcoholic or sexual, did not interfere with or seriously endanger the discharge of his public duties, a man was entitled to his privacy."[74] The press corps extended to Kennedy all the traditional courtesies enjoyed by presidents, and then some. As with FDR's polio, Kennedy's crippling back pain (caused by Addison's disease) was kept from the public, along with the regimen of pills and painkillers JFK took. While the stories that were published and broadcast drew attention to Kennedy's heroism in the navy or to his wife's leopard-skin pillbox hats, the stories that were *not* published or broadcast kept the public in the dark about Kennedy's many extramarital affairs.[75]

The reporters who covered Kennedy were enablers of such behavior every bit as much as his doctors, his brother Robert, or the many presidential aides who all covered up for Kennedy. Such protection of the president may have stemmed in part from journalists' professional aspirations, expressed in their disdain for what were known as "keyhole" reporters like Winchell, who published anything and everything. By the time a reporter makes it to covering the White House, he or she usually hopes to be focused on bigger issues than the president's sex life. At the same time, the protection of the president may also have stemmed from reporters' traditional concern about access, an issue that bedevils all reporters who cover powerful people, from presidents to corporate tycoons to home-run kings. The powerful person almost always controls who gets how close, and reporters are usually suckers for the feeling of being in the know that comes from getting close to powerful newsmakers. For his part, Kennedy had an unerring sense of what reporters wanted—and what they were willing to overlook in order to get it.

During the Kennedy presidency, television news became more powerful than ever. In the years since the quiz show scandals of the 1950s, television executives had been atoning by lavishing resources on their news divisions. Television sets were in the vast majority of homes by 1960, and the audience for the TV networks dwarfed that of any newspaper and even the readership of the entire Time-Life empire. The media president, Jack Kennedy, also introduced live television coverage of presidential news conferences and proceeded to thrive in the new forum. Television carried more news than ever, to more people.

On November 22, 1963, television was the medium by which many Americans first got the news about the shooting.[76] There it was, right on TV. The president and his wife were in a motorcade with Governor John Connally and his wife. Shots rang out, and the president was rushed to the hospital. No word on the shooter's identity. It may not have been apparent to viewers, but television executives were scrambling to keep up. The networks did not have the equipment and staff needed to "go live" and put news on the air as it was unfolding. Just off camera it was pandemonium, as executives met to decide how to cover a presidential shooting in the new medium. Eventually they reached a consensus: they would stay with the story, without interruptions and without ads, for the duration.[77] So it was that for three or four days the American people did something they had never done before: they stayed home and attended a funeral via television. If they were watching CBS, they saw Walter Cronkite dab at his eye when he announced the bulletin confirming Kennedy's death (fig. 10.5). No matter what network they watched, viewers saw Jack Ruby shoot Lee Harvey Oswald; they saw the flag-draped caisson and the riderless horse; and they saw the salute given by the president's young son. For the first time (and almost the last, as it happened), nearly the entire country had nearly the same experience at the same time.

In the *New York Times,* on Monday, November 25, 1963, the front page featured a banner headline across the entire page, stacked three decks deep:

PRESIDENT'S ASSASSIN SHOT TO DEATH
IN JAIL CORRIDOR BY A DALLAS CITIZEN;
GRIEVING THRONGS VIEW KENNEDY BIER

The funeral was planned for later that day. Below the big headline was a photo (from the AP) of Jackie Kennedy and Caroline kneeling next to the president's flag-draped casket. Underneath was a little single-column story headlined:

JOHNSON AFFIRMS
AIMS IN VIETNAM

Then, this ominous subhead:

Retains Kennedy's Policy
of Aiding War on Reds

10.5 CBS NEWS ANCHOR WALTER CRONKITE struggles to keep his composure on camera as he announces the news of the death of President John F. Kennedy live on the air on November 22, 1963.
—*Getty Images.*

At the end of World War II, the publishers, editors, news directors, reporters, and photographers working for the mainstream news organizations in America did not see themselves as members of a vanguard that would soon contribute to significant social turmoil, conflict, and change. Like most of the soldiers and sailors who were busy demobilizing, the journalists who had covered the war were streaming back home, taking up their old jobs, and looking forward to regaining some semblance of normalcy. In many newsrooms the return of all those reporters and cameramen meant that some of the women hired during the wartime labor shortage now had to be let go, although many managed to hang on. Even as they withdrew to the "women's page," covering parties, recipes, and hairstyles, they provided a toehold in the newsroom for the coming generation of women journalists.

In this period, which is often described as a "Great Consensus," there were actually some serious conflicts in America, and two of the most significant were the struggles over civil rights and over communism. In both of those conflicts, the dominant news media (newspapers, the national news magazines, radio, and, increasingly, television) played a role. In both cases, that role was similar: they were reluctant agents of change. Not all the media; not all the time. But in key ways, at key stages, some individual journalists and certain news institutions exerted themselves in ways they did not have to, and those exertions had distinct consequences. Murrow (and others) did help to topple Joseph McCarthy. About a dozen news operations with nationwide reach made a vital difference in the outcome of the civil rights movement.

There were other cross-currents, too, during the period from 1945 to 1963, accelerating toward the end. The crusading reporter I. F. Stone established his muckraking weekly newspaper, taking up the tradition of self-published advocacy reaching back to William Lloyd Garrison. Socialist Michael Harrington published his investigation into poverty, *The Other America,* in 1962, reviving the social reform tradition reaching back to Jacob Riis. The scientist and writer Rachel Carson published *Silent Spring* (first as a series in the *New Yorker,* then as a book in 1962), adding a new note of alarm over chemical pollution to the grand tradition of American nature writing. In 1963, Betty Friedan published *The Feminine Mystique,* reigniting the feminist tradition reaching back as far as Margaret Fuller.

But these works, great as they were, remained cross currents in the dominant tide of the period. During the Cold War, the solidarity that many Americans had felt during World War II was reinforced by postwar anxiety over communism. Never was the mainstream more mainstream. Almost all the major institutions of news—the big daily papers, the news-oriented magazines, the news divisions of every major broadcast network—were in the hands of middle-aged white men, and almost all of them were part of a broad conservative-centrist consensus. The decision makers were not just white and male, they were almost all heterosexual, Christian, and increasingly well off. A tremendous number worked within a few blocks of one another in midtown Manhattan. It was a brief phase, a moment in which the business model and the culture were poised in a rough equilibrium. One fateful change, flagged by A. J. Liebling, was beginning to undermine that equilibrium: the start of the movement toward consolidation of ownership in the news business and the shift toward local monopolies in the newspaper business. These two (often overlapping) trends only gathered momentum in the coming decades, changing most of the vehicles that carried American journalism.

Some people consider it a tragedy that this mainstream hegemony ever changed. Many conservatives in particular seem to have this period in mind as the template of a prelapsarian Golden Age, and they regard the next two decades as a time of decline. Some now seek a restoration to a pervasive conservatism. They don't see anything wrong with bias (or even monopoly) in the mainstream media, provided that it supports a Christian, capitalist, conservative consensus. In retrospect, it can be argued that the period of comparative liberalism in the media just dawning in the mid-1960s was the aberration, not the norm.

When Edward Murrow left CBS in early 1961 to join the New Frontier, he was leaving his first love—news. As director of the U.S. Information Agency, he was in a new and uncomfortable position. For the first time in his life, he was selling something. This time it was the entire United States of America, and it was his job to sell it to the rest of the world. It must be said that he tried. He even tried to censor one program in particular that he thought would hurt the image of the United States abroad: none other than "Harvest of Shame," starring himself. He tried to sell the idea of opposing Castro, and he even tried to sell the idea of supporting the Diem regime in Vietnam. He kept smoking, several packs of Camels a day, and he stepped up his drinking.

Then in late 1963 came bad news: lung cancer. He had one lung removed and underwent radiation. By the fall of 1964 he was well enough to go to Washington to receive the Presidential Medal of Freedom, the country's highest peacetime honor for a civilian. On April 27, 1965, Murrow died, at the estate in Pawling, New York, that his earnings from television had paid for. He was fifty-seven.

CHAPTER 11

Rocking the Establishment, 1962–1972

Believe half of what you see
And none of what you hear.
—*"I Heard It Through the Grapevine," as sung by Marvin Gaye, 1968*

I**N THE FALL OF** 1962, a young correspondent arrived in Vietnam to take over the Saigon bureau of the *New York Times*. The new man was David Halberstam, and he was succeeding a reporter who was a living legend: Homer Bigart. Having covered both World War II and Korea, Bigart had seen more combat than most of the U.S. military officers serving in Vietnam. Bigart was eager to leave, but first he sat down and typed out a three-page letter to Halberstam. It was a classic handoff from a veteran to a rookie, full of advice on everything from news sources to food.

> Dear Dave:
>
> I am very glad you're going to Saigon. . . . The Caravelle is a good hotel, and the food is better than in New York. . . .
>
> A good guy at the Embassy is Barbour, in the political section. The Ambassador [Frederick Nolting] is rather complicated; sometimes he won't tell you anything, at other times he will drop a few clues in an offhand way. He's no genius, but I've seen worse. . . .
>
> The city is full of American spooks trying to silence the few honest Americans who will level with correspondents. Never reveal your sources of information. . . .
>
> The climate is like West Africa, except for some pleasant months in mid-Winter. Take a sweater for the highlands. You can have some bush

jackets made up in Saigon (the 55 Tailor) in a few days and quite cheap.
I left a lot of essential gear, canteen, messkit, belt, etc. . . .

[Signed]
Homer Bigart

PS: I never really got to know the new Vietnamese chief of information, but I hear he is a decent fellow, not like the crummy bastard that
tried to throw me out.[1]

In a sense, it was a handoff not just from Bigart to Halberstam but from the
World War II generation to a rising group of younger reporters. Bigart, who
had seen a lot of action in the Second World War and won a Pulitzer Prize for
his Korean War reporting, was then fifty-five years old; Halberstam was just
twenty-eight. Halberstam was part of an in-between generation—too young for
World War II and even Korea, but too old to be counted among the baby boom-
ers, the first of whom were born in 1946. Halberstam turned out to be a pioneer
for many of the younger American journalists who came after him in the 1960s
and 1970s, a fearless reporter who would fight for stories and fight just as hard
to keep his stories from getting suppressed by the regime in Vietnam, by certain
editors back home on the *Times* foreign desk, or even by the president of the
United States. Halberstam's reporting from Vietnam not only set the standard
for those who followed but also provided the wedge that resulted in a cultural
and political trend that would come to mark the era: the "credibility gap." This
in turn opened up American journalism to an approach that was much more
skeptical, often more honest, and ultimately more creative than it would have
been otherwise.

Even in 1962, when he took over the Saigon job, Halberstam was already a rising
star. Born in 1934 in the Bronx to a doctor father and schoolteacher mother, Halberstam grew up in the small town of Winsted in northwestern Connecticut and attended the local schools (where one of his classmates was Ralph Nader). In 1951 he
entered Harvard and stepped onto a new trajectory when he joined the reporting
staff of the independent student newspaper, the *Harvard Crimson*. After graduating in 1955 with a degree in history, Halberstam did something very unusual for a
talented, well-connected young Harvard grad from the Northeast: he went to Mississippi and got himself a job on the smallest daily newspaper in the state, the *West
Point Daily Times Leader,* where he banged out as many as a dozen stories a day. The
next year he moved up to the *Nashville Tennessean,* a progressive paper in the thick
of covering the civil rights movement. The lunch counter sit-in campaign was gathering force in Nashville just as Halberstam arrived, and he was assigned to cover it.
As a young Northerner in sympathy with the movement's goals, Halberstam was
trusted by the demonstrators, who granted him more access than any other reporter.[2] In the process, he was learning the ropes in covering conflict. During these

years Halberstam also satisfied his military obligation by spending six months in infantry training with the army, picking up some more valuable experience.[3]

In 1960 he was hired by James Reston to join the Washington bureau of the *New York Times*. After less than a year, Halberstam shipped out to cover a sizable chunk of Africa for the *Times* from a bureau in the Congo, one of many Third World flashpoints in the global conflict between the United States and the Soviet Union. There and in the surrounding countries, Halberstam got his chance to report on the central issues of Cold War journalism in the Third World: coups, communism, and combat (usually involving guerrilla tactics).

When he arrived in Vietnam in 1962, Halberstam, who would later become famous as a critic of U.S. policy, was very much a creature of the Cold War and therefore wanted the U.S. mission in Vietnam to succeed.[4] By training and perhaps by temperament he was a skeptic, but he was no rebel. He was not an anti-imperialist, and he was certainly not anti-American. In an early dispatch from Vietnam, Halberstam cabled: "young american officers have been highly impressive here comma and are admired not only for their conduct in the field but their conduct as unofficial diplomatic representatives of their country stop they and their younger vietnamese counterparts generally enjoy good personal relationships."[5] He was, by his own account, "probably a Democrat," and to that extent was inclined to support Kennedy's efforts in Vietnam. His gripes were about tactics, not strategy—about how to succeed, not about how to define success. But presidents and their aides rarely make such nice distinctions. They tend to see reporters as for them or against them. In Halberstam's case, it appears that the American mission in Vietnam took a reporter who wanted to be for them and left him nowhere to go but into the opposition.

Almost from the beginning, something about Vietnam wasn't quite right. Normally, a foreign correspondent for a prestigious newspaper like the *New York Times* would immediately be welcomed by the American elites abroad and become a fixture in the American establishment in that country. The correspondent would know the U.S. ambassador, the CIA station chief, and everyone else who mattered. In fact, it was routine practice for American journalists in the years after World War II to coordinate with the CIA when heading abroad or returning home. At a minimum, reporters could count on a briefing by the CIA about the country or region they would be covering; when they got back, it was expected that the journalists would return the favor by meeting with CIA officers to divulge anything of interest that had not already been made public in their stories or columns.[6] Not surprisingly, then, soon after Halberstam arrived in Saigon in 1962, one of his first stops was lunch with John Richardson, the CIA chief for Vietnam.

The real friction arose between Halberstam and the two most visible officials responsible for U.S. policy in Vietnam: the ambassador, Frederick Nolting, and the ranking military officer, General Paul Harkins. Halberstam expressed his views of both men in a memo he wrote to a reporter from *Esquire* magazine who was preparing a profile of Halberstam, titled "Our Man in Saigon." Halberstam referred to Nolting as "a fool, mind you, but worth talking to" and observed that he was "never invited to Nolting's house for any meal." As for the general and his relations with the press corps, Halberstam wrote, "Harkins hated our guts and tried to have our sources investigated." Halberstam came to loathe both men, but there was far more involved than personal pique. Long before most other Americans saw it, Halberstam pointed to deeper sources of antagonism between the U.S. mission and the press corps: "Some of it was an all-out attempt to keep a nice easy unruffled relationship with the [ruling] Ngo family—our stories traditionally ruffle that relationship—and part of it was that they themselves were reporting this optimistic crap [to Washington] and they didn't want any other stuff getting out."[7]

But the fundamental problem was that Nolting and Harkins were doing their damnedest to execute a policy that was unworkable, under conditions in which they felt they could not level with any correspondent. This reality created two specific sore points with Halberstam and the other reporters in Vietnam. One was a denial of access. Although reporters expect to be in the know, the ambassador and the general could not oblige them, a stance that simply sent the correspondents off in search of other sources, which they found among the junior officers and the regular foot soldiers, or "grunts." Second, the Kennedy policy of sending military "advisers" to prop up the capacity of the Diem regime to resist the communist insurgence was not working. Ngo Dinh Diem, a reclusive bachelor, was a corrupt dictator and a Catholic in a majority-Buddhist country. He had become the leader of South Vietnam after the 1954 Geneva Accords divided the country. (Among other provisions, the accords forbade outside intervention.) Diem was never a popular figure; the United States was backing him only because he was anticommunist. The South Vietnamese army, under Diem's direction, existed not to fight communism but to keep Diem in power by preventing a coup. If anyone was going to fight effectively against communism in Vietnam, it would have to be regular U.S. combat forces. But that was not the stated U.S. policy as of 1962–63, so no one could acknowledge it. Instead they stuck to the official line, which was an insult to any reporter with eyes and ears. The political imperatives of those in charge (to sell the program) were at odds with the professional imperatives of Halberstam and the rest of the press corps (to find out what was really going on). Fundamentally, the U.S. mission in Vietnam and the American correspondents stationed there were on a collision course.

In the early 1960s Halberstam was the only full-time reporter working in Vietnam for a U.S. newspaper, and since that paper was the *Times*, he was destined to become the most visible journalist in the country. But Halberstam was not the only American correspondent based in Saigon. There was a small contingent of other journalists, who were followed later by hundreds of reporters, photographers, television cameramen, producers, columnists, feature writers, spies, adventurers, and poseurs, along with brigades of military "public information officers" whose mission was the care and feeding of the vast and hungry press corps. But all that was still far off. In the early 1960s the Saigon press corps could have easily fit into one helicopter.[8] They had a lot in common, this band of friendly rivals; as was typical of the era, they were all white and all male, and no one spoke Vietnamese.

Among the news agencies with a presence in Vietnam, two of the most important, because of the enormous size of their audiences, were the U.S.-based wire services the Associated Press and United Press International. The AP bureau was led by Malcolm Browne, who was raised a Quaker and began a career as a chemist but then was drafted into the army in 1956 and ended up driving tanks in Korea. He came home and worked for several newspapers in the States (including the *Record* in Middletown, New York, where he briefly worked alongside a young reporter named Hunter S. Thompson) before joining the AP and getting his wish—to become a foreign correspondent—in his early thirties. Tall, thin, and pensive, Browne might have been mistaken for a professor if not for his wide array of sources and the bright red socks he always wore. He shared a cramped office with Horst Faas, AP's Saigon photo editor (who insisted that all AP reporters in the country carry cameras, just in case), and a young AP reporter from New Zealand, Peter Arnett. Fearless and relentless, Arnett became a legend in Vietnam. "He stayed longer, took more chances, and wrote more words read by more people than any war correspondent in any war in history," notes one observer.[9] At UPI, the AP's major competitor, the bureau consisted of a single correspondent, Neil Sheehan, who had worked his way out of the old factory town of Holyoke, Massachusetts, and into Harvard, graduating three years after Halberstam. He then joined the army, went to Korea, and worked at Stars and Stripes before joining UPI. Like his rival Browne at AP, Sheehan was young and hungry. Nobody had ever heard of either reporter in 1962, but they would before it was all over (fig. 11.1).[10]

As these correspondents went about their reporting in the early 1960s, they were on a fairly long leash. Given the state of communications, they were often hard to reach, so if their editors in New York had some brilliant idea, they might as well forget it, because by the time it arrived in Saigon, the reporter would probably be off somewhere else covering the action. Reporters thus had the happy burden of making up their own assignments. They also had pretty much the run of South Vietnam and could almost always get to the scene of any action. Sometimes the war would take place right in front of them, even in the middle of Saigon. In a guerrilla war, reporters soon realized, the battle was everywhere and nowhere. There was certainly no "front line," as there had been since time immemorial. When fighting did break out, the U.S. military usually obliged with transportation, putting reporters into any available space aboard jeeps, armored vehicles, helicopters, ships, and jets. At other times, reporters could hire a car and driver or literally take a taxi to cover the news.

On the whole, there was remarkably little censorship in Vietnam.[11] Officially,

11.1 **THESE THREE YOUNG AMERICAN JOURNALISTS** played significant roles in covering the early stages of the U.S. war in Vietnam. *Left to right:* David Halberstam of the *New York Times,* Malcolm Browne of the Associated Press, and Neil Sheehan of United Press International (who later worked for the *Times*).
—*Photo courtesy of Horst Faas.*

there was no military censorship in the traditional sense, although the United States did issue "guidelines" to all correspondents that covered the basics.[12] To be sure, first Kennedy then Lyndon Johnson tried to have individual reporters fired, and they counted on the South Vietnamese government to expel any real trouble-makers. Especially in the early years, the Diem regime made life miserable for correspondents, particularly if their reporting was critical of Diem's government. But the fact was that the United States, as a guest in an undeclared war, fighting for freedom against totalitarian communism, was in a bind and could not impose official censorship.[13]

As a result, the Pentagon brass and officials in the Kennedy and Johnson administrations felt the need to try to *sell* the war, using the techniques of public relations and news management. One approach involved the selective withhold-ing of information. Until 1967, for example, American officials did not provide a total count of U.S. troops killed and missing. At the same time, officials made a great effort to encourage reporters, especially in the early years, to "get on the team," as generations of journalists had done in previous wars.[14] They also bor-rowed techniques from public relations to try to convey the message that the United States was winning and the enemy was losing. Halberstam, for one, had seen enough of the war firsthand so that he was not buying what they were sell-ing. Neither were most of the other young resident correspondents.

Stories revealing the conflict between the military and the press abound. To take one notorious case, in December 1961 the U.S. aircraft carrier *Core* docked at the foot of Tu Do Street in Saigon, towering over the nearby buildings. Plainly vis-ible on the deck were dozens of olive drab Sikorsky H-21 helicopters. Mal Browne was among a half-dozen reporters who wanted to know what was going on, since the United States was officially only advising South Vietnam, not arming it. The reporters went to the U.S. Information Service office and asked the director about the massive ship.

"Aircraft carrier?" he asked. "What aircraft carrier? I don't see any aircraft carrier."

V.C. spies, of course, managed to see the ship and even record the serial numbers of the aircraft as they were unloaded.[15]

But there is no better example of the tensions between the military and the press than the battle of Ap Bac.[16] In February 1963, American "advisers" finally had their wish granted: they got to fight regular enemy forces, in the daytime, using armor and air support. From the beginning, U.S. military experts had been frustrated by the guerrilla tactics used by the communists: ambushes, hit-and-run attacks, booby traps, night raids. Vietcong forces usually picked their spots, assembled quickly to strike, then broke off and melted back into the jungle or the rural villages. The Americans, with their technological edge and their legacy of victory through massed forces, were spoiling for what they considered a fair fight.

When the moment arrived at Ap Bac, there was one serious problem: the army doing the fighting was not America's own. Instead the Americans were mere advisers, limited to supporting, cheering, and even cursing out the Army of the Republic of Viet Nam (ARVN, pronounced "Arvin"), the military force of the Diem government in Saigon. ARVN was supposed to be taking the lead role in defeating the Viet Cong, the communist guerrilla movement (usually referred to as the V.C.). No one tried harder to get ARVN to fight than Lieutenant Colonel John Paul Vann, then a rising star among the hundreds of U.S. military advisers in Vietnam. In the battle of Ap Bac, the ARVN forces eventually had a V.C. regiment hemmed in on three sides and needed only to call in reinforcements to seal the enemy troops in and wipe them out. In the end, the Vietnamese commander, fearing casualties, dropped his men on the wrong side, leaving the Vietcong an escape route, which they took as soon as darkness fell. ARVN did inflict some casualties that day, but it was hardly the great victory that the Diem government claimed. In fact, as Vann insisted to Halberstam and Sheehan and anyone else who would listen, it was a wasted opportunity. As the reporters told the story, it was hard to miss the point that America was trying to fight a war with an ally that did not want to fight. It was like pushing on a chain.

As the reporters in the Saigon press corps could see, the strategy was not working. More evidence came in 1963 in a series of events known as "the Buddhist crisis." The crisis began in May, when Diem traveled to Hue to celebrate the twenty-fifth anniversary of his brother's elevation to the Catholic hierarchy. For the occasion, the streets of Hue were festooned with flags, both the Vietnamese national flag and the Vatican flag. The problem was that a majority of Vietnam's people (70 to 80 percent) were Buddhists. A few days later the Buddhists of Hue were celebrating the 2,587th birthday of the Buddha, and they wanted to fly their own flag. When the Diem government said no, the Buddhists took to the streets. Someone threw a grenade, and the conflict rapidly escalated. Monks began to venture out from their pagodas, and they quickly spread the protests to Saigon

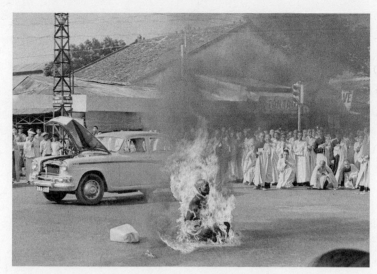

11.2 **A SHOCKING IMAGE OF PROTEST IN VIETNAM** was shot by Malcolm Browne of the Associated Press, covering the rising anti-government movement of South Vietnam's Buddhist monks. Browne took his camera to a demonstration on June 11, 1963, and captured the moment as a monk, Quang Duc, immolated himself in protest against the regime.
—*AP Photo/Malcolm Browne.*

and other cities. The Diem regime embarked on a series of clumsy crackdowns, which only made matters worse. Halberstam pounced on the story and pushed it onto the front page of the *New York Times*.

In the White House, President Kennedy, an avid reader of the *Times*, was still learning about Vietnam. After reading Halberstam's report about the Buddhists, Kennedy asked an aide: "Who are these people? Why didn't we know about them before?"[17]

On June 11, 1963, the Buddhist monks of Vietnam took center stage.[18] For weeks as the crisis built, the AP's Mal Browne had been filing stories, and he had spent a lot of time in pagodas, interviewing monks and getting a good understanding of their cause. On the night of June 10 Browne got a call from a contact among the monks, telling him there would be an important development the next morning at a small Saigon pagoda. Several Western correspondents got the same tip, but only a few showed up, including Browne and, later, Halberstam. Only Browne, under the AP photo policy, was carrying a camera.[19] After a while, a seventy-three-year-old Buddhist monk, Thich Quang Duc, went to a busy Saigon intersection and sat down in the lotus position, ringed by hundreds of other monks. Several monks doused him with gasoline, then he struck a match (fig. 11.2). As the flames rose, the monk never flinched. Browne kept working. "Numb with shock," Browne later recalled, "I shot roll after roll of film, focusing and adjusting exposures mechanically and unconsciously, almost as an athlete chews gum to relieve stress. Trying hard not to perceive what I was witnessing I found myself thinking: 'The sun is bright and the subject is self-illuminated, so f16 at 125th of a second should be right.' But I couldn't close out the smell."[20] Browne probably could not have intervened once the match was lit, even if he had been prepared. The hundreds of monks would have stopped him.

This incident, like much else that correspondents saw in Vietnam, dramatizes a problem that might be called the Journalist's Dilemma. For obvious reasons, journalists often witness tragedies and catastrophes. In the course of reporting or shooting photos, they are sometimes confronted by an apparent conflict between continuing to work or stopping to render assistance. Should the journalist step out of the traditional role of observing news and try to help? If the journalist intervenes to prevent a tragedy or to offer aid and comfort to victims, does he or she thus enter the story as a historical actor and give up any claim to practicing journalism (and along with it, perhaps, any First Amendment rights)? Close examination of many cases reveals that the Journalist's Dilemma is often an illusion. In most instances, the action unfolds so quickly that there is no time for decision making, while in others, the journalist is in fact able to observe the news, record it, and still rise to at least a basic level of humanitarian action. Still, it is in the nature of a dilemma to have no ultimate solution.

Browne's photos, which were flashed worldwide, dominated the coverage and reached the desk of President Kennedy, who was clearly upset by what he saw. The president turned to a visitor and said, "We're going to have to do something about that regime."[21]

While Kennedy pondered his relations with Diem and the Buddhists expanded their campaign against the government, Browne and Halberstam and the rest of the reporters in Saigon pressed on. Soon they were coming under attack from an unlikely quarter: the journalism establishment. Leading the criticism were a number of older columnists, reporters, and editors who made only occasional forays to Vietnam yet considered themselves more informed—on the basis of their chats with their high-ranking sources in the White House and the Pentagon—than the reporters who were there on the ground. In what became known as the "press crisis" of 1963, the Saigon-based reporters found their reporting challenged, their motives questioned, and their patriotism attacked.

One of the most prominent of the critics was a veteran of reporting World War II and Korea, Maggie Higgins. Now married to an air force general, Higgins saw Vietnam in the same frame as those two earlier wars—a straight-up military confrontation in which the United States must prevail. In late August 1963 she began a series in the *New York Herald Tribune* that ran under the logo "VIETNAM—FACT AND FICTION." In a thinly veiled assault on Halberstam, she relied on the top U.S. military officer as her chief informant. Not surprisingly, she concluded that all was well in Vietnam. "Contrary to recent published reports that the situation in the rich Mekong River delta has 'deteriorated,' Gen. Paul Harkins insists that the opposite is true," Higgins wrote. She lamented that Vietnam's image was being tarnished "at a period when the war is going better than ever." Still not finished with the young correspondents in Saigon, she slipped one in below the belt: "Reporters here would like to see us lose the war to prove they are right."[22] Her series in the *Trib* was read closely by *Times* editors back in New York, especially by the night foreign editor, Nathaniel Gerstenzang, one of Halberstam's bosses. Gerstenzang fired off a series of critical cables (known as "rockets") demanding that Halberstam justify his reporting. Eventually Halberstam blew his stack, cabling back: "GERSTENZANG IF YOU SEND ME ONE MORE CABLE REFERRING TO THAT WOMANS COPY YOU WILL HAVE MY RESIGNATION FORTHWITH BY RETURN CABLE AND I MEAN IT REPEAT MEAN IT HALBERSTAM."[23] One reason why Halberstam may have felt free to be so bold in pushing back against his editor can be found in a back channel that Halberstam had to his publisher. Even while he was fielding rockets from the foreign desk, Halberstam was also drawing a lot of support from the highest echelons at the *Times*, including raises, bonuses, and private messages of encouragement and praise (which Gerstenzang did not see). In August 1963, for example, the publisher himself, Arthur "Punch" Sulzberger, cabled Halberstam: "ALL OF US ARE REALLY PROUD OF THE OUTSTANDING JOB YOU ARE DOING UNDER SUCH ADVERSE CONDITIONS. SINCEREST CONGRATULATIONS."[24] So while Halberstam may have been under fire, he was never in any serious professional danger.

Others were not so fortunate. The most direct attack on the Saigon press corps came from *Time*, whose sniping did not spare the magazine's own correspondents. In the early 1960s Luce was getting reports from Charley Mohr and Mert Perry telling him that the communists were gaining in South Vietnam. Still determined to see Asia through the lens of his Christian anticommunism, Luce would not tolerate news he did not want to hear. So the dispatches from the field were rewritten in Manhattan. Mohr submitted a lengthy file that opened, "The war in Vietnam is being lost."[25] After it was edited in New York, it included statements such as "Government troops are fighting better than ever." Luce's top foreign editor, Otto Fuerbringer, not only rewrote the files from Vietnam but also commissioned a "Press" column attacking the messengers. The column granted that the resident reporters in Saigon competed in print against one another. "But when they meet and unwind—in the field, in their homes or in the camaraderie of the Hotel Caravelle's eighth-floor bar—they pool their convictions, information, misinformation and grievances. But the balm of such companionship has not been conducive to independent thought. The reporters have tended to reach unanimous agreement on almost everything they have seen."[26] The column went on to call the Saigon correspondents defeatists, saying that they gave short shrift to military victories by the Diem forces while harping on setbacks. For Mohr and Perry, this burst of friendly fire was the last straw, and both soon quit *Time*. As for the rest of the press corps, all they could do was seethe.

In Washington, the president was seething too. In the fall of 1963, Kennedy invited the new publisher of the *New York Times*, Punch Sulzberger, to a private session at the White House, accompanied by his Washington bureau chief, James "Scotty" Reston. Sulzberger, who was just thirty-seven and had been on the job only five months, was nervous as he headed to the meeting in late October. Instead of a friendly chat, Sulzberger found himself getting a dressing-down from the president over his paper's coverage of Vietnam. The meeting turned tense.

> "What do you think of your young man in Saigon?" Kennedy began.
> "We like him fine," Sulzberger said, somewhat taken aback.
> "You don't think he's too close to the story?" the President asked.
> No, said Sulzberger, he did not. . . .
> "You weren't," suggested the President, "thinking of transferring him to Paris or Rome?"[27]

Sulzberger may have been nervous, but he did not buckle. It was clear to him that Kennedy was trying to intimidate him and that he would have to assert his journalistic independence. The publisher told the president that his correspondent would be staying put. To make the point clear, Sulzberger instructed Halberstam to cancel an impending vacation—just so that no one would get the wrong idea and think the *Times* had caved in to pressure.

As it turned out, the press and the military were stuck with each other. After the strained start in 1962–63, the relationship only deteriorated. Although many correspondents had warm personal friendships with individual U.S. soldiers, sailors, and airmen (who were often the best sources), the fact was that relations between most of the in-country correspondents and the military brass spiraled downward into mutual distrust and even loathing. One source of constant friction was the military's campaign to sell the idea of success in Vietnam. A flashpoint was the daily news briefing in Saigon. Halberstam described the ritual this way:

> By 1965 the [U.S.] embassy was offering a briefing every afternoon at 5 p.m. It became known as the Five O'Clock Follies. An American military spokesman, usually a major, put forth what were said to be the day's military developments. The briefing officer had never been to these battles, he could not vouch for the information he was giving out, he had no sense of what really happened, but he gave it out anyway. Most of the information was based on what American officers *said* had happened and what South Vietnamese officers *said* had happened. It was a known fact of Saigon life that as the information went up from company to battalion to division and to Saigon the statistics changed. Vietcong casualties tended to rise dramatically. All of these battles were victories.
>
> It was a cynical performance. . . . In terms of news management, it was a great success. In terms of dealing with the Vietnamese Communists, it had no effect at all.[28]

Obviously, a reporter would do well to approach a briefing like the "Five O'Clock Follies" with even more than the customary professional skepticism.[29] Many reporters simply stopped going, but whether they went or not, they were all learning a lesson that became a motif of the war in Vietnam: you can't trust anyone—not even, or perhaps *especially* not, a high-ranking U.S. military officer. Forget about glory or honor. The military was, despite all the charts and statistics, losing its reputation for knowing the score. The result was the "credibility gap," a phrase that contained a sardonic echo of Kennedy's 1960 campaign charge that the Republicans had allowed a "missile gap" to develop between the United States and the Soviet Union. As much as anything else, the credibility gap was the result of a clash between the professional values held by the journalists (such as skepticism and independence) and the political values held by the policymakers and reinforced by the military values of loyalty and obedience. By 1967 the term "credibility gap" was coming into general use, as noted by correspondent Richard Harwood, who observed in the *Washington Post* that a "substantial majority" of correspondents in Vietnam had come to believe that the war was going badly, and their reporting was beginning to reflect that gloomy conclusion. The military, naturally, disagreed. Harwood wrote:

> One result of this conflict is public confusion, which the opinion polls reflect. Another result is mistrust between the press and American officialdom involved in the war in Vietnam. At a social gathering in Honolulu a few weeks ago, a correspondent was introduced to an admiral, who curtly announced, "If I'd known you were a newspaperman, I wouldn't have shaken your hand." The press corps, at times, has been no more gracious. Many of the statements issued by the American establishment in Saigon these days are challenged bluntly as propaganda or self-delusion.
>
> This "credibility gap" is a product of many factors.[30]

The long-standing partnership between the military and the press was breaking up. Gone was the candid exchange of information and views between the officer corps and the press corps of the World War II era. The two groups were no longer on the same team, and they would not be again for at least a generation. Vietnam was the wedge that opened a widening split between the news media and a growing number of institutions.

*   *   *

BY THE MID-1960S TELEVISION HAD become nearly universal in U.S. homes, and it was that change that made Vietnam the first "living room war." Television also shaped the thinking of policymakers, including President Johnson, who had three TV sets installed in the Oval Office so he could keep an eye on the network news reports, which were reaching a combined audience of some 35 million Americans every evening. From the correspondent's point of view, the technology of television was still crude. Mal Browne, after leaving the AP, worked for a few years for ABC Television and continued to cover Vietnam. Although his photos of the burning monk became a famous symbol of the war, Browne never considered himself a photographer, and he quickly came to appreciate the television cameramen, the guys who humped around the heavy equipment that made it possible to film the fighting in the field. He wrote: "A network of electric umbilical cords connected the Auricon to the soundman and his recording controls, and to a microphone clutched in the hand of the correspondent. Joined together as a cursed trinity, a television crew would leap together from an alighting helicopter and run in cadence through ground fire like three monkeys holding each other's tails."[31]

Color television was becoming commonplace in the second half of the 1960s, and the camera's eye left little to the imagination: viewers saw death and destruction on a regular basis, red blood on green uniforms, right in their living rooms.[32] One shocking early television report that became an iconic image of the war in Vietnam was done by Morley Safer of CBS. Safer, a Canadian still in his early thirties, had already covered Europe, Africa, and the Middle East before arriving in Saigon in 1965 to open a bureau for CBS, part of the influx of full-time television correspondents that coincided with Johnson's huge escalation of U.S. combat forces in Vietnam that same year. CBS executives told Safer to plan to stay for six months, tops—because American troops would not be remaining long in Vietnam.

That August, looking for action to cover near Da Nang, Safer accompanied a marine unit to a village called Cam Ne.[33] When he asked a captain about the nature of the mission, he was told that the marines had drawn some fire from the area. "We've had orders to take out this complex of villages," the captain told him. Safer was puzzled by the term "take out" in that setting. Were they going to eliminate a whole village, which appeared not to be a major enemy military installation? Or was the captain perhaps exaggerating?

As the troops approached the village, firing broke out. Then the marines set fire to the houses, using flamethrowers or, if need be, their own cigarette lighters. As Safer watched, a marine with a flamethrower approached one thatched house. He heard his Vietnamese cameraman shout, trying to point out that there were people inside. Sure enough, there was a family in the house, crouched in a tiny shelter. As soon as the cameraman coaxed them out, the marines went back to work. As Safer recalled, "The house was torched, as every house along the way was torched, either by flamethrowers, matches, or cigarette lighters—Zippos," specifying the brand that so many troops carried. Despite the pleas of the villagers, marines burned every house in Cam Ne, along with the contents and rice supplies. Four prisoners were captured—all old men. When the piece aired on CBS on August 5, 1966, it had a tremendous impact. Marine Corps officials, according to Safer, went ballistic, denying that any such thing had happened, despite the filmed evidence.

At the White House, the president was furious too. CBS president Frank Stanton was awakened by his telephone ringing:

"Frank, are you trying to *fuck* me?" asked the angry voice.

"Who is this?" a groggy Stanton replied.

"Frank, this is your president, and yesterday your boys *shat* on the American flag!"

Johnson continued to berate the CBS executive, demanding to know if Safer was some kind of communist and threatening an investigation of the CBS newsman.[34]

For American TV viewers, the CBS report from Cam Ne was also troubling, but for a different reason. They could see U.S. soldiers inflicting what looked like egregious damage on civilians. For American veterans of World War II and their admiring children, this was something new: American soldiers acting like bullies rather than liberators.

What was going on over there?

* * *

IN THE MID-1960S PUNCH SULZBERGER was facing plenty of problems running the *New York Times* that had nothing to do with Vietnam. As publisher and steward of the family business (which, because of its prominence in the journalistic Fourth Estate, was considered something of a public trust), Sulzberger faced numerous pressures. Not only had he inherited the family's sense of duty to journalistic excellence, but also he bore a burden that no one in the newsroom shared with him: he had to make sure that the *Times* remained afloat as a business enterprise. The paper had to make money, and ideally lots of it, in order to subsidize all its other goals. As publisher, Sulzberger was the only person in the entire company with responsibilities that crossed the line between the news side and the business side. The paper's hundreds of reporters, photographers, and editors were supposed to focus only on the journalism, while its many printers, drivers, ad sellers, circulation managers, accountants, lawyers, and executives were all supposed to focus on making the money to pay for the journalism. The two camps were entirely separate, each with its own chain of command. The arrangement, often referred to as a "separation of church and state," and widely imitated throughout the news business with varying degrees of success, was intended to protect the newsroom from any undue influence by advertisers or anyone else. Ultimately, everyone on both sides of the divide reported to Sulzberger.

The *Times* was making money in the mid-1960s, but the question facing the publisher was how to protect its legacy and extend the franchise into future generations. One challenge had been the 1963 New York City newspaper strike, in which the printers and other craft unions forced the shutdown of every big daily in the city for 114 days. The *Times* and the other papers lost advertising revenues during the strike, then had to accept an expensive settlement. In 1965 the *Times* caved in again to the unions in another expensive settlement. The only way Sulzberger could see to maintain the paper, fund the union contracts, and prepare for the future was to diversify into other fields besides the flagship newspaper. "It became so obvious that having all our eggs in one basket was a dangerous business philosophy," he once said.[35] Sulzberger began to diversify modestly in the mid-1960s, but to continue that policy, especially if he wanted to acquire bigger companies, he would need lots more cash. To get that kind of money, there was one obvious source: the stock market.

So, responding to a variety of pressures, Sulzberger came to the conclusion that he would have to sell stock in the Times Company to the general public. Going public was a proven means of raising capital, but it brought certain risks. A major issue was control of the company, which had been in the family since the purchase by his grandfather, Adolph Ochs, back in 1896. Ordinarily, when a company goes public, it changes ownership and ends up in the hands of the thousands—or millions—of strangers who buy the stock. The new shareholders typically care about one thing only: they want the company to make as much money as possible so that the company will pay them nice dividends and the price of the stock will rise. Along with their share of the company, the shareholders also get the power to approve the top management and the right to sue those managers if they don't perform. How would that ownership model fit with the idea of stewardship that Punch Sulzberger had inherited? How could he keep faith with past and future generations and ensure that the family's values would continue to guide the enterprise? How could he follow the journalistic imperative to provide all the news that's fit to print and do it without fear or favor? Would the new shareholders see the business that way? Maybe people who didn't care about journalism would buy the stock. What then?

Such were the issues he was facing in 1968 as he neared the decision to go public. There was also an immediate practical problem: the American Stock Exchange would not list the stock because it came with a proviso that denied the shareholders the right to vote on the management. People were supposed to buy the stock but get no say in running the company. All the control was to stay with the Sulzberger family, who would hold a special category of Times stock called Class B shares. In the end, under terms of a compromise, the company was allowed to offer Class A shares to the public with limited voting rights (capped at electing 30 percent of the Times Company's board members), while the family could keep the Class B shares and control 70 percent of the board. As long as family members held onto the Class B stock or traded it only among one another, they could control the paper forever. At the same time, they would enjoy the infusion of fresh capital that came from selling stock to the public. It seemed like the perfect solution. On January 14, 1969, New York Times Company Class A stock went on sale, opening at $42 a share.[36]

The *Times* was not the first newspaper to go public. That had been done a few years earlier, in 1963, by the business-oriented Dow Jones Company, the publisher of the *Wall Street Journal*. This started a trend among American newspapers, which had been in private hands for generations.[37] The chains built by Hearst, Scripps, Pulitzer, and others were all private companies, usually owned by one person or several family members. As the founders died, many families discovered that they needed cash to pay estate taxes, or they realized that the next generation

TABLE 11.1

Newspapers go to Wall Street to raise funds

DATE OF PUBLIC OFFERING	COMPANY
1963	Dow Jones
1964	Times Mirror
1966	Richmond Newspapers (later Media General)
1967	Gannett Corporation
1969	New York Times Company, Knight Newspapers, Ridder Publications
1971	Washington Post Company
1981	A. H. Belo
1983	Tribune Company
1986	Pulitzer
1988	McClatchy
1994	Hollinger
1997	Journal Register
1998	E. W. Scripps

had no interest in the news business. Then, too, all these companies needed more capital if they were to grow and expand in the late-twentieth-century economy. For some combination of these reasons, one newspaper company after another began going public in the late 1960s, including Gannett and the company produced by the merger of the Knight and Ridder chains. Most other large papers and newspaper chains followed suit in three flurries of activity—one lasting from the mid-1960s to the early 1970s, the next in the mid-1980s, and the last in the late 1990s (see Table 11.1).

Going public was a fateful step for newspapers, because it meant a change in the business model that had supported most American journalism for more than a century. Just as the original model of the colonial print shop gave way to the partisan press of the early republic, the subsidized party papers gave way to the new dynamic of the penny press. Those commercial papers tried to pay for newsgathering by appealing to a mass audience, which would not only pay for the paper but also attract advertisers. That model, dramatically expanded to an industrial scale in the late nineteenth and early twentieth centuries, turned out to be a mighty engine of profit. Although newspapers were now operating on a larger scale than ever before, ownership remained in the hands of individuals and families. They generated new capital out of earnings, or they borrowed money from banks. Until Dow Jones went public, no newspaper company had resorted to the stock market.

Generally those family-run newspapers were moneymakers, sometimes creating large private fortunes. There had always been exceptions, of course, such as the nonprofit Associated Press, or the occasional money-losing publication that was kept afloat by a generous patron or some backer with non-economic motives, such as a church or labor union. Then, starting in the 1920s, some of the leading institutions in American journalism introduced the "public company" model into the news field. Among the earliest were radio companies such as CBS and NBC, as well as the magazine empire founded by Henry Luce. But while those companies sold stock to the public, they remained the creatures of their founders as long as they were alive. Bill Paley, David Sarnoff, and Harry Luce all owned enough stock and carried enough clout so that they were able to run their companies almost as if they were the sole proprietors. With the passing of that generation, however, those companies too began to conform to the public model and to behave like typical big corporations.[38]

As more and more news businesses became big businesses in the 1960s and 1970s, they grew in scale and in influence. They usually made their founders very wealthy, and they often made money for their shareholders; sometimes they made some of their employees quite wealthy too. Luce, for example, had a personal fortune of about $100 million; Paley's holdings of CBS stock were worth about the same.[39] But all that came at a cost. Most of the major news organizations were losing control of their own destinies. As publicly traded companies, they were subject to regulation by the federal government's Securities and Exchange Commission. They were vulnerable to shareholder lawsuits and hostile takeovers. They were legally bound to seek the highest possible return on their shareholders' investments. They could be bought and sold just like a company that made nails or soap, cigarettes or jet engines. They could be combined and recombined with other companies, captured like so many pieces on a corporate chessboard. From now on they could be owned by people who didn't care about journalism, or who didn't even like journalists.

* * *

THE TRUTH ABOUT THE NEW JOURNALISM, which seemed to burst onto the scene in the mid-1960s, is that it actually had roots in the old journalism. John Hersey, for one, had pioneered many of the trademarks of the New Journalism nearly twenty years earlier. He had already written the acclaimed novel *A Bell for Adano* before tackling the immense devastation of Hiroshima. In his reporting on the A-bomb's impact on the ground, Hersey immersed himself in the lives of his six protagonists, accumulating detail upon detail. When it came time to write, Hersey reached into the toolbox of the novelist and developed his masterpiece through scenes, dialogue, and character. In his telling of *Hiroshima,* Hersey did not break his narrative stance and pull back into the point of view of the neutral observer. The entire story is related through its characters, scene by scene, just as in a novel. Hersey's piece was, of course, extraordinary—both for its content and for its technique.

The fact was that by the 1950s and early 1960s American journalism had a serious problem: most of it was boring. From time to time there were startling, great works written by immensely talented individuals—writers like Michael Harrington (*The Other America,* 1962), Rachel Carson (*Silent Spring,* 1962), Jessica Mitford (*The*

American Way of Death, 1963). There were some lonely outposts such as the weekly *I. F. Stone Reader* and the *Village Voice.* These had a lot of impact on the public, and they stand tall in the ranks of progressive muckraking, but they did not do much to change the practice of journalism itself. On the whole, the news business was still rather plodding—familiar beats, familiar styles, familiar white guys working the usual tropes of politics, business, sports. Journalism was like a horse wearing blinders, making its regular rounds oblivious to all sorts of activity just outside its field of vision: black Americans showed up in its pages only when they committed crimes against white people, women only when they gave birth, got married, or held a fashion show. The whole enterprise was ossified, rigid, running on inertia.

At the high end, though, some really ambitious craftsmen were pushing the limits. One of them was a genre-bending young writer, Truman Capote, who first began to cross literary boundaries in the early 1960s. Born in New Orleans, young Truman had been sent to live with relatives in the tiny town of Monroeville, Alabama. Lonely and bookish, he had one close friend there, a tomboy about his age named Nelle Lee. When Truman was a teenager, his mother remarried and retrieved the boy, moving to New York. After a long literary apprenticeship, he established himself as a dramatist and novelist during the 1950s; his *Breakfast at Tiffany's* cemented his reputation in 1958. Then, in late 1959, Capote happened to notice a small wire-service item in the *New York Times* about the murder of a perfectly respectable wheat farmer and his family in Holcomb, Kansas. Although he was hardly a crime writer, Capote found something about the case absorbing. So off he went—to the heart of the heartland, to a tiny town of unpaved roads and unlocked houses. "It was as strange to me as if I'd gone to Peking," Capote recalled.[40]

For his part, Truman Capote must have been one of the strangest sights ever to greet the plain people of Holcomb. A pale, gnomish figure, Capote had enormous eyes and a high, sometimes whiny voice. He favored bow ties, and he had a large collection of stylish hats—not just gimme caps from John Deere or fertilizer companies, but beautiful fedoras, Stetsons, and other serious headgear. He was frankly effeminate, probably the first gay man most folks in Holcomb thought they had ever met. At the same time, most of the farmers and townspeople in western Kansas had never met a writer from New York City, either, especially not one who was obsessively interested in them. In any case, Capote immersed himself in the crime, the town, and the people. He spent enormous amounts of time with the two convicted killers, conducting lengthy interviews in their jail cells. On many of his long visits to Holcomb, Capote had the assistance of his old friend Nelle Lee (who was also a writer, and who decided to use her middle name, Harper, for literary purposes). Truman, who was already successful as a writer, invited Nelle—who was finishing her masterpiece, *To Kill a Mockingbird,* but was still unknown to the general public—to be his research assistant.[41] Toting her Underwood typewriter, she took abundant notes and helped break the ice with many residents of Holcomb and the nearby county seat, Garden City. Capote worked on the murder story for six years, right through the executions of the two killers. Then, in September 1965, the results began appearing in a four-part "Annals of Crime" series in the *New Yorker*. In January 1966, Random House published the book version, *In Cold Blood*, which had a mammoth initial printing of 100,000 copies; it had already been sold to the Book of the Month Club and to Hollywood.

In terms of traditional journalism, Capote was certainly an innovator, and like many innovators, he was a focus of criticism from the old guard. One objection had to do with his reporting technique. Not only did he not use a tape recorder, but also he did not even take notes. Capote claimed that he did not need to take notes because he had trained himself, through many hours of practice, to remember what people told him. After a day of interviews, he would go back to his room and write down all the verbatim quotations he could recall. (Nelle Lee used the traditional method of taking notes.) Skeptical journalists and others questioned how accurate such recollections could possibly be. One critique appeared in *Esquire* in June 1966 under the mocking title "In Cold Fact."

With *In Cold Blood*, Capote was also innovating in terms of the essential nature of the work he was doing. He claimed to have invented a new literary form, which he called the "nonfiction novel." In a series of interviews, he expounded on what that paradoxical term might mean.[42] Capote made clear that he was self-consciously forging a new art form. With that in mind, he said it was essential, first, for the writer to pick a subject that will not become dated; it should be a recurring problem or a timeless situation. Then the challenge is to take the techniques of the novel—a deliberately chosen point of view; a narrative structure; a concern for pacing, tone, and other purely aesthetic issues—and raise the degree of difficulty by limiting the possible topics to things that had actually happened. His goal was for his book to read just like a novel but for nothing to be made up:

> My theory, you see, is that you can take *any* subject and make it into a nonfiction novel. By that I don't mean a historical or documentary novel—those are popular but impure genres, with neither the persuasiveness of fact nor the poetic attitude of fiction. . . . What I have done is much harder than a conventional novel. You have to get away from your own particular vision of the world. Too many writers are mesmerized by their own navels. I've had that problem myself—which was one reason I wanted to do a book about a place absolutely new to me, one where the terrain, the accents, and the people would all seem freshly minted. I thought it would sharpen my eye and quicken my ear.[43]

Capote was not alone in chafing at the bounds of genre in the mid-1960s. Around the same time, other writers were also trying to escape the gravitational pull of traditional journalism. A young reporter at the *New York Times* named Gay Talese was doing something similar in a series of magazine-length profiles.

Talese, the son of an immigrant tailor (and quite a snappy dresser), had begun to make a name for himself with meticulously reported articles, often written for *Esquire* magazine on top of his duties at the *Times*. In late 1965 he tackled one of the most difficult journalistic subjects in the country: Frank Sinatra. As he neared age fifty, Sinatra was the biggest, most elusive, and most menacing of all the big game that reporters stalked, and he made it clear that he did not like report- ers and had no intention of cooperating. None of this mattered to Talese, who burned through something like $5,000 in expenses while interviewing all of the coat-holders, flaks, ex-wives, pals, producers, and other members of the Sinatra entourage who *would* talk to him. The result was a piece for *Esquire* in 1966 titled "Frank Sinatra Has a Cold," which almost immediately became a landmark in journalism. The much-talked-about article (for which Sinatra never did consent to an interview) was told almost entirely in a series of scenes, set in Beverly Hills, New York, and Las Vegas. In the piece, the singer's character is slowly revealed, as it might be in a short story, through the things he says and does and through the way those around him relate to him or talk about him. By using action, dialogue, and description, Talese bagged the big one. Many writers who came after him could recall the first time they read a piece by Gay Talese the way baseball fans remember a certain pennant-winning home run.[44]

The movement also got a goosing from Tom Wolfe, a young feature writer at the *New York Herald Tribune* who dreamt of writing the Great American Novel. Working in his spare time as a freelancer for *Esquire* magazine, Wolfe profiled a young boxer named Cassius Clay, then talked his editor, Byron Dobell, into let- ting him cover the Kustom Kars craze in southern California. The result was a tour de force of intense observation and bravura storytelling. In the November 1963 *Esquire*, the piece appeared under the memorable headline:

> There goes (VAROOM! VAROOM!)
>> that Kandy-Kolored (THPHHHHHH!)
>> tangerine-flake streamline baby (RAHGHHHH!)
>> around the bend (BRUMMMMMMMMMMMMMMMM . . .)

By the mid-1960s the movement was starting to reach escape velocity. In part the success of what was coming to be known as the New Journalism was due to the sheer talent of its founders. They inherited a problem in their field, which was becoming set in its ways, and they tackled it with style and verve.[45]

Another reason for the success of the New Journalism was institutional. Like the innovators of any new creative movement, the practitioners of this hybrid form of journalism needed patrons. They did not find them among the lords of the newsroom, the editors of America's daily newspapers, who mostly thought these writers had lost their bearings (and maybe their sanity). Instead the New Journal- ists found sympathy, encouragement, expense accounts, and pretty good pay at a handful of magazines with extraordinary editors. One of the most influential was Clay Felker, who edited the Sunday supplement published by the *Herald Tribune*.[46]

It was an incubator for the talents of the young Tom Wolfe and a columnist named Jimmy Breslin. Felker, who had previously worked at *Esquire,* stayed at the *Trib,* cultivating good new writers—such as Gloria Steinem—wherever he could find them, until the newspaper folded in 1967. Then he took the nameplate of the *Trib*'s Sunday magazine, *New York,* and turned it into the prototype "city magazine." In the early days, *New York* magazine also served as one of the unofficial headquarters of the New Journalism.[47] A second clubhouse was not far away in Manhattan, at the offices of *Esquire* magazine. Under editor Harold Hayes, *Esquire* published many of the foundational pieces of the New Journalism, including Norman Mailer's 1960 meditation on JFK, "Superman Comes to the Supermart," and Gay Talese's famous profiles of Joe DiMaggio and Frank Sinatra. Elsewhere in Manhattan, literary agents and editors at book publishing houses were starting to talk to some of these hotshot young writers, and some of those journalists quit their newspaper jobs to become full-time *writers.*

At the same time, other people, operating far from Manhattan and its slick, high-paying magazine world, were creating new publications around the country that would also help to sustain the New Journalism.[48] Here and there, these newspapers were cropping up in the mid-1960s, often modeled on the *Village Voice* and offering a mix of arts coverage, left-wing politics, and notes on the emerging counterculture. These "underground" or "alternative" papers were usually printed on cheap newsprint, and they were often sustained by ads for rock concerts, rolling papers, and head shops. In every issue they carried an implied challenge to the straight media: Why are you so dull? Of all the alternative, rock-oriented publications of the mid-1960s, none was more important than the one started in San Francisco in late 1967 by a young Berkeley dropout named Jann Wenner. He called his new magazine *Rolling Stone,* and he had one supreme goal: to capture the energy and wonder of the new music being made by the likes of the Beatles, the Rolling Stones, Bob Dylan, and the Grateful Dead. Wenner wanted to write about rock music, for sure, but he also wanted his magazine to capture the broader zeitgeist of the emerging youth culture. One of his most fruitful partnerships was with a singular figure, Hunter S. Thompson.

A native of Louisville, Thompson wound up in the air force in the mid-1950s and became the sports editor of his base newspaper. Criticized for his "rebel and superior attitude," Thompson was soon drummed out of the military, and he made his way to New York to seek his fortune in journalism.[49] Somehow he got himself to South America and sold a handful of articles about it to *National Observer,* a weekly paper owned by the Dow Jones company. In 1965 Thompson read Tom Wolfe's anthology of magazine articles titled *The Kandy-Kolored Tangerine-Flake Streamline Baby.* Thompson was wowed by Wolfe's writing, and he wrote a rave review for the *Observer.* His editor disapproved of Wolfe and spiked the review. Thompson (characteristically) flew into a rage and swore he'd never write there again. Around the same time, the strangest thing happened: Thompson, who was living hand-to-mouth in the Haight district in San Francisco, got an inquiry from the editor of *The Nation* magazine asking if he would be interested in writing an article about a band of outlaws in California who rode motorcycles.

Thus began one of the great pairings of writer and subject: Hunter S. Thompson and the Hells Angels. Thompson plunged into the story—not just reporting on the Angels but hanging with them, drinking with them, and riding with them. The magazine article turned into a book contract, which allowed him to spend many months with some of the most unpredictably violent men in the country who were not already in prison. Ultimately, Thompson said the wrong thing to the wrong guy. He suffered a serious beating and nearly got his skull bashed in. Thompson put it all into his book, which was scheduled for publication in February 1967. At the time, the twenty-one-year-old Wenner was working as an assistant editor at *Ramparts,* and he saw the magazine's advance copy of Thompson's book. "It knocked me out," Wenner said later. He decided to pursue the writer and get him into the new magazine that Wenner was about to launch.

Meanwhile, Thompson kept writing. In 1970 he accepted an assignment from Warren Hinckle at *Scanlan's Monthly* magazine to cover the Kentucky Derby. The magazine teamed him up with a satirical British cartoonist named Ralph Steadman. The result was a minor masterpiece. The article, titled "The Kentucky Derby Is Decadent and Depraved," showcased a full-throated Thompson writing with absolutely no inhibitions. It is also considered the piece that launched a subgenre of the New Journalism known as "Gonzo journalism." One of the defining features of Gonzo was Thompson's shrewd discovery that his greatest character was himself. By processing all his sensory experiences and reflections through his own (altered) consciousness, Thompson turned most of his reporting into an investigation of his internal states, often flamboyantly distorted by illegal drugs. This was a brilliant move because it allowed him to explore uncharted territory, and it allowed him to say the most outrageous things without fear of a libel suit from the other people in his stories. Jacked up on amphetamines and bourbon, Thompson could entertain the most outrageous thoughts and "report" it all as straight interior monologue. The technique served him well through the piece about the Derby and his two book-length masterpieces, *Fear and Loathing in Las Vegas* and *Fear and Loathing on the Campaign Trail '72.* In his book about the 1972 presidential election, Thompson revealed something else, something unexpected: underneath that drug-crazed, cynical, menacing exterior, it turned out that Hunter S. Thompson was an idealist, a patriot who felt really disappointed that his country so rarely lived up to its promise.

In the nick of time, the New Journalists sent a jolt through American journalism. Gone was the understatement and detachment of Lippmann or Murrow. Instead, journalists could have feelings. They could get mad, they could get happy. They could appear in their own stories. (How else could Gloria Steinem have possibly captured what it felt like to work as a Playboy bunny than to write about her own bra-stuffing, tail-pulling experience?)[50] They could use every key on the keyboard, as Wolfe did, tap-dancing through QWERTY and hammering

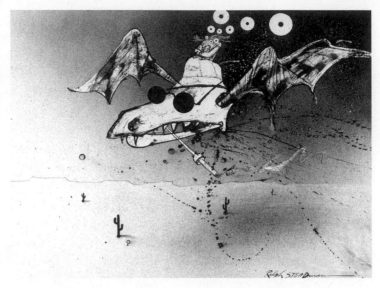

11.3 THE "SPIRIT OF GONZO" floats over the desert in this drawing by Ralph Steadman—the colleague, collaborator, and occasional co-conspirator of journalist Hunter S. Thompson. Steadman's drawings and Thompson's writings combined to produce extraordinary effects. —*Illustration by Ralph Steadman.*

on the exclamation point !!!!!!!!!!!!!!!!!!!! (It's still fun to do, but it was a lot more athletic in the days of manual typewriters, when you could set the shift key and then whale away.) Writers could now tackle all kinds of topics, straying far from the well-marked terrain of cops, pols, Wall Street, and sports. If you could write about Kustom Kars, why not write about hippies? If you could write about Hells Angels, what about astronauts? What about the last guy in America who makes canoes out of birch bark? How about the war? What about vaginas? What the hell? Why not write about everything??? Yes, yes, yes!!!!!!!

Funny thing: despite the resistance by many in the old guard, the New Journalists swept all before them. In the end, just about everybody wanted to get on that bus (fig. 11.3).

* * *

BY TURNS AMAZING, SHOCKING, DEPRESSING, inspiring, and enraging, the news in 1968 seemed to have entered some uncharted realm. Things started normally enough. Americans woke on the first day of the year to read a UPI story reporting that the Census Bureau put the U.S. population at just over 200 million. By the end of the year, the country had seen and read about shocking reversals in Vietnam, two major assassinations, rioting at the national political conventions and in the streets of many urban ghettoes, hippies, Yippies, miniskirts, dope, and free love. To top it off, in November, Republicans Richard Nixon and Spiro Agnew crushed the Democrats, Hubert Humphrey and Edmund Muskie. Weeks later the Beatles released their latest album. It had no name, just a white cover, and it included two versions of a song called "Revolution." *Did they mean it?*

That same year, the music that fueled youth culture got a major media partner in the form of that new magazine from San Francisco, *Rolling Stone*. It had been founded the year before, but in 1968 it really began to take off, gaining national circulation—in part on the strength of young vagabonds who crisscrossed the country, following rock bands, going to concerts, always heading farther down those long, long roads. They carried *Rolling Stone* with them from Berkeley to Boston and from Austin to Madison, sharing it with friends, turning them on to a new voice that was right on their wavelength. *Rolling Stone* had caught the wave of hip culture, youth culture, and rock 'n' roll. It was not the first "alternative" paper, and it was far from the only one; it was not even the only one covering the music scene. But *Rolling Stone* was one of a kind. It was not spying on the scene like *Time* or *Newsweek*; it was *part* of the scene. Like the music itself, each new issue of *Rolling Stone* was something of an adventure. Who would be on the cover? What taboo might fall? Whose weird new writing style might emerge from those acres of prose?

Out with the old.

Change came in 1968 to television, too.[51] Network television had reached a plateau by the late 1960s. The evening newscasts were now thirty minutes long, but gone were the days of a multihour prime-time news special like *See It Now* or a documentary report like "Harvest of Shame." Under the rules of the FCC and the demands of stockholders, the new generation of corporate executives who followed Sarnoff and Paley at the top of the television networks were cautious men whose goal was to make money by renting audiences to advertisers. To the well-paid executives who ran the networks, the news divisions of ABC, NBC, and CBS were potential headaches. They always lost money, and they could anger any number of people with all those images of dead soldiers in Vietnam, assassinations at home, riots in the cities, protests on campus. The major redeeming feature of TV news, as far as the corporate brass were concerned, was that it seemed to satisfy the FCC requirement that broadcasters operate in "the public interest," and the news divisions generated a certain amount of goodwill, even prestige.

That world was turned upside down in 1968, and from an unlikely source—from within the ranks of CBS News. The still-young news producer Don Hewitt (who had handled the Nixon-Kennedy debates in 1960) had a new idea, which he pitched to Dick Salant, who had replaced Fred Friendly as head of CBS News: "Why don't we try to package sixty minutes of reality as attractively as Hollywood packages sixty minutes of make-believe?"[52] In other words, what about putting news on the air in prime time? Until then, the forms of journalism on television were fairly few and firmly fixed. The evening newscast was an attempt to put the day's newspaper on the air. The occasional one- or two-hour documentary was an attempt to put the equivalent of a book on the air. Hewitt found a sweet spot in between these models by doing what amounted to putting a magazine on the air. He called it *60 Minutes,* and it debuted on CBS on September 24, 1968, featuring the television journalists Mike Wallace and Harry Reasoner (fig. 11.4).[53]

11.4 **CBS NEWS PRODUCER DON HEWITT** spearheaded the creation of the prime-time weekly television news "magazine" called *60 Minutes* in 1968. Hewitt is shown (*seated in foreground*) with the show's early team of on-air journalists: (*left to right*) Morley Safer, Dan Rather, and Mike Wallace.
—*Getty Images.*

By this point, journalism had been practiced long enough that it had the equivalent of a big attic that Hewitt could rummage around in. From the news-oriented print magazines like *Time* and *Life,* he took the basic pacing and rhythm for *60 Minutes,* which meant covering a variety of subjects each week. The show would be topical and timely, but it did not have to rehash all the news. From the old Hearst press he took the idea of casting his correspondents as the real heroes of most pieces. Mike Wallace and Harry Reasoner would not be distant observers; they would be present in every piece, on camera—asking questions, getting answers, busting frauds, and righting wrongs (even if they did not personally do all of the reporting they appeared to have done). From the muckrakers Hewitt took the drama of the righteous quest with a social purpose. From the old Murrow show *Person to Person* he took the gloss and lift that would come from spending time with celebrities. And from his own head, he pulled the overall look and feel of a program that would become the most popular in the history of television news. Not only did *60 Minutes* invent a new genre, but also it transformed the economics of television news. It did that by doing something television news had not done before: it made money. Slowly at first as it jumped around the schedule in the early years, but then increasingly after settling in at 7:00 p.m. on Sundays, *60 Minutes* began making lots of money. Over the next two decades it earned well over $1 billion for CBS, and Hewitt went so far as to boast that over its long run, the show was "the biggest money-maker in the history of broadcasting."[54] No longer was news just a loss leader, a prestigious public service; now the news division could be a profit center for the network as well, just like the entertainment division. Confirmation arrived in the form of imitation: ABC came along with a weekly news magazine called *20/20,* and NBC came up with *Dateline.* TV news was now a business, and a big business at that.

There was one exception to profit-driven television news—not very significant at first, but eventually a major one. That exception proved that there could be news on television that was not merely *not* making a profit but was not even trying to. That exception was public broadcasting. It was an idea that had been around for a while, mainly espoused by professors and by the people who worked at the old-line foundations. Then quite abruptly, in late 1967, Lyndon Johnson took a shine to it, and before you knew it, he'd rammed a bill through Congress creating the Corporation for Public Broadcasting (CPB). At the signing ceremony Johnson took a characteristically expansive view. He invoked the memory of Samuel F. B. Morse and the $30,000 subsidy Morse had received from Congress to establish the first working telegraph line back in 1844. "Every one of us should feel the same awe and wonderment here today," the president said. He envisioned public TV as part of the Great Society, the part that would try to transcend economic security and reach for culture, education, and uplift. He explained:

> It will get part of its support from our Government. But it will be care-fully guarded from Government or from party control. It will be free, and it will be independent—and it will belong to all of our people.
>
> Television is still a young invention. But we have learned already that it has immense—even revolutionary—power to change, to change our lives. I hope that those who lead the Corporation will direct that power toward the great and not the trivial purposes.[55]

Johnson did not spell out exactly how the new, public corporation was supposed to be independent, objective, balanced, and responsible all at the same time. Nor did he explain how an institution that was spending the tax money of all the American people was supposed to make all of them (and their representatives in Congress, from both parties) happy. That was for the future.

For now, the CPB spent 1968 building a staff and creating the two major sub-sidiaries that would carry out the actual work of public broadcasting: National Public Radio and the Public Broadcasting System. Here was another new business model in mass media. Public radio and television would be noncommercial—no advertising, no stockholders, and no profits. Instead they would have three major sources of funds. One was the public subsidy funneled from the U.S. Treasury to CPB and thence to NPR and PBS. A second source was foundations. The third source would be the viewers and listeners themselves, who would be getting rid of ads but winding up with pledge drives instead. The ratio of those sources has var-ied over the years, although the taxpayers' share has consistently declined. From the beginning, public broadcasting waded into the troubled waters of presenting news and public affairs programming.

Also from the beginning, most Republicans in Congress hated public broad-casting and tried to eliminate it. Part of the objection was philosophical, based on the principles of free enterprise. They argued that if there was a market for such highbrow fare on television or radio, then some profit-seeking business would cater to it. There was no need for the government to involve itself in business, period. Then, too, there were the political suspicions. Some Republicans worried that if they set up a national TV and radio network and cut it loose from the need to make money, it would attract liberals and Democrats and all kinds of artists, poets, and other people who are likely to criticize those in power. To address such concerns, executives at PBS made an early decision to include the interview and debate show *Firing Line,* which William F. Buckley Jr. had already created for commercial TV. The program by the ultraconservative Buckley—which some Republicans suspected was only a gesture, or a form of political protection—ran weekly on PBS from 1971 to 1999, giving an enviable pulpit to the most prominent right-wing public intellectual in the country. PBS added other conservative programs from time to time over the years, but most Republicans remained wary or outright hostile. As they looked over the offerings of shows—including children's programming that inculcated values such as tolerance for differences—those Republicans saw and heard their worst fears come true. One day, if they could, they would pull the plug on public broadcasting.

*   *   *

BY THE LATE 1960S AMERICAN journalism had a long tradition of advocacy, and there was also a long tradition of writing by, for, and about women, but still something was missing. The tradition of journalism that expressed advocacy for women was thin and erratic. In 1868 the pioneering suffragists Susan B. Anthony and Elizabeth Cady Stanton had founded a magazine called *The Revolution,* which expressed many of the most militant demands that women were making. But it did not last long: four years later it was out of business. There was a large volume of journalism aimed at women which presumed that women's interests began and ended with the domestic sphere. Going back at least as far as *Godey's Lady's Book* in 1830, magazines catered to women by focusing on food, fashion, child-rearing, and the like. For most of the twentieth century, women were visible in the mass media mainly through the "seven sisters" magazines: *Ladies' Home Journal, Better Homes and Gardens, Good Housekeeping, Family Circle, Redbook, Woman's Day,* and *McCall's.* All vied to be the housewife's best friend. Then, in 1962, Helen Gurley Brown published a landmark book with the provocative title *Sex and the Single Girl.* In it she made the case that a woman could have a career, a bank account, and a sex life—all outside of marriage. Three years later she became editor in chief of *Cosmopolitan,* the venerable Hearst Company magazine that had been a force in the muckraking movement. Under Brown, *Cosmo* got a real makeover and began telling women that they could have it all—love, sex, and money.

For all the ground that it broke, though, even *Cosmo* did not keep up with the changes that American women were making in the late 1960s. Most of the mainstream news media were either bewildered or downright hostile to the emerging "second wave" of feminism. One instance occurred in 1968. The setting was the Miss America beauty pageant, the epitome of the process of reducing women to objects to satisfy men. Demanding an end to women's "enslavement," a group of radical feminists picketed the pageant in Atlantic City, setting up a "freedom trash can" on the Boardwalk which they filled with girdles, bras, high-heeled shoes, hair curlers, copies of *Playboy,* and other things that pinched or demeaned women. The media went berserk, seizing on the alliterative image of feminists as "bra-burners."[56] When it came to understanding this new wave of feminism, there was a long way to go.

One of the most prominent and influential women who changed the perception of feminism was a journalist and political activist who helped found a magazine that captured the new zeitgeist—Gloria Steinem. With obvious talent, intelligence, and (as was always remarked) good looks, Steinem became a highly visible figure who helped to lead both a magazine and a movement.[57]

After a difficult childhood in Toledo, where she saw firsthand the vulnerability of women in traditional roles after her father left her mother, Steinem went to Smith College. Following her graduation in 1956, she traveled around India before landing in New York City, where she began to work as a freelance magazine writer. She worked hard and took all kinds of assignments. In an effort worthy of Nellie Bly, Steinem even went undercover for an article about working as a Playboy bunny.[58] She thrived as a freelance writer, and she became a rising star. But still, as a "girl reporter," she knew there were limits. (The low point: a piece for the *New York Times* magazine about textured stockings.) Over the course of the decade, even as she kept writing, Steinem became an activist in the civil rights, antiwar, and farm workers' movements.

She found a congenial base at *New York* magazine, where editor Clay Felker allowed Steinem to tackle bigger and better assignments. Eventually she wrote the magazine's "City Politic" column, which meant she was covering national politics and all the major issues. She liked Felker, and he advanced her career immeasurably, but in the end they came to an impasse: he was interested in pro-feminist articles only if they were paired with articles from an opposing point of view. "That's why I gradually stopped writing for *New York,*" Steinem later explained. "It was just too painful to be only able to do it in the context of two women fighting."[59] As a single working woman, she was naturally drawn to thinkers who were reexamining women's roles, and she was beginning to make contributions to that discussion. In 1968 she wrote a lament from the heart in a *New York Times* review of Caroline Bird's *Born Female:* "In fact, women who write, like Negroes who write, are supposed to be specialists on themselves, and little else. Newspapers and magazines are generous with assignments on fashion, beauty and childbirth. (Would men like to write about hunting, shaving and paternity?) But scientific or economic or political stories have a way of gravitating somewhere else. The rule Henry Luce invented 30 years ago still applies: . . . women research, men write."[60]

By Steinem's own reckoning, a pivotal moment came in 1969. The occasion was a hearing on abortion by the New York State legislature in which the fifteen official witnesses included fourteen men plus a nun. Members of the radical women's group called the Redstockings tried to get to the microphone, but the meeting was adjourned. Instead the group organized a feminist hearing shortly afterward, at which a dozen women testified publicly about their own abortion experiences. According to Steinem, who had had an abortion herself, the event was like a thunderclap. It was the moment when she realized that she was not just observing the movement, she was *of* it. Soon she began touring the country with other women, speaking as well as writing.

It was a time of ferment. As women continued theorizing, debating, investigating, and agitating, the late 1960s and early 1970s saw a proliferation of new feminist publications. By one estimate there were 560 new titles, many of them short-lived, launched during a five-year period. Most were local newsletters. What the movement needed was a good-looking national magazine, by women and for women. Steinem was among a group of women in New York who began to wonder, why not start one? Several of the organizers liked the name *Sisters,* but Steinem kept pushing for *Ms.,* the title that freed women from being defined by their relation to a man. At an early stage they got some critical help from a financial angel, Katharine Graham, publisher of the *Washington Post,* who put up $20,000. But there was still a long way to go. Then, in the summer of 1971, Felker had an idea. He was at a loss for a theme for his annual year-end special double issue of *New York.* He offered to publish a sample issue of *Ms.* as a one-time insert in the magazine. They would split any profits, and *Ms.* would be on its own after that.[61] Steinem and the other editors plunged in. By December they were ready. The inserts were tucked into the *New York* double issue, and another 300,000 copies of the inaugural issue of *Ms.* were distributed around the country to see how they would sell. It turned out that they didn't just sell, they were treasured. After the initial press run sold out in little more than a week, women passed their copies around to friends, took them to meetings, and saved them as mementos. They also signed up, in huge numbers, for regular subscriptions. And they wrote—oh, did they write. That initial run of 300,000 copies yielded an amazing twenty thousand letters to the editors.

By the time the first regular issue came out in July 1972, Steinem and her sister editors had lined up financing. Executive Steve Ross at Warner Communications put up $1 million in return for preferred stock in the new Ms. Magazine Corporation. Most of the rest would be owned by Steinem, who would function as editor in chief, and by Patricia Carbine, who would function as publisher. (*Ms.* did not embrace hierarchy or titles; the masthead was alphabetical.) The magazine was organized as a for-profit venture, so the staff started selling advertisements, subject to a few guidelines. "*Ms.* won't solicit or accept ads . . . that are downright insulting to women," the editors wrote in the summer edition, which contained ads for liquor and cigarettes (just like a men's magazine!) as well as such "women's magazine" staples as deodorant and nail polish, along with a few surprises, such as full-page "goodwill" ads from AT&T saying the company was looking to hire more women telephone installers.

The articles ranged from a cover story about what it would mean to have a serious woman candidate for president to a review of sex manuals and an article headlined "Body Hair: The Last Frontier." Other articles offered practical advice on how to fix a car by yourself, as well as poetry and exemplary stories for children. The issue also included many, many letters, in keeping with the idea that *Ms.* should function as a nationwide town meeting/consciousness-raising session. In the coming years, *Ms.* launched the careers of many women writers, and it spun off dozens of conferences and books. It was never ignored.

Like Garrison and Douglass, Steinem and the other editors at *Ms.* soon began to address the specific challenges which face a publication that is trying to provide leadership and direction to a political movement. A major issue was factionalism: Would the magazine be flexible or doctrinaire? Would it be gradualist and reformist, or would it be radical and extreme? Should the magazine endorse political candidates? And what about politicians who happened to be male but who were sympathetic to women's issues? Is every female candidate superior to every male candidate? *Ms.* drew criticism at first not just from the usual quarters but also from more moderate feminists like Betty Friedan. At the same time, the women's movement made demands on the magazine, whose editors had set a goal to make enough money from *Ms.* so that they could donate to women's causes. Some women thought *Ms.* should go faster; others said go slower. Some thought it should serve as a cheerleader; some thought it should be a critic; some thought it should be an employment agency.

In the end, of course, Steinem and the rest of the *Ms.* editorial team could not be all things to all people all the time. But over the next two decades, they produced journalism that was at the same time professional, personal, and powerful. Above all, *Ms.* succeeded in its ultimate goal: to change women's lives.

CHAPTER 12

The Establishment Holds, 1967–1974

"Follow the money."

—*The informant "Deep Throat" in the film* All the President's Men, *1976*

"What really hurts is if you try to cover it up."

—*President Richard Nixon, 1972*

B Y 1967 THE UNITED STATES was deeply involved in Vietnam. Since the big buildup of forces ordered by President Johnson in 1965, the number of U.S. combat troops had grown to exceed half a million. No longer just advisers, Americans were now fighting the war themselves, and throwing everything they had at it. The press corps was growing, too. From the small handful of correspondents in 1962, the number of journalists of all types—U.S. and foreign, print and broadcast, freelancers and full-timers—was building to a peak in the late 1960s of about 650.[1] Some seventy women—including the writers Gloria Emerson and Frances FitzGerald, as well as the photographer Dickey Chapelle—were among the press corps during the war years, taking photos, writing stories, or reporting for TV.[2] More and more often, these correspondents were not the optimistic cold warriors of the first wave, impatient for U.S. success. Reporters were starting to arrive in Saigon with questions, sometimes deep questions, not just about the progress of the war but about its fundamental rationale, even its moral basis. Back at home, on the "desks" that made assignments and planned coverage, many of the senior editors still supported the war. And on most editorial pages it was seen as a necessity. President Johnson once observed—even while the reporting was turning critical—that the editorials in the *Washington Post* still supported his policies, and he considered those editorials worth as much as having another division on the ground in Vietnam.[3] It was the reporters, however, especially the ones in the field, who were souring on the war.

Among U.S. officials, the can-do attitude certainly prevailed. The top U.S. military commander was now General William Westmoreland, a bolder and more confident leader than his predecessor. Westmoreland's assignment from Washington was to defeat the communists and keep South Vietnam a "free" country, and he was bound and determined to carry out that policy. In 1967 the coverage reflected Westmoreland's confidence. Although the general sometimes hedged his predictions and warned that the war could still take a long time, the headlines glossed over any reservations. In May, Westmoreland was the subject of a *Time* cover story focusing on his appearance before a joint session of Congress. "Backed at home by resolve, confidence, patience, determination and continued support," he assured the legislators, "we will prevail in Viet Nam over the Communist aggressor!" In the mode of his boss, Defense Secretary Robert McNamara, Westmoreland rattled off statistics:

> Two years ago, the Republic of Viet Nam had fewer than 30 combat-ready battalions. Today it has 154. Then, there were three jet-capable runways in South Viet Nam. Today there are 14. In April 1965, there were 15 airfields that could take C-130 transport aircraft. We now have 89. . . . During 1965, the Republic of Viet Nam armed forces and its allies killed 36,000 of the enemy at a cost of approximately 12,000 friendly killed—and 90% of these were Vietnamese. During recent months, this 3-to-1 ratio in favor of the allies has risen significantly, and in some weeks has been as high as 10 or 20 to 1.[4]

Later that year, the Johnson administration gave the public the impression that the war was nearly won, that there was "light at the end of the tunnel." As late as November, Westmoreland was saying that the enemy was having trouble finding new recruits and could not feed the V.C. forces in the field. "I have never been more encouraged in my four years in Viet Nam," declared the general, who, with his wife and daughter, spent the week as a guest at the White House. On November 21, 1967, he gave a major speech at the National Press Club that resulted in this *Washington Post* headline the next day: "War's End In View—Westmoreland."

So it came as quite a shock to most Americans when communist forces launched an all-out offensive in late January 1968 at the Vietnamese New Year, known as Tet. In a dramatic shift in tactics, the enemy fought, for the first time, by conventional means—striking in the daytime, in the open, and in regular units. Communist forces captured large areas of South Vietnam, attacking almost every provincial capital and rolling right up to the front lawn of the U.S. embassy in Saigon before being repulsed. Eventually, after weeks of fierce fighting, U.S. troops forced the Vietcong back. During that phase of the combat, AP correspondent Peter Arnett traveled to the Mekong Delta to report on the heavy fighting that was driving communist forces out of Ben Tre. There, Arnett reported one of the signature comments of the entire war when an unidentified U.S. officer told him, "It became necessary to destroy the town in order to save it."[5]

The meaning of the Tet offensive remains bitterly contested. Some argue that the news media (willfully or not) took a military defeat for the communists and turned it into a propaganda bonanza for them. But that misses the deeper point. What the attacks revealed was that the regime in Saigon and the U.S. Military Assistance Command–Vietnam (MACV) had made little progress in gaining popular support in the countryside of South Vietnam. That was, after all, what the war was all about. Five or six years in, Tet showed that no matter what the outcome of a given military engagement, the political challenge in Vietnam was going nowhere. Success in arms was not the issue. So although in military terms the Tet offensive proved to be a victory for the Americans, in political terms it was a disaster. After years of being told that we were winning the hearts and minds of Vietnam and that victory was just around the corner, Americans back home could see that there was not an inch of soil in Vietnam that was secure. The entire country was up for grabs, as if all the previous fighting had been for naught.

Tet also yielded another image that came to symbolize the brutality of the war. On February 2, 1968, General Nguyen Ngoc Loan, the chief of the South Vietnam National Police, came upon a newly captured Vietcong officer, who was accused of killing "many Americans" as well as South Vietnamese. The Vietcong suspect was handcuffed and wearing civilian clothes. As an NBC television crew filmed, Loan dispensed with formalities, raised his pistol to the prisoner's head, and fired. Also present was AP photographer Eddie Adams, who snapped off a still photo just as the bullet entered the prisoner's right temple. The AP photo appeared in almost every major newspaper in the United States and many others world-wide.[6] The offhanded summary execution imparted the message that the war had reached a new depth of savagery, and that image would be used by opponents of the war again and again to make the point.

There is debate over the impact of Tet on U.S. public opinion, but there is no doubt that it had one very specific impact: it demonstrated to the editors at home exactly what many of the reporters in the field had been saying. Now, some of the key figures in the American journalistic establishment—editors like Ben Bradlee at the *Washington Post* and Hedley Donovan at *Time*—were joining the ranks of the doubters.

The most public change of heart came from Walter Cronkite, the longtime anchor at CBS. A veteran of combat coverage in World War II and Korea, Cronkite was the successor to Edward R. Murrow at the premier broadcast news operation in America and the most respected newsman in the country. After reading the early wire-service reports about Tet, Cronkite was flabbergasted. He asked the question that was on a lot of minds in the CBS newsroom: "What the hell is going on? I thought we were *winning* the war."[7] Cronkite decided to go to Vietnam and see for himself. Leaving the comfort of the anchor chair (an almost unheard-of step at the time), he once again put on a helmet and a flak jacket and humped along with the grunts to the front lines. What he saw there shook him. He returned to New York and put together what turned out to be a historic prime-time broadcast. On February 27, 1968, he presented a special CBS report, *Who, What, When, Why.* Cronkite reported on his findings. Then he stepped out of his role as a reporter, looked straight at the camera, and told Americans what he personally believed about the war:

> It seems now more certain than ever that the bloody experience of Vietnam is to end in a stalemate. . . . To say that we are mired in stalemate seems the only realistic, yet unsatisfactory, conclusion. . . .
>
> It is increasingly clear to this reporter that the only rational way out will be to negotiate, not as victors, but as an honorable people who lived up to their pledge to defend democracy, and did the best they could.
>
> This is Walter Cronkite. Good night.

At the White House, President Johnson watched a taped version a short time later in a grim mood. At the end he supposedly turned to an aide and remarked, "If I've lost Cronkite, I've lost middle America."[8] Indeed, the reporting about Tet by Cronkite and many others had the effect of eroding support for the war among key constituencies in the Democratic Party. For the time being, Johnson kept a public silence as he absorbed the impact of the news about Tet. A little more than a month after Cronkite's report, with his approval ratings at rock bottom and with concerns growing over his own health, Johnson went on television and told his fellow Americans that he was finished. He would not seek a second term.[9]

Through the coverage of the Tet offensive, Americans began facing up to a key fact about Vietnam: the United States was probably not going to win, and not just because the media said so. It simply wasn't working. A short time later came the knockout punch, the one that flattened American hopes and idealism and inflamed the antiwar movement.

On March 16, 1968, a company of U.S. soldiers in the Americal Division entered the village of My Lai (which Americans pronounced "mee lie"), near Da Nang in South Vietnam. There had been reports of hostile fire coming from the area, and several U.S. soldiers had been killed near there in recent days. The men in C Company were being led by Lieutenant William L. Calley Jr. Under orders from Calley, troops gathered villagers into groups and "wasted" them with machine-gun fire. Anyone who survived was picked off with rifle fire. At least 90 people, and possibly as many as 130 or more, were killed—all civilians. The army even had a combat photographer on hand that day, who took plenty of pictures. Afterward, nothing happened.

More than a year later, the stories and rumors about the events at My Lai reached a soldier named Ronald Ridenhour. Just on the basis of what he'd heard, Ridenhour was so disturbed that he started writing letters. He wrote to the president, members of Congress, anyone he thought might do something. Again, nothing happened. Then a single congressman, liberal Democrat Mo Udall of Arizona, promised to look into the matter. He prodded the army to do so.

In September 1969, just days before Calley was due to be discharged, the army filed charges against him, accusing him of the murder of "more than 100 Oriental human beings." The army, seeking to minimize the impact, released the news about the impending court-martial out of Fort Benning, Georgia, where Calley was being held pending trial. The Associated Press ran a brief item, picked up by a few newspapers and printed on inside pages. The *New York Times* carried it on September 8, at the bottom of page thirty-eight. And that might have been the end.

Except a reporter named Seymour Hersh got a call from a friend alerting him to the case. Sy Hersh, who was then thirty-two, had cut his teeth in Chicago and the famous City News Bureau. He went on to work for the Associated Press, where he spent some time covering the Pentagon. In the fall of 1969 he was working as a freelancer. As a result of that career path, he was in a rare position to report on My Lai: he knew his way around the Pentagon, but he was not bound by the institutional culture or the editorial caution of the major news organizations, which probably kept journalists employed by those organizations from seeing the massacre for what it was. Most news organizations were very wary of saying such damning things about the military, and many in-country correspondents knew all about similar atrocities in Vietnam but had never reported them because they did not seem like "news."

In any case, Hersh, who opposed the war, dropped everything and plunged into the My Lai story.[10] He made a lot of phone calls before he found Calley's attorney, who agreed to talk with him. Fortified by a grant of $2,000 from the Fund for Investigative Journalism, Hersh kept digging. At the same time, he called *Life* to see if the magazine was interested. The editors turned him down flat, saying a massacre story was out of the question. He tried *Look* and got the same answer. Even so, Hersh pressed on, flying to Georgia so he could try to find Calley in the vastness of Fort Benning. After a lengthy runaround, during which Hersh used every trick in his bag (schmoozing, impersonating, bluffing), he finally located him. After a lengthy face-to-face interview, Hersh banged out a 1,500-word story about the My Lai massacre and found a buyer, the obscure left-wing Dispatch News Service, which sent the story out to its client newspapers. Some three dozen papers, including the *Boston Globe* and the *Times* of London, bought the story (paying $100 apiece for it) and ran it on page one on November 13, 1969. And that seemed to be that. The story got little attention at first, especially compared to the Apollo 12 space mission and Vice President Spiro Agnew's attacks on the media's supposed liberalism. My Lai got another bump when Hersh sent out a second story based on interviews with members of C Company.

1st Photos of Viet Mass Slaying

THE PLAIN DEALER

OHIO'S LARGEST NEWSPAPER

WEATHER

FINAL
Stocks & Races
Dow-Jones off 5.21

128TH YEAR—NO. 324 ★ ★ ★ ★ ★　　CLEVELAND, THURSDAY, NOVEMBER 20, 1969　　　96 PAGES　　10 CENTS

Exclusive

A clump of bodies on a road in South Vietnam.

Cameraman Saw GIs Slay 100 Villagers

By JOSEPH ESZTERHAS

12.1 DISTURBING PHOTOGRAPHS OF CIVILIANS MASSACRED BY U.S. SOLDIERS first appeared on the front page of the *Cleveland Plain Dealer* on November 20, 1969. The photos were taken the year before by army photographer Ronald L. Haeberle. The story of the My Lai massacre had been broken earlier by journalist Seymour Hersh, but Haeberle's photos added to the impact.

—©1974, The Plain Dealer. *All Rights Reserved. Used with permission of the* The Plain Dealer.

One thing the story lacked was photos. Without dramatic pictures, the facts of the massacre did not seem to register with the public. But as it turned out, there *were* photos. They were in the possession of former sergeant Ronald Haeberle, the army combat photographer who had been at My Lai during the massacre. Haeberle had had his official army camera with him that day, but he'd also had his personal camera on a strap around his neck, and he had brought some of his own photos home with him. When he heard about the interest in My Lai, he approached his local newspaper, the *Cleveland Plain Dealer*. On November 20, 1969, the paper published the first photos of the massacre (fig. 12.1). They were gruesome, but what was most troubling was that they clearly showed the bodies of Vietnamese civilians—lots of them, jumbled atop and beside one another—but no enemy soldiers. Suddenly *Time, Life,* and *Newsweek* were all interested, and the story became a certified big deal. The December 5, 1969, issue of *Life,* for example, featured an extensive display of Haeberle's photos, plus a story by Joe Eszterhas, a young reporter for the *Plain Dealer*.[11] Next, television joined the pack, offering dramatic interviews with members of C Company. One former soldier went on television to confess his role in My Lai and to say he was sorry. His mother blamed the army. She looked into the camera and declared, "I sent them a good boy, and they made him a murderer."[12]

In the following months, as the Calley court-martial unfolded, the My Lai case kept the issue of atrocities on the public agenda. Some in the military and their supporters in the media tried to downplay the charges, or to chalk the incident up to the "war-is-hell" philosophy.[13] But the vast majority of editorial commentary was critical, blaming the army and raising new questions about the nature of the war in Vietnam. Coming after the coverage of Tet the previous year, the My Lai story was another hammer blow against American enthusiasm for the war.

12.2 ONE OF THE FEW "GOOD NEWS" STORIES in the late 1960s occurred in July 1969, when the crew of Apollo 11 landed on the moon, drawing saturation coverage in all news media. A U.S. astronaut left this footprint in the lunar soil. —*NASA.*

The My Lai story not only caused a sensation but also broke a journalistic taboo. In almost all previous wars, it was unheard of for any country's press to report on its own side's atrocities, especially while the fighting was still going on. *Reader's Digest,* for example, offered Americans a steady drumbeat of stories about atrocities blamed on communists in Vietnam but never found a single case among U.S. troops. My Lai changed that, too. Suddenly, there were stories appearing everywhere in the media about U.S. atrocities in Vietnam—rape, murder, torture, and a particularly shocking form of execution: pushing a prisoner out of a helicopter. There were stories that some American soldiers made a practice of cutting the ears off dead VC soldiers, drying them, and stringing them into ghoulish necklaces. In July 1970, Americans learned about the notorious "tiger cages," a brutal prison maintained by South Vietnamese authorities on an offshore island. When a congressional delegation visited, a young aide took photos, which were promptly published in *Life* magazine.

*   *   *

BY THIS TIME, VIETNAM WAS Richard Nixon's problem. Late in his first year in office, the Republican president began waging a campaign in the news media to put his stamp on the war. He did not expect any help from the media, with which he had a famously fraught relationship (fig. 12.2). Nixon had long before developed a distrust of the media as an institution and a dislike of most journalists as individuals. One irony in all this was that the Nixon White House was obsessed (even more than most administrations) with its image and was staffed to an unprecedented degree by advertising executives, p.r. experts, former journalists, and other practitioners of the emerging discipline of spin control. Some of Nixon's closest and longest-serving aides were media types, though none had ever actually worked as a *reporter:*

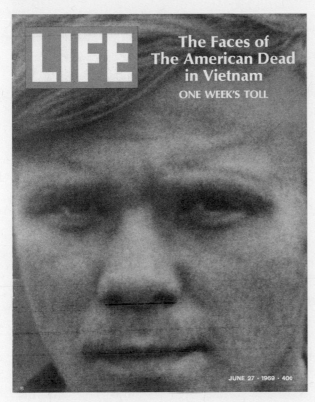

12.3 *LIFE* MAGAZINE SHOWED THE POWER OF PHOTOS in a special project published in 1969. A photospread showed individual portraits of each of the 242 U.S. soldiers killed in Vietnam between May 28 and June 3.
—*Getty Images.*

PATRICK BUCHANAN, a conservative young Catholic, was the first staffer hired for Nixon's run for the presidency, and he became a White House aide and speechwriter.

ROGER AILES was a producer for the Mike Douglas daytime television talk program when he met Nixon in 1967 and told him that if he thought it was undignified for a presidential candidate to go on daytime TV, then he didn't deserve to win. Ailes pioneered the stage-managed televised "town meeting" for Nixon and stayed on as a White House aide.

WILLIAM SAFIRE, the oldest of the three, had been a public relations agent when he met Nixon in Moscow in 1957, then joined the 1960 campaign. In 1968, Safire was back, and he became one of Nixon's most important speechwriters.

Together these three helped plan, script, and execute Nixon's strategy. To a large extent, that consisted of waging war on the news media themselves (fig. 12.3).

Resentful and cunning, paranoid and quick to anger, Nixon made his feud with the media a war of one against all, taking on the major newspapers, the big weekly magazines, and (his ultimate nemesis) the network television news divisions. He had never given up on his quest to get around the network news divisions, full of smarty-pants like David Brinkley, Eric Sevareid, and John Chancellor—liberals all, Nixon said, who sanctimoniously insisted that they didn't have a biased bone in their bodies. The key to using television, in Nixon's view, was to bypass the TV journalists and speak directly to the audience, the way advertisers do. The key moment came early in his first term. On November 3, 1969, Nixon gave a televised prime-time speech about the war in Vietnam. He had prepared for weeks, and he threw himself into it. Still, the fact was that he did not have much to say that was new, dramatic, or persuasive. One of the few notable points in the speech was his introduction of a new political image, the "Silent Majority" (in Buchanan's phrase), those loyal and patriotic Americans who were not demonstrating in the streets, burning flags, or giving antiwar speeches. Not only did Nixon not offer anything of substance in his prime-time address, but also, to make matters worse, he spoke for thirty-two minutes.[14] If he had stopped at twenty-seven or twenty-eight minutes, the networks could not have done much more than recap his major points and sign off, returning to the regular schedule. But by running over into the next block of prime time, Nixon left the networks with nearly half an hour to fill. What they filled it with was commentary and analysis, which infuriated Nixon and his team.

It was time to quit pretending; it was time to shoot the messenger, or at least to start shooting *at* the messenger. Ten days later, at Buchanan's urging, the White House struck back, unleashing Vice President Agnew, who commenced a series of attacks on the media at a regional Republican conference in Des Moines. "A raised eyebrow, an inflection of the voice, a caustic remark dropped in the middle of a broadcast, can raise doubts in a million minds. . . . What do Americans know of the men who wield this power?" demanded Agnew. "Little—other than that they reflect an urbane and assured presence, *seemingly* well-informed on every important matter. . . . To a man, these commentators and producers live and work in the geographical and intellectual confines of Washington, D.C., or New York City." He went on to spell out his point, urging Americans to question the concentration of power in the hands of "a tiny and closed fraternity of privileged men, elected by no one, and enjoying a monopoly sanctioned and licensed by government."[15] In a regulated industry like television, those words were ominous. A week later Agnew struck again, adding the leading institutions of the print media to his list of targets. In a speech delivered in Montgomery, Alabama, he proclaimed, "The day when the network commentators and even gentlemen of the *New York Times* enjoyed a form of diplomatic immunity from comment and criticism of what they said—that day is over." Agnew called out the Washington Post Company specifically "as an example of the trend toward monopolization."[16]

Agnew kept right on attacking the media. His famously alliterative denunciation of the "nattering nabobs of negativism" dates from 1970, in an address (written by Safire) to the California Republican state convention. From the context, it appears that Agnew was aiming the barb at Democrats, not at journalists, but the phrase later became widely associated with his sustained attacks on the news media.[17] In any event, it is unclear whether Nixon or anyone around him really thought through the long-term implications of this assault. After all, by declaring war on the press, Nixon and Agnew pretty much ensured decades of unfavorable coverage for the Republican Party. Nevertheless, a good measure of Agnew's antagonism was personal. When Agnew was added to the ticket in 1968, the journalist Ward Just wrote in the *Washington Post,* "Nixon's decision . . . may come to be regarded as perhaps the most eccentric political appointment since the Roman emperor Caligula named his horse a consul."[18]

Those assaults by Agnew eventually paid a short-term dividend in 1973, when Bill Paley suddenly issued a memo banning "instant analysis" from CBS News.[19] That same year, of course, brought another development in the war against the media: the resignation of Spiro Agnew himself, on corruption charges.

In the end, there were limits to what the president's men could do about the media, especially the coverage of the war. From Vietnam, the news remained mostly negative. A place at first just ghastly turned a darker shade of hell.

On June 8, 1972, a Vietnamese photographer working for the Associated Press, Nick Ut, boarded an AP minibus and headed northwest up Route 1. Near Trang Bang he halted to photograph fighting between South Vietnamese units and communist forces. Around noon, the ARVN commander called for air support, and the South Vietnamese air force responded, dropping napalm at the edge of the village. Suddenly, Ut saw a group of burned and wounded villagers streaming down the road, right toward him. One of his photos would haunt a generation. It showed several terrified children fleeing in agony. In the center, a naked young girl, badly burned, ran with her arms drooping by her sides and her mouth fixed in a scream. Her name was Kim Phuc. When she got near Ut, the photographer poured water on her wounds, then carried her to his waiting vehicle. Several of her family members piled in, and Ut sped off with them toward a hospital. Kim was wailing: *"I am thirsty. I am thirsty. I need water."* At the hospital, Ut pleaded with the doctors to try to save her. Once she was on the operating table, Ut headed to Saigon to develop the film (which won a Pulitzer Prize) (fig. 12.4).[20]

That photo brought home the brutality of the war and made people wonder what could possibly justify it. More and more Americans had more and more doubts about the war. By the millions, they took to the streets, marching in protest and demanding a swift end to a conflict that now seemed not merely ineffective but senseless. Not only was America not winning in any traditional sense, but also it now seemed as though the war was destroying something precious about America in the process. All the coverage tended to reinforce the antiwar message: Get out of Vietnam.

Publicly, President Nixon embraced that goal, although he would take years to do so and widen the war in the process. Many news organizations, however, began to pull out of Vietnam long before the fighting ended. The number of reporters accredited by U.S. officials in South Vietnam plunged from a high of 637 in 1968 to 355 in 1971, then plunged again after most U.S. troops left in 1973. By mid-1974 there were only about three dozen left, and there were just a handful on April 30, 1975, when communist troops took over Saigon, the last U.S. helicopters lifted off

12.4 IN ONE OF THE MOST HORRIFYING PHOTOS FROM THE WAR IN VIETNAM, terrified children run from an accidental bombing by South Vietnamese forces, which dropped the burning gel napalm on civilians in June 1972. Near the center is a young girl named Kim Phuc, who survived the attack—in part through the aid she received from the photographer, Nick Ut of the Associated Press. —*AP Photo/Nick Ut.*

jammed with refugees, and looters stripped the U.S. embassy. Among those at the end were the reporters in the lonely outposts maintained by the Associated Press and the *New York Times*.

*   *   *

EARL CALDWELL GREW UP IN the late 1930s and 1940s in Clearfield, Pennsylvania, in coal country, far from the struggles to end Jim Crow in the Deep South, far from the growing urban centers of black population in the North and West, indeed far from just about any contact with other black people. His parents worked with their hands, and young Earl probably figured he would too. After high school he got a job in a steel mill in Buffalo. But Earl had always been a good reader, and he enrolled at the University of Buffalo, studying business. He got a summer job at an insurance company in Philadelphia, where he was told the facts of life: because he was black, he could work for the company only in the South, a prospect that horrified him. Later a friend from high school helped him get a job as a sportswriter on a paper in his hometown. From then on, Earl Caldwell knew what he wanted to do. He began a classic newsroom apprenticeship, moving from Clearfield to bigger and bigger papers in Lancaster, Pennsylvania, and Rochester, New York, breaking the color barrier time and again. "I was the Jackie Robinson of every place I worked until I got to New York [City]," he recalled many years later.[21]

In 1964 there was a riot in Rochester that attracted out-of-town reporters. One of the visitors was also one of Caldwell's journalistic heroes—Jimmy Breslin, then of the *Herald Tribune*. Caldwell helped him make his way around Rochester, and later Breslin helped the younger man get a job at the *New York Post*. Caldwell's next move was to approach the *New York Times*—as it happened, at just the moment when the paper was beginning to hire black reporters. The *Times* was famous for having plenty of black elevator operators, but when Caldwell started in March 1967, he was just the second black in a newsroom position at the *Times* (following Tom Johnson). On his first day, Caldwell wore a Brooks Brothers suit and declared that he wanted to write like Gay Talese. For the first few weeks he did what most newly hired reporters did at the *Times:* cover New York City. At times he served as something like a foreign correspondent, exploring Harlem for the *Times'* white readers and describing the sights, sounds, and folkways of people who lived only a few blocks away. Once a *Times* editor asked Caldwell for James Baldwin's telephone number, evidently assuming that all black people knew all other black people. Soon, though, cities across America began erupting in race riots, and the *Times* tapped the new guy to help out, often teaming him with Gene Roberts, an experienced white reporter who was the paper's chief Southern-based civil rights correspondent in the late 1960s.[22] Over the next months, the headlines from Caldwell's stories in the *Times* serve as a summary of the era's social history:

GUARD IS CALLED INTO CINCINNATI AS RIOTS SPREAD

*

BLACK NATIONALISM GROWS IN WATTS

*

BLACK POWER PARLEY TO SEEK NEGRO UNITY

*

FOCUS ON RAP BROWN
'HE SCARES THEM A LITTLE BIT'

*

FEWER WHITES ARE TAKING
THE 'A' TRAIN TO
HARLEM'S NIGHT SPOTS

In the spring of 1968, Caldwell traveled to Memphis to cover the strike being waged by the city's sanitation workers, supported by the Reverend Martin Luther King Jr. Caldwell was in the Lorraine Motel on April 4 when a loud shot rang out. The only journalist present at the scene, Caldwell immediately called the *Times* newsroom and began dictating details of the King assassination, which the editors spread across the top of page one. According to Caldwell, King had spent most of the day in his room, then emerged around 6 p.m. onto the balcony, wearing a black suit and a white shirt. Caldwell's report continued:

> Dr. King, an open-faced genial man, leaned over a green iron railing to chat with an associate. . . .
>
> The Rev. Ralph W. Abernathy, perhaps Dr. King's closest friend, was just about to come out of the motel room when the sudden loud noise burst out.
>
> Dr. King toppled to the concrete second-floor walkway. Blood gushed from the right jaw and neck area. His necktie had been ripped off by the blast.[23]

King's murder touched off a fresh round of violence in cities across America, and Caldwell returned to the "riot beat" for much of the summer (fig. 12.5).

That fall, Caldwell went to San Francisco to become a West Coast correspondent for the *Times*. Through his contacts among the few black reporters in the Bay Area, he gained access to Black Power advocate Eldridge Cleaver, and by the end of 1968, Caldwell was the most knowledgeable reporter in the mainstream press about the emerging Black Panther Party, based across the bay in Oakland. As it turned out, the Panthers were shrewd enough about the media to want coverage in the *New York Times,* and they gave Caldwell access, as well as what reporters call "color" (atmospheric details), on-the-record interviews, just about anything he might want. His stories established that the Panthers were heavily armed and were talking about violent revolution. Caldwell worried about how Cleaver and the other Panthers would react to his reporting, but he didn't need to. "The Panthers *wanted* people to know what they were doing. They *wanted* me to write in the paper about them having guns."[24] His reporting also attracted the attention of the FBI, which was waging a nationwide campaign of surveillance and intimidation against radical groups both black and white. That attention would develop into one of the landmark Supreme Court rulings affecting reporters and their ability to protect confidential sources.

The legal case began when FBI agents paid a visit to Caldwell and told him that they wanted a lot more information about the Panthers. Caldwell told the agents that everything he knew was right there in the newspaper, including the fact that the Panthers were armed and that they were threatening to kill the president. Even so, the government wanted more from Caldwell. He refused to talk, however, believing that any appearance in secret before a grand jury would make him look like an informant and dry up his sources. The agents were not satisfied, and the Bureau turned up the pressure, warning him that he would be forced to testify in court—a step that would not only destroy his relationship with the Black Panthers but jeopardize his value as a reporter on any other beat as well. Facing a possible court appearance, Caldwell destroyed most of his Panther files, but there was still the matter of his testimony. In February 1970 he was served with a subpoena ordering him to appear before a federal grand jury investigating the Black Panthers. The subpoena did not name the *Times,* but the newspaper hired a prestigious San Francisco law firm to represent Caldwell. Their advice: cooperate. Hearing that, Caldwell tapped his network of black journalists, who steered him toward a Stanford law professor, Anthony Amsterdam, a brilliant defense lawyer, who agreed with Caldwell's decision not to testify and offered to represent him pro bono.[25]

After he continued to refuse to testify about his news sources, Caldwell was found in contempt of court and ordered to jail, but he was allowed to remain free while his case went to the Ninth U.S. Circuit Court of Appeals. The higher court sided with Caldwell, but then the federal government appealed that ruling. En

12.5 *NEW YORK TIMES* **REPORTER EARL CALDWELL** (*at left*) trails Rev. Martin Luther King Jr. up stairs in the courtyard of the Lorraine Motel in Memphis, shortly before King's assassination on April 4, 1968. Caldwell was the only reporter in a position to provide an eyewitness account.
—*Memphis Commercial Appeal.*

route to the U.S. Supreme Court, Caldwell's case was combined with two others and filed under the heading *Branzburg v. Hayes.* Paul Branzburg was a reporter for the *Louisville Courier-Journal* who had been an eyewitness to a drug crime. (Thus he was not, strictly speaking, protecting a confidential source.) Paul Pappas was a television news photographer working for a TV station in New Bedford, Massachusetts, who had gone to nearby Providence to cover the local Black Panthers chapter and spent several hours inside their headquarters. Like Caldwell, Branzburg and Pappas were both journalists who had been ordered to testify before grand juries; like Caldwell, they had refused on professional grounds.

In all three cases, the issue was not a classic instance of protecting the identity of a confidential source. It was more a matter of preserving the journalists' *access* to sources, which would be destroyed if the people who were being reported on suspected that the reporters had cooperated with law enforcement. All three cases involved a constitutional claim that the First Amendment includes not only the right to publish (and withhold) information freely but also the right to gather news freely. Recognizing the stakes, news executives threw their institutional weight behind Caldwell and the other reporters. Supporting briefs were filed by the Washington Post Company, the Chicago Tribune Company, the American Newspaper Publishers Association, the American Society of Newspaper Editors, the American Newspaper Guild, the Radio and Television News Directors Association, the Press Photographers Association, and the ACLU—along with affidavits from such respected journalists as Anthony Lukas, Walter Cronkite, and Marvin Kalb.

In a decision handed down on June 29, 1972, the Supreme Court narrowly ruled against the journalists.[26] Writing for the 5–4 majority, Justice Byron White held that the First Amendment had to be balanced against the Fifth Amendment, which guarantees criminal defendants the right to have their cases presented to a grand jury before indictment. In his opinion White invoked the ancient legal doctrine that "the public . . . has a right to every man's evidence." The only exceptions, he said, are those instances in which the states have adopted laws specifically granting certain categories of people a legal privilege against having to testify. Such a "testimonial privilege" might protect a wife from testifying about her husband, a doctor about a patient, or a priest about a penitent. In such cases, legislatures determined that some other social good was worth the cost of allowing the privileged category of people to avoid the grand jury. But, White said, the Court could not take seriously the idea "that it is better to write about crime than to do something about it." If reporters know things that prosecutors want to find out, they must tell what they know. Besides, the justice wrote, if the Court created a special privilege for journalists, it would soon have to define who is (and is not) a journalist—a task that raised the specter of government licensing of journalists, which would be far more murky than determining who is a doctor or a priest. "Almost any author may quite accurately assert that he is contributing to the flow of information to the public," White wrote, warning that just about anybody could claim to be a journalist of one variety or another. Finally, White observed that the U.S. attorney general had written a set of guidelines governing the issuance of subpoenas to reporters, which the high court thought ought to suffice for the bulk of cases.[27] The majority opinion also included an invitation to legislatures to create a "testimonial privilege" for reporters, and many state legislatures went ahead and passed versions of what are known as "shield laws."

In a brief concurring opinion, Justice Lewis Powell, though voting with the majority, very nearly came down on the other side.[28] He warned prosecutors that "no harassment of newsmen will be tolerated," and he wrote that if reporters feel they are being abused by overzealous prosecutors seeking the names of confidential sources, then those reporters should go to court and seek a protective order. "The asserted claim to privilege should be judged on its facts by the striking of a proper balance between freedom of the press and the obligation of all citizens to give relevant testimony with respect to criminal conduct," Powell wrote, saying it is up to the courts to handle such claims on a case-by-case basis. Nevertheless, his joining with the majority had the effect of denying journalists' claims to a constitutional privilege.

Among the dissenters, Justice William O. Douglas wrote one of the most eloquent statements of press freedom in history. Having staked out a position as a First Amendment fundamentalist, Douglas saw the Caldwell and related cases in clear-cut terms. "My belief is that all of the 'balancing' was done by those who wrote the Bill of Rights," he said, adding that "by casting the First Amendment in absolute terms, they repudiated timid, watered-down, emasculated versions of the First Amendment. . . ." The key to understanding the First Amendment, Douglas argued, is to recognize that it exists for the benefit of the American people as a whole. If the people are to govern themselves, they must have reliable, independent sources of information. "Effective self-government cannot succeed unless the people are immersed in a steady, robust, unimpeded, and uncensored flow of opinion and reporting which are continuously subjected to critique, rebuttal, and re-examination," he wrote. In Douglas's view, the free press cases that come before the Court are not really about the press per se; they are about the rights of the American people, the ultimate sovereigns of our system. The press, which serves as the agent of its audience, is incidental to the greater purpose of self-government. Douglas continued: "The press has a preferred position in our constitutional scheme, not to enable it to make money, not to set newsmen apart as a favored class, but to bring to fulfillment the public's right to know. . . . There is no higher function performed under our constitutional regime. Its performance means that the press is often engaged in projects that bring anxiety and even fear to the bureaucracies, departments, or officials of government." He concluded by warning that the Court's majority opinion would reduce journalists to stenographers, and that without the right to protect confidential sources, "the reporter's main function in American society will be to pass on to the public the press releases which the various departments of government issue."

The majority, however, did not see it that way. As a result of the Court's 5–4 ruling against the journalists, reporters and their sources have operated in legal jeopardy ever since, at least in federal courts.[29] On the state level, the *Branzburg* ruling had the effect of spurring many legislatures around the country to enact shield laws to protect reporters in state courts, but Congress has steadfastly refused to recognize the same right on the federal level. Ironically, the *Branzburg* ruling also had another impact: it dried up what was probably the FBI's greatest source of information about the Black Panthers—the reporting that anybody could read in the pages of the *New York Times*.[30] Of course, by the time Caldwell's case was resolved, the Justice Department had lost much of its interest in the Black Panthers. Most of Caldwell's contacts were in jail, in exile, or dead.

* * *

MEANWHILE, BY THE LATE 1960S, more and more people were asking new and troubling questions about the war in Southeast Asia. No longer was the issue *How are we doing in Vietnam?* Now the question was *What are we doing in Vietnam?* Even the secretary of defense had questions. Robert McNamara, the ultimate whiz kid, the brightest of the best and brightest, was determined to get answers. He fell back on the tools he knew best: data, reason, and analysis. In 1967 he commissioned an internal study of U.S. involvement in Vietnam, tapping vast archives of government documents and a large team of military veterans, historians, security experts, and analysts. Among those recruited to work on the secret project—known by its nickname, the Pentagon Papers—was a former marine with a Harvard doctorate: Daniel Ellsberg.[31]

Ellsberg, an expert in decision-making theory, was a civilian working at the Rand Corporation, a private think tank that did a lot of analytical work for the U.S. government, especially the Defense Department. While he was working on the Pentagon Papers, Ellsberg underwent a profound personal conversion about the war—from enthusiastic hawk to passionate dove. Part of the reason for this change lay in the papers themselves. Studying the mountains of documents (which he read in their entirety, even in areas where it was not his role to contribute), Ellsberg came to believe that the problem was not the one he expected—that presidents lacked solid information about Vietnam. They had plenty of information. The problem was that those presidents had all chosen to lie about it. At the same time, Ellsberg was meeting leaders of the growing and increasingly vocal antiwar movement, who were posing questions that he found troubling: What right does the United States have to intervene in the lives of faraway peoples who pose no threat to us? What is the moral justification for prosecuting a war in which the deaths of Asian people are not even a factor?

In his newfound determination to help stop the war, Ellsberg started to think that perhaps the Pentagon Papers themselves could make the difference. If the American public only knew what was in that study, they would see what he had seen—that Vietnam was a disaster, one that president after president had led us deeper and deeper into, always claiming that victory or "peace with honor" was just around the corner. With the idea of divulging its contents, he began secretly photocopying the study in October 1969. It was a daunting task. With help from a friend, Ellsberg developed a system. At the Rand offices in Santa Monica, California, he would put in his briefcase as many pages as he could carry. At the end of the day, he would wave to the security guard and leave with the briefcase, then head to another friend's advertising agency, where he had permission to use the Xerox machine all night. This meant that Ellsberg had to lay each page facedown on the glass plate, push a button, wait, remove the original, replace it with another, push the button again, and so on. Each night he would wrap up, catch some sleep, and then in the morning return the batch of documents to Rand. "I took it for granted that what I was doing violated some law, perhaps several," Ellsberg recalled years later.[32] As a contributor to the study, Ellsberg had top-security clearance, and he was authorized to have access to the set of the Pentagon Papers at Rand. Whether he had any right to make copies and distribute them remained to be seen. Under the circumstances, however, it is debatable whether Ellsberg "stole" anything.

Aside from the legal issues, copying the Pentagon Papers was a physical challenge. The study was massive. Each set ran to forty-seven volumes, about seven thousand pages in all. Just fifteen official copies had been made, and most of those were stored in a vault at the Pentagon. The whole thing was classified "TOP SECRET—SENSITIVE" and bore warning stamps on the front and back covers and on every page. Under the protocols of the federal classification system, a document must be classified at the highest level of its most sensitive contents. Thus, if a volume of the Pentagon Papers consisted of analysis written by a historian buttressed by secret diplomatic cables or orders to units in the field, then the whole volume was treated the same as its most secret components. And as Ellsberg well knew, the Pentagon Papers were packed with secrets—everything from the fruits of U.S. spy agencies to private exchanges between world leaders, and from plots to carry out coups to estimates of other countries' intentions.

In terms of domestic U.S. politics, the Pentagon Papers also posed a threat. As of 1969, only a handful of people had read the whole study, and Ellsberg was one of them.[33] He'd seen document after document proving that one American president after another had lied to the American people by telling them that the U.S. role in Vietnam was minimal and successful, when in fact that role was growing and stalemated. The study also cast major doubts about the part played by the United States in the Tonkin Gulf incident of 1964, which had provided the justification for the congressional resolution authorizing a U.S. combat role in Vietnam. The Pentagon Papers provided a detailed, damning indictment of a generation of policy and policymakers about a war that was still very much in progress. It was never meant to be read by more than a few dozen people at the very summit of power. What Ellsberg was contemplating was, according to a leading expert, "probably the single largest unauthorized disclosure of classified documents in the history of the United States."[34]

As Ellsberg considered his options in late 1969 and early 1970, his first thought was to get the papers released through a member of Congress. He hit upon Senator J. William Fulbright, the Arkansas Democrat who chaired the Foreign Relations Committee and who was the most prominent congressional critic of U.S. involvement in Vietnam. Ellsberg also approached Senators George McGovern of South Dakota, Mike Gravel of Alaska, and Charles Mathias of Maryland, hoping that one of them would use his congressional immunity to introduce the papers into the Congressional Record. In the end, after taking more than a year to decide, they all found reasons to decline. So Ellsberg turned to his fallback position and thought about giving a set of the papers to the press. In his mind there was one obvious choice, one newspaper with the resources, the sense of history, and the track record: the *New York Times*. And at the *Times*, the obvious choice was Neil Sheehan. Sheehan, who had been the Saigon bureau chief for UPI in the early 1960s, knew as much about Vietnam as anyone. He had since joined the *Times*, where he was a Washington correspondent, still very much involved in covering the war. One thing that impressed Ellsberg about Sheehan was a piece the reporter had recently written for the *Times Book Review* on the subject of war crimes and the application of war crimes doctrine to U.S. actions in Vietnam. Ellsberg was struck by the passion Sheehan showed in his writing, the urgent desire to end the fighting and bombing.

So, late in the evening of March 2, 1971, during a visit to Washington, Ellsberg called Sheehan at his home. Sheehan invited him over, and they stayed up all night while Ellsberg described the mammoth McNamara study and drew Sheehan into the plan. The journalist could not promise that his newspaper would use it just as Ellsberg wished, but Sheehan himself was eager to see it and optimistic about publishing. What happened next remains shrouded in a good bit of secrecy. Sheehan, in keeping with the reporter's code of *omertà* in protecting confidential sources, never identified Ellsberg as his source and has never explained in detail how he acquired the Pentagon Papers for the *Times*. In all his public statements he has said simply that he "got" or "obtained" the study—which is true as far as it goes. According to Ellsberg, it was more like a dance.[35]

Around this time Ellsberg left California for Cambridge, to begin a fellowship at MIT, and he continued making photocopies. Since he first started copying the Pentagon Papers in 1969, he had made several sets for the senators he hoped would make them public. He now decided to salt away several extra sets in the apartments of various friends, to thwart any attempt by the government to silence him. Ellsberg assumed that the FBI was watching his apartment, on a side street just off Harvard Square, so he kept his own copy nearby, in a box at the apartment of his brother-in-law. While Ellsberg organized the contents of the box, his wife, Patricia, took batches to different copy shops in Harvard Square. These shops had fairly powerful commercial copiers, but it still took a long time. Ellsberg had clipped out the TOP SECRET stamp from every page of his set before making additional copies from it, but still, he had to wonder what might happen if a clerk at a copy shop read some of the contents and decided to drop a dime into a pay phone and call the authorities to see if they'd like their secrets back.

Ellsberg and Sheehan continued to discuss the ground rules for a handoff of the giant secret study. Oddly, perhaps, one issue they did not discuss was confidentiality. Ellsberg just assumed that Sheehan would protect his identity, but nothing was ever spelled out. Of greater concern to Ellsberg was the political goal of stopping the war. To that end he wanted a definite commitment that the *Times* would publish and that the newspaper would include in its reports some of the actual documents contained in the Pentagon Papers. As a mere reporter, Sheehan was in no position to make promises that would bind the newspaper, but he pledged to do his best. Ellsberg met him halfway, saying that Sheehan could inspect the papers (in fact, Ellsberg withheld four volumes of diplomatic history that contained many still important secrets) and take notes on them, to give Sheehan the evidence he would need to try to persuade his superiors at the *Times*. Ellsberg even gave Sheehan a key to his apartment so he could come and go as he set about the tedious business of reading and taking notes. Sheehan asked for his own photocopies, but Ellsberg was not ready yet to take that step. After a few days, Sheehan headed back to Washington to begin the process of pitching the idea to his editors.

Not too long afterwards it appears that, unbeknownst to Ellsberg, Sheehan returned to Cambridge, this time with his wife, the journalist Susan Sheehan. On a weekend when they knew that Ellsberg would be away, the Sheehans checked into a hotel near Harvard Square under false names. Using the key to the apartment, which Neil had kept, the Sheehans (according to Ellsberg) let themselves in and removed an entire set of the Pentagon Papers. At some point that weekend, Sheehan used a pay phone to call the Boston bureau of the *Times* and asked the local correspondent, Bill Kovach, for some expense money. Kovach, in turn, called New York and got $1,500 wired to him.[36] The Sheehans took the study to a nearby copy shop and got a complete duplicate made. Then they returned the first set to the apartment and slipped out of town. In this way, Sheehan may have broken trust with Ellsberg, but he may also have done him a big favor. If it all ever came out in a criminal trial, Ellsberg could assert that he had not actually "given" the study to Sheehan. The reporter was, in other words, taking the whole potential liability upon himself.[37]

After spending several weeks examining the papers in Washington, Sheehan was making headway in getting the newspaper's top executives to commit. The most important figure on the news side was the managing editor, A. M. "Abe" Rosenthal, who was no dove when it came to the war in Vietnam. Rosenthal, however, determined that the project was potentially significant and took over close supervision himself. He had Sheehan's photocopied set brought to the *Times* newsroom on West Forty-third Street in Manhattan, but soon thought better of it. He did not want the FBI storming that hallowed journalistic ground to seize files. Instead, Rosenthal ordered the establishment of a separate command post in several suites at the midtown Hilton Hotel. Everyone involved (which ultimately ran to about seventy-five reporters, editors, clerks, and design personnel) was ordered to keep mum about "Project X."[38] They had reason to be careful.

The set held by the *Times* represented an unprecedented breach of the national security classification system, and anyone in possession of the report could face criminal charges, not merely of stealing government property but perhaps even of espionage or, ultimately, treason. Indeed, that was the opinion reached by the *Times*' longtime law firm, Lord Day & Lord. Senior partner Louis M. Loeb objected to the idea of publishing leaked military secrets in wartime, which he considered irresponsible and unpatriotic, and he warned that the government would be sure to prosecute the newspaper and its top executives. He urged the editors to return the papers to the government.[39] Punch Sulzberger decided to listen instead to the company's in-house counsel, Jim Goodale, who was more sanguine about keeping everyone out of jail. With that question still unresolved, Sulzberger decided to let the project move forward but to proceed carefully. By now, he had eight years as publisher under his belt, and he felt a lot more confident than he had in his first year, when JFK had tried to bully him into transferring Halberstam out of Saigon. Still, confronting the president of the United States would be a challenge.

In one room at the hotel, Sulzberger assembled the newspaper's lawyers to help him decide whether to publish anything at all. They argued over issues of sedition, corporate liability, and professional responsibility. In another room he assembled a select group of the newspaper's senior editors and top reporters to wade into the documents and help him determine what to publish. It was tough going in both rooms. In the roomful of journalists, the Pentagon Papers were providing dozens of leads and tantalizing revelations. But the report as a whole was so vast that it would take a long time to find a storyline in there. What was the upshot? What was the headline? Week after week, debates raged in both rooms. Was the *Times* about to break the law by publishing classified information during wartime? Would the government bring a charge of treason? If so, could the paper survive? Finally, the stories were ready.

It all came down to Sulzberger. It was time to say yes or no, time to put all his chips—the paper he loved, his family's legacy, the good of his country—on the table. His answer was yes. So on Saturday, June 12, 1971, while President Nixon was dancing in the White House at the wedding of his daughter Tricia and enjoying what he called the happiest day of his presidency, the typesetters and pressmen at the *Times* started printing the stories that would bring about a first-order constitutional crisis.[40]

Early on June 13, the first edition of the Sunday *New York Times* began to circulate. In Harvard Square, after seeing a late movie, Daniel Ellsberg went to an all-night news kiosk and bought a couple of copies. As he walked home, he broke into a smile. In 24-point type over the four columns on the upper right of page one ran this headline:

VIETNAM ARCHIVE: PENTAGON STUDY TRACES
3 DECADES OF GROWING U.S. INVOLVEMENT

The lead article, written by Neil Sheehan, reported that a "massive" study commissioned by Defense Secretary Robert McNamara showed that four presidential administrations "progressively developed a sense of commitment to a non-Communist Vietnam, a readiness to fight the North to protect the South, and an ultimate frustration with this effort to a much greater extent than their public statements acknowledged at the time." The story went on in that vein—not exactly a bombshell; more like the pebble that starts the landslide. The *Times* promised more articles and more documents in the following days.

The news caught the White House off guard. In all the months of deliberations at the *Times,* no one had contacted the White House for comment, so the initial report came out of the blue. At first, the president decided to do nothing. In telephone calls that Sunday, Nixon told General Alexander Haig and Secretary of State William Rogers that he had not even read the *Times* story. He seemed more interested in the political impact than in the security breach, although he did call it "treasonable action on the part of the bastards that put it out."[41] To Nixon's mind, the salient feature was that the series criticized Democrats—Kennedy and Johnson—and not him. Then his national security adviser, Henry Kissinger, went to work on him. Even though he himself was one of the most astute and prolific leakers in history,

Kissinger argued that the conduct of U.S. diplomacy depended on plugging the leaks. Then he played his trump card, warning Nixon that if he tolerated this massive security breach, "it shows you're a weakling."[42] That did it. If there was one thing Nixon feared, it was showing vulnerability. So he began to weigh other options.

On Tuesday, June 15, 1971, government lawyers went into federal court in Manhattan and asked the court to enjoin the *Times* from publishing anything further about the Pentagon Papers. That was a momentous step. It was the first time since the adoption of the U.S. Constitution that the federal government had tried to impose "prior restraint" on a newspaper, on grounds of national security. Not since the British Crown ruled over the land had a publisher of a newspaper been told by the government in advance what it might or might not print. That was the essence of the constitutional crisis. Did the president have such power? If so, the Constitution did not grant it explicitly. From the newspaper's point of view, the issue was the plain meaning of the First Amendment, with its sweeping ban on abridging the freedom of the press. From the president's point of view, the issue was his duty as commander in chief to safeguard the nation by keeping its military, intelligence, and diplomatic secrets, particularly in time of war. Citing the Constitution, both sides prepared for a legal showdown.

At the outset, the case did not look promising for the newspaper. The matter was assigned to Judge Murray Gurfein, a veteran of army intelligence in World War II and a Republican who had just been appointed by Nixon himself.[43] It was Gurfein's very first case as a judge. After a brief hearing, Gurfein granted the government's request for a temporary restraining order and set a hearing for Friday. Significantly, the *Times* obeyed the court order and suspended the series about the Pentagon Papers. Some members of the *Times* staff wanted to print the following day's paper with a big chunk of white space where the story would have been as a mute protest against censorship, but the paper appeared as usual. For the time being at least, the government had succeeded in imposing prior restraint.

At the *Washington Post,* editor Ben Bradlee and his team had been hearing rumors of a big project at the *Times* but could not crack the secret. When the Pentagon Papers story hit on Sunday, Bradlee was beside himself. His immediate goal was to match what the *Times* had. He threw all his resources at it. Meanwhile, with the *Times* now enjoined from publishing anything further, Ellsberg became concerned that the momentum of the initial disclosures would evaporate and that the remaining documents might be successfully suppressed in court. Using a series of intermediaries and pay phones, he placed a call on Wednesday to an editor he knew at the *Washington Post,* Ben Bagdikian. If the *Post* could commit to publishing, Ellsberg said, Bagdikian should fly to Boston—and bring a large suitcase. So Bagdikian flew to Boston on Wednesday and got his own set of most of the documents.

Wednesday was also the day Ellsberg and his wife, Patricia, went on the lam, at first moving in and out of a series of motels in the Boston area. At the same time,

Ellsberg worked feverishly to stash more copies of the papers in various locations to prevent FBI agents from gathering them, and he contacted more journalists to offer them copies, operating on the theory that if more newspapers published the documents, the government would have a harder time persuading a court to attempt to put the milk back in the bottle.[44]

With its own version of the Pentagon Papers in hand, the *Post* now swung into action, setting up a command center at Bradlee's house in the Georgetown section of Washington. In one room the writers got to work. In another room the editors and lawyers got busy trying to decide whether to publish at all. They had twelve hours to do what had taken the *Times* three months. In some ways their challenge was more difficult than the one faced by the *Times*. For one thing, the lawyers pointed out, the *Post* (unlike the *Times*) was contemplating publication in an environment in which a federal court had already issued a restraining order. The order did not apply to the *Post*, but that was something of a technicality; the lawyers could hardly maintain that they did not know how the executive and judiciary felt about publication. *Post* executives also had another worry that had not concerned the *Times*. The Post Company owned several television stations, and the Nixon administration could be expected to seek revenge by using its majority on the FCC to block the renewal of those lucrative broadcasting licenses. What's more, the Post Company, strapped for cash, had just decided to join the trend toward selling stock to the general public. If the publisher, Katharine Graham, were charged with a felony for publishing the Pentagon Papers, the brokerage house underwriting the sale of the stock could back out of the deal; if convicted of a felony, she could be stripped of her television licenses. Either one might mean the end of the *Post* as a business enterprise.[45]

Finally, after frantic debate, the editors reached Mrs. Graham, who was hosting a dinner party at her home. On a conference call, she was told that it was now or never. She quickly gave her answer: "Go ahead, go ahead, go ahead. Let's go. Let's publish."[46] Like Arthur Sulzberger, Katharine Graham was betting the house—the company, the newspaper, the family's reputation. Like Sulzberger, she did so not only because she had good journalistic instincts but for another key reason as well. The fact was, she could. She owned enough of the paper to do whatever she wished. For better or worse, the publishers of the *Times* and the *Post* were answerable to no one. No less than Pulitzer, Hearst, or Luce in their day, they were at the peak of their personal power. They were operating at a time when their newspapers were profitable and the publishers were about as autonomous as they ever had been or would be. If they chose, they could even stand up to the president himself.

So the copies of the *Washington Post* that appeared on Friday morning carried a front-page story about the massive Vietnam study, revealing that the *Post* had obtained the same classified materials as the *Times*. Government lawyers swiftly went into U.S. District Court in Washington, D.C., seeking this time to impose prior restraint on the *Post*. Judge Gerhard Gesell refused to issue a restraining order, prompting the government to appeal. The appellate court reversed, and the *Post* was now in the same position as the *Times*, possessing the classified documents but muzzled from sharing them with the American public.

Meanwhile, all eyes were on the U.S. District Court in Manhattan, with Judge Gurfein presiding over a session to argue the merits of maintaining the injunction against the *Times*. The newspaper's lead attorney was Alexander Bickel, a Yale Law professor. (When the paper's longtime law firm balked, in-house counsel Jim Goodale recruited Bickel and a young First Amendment expert, Floyd Abrams, to help with the case.) He opened by noting that the *Washington Post* had published details from the secret report that very day and shared the story with the clients of the *Post*'s syndicated news service. The cat was out of the bag. There was no reason to go on enjoining the *Times*. Besides, Bickel continued, even after the disclosures by the two newspapers from the secret report, the sky had not fallen. "The Republic stands and it stood for the first three days," he declared, drawing cheers from the crowd in the courtroom.[47] Gurfein banged his gavel for order and later cleared the courtroom entirely for a closed session to hear the substance of the government's claim that the Pentagon Papers contained secrets that, if revealed, would threaten national security. The hearing went on for hours, followed by more arguments in open court until well past 11 p.m.

The next day Gurfein issued a ruling that shocked just about everyone. He ruled against the government. He said the Justice Department had failed to offer any "cogent reasons" for continued secrecy, and he went on to offer a stirring defense of press freedom: "The security of the Nation is not at the ramparts alone. Security also lies in the value of our free institutions. A cantankerous press, an obstinate press, a ubiquitous press must be suffered by those in authority in order to preserve the even greater values of the freedom of expression and the right of the people to know."[48] In one concession to the government, however, the judge extended the restraining order against the *Times* until the government had a chance to appeal.

On Friday evening, ruling in the government's case against the *Post*, Judge Gerhard Gesell in Washington had reached a similar conclusion and refused to impose prior restraint on the *Post*. The government promptly appealed (and secured a temporary restraining order), which meant that the two cases went to different circuits of the U.S. Court of Appeals. While lawyers argued, Ellsberg's strategy of diversifying the outlets for publication bore fruit. Excerpts from the Pentagon Papers began appearing in some twenty newspapers nationwide, including the *Boston Globe*, the *St. Louis Post-Dispatch*, and the *Christian Science Monitor*, papers Ellsberg chose for their opposition to the war. Meanwhile, the *Times* and the government both appealed to the U.S. Supreme Court. The legal stakes were as high as they get. There was essentially no case law on this legal question, so the judges lacked almost any precedent. On Friday, June 25, the high court, acting with rare speed, agreed to review both cases and ordered oral arguments the very next morning.

On Saturday the nine justices of the Supreme Court assembled in an open session, and lawyers for both sides were invited to make their arguments. As each side did so, the justices peppered them with questions. The interchanges went on for hours. At the end, Chief Justice Warren Burger thanked the lawyers, then adjourned.

On Wednesday, June 30, just fifteen days after the government had initiated the case, the justices assembled again. The chief justice read the court's ruling. Although the justices wrote nine separate opinions, it was a clear-cut victory for press freedom. By a 6–3 margin, a majority had decided that the *Times* and the *Post* could resume publication of their series. When word reached the two news-rooms, reporters broke into cheers (which doesn't happen very often), cham-pagne flowed, and stories that had been frozen by the Nixon administration were quickly readied for publication in the next day's papers.

Because of the stakes involved, the high court's ruling deserves close attention.[49] Among the nine justices, there were three distinct schools of thought. One group of three (Justices Hugo Black, William O. Douglas, and William J. Brennan Jr.) took a view sometimes known as "First Amendment absolutism." That is, they believed that when the Constitution says Congress shall "make no law . . . abridg-ing the freedom of the press," it means just that: the government may not restrain the press, no matter what. Accordingly, Black found that "every moment's con-tinuance of the injunctions against these newspapers amounts to a flagrant, in-defensible, and continuing violation of the First Amendment." In this view, press freedom exists to serve the American people, the ultimate sovereigns in a system of self-government. "The press [is] to serve the governed, not the governors," as Black put it. If the press causes some harm, then the remedies have to come after publication and not before.

Another group of three (Chief Justice Warren Burger, along with Justices John Marshall Harlan and Harry Blackmun) sided with the government. Burger objected on procedural grounds; he thought the Court was being stampeded and wanted more time to consider. Harlan objected to the rush as well, but he ruled on the merits anyway. His main point was that the president has the exclusive power to handle foreign relations for the United States and therefore must be able to maintain secrets. In his opinion, Blackmun wrote that the case required balancing different portions of the Constitution: "The First Amendment, after all, is only one part of an entire Constitution. Article II of the great document vests in the Executive Branch primary power over the conduct of foreign affairs, and places in that branch the responsibility for the Nation's safety. Each provi-sion of the Constitution is important, and I cannot subscribe to a doctrine of unlimited absolutism for the First Amendment at the cost of downgrading other provisions."

With such a 3–3 split, the three remaining justices (Potter Stewart, Byron White, and Thurgood Marshall) held the balance. In answer to the question whether the government could ever impose prior restraint, they said, in effect, it depends. To begin with, the government faces a heavy burden of proof in such cases. More important, they went on to spell out the conditions under which prior restraint might be justified in the future: the government would have to show that publication would present an immediate, serious, and irreparable harm to the national security. The threat could not be far off or hypothetical; it could not be a matter of politics or mere inconvenience or embarrassment. In the case at hand, they ruled, the government had not met the standard they had just invented. On that basis, they joined with the absolutists and held that publication could resume.

Naturally, the press hailed the ruling as a great victory, which indeed it was. But newspapers, which are averse to stories about complicated legal issues and allergic to stories about themselves, quickly changed the subject and moved on. In that, they may have been hasty, because the consequences of the Pentagon Papers case were many, sometimes subtle, and sometimes roundabout.

First and foremost, of course, the 6–3 ruling was a tremendous legal win for the news media, on the scale of an earthquake that reshapes the landscape for a long time to come. The verdict remains the law of the land some four decades later and may stand for a good deal longer. In the first showdown over prior restraint, the press won and the government lost, an outcome that pretty thoroughly repudiated the whole idea of prior restraint and created a de facto moratorium on its use.[50] That much is clear. What is more difficult to measure is the psychological impact. To judge by the record, though, it seems fair to say that the press as an institution was emboldened by the Pentagon Papers case. The experience of taking on the president (which in this case also meant Defense, Justice, and State) and coming out on top was a heady one. It would be only natural for a publisher, editor, or reporter to think that maybe the press really was a Fourth Estate, that the media could tackle other powerful institutions, that journalism could do more than record the things that other people say and do.

The Pentagon Papers also vindicated the early reporting out of Vietnam, by Halberstam and others, which had tried to point out that the war effort was not working. Particularly when the papers were printed in book form, as they quickly were, the government's own documents could be used to settle some of the debates over the war. All the reporting that had caused so much controversy and bitterness for the Saigon press corps in the period from 1962 to 1965 was fully documented. In fact, if anything, the Pentagon Papers indicated that the situation had been worse—and more duplicitous—than even the most critical reporting had indicated. If they were going to report on the government, reporters concluded, they were going to have to become a lot more cynical.

The case also had an impact on American culture and politics. In terms of the "credibility gap," the Pentagon Papers blew it wide open. The gap now became a chasm that threatened to swallow up every powerful institution in the country. No one could read the documents, or even the stories about them, without taking away a deeper message: the officials who run the White House and the Pentagon do not level with the American people. They exaggerate, they prevaricate, they even lie—all in pursuit of their own agendas. In terms of domestic politics, the Pentagon Papers provided fresh fuel for the antiwar movement. The release of the papers also gave evidence that the government routinely abused the power to classify information, hiding materials from the public because of convenience or politics rather than national survival, and it showed that officials rarely caught up with the need to declassify information.

In a narrower political sense, the Pentagon Papers had the effect of ratcheting up the war between Nixon and the press. Nixon had always resented and loathed the press, and the outcome in this case left him apoplectic. One result was a desperate attempt to control information by plugging "leaks." Nixon had found that the FBI did not share his sense of urgency about the problem, so he started to demand new ways of stopping leaks. In doing so, he was heading down the road to perdition, a path that would ultimately doom his presidency at a place called Watergate.

It is also important to note what the Pentagon Papers case did not do. One thing it did not do was to affect combat operations. Not a single U.S. casualty in Vietnam was ever blamed on any of the revelations. The papers did not contain current operational details. If they had, it is almost certain—given a track record stretching over decades—that the press would have voluntarily censored anything of the kind.

In terms of defining the relationship between government and the press, the Supreme Court ruling left many questions unanswered. It did not define what legal protections, if any, might be enjoyed by government employees who divulge secret or classified information. Were these "leakers" to be treated like villains or heroes? Were they reformist "whistleblowers" . . . or disloyal sneak-thieves? The case also did not address the status of the journalists who collaborate with leakers. Do the journalists have any legal claim of confidentiality? Do they enjoy any of the privileges that protect clergymen or doctors from having to testify about the things people tell them in confidence? On these matters the Court was silent, leaving them to future courts and Congress to argue over.

Specifically, the high court also sidestepped the matter of Daniel Ellsberg, whose case was not before them. Instead, he was facing criminal charges, which had been brought just one day before the Supreme Court ruling. Almost as soon as the Pentagon Papers appeared in print, Ellsberg had been "outed" by a journalist who was not involved in the case: former *Times* reporter Sidney Zion. Although Zion had no firsthand information, he publicly identified Ellsberg on a radio show in New York. (Ellsberg fully expected that the FBI would know it was he who had leaked, so he was not particularly upset with Zion.)[51] Nixon was furious at Ellsberg and wanted him destroyed. "Let's get the son-of-a-bitch in jail," Nixon told aides on the afternoon of June 30 as he began to outline a smear campaign against Ellsberg. "Don't worry about his trial. Just get everything out. Try him in the press. Everything . . . get it out, leak it out. We want to destroy him in the press. . . . Is that clear?"[52] He apparently drew a major distinction between authorized leaks and unauthorized leaks. The former were a tool of governance; the latter were a personal affront and an abomination. But beyond that, Nixon, a lawyer, had little use for the law. To him it was all politics. And in politics, what better weapon than a leak?

As it turned out, Nixon's determination to play rough with Ellsberg backfired. Eventually Ellsberg was brought to trial in a federal court in California, represented by radical attorney Leonard Boudin. Ellsberg was charged with stealing government property, conspiracy, and violating the Espionage Act. After months of proceedings, his trial was suddenly halted. Judge Matthew Byrne got word from the government's lawyers about something he just could not stomach. Not only had the Nixon administration tapped Ellsberg's phones. Not only had the government hired goons to break up a rally where Ellsberg was speaking. Not only did the White House dangle the offer of making Judge Byrne the head of the FBI while he was still presiding over the trial. The real bombshell was that two men hired by the White House to plug leaks for Nixon—known by the nickname "Plumbers"—had taken the president at his word that they should find a way to disgrace Ellsberg. What these plumbers, ex-CIA man Howard Hunt and ex-FBI man G. Gordon Liddy, decided to do was to burglarize the office of Ellsberg's psychiatrist in hopes of finding something they could use against him. When Judge Byrne heard about the burglary of a doctor's office carried out by government agents, he had had enough. "The totality of the circumstances of this case," he declared, "offend 'a sense of justice.'"[53]

Case dismissed.[54]

* * *

KATHARINE GRAHAM WAS AN UNLIKELY choice to topple a president. The insecure, awkward daughter of a wealthy businessman, she had never been prepared to run anything more complicated than a dinner party. Her role in life was all set at birth: as with Iphigene Ochs, daughter of *New York Times* publisher Adolph Ochs, Katharine's task was to marry a man who could inherit her father's newspaper, the *Washington Post.*[55]

Katharine was born to wealth and privilege. Her father, Eugene Meyer, the son of an immigrant from Alsace, went into investment banking and made a fortune on Wall Street. Her mother, Agnes Ernst, grew up outside New York City in more modest circumstances; she went to Barnard College on a scholarship (over her father's objections), then did some freelance reporting for the *New York Sun.*[56] Agnes's life changed when she met Eugene Meyer. A non-observant Jew, Meyer married Agnes in a Lutheran ceremony. By the time Katharine was born in 1917, Meyer's personal fortune, derived from the Wall Street investment company he had founded, was estimated at $40 to $60 million. With the coming of war in 1917, Meyer decided to offer his services to the Wilson administration as a "dollar-a-year" man—the first in a series of public service appointments, under both

Democrats and Republicans, that would culminate in his running the Federal Reserve Board and then the World Bank. While working in Washington, Meyer attempted to buy the failing *Washington Post* in 1929, but the owner rejected his $5 million offer. After more losses, the paper went bankrupt, and Meyer was able to buy it at auction in 1933. When William Randolph Hearst dropped out of the bidding at $800,000, Meyer got the paper for $825,000.

Young Katharine Meyer, meanwhile, grew up in high style, spending much of her childhood in Mount Kisco, outside New York City, where the family had a vast mansion. She attended the exclusive Madeira School, then entered Vassar before transferring to the University of Chicago. Upon her graduation, her father arranged for Katharine to work on the *San Francisco News,* where she started at the bottom, helping to cover labor brawls on the waterfront and learning to drink boilermakers. (Still, she remained a Meyer. Once, after a day of covering the long-shoremen, she went with her aunt to the opening of the opera season, wearing a long black velvet gown with leopard-skin straps that had been sent from back East.) After a year, she headed to Washington in 1939 and went to work at her father's paper, on the editorial page. She soon met the brilliant, handsome Phil Graham, who had risen from hard times in Florida to the front ranks of the most ambitious young men of his generation. He had been editor of the *Harvard Law Review* and was now clerking at the U.S. Supreme Court.

When Phil proposed to Kay, he had one condition: that they live on his salary and take nothing from her father. On those terms (more or less), they married and began making plans. Phil pursued the law, and Kay went back to work at the *Post,* writing items for a Sunday section called "Brains." During World War II, while Phil was in the Army Air Corps, the *Post* finally began to make money, and Eugene Meyer started thinking about a successor. Everyone assumed that it would have to be a man, and Meyer turned to his son-in-law. Phil raised objections, but eventually Meyer overcame them, and Philip Graham became associate publisher of the *Washington Post* on January 1, 1946, moving up to publisher soon after. Kay, meanwhile, played an affluent woman's domestic role—looking after the children and supervising a household staff that included a nurse, a cook, and a laundress. Although she continued to write for the *Post,* she and Phil had a very traditional marriage.

Phil Graham did not know much about journalism, but he learned quickly. He also discovered that the part he liked best was making deals. In 1948 he bought an interest in the CBS radio station WTOP, bringing the Post Company into broadcasting. In 1950 he built a new headquarters for the *Post* in downtown Washington. In 1954 he helped engineer the purchase of the *Washington Times-Herald,* a move that gave the *Post* a monopoly in the city's morning newspaper market, and thus ensured the paper's financial future as far ahead as anyone could see. In 1961, Phil took the advice of the assistant Washington bureau chief of *Newsweek,* Ben Bradlee, and bought the weekly newsmagazine for some $8.9 million. In all these moves,

Graham had wide latitude. The company had been incorporated, but it was entirely in the family's hands. When the *Post* needed money for building or acquisitions, Phil asked his in-laws for it, or he raised cash by selling assets. After Meyer died in 1959, Phil was fully in command. He was building a media empire under his own control.

During the Kennedy years, the Grahams were reaching an apex of early success. Still in their forties (just like their friend the president), they were rich, powerful, and connected. Outwardly they seemed like a golden couple. But there were clouds, sometimes quite dark. The problem was Phil. Always a heavy drinker, he had become increasingly erratic during the previous decade, swinging between periods of high energy when he was making business deals or brokering political alliances, then plunging into gloomy spells when he would lie nearly catatonic for weeks at a time. In an era that valued stoicism and dreaded mental illness, Phil and Kay always managed to keep his condition quiet. Once, in 1957, he had snapped, weeping uncontrollably. Kay was panic-stricken, struggling not only with her husband's collapse but also with her own ignorance about mental illness and her sense of shame at the stigma. Phil took about a year to recover, spending much of his time at their country place, Glen Welby, in Virginia. Under the care of Dr. Leslie Farber, a devotee of "existential psychology" and a follower of Rollo May,[57] Phil had his ups and downs, but the trend was largely downward. He became abusive, and he began an affair with a young *Newsweek* staffer, Robin Webb.

In early 1963, Phil's condition became public. He and his girlfriend flew to Phoenix to attend a meeting of the Associated Press. There, in a ballroom full of the nation's top publishers, Phil Graham lost it. He stormed the podium and berated the audience, telling them that they were all fat bastards and promising to wipe his ass with their papers. Then he started taking off his clothes. Roused from a state of stupefaction, Otis Chandler (publisher of the *Los Angeles Times*) and others stepped in and hustled Phil off to a nearby room. Eventually Dr. Farber flew out to Arizona, administered a tranquillizer, and put Phil aboard a presidential airplane dispatched by Jack Kennedy. Phil was admitted to Chestnut Lodge, a private mental hospital in suburban Washington, where he seemed to get better. He announced his intention to divorce Kay, marry Robin, and take the *Post* away from the Meyer family. For Kay, this was rock bottom: she could see that Phil was slipping away from her, but she was determined to hang on to her family's newspaper. By June, Phil was much improved. He declared that the affair with Robin was over and that he wanted to return to Kay, who welcomed him back. He was staying at Chestnut Lodge again, but he talked the doctors into letting him out for a weekend in August. He and Kay had lunch on the back porch at Glen Welby, then went upstairs for a nap. Phil got up and went out. A few minutes later there was the sound of a shotgun blast. Kay bolted up and raced around the house looking for Phil. She found him in a bathroom. There must have been blood everywhere.

Now she was alone. After Phil's suicide, everything depended on her; she was responsible for the kids, the houses, the staff, the family fortune, plus a potentially great newspaper. It was a daunting array of challenges of very different sorts. In many ways, the most difficult was the *Post.* In 1963, women in American journalism were few in number and low in prestige. Despite some prominent exceptions such as the syndicated columnist Dorothy Thompson or the reporter Maggie Higgins, very few women had managed to move beyond what were still known as the "women's pages" (or "society pages"), where they wrote about weddings, fashion, and casseroles.[58] A young woman might work for a while for a newspaper or magazine taking photos, as Jacqueline Bouvier had done (that was how she met Jack Kennedy), or she might work as an assistant to an editor or publisher. But almost no women wielded any real power in the newsrooms. Nor did they wield much power in any other industry; in 1960 only 5 percent of all working women were in management. When Mrs. Graham (as all her employees called her) took over the *Post,* she was a pioneer at every turn. The boards she eventually joined—of the American Newspaper Publishers Association, the Associated Press, and the Washington Post Company itself—had never had a woman member before. In 1963, Mrs. Graham could not even join the National Press Club, just a few blocks away from the *Post,* because it was still all male. Even the *Post* itself would be the focus of an antidiscrimination action by women employees, which resulted in a settlement shared by everyone in the category, including Kay Graham. In that setting, it was widely assumed that she would sell the paper or turn it over to someone else to run.

So what she did next came as a surprise. She decided to run the *Post* herself. Though terrified of what she was getting into and almost entirely unprepared to lead a large enterprise, Kay Graham became president of the Washington Post Company in late 1963 and set about making her mark. In 1965 she brought Ben Bradlee over from *Newsweek* and made him managing editor of the *Post.* She helped him become a great editor, not only by supporting him professionally but also by presiding over a business that was practically printing money. These were boom years in Washington. Under Johnson, the Great Society programs were staffing up, bringing thousands of middle-class, white-collar jobs to the city and its increasingly far-flung suburbs. This was the target audience for the *Post,* and for every advertiser in the region. Money came rolling in. During the three years after Bradlee took over, the budget for the *Post* newsroom more than tripled, leaping from $2.25 million a year to almost $7.3 million.[59] Bradlee got to add fifty new slots in the newsroom, and he went on a hiring spree. In the process, he transformed the paper, creating a star system (known famously at the *Post* as "creative tension") in which reporters had to jockey for space in the paper and for favor in Bradlee's inner circle.

But that was not Mrs. Graham's domain. She visited the newsroom from time to time, and she was delighted with Bradlee, but her real duties were upstairs, in trying to run the whole business. Some time after Phil's suicide she also began to return to her social life, often on the arm of former Illinois governor and twice unsuccessful Democratic presidential candidate Adlai Stevenson. Her role was a

12.6 **JOURNALIST TRUMAN CAPOTE AND** *WASHINGTON POST* **PUBLISHER KATHARINE GRAHAM** enter the Plaza Hotel in 1966. Capote planned the masked "Black and White Ball" to cheer up his friend Graham. It became a social and media sensation.
—*Getty Images.*

busy one. She had many friends in Washington and another roster in New York, where she and Phil had gone regularly for years to keep tabs on *Newsweek,* which was based in midtown Manhattan. She became quite friendly with Babe Paley, wife of the CBS chairman. Through Babe, Kay met Truman Capote in the early 1960s, and they became friends as well. In 1966, now that she was resuming her social life, Capote told Kay that he was going to host a ball to cheer her up—"the nicest party, darling, you ever went to." Capote thought it would be fun to hold it in the Grand Ballroom of New York's Plaza Hotel and that it would be extra special if the guests wore masks and dressed all in black and white. Kay would be the guest of honor. The Black and White Ball, held on November 28, 1966, became a phenomenon, a who's who of the worlds of media, business, the arts, and the burgeoning field of pure celebrity. Anyone who was fabulous simply *had* to be there. Later, Kay would say that she felt like "a middle-aged debutante" and a bit like Cinderella.[60] The media, naturally, had a field day (fig. 12.6).

While Kay Graham was emerging from tragedy, the man who would become her greatest antagonist was not far away, busy carrying out plans for a comeback of his own. Richard Nixon and Kay Graham could not have been more different. She came from a world of wealth, grace, and entrée. He came from a world of poverty, striving, and a lack of entrée. She was the Washington establishment; he was the ultimate outsider. She was ostensibly bipartisan but a registered Democrat; he was as partisan a Republican as you could find. She was a creature of the news media, surrounded by journalists; he was surrounded by guys from advertising and p.r., and he distrusted, feared, and loathed the news media. And yet their lives were unfolding along oddly parallel arcs: early success, followed by tragedy, followed by a second act of even greater heights. Neither one could have had an inkling on the night of Capote's ball in 1966, but their paths were about to cross.

SCENE: NEW YORK CITY.

Nixon had left Washington in defeat after losing the presidency in 1960 to Mrs. Graham's rich, connected, handsome friend Jack Kennedy, and he had left electoral politics in disgrace, telling reporters after he lost the 1962 race for governor of California, "You won't have Nixon to kick around any more, because, gentlemen, this is my last press conference." But now he was on his way back. He was living in New York and working as a lawyer. (That very year, 1966, he argued his first case before the U.S. Supreme Court.) But a law practice was not what Nixon had in mind as his final act. He was planning to make it all the way back, to win the ultimate prize, the White House. He was in exile, and Manhattan was his Elba. While Mrs. Graham had been having dress fittings (including a mask made by Halston) that fall, Nixon had been humping around the country campaigning for Republican candidates for Congress. Two years later he was ready to campaign for himself.

When Nixon won the Republican presidential nomination in the summer of 1968, a Post *editorial observed, "As well as we ought to know him by now, he remains remarkably unknown."*[61] *When Nixon won the presidency and returned to Washington in January 1969, he must have felt that he was entering enemy territory, full of Kennedy people and Johnson people. From the get-go, he decided that most of the press—including, of course, those snide bastards at the television networks—were against him. Soon he had so many enemies that he felt he needed to keep a list. He was going to push back, hard. After losing the Pentagon Papers case, Nixon gave the order: Stop the leaks. He didn't care how—just* STOP THE GODDAMN LEAKS.

The first Mrs. Graham heard about the Watergate break-in came when she got a call at home on the morning of Saturday, June 17, 1972.[62] It was from Howard Simons, the *Post*'s managing editor.[63] First, though, he had to tell her about a pip of a story: a car plowed into a house and pushed a sofa right out the far side—*with a couple on the sofa having sex!* Oh, yes, there was also another local story: five guys were arrested breaking into the Democratic National Committee headquarters at the Watergate complex.

Hmmm . . . *that* might be something.

According to police reports, five men were caught trying to burglarize the Watergate offices of the DNC. That would be small potatoes, hardly more than a local news brief, except that there were a couple of details that weren't quite right, details that put the break-in story on page one. These burglars wore suits and surgical gloves. They were carrying a walkie-talkie, which might make sense, except that they had only one. Where was the other one? Who were they coordinating with? Not only that, but also, when they showed up in court first thing the next morning, they already had a lawyer. Very strange.

On June 18, 1972, the first piece in the drama that would become known as Watergate appeared on the front page of the *Washington Post*. It carried the byline of longtime cops reporter Alfred E. Lewis and bore an italicized credit line at the bottom adding the names of Bob Woodward and Carl Bernstein (along with six others, making a total of nine reporters on one story, plus photographers and editors—*that's* resources).[64] The story began:

> Five men, one of whom said he is a former employee of the CIA, were arrested at 2:30 a.m. yesterday in what authorities described as an elaborate plot to bug the offices of the Democratic National Committee here.
>
> Three of the men were native-born Cubans and another was said to have trained Cuban exiles for guerrilla activity after the 1961 Bay of Pigs invasion.

Nixon, who was in the midst of a reelection campaign that year, one in which he really wanted to run up the score against the Democrats, made no official comment on such a minor matter. His press secretary, Ron Ziegler, pooh-poohed the incident when he was asked about it at the Florida White House in Key Biscayne: "Certain elements may try to stretch this beyond what it is." It was, Ziegler asserted, nothing but "a third-rate burglary attempt."[65]

SCENE: THE WHITE HOUSE.

In private, Nixon was worried.[66] Within days of the break-in, he was plotting with his top aides about how to handle the mess. He knew that his top campaign aide and former attorney general, John Mitchell, had approved "Operation Gemstone," which included bugging the DNC headquarters, so Nixon wasn't learning anything from the Washington Post *about Watergate that he didn't already know. On June 20, chief of staff Bob Haldeman informed Nixon that Howard Hunt had been posted across the street from the Watergate with binoculars and the equipment needed to receive any signals sent by the electronic "bug" that the burglars had planted at the DNC. In Nixon's view, Plan A should be to keep denying everything. "My God, the committee isn't worth bugging in my opinion. That's my public line." Three days later Nixon had a better idea. He knew that if the FBI conducted an even routinely competent investigation, it would lead directly to the White House. So he had to thwart that lawful criminal investigation. How about the CIA? Yes, that was it! He could tell the CIA to call the FBI and say, You guys have to back off this Watergate thing because it involves the Cubans from Miami and that points back to the Bay of Pigs, and that means it's international and not really an FBI matter after all. Yes, that would work. So he told his top aides: "When you get in these people . . . say: 'Look, the problem is that this will open the whole, the whole Bay of Pigs thing, and the President just feels that'—without going into details—don't, don't lie to them to the extent to say there is no involvement, but just say this is sort of a comedy of errors, bizarre, without getting into it."*

That should fix it.

The *Post* assigned the break-in story to Bob Woodward, a former navy man who

at age twenty-nine was a rookie in *Post* terms, hardly a reporter at all. He was
soon joined by Carl Bernstein, twenty-eight, a young guy with tons of experience
but a reputation as something of a flake. Bernstein didn't know it, but he was on
the verge of being fired when he shoehorned his way onto the Watergate story.
Significantly, the *Post* editors did not assign the story to one of the paper's many
talented National staff reporters, the kind who are very good at seeing the big picture, who would have known all the key players, but who were not in the habit of
working a crime story. Instead, the Watergate story stayed with the local reporters on the metro desk, and that may have made all the difference. Woodward and
Bernstein started asking questions, and that simple fact was the key to their entire
success. They had no master plan, no special technique. They started asking questions, and they didn't stop until they had answers. They wanted to know why the
burglars had crisp $100 bills in their wallets, in sequence. They wanted to know
why one of the burglars had an entry in his address book that referred to Howard
Hunt and the White House. Who was Howard Hunt? They wanted to know what

it meant that one of the burglars was retired from the CIA. So many questions. It could take months . . . (fig. 12.7)

One of the answers appeared in a story that ran on August 1, 1972: "Bug Suspect Got Campaign Funds." In it, Bernstein and Woodward (they alternated the order of their bylines) reported that a $25,000 cashier's check that was supposed to go to Nixon's reelection campaign fund (the Committee to Re-elect the President, with the hapless acronym CREEP) had ended up in a bank account belonging to one of the Watergate burglars. There it was—the first break that pointed from the burglary toward the president and his political team.

Publicly, Nixon denied everything, as did his aides and allies. Later in August, Nixon announced that his legal counsel, John Dean, had looked into the Watergate matter. "I can state categorically that his investigation indicates that no one in the White House staff, no one in this administration, presently employed, was involved in this very bizarre incident," Nixon intoned, then added, "What really hurts is if you try to cover it up."[67] His bluff almost worked. Most of the press showed little interest in the case, and the story seemed to be petering out.

SCENE: THE OVAL OFFICE
Meanwhile, Nixon was furious at the Post *and threatened retaliation. His weapon of choice: challenging the FCC's renewal of the broadcasting licenses held by the two Post Company television stations. On September 15 he told his lawyer, John Dean, and his chief of staff, Bob Haldeman: "The main thing is, the* Post *is going to have damnable, damnable problems out of this one. . . . The game has to be played awfully rough."*

On September 28, 1972, another bombshell: Woodward and Bernstein had discovered that John Mitchell, the chairman of CREEP, had, while serving as attorney general, controlled a secret slush fund that was used to spy on Democrats. Citing anonymous sources, the story said that some of those funds had been used by the Plumbers, the president's private political hit squad. As any conscientious reporter must do, Bernstein called the target of the story to invite him to comment. When he phoned Mitchell, the president's man exploded: "All that *crap,* you're putting it in the paper? It's all been denied. Katie Graham's gonna get her tit caught in a big fat wringer if that's published. Good Christ! That's the most sickening thing I ever heard."[68] To his great credit, Bernstein followed one of the basic tenets of reporting: when people get mad at you, don't take it personally, but *do* take notes.

At other times, the pressure of Watergate was more diffuse. For months during the summer and fall of 1972 the *Post* was driving the coverage, setting the pace of revelations, providing what journalists call the "enterprise" for the story. Once in a while someone else added a tidbit, and CBS did a very welcome two-night special report in October, lavishing credit on the *Post.* In two lengthy segments on the *CBS Evening News,* Walter Cronkite brought together many details from the *Post*'s reporting in the previous four months, as well as some original material. Up until then, Watergate had proven too complicated and lacking in "visuals" to qualify as a television news story. The first segment ran about twenty minutes on a Friday evening. Before the second segment could be aired on Monday, Nixon aide Chuck Colson called CBS chief William Paley to berate him for biased coverage, and Paley prevailed on the news division to shorten the second segment. Still, Cronkite's coverage helped give the story the imprimatur of the most trusted journalist in the country.

Even so, it was a bit unnerving to the journalists at the *Post* that no one else in the news media was doing any original reporting on Watergate. As Bradlee recalled, Mrs. Graham used to stroll through the newsroom at times during the early months of Watergate and ask a question: If this is such a great story, where's the rest of the media? It was a hard one to answer.

Despite the pressure, Mrs. Graham hung in there. At the other end of the *Post* hierarchy, Woodward and Bernstein kept banging away at Watergate, trying to fit pieces together in a giant puzzle whose overall pattern they couldn't yet perceive. They had their own reasons for soldiering on. For one thing, they were, of course, ambitious young reporters who could see that these stories were getting them onto page one. They also had another reason for proceeding, or at least Woodward did. That was a special friend of his, the man who became the most famous anonymous source in Washington, the one known for decades by the nickname "Deep Throat." The role of Deep Throat began early on in the Watergate story. Woodward had met him a few years earlier, while Woodward was in the navy, handling coded communications for the Pentagon, a duty that occasionally involved carrying sealed courier bags to the White House. There, in a waiting room, Woodward had once spoken with a man a good twenty years older than himself, who proved to be one of the best sources a reporter could hope for.

Woodward guarded the man's identity scrupulously. He told Bernstein who he was, but he never included Bernstein in his meetings with the source. Even Bradlee didn't know Deep Throat's real name—at least not at first. He only knew what kind of position Deep Throat held. For Woodward, Deep Throat was a guide and a tipster but not a true source in the usual sense, since nothing he said could be used in print. He was not a leaker like Ellsberg (or Kissinger, for that matter).[69] He provided no quotes, no documents. He did provide invaluable guidance, but anything he told Woodward had to be confirmed with at least two other, independent sources (under a policy formalized by Bradlee after dealing with a rash of anonymously sourced stories). Along the way, Woodward and Bernstein had many hundreds of other sources. But none was as helpful as Deep Throat in suggesting the outlines of the puzzle they were trying to solve.

The nickname Deep Throat was suggested by *Post* managing editor Howard Simons, a play on words with the ground rules of anonymous briefings in Washington known as "deep background" and a reference to the then current porn film *Deep Throat,* which featured fellatio. Amazingly, Deep Throat's true identity was kept secret for more than thirty years—one of very few secrets to last that long in

Washington. In 2005, Deep Throat finally revealed himself. It turned out that he was Mark Felt, who had been deputy director of the FBI throughout the Watergate investigation and was therefore in a position to see every scrap of evidence turned up by the government. Feeling alienated when he was passed over for the job of FBI director, he found a way to settle the score.[70]

Felt probably never uttered the brilliant line "Follow the money," made famous by the film version of *All the President's Men* (Woodward has acknowledged that the phrase does not appear anywhere in his notes of their conversations). But the phrase perfectly encapsulates the thrust of his advice, which was to follow the trail of evidence left by CREEP's financing of the burglars. In any case, it has been adopted as something of a First Commandment for journalism, especially for investigative reporting.[71]

On November 7, 1972, Nixon was reelected in one of the biggest landslides in U.S. history, taking every state but Massachusetts.[72] (*So much for the power of the media,* Mrs. Graham thought.) His mission accomplished, Nixon could now turn to revenge and to those "damnable, damnable problems" he planned to visit on his tormentors at the *Washington Post.* It didn't take long. In the closing days of 1972 and the first week of 1973, there was a flurry of challenges to renewals of the licenses held by two TV stations in Florida, which just happened to be owned by the Post Company. Out of the thirty stations around the country up for renewal at the time, only the *Post's* two licenses were challenged. Not only that, but also the Watergate story seemed to dry up again. For the rest of November and December, nothing. It looked as though Nixon was going to get away with it—the secret funds, the Plumbers, the dirty tricks, the cover-up, the whole enchilada.

Then, in January 1973, the Watergate case took on fresh momentum. One big break came when the *New York Times* weighed in. The paper had a large Washington bureau, but it was full of pipe-smoking experts, distinguished senior correspondents who covered the State Department or arms control or Congress, not the local D.C. cops and courts. But feeling the Watergate story slipping away, the *Times* had hired Seymour Hersh, the reporter who broke the My Lai story in 1969, and turned him loose on Watergate. On Sunday, January 14, 1973, Hersh came up with a page one doozy: the Watergate burglars, who were facing criminal charges, were keeping their mouths shut not because they were such stand-up guys but because Hunt was shaking down the White House for hush money. The burglars were being paid up to $400 a month to maintain silence (a further obstruction of justice). Now the *Times* had put its institutional heft behind the Watergate story, and the *Post* would never be alone again. As if on signal, the rest of the press corps felt a sudden resurgence of interest.

In addition, January 1973 was the month when the wheels of government finally started to turn. One wheel was judicial. In the U.S. District Court in Washington, Judge John Sirica was presiding over the trial of the burglars. Prior to sentencing, burglar James McCord decided to break his silence in hopes of getting a lighter sentence. He began telling the judge what he knew, and he knew a lot. Another wheel was congressional: the Senate voted that same month to establish a "select committee" to look into the Watergate matter, under chairman Sam Ervin, a Democrat from North Carolina, who used his folksy Southern manners to disarm the unwary. From here on out, Nixon was caught in the official investigative machinery, and the initiative passed from the *Post* to the federal government. The Ervin committee and others began staffing up, hiring hundreds of extra investigators and lawyers,[73] who inevitably started leaking the fruits of those investigations to the media.

Step by step, the wheels of government ground more and more finely, producing a series of shocking disclosures. In April 1973 the momentum shifted against Nixon decisively. Presidential advisers Bob Haldeman, John Ehrlichman, and John Dean all lost their jobs, along with Attorney General Richard Kleindienst. That same month the *Post* won the Pulitzer Prize for its 1972 Watergate reporting, the ultimate professional vindication. As Ben Bradlee later recalled:

> The air was thick with lies, and the president was the lead liar. In April 1973, Nixon said he "began intensive new inquiries." That was a lie. In the same statement, he said he condemned "any attempts to cover up in this case, no matter who is involved." That was another lie. He, himself, was leading the cover-up of Watergate. [Press secretary Ron] Ziegler was lying so often, he had to coin the expression "inoperative statements" when he needed to find the euphemistic way to admit that he had lied.[74]

In May, the Ervin committee opened its hearings, which the TV networks covered live. Viewers wondered along with senators, in the era's famous phrase, "What did the president know, and when did he know it?" Americans debated whether there was a "smoking gun"—some piece of evidence that would put the case beyond politics and establish Nixon's guilt even to the satisfaction of his diehard supporters. Now the bombshells came tumbling out, exploding almost daily. In June, Dean testified. The president's own lawyer accused the Nixon White House of engaging in wiretapping, burglary, manipulating secret funds, laundering money, using enemies lists, pulling dirty tricks, and maintaining the "Plumbers." In July, the ultimate revelation: an obscure White House aide named Alexander Butterfield told the committee about a secret tape-recording system in the Oval Office. Amazing, stupendous. *Everything on tape?* The whole country wanted to listen.

From that point on, until the final tawdry details were pried from Nixon's control, the Watergate story was driven by the principal legal and political actors, not by journalists like Woodward and Bernstein. The media certainly carried the story, trying to meet what became an insatiable public demand, but did not drive it. From the moment the existence of the tapes was revealed, according to Bradlee, "the courts and the Congress had the president in their sight, and he couldn't hide."[75]

Much of late 1973 and early 1974 was spent in a constitutional showdown involving the executive, legislative, and judicial branches over those Oval Office tapes. In July 1974, the House Judiciary Committee approved three articles of impeachment against Richard Nixon—on charges of obstruction of justice, abuse of power, and contempt of Congress. On August 5, the White House was forced to release the tape from June 23, 1972. That did it. This proved to be the long-sought "smoking gun." The whole country could now hear Nixon plotting with his top aides to divert the FBI's lawful investigation of Watergate. Americans could also figure out that every public statement Nixon had made about Watergate since then had been a lie. Mrs. Graham, vacationing on Martha's Vineyard off the Massachusetts coast, sensed that the end was near and flew home to Washington. Overnight, the remnants of Nixon's support vanished, and the president announced that he would do the one thing he had always said he would never do.

The next day, the *Washington Post* ran a banner headline:[76]

NIXON RESIGNS

In the *Post* newsroom, Bradlee braced for the final act. He wanted to be sure there was no gloating, and he banned all outside reporters from the premises. Mrs. Graham felt a great sense of relief, and she promptly returned to the Vineyard. On television, she could hear the new president, Gerald Ford, announce the end of "our long national nightmare." Years later she would observe, "The relief came from having a *nice,* open, honest and nonthreatening president."[77] Not like that horrible, secretive Nixon.

The coverage of Watergate has loomed large ever since 1974 in the national memory of the period.

On any assessment of the reporting, it must be noted first that Woodward and Bernstein were, on the overwhelming majority of matters large and small, right. Certainly there were individual stories that were fragmentary, confusing, and tendentious. But in the end, their reporting stood up. Second, it must also be observed that it is too glib to say that Woodward and Bernstein, or Ben Bradlee and Kay Graham, or the *Washington Post* as a whole "toppled a president." Nixon was forced to resign, manifestly, by the actions taken by Congress and the courts, as contemplated by the Constitution itself. His own deeds amply justified the result. But that is not to say that the reporting played no role. In fact, the *Post's* coverage played a key role. Bradlee was correct in his evaluation of the coverage when he wrote that Woodward and Bernstein played a decisive part in the summer and fall of 1972, when it was their reporting alone that kept the Watergate story on the national agenda long enough to force a response by the political and legal system. According to one tally, the *Post* ran more than twice as many stories about Watergate between June 17 and December 31, 1972, as the nearest competitor, the *New York Times*.[78] In this period and in this way, it can be said that the practice of journalism *made* history rather than just reflected it.

Watergate also left a major legacy in the practice of journalism in the United States. Whether by foresight or plain luck, Woodward and Bernstein captured the narrative about Watergate for a generation. In their first draft of history, especially as laid out in their 1974 instant history, *All the President's Men,* and in the 1976 Hollywood version, Watergate was depicted as a tale of two plucky, idealistic reporters fighting for truth and justice who bring down a venal, corrupt dictator. That is a narrative with immense emotional appeal—especially for journalists, who mostly embraced it—and there is some truth to it, but it is far from the whole story. The Watergate reporting also represented the convergence and the culmination of much broader trends and issues. For one thing, it was never just a tale of two Davids against one Goliath; it was an institutional story, one that pitted the *Washington Post* against the executive branch. In that sense it is vital to note that in 1972 the *Post* was at the peak of its power as an institution. For years, profits had been rolling in, giving Bradlee the deep bench he needed to allow Woodward and Bernstein to disappear for days and weeks at a time while they pursued leads. Those profits also meant that Mrs. Graham arrived at the start of Watergate in a position of immense strength. That was the necessary condition—not a sufficient condition, to be sure, but a necessary one.

The Watergate coverage also reflected the professional imperatives of twentieth-century American journalism. As to purpose, the *Post* was acting very much as a watchdog, allowing the American people, as John Adams had hoped, to gain information about the character of their rulers. As to technique, it was perfecting the sourced investigation. Then, too, although all the journalists involved always denied it, there was also a partisan edge to the Watergate story. The fact was, all the key players despised Nixon, his agenda, and his administration. But those feelings were aligned with professional imperatives: get the facts, act independently of party or faction, serve the public good.

Across the field of journalism, Watergate provided a jolt. In its wake, journalism suddenly seemed very glamorous, and it started drawing people who were more ambitious and better educated than ever before. It is often said that enrollment at journalism schools shot up in the aftermath of Watergate, though there is little evidence for that claim, in part because the number of seats in such programs could not expand overnight. Instead, the impact seems to have been more roundabout. Watergate gave journalism a much greater cachet and sense of purpose, which in turn drew some very talented people into the business who might otherwise have gone into other professions. This trend meant pretty much the end of reporting as a blue-collar job; instead, a new generation brought professional aspirations and lifestyles (which spelled the end of most of the smoking and hard drinking as well).

At the same time, the example of Woodward and Bernstein touched off a vogue for investigative reporting. Plenty of people, perhaps including Nellie Bly, would say this was nothing new, and Woodward and Bernstein would be the first to agree: all they were doing was old-fashioned reporting, reporting, and more reporting. On the whole, the trend toward a more inquisitorial approach was beneficial, because it brought to light all sorts of scandals, and it extended the techniques of investigative reporting to beats such as business and sports, which proved to be target-rich environments. Many newspapers created special units dedicated to carrying out investigations, and in 1975 the movement was formalized in a national organization called Investigative Reporters and Editors. Along with the new prestige for exposé came the spread of a new bedrock belief among reporters and editors: that all politicians are sleazy and dangerous. Henceforth they would all be considered guilty until proven innocent. In its most extreme form, this view hardened into the conviction that the only real measure of a news organization is how many trophies are hanging on the wall in the form of powerful people who have been "bagged."

At the *Post* itself, Watergate certainly produced several trophies. Just off the main newsroom in the building on Fifteenth Street, there is a conference room where the daily meeting is held to determine the front page of the following day's paper. As of the 1990s, one wall held a map of the world, another an aerial view of Washington. On the third was the chase that still holds the metal type for printing the front page of August 10, 1974. Even in reverse, it is easy to read the headline "Nixon Resigns." There was also a photo of Gerald Ford with a speech bubble that has the president saying, "I got my job through the *Washington Post*!"

Finally, in terms of American culture, Watergate completed what might be called a "loss of innocence." Beginning with the "credibility gap" of the early 1960s, the era of Vietnam and Watergate shook Americans' faith in the military and in the presidency. Especially with the release of the Oval Office tapes, people who had any remaining illusions about the nobility (or even the decency) of their elected leaders had to abandon all hope. Quite apart from the content of the tapes, there was an overall quality to them that was profoundly disappointing. Nixon could be heard swearing all day long, lashing out at blacks and Jews, sitting in the office used by Jefferson, Lincoln, and Roosevelt sounding not like a statesman but like a punk.

During the 1970s, the defining episodes for the American news media were Vietnam and Watergate. In both cases, the media acted independently to challenge powerful institutions. Not to take away from individual abilities and initiative, but the most important fact was that the media were just powerful enough and still independent enough to undertake serious challenges to power centers like the Pentagon and the White House. In particular, the *Times* and the *Post,* in reporting the Pentagon Papers and the Watergate scandal, distinguished themselves as institutions that, for all their faults, were able and willing to seek the truth and tell it, and damn the consequences. In breaking ranks with the rest of the American establishment, they showed a willingness to antagonize the most powerful people and institutions in the country in pursuing truth and exercising the professional virtue of independence. It was no accident that those two newspapers were at the forefront. Both were profitable, so they had plenty of resources to throw into the fight. Both also were controlled by newspaper families, not by stockholders.

Punch Sulzberger and Katharine Graham enjoyed a degree of autonomy that may never be seen again. The fact that they risked as much as they did is a tribute to their personal character and professional commitment. But it is important to note that they were acting under a very specific set of conditions which are now gone and not likely to recur. Their actions stand as the apotheosis of the journalism that began in 1833 with the penny papers: build a big enough audience so that you can make enough money to tell anyone to go to hell. The risk of such an attitude is sounding arrogant, but without it there is no real journalism.

For all their personal integrity, it is also important to note that Sulzberger and Graham were not alone. Something deeper was happening in the 1960s and 1970s. The transition of key segments of the news media from a sustaining institution of the American establishment into a key part of the oppositional culture is a critical feature of this period. From the "credibility gap" of the early 1960s to the first presidential resignation in history, more and more journalists, starting in the alternative press and spreading into the highest ranks of the journalistic elite, came to doubt and challenge the traditional institutions and holders of power. Those challenges in turn provoked a sharp reaction that was little noticed at the time: conservatives were infuriated by what they saw as growing liberal bias in the media, and they began to mobilize a counterattack that would play out in the following decades.

The death toll in Vietnam included not only 58,195 American military personnel, along with millions of Vietnamese soldiers, guerrillas, and civilians, but also forty-five journalists. In many cases, those journalists died as a result of the very access that so marked their reporting. Slogging through the boonies with the troops, coming under fire, taking risks—all of it took a toll, including veterans such as Larry Burrows, Dickey Chapelle, François Sully, Bernard Fall, and Maggie Higgins (who died of the tropical disease Leishmaniasis, which she contracted while reporting in Vietnam).

*As for David Halberstam, he emerged from Vietnam as one of the most respected and prolific journalists of the era. He was admired not just for his reporting on combat and on the political intrigues of Saigon in the early 1960s, but especially for his two books about Vietnam—*The Making of a Quagmire *and* The Best and the Brightest*—which became indispensable works. He later left the* Times *and spent the next three decades working as a self-employed journalist, doing occasional stories for magazines and writing a book almost every other year. Halberstam developed a pattern of alternating a "serious" book and a "fun" book (usually about sports). In all, he wrote more than twenty books, on subjects ranging from war to the media and from automobiles to basketball.*

In April 2007, after speaking about journalism at Berkeley, Halberstam was riding in a car driven by a UC-Berkeley grad student, heading to his next stop. In Menlo Park, the car was involved in a crash. Halberstam was killed almost instantly. He was seventy-three.

Up to the very end, Halberstam was still reporting. He was working on a book about football and was on his way to interview the great Giants quarterback Y. A. Tittle.

CHAPTER 13

Big Media Get Bigger, 1980–1999

Information wants to be free. Information also wants to be expensive. Information wants to be free because it has become so cheap to distribute, copy, and recombine—too cheap to meter. It wants to be expensive because it can be immeasurably valuable to the recipient. That tension will not go away.
—*Stewart Brand, 1987*

B Y THE END OF the twentieth century, the news business was, in economic terms, beyond mature. It was almost senescent, having begun in the fifteenth century and having long ago brought to a point of logical fulfillment a business and professional model that appeared to guarantee high profits in perpetuity. After a shakeout in the middle of the century, the newspaper industry had mostly slipped the bonds of competition. Most daily papers serving small and medium-sized cities existed as local monopolies, and a fair number of papers serving bigger cities had no real competition either. Even the *New York Times,* operating in an apparently crowded newspaper market, enjoyed an effective monopoly within its circulation area, because the *Times* was not competing with the other New York–area dailies, nor did they dare challenge the *Times.* For educated, affluent readers in the tri-state area who wanted to know about national and international affairs as well as business news, sports, arts, and "style," there was essentially no alternative.

The big newsmagazines *Time* and *Newsweek* constituted a "duopoly." Radio, a formerly diverse industry, was consolidating as fast as possible in the 1990s, resulting in such continent-straddling behemoths as Clear Channel Communications. The television business was not (strictly speaking) a monopoly but an oligopoly, a situation in which a limited number of sellers dominate a market for millions of buyers. Like the Big Three automakers, the big three networks spent the middle and later years of the twentieth century battling one another at the margins over their huge slices of the American pie, scorning at first the new business of delivering TV signals by cable. And in all media, the big kept getting bigger. In just a few years during the second half of the 1980s, Capital Cities Communications bought ABC; News Corp. launched Fox TV; GE announced that it was buying NBC; the FCC repealed the fairness doctrine, facilitating the rise of talk radio; and Time Inc. merged with Warner Bros. to create the biggest American media conglomerate of them all, Time Warner.

In this setting, it is no surprise that the professional values of American journalism (the ideals of independence, truthfulness, diversity) came under pressure. A major portion of that pressure arose from the tensions inherent in trying to house a critical professional institution like journalism inside the big modern corporation. This tension became especially acute during the conglomerate phase. There was a "cultural contradiction" in the news business between news values and business values. Media executives were making business decisions that were normal for large, profitable, publicly traded corporations seeking to prosper *as businesses.* One goal they sought was to create monopolies wherever they could. In this they were so successful that profit margins began to rise, then soared to 20 percent a year and higher. The problem for journalism is that while monopolies are profitable, they represent the fulfillment of a commercial value, not a professional one. Indeed, the values of journalism lean toward competition and a multiplicity of views, not toward the arrogance and narrowing of views associated with monopoly. The reality of monopoly is corrupting in another way, too. As Liebling warned many times, in a one-paper town, the readers get only as much news as the publisher feels like paying for. With no competition, there is less incentive to spend money on reporting.

Another source of conflict in the misfit between news and business is the issue of size. The goal of most business executives is to expand; in the news business, executives expand by launching or acquiring more and more newspapers, magazines, radio channels, and television stations. If a media company already owns all those things, its executives might venture into other areas, such as companies that coach young people on how to take standardized tests (as the Washington Post Company did in acquiring Kaplan, Inc., which eventually came to provide the majority of the company's revenues, transforming the enterprise into a test-prep company that publishes a newspaper as a sideline). The news business was becoming part of Big Media. In order to make all those acquisitions in the late 1980s and into the 1990s, managers needed cash, so they borrowed it. The result was debt, which is the enemy of innovation. Thus, success in business terms threatened to undermine the news media in journalistic terms.

At the same time, the news media came under attack from the political Right. Conservatives railed against a media system they said favored big government, welfare, immigrants, and alternative lifestyles while denigrating family, country, and God. In part, many conservative critics were misreading the media—finding an *ideological* intention where journalists were actually asserting their *professional* values. Often, critics on the Right interpreted the *journalistic* ideals of independence and skepticism as *political* commitments to antiauthoritarianism or partisan liberalism. In either case, the result was the same: a growing conservative resentment of the news media.

Another cause for conservative resentment arose from changes affecting the media landscape which had the unintended result of making journalism more interpretive and therefore more open to charges of bias. One was the rise of television as a headline service. Beginning with the widespread use of the remote control in the late 1970s, the pace of television began increasing. Viewers who could jump to another channel with a tap of a finger had to be wooed second by second. In television news, this meant a dramatic increase in the pacing of delivering the news, which meant, in turn, a shortening of the amount of time devoted to any one topic. As a result, television news offered "the shrinking sound bite," forcing newsmakers to have their say in as little as ten seconds of air time.[1]

At the same time, television news was getting better at covering breaking stories. With mobile units, television crews could go to the scene of events and report live. In response, newspaper reporters and editors realized that by the time the paper came out, their audience had already seen "the news" on television. So newspapers became more interpretive, telling readers not what had just happened but what it *meant*. As journalism became more professional and better paid, it also started attracting more college graduates and, eventually, an unprecedented number of entrants into journalism from the nation's elite colleges, including some with advanced degrees. These very well educated people took to interpretive journalism, which drew on their analytical and rhetorical skills. They relished the chance to be interpretive, which is to say, opinionated. As it turned out, a lot of their opinions were (broadly speaking) liberal, which antagonized a lot of people who did not share those views. In their frustration, some conservatives and "culture warriors" decided they wanted to create new, right-wing media institutions to match or supplant the "liberal media."

Even so, the trends sweeping through journalism produced something like a heyday in the late twentieth century. The key was profit. The money that flowed in from advertising and subscriptions gave owners who chose to engage in serious journalism the resources to do so. As the journalist Steve Coll put it in testimony before Congress:

> Uniquely in the history of journalism, the United States witnessed the rise of large, independently owned, constitutionally protected, civil service–imitating newsrooms, particularly after the 1960s. These newsrooms and the culture of independent-minded but professional reporting within them were in many respects an accident of history.

At newspapers, demographic, economic, and technological factors created an era of quasi-monopolistic business models; to preserve their quasi-monopolies, owners of these properties had incentives to create journalism that would be seen as credible and attractive by the greatest numbers of readers. Thus the owners invested in "objective," politically neutral reporting. They also enjoyed high profit margins that allowed the more public-minded among them to invest in expensive foreign bureaus, national bureaus, and investigative teams.[2]

The profits from monopolies and near-monopolies paid for some terrific reporting—at least sometimes. There was a brief period when big money and high professional standards could, if executives allowed it, work together to produce some great results. But it couldn't last, even if the World Wide Web had never been invented. It couldn't last because of the growing conflict at the heart of the news business.

As businesses, the news media generally behaved according to the imperatives of business: they sought growth, market share, and profit. In this they were very successful. But in that pursuit of business success they created the conditions for their professional demise. This is the true crisis of the traditional news media. Size matters. As media companies grew into conglomerates, they became entangled in an endless series of ethical conflicts. The growth in the scale of the business also aggravated a perennial problem: the barriers to entry. By the 1990s it cost a fortune—about $1 billion—to launch a traditional media venture. Unless you were already a mogul, you could not begin to compete with the big players. So for Big Media, the window for experimentation was closing. In evolutionary terms, it was unclear whether such organizations could adapt quickly enough to have a future.

Then the Web came along. It could have been seen as a solution to these problems. Instead, many Big Media executives chose to ignore the Web, while others saw it either as a threat or as, potentially, a separate profit center, to be kept apart from the main newsroom—all of which only worsened the trends that were already threatening most traditional media. Granted, it was hard to see all of this at the time. In the 1980s and 1990s, Big Media were prospering, a condition in which it is always difficult to make the case for change. Prosperous, proud, and ponderous, the media behemoths saw no reason to change. They had become dinosaurs.

*   *   *

ONE MILESTONE IN TRADITIONAL NEWS media history was the creation of *USA Today,* the largest general-interest newspaper in the country. Like many previous media ventures, this one began with one individual with an idea. But in the corporate media world of the 1980s, one person with an idea, even a great idea, could hardly expect to launch a media venture. It would take hundreds of millions of dollars. The reason *USA Today* succeeded was that its founder happened to be a powerful, stubborn executive who was well ensconced in Big Media—Al Neuharth, the head of the biggest, most profitable chain of newspapers in America. As the CEO of the Gannett Corporation, Neuharth oversaw dozens of newspapers, most of them situated in medium-sized U.S. cities, nearly always in a monopoly situation. Gannett churned out record profits, quarter after quarter. As one Wall Street analyst concluded: "Gannett's basic media business is awesome. It is virtually an unregulated monopoly."[3] While running the company, Neuharth also harbored a dream: to create a new newspaper. It would be not just a new newspaper but a new *kind* of paper, nationwide, popular, and innovative. "We'll reinvent the newspaper," he declared.[4]

In 1979 he began working on it. The timing was propitious, in that Gannett had just racked up its first year of more than $1 billion in annual revenues (which was a good thing, because this idea was going to be expensive). From the start, Neuharth knew what he wanted: "*USA Today* had to be different, in appearance and content. Wrapped in color. Four sections. Everything organized and in a fixed place. Short, easy-to-read stories. Lots of them. Heavy use of graphics and charts. Heavy emphasis on sports, TV, weather. News every day from every state."[5] In planning a general-interest national daily, Neuharth faced a central problem: unlike every other newspaper, it would have no "hometown." For one thing, that meant there was no local department store that would be regularly buying full-page ads as Bloomingdale's and Saks did in the *Times*. *USA Today* would have to find national advertisers. It would have no built-in hometown readership, either, and since it needed at least 1 million readers to break even, it would have to find them somewhere—in the nation's airports, hotels, and convention centers. And it would have no local sports teams to root for, so it would have to cover most pro sports from a neutral point of view or focus on "national" sports like golf or NASCAR racing.

On the plus side, *USA Today* had some important assets. It could draw on Gannett's entire chain of about eighty newspapers, both for temporary staffers and for printing presses that were already in place all over the country. It could also tap the vast financial strength of a parent company that was making record profits. Gannett had gone public in 1967 (it then had twenty-eight papers and $250 million in annual revenues), becoming the third U.S. newspaper company to sell stock. With cash from Wall Street, it continued to grow. In the eighteen years from 1967 to 1985, it posted a gain in profits every quarter—seventy-two new records in a row. The company averaged 21 percent return on stockholder equity; some of the papers in the chain made 30 to as much as 50 percent profit a year.[6] *USA Today* also had the advantage of being the pet project of Neuharth, a man willing to call himself an S.O.B. in the title of his own autobiography.

After more than two years of plotting to win over the Gannett board, polling potential readers, and designing prototypes, Neuharth was ready for the rollout

13.1 **THE FIRST EDITION OF** *USA TODAY* challenged the conventions of U.S. newspaper design when it debuted on September 15, 1982, with generous doses of color ink, photos, and graphics. Originally mocked by the journalistic establishment as "McPaper," *USA Today* eventually changed the look of most newspapers.
—*USA Today.*

(fig. 13.1). On September 15, 1982, the launch party was held, on the National Mall in Washington, D.C., attended by no less a figure than the sitting president, Ronald Reagan. When *USA Today* first appeared, it was clear at a glance that this was not just another newspaper. It had the color, pacing, and style of television. The writing was light, tight, and bright. The organization was strict; features were put in their places and stayed there, and there was a prominent, detailed index to aid in navigation. No longer did readers have to search for the sports or weather or the crossword. At first, most Americans caught a glimpse of *USA Today* in an airport or hotel, where it was usually given away free in the early days in an effort to build readership.

Most professional journalists reacted negatively. Ben Bradlee of the *Washington Post,* for example, observed that if *USA Today* was a good newspaper, "then I'm in the wrong business."[7] The critics thought the stories were too short. They thought the graphics were too big. They accused Neuharth of pandering to his readers, of publishing the journalistic equivalent of junk food. They called his creation "McPaper." In the end, though, Neuharth had something like the last laugh, as newspaper after newspaper began to imitate the innovations found in McPaper. Twenty years later it was impossible to find a major U.S. daily that was not using color inks, color photos, giant weather maps, more and more "info-graphics," and fewer and fewer "jumps." Even the staid *New York Times,* the "great gray lady" herself, joined the bandwagon. In 1993 the *Times* started using full color in the book review section and later in other sections, and on October 16, 1997, the *Times* printed the first page one color photograph in its history, a shot of the game-winning home run in the World Series.[8] One *USA Today* editor summed it up: "They call us McPaper, but they are stealing our McNuggets."[9]

The Gannett Corporation lost an estimated $200 million a year for five years getting *USA Today* started and nurturing it to profitability.[10] In all likelihood, the $1 billion figure will stand as the all-time highest barrier for entry into the news business, if for no other reason than that there will probably never be a launch of a daily newspaper on that scale again. In retrospect, *USA Today* appears likely to be the last new major printed newspaper, the end of a line that began in 1704 with the *Boston News-Letter.* It was the culmination of Big Media in its oldest form.

* * *

IF A CHARACTER LIKE TED TURNER appeared in a novel, an editor would probably insist on toning him down. He just doesn't sound plausible. Born in Cincinnati in 1938, he was sent to Georgia Military Academy near Atlanta, where he took up boxing, sailing, and debating. Ted went north to Brown University and decided to major in classics, only to have his father denounce him as a "jackass" for doing so and refuse to pay any more tuition.[11] In response, Ted dropped out, went home, and joined his father in his billboard advertising business. As a young man, Ted Turner was a whisky-drinking Goldwater conservative. He went into business and became a multimillionaire. He went into sailing and won the America's Cup (and the nickname "Captain Courageous"). He went into sports, and the baseball team he bought, the Atlanta Braves, won the World Series. He took up conservation and became the largest private landowner in the United States. Initially dubious about news, he has acknowledged watching the film *Citizen Kane* (to which he bought the rights) more than one hundred times.[12] A onetime Republican, he would eventually marry the former radical Jane Fonda. With Ted, it was always all-in.

But most of that lay ahead. In the late 1970s Turner was a businessman based in Atlanta who had made a fortune in billboards and was getting involved in television. He had a reputation as outspoken, impulsive, and hard-charging—the "Mouth of the South," people called him. He was using his ownership of Atlanta sports teams to help build his "SuperStation," the first television operation to take advantage of satellite relay to reach the whole country inexpensively. One thing he did *not* care for was network TV. In fact, he *hated* the networks. He resented their riches and their arrogance. He didn't like their politics, either, considering them far too liberal. No one associated Ted Turner with journalism, and with good reason: he didn't care too much for it. He found the news depressing and rarely watched or read much of it. In 1977, while attending a cable television convention, Turner got into an exchange with Reese Schonfeld, who would later become the president of CNN. Schonfeld, then the head of a syndication service that provided video news to television stations that were not affiliated with the Big Three networks, tried to interest Turner in buying news from him for his station. "News is nothing," Turner said, theatrically. "*Nobody* watches news. Ain't you *tired* of all that news? Don't it just make you *sick* after watchin' that stuff? Listen, Reese, you know what my motto is? *No news is good news!*"[13] At his "SuperStation," the news was a poor relation. The only local news was presented after midnight, and the anchor sometimes delivered the news while wearing a bag over his head or accompanied on-screen by a German shepherd.[14]

Still, Turner had an idea: What if you put news on television and kept it on twenty-four hours a day? Not just the twenty-two minutes a day that the networks deigned to show people, but *all news all the time*—like news radio, but with video. He liked the idea so much that he refused to let go of it. He even started to worry that someone might beat him to it, maybe even one of the networks. He could see the success already being enjoyed by HBO in bringing movies to cable TV and by ESPN in bringing sports to cable. Why not news? At this point Turner had amassed a personal fortune of about $100 million, and there was nothing stopping him. He decided to go for it—to put all his chips on cable news.

In November 1978, Turner called Reese Schonfeld and signed him up. In his memoir *Call Me Ted*, Turner claims that twenty-four-hour cable news was his own idea. Schonfeld has written his own memoir in which he says he'd already had the same thought and calls himself a "co-founder" of CNN with Turner. Whatever the case, Schonfeld was a smart choice for Turner because he had the major qualification that Turner lacked: vast experience in non-network television news. From the early years of his career in wire service news, Schonfeld had an understanding of the tremendous volume of news that is reported each day, and he knew that only a tiny fraction of that made it into the prestigious evening newscasts on CBS, NBC, and ABC. From his years at the Independent Television News Association, which he had founded, Schonfeld knew about as much as anyone about how to get large amounts of inexpensive television news footage without relying on the networks. And Schonfeld had his own reasons for wanting to beat the networks. He had battled for years to compete with them, only to end up stymied by their cozy relationship with AT&T, which gave them a virtual lock on television distribution.

The timing was right for the new venture, which Turner was calling Cable News Network. The cable TV business was wiring up some 200,000 new homes a month, and by 1978 Nielsen estimated that cable TV had penetrated into some 13 million American homes, accounting for about 18 percent of all TV sets.[15] The next decision was where to locate CNN. For more than a century, the unofficial capital of news in America had been New York City, and for generations, young people who wanted to make it big in journalism had been moving to Manhattan to fight for recognition. Not Ted Turner. He had no use for New York, and he could see plenty of reasons to stick to his native southland. By locating his cable news operation in Atlanta, he could keep costs down, which would be critical. Everything from real estate to office supplies cost less in Atlanta than in New York. By settling in Atlanta, he could also take advantage of Georgia's "right-to-work" law and exclude unions, thus cutting his labor costs to a fraction of the networks' payroll.

Another key decision, which also helped save money, was to avoid the traditional star system of network news, at just the moment when salaries for TV news anchors were beginning to pass the $1 million mark. Barbara Walters had the distinction of being the first TV news anchor to earn $1 million a year, when she jumped to ABC in 1976. At the time, Cronkite was earning a reported $500,000. Once Walters broke the barrier, there was no turning back, as the networks engaged in a bidding war for talent.[16] Turner's only concession to the TV news establishment was to hire Dan Schorr, the respected CBS news veteran, to give his new venture some instant heft. Otherwise, Turner operated on the principle that at CNN, the news itself would be the star, not the anchors or reporters. Over the years, CNN stayed out of the bidding wars for network stars and instead developed a roster of its own: Bernard Shaw, Kathleen Sullivan, Bobbie Batista, Christiane Amanpour, and many others. In preparing to launch, Turner saw himself as an underdog, a real capitalist trying to upset the cozy arrangements of the oligopolists and elitists in the journalistic establishment.[17]

By approaching cable news this way, Turner was coincidentally creating a new business model for TV journalism. Unlike the networks, CNN did not plan to build a huge entertainment division that would have to create or bid for programs. And unlike public television, CNN was not dependent on public subsidies, foundation grants, or donations from the audience. Instead, Turner was adapting an older business model from newspapers. In the CNN approach, TV news would be paid for through a "dual revenue stream." Just as newspapers made money from two sources—advertising and subscriptions—so would CNN. The company would sell ads, and it would also have a steady stream of revenue coming in from the cable operators, who had to pay CNN a few pennies per customer per month, reflecting CNN's share of the monthly cable TV bills that Americans were getting used to paying. With low costs and two fairly reliable streams of revenue, news on cable just might work.

Ready or not, on June 1, 1980, CNN made its debut. There were the inevitable mishaps (the cleaning lady who walked across the set behind the anchor while the cameras were rolling), but the impressive thing was that it worked. CNN started covering the news that day and has done so continuously ever since—days, nights, weekends, holidays. Only the AP could make a similar claim, (though it supplies news to the industry rather than directly to the public). Soon, Turner was showing the skeptics that it was in fact possible to put news on television round the clock. Yes, it was sometimes raggedy. And yes, there was a lot still to accomplish—including hammering out reciprocal video-sharing agreements with affiliates, hiring more and more staff, opening bureaus around the world. But it worked.

By the end of 1981, CNN was getting established. It was reaching 10 million households and was clawing its way to journalistic parity with the network news divisions.[18] One key issue was what is known as "pool coverage." This occurs in many settings when there is not enough room to accommodate all the media people who wish to cover some location or event, such as a courtroom, a presidential appearance with limited access, or the like. In those cases, the answer is a pool, in which all the journalists in each medium agree to cooperate. Typically, each medium gets to put one representative at the scene. In return for that access, the chosen journalist agrees to share the results with all the other members of the pool in the same medium. In addition, each member of the pool agrees to take a turn in providing the feed. This arrangement assumes, of course, that anyone participating in the pool will produce work of high enough quality to satisfy all the others. CNN was originally scorned by the networks, which refused to let CNN crews participate in the White House television pool coverage. It took a lawsuit (which cost Turner another $1 million), but eventually CNN was allowed in.

One of the early tests of CNN as a news organization came on March 30, 1981. President Reagan gave a speech that day to the AFL-CIO at the Washington Hilton. CNN covered the speech live and then, when it was over, switched to some filler material, about sewing in China. While that was airing, the police scanner in CNN's Washington bureau barked: "*Shots fired . . . Hilton Hotel.*" Almost immediately, the veteran newscaster Bernard Shaw sat down in the anchor chair in the CNN Washington bureau and began reporting that shots had been fired at the president—a full four minutes before the networks. Shaw stayed in the chair for more than seven hours, and, with help from Dan Schorr, proved that the fledgling news service could keep up with the established networks. Through the evening,

CNN kept breaking in with new details: a picture of the shooter's home, a report on his motive, pictures of the vice president in Texas heading to Washington. According to one account of that day: "Such details were hitting the air in no particular sequence. CNN's viewers got the story in the jumbled way a journalist receives fragments of information before transforming them into an orderly, polished report. The 'process' of gathering news determined the form in which that news was delivered."[19] Before CNN, viewers had received their news in measured doses at fixed times; now they were drinking straight from the fire hose.

For years, CNN cost more to produce than it brought in through the combined revenues of cable subscriptions and advertising. The network was burning through Ted Turner's personal wealth at an unsustainable rate. The early years were a desperate race to get CNN included in enough viewers' basic cable packages to pay for itself. Most of the costs of gathering and disseminating the news by cable were fixed; the great variable was the size of the audience. Beginning in 1978, from the pre-launch investments in people, property, satellite time, and equipment, CNN lost an estimated $77 million through 1984.[20] But then in 1985, CNN began posting profits: $20 million that year and more in the coming years. In the grow-or-die spirit of modern capitalism, Turner soon started thinking about acquiring other businesses. At the same time, a profitable CNN was looking more attractive to other investors, who might try to take it over. By the end of the decade, CNN was earning almost $90 million a year and had an estimated value of $1.5 billion. At the decade mark, on June 1, 1990, it could be seen in 53 million homes in the United States and in eighty-four countries worldwide. CNN had nine U.S. bureaus and another eighteen overseas, with a global total of some 1,800 employees. CNN had arrived.

Along the way, Turner was undergoing a makeover in his political views, embracing environmentalism, the United Nations, and a number of other liberal causes. He also became much more internationalist in his outlook, forming the first truly global television news operation. Always outspoken, he often found ways to shock people and antagonize his opponents. Not for him the mealy-mouthed, straddling, corporate-style diplomacy of most network executives or, for that matter, most executives of any large corporation seeking to please the general public. In a typical outburst, Turner once addressed a gathering of television critics and unloaded on antiabortion activists: "The pro-lifers say they don't want people to have sex for fun, only to have babies. '*Sex is sinful.*' Well, that's fine if those people don't want to ever have sex. Swell. I happen to enjoy it. I don't get near as much as I want to." Perhaps realizing that he was shocking the assembled critics, Turner promised to offer rebuttal time to the other side of the abortion issue, but he could not help himself: "We'll give the other bozos a chance to talk back."[21] Those other bozos were not amused; someday, they would come after him.

In 1991, CNN broke more new ground in journalism. For the first time in history, the cable news channel provided real-time video coverage of a major armed conflict. During the preceding summer, Turner had needed to find a new president to run CNN, and he picked Tom Johnson, a former publisher of the *Los Angeles Times,* after just a fifteen-minute interview. Johnson took over on August 1, 1990, and the next day, Iraq invaded its neighbor Kuwait. That action prompted an outcry from President George H. W. Bush, who announced that he would form an international coalition to liberate Kuwait. As the world braced, journalists planned their coverage. Quickly, Johnson prepared a range of proposals for CNN's potential expenses in covering such a war, from a low of $5 million to a high of $36 million, and presented them to Turner. "What am I authorized to spend?' Johnson asked. Turner, the ultimate news buccaneer, didn't hesitate: "You spend whatever you think it takes, pal." The startled Johnson proceeded to do just that, posting news teams in Baghdad, Jordan, Saudi Arabia, and Israel, and adding extra people at the White House, the Pentagon, and the State Department. CNN's international news chief, Eason Jordan, spent some $52,000 just to equip the Baghdad team with a satellite telephone. In all, Johnson reckoned that CNN spent $22 million on covering the Gulf War. When journalists talk about "the good old days," this is the kind of thing they have in mind.[22]

The most dramatic demonstration yet of the power of cable news came on January 17, 1991, when U.S. forces launched rocket attacks on Baghdad. There were few American correspondents left in Iraq's capital city, but there was a three-man crew from CNN. One was the Washington anchor Bernard Shaw; another was the veteran war correspondent Peter Arnett, who had been in and out of war zones since the early 1960s, first for the AP and then for CNN. Also on hand was reporter John Holliman. When the attacks came, sure enough, that satellite phone was the only telephone in Baghdad that still worked after U.S. forces took out Iraq's communications system. The CNN reporters transmitted live from the roof of the al-Rashid Hotel, allowing the world to see the impact of the U.S. bombing while it was happening. For CNN, the investment in covering the news paid off handsomely in terms of the highest ratings in CNN's existence. The cable news channel was suddenly the prime source of live reporting about the war— and not just for viewers at home but also for policymakers, politicians, generals, and even heads of state. For the first time in world history, all these actors were receiving the same information and responding to it at the same time. Wartime leaders had always had spies and intelligence agencies to tell them how a war was going, but those reports were well-guarded secrets. Not anymore. Now the whole world really was watching (fig. 13.2).

For all its success, however, CNN still had critics, because it still had flaws. One was the inherent susceptibility of television news to the power of pictures. Television is different from all other news media in that it combines sound with moving pictures, and the pictures are often the determining factor when it comes to deciding what makes a "good story." That is why the self-mocking motto of local

13.2 CNN EXPANDED ITS GLOBAL IMPACT during the Gulf War in 1991 when its correspondents supplied live accounts to all parties. Shown here are three women who covered the war for CNN (*left to right*): photographer Maria Fleet, correspondent Christiane Amanpour, and photographer Jane Evans. —©*Annie Liebovitz (Contact Press Images).*

television news is "If it bleeds, it leads." That is, if there is gory video available, that story will begin the newscast, regardless of its real news value. Conversely, a great story like Watergate, for example, which had no visual side, almost did not exist in television terms. Meanwhile, a story of slight significance in the greater scheme of things that offers dramatic video is a natural on television, such as a live police chase of a speeding vehicle, shot from a helicopter. That was exactly what unfolded on CNN in 1995, when the former football star O. J. Simpson, wanted as a suspect in the murder of his former wife, led police on a low-speed tour of Los Angeles in a white Ford Bronco while trying to make up his mind whether to surrender to authorities. Yes, it was inane, but the chase was dramatic, it had "great visuals," and it addressed a problem that was unique to CNN: how to fill twenty-four hours a day, day in and day out, with fresh news. That chase, along with Simpson's ensuing murder trial, has become notorious as an example of the problems that arise in a nonstop media environment: the questionable news judgment, the obsession with celebrity, the excessive coverage of one story to the neglect of others.

As CNN approached the end of its third decade, it became possible to appreciate what Ted Turner had brought to journalism. CNN was, if nothing else, a historic first: the original round-the-clock cable news channel, the experiment that proved it could be done. From the start, though, it has also had a broader effect on journalism, reaching well beyond television. Perhaps the greatest impact CNN has had was unintentional: it redefined the meaning and experience of news itself. Before CNN, news was almost always presented to an audience as a finished *product,* that is, as a "story" or "report," whether in a newspaper, a magazine, a radio show, or a TV program (where it is usually known as a "package"). The story was the result of certain steps taken by the journalist, usually with help from an editor. Someone had to make inquiries, gather the results, distill them into a familiar format, double-check the facts and spelling, and put them before the audience. Usually this was done according to a set timetable: monthly, weekly, daily, hourly. CNN changed the basic premise of journalism by presenting it as a *process* rather than a product. In a live, twenty-four-hour format, news is whatever information or pictures you have *right now.* If the information is incomplete, so what? You can always come back on the air in a few minutes or hours with an "update" to supply the missing denial, counterpoint, or fact. This approach puts pressure on editors and other media "gatekeepers" to suspend much of their professional judgment in favor of getting material on the air as quickly as possible. It becomes less important to double-check facts, weigh their significance, and polish the final story. As a result, more of the material that reaches the public is partial, fragmentary, often speculative, and sometimes hearsay.

For viewers, this was a profound change. Accustomed to seeing Walter Cronkite or John Chancellor precisely at 6:30 p.m. for a half hour of highly polished, produced "pieces," viewers could flip to CNN at any time of the day that was convenient and jump into the river of news flowing by. By doing so, they got a lot closer to what the practice of journalism actually looks and feels like: tracking down parts of a story over a day or longer, conducting one interview after another from the various parties or "newsmakers," waiting for confirmation of key details, passing along rumors, getting lied to, going back to the original newsmaker with new questions, and so on. On CNN, viewers got to see just about everything but the bathroom breaks. And as with watching legislation or sausage being made, the process is not always appealing.

A related phenomenon became known as the "CNN effect"—the tendency for a certain kind of intensive, highly emotional coverage to drive public policy. If CNN focuses on certain poignant or horrifying topics and frames them in a certain way, the public reaction will be so strong that a political response will follow. So, for example, if CNN shows dramatic photos of a dead soldier being dragged through the streets of Mogadishu, policymakers cannot sit tight and say, "Well, war is hell." They have to *do something.* They have to present options to the president that will allow him to appear to be taking action. According to this theory, the president will want to announce some forceful response to the news—ideally, on CNN. That is not to say that CNN dictates the *content* of the policy, only that its coverage dictates the *necessity* of a policy.

The rise of CNN had an impact in another area as well. Traditionally, top policymakers were sources of information for the news media. Generals, diplomats, global bankers, and the like made decisions and, when it suited them, favored the expectant press corps with tidbits. Never mind that those tidbits might be deceitful, tendentious, or self-serving; they were authoritative, or at least official, and could therefore be presented as "news." This reality was never expressed better than by the great journalist and humorist Russell Baker. He was covering Capitol Hill for the *New York Times,* and one day his duties involved sitting on the floor of the Senate Office Building waiting for a closed-door session of the Armed Services Committee to end. The marble floors reminded him of his father, who had been a mason and therefore had built useful things that endured. "Instead, I spend my life sitting on marble floors, waiting for somebody to come out and lie to me," Baker observed.[23] The existence of all-news television often turned that traditional relationship between leaders and journalists on its head. With the coming of CNN, the media became sources of information for top policymakers. In 1989, for instance, the *New York Times* reported on the way top officials in George H. W. Bush's White House were handling the latest crisis: "Early last week, when the administration was immersed in deciding how to respond to the threat to American hostages in Lebanon, a Bush aide was asked how the president was spending his day. 'He's been in his study a lot watching CNN,' the aide replied."[24]

He was not the only one. Watching cable television news became de rigueur for policymakers during all major crises. In 1991, *New York Times* reporter Maureen Dowd wrote a behind-the-scenes "Reporter's Notebook" piece in which she observed that many top Bush aides involved in the Persian Gulf War had given up on the traditional intelligence mechanisms in favor of watching CNN: "'The problem is that it's hard to sort out the information because the CNN stuff has a way of trickling into the intelligence,' another Bush adviser said, referring to Cable News Network, the potent new entry in Washington's alphabet soup. 'We get the intelligence reports, and they include the stuff that's on CNN. Then we get another report that seems to confirm what the first report said, but it turns out that they're just using a later CNN broadcast. CNN confirming CNN'" (fig. 13.3).[25]

Ultimately, Turner won the highest compliment of all—imitation. Although CNN was profitable from 1985 on, for years no one dared try to do the same thing. Like many first movers, Turner enjoyed one benefit of getting into a new field early, high name recognition, which intimidates many others from jumping in. For years, CNN was practically synonymous with breaking news on TV. In fact, it was sixteen years before CNN faced competition in round-the-clock cable news. But then, in 1996, two new entrants arrived: MSNBC and Fox News.

13.3 **A LONE FIGURE CON-FRONTS A ROW OF TANKS** in Tiananmen Square in Beijing during a government crackdown on pro-democracy demonstrations in June 1989. He became famous as "tank man" in this widely reprinted image. —*AP Photo/Jeff Widener.*

* * *

WHILE THE BIG MEDIA COMPANIES were busy expanding, some Americans found the news media very upsetting—not the content of the news, although that could be upsetting too, but the media as an institution. For conservatives, who saw their grip on national power slipping away with Nixon's resignation, it seemed that the news media were not neutral observers but active partisans. Look at *Time* magazine, they said; since Henry Luce retired, year by year it was getting more liberal, more anti-war, more anti-Establishment. Look at the *New York Times* since the ascendancy of Sulzberger cousin John Oakes. He was pushing the editorial page further and further to the left, embracing every new cause to come along, from civil rights to the environment, from peace in Vietnam to women's rights. Where was the sensible, predictable, centrist paper of his uncle Adolph Ochs? The *Washington Post,* after that Watergate episode, was hopeless. And then there were the TV networks—all in love with Democrats, peaceniks, feminists, welfare queens, you name it. And to make matters worse, the liberals who ran all these places would not even admit that they *were* liberals. If you tried to call them on it, they would scurry for cover under the banner of Journalism or Objectivity or some other shibboleth. For conservatives, it was all quite maddening.

Some of these objections were the result of a short memory. The media had been overwhelmingly conservative for most of the twentieth century, and many media outlets remained so, including the Chicago and Los Angeles papers, the *Wall Street Journal,* the mass-circulation *Reader's Digest,* and a number of journals of opinion. So in part the conservative outrage was based on a perception that the media were rightfully theirs, and therefore that the liberal trend among some media outlets in the late 1960s and 1970s was an affront to the natural order of things. Of course, from a radical Left perspective, the overwhelming majority of the media are conservative in the sense that they all tend to strengthen the view that free-market capitalism is such a good idea that it isn't even open to discussion.

Whatever the case, journalism was ripe for a critique. This was partly the fault of journalists themselves. By promising to meet an impossible standard ("objectivity"), the media had set themselves up to fail and thereby antagonize people.

One media crisis for conservatives occurred in the early 1980s, when the *Washington Star* folded, leaving the nation's capital in the hands of a single daily paper, the despised *Washington Post*. It was intolerable to think that the entire national government and the federal workforce would be under the influence of Katharine Graham, Ben Bradlee, Sally Quinn, Art Buchwald, and the rest of that big-government crowd. Still, no one would step up and buy the *Star*. So conservatives felt some sense of relief when a new, frankly right-wing paper was founded there in 1982. Conservatives had to swallow hard to accept that the creator of the new *Washington Times* was the outré Korean religious leader the Reverend Sun Myung Moon, who was criticized for running a cult that turned followers into robotic "Moonies." As the founder of the Unification Church, Moon did not have any obvious qualifications for running a big-city American newspaper, except perhaps one: he had vast amounts of money available through his church to underwrite losses at the *Washington Times*. In the twenty years after its launch in 1982, those losses were estimated to be in the range of $1 billion (by Moon himself) to perhaps $2 billion (by the *Columbia Journalism Review*). Moon's great appeal for conservatives was his staunch anticommunism. With its conservative slant, the *Washington Times* quickly became the favorite local paper of the Reagan administration, whose members rewarded it with news leaks. With its location in the capital, the *Times* could also supply editors to appear on Washington-based television programs and "balance" liberal guests. Even though its circulation was only about 10 percent of the *Post*'s, the *Washington Times* proved invaluable to conservatives as a counterweight to the liberal *Post*.

The Reagan years changed U.S. journalism in other ways as well, some quite far-reaching. One important change arose from Reagan's great ambition to deregulate the American economy. When it came to the news media, the natural target of the Reagan reformers was the most regulated portion of the field: broadcasting. After decades of attempting to ensure diversity and local control in radio and television, the FCC began to reverse course. In terms of radio, there were two key decisions. One was to relax (and eventually almost eliminate) the traditional limits on ownership. This allowed a company like Clear Channel Communications to start buying up radio stations (eventually more than one thousand of them) and dominate the market. Just a few years after deregulation, it would be possible to drive from Medford, Massachusetts, to Medford, Oregon, constantly adjusting the car radio dial, and pull in only stations owned by Clear Channel. All the programming would come from Clear Channel headquarters in San Antonio. This corporate takeover of radio had the result of centralizing programming decisions to an unprecedented degree, often in the hands of conservative big-business executives.[26]

The other crucial step in the deregulation of broadcasting was the repeal of the fairness doctrine, which had governed radio since 1949. Under that policy, the FCC encouraged broadcasters to take positions on matters of public concern, but it also required them to seek out people with different points of view and give them equal air time—for free. Radio station owners mostly hated the fairness doctrine and had been trying for decades to scuttle it. They finally succeeded under Reagan when the FCC voted to drop it in 1987. When Congress tried to restore the doctrine by enacting it into law, Reagan vetoed the bill, and Congress failed to override. As a result, radio and television stations no longer had to present balancing comments on an issue; they were as free as a newspaper or a magazine to propound one point of view all day long. That change opened the door, in turn, for the "talk" format, especially on AM radio. In 1987, fewer than 240 radio stations in America relied on a talk format, according to *Broadcasting* magazine; five years later, the number was approaching 900.[27]

Taken together, those changes give rise to the phenomenon known as Rush. Born in 1951 in Cape Girardeau, Missouri, Rush Hudson Limbaugh III came from a family of distinguished lawyers and prominent judges. He got involved with radio in high school and became so enamored that he made it through only one year of college at Southeast Missouri State before dropping out to go into radio full-time as a disc jockey. Using professional pseudonyms such as Jeff Christie and Rusty Sharp, he played music, read the news, and ran call-in shows for a succession of small radio stations. He moved a lot (and married a few times), then worked for a few years in marketing for the Kansas City Royals baseball team. In the mid-1980s he ended up in Sacramento, where he experimented with hosting a radio program without guests. In 1987 a former ABC executive who ran a syndication service came to Sacramento to listen and decided to sign him up. Limbaugh moved to WABC in New York City and launched his nationally syndicated daily talk show on August 1, 1988.

Starting with about 250,000 listeners on a few dozen stations, Limbaugh quickly expanded. The essence of his show was Rush himself. There were no guests, no "experts," no debates, and no on-the-one-hand/on-the-other-hand. His listeners loved the program, and they loved Rush. It turned out they agreed with him so much and so often that he had to come up with a shorthand way for them to acknowledge that they shared his philosophy—hence, the "ditto-head" and "mega-dittoes" phenomenon. Part of his success was due to the fact that his was one of the few national media programs to break out of the traditional one-way or "lecture" format. Traditionally, readers of newspapers and magazines, listeners to radio, or viewers of television were on the receiving end of one-way communication. The media outlet (usually based in New York) created the entire product, and the audience could either take it or leave it. The call-in feature of Limbaugh's program allowed listeners to interact, to comment, and even (once in a great while) to disagree with the great "El Rushbo." It was not as interactive as the Web would prove to be, but it was an antidote to the (sometimes insufferable) top-down pose of traditional print and broadcast media.

Limbaugh also tapped into a huge reservoir of conservative outrage, which had previously gone pretty much unnoticed by the national media. As it turned out, there were a lot of Americans who did not share the values and outlook of the *Times, Newsweek,* Dan Rather, or NPR. Soon, millions were tuning in three hours a day to hear their views expressed by Limbaugh, including disproportionate numbers of white, conservative male listeners.[28] Freed from the constraints of the fairness doctrine, Limbaugh could hammer away with his personal doctrine, undiluted by any guests or any journalistic conscience demanding balance or a sampling of a range of viewpoints. His show was all Rush, all the time.

One of Limbaugh's biggest bugaboos has been the rest of the media. Although he lives inside the glass house himself, Limbaugh has always thrown a lot of stones at what he calls "the mainstream media" or (in his coinage) "the drive-by media" or (since the election of Barack Obama) the "government-run media." In his view, the major media are just another elite looking down on average Americans. "The media is now considered just another part of the arrogant, condescending, elite, and out-of-touch political structure . . . engaging in the abuse of power," he has said.[29] Although his position in the media was making him quite wealthy and powerful in the 1990s, Limbaugh positioned himself as a perpetual "outsider" whom listeners could therefore trust. In this he was acting a bit like a veteran politician who runs as the "outsider" taking on Washington.

In the process, it also became obvious that Limbaugh was very, very talented. He worked hard and did his homework before shows. He had a magnificent radio voice, with superb delivery. He could also be extremely articulate and often quite funny. And he had a kind of political perfect pitch for his audience, which was, like himself, predominantly white, male, and conservative. He has also proved to be a master of more than one medium. Limbaugh's book *The Way Things Ought to Be* spent a year in the early 1990s on the *New York Times* best-seller list, selling close to 3 million copies. Rush was, in short, a full-blown media phenomenon.

Is Rush Limbaugh a journalist? In one sense, of course, he is not, because he does almost no original reporting. He does not set out each day to find and verify information that will add to the world's storehouse of facts, images, and quotations. He does not cover *news.* In another sense, though, Limbaugh is a journalist in the long tradition of analysis and advocacy. From its inception, journalism has consisted of activities that can be arrayed along a continuum stretching from "news" to "views"—that is, from facts to opinions. What Limbaugh offers listeners is a point of view about the news, and many people want to hear his take on what others are reporting. At times, he seems to get help in establishing his take on the news from sources such as the Republican Party, conservative think tanks like the Heritage Foundation, and in the early 2000s the George W. Bush White House. At other times, he's clearly improvising, as when he grabs a fresh news item from the Associated Press and begins, live on the air, to analyze it and coach his audience about what sort of attitude they should take toward this or that recent development. During periods

13.4 **CONSERVATIVE TALK-RADIO HOST RUSH LIMBAUGH** appeared on the cover of the *New York Times Magazine* on July 6, 2008. —*New York Times.*

when the Republican Party has lacked clear leadership, Limbaugh has filled the void. Like a partisan editor of the early 1800s, he keeps the faith when his party is out of office, vets up-and-coming politicians, and shepherds the flock (fig. 13.4).

Conservative media got another jolt in the 1990s from Rupert Murdoch, the Australian who had built a global media conglomerate known as News Corp., which stretched from Melbourne to Beijing to London to New York. Journalism, which had always been a homegrown affair in America, was about to change again and get its first dose of foreign ownership on a large scale. Murdoch had entered the U.S. media market in the 1970s, having amassed a fortune and acquired a reputation as a modern master of tabloid journalism. After buying a couple of papers in San Antonio, Murdoch made a splash by moving into the U.S. media scene big-time when he bought the *New York Post* in 1976. The *Post* had begun life as a partisan paper with its founding by Alexander Hamilton in 1801 as a vehicle for Federalist views; in the nineteenth century, it emerged as a leader of progressive thought. Later it was owned by the liberal Dorothy Schiff, who sold it to Murdoch, who turned it into a conservative paper and a sensational tabloid. (A classic *Post* headline from April 15, 1983: "HEADLESS BODY IN TOPLESS BAR.") As one Murdoch biographer noted in 2003: "For more than thirty years the Post has been News Corp.'s flamboyant, money-losing (up to $50 million a year), and eccentric flagship property in the United States. It has no business reason for being other than to prosecute political and business grudges and to entertain Murdoch himself, but it remains the sentimental heart of News Corp."[30]

The American journalism establishment loathed Murdoch. In 1980 the *Columbia Journalism Review,* the ultimate arbiter of professional standards and journalistic good taste, asserted that "the *New York Post* is no longer merely a journalistic problem. It is a social problem—a force for evil."[31] The *Post* was pure journalistic id, but it also provided Murdoch with another advantage, an editorial page that he could use to take stands on American political issues. Editorially, the *Post* became muscularly conservative and militaristic. In 2003–4 the paper enthusiastically embraced the Bush invasion of Iraq, both on the editorial pages and in the news pages. Even years later the *Post* remained militant on the subject. In 2006, to cite a notorious example, the *Post* superimposed the faces of the two moderate leaders of the Iraq Study Group, which was offering the Bush administration a much-needed out, onto the bodies of two chimpanzees and ran their images under the headline "SURRENDER MONKEYS."

Murdoch launched another major conservative outlet in 1995 when he bankrolled the *Weekly Standard,* a new conservative magazine. The *Standard* was hardly the first conservative journal of opinion. In fact, the modern conservative movement practically began with a journal of opinion—*National Review,* the influential biweekly launched by William F. Buckley in 1955. The field expanded in 1965, when one of the founders of the neoconservative movement, former Democrat Irving Kristol, launched *The Public Interest,* a quarterly that featured the nonscholarly writing of many conservative academics. In the late 1960s R. Emmett Tyrell Jr. launched a conservative monthly, the *American Spectator,* which found new life in the 1990s attacking the Clintons (and new money from Richard Mellon Scaife, the billionaire heir to the Mellon fortune, who has bankrolled dozens of right-wing causes).

Then, in 1995, Kristol's son William, a Republican who had been the chief of staff to Vice President Dan Quayle (he was referred to as "Quayle's brain"), launched the *Weekly Standard,* with financial backing from Murdoch. William Kristol was joined on the new magazine's masthead by former Reagan speechwriter John Podhoretz (who, like Kristol, was the son of a prominent neocon, Norman Podhoretz, who had been the editor of *Commentary* for thirty-five years). By publishing weekly, the *Standard* could be more timely than most other conservative magazines, and by being located in Washington, it could focus on policy matters and tap into a growing network of conservative think tanks, commentators, and political activists. The *Standard* took up the anti-Clinton cause, then embraced Bill Clinton's Republican successor, George W. Bush. It became one of the loudest voices demanding U.S. retaliation for the attacks of September 11, 2001, and supporting the Bush invasion of Iraq. It was also another money loser for Murdoch. The magazine made no sense as a business proposition; Murdoch must have had some other goal in mind. And indeed the *Weekly Standard* has a clear focus: promoting the success of conservative ideas and Republican candidates.

Far more important in terms of its impact on the American media landscape was the move Murdoch made in 1996, the year after he had agreed to underwrite the *Weekly Standard*. That was the creation of a second all-news channel on cable television, a conservative challenger to CNN. In the sixteen years since its launch, CNN had enjoyed a near-monopoly in nonstop cable news, and it had developed a reputation as a liberal-leaning news organization that shared many of the assumptions (and some of the same personnel) as the Big Three broadcast networks. No one would ever accuse Fox News of that. Murdoch had already entered the U.S. television market when he started Fox Broadcasting Company in 1986, offering mainly entertainment such as *The Simpsons* and *Married . . . with Children*. Fox Broadcasting would become a powerhouse as it moved into televising major sports events in the mid-1990s and added the prime-time phenomenon *American Idol* in 2002. Within just a few years, Fox Broadcasting had become both a ratings success and a financial success. What it lacked was a news division. Instead of creating one within Fox Broadcasting, Murdoch set up a separate cable channel for Fox News. His first key decision was to hire Roger Ailes to run it.

Ailes's background was in television and in conservative politics, not in journalism. After graduating from Ohio University, where he had worked for the radio station, Ailes got a job in television and soon rose to the position of executive producer for *The Mike Douglas Show*, a pioneering syndicated afternoon talk and variety show. One day in 1967, one of the guests on the show was a belly dancer named "Little Egypt," who performed with a boa constrictor. The other guest was former vice president Richard Nixon, who was trying to raise his profile for the 1968 presidential campaign. To keep the two guests apart, Ailes used his own office as an impromptu "green room" for Nixon.

"It's a shame," Nixon said, referring to his appearing with the belly dancer, "that a man has to use gimmicks like this to get elected." Ailes, just twenty-six years old, rebuked Nixon, telling the older man that if he did not understand television, he would never win the White House.[32] Ailes went on to explain the mistakes he thought Nixon had made on television in the 1960 campaign. A few days later a Nixon aide called Ailes, inviting him to join the team. He went to work devising a Nixon television strategy for the 1968 presidential campaign. Debates were out of the question (*No reruns of 1960!*), and so were speeches. Instead they would shoot Nixon taking questions and jawing with apparently regular folks—all carefully screened in advance—and carefully edit the results to show Nixon as a relaxed, informed master of the issues. Following Nixon's victory in 1968, Ailes went on to become a Republican political consultant and worked for Ronald Reagan and George H. W. Bush. In 1988, Ailes worked for Vice President Bush in his run against Democrat Michael Dukakis, one of the most squalid campaigns of recent times. During the 1990s Ailes briefly tried to bring Rush Limbaugh to television, but the show flopped. Ailes was recruited by NBC, and he oversaw the launch of CNBC, the network's successful and profitable all-business cable channel.

In 1996, Ailes teamed up with Rupert Murdoch for the ambitious launch of Fox News. Jowly, self-assured, and inclined to crush his rivals, Ailes had the chance of a lifetime: using Murdoch's money and support, he could establish a conservative alternative to CNN. It has been said that if CNN was an attempt to translate all-news radio into television, then Fox News was an attempt to translate talk radio into television.[33] Compared to CNN, Fox would be faster, sharper, and much, much more overtly ideological. From day one, Fox was also committed to a conservative political agenda that suffuses every hour of its programming, whether a show is labeled news or talk or analysis. In planning for the Fox News debut, Ailes came up with two bumper-sticker-size slogans that have come to stand for the Fox approach and for what critics call the "Foxification" of news. Long resentful of the liberal bias he detected in the mainstream media, Ailes famously declared that Fox would be "fair and balanced"—implying, of course, that it differed from all other news operations in that regard. His other slogan was "We report. You decide." Again, the meaning was clear: unlike all those *other* news organizations, we will stick to factual reporting so that viewers can make up their own minds about events. Like Henry Luce's promise that "no article will be written to prove any special case," this was a pledge that Fox News has violated every day of its existence.

From its public launch on October 7, 1996, Fox News had an uphill climb against the better-established CNN. It was received in fewer homes, and it had to spend much more than Turner's $100 million to build studios, hire technical and on-air talent, and open bureaus. From the start, Fox News expressed a conservative point of view. Ailes and other spokesman have presented two rationales for the Fox approach. Sometimes they insist that Fox really is fair and balanced; at other times they admit that it is conservative but argue that Fox thus provides a necessary antidote to the networks and the rest of the "mainstream media." Most decisively, perhaps, Murdoch himself has insisted that Fox would be an alternative to CNN's legion of suspected liberals. "They reflect the almost monolithic attitude of the press coming out of the *New York Times,* the *Boston Globe,* the *Washington Post,* and the three networks follow it exactly," Murdoch said of his rivals at CNN shortly after the rollout of Fox News in 1996.[34] In recent years, Fox executives have offered another rationale for the Fox approach: Fox News presents opinion shows in the morning and in prime time (*Fox and Friends, The O'Reilly Factor, The Sean Hannity Show*) and offers "straight news" during the daytime (*America Live with Megyn Kelly, Studio B with Shepard Smith*). Furthermore, Fox defenders insist that viewers know the difference.

There was little reason for Fox staffers to be in any doubt where the cable channel stood. The network proudly (and almost exclusively) recruited high-profile conservatives. The owner was a globally prominent conservative. The company president had worked for Nixon, Reagan, and Bush Sr. In recent years the Fox News channel has served as a haven for out-of-work conservative politicians like Sarah Palin and Republican operatives like Karl Rove, who appear on Fox under contract as "analysts" and keep their views before the public. With all those conservatives in the house, a writer or producer who went to work at Fox would have to be awfully naïve not to understand the ground rules. One episode of possible confusion arose in January 2001, when Republican George W. Bush took the oath of office. At that moment, Fox suddenly made an about-face: since its birth, it had been one of the most anti-administration voices in all U.S. news media, as long as the White House was occupied by Democrats Bill and Hillary Clinton. With the arrival of Bush, however, Fox faced a serious dilemma: Should it follow its journalistic instincts and remain a skeptical outsider? Or should it follow its ideological instincts and rally around the new administration? Fox decided.

Just in case anyone at Fox was unsure, the vice president for news, John Moody, began bombarding the staff with memorandums about how to cover conservatives when they are in power. His morning memos outlined the theme of the day, much like a party line. They were divulged publicly by a former Fox editor and producer, Charlie Reina, who said the memos gave daily political guidance that consistently bolstered the Bush message. Moody could always find something to admire in Bush. A memo from June 3, 2003, read: "The president is doing something that few of his predecessors dared undertake: putting the US case for Mideast peace to an Arab summit. It's a distinctly skeptical crowd that Bush faces. His political courage and tactical cunning are worth noting in our reporting through the day." Anticipating criticism of Bush from the bipartisan 9/11 Commission, Moody had a warning for his staff on March 23, 2004: "Do not turn this into Watergate. Remember the fleeting sense of national unity that emerged from this tragedy. Let's not desecrate that." As fighting in Iraq continued, he instructed on April 4, 2004: "Into Fallujah: It's called Operation Vigilant Resolve and it began Monday morning (NY time) with the US and Iraqi military surrounding Fallujah. We will cover this hour by hour today, explaining repeatedly why it is happening. It won't be long before some people start to decry the use of 'excessive force.' We won't be among that group."[35]

The Moody memos, which eventually stopped, are more reminiscent of life inside a political campaign than in a newsroom. Most large news organizations, like most large bureaucracies of any kind, run on memos. But Moody's daily directives were unlike anything any journalist had ever seen at the wire services, the big papers, the newsweeklies, or the network news divisions. Occasionally one of those institutions would experience an internal debate over a question such as how to define who is a "terrorist." When the issue was settled, it might be written down and circulated so that coverage was consistent. Typically, there might be a handful of such pronouncements in a year. Moody's memos were highly unusual in that they appeared so often and gave such explicitly political guidelines for coverage. Unlike most news executives who react to events, Moody had an uncanny sense of what the news should be *even before it happened*.

One of the most clear-cut illustrations of Fox's sympathies occurred during the 2003 invasion of Iraq—or as Fox chose to label it, adopting a slogan straight from the Bush administration, "The War on Terror." It should be noted that the journalism of that time was so politicized that even the use of the word "invasion," which denotes the movement of one nation's armed forces uninvited into the territory of another, was considered unpatriotic, and most U.S. news organizations shunned the term. From the moment of the terror attacks on September 11, 2001, by Islamic extremists from Saudi Arabia, Fox supported the Bush plan to retaliate against the non-religious regime in Iraq. Fox reporters and commentators embraced each successive rationale for the war, from stopping "terror" to eliminating weapons of mass destruction. During the run-up, Fox commentator Bill O'Reilly threw down a challenge: "Once the war against Saddam begins, we expect every American to support our military, and if they can't do that, to shut up. Americans, and indeed, our allies who actively work against our military once the war is underway will be considered enemies of the state by me."[36] During the shooting phase of the Iraq war, Fox went so far as to install a special logo in the upper part of the TV screen showing a waving flag (reminiscent of Hearst's attempt to wrap his paper in the flag during World War I; see chapter 6).

Fox executives dug deep to match the resources of more established media. In the end, Fox News had fifteen correspondents in the region (including the flamboyant Geraldo Rivera and former marine Lieutenant Colonel Oliver North, a genuine hero to American conservatives). The fifteen Fox correspondents were matched up against forty-nine correspondents for CNN and more than one hundred each at the major networks. But the scrappy underdog made up for the lack of resources with a surfeit of enthusiasm. For instance, during the invasion, Rivera—better known by just his first name, as "Geraldo"—did a notorious live shot in which he knelt down and sketched a map in the sand, showing the planned movements of U.S. troops. He was denounced by the U.S. military but—perhaps because of Fox's ties to the administration—was not expelled from Iraq. Fox emerged from the war with the highest ratings in its history, allowing the network to move ahead of CNN and into first place in cable news.

Does this kind of partisanship matter? Yes, it does—especially in wartime. Covering war is not the same as covering a Wimbledon tennis match, or a fashion show, or even a campaign for governor. In wartime, with lives at stake, journalists take on the ultimate responsibility to find—and tell—the truth. Doing so may not prove very profitable or popular, but so be it. In the case of the Iraq invasion, the coverage by Fox had serious consequences. A study conducted in 2003 by the Program on International Policy Attitudes at the University of Maryland points to some of those consequences. The researchers looked at how Americans perceived several of the key issues involved in the war. Specifically, they polled the public to determine how widespread were three misperceptions:

1. that there was a link between al-Qaeda and the Iraqi government (there was not)

2. that weapons of mass destruction were found in Iraq (they
were not)
3. that most people around the world thought the U.S. invasion
was a good idea (they did not)

The researchers reported that the more often people watched Fox News, the more
*mis*informed they were about the war. Among Fox viewers, 80 percent believed
one or more of these misperceptions, while results for viewers of other media
trailed off, down to just 23 percent for the audiences of NPR and PBS.[37]

In dealing with their success, Fox News executives seem to be of two minds.
On the one hand, in their own advertising they emphasize that Fox News is the
top-rated channel in cable television. So in that sense Fox has become a significant
part of the media "mainstream" that is one of its major targets. On the other hand,
Fox executives and on-air commentators like to depict themselves as a plucky
embattled minority, fighting for bedrock American values. At Fox News, every
day feels like the Alamo or the siege of Bastogne. At the same time, Fox executives
also claim that the rest of the media is biased in favor of liberals. If that's true, then
the Fox News audience is in fact tiny compared to the combined news audiences
racked up by ABC, NBC, CBS, MSNBC, CNN, NPR, and PBS. On any given day,
the other television news outlets combined draw at least ten times the Fox audience. Still, Fox has an impact out of all proportion to the size of the audience. It
is more partisan and ideological than anything Americans ever saw on television
before it—or indeed since the partisan era of two hundred years ago.

* * *

FOR MORE THAN A HUNDRED years, from the early nineteenth century to the late
twentieth century, white news media and black news media existed in separate markets. They might as well have been in separate countries. The white media (including daily and weekly papers, magazines, newsreels, radio, and television) looked
at African Americans only intermittently, usually as objects of curiosity, concern,
or scorn. When they appeared in the white media at all, blacks were presented as
"problems" (most often as criminals) or as amusements, in the form of entertainers
or athletes. Blacks appeared quite differently, of course, in their own media—the
weekly newspapers as well as the big post–World War II magazines like *Ebony* and
Jet. There, blacks got married, raised families, ran businesses, and otherwise led full
lives. Whites who appeared in the black press usually appeared as problems themselves—as lynch mobs, as bigots, or as The Man. The media treatment of race did
little to bridge the gap between the two separate societies living side by side. As the
Kerner Commission concluded in 1968, the media were "basking in a white world,
looking out of it, if at all, with a white man's eyes and a white perspective."[38] In the
late twentieth century, however, two trends emerged that began to change those
cultural patterns.

One was the gradual process of desegregating the newsrooms of the mainstream media. Starting with the urban riots of the mid- and late 1960s, more and more newspaper editors—who are in charge of almost all newsroom hiring—began to realize that they needed black reporters on their staffs. At first this was entirely pragmatic: they needed reporters who could gather news in the urban ghettoes and come back with a story. Whatever the motive, this change was over-due in almost every newsroom. Almost no white-owned newspaper had more than one or two black reporters as of the early 1960s, and the vast majority had none. Over time, editors could see that there was an inherent value in having a reporting staff that represented all the social groups of America, or at least all the social groups in the paper's circulation area. So, starting essentially from scratch, the mainstream media began integrating newsrooms.

The best evidence of social change, at least as far as newspapers are concerned, comes from an annual census of the newsroom population conducted since 1978 by a powerful professional group, the American Society of Newspaper Editors. On the basis of its first survey, the ASNE estimated that minorities of all kinds made up only 3.95 percent of the editorial workforce at U.S. newspapers. The survey then presented the results at ten-year intervals (see Table 13.1). The overall trend is clear. Over the thirty-year period from 1978 to 2008, a steadily increasing number of minorities found work in the nation's newsrooms, and they held on to most of those gains even when total employment began to drop in 2007. On a percentage basis, minorities more than tripled their representation as reporters, editors, pho-tographers, and other newsroom staff. At the same time, of course, it should be noted that these figures reflect all minorities combined. The percentage for African Americans in 2008 was 5.3, compared to 13.4 percent of the total U.S. population. So it must also be said that black journalists remain seriously underrepresented in the newsrooms of American newspapers, especially those in smaller towns. While all of the papers with circulations above fifty thousand employed one or more minority journalists by 2008, about three-quarters of all the papers with circula-tion below ten thousand still had no minorities at all in their newsrooms.[39] Figures for Hispanic, Asian, and Native American journalists all show similar patterns: significant gains over those thirty years, but a persistent underrepresentation.

TABLE 13.1

Minorities in U.S. newsrooms at ten-year intervals, 1978–2008

YEAR	TOTAL	ALL MINORITIES	PERCENTAGE OF NEWSROOM
1978	43,000	1,700	3.95
1988	55,300	3,900	7.02
1998	54,700	6,300	11.46
2008	52,600	7,100	13.52

Source: American Society of News Editors, http//ASNE.org.

Since the late 1970s African Americans have made gains across all white-owned news media *as employees.* Following pioneers such as Milton Coleman, William Raspberry, and Charlayne Hunter (later known by her married name, Hunter-Gault), enough African American journalists were employed by 1975 to found the National Association of Black Journalists. In the following years, one milestone after another was reached. In 1978, Max Robinson became the first black co-anchor of an evening network news program, on ABC. In 1981, Ed Bradley joined *60 Minutes* after covering the White House and serving as weekend anchor at CBS. In 1982, Bryant Gumbel became the first black co-anchor of a network morning news program, and for most of his fifteen years at NBC's *Today Show* he was teamed with a white woman. In 1988, CNN co-anchor Bernard Shaw became the first African American to moderate a presidential debate. Despite all the "first black" moments, it would be an overstatement to say that the change was smooth, steady, or inevitable. It was sporadic and contentious. Nevertheless, the newsrooms of major metropolitan newspapers and television stations, as well as a growing number of rural news operations, became far more diverse than those of a generation earlier.

Another important trend of the late twentieth century was the rise of African Americans as *owners* of major media properties. If ownership is the true foundation of press freedom, then perhaps this is the most critical measure of black participation in the media. Since the 1820s, of course, blacks had owned media aimed at a black audience; most often those were weekly papers such as the *Chicago Defender* and the *Baltimore African-American.* The most successful black owner of black-oriented media was John H. Johnson, founder of Johnson Publishing, who became the first African American to appear on the *Forbes* magazine list of the "400 Richest Americans," breaking that barrier in 1982—before any black athlete or entertainer. The basis of his fortune was the magazine empire he founded, beginning in 1942 with the *Negro Digest,* modeled after *Reader's Digest.* Three years later he launched his most successful title, *Ebony,* which resembled *Life* in its array of topics and use of photography. In the early 1950s he added *Jet,* which was more focused on news. Johnson also built a Chicago-based business empire that included three radio stations, a book publisher, and a television production company, as well as non-media companies selling cosmetics and life insurance.[40]

Another milestone in black media ownership came in the early 1980s, when Robert Maynard became the editor, president, and major owner of the *Oakland Tribune.* It was the first time that an African American owned a general-interest newspaper serving a big U.S. city; although Oakland has a substantial black population, it had a white majority at the time. Maynard became editor in 1979 and bought the paper four years later in a leveraged buyout. Seven years later the *Tribune* won a Pulitzer Prize. In television, the first African American to have a major ownership position was Robert L. Johnson (no relation to John H. Johnson), who founded Black Entertainment Television in 1980. BET was the first cable television network aimed at a black audience, although it attracted a sizable minority of white viewers over the years, drawn to its hip-hop music programming. Johnson took the company private in 1998, then sold it the following year to Viacom for $3 billion, making Robert L. Johnson the first African American billionaire and landing him on the *Forbes* magazine list of the richest people in the world.

Above all, there is Oprah—the ultimate high-impact, crossover, all-platform media mogul. So vast is her reputation, so familiar her likeness, so pervasive her reach that she can be identified by just one name (like Cronkite, or Cleopatra). Every weekday, for twenty-five years, she had a chat with the millions of American viewers of her TV show—mostly women, mostly white (and millions more in the 119 other countries where it appears).[41] Every month her magazine, *O,* promises to coach readers on how to "Live Your Best Life." When she endorses a book, it invariably rockets onto the best-seller list. Author, editor, publisher, broadcaster, tastemaker, entrepreneur—her numbers certify the arrival of black media. On the strength of her media interests, she became the first African American woman on the *Forbes* magazine list of wealthiest Americans. Her ratings, sales, and earnings are so vast that they make the case for at least the beginnings of a postracial media universe in America. Even Oprah never could have amassed such a record if it were based on black readers or watchers alone. From the start, she has appealed across the color line.

If race, class, and gender are the great parameters of social life in America, Oprah Winfrey started with three strikes against her.[42] She was born in 1954 in Kosciusko, Mississippi, a small town north of Jackson. Her mother had a one-night stand with a soldier stationed at a nearby military base and gave birth to the girl she called Oprah. Raised on a farm by her mother's mother, Oprah learned to read at three, and she could memorize and deliver speeches from a young age. People would say, "Whew! That child can speak!"[43] At age six she was taken by her mother to live in Milwaukee. Years later Oprah revealed that, starting at age nine, she suffered years of sexual abuse, sexual assault, and incest by relatives and family friends. During this period Oprah was sent to Nashville to live with her father, who had left the military and was working as a barber. He ran a strict household and demanded good grades, which Oprah managed to earn at her integrated high school. While still a teenager, Oprah got her first taste of working in the media when she was hired by a local radio station and then by a television station as a news anchor and reporter. A top student, she won a scholarship to attend the historically black Tennessee State University, where she majored in speech and drama before switching to media studies.

After college, Oprah moved to Baltimore to take a job as a co-anchor of the news program on WJZ-TV, but she was never entirely comfortable in a hard-news setting. Two years later she became a co-host of the station's local talk show and declared: "Thank God! This is it. I've found out what I was meant to do."[44] In

13.5 **OPRAH WINFREY BROKE INTO JOURNALISM EARLY,** then discovered her flair for hosting talk shows. She is shown taking a break in her studio office in Chicago on December 18, 1985, just after finishing an episode of her television show *A.M. Chicago,* later renamed *The Oprah Winfrey Show.*
—*AP Photo/Charlie Knoblock.*

1984 she made a fateful move to Chicago. There she took over a faltering morning talk show, *A.M. Chicago* on WLS-TV, and turned it into a hit (fig. 13.5). Within a year she was already bringing in more viewers than her cross-town rival Phil Donahue, who was a pioneer of the television talk show. In both cases, most of the viewers were women who were watching television at home during the workday. What Oprah had over Donahue, of course, was her experience as a woman, which gave her a fluency and sureness about issues of interest to women that no man could approach. In Chicago, she met (and for a while dated) the movie critic Roger Ebert, who informed her about the advantages of syndication. She also met a lawyer, Jeffrey Jacobs, who represented a number of athletes and entertainers. Taking Ebert's suggestion, and using Jacobs as her agent, Oprah bought her show—now renamed *The Oprah Winfrey Show*—from ABC. Then, coming off her newfound fame after her performance in the film version of Alice Walker's novel *The Color Purple,* Oprah negotiated a deal with King World, Inc., to syndicate her television program nationally. And she created a company, Harpo, Inc., to oversee her new production company, her studio, and other ventures. With those key decisions, Oprah lifted herself from the ranks of employees and into the ranks of media owners, a move that laid the basis for her later fortune. The payoff came right away: after earning $200,000 in salary from ABC in 1984, she made $30 million from her show's syndication in 1986. Four years later, she was worth an estimated $250 million.

What was unusual about Winfrey was that even as she was becoming a major media mogul, she stayed involved in the creation of content. In a sense, perhaps, she had no choice, because she herself was the big heart and warm soul of the *Oprah Winfrey Show*. Day after day she displayed her ineffable talent for empathy. She was warm and funny. She related to people. She could sympathize and she could empathize. She could dish, cry, hug, laugh. She could be a good questioner and a good listener, but she was also happy to be in the spotlight. In TV terms, she had perfect pitch. She took the daytime TV talk format pioneered by Donahue and pushed it to its limits. Oprah is sometimes faulted for turning her show into "confessional" or "therapy" television, but the charge does not seem to bother her. In part that may be because the show is not *merely* confessional. While most of the episodes have a high emotional quotient, they also usually have another purpose as well. Many of her shows are quite informative and shed light on issues that other programs avoid, such as homosexuality, sexual abuse, and the power of prayer.

In 1999, Oprah branched out again, this time launching *O: The Oprah Magazine*. In a partnership with Hearst Publications, she created a glossy lifestyle magazine that propounded one of Oprah's core beliefs: You should "Live your best life." Like her television show, the magazine appeals overwhelmingly to women; and like her television audience, the magazine audience is white as well as black. *O* offers up generous doses of information about fashion, homemaking, and weight loss. Each month the cover features a dramatic, flattering photo of Oprah herself, and the contents are consistently upbeat and solution-oriented. In the words of a highly accomplished professional woman who is a longtime subscriber, picking up each new issue is like getting a hug from Oprah herself. The magazine was considered the most successful launch of a print publication in the first decade of the twentieth century and may (given the outlook for printed media) go down in history as the last successful launch of a glossy national magazine.

With her interests in television, film, and publishing, Oprah has emerged as a full-fledged media mogul on a scale that rivals the stature of any other self-made media figure. At the same time, Oprah is a tastemaker and trendsetter, and she navigates across multiple boundaries. She is a classic American success story, having risen from poverty so deep that she had to wear sacks for dresses to the ranks of billionaires by achieving fame, influence, and status. She eventually replaced Katharine Graham on the lists of most admired women. In 1998, *Time* magazine named Oprah one of the "100 Most Influential People of the 20th Century."

Is there another meaning to her success? Unlike all earlier press lords and broadcasting titans, Oprah is neither white nor male. She had perhaps the least privileged upbringing of any prominent media figure. Yet her success was built on an upbeat outlook that millions wanted to share. It was also based on her capacity to cross racial lines. Like the pan-ethnic Tiger Woods or the "post-racial" Barack Obama, Oprah transcends the categorizations that have long defined (and limited) American lives. Like Robert L. Johnson, she proved that an African American could make a fortune in the media. But Oprah went far beyond Johnson in building a brand around herself and doing so in a way that crossed old racial boundaries. The success of Oprah (and others) suggests that it may be time to ask whether the categories of "white media" and "black media" still apply.

*   *   *

WHAT WAS IT LIKE INSIDE Big Media in the glory days? Here's an account from the journalist John Podhoretz, reminiscing about the 1980s:

> Time Inc., the parent company of *Time,* was flush then. Very, very, very flush. So flush that the first week I was there, the World section had a farewell lunch for a writer who was being sent to Paris to serve as bureau chief . . . at Lutèce, the most expensive restaurant in Manhattan, for 50 people. So flush that if you stayed past 8, you could take a limousine home . . . and take it anywhere, including to the Hamptons if you had weekend plans there. So flush that if a writer who lived, say, in suburban Connecticut, stayed late writing his article that week, he could stay in town at a hotel of his choice. So flush that, when I turned in an expense account covering my first month with a $32 charge on it for two books I'd bought for research purposes, my boss closed her office door and told me never to submit a report asking for less than $300 back, because it would make everybody else look bad. So flush that when its editor-in-chief, the late Henry Grunwald, went to visit the facilities of a new publication called *TV Cable Week* that was based in White Plains, a 40 minute drive from the Time Life Building, he arrived by helicopter—and when he grew bored by the tour, he said to his aide, "Get me my helicopter."[45]

In the same period, *Time* was paying its top freelancers in the range of $10 a word (which certainly adds up!). And it was not just *Time* magazine. At the *New York Times,* the journalist R. W. "Johnny" Apple Jr. made a reputation not only for his stylish front-page pieces but also for his outlandish expense accounts, brimming with $400 bottles of wine (followed by expensive brandies) and the best rooms at the best hotels. At the *Washington Post,* the newspaper employed two full-time in-house travel agents just to handle transportation and housing. When reporters needed to go somewhere, they just called the travel desk and let them know. A short while later, a big envelope full of tickets and vouchers would appear. *Have a nice trip.*

Throughout the 1980s and 1990s, the big media grew much bigger, partly on the strength of their growing audiences, but mainly by taking a page from Wall Street's book and engaging in the frenzy of mergers and acquisitions that was then sweeping through the rest of the economy. The media consolidation began in earnest in 1985, placing more and more journalism properties inside giant companies that sometimes had little interest in news. That year, Capital Cities Communication (a company previously unheard of in the news media) bought ABC for $3.5 billion, and General Electric bought RCA and its NBC division for $6.3 billion.[46] In 1986, CBS underwent a friendly takeover by Laurence Tisch and thus passed out of the effective control of William Paley. In 1989, Time Inc., seeking to become too big to take over, merged with Warner Bros. film studios in a record-setting $14 billion deal. The pace quickened again in the mid-1990s. In 1995, CBS changed hands again, bought by Westinghouse for $5.4 billion. The next year brought the purchase of Cap Cities/ABC by Disney Corp. for some $19 billion. In October 1996, Ted Turner took his Turner Broadcasting System into a merger with Time Warner, Inc., creating the biggest media conglomerate to date and combining the newsgathering companies CNN and *Time* magazine, along with dozens of entertainment properties. In 1999, CBS changed hands yet again when it was bought by Viacom for $37 billion. (It was later spun off and emerged once more as an independent company.) The mentality was simple: grow or die.[47]

Even the giants wanted to get bigger. In 2000, Time Warner merged again, this time teaming up with the Internet phenomenon America Online. Gerald Levin of Time Warner (who never worked as a journalist) was now hitched to Steve Case of AOL (who also never worked as a journalist) in an arrangement that was awkward to begin with and spiraled downhill as AOL began losing money. One casualty of the merger was Ted Turner. When he had brought TBS into the Time Warner fold, Turner solidified his personal fortune, but he was no longer his own boss. Instead, he was given profit targets, just like the heads of other divisions at Time Warner. "For the last four years we were asked to grow 20 percent a year compounded profits for our division. We've done it," Turner said in 2004, but he lamented that the only way to hit those profit targets was to forgo one of his pet projects: hard-hitting documentaries on subjects like the Soviet nuclear program.[48] For a buccaneer with a taste for news, it proved a deal with the devil. On the day of the AOL–Time Warner merger in 2001, Turner's personal stake in the combined company was worth more than $7 billion. What none of the principals knew was that the stock price was just about at its peak. In less than three years, Turner's stake would shrink to less than $2 billion. As more and more Internet users discovered how to browse the Web on their own (especially once Google started helping them), they no longer needed to pay AOL a monthly fee to hold their hand. So AOL stopped growing and began imploding financially, threatening the very existence of the company that Henry Luce had founded in 1923. The Time Warner–AOL merger was shaping up as a case of grow *and* die.

The results of all these corporate mergers and acquisitions was not a net benefit to the practice of journalism. For one thing, most of the deals were, in Wall

Street parlance, highly leveraged. That is, the dealmakers used debt rather than cash to buy the properties. As a result, the management was obligated to pay the bankers and bondholders on a relentless schedule. Management issued quarterly profit demands to the heads of divisions for a simple reason: they needed the money. To make matters worse, the stockholders wanted dividends, which also came out of profits, and they wanted to see the value of their shares increase. Under those constraints, big media companies came under tremendous pressure to cut costs and to keep looking for deals that would allow them to borrow even more money to make the company even bigger. The executives who planned and executed these financial maneuvers were not journalists; they were bankers, lawyers, arbitragers, dealmakers. News was not their business; *business* was their business.

At the same time, there were some notable exceptions. Two important ones in the newspaper business were the *New York Times* and the *Washington Post.* Using slightly different techniques, both papers were organized in such a way that the families who owned them exercised effective control over the newspapers at their cores, and both companies were protected from takeovers by outsiders. This meant that the Sulzbergers and the Grahams continued to own (and manage) the two most important daily papers in the country. As long as the money flowed in from circulation and advertising, they could poke a finger in the eye of the federal government, big companies, or almost anyone they thought deserved it. They could maintain costly bureaus in distant places and not have to justify the expense to anyone else. They were not infallible, of course, but they were not subject to corporate overlords, either. The question about both papers at the turn of the century was: How long could it last?

There were other notable exceptions to the corporate takeover of American journalism. Among magazines, several small but important journals of opinion, like *The Nation* or the *New Republic,* had patrons with deep pockets who kept them alive for noneconomic reasons. The *New Yorker* had survived its first few years courtesy of the largesse of Raoul Fleischmann. Then, for decades, it was immensely profitable, right up until 1967, when the number of advertising pages began to drop precipitously.[49] Then followed years of turmoil and turnover, including the sale of the magazine by the Fleischmann family to the privately held Advance Publications, owned by S. I. Newhouse. The *New Yorker* lost money for eighteen years until it was folded into Condé Nast (a division of Advance Publications) in 1999,[50] and it became modestly profitable again under editor David Remnick while continuing to win prizes and astound readers.[51]

Another major exception to the Wall Street model was National Public Radio, which flourished during these years as a nonprofit. With a growing budget, NPR strengthened its newsgathering capacity, both at home and abroad, and emerged as a major source of news and commentary. The government's contribution to its budget continued to shrink, as NPR came to rely more and more on sponsors and

on "listeners like you." By 2010 the biggest single source was the voluntary donations from the audience.[52] In addition, another major source of news in America was that venerable cooperative the Associated Press, which supplied a vast
amount of hard news (along with sports and business reporting, as well as photos
and video) to nearly all of the nation's news outlets. It remained nonprofit as well.

The most powerful trend in the news business in the late twentieth century was
the reorganization of most news outlets into parts of large, publicly traded corporations, often without the ultimate consumers even noticing. In the newspaper field, chains like Gannett, Knight-Ridder, and McClatchy—hardly household
names to most readers—gobbled up formerly independent papers. In radio, Clear
Channel bought its one thousandth radio station in 2000. Television ownership
actually expanded a bit with the arrival of Fox News (a division of News Corp.),
but the industry remained one of limited sellers and enormous barriers to entry. The magazine business, too, followed a similar pattern, except that most of
the biggest players—Advance Publications (which owns Fairchild Publications
as well as the Condé Nast group) and Hearst Corporation—were both privately
held companies.

It might be asked: So what? What difference does it make if the news business
is, like most of the rest of the economy, in the hands of big corporations? Isn't the
publicly traded corporation the engine that drives the U.S. economy, giving it the
dynamism that makes it the envy of the world? It's a fair question. In the history
of the news business, the form of ownership has always mattered, from the colonial print shop through the industrial, family-owned era, to the corporate phase.
In the transformation of the news business into a corporate form and then into a
conglomerate form, the changes have not been neutral for journalism. The older
forms were not perfect—far from it, as the record indicates. But the transformation of traditional media in the late twentieth century also came at a high cost in
several respects.

One problem was the drive toward monopoly—or if not monopoly, then what
economists call "concentration." As the number of different owners in any industry
shrinks, that industry changes. The survivors face less competition, and they often
find it easier as a result to raise prices. If there is a single survivor in the field, then
the winner can take all. In the news business, this pattern threatens the very existence of diverse, and local, points of view. Clear Channel replaced more than one
thousand individual owners, with different aspirations, different ideas about their
civic roles, and different ideologies. The number of U.S. cities with healthy, competing daily newspapers, once in the hundreds, fell to about a dozen. By the year 2000,
in American cities that had a daily newspaper, 99 percent had only one management in town.[53] The fifteen biggest newspaper chains account for more than half the
nation's total circulation. In all, there were about 1,500 daily newspapers remaining
in America. Of those, only about 350 were independently owned, and most of those

were very small. The whole industry was heading in a direction that was at odds with the journalistic values of independence, localism, and competition.

Housing news operations inside such huge conglomerates gave rise to prob-lems. One was the ethical quandary known as conflict of interest. For decades, journalists sought to be independent so that readers and viewers could trust that they were getting the straight dope—about government, about business, even about sports. The idea was that journalists should be able to tell it like it is, without worrying about who benefits or suffers from what their reporting turns up. Independence was the professional ideal. But inside conglomerates, no news operation could be even close to independent. In a notorious example, ABC investigative reporter Brian Ross came across a juicy story. Officials at Disney-world in Orlando were so hard-pressed to find security guards that they were hir-ing convicted sex offenders to look after the safety of children visiting the theme park. But his superiors at ABC News decided to sit on the story for fear of offend-ing their own superiors at Disney corporate headquarters. (Those ABC execs had not actually been threatened or told what to do; they were just anticipating the reaction.) All of the paychecks at ABC News come from Disney Corp., so why bite the hand that feeds them? If ABC had still been independent, Ross could have reported his findings and let the chips fall where they may.[54]

Even when there is no pressure (or anticipation of pressure), the ethical prob-lem persists inside big conglomerates. The problem that cannot be eliminated is the *appearance* of a conflict of interest, which can be just as damaging to an insti-tution's credibility as an actual conflict. Under parent company GE, for example, every reporter and every editor at NBC News knew that GE made heavy indus-trial products like jet engines and wind turbines. How aggressive could they have been in looking into problems in those industries? And even if they were profes-sionally aggressive in pursuit of news in those fields, some number of members of the audience were surely aware that NBC's parent company made those products and would, as a result, have remained suspicious. Or to take another example: the Washington Post company owns not only the *Washington Post* newspaper but also Kaplan, Inc., which coaches students on how to pass standardized tests. How aggressive can *Post* reporters be in evaluating the test-prep business? And even if they do their best, why should readers believe anything they say about Kaplan? Especially since the test-coaching division surpassed the newspaper as the big-gest producer of revenue for the parent company. No corporation that includes news and non-news divisions can entirely escape the question of apparent (or structural) conflicts of interest. The problem is inherent in the model.

There are other problems with conglomerate news. While the news divisions may enjoy a measure of independence and First Amendment protections, the likelihood is that some other part of the company is regulated by one or more government agencies. All broadcasters, for example, are regulated by the FCC. Moreover, if the parent company is big enough, there is a likelihood that it sells products or services to the federal or state governments. In that case, how aggressively can the news division be expected to carry out its traditional watchdog role? In fact, most large corporations are inherently unsuited to the practice of journalism. There is an innate caution that is part of the DNA of any large corporation. Large corporations employ large numbers of people—including legions of attorneys, consultants, accountants, and executives (the people known as "the suits")—who all have perfectly sane and logical reasons for *not* doing a particular investigation, satire, or routine news story. It is not part of their makeup to go around antagonizing other powerful institutions. Why would a division of GE want to pick a fight with the Pentagon? Why would a company like Westinghouse, which hopes to sell products to the largest possible number of customers worldwide, want one of its divisions, CBS, to investigate an institution like the Catholic Church, or even the Mafia? As a business matter, such an investigation is suicide. But as a journalistic matter, it is essential.

*   *   *

WHEN TROUBLE CAME, IT CAME fast. Newspapers that measured their lives in centuries, magazines that rounded their circulations to the nearest million, networks that had annual revenues in the billions, all of them thinking that they were on a never-ending upswell of money, power, and sway—all of them went over the cliff together. At the very end of the twentieth century, in December 1999, the value of a share of stock in Time Warner, Inc., one of the mightiest of the Big Five media conglomerates, hit its all-time high: $254 a share. Ten years later it was trading at about $25 a share. In a decade, 90 percent of the value of the company had vaporized. It was not an isolated case (see Table 13.2).

TABLE 13.2

Big Media stock performance, 1999–2009

COMPANY	PEAK PRICE/SHARE	DATE	LOW PRICE/SHARE	DATE	% CHANGE
		The Big Five			
Time Warner	254	Dec. 1999	24	July 2009	-90
CBS/Viacom	71	Aug. 2000	6.7	March 2009	-90
GE	56	Aug. 2000	7.06	March 2009	-87
News Corp.	31	March 2000	6	Feb. 2009	-80
Disney	41	March 2000	17	March 2009	-58
		Selected Others			
New York Times	51.8	July 2002	5	Nov. 2008	-90
Washington Post	983	Dec. 2004	322	March 2009	-67
Gannett	90	April 2004	3.54	Feb. 2009	-96
McClatchy	74	March 2005	0.44	July 2009	-99
				Avg.	-84

Source: Google Finance (calculations by author)

13.6 **THE TERRORIST ATTACKS ON SEPTEMBER 11, 2001,** made headlines around the world. The destruction of the twin towers in New York City's World Trade Center took place near the capital of the U.S. news media, and writers and photographers flocked to the scene. —*AP Photo/Shawn Baldwin.*

No sooner had the new millennium arrived than gloom settled over most traditional news media. All of a sudden, revenues were flat or down. Budgets were tighter. Part of the problem was the "dot-com" economic bust, which was causing the high-flying computer-related companies to slash or eliminate their advertising budgets. Those companies also stopped their initial public offerings of stock, so there were no more of those full-page IPO announcements in the business press. Then came September 11, and suddenly the news mattered again (fig. 13.6). Americans flipped on their radios and TVs and kept them on. The day after and the day after that, newsstands were sold out of papers. Maybe the news was important after all. Then came the economic aftershock, a mini-recession that made everything even worse. But, the thinking went, maybe this was just temporary and things would turn around. Still, the fact was that the money just wasn't there. Cuts would have to be made. First came the easy things: expense accounts, part-timers, freelancers, stringers. But those didn't add up to much. Then came bigger cuts: foreign bureaus, then domestic bureaus, even the Washington bureau. At television news divisions, at the big news-oriented magazines, and at big newspapers, the story was the same.

The economy recovered, but not the news business. By 2004–5 there was a steady drumbeat of cuts, contraction, and worry. Now the cuts were reaching into the heart of most operations, into the newsroom itself. News managers tried to shrink their budgets by offering "buyouts"—in effect, a severance package to pay senior staffers (the ones who were making top pay and who had earned the longest vacations) to go away. When that didn't solve the problem, the next step was out-and-out layoffs. Many a newsroom became the scene of tearful good-byes, as security guards watched reporters and editors box up a career's worth of mementos and junk, then escorted them out of the building. Still, things got worse. In 2008–9 the news was about bankruptcies—the Tribune Company, Philadelphia Media, the Sun-Times Company. Five major newspaper companies filed for bankruptcy between December 2008 and March 2009 and kept publishing while they sought to reorganize their debts.[55]

A few newspapers took the ultimate step and closed up shop altogether, or they abandoned print and became available only online.[56] The wolf was not just through the door, it was also devouring institutions that had been decades, even centuries in the making.

The most endangered of the "legacy" media was also the oldest: the daily newspaper. The problems besetting the typical newspaper by the end of the first decade of the twenty-first century were many and serious. One was a cost structure that was in part the result of having been in business so long. Like the Big Three automakers, which were also facing extinction at the same time, most large newspapers had enormous "fixed costs." That is, they were committed to spending a certain large amount of money every day that they did business. Among newspapers at this time, the first fixed cost a publisher faced was the debt incurred in growing to the size of a chain or conglomerate. Just paying the interest on the debt could be crushing. Then there were pensions—legal obligations to keep paying people who hadn't worked at the paper for years or decades, people hired before the current executives were even born. Those were costs that startups, like all those brand-new news sites and aggregators on the Web, did not face. Plus there were health care costs, and the price of buying health insurance was going through the roof. On top of that there was the payroll, and at most big newspapers that meant union contracts—covering pressmen, drivers, photographers, reporters, you name it—that spelled out how much everyone had to be paid, including overtime in a lot of jobs, and all the vacation, sick leave, and other benefits dreamed up in the good times. To make matters worse, a newspaper company operates what is, in effect, a manufacturing plant. Every day it needs large amounts of raw materials. Tons of paper and buckets of ink have to be fed into enormous presses. Out the other end come hundreds of thousands of objects that have to be placed on a fleet of waiting trucks (no matter how high the price of diesel fuel) and hauled through the crowded streets of the home city, through every suburb round about, and hundreds of miles away to the far reaches of the circulation area. The next day, it all has to happen again.

That kind of operation, with its vast overhead, is utterly dependent on seeing a large and steady stream of revenue coming in to support it all. But in recent years, while most of the costs remained fixed, the revenue went steadily downward. Department stores, once the mainstay of big-city papers, with their full-page ads spreading over multiple pages several days a week, consolidated and stopped competing against one another. In the process, they cut way back on their newspaper advertising. In the classified ad department, long an important profit center at most papers, the phones stopped ringing. The people who needed to sell stuff and the people looking to buy stuff met up on Craigslist or eBay or some other online site and didn't need the newspaper any more. There went another major source of revenue. Finally, young people mostly stopped reading newspapers—or they stopped reading the *print* version. Survey after survey showed publishers that the print audience was shrinking and aging. The people in nursing homes were not the demographic that was going to keep the business afloat. But it seemed that almost everyone else was flocking to the Web, where they could get news for free, and letting their subscriptions expire. There went another big revenue source.

Another problem besetting newspapers (and, to a great extent, magazines and television news as well) was even more existential. When seen against the backdrop of the Internet, one fact about newspapers becomes painfully obvious: a newspaper is a fixed bundle of coverage that is good but ultimately second rate. Offering readers no choice, a newspaper presents coverage of a set matrix of topics: politics, crime, business, sports, arts, and something called lifestyle. In each case, though, people who really know or care about those fields understand that they are not going to find the absolute best, most detailed, most passionate coverage of their favorite topic in a daily newspaper. They know that the best coverage will be in some niche on the Web where obsessive amateurs or professional experts gather. And with the coming of the Web, the absolute best coverage is available to everyone, everywhere, all the time, for free.[57] In politics, for example, readers can find pretty good coverage in the *Times* or *Newsweek*. But if they really live and breathe politics, they will want it faster and at a much higher level of granularity, so they will log on to a site like Politico or Real Clear Politics instead and get what they are looking for. The same is true for business, sports, even crosswords and recipes. Thus the question arises: What is the remaining value of reading merely pretty good coverage (and paying for it) when readers can unbundle the newspaper, go online, and plunge into first-rate coverage, written by real aficionados and provided at a price of zero?

One way to understand the decline of the newspaper is to ask the ultimate question: If newspapers did not exist, would it make any sense to invent them?

CHAPTER 14

Going Digital, 1995–

"If the news is that important, it will find me."
—Anonymous college student, 2008

B Y THE 1990S, THE news media had entered something like a Late Cretaceous period: enormous dinosaurs, having evolved to unprecedented sizes, roamed the landscape. They had adapted magnificently to their environment, and they appeared to be the crowning achievement of all creation. They filled almost every niche. Their sheer mass was astonishing. They seemed to be the greatest accomplishment that Earth was capable of.

But . . . what if that environment changed?

What if, say, an asteroid struck and the climate changed very rapidly?

In that case, the dinosaurs would not survive. The great hulks would come crashing down into the dust or muck or snow. With their bloated bodies, their thermal demands, and their tiny brains, they would be doomed. Even their vast size could not save them. Because when it comes to survival, size alone is no guarantee; the issue is fitness—that is, the ability to adapt to a given environment. If economic dinosaurs like the giant media conglomerates could not adapt, they would die.

As the dinosaurs were falling, however, far below their majestic heights, down in the underbrush, another life form was emerging. Down at the dinosaurs' feet were the earliest indicators of a new species: mammals. Bright-eyed and quick, they didn't look like much at first. Scientists call them nocturnal and hairy. In the new climate, they learn to forage. They adapt to their environment. And when that environment changes, the mammals find that they are able not just to survive

[435]

but to adapt and move into some of the niches abandoned by the dinosaurs. The mammals, as we know, rise.

In early 1995, during the first term of President Bill Clinton, hardly anybody had heard of the World Wide Web, much less used it.[1] The president (and his very busy vice president, Al Gore), talked about building an "information superhighway," but that sounded like a metaphor, just talk by politicians. That same year, though, a software engineer named Dave Winer was way ahead of the curve. Not yet forty, Winer was already a veteran of several software startups and was something of a legend in California's Silicon Valley. After a sour experience with a personal-computer software project, he started thinking about what to do next. What about the Web? Yes, that was it! He took a long look ahead, and he shared his vision with the readers who were on the mailing list of the regular thought-bulletins that he called DaveNet, which he e-mailed to more than one hundred recipients. In the future, Winer wrote in 1995, "everyone gets their own personal website." Someday, he predicted, there would be billions of them. "Every new website begets more websites. If I have one, I want my friend to have one, so I can point to it," he wrote. "Someday I'll be able to walk a network of friendships, automatically knowing that each of us has mutual friends. It'll be cool."[2]

The change that threatened the media dinosaurs was the same thing that inspired Dave Winer: computers and the systems that linked them together. Specifically, the great change sweeping through communications and many, many other fields in the 1990s was swelling to an irresistible force thanks to two components, the personal computer and the Internet. The personal computer, or PC, brought the power of computing into the realm of ordinary people, and it did so in a way that did not limit what it might be good for. If you bought a toaster, you wouldn't try to use it to talk to people thousands of miles away. Toasters make toast, and that's about it. But if you bought a PC, who knew what you might be able to do with it? Send e-mail? Sure. *(You've got mail!)* Calculate what would happen to your business if sales increased? Oh, wow. Look at porn? Easy. Compose music? Why not? Combine words, photos, and video and share the results with people around the world? Cover news that way? Oh, *wow!* Software could turn any PC into a device that could do all those things. But what really turned the PC into a revolutionary device was the Internet. Without PCs, the Internet would be limited in its use. Without the Internet, a PC is a versatile tool, although standing alone, it is as isolated as a single telephone. But if you combine the Internet and the PC, look out! Together, they constitute a new environment.

Together, the PC and the Internet have brought about the digital revolution, which in turn has brought pervasive change to the news media. Previously, all forms of mass communication were tangible: ink on paper, light on film, sounds stored on tape. Then came a great divide. In the "digital" era, real things with a physical existence can be represented, stored, or described in terms of codes read by computers. These codes typically consist of numbers—or "digits"—and usually strings of just two digits: 1 and 0. With the hardware of a computer operating a set of instructions known as software, digits can express ideas, words, symbols, and images with almost limitless flexibility. In the world of banking, for example, you do not need wheelbarrows of coins to create an analog of your wealth; a series of 1s and 0s in the bank's computer tallies your account. In media terms, the digital revolution means that data can replace all those physical media that used to be needed to express or record words and images. No more ink, no more paper, no more film. Instead, computers can process words; digital recorders can capture speech without audiotape; and digital cameras can "take" pictures—even moving pictures, which are still called "video" even though there is no videotape involved—and store them without film. With computers connected to the Internet, the final step is possible: all the data can be transmitted to anyone on earth with an Internet connection—almost instantly and practically for free.[3]

To the Big Media of the late twentieth century, the digital revolution was the convulsive change that reshapes the landscape, the asteroid strike that alters the climate, which in turn determines who will evolve and survive and who will not. In terms of journalism specifically, the digital revolution is the most sweeping set of changes in centuries, perhaps ever. It is practical magic.

The effects of the digital revolution can be traced along all five of the dimensions that define the news media, each one amplified by the fact that change is occurring along all of these dimensions *at the same time.*

1. TECHNOLOGY. Some of the most obvious changes in the news media brought about by the digital revolution are technological. Almost every tool in the newsroom has been outmoded or updated. That changes the way journalistic work is organized and conceived. Since the coming of the digital revolution, it is possible for a single reporter carrying a backpack (and a lot of charged batteries) to travel to virtually any spot on the planet with a laptop computer, a satellite telephone, a digital camera, and a digital audio recorder and become a roving news bureau. That single person embodies skills and capabilities that were, until very recently, discrete. Under the traditional division of labor in the news business, every item in that journalist's backpack once belonged to a different person, with a different degree or skill set, and a separate trade union. Reporters were forbidden to pick up cameras. Photo editors could not write stories. The engineers who handled "traffic" of words or photos never generated any content. With the digital revolution, the strict guild lines that followed those separate analog technologies began melting into air.

2. ECONOMICS. The digital revolution overturned almost every economic reality of the Big Media. The financial barriers to entry, which had risen steadily over

the centuries from Franklin's bright penny to the hundreds of millions of dollars involved in launching CNN or Fox News, fell in the new millennium into the range of just about anyone. With a couple of thousand dollars for a decent computer, a digital camera, and an Internet connection, the world belongs to anyone with a modem. The digital revolution has also smashed the idea of monopoly because it has made the traditional boundaries of physical geography irrelevant. In the digital landscape, everyone competes against everyone else. No one "owns" (in a journalistic sense) any physical space.

In the newspaper field, the long-established "dual revenue" model—in which papers could count on one stream of revenue coming from subscribers and another stream from advertisers—was suddenly in jeopardy.[4] In the mid-1990s, an I.T. professional named Craig Newmark working for Charles Schwab Investment Services in San Francisco started an e-mail list that let his friends buy and sell things. In a few years, newspapers started noticing that one of their revenue streams was drying up because Newmark had taken his "Craigslist" to the Web, and now everybody who wanted to sell an old boat or look for a job or buy a gun was going to a free website instead of paying for a classified ad in the local paper. To make matters worse, advertisers began cutting back on the amount of "display" advertising they placed in traditional media. This was partly due to the concentration of ownership in retailing,[5] but mainly due to the diversion of advertising dollars from traditional print media to the Web.

At the same time, the Web was overturning the traditional sales model of the media. The whole idea was based on scarcity: if you wanted to know what was going on, there was only one local paper (or maybe two) that would let you stay informed. So if you wanted a copy, you had to pay. If you wanted to watch the news on television, there were just a few networks, and they all required that you sit through advertising to get to the news. You had no choice. But not on the Web. On the Web, almost everything is free and instantly available. If one door is locked, there are thousands more that are wide open. As a result, the other great river of money flowing into newspapers began to dry up. Subscription revenues plummeted. Similar changes upset the economic models on which magazines, television news, and other traditional media were founded.

3. SOCIOLOGY. From the start of the digital revolution, the sociology of news began to evolve. On one end, the sociology of the newsroom was transformed decisively in the 1990s as the traditional distinction between journalist and non-journalist simply evaporated. For more than a century there had existed a broad consensus in America about who was a journalist. Because of the First Amendment, there was no history of issuing government licenses to journalists, comparable to the licenses to practice law or medicine or plumbing. Sometimes the state police or some other agency would issue a press pass, a kind of badge that reporters and photographers could wear around their necks, but those press passes had no real legal standing. Instead, the rough equivalent of a license to practice journalism

was based on *employment* by a company in the news business. If you worked for a news company, then you were in; if not, you were out. But what about people who didn't work for a news organization but who had a computer with an Internet connection *plus* really good information? If someone had the inside scoop on a new Apple release or a copy of a celebrity arrest record, wasn't that news, no matter where that person worked? In short, an army of bloggers began proving their worth and demanding a place at the table. They showed that in America, the new way to become a journalist is to act like one: if you seek facts and verify them and intend to share them with an audience, you're in.

Another challenge to the definition of a journalist arose with the movement known as "citizen journalism." This movement quickly took several forms, all of them involving people who do not draw paychecks from traditional news organizations. One form of citizen journalism involves people who happen to be on the scene when something terrible or amazing occurs. Thanks to the digital revolution, a fair number of those eyewitnesses are likely to have cell phones or digital cameras that will allow them to record the news, often while it is still happening. When a bomb blows up, or deranged loners start shooting up a high school, there is virtually no likelihood that a trained professional reporter will be on hand. In the absence of professional journalists, plenty of other people are quite capable of stepping up and laying down the "first rough draft of history." In addition, thanks to computers and the Internet, new institutions have grown up that take advantage of the power of "distributed reporting"—the impressive ability of thousands of people to cooperate on a journalistic project that would defeat even the largest newsroom. When Congress pumps out a bill running to thousands of pages, secure in the belief that no one will read it, the Web allows a whole lot of people to read bits of it and combine forces. These examples of "citizen journalism" have sometimes been dismissed by traditional journalists as the equivalent of "citizen surgery," but that disdain already seems dated.

At the same time, the digital revolution has transformed another social grouping: the "people formerly known as the audience."[6] For centuries, the role of the audience in news was twofold: they were expected to *receive* information, ideas, and images passively, and they were expected to *pay* for it. The flow of communication was essentially one-way, like a lecture. The journalist compiled a package of information and sent it off to the recipients. At a newspaper, a handful of readers might be allowed the privilege of having a letter to the editor published, but these were few and far between. In most cities there are more lightning strikes in a year than published letters to the editor.[7] On radio and TV, input from regular people about the news was practically unheard of. With the coming of the Internet, however, people would no longer tolerate being lectured to. They expected to interact with journalists, just as they did with everyone else online. What was once a lecture was turning into a conversation, a two-way interchange, not always civil, in which the professional journalist did not always get the last word.

4. POLITICS. If politics is defined broadly as the relationships of power in a society, then the digital revolution has also brought profound change in media politics. The open architecture of the personal computer and the Internet gave rise to a new media era that, so far at least, has more in common with the print tradition of comparative freedom than with the broadcast tradition of government regulation. A typical Web transmission of material is an entirely private affair. A content creator cooks something up on a personal computer. The resulting packet of data is transmitted by an Internet service provider (or ISP, a private company), then relayed through a constantly shifting array of servers and routers in a privately owned network of fiber optic cables and computers. In the American setting, there is no government involvement (and, theoretically, no government spying on domestic communications). In principle, that is all fine. But almost from the start of the Web in the mid-1990s, there have been legislative and legal struggles over the degree and quality of the freedom of online communication. One source of conflict involves the sending of messages or images that are inherently criminal: selling or swapping child pornography, for example, or using Craigslist to solicit prostitution. These issues are fairly straightforward and do not send most Web advocates to the barricades. Another, much more challenging set of issues has arisen over attempts to define and enforce copyright and intellectual property rights. Many parties have attempted to draw government onto their side against people they believe are stealing their work.

Other issues create direct conflicts between the media and governments. One involves censorship. It is an open question whether the United States government ever would (or could) directly censor civilian communications via the Web. Americans may never find out the answer to that question. But residents of other countries have cautionary tales. In China, for example, the government in Beijing routinely censors individual sites and categories of websites that are seen as threats to stability and party rule. American journalists who travel to China soon experience the reach of a motivated government, even when they are covering a global showcase such as the Olympics. In Myanmar, the regime has gone so far as to attempt to pull the plug on all Internet service nationwide, just to prevent some unwelcome communications. Multiplying cases from around the world give cause for concern about the future of freedom for journalists (and others) on the Web. A related concern involves spying, another form of direct government action that is hostile to communication freedom. Unlike censorship, which is usually obvious, spying can be very difficult to detect.

In addition, the Web is sometimes a focus for lawmakers who want to legislate some of the terms and conditions of Internet access. The way is open because the companies that build and operate the "pipes" of the system—telecommunication companies like Comcast and Verizon, which supply the routers and cables that carry data—are regulated utilities. As common carriers, they are subject to a host of regulations, and they are targets for politicians seeking to favor one interest group or another. One particular flashpoint involves "net neutrality," the idea that broadband networks should impose no restrictions on contents, platforms, or equipment that users attach at their end. In some cases, the carriers want to block or slow services delivered by their business rivals. In other cases, the carriers want to be able to charge different rates to individuals or companies that use a lot of capacity, for example, by uploading and downloading large video or audio files. Courthouses, state legislatures, and Congress are filled with people seeking to gain something or thwart something.

In terms of electoral politics, the digital revolution has had a dramatic impact by reviving the tradition of partisanship in American journalism. Websites like anncoulter.com and dailykos.com have raised the level of political vituperation to heights not seen since the early nineteenth century. And the common online practice of adding anonymous comments to Web postings has unleashed the barbaric yawp of the most angry, bitter, and resentful people on the planet. In traditional media, those notes were almost never struck. In broadcast television, the public was rarely invited in. In newspapers and magazines, editors serving as gatekeepers zealously enforced their notions of taste, fairness, and decorum. Thus, even the old-fashioned published letters to the editor stayed within fairly narrow bounds of expression. As it turned out, when those gates came down, there were a lot of ticked-off people just waiting to "flame" someone.

5. PHILOSOPHY. Finally, the digital revolution struck at the very definition of journalism itself. For more than a century, the philosophy of journalism went something like this: Journalism is the gathering and disseminating of information, images, and ideas by trained practitioners, who deserve a constitutionally privileged position because their work is essential to informing the people, so that the people can carry out their duties as informed citizens. Traditionally, the distribution of news was a one-way guess by editors about what audiences wanted or needed to know. In the new media environment, many of those assumptions have been upset. In the resulting turbulence, professional journalists, critics, and non-traditional journalists are all contending to define the new meaning of "news." If news is no longer a lecture, is it really a conversation? If so, who gets to talk and under what ground rules (if any)? For a while, journalists resisted the idea that bloggers (dismissed as kids in pajamas) could contribute anything of value to the world's storehouse of information and arguments. As it turned out, the digital revolution showed that timely and reliable information can come from just about anywhere.

The digital revolution also changed the very definition of "media." Before the Web, newspapers, magazines, radio, and television coexisted, each medium distinct from the others, defined by its mode of transmission. In the digital era, though, all media meet all other media on the Web. Thus National Public Radio, while continuing to broadcast, devotes considerable resources to its online operations, including the posting of many written stories. In other words, the biggest radio news operation is also deeply engaged in a "print" medium. Most newspapers maintain elaborate websites, where they offer not just text and photos but audio and video as well. In other words, the print media are now engaged in what was once called "broadcasting." In many ways, the issue of which medium a journalist works in (which was once a definitional question) has become practically irrelevant.

In addition, the digital revolution sparked a new mode of organizing and disseminating information known as "aggregation." As the number of sites on the Web proliferated to an unmanageable scale, some sites began offering "news" that was not original but was collected from other newsgathering sources; the "news aggregators" typically offered a headline or brief summary (usually the first paragraph, or "lede," of the story) and a hyperlink connecting interested readers to the full-length original. In this way, sites like the Drudge Report and Yahoo! News became important disseminators of news even though they did not generate any original reporting. This caused consternation and anger within traditional media, for at least two reasons. First, although the online aggregators contributed nothing in the way of their own reporting, they gave the impression that they were in the news business. This raised the existential question: Is it still journalism if there's no reporting? Second, the aggregators provided links to free material, making it that much more difficult for news-reporting sites to charge for their own content. This raised the financial question: Is it a sustainable business if you give your product away? Who will pay for reporting? On their side, the aggregators argue that those are the wrong questions. In the online economy, real value is created by the volume of visitors to a site. By providing links to the news-generating sites, the aggregators claim, they are actually doing those sites a favor. That argument shows no signs of ending soon.

How did all this happen? How did all this profound, multidimensional change sweep across the globe? In the digital revolution, there was no single moment of conception, birth, or maturity. Even so, the digital age is well enough established that the history of its key figures, ideas, and milestones is coming into focus. In terms of its impact on the news media, much of that history can be compressed to a few key events. One certainly was the "invention" of the World Wide Web by Tim Berners-Lee in 1989. Another was the "invention" of the first graphical interface browser, Mosaic, by Marc Andreesen in 1992. Like the halftone process of the late nineteenth century, which allowed the combining of print and photos on a single page, the browser enabled an online merger of text and graphic elements. In 1993 a new magazine—called, appropriately, *Wired*—was founded just to focus on this new wired world. (Soon, however, the leading edge of that world would go wireless, and the magazine would migrate to the Web.) Then the pace quickened with a cluster of uncoordinated initiatives by unaffiliated individuals in the mid-1990s that, taken together, brought the digital revolution directly to bear on traditional news media.

A big step was the creation of the blog.[8] The practices now known as blogging were worked out among a community of software engineers, high-tech entrepreneurs, computer programmers, and like-minded "techies," many of them in Silicon Valley and other high-tech hotspots, during the mid-1990s.[9] One of the earliest and most influential bloggers was Dave Winer.

A native of Brooklyn, Winer was the son of two Ph.D.s. He graduated in 1972 from the Bronx High School of Science, majored in math at Tulane, then got a master's degree in the new field of computer science at the University of Wisconsin in 1978. During the 1980s he founded and ran a software company in Mountain View, California, in the heart of the emerging computer industry. In 1988 he founded a company called UserLand Software and became known as a consistent innovator. As he became more prominent, he and his products received a growing amount of coverage from newspapers and other media. From his firsthand knowledge, he could see that most journalists made a hash of it. They did not know what they were talking about. It was disillusioning. "Ask any expert who's been interviewed on a subject of any subtlety or complexity," he wrote later. "The reporter mangles it."[10] There had to be a better way.

One way he found in 1994 was an e-mail list, which he used to send his thoughts out en masse to friends and colleagues in the high-tech field. After a while, he gave his list a nickname, DaveNet, and started writing several times a week.[11] He had discovered a way around the traditional media that allowed him to reach a sizable audience without filters or editors. If he got a really interesting reply from someone, he would send that along to the group as well. One growing focus of DaveNet was a topic of personal interest to Winer: the World Wide Web and its possible paths of development. Winer was a fluent writer; he knew almost everyone who mattered in the high-tech world; and he was a veteran computer programmer. He was thus just about perfectly situated to take the next step: figure out a way to move the e-mail version of DaveNet right onto the Web. He made a first pass in 1996 with a UserLand product called Frontier, which could serve as an online meeting place for software developers. The following year he changed the name to Scripting News (which has remained in use continuously ever since), and he continued to improve the software. Soon, some key features were recognizable. For example, the "new stuff" always appeared at the top, and there were links to other pages on the Web (lots of them, in fact). It was relatively word-heavy, compared to sites with lots of bells and whistles, but it served his purpose, which was to speak his mind. In Winer's view, that was key: the essence of a Web log was "the unedited voice of a person."[12]

Around the same time, a small but growing number of people were creating their own Web logs, adding a feature here and coining a phrase there. For a while, most bloggers could plausibly consider themselves part of a community. After all, a lot of them actually knew one another off-line, having worked together at Apple, Microsoft, or any of a few dozen other companies, or having met at conferences and trade shows. Most were white men with advanced degrees, although a few women like Esther Dyson and Meg Hourihan were also part of the club. Most traditional media considered blogs a curiosity, a hobby for techies. But that was about to change, rather abruptly. The change came from a blogger who was not part of the Silicon Valley/high-tech crowd. In fact he was a loner, a misfit in a lot of ways. His name was Matt Drudge.

Drudge had grown up in the Washington, D.C, area and he became something of a slacker, working nights at a 7-Eleven store. In 1989 he moved to Los Angeles and found a job working in the gift shop at CBS Studios. In 1994, in an effort to get him off the couch, his father bought him a Packard Bell computer. Soon, Drudge began sending out a group e-mail to his friends, often passing along gossip about celebrities that he picked up at the CBS gift shop. Within a few years, Drudge moved his newsletter to the Web and added more politics, with a conservative bent. His site really took off in January 1998, when Drudge revealed that Michael Isikoff, an actual investigative reporter at *Newsweek,* was looking into the Monica Lewinsky case and that *Newsweek* was balking at printing the story. Drudge "published" that information on his website on January 17, 1998, effectively forcing *Newsweek*'s hand. Here was something new: a pillar of the establishment media was being made to jump (and being told how high) by a guy with a modem. The media world (not to mention the Clinton administration) would never be quite the same again (fig. 14.1).

Meanwhile, the Web was becoming home to several noteworthy ventures that were hybrids—attempts to take traditional forms like the magazine and translate them to the new medium. In the mid-1990s the Web got its equivalent in the form of two new online magazines (or e-zines, or just 'zines) which appeared on the Web and on the Web only: *Salon* and *Slate.*

On November 25, 1995, *Salon* made its debut. It began with two handfuls of staffers working over two tables in an architect's office in San Francisco, a scene reminiscent of the early days of the penny papers.[13] The founder was David Talbot, a journalist who had learned his trade at the old *San Francisco Examiner,* where he had worked as editor of the arts section and of the paper's Sunday magazine.[14] Talbot itched to run his own magazine, and his first thought ran to print, but the startup costs were prohibitive. So along with several *Examiner* colleagues and others, he turned to the low-cost alternative, the Web. With $60,000 in hand from an executive at Apple Computer, Talbot started planning and hiring. Apple got cold feet, but Talbot found $2 million from Adobe Ventures, and *Salon* was a go. The first issue included an interview with author Amy Tan, along with pieces by Camille Paglia, Armistead Maupin, and Amanda Spake, as well as a cartoon by Tom Tomorrow.

As with many other early Web publications, the editors operated on the

14.1 **THE ONLINE NEWS-AGGREGATING SITE DRUDGE REPORT** has stuck with the distinctively spare look of its home page, featuring a typewriter font, almost from its inception in the mid-1990s. This array of headlines appeared a few days after the terrorist attack on the World Trade Center on September 11, 2001.—*The Drudge Report.*

assumption that they would produce "editions" on a fixed schedule (originally, every two weeks), just like a print magazine. That didn't last long. By 1997, *Salon* was operating at Internet pace and updating daily. One early discovery of online publishing was an end to any self-delusion about how much each story actually appealed to readers. Online, there was no mystery and no guesswork; computer servers kept a tally of readers, which could be shown to the writer, or to the advertiser whose ad appeared on that page. As *Salon* editor Gary Kamiya wrote in 2005 in a ten-year retrospective: "To this day, whenever we run some . . . sexy, gossip-ridden story . . . readers send in angry letters denouncing our lowbrow, vulgar sensibility and threatening to cancel their subscriptions. Meanwhile, our servers melt under the demand and the page views soar into the stratosphere . . . The server, like a gentleman's valet, knows all."[15] Over the years, *Salon* made a stock offering, only to watch its stock dive from $15.13 a share to a penny after the dot-com bust of 2000, which almost turned out the lights. But the site survived long enough to see advertising return—in part because it created *Salon Premium*, offering readers special treatment if they were willing to pay; for a fee, readers could get extra material, or they could be spared from having to look at ads.

At just about the same time that *Salon* was starting up in the mid-1990s, the journalist Michael Kinsley got a phone call. A Rhodes Scholar and Harvard Law grad, Kinsley was an aging boy wonder. He had already held the job of editor of the *New Republic* and had given that up to appear on CNN's *Crossfire* show as the tire swing for Pat Buchanan's eight-hundred-pound gorilla. The caller invited Kinsley to Seattle in August 1995 for a secret meeting at Microsoft. At the time, the software giant was looking for ventures to expand its presence on the Web, and Kinsley was still dreaming of founding his own magazine. He even wrote a memo outlining how an online magazine would work. (Never mind that, as he would write later, "almost everything in the memo was completely wrong." The fact was, no one knew how to launch an online magazine.)[16] The new magazine, called *Slate* and based on the Microsoft campus in Redmond, Washington, went online in June 1996. Like the editors at *Salon,* Kinsley at first planned to "publish" on a regular schedule but soon scrapped that premise in favor of posting items whenever they were ready. From the beginning, Kinsley's financial goal was to break even. Although Microsoft had enormous amounts of free cash, the company had no intention of pouring it down an online rat hole. Besides, and far more important, Kinsley believed that the ability to make money is essential to independent journalism. It is what allows an editor to say "Screw you"—to say it to pressure groups, to advertisers, even to readers, if need be. One early mistake Kinsley admitted to in pursuit of making money was to try to charge readers for the privilege of reading online. For about a year, *Slate* charged $19.95 for twelve months' access, which resulted in 20,000 subscribers paying for premium material while some 400,000 were helping themselves to the free content. In the end, *Slate* managed to break even by keeping costs low and by building up its (free) readership to the point where revenue from online ads would pay the bills—or *almost* pay the bills.

While *Salon* and *Slate* were launching, the traditional media were tentatively beginning to call meetings and hire consultants to try to figure out what exactly to do about this Internet thing. Was it a fad? Was it the CB radio of the decade? What was it *good for*? (So far, they thought, not much—although e-mail seemed like a fine idea, especially as a way to cut expenses on phone bills.) The Internet seemed to executives of traditional media like a toy for kids. Why worry? Everyone knows that smart, sensible people will always read a thick morning paper and a glossy weekly magazine or two. What publishers and editors at the elite media wanted to know in the mid-1990s was: What was this Internet thing going to do to help *them*?

So, sometimes against their better judgment, they authorized a series of experiments. Time for the dinosaurs to learn to ice skate!

At the *Washington Post* a project got under way in October 1993. The idea was to set up a separate operation and give it what sounded like a snappy Internet era name: Digital Ink. The idea also included a plan to herd readers to the site through a tollbooth (run by a venture known as ATT Interchange) and make them pay for very slow downloads. That model was partly the result of a culture gap. As Melinda McAdams, the "content developer" for Digital Ink, tried to explain in June 1995: "A journalist with little online experience tends to think in terms of stories, news value, public service, and things that are good to read. These are the staples of a one-way medium. But a person with a lot of online experience thinks more about connections, organization, movement within and among sets of information, and communication among different people. Online is bi-directional."[17] Digital Ink was a start. But three years and millions of dollars later, the *Post* gave up.[18] Not only did people not want to pay for slow downloads, but also the paper was squandering one of the greatest brand names in journalism. Online, users were supposed to find *Washington Post* content under that other name, the one nobody could remember. After two years in development and a year online, *Post* executives pulled the plug on Digital Ink in 1996 and moved their online news efforts to a new website. Taking advantage of the company's brand name, the new site was called washingtonpost.com.

At mighty Time Warner, Inc., the first foray onto the Internet did not go any better. In the mid-1990s, Time Warner wasted millions of dollars, and (more important) precious years in the life of the online world, on a venture it called Pathfinder. The idea was to create a single portal to guide online readers to the dozens of magazine titles owned by Time Warner. Never mind that most of those titles were already household names. What could be more familiar to most Americans than *Time, People,* or *Sports Illustrated*? Time Inc. had long ago sunk millions into establishing those brands. Why make people hunt for them behind a name nobody had ever heard of and did not associate with the thing they were looking for? (*Pathfinder? What's that—a new Deerslayer novel? A car? A what? Where's* Time?) In desperation, Time Warner changed management and brought in the brilliant magazine editor Dan Okrent to oversee Pathfinder. He could not make it work either. Eventually Time Warner killed it.[19]

At the *New York Times*, editors took a similarly wary approach. At the *Times*, change is never taken lightly. The burden of history haunts the paper of record and contributes to a culture that despises fads and looks askance at trends. The *Times* did not switch to offset printing until 1981, and the paper would not print a color photo on page one until 1997. Still, the paper was in the news business, after all, and story after story kept touting this Internet thing. So the *Times* faced facts and began its own tryout. In June 1994 the paper introduced a service it called "@times," which was limited to arts and entertainment pieces that it licensed to AOL, which made them available to its growing customer base. Finally, in January 1996, the *Times* launched a truly Web-based version, under its own name, called nytimes.com. The new website gave readers anywhere in the world access to something a lot of people wanted: a look at the full content of the *New York Times* on the night of publication. It was a start.

Like the leaders of other "legacy media," however, *Times* executives could not figure out how to make money on the Web; that is, they could not figure out how to make *lots* of money. Online advertising brought in some money, and the amount rose every year. But it started from such a low base that even spectacular annual growth still left online revenues lagging well behind the income from the printed version. Eager to increase the online contribution, the *Times* tried an experiment in 2005, a program called Times Select, in which certain content, including the marquee op-ed columns, would be removed from the public website and placed behind a "paywall," forcing people who wanted to read celebrated columnists like Thomas Friedman and Maureen Dowd to pay for it. Times Select lasted two years. It turned out that the paper was chasing away so many readers from the website, thus reducing the value of online advertising, that it was not worth the money coming in courtesy of the paywall. In 2011, *Times* executive tried again, launching a "metered model," in which online readers get a certain number of free page views in a given period and must pay for access beyond that threshold.

In the buzz phrase of the time, the traditional media "just didn't get it" when it came to emigrating to the Web.[20] What they did not get was that the Internet was a game changer. While the executives at most traditional media were wasting precious time ignoring the Web—or treating it as an enemy and blaming young people for not reading enough—the Web was already forcing change, deep inside the newsrooms of even the biggest and oldest news media (fig. 14.2).

*   *   *

IT IS NOT KNOWN FOR sure if there was much contact between the last dinosaurs and the first mammals. As reptiles, the dinosaurs needed to thermoregulate, so most of them were active in the day. At night, the warm-blooded mammals came out. They did not cause the dinosaurs to go extinct. Dinosaurs died off because they could not adapt to changes in their environment. Mammals did not kill them off. Mammals just *replaced* them. When the opportunity arose, when environmental niches became available, mammals flooded into them. The mammals were more adaptable.

Similar patterns of collapse and replacement in the economic realm have been identified as the phenomenon of "creative destruction." The great theorist Joseph Schumpeter, who coined the phrase, considered it an essential feature of capitalism.[21] In this scheme, economic life is marked not by equilibrium but by turbulence. As soon as one technology or corporation becomes dominant, an entrepreneur comes along with a new technology or a radically different cost structure and threatens to topple today's dominant structures. Economists tend to view "creative destruction" with equanimity or even with pride, pointing out that the collapse of a firm like Polaroid opens the way for new forms of instant photography. Carriage makers learn to make automobile bodies, or else they go

14.2 *THE NEW YORKER* took a wry look at one kind of response to the rise of digital news.
—*David Sipress/The New Yorker.*

"I'd like to see you do this online."

out of business. At the same time, however, it is important not to brush past the "destructive" half of creative destruction. The process is two-sided: there are winners in economics, to be sure, but there are also losers. Among the most obvious losers in the transformation of the news business were the veteran journalists from the pre-Internet era who were bought out, laid off, or simply fired. But they were not the only losers in the process. Beyond them were the readers and viewers who enjoyed their work or depended on it. Included within the audience for mass media was nothing less than the bulk of the citizenry. Without newspapers, magazines, and television, how would they stay informed? If all the "legacy media" were to collapse, there would be a substantial loss of skilled, experienced newsgatherers. Who would serve as the watchdogs and keep an eye on the thousands of local governments and dozens of state capitals and the Congress? Who would keep an eye on Africa, or know the difference between tribes in Afghanistan? Along with all the gains, what would be lost?

From the viewpoint of the legacy media, the Internet and the online news sites that were claiming "their" readers and "their" ads were often seen as a destructive threat. But that is far too limited a viewpoint, even within the field of journalism. There is another perspective, one that is ultimately likely to prove decisive: that of the digital natives.[22] The digital natives are defined as those people born after 1980 or so who have come of age with the Internet and consider it second nature, a utility like running water or electricity. To them, the printed newspaper or the 6:30 p.m. national news broadcast were relics from an earlier period—the journalistic equivalent of buggy whips in an automotive age or tea cozies in the Starbucks era. The digital natives did not miss the legacy media because they never really depended on them. In a dynamic process, the new producers of journalism and the new consumers of journalism were driving a transformation of the field. That is the creative side of creative destruction, and it too commands attention.

One emerging journalistic form is the online news site, such as the Huffington Post. Round the clock, "HuffPo" offers a mix of material—some original reporting, lots of inexpensive commentary and analysis, combined with constantly updated feeds of hard news from traditional sources and regularly updated blogs commenting on all of the above. It was successful, at least by the lights of the online world. Founded by Arianna Huffington in May 2005, the Huffington Post had within a few years achieved the top rating on the website Technorati, the authority of online clout and popularity. By early 2010, "HuffPo" had achieved a traffic milestone of 13 million unique users a month, ranking it second behind the *New York Times* site.[23] Among professional journalists, Huffington became notorious for not paying (or underpaying) her contributors, but no one could argue with her success. Part of the reason her site flourished was that its costs were a fraction of what a "legacy" news organization would face to produce the same kind of daily page. The general focus is on national politics and the general cultural zeitgeist. Although it had a small salaried staff who produced some original material, Huffington Post functioned primarily as a news aggregator, presenting online content created by others in an attractive package (fig. 14.3).

The package proved to be so attractive that AOL bought Huffington's site in early 2010 for $315 million—an enormous return on a very modest initial investment. The sale settled one question about digital journalism by proving that it could be lucrative, at least for owners. The big question that remained was whether online journalism could employ significant numbers of skilled reporters and pay them decent wages. Indeed, prompted by the thought of $315 million changing hands, HuffPo's legions of bloggers and writers who contributed for free for the first six years, suddenly began demanding compensation.

Another type of successful online news site is more specialized. One of the most popular of the "niche" sites was TMZ.com (for "Thirty Mile Zone," which describes the founder's original scope: thirty miles around Hollywood). Updated continually, TMZ carved out a reputation as the primary source for news about celebrities behaving badly, especially those connected to Hollywood. Although it often seemed that the site could be more appropriately named TMI (for "too much information"), it stood as proof of the unquenchable thirst for minutiae about the lives of the famous, the formerly famous, the near-famous, and the would-be famous. TMZ also became known for breaking news that ended up in more highbrow media. In addition to celebrity news, sports journalism has also flourished online. In the realm of sports, some of the most important sites included online versions of legacy media such as the *New York Daily News* or ESPN, which existed on television and in magazine form before going online. Other sites such as "RichieBaseball" and "StatsGuru" were operated by lone sports-mad individuals. In the business world, sites cater to investors or real estate speculators or entrepreneurs.

14.3 **ARIANNA HUFFINGTON**, founder of the online blogging and news site Huffington Post, pauses in her company's Manhattan newsroom. She announced in 2011 that her site was being acquired by AOL for $315 million, making it the biggest acquisition by AOL since it was spun off from Time Warner in 2009. —*Countour/Getty Images.*

Of all the digital news and opinion sites, one in particular achieved an unprecedented degree of both professional stature and business success. For those reasons, the site known as Talking Points Memo, founded by Joshua Micah Marshall in 2000, may point the way to one version of the journalistic future. At his site, Marshall has managed to combine two important activities: doing original reporting and making enough money to pay for it. That is a rare combination in the online world, which is what makes TPM worth examining.

Josh Marshall is not, strictly speaking, a digital native; he was born too soon.[24] Nevertheless, he adapted to the online environment and managed to flourish there. Born in St. Louis in 1969, he attended the Webb Schools in Claremont, California, in the San Gabriel Mountains, then went to Princeton. After his graduation in 1991, he entered a Ph.D. program in American history at Brown University, where his dissertation adviser was the eminent scholar of the American Revolution, Gordon Wood. While he was studying at Brown, Marshall began writing for the liberal (print) magazine *American Prospect*, then based in Boston, and he was soon hired as an associate editor. Without giving up on his dissertation (which had to do with the role of violence in relations between native peoples and English settlers in seventeenth-century New England), he became the *American Prospect*'s Washington editor. During the vote-counting fiasco in Florida in the 2000 presidential election, Marshall began blogging about the furor over the tally. He called his blog Talking Points Memo. In 2001 he left the *Prospect* and worked as a freelancer while continuing his blog. He was successful as a freelancer, writing for the *Atlantic,* the *New Yorker, Salon,* the *New Republic,* and the *Washington Monthly.* Still, now that Marshall was in his early thirties, it could appear that he was something of a vagabond in both academic and journalistic circles.

Then he began making a name for himself. In 2002 the powerful conservative senator Trent Lott gave a speech in which he praised the segregationist views of his fellow Southerner Strom Thurmond on the occasion of Thurmond's one-hundredth birthday. The mainstream media gave Lott a pass, dismissing the incident as a lame attempt to make an old man happy. But Marshall kept banging away on his blog at the issue of Lott's racist comments, and Marshall's page views suddenly jumped from eight thousand a day to twenty thousand. As anyone who had ever worked in any medium would agree, a shift like that tells you that you're onto something. Eventually, Marshall's blog pushed the issue into the limelight, Lott was forced to resign as Senate majority leader, and a lot more people knew the name TPM.com. In a sense, Marshall had repeated the maneuver first used by Matt Drudge in making the mainstream media pay attention to an issue they preferred to avoid. The agenda-setting function of the traditional news media was vanishing. In 2003, Marshall tried to "monetize" the extra traffic that the Lott incident had brought to his site by selling ad space. From that point on, extra visitors translated directly into extra revenue. He also completed his dissertation and got his Ph.D.

Meanwhile, his core readership continued to expand, drawn to his mix of brains and left-leaning sympathies. He tartly tracked every blunder and scandal of the George W. Bush years, updating the site many times a day to keep his readers satisfied. He served as a one-man opposition party, decrying Bush's handling of Iraq, Hurricane Katrina, the outing of Valerie Plame, the campaign to privatize Social Security, and the outrage du jour. A hard-driving person, he set a grueling pace. In 2005 he married Millet Israeli, whom he had known since his Princeton days. She had gone to Harvard Law School, then worked as a lawyer for Dow Jones. Eventually she joined Marshall in working full-time for TPM, where she became general counsel and general manager. Over time, the revenue from the online ads grew to the point where they could not only afford the rent on modest office space in lower Manhattan but also hire a few people to join TPM as full-time reporters and bloggers.

It was still a pretty modest operation in 2007, when Marshall tackled another major story. He was not the only one to notice the role of politics in the decisions to vet and fire U.S. attorneys in the Bush Justice Department, but he was the most tenacious in getting to the bottom of the scandal. TPM became the pace-

14.4 **ONLINE JOURNALIST JOSHUA MICAH MARSHALL** began his "Talking Points Memo" as a blog so that he could comment on the controversy over the Florida vote-counting in the 2000 presidential election. Marshall, shown here in his Manhattan newsroom, built TPM into a prize-winning (and money-making) online news site by offering a mix of original reporting, political commentary, and links to other news sites. —*Andrea Mohin/The New York Times/Redux.*

setter in demanding (and receiving) answers about the process for hiring federal prosecutors, usually a fairly straightforward professional matter. At TPM, as at most blogs, the whole idea of a "story" is irrelevant. The site offers a constantly revised stream of posts, including links, comments, questions, updates on developing themes, and random jottings. TPM's approach to the attorneys scandal was typical: there was no single blockbuster story or series, but instead there was a steady accumulation of evidence and analysis. By the time Marshall was done, U.S. Attorney General Alberto Gonzalez had been forced to resign. The next year, Marshall was rewarded for his work on the hiring scandal with one of the leading prizes in professional journalism, the George Polk Award for legal reporting. *Time* magazine named TPM the best blog of 2009. Such accolades were acknowledgment that a serious blogger could drive the national agenda, force the mainstream media to pay attention to an issue they were prepared to ignore, and back it all up with solid reporting. Indeed, the reason for Marshall's professional success in the U.S. attorneys scandal was simple: he had the goods. He could have conformed to the stereotype about bloggers and stayed at home in his pajamas and used his site to whine about politics or issue flaming insults to politicians he didn't like. While TPM is certainly opinionated, the important thing is that it is not *merely* opinionated (fig. 14.4).

Marshall's other accomplishment was to make money online. He made enough not only to be able to move to bigger quarters in the Chelsea neighborhood of Manhattan but also to expand the paid staff to eight and add a Washington bureau, while—above all—remaining independent. With some 99 percent of revenues coming from online ads, the site's financial health was dependent on traffic from visitors. The number of visitors to TPM continued to grow, reaching 1.5 million unique visitors in 2009.[25] One key was to keep costs down. Marshall was not building any skyscrapers, nor was he borrowing money from banks or from venture capitalists. He has operated on a pay-as-you-go basis, spending money only after he had it in hand. Salaries were modest—ranging from $24,000 to $40,000 a year (which in New York City is barely enough). Staffers who burned out or who needed to earn more have found jobs at prestigious legacy news media such as the *Washington Post* and ABC News. Just as significantly, Marshall found that when he had a job opening and advertised for journalists, he had his pick of highly skilled veterans who were eager to bail out of troubled legacy media such as daily papers and weekly magazines, including some applicants he described as "household names."[26] By 2011 he had a staff of twenty, posting verified information by real journalists using real bylines. It was, in short, a real news operation.

Conclusion

IN RECENT YEARS, THE economic problems facing most of the mainstream news media grew so severe that many people began to ask, Does journalism have a future? Were we seeing the "end of news"?[1] Beneath the "froth and scum" of each hour's headlines about the news field—the latest merger or bankruptcy, the freshest outrage over partisanship, the newest online startup—there ran deeper currents and tidal movements. If we look at the history over a long enough stretch of time, we can see some of these larger patterns. In my view, the three hundred years and more of human struggle to build, define, and control the news media in America can be thought of in terms of fairly coherent phases—substantial periods of time when a particular pattern or problem predominates. Throughout this lengthy narrative I have maintained that, despite the historical constraints of their times, a series of innovators have changed journalism in profound ways. Their innovations define the contours of those historical periods. Thus far there have been five major eras in the history of journalism in America (see the Appendix for a summary). Each one is marked by efforts to reconcile a philosophy of journalism (that is, a set of operating principles) with the emerging or dominant economic model of the time. In each of those episodes of convulsive change, significant innovations can be seen occurring across all the major indexes of change—economic, technological, political, sociological, and philosophical—at about the same time. Not all of these periods have a clear starting bell or finale. In fact, in many instances a given technology or ideology persists long after a new one has arrived. The story contained in this book is not one of an orderly succession. Instead it is the tale of an often messy proliferation of ideas, tools, and business models. Even so, amid all the details and individual stories, patterns are visible.

Journalism in America began as a tiny and timid affair conducted by a handful of people in a remote backwater of the great British Empire. The first period in that history can be said to have started in 1704 with the founding of the first successful newspaper (see chapter 1). The colonists had had ways of gathering and disseminating news before then, but news in the sense of regular communications to a substantial audience really got under way with John Campbell's *Boston News-Letter*. In the following decades, while individual newspapers came and went, the industry as a whole flourished as papers grew larger, appeared more frequently, and spread to more and more cities and towns. Still operating along the lines of the shop, with hand-powered presses of limited speed, printers like Ben Franklin who launched newspapers in the American colonies faced a number of problems. Chafing under the practice of censorship and the law of sedition, they articulated a philosophy of press freedom, then challenged authority in order to enlarge the "public sphere" in which their traffic in ideas could take place. Under pressure from their readers (sometimes in the form of mobs), colonial editors found that they had to abandon their original stance of neutrality and move to one side or the other in the great argument over the proper relation between colonies and Crown (see chapter 2). In fighting for their economic survival, they turned to politics. In the process, the pages of newspapers became increasingly bold and increasingly polarized. Whigs read Whig papers, and Tories read Tory papers. As the conflict sharpened, pamphleteers like Thomas Paine joined the debate and pushed journalism to new polemical heights. In the aftermath of the Revolution, printers continued their central role in politics by helping to organize the original political parties. They also found themselves in a newly advantageous social role—as constitutionally favored catalysts in the great experiment in self-government and as economically privileged players enjoying government subsidies such as free postage and lucrative printing contracts. They had solved their financial problems by embracing politics and thereby taking on a central role in the new party system.

The next major period in journalism history began in the 1830s and played out over the rest of the nineteenth century in a trend that has been called "the commercialization of news" (see chapters 3 and 4). In this era the key driver of change was, once again, primarily economic. The basic business model changed from the shop to the factory, as printers took a leading role in a historic and contentious reorganization of the workplace, giving up the traditional role of master in favor of the new role of publisher. As publishers, they began to institute a division of labor that allowed for the introduction of new technology, which in turn, made possible operations on an unprecedented scale. At the start of this period, the biggest daily papers in America sold in the low thousands; by the end, they would pass a million copies a day. Using the latest steam-powered presses, publishers like Benjamin Day and James Gordon Bennett (and, later, Joseph Pulitzer and William Randolph Hearst) took aim at the urban masses, pioneering a mix of nonpolitical news that featured riots, fires, and scandals, supplemented in later decades by stunts, photos, cartoons, coverage of sports and celebrities, and anything else the editors could concoct to get people to part with a penny or two. Taking advantage of the telegraph, the AP wire, the telephone, and the photograph, they consistently pushed journalism in the direction of greater speed and greater visual appeal. Using the resulting profits to declare their independence from the political parties, these publishers staked their own claim to representing the masses and asserted their right to pass judgment on the performance of those in power. Operating on the philosophy that journalism is news that passes the test of the marketplace, they turned the big-city daily newspaper into a juggernaut of profit and power.

As the twentieth century opened, journalism came under new stresses. In the third major period of our history, journalists had to find new ways to reconcile the culture of news with the business of news (see chapter 5). At a quickening pace after 1900, newspaper publishers began building the first chain enterprises, linking several (and, later, many) newspapers together. As new forms of communicating arrived, an innovator like Hearst could yoke a newspaper chain to a wire service, a feature syndicate, a rack of magazines, a newsreel company, and the latest thing: radio. With the coming of radio, and then television, the broadcasting of information and opinions quickly expanded the definition of the "news media." Radio also introduced the first entry of a new business form into news: the publicly traded corporation. Although it would ultimately triumph, the corporate form took hold slowly in a field traditionally dominated by individuals and families. At the start of the twentieth century, the success of "yellow press" publishers like Pulitzer and Hearst threatened to degrade journalism into a cynical, sensationalistic quest for profit. Against that threat, a growing number of journalists fought to define and enforce higher standards and tried to emulate the established professions (see chapter 6). Led by Adolph Ochs at the *New York Times,* this group of publishers, educators, and critics advanced a vision of journalism that was factual, independent, and reliable. Often referred to as "objective" (especially by outsiders), this style of journalism emphasized reporting on the things that serious and important people said and did. For those journalists who embraced the professional model—with its standards, schools of journalism, and professional organizations—it proved successful in attracting elite audiences and in sheltering many journalists from the century's great ideological battles over fascism and communism. It was this professional ideology, operating in a setting of financial success, that created the climate in which a handful of people were able to achieve what many consider the apotheosis of independent journalism in the Pentagon Papers and Watergate stories (see chapters 7–9).

Such a heyday, however, proved brief. The corporate-professional model ulti-mately gave way in the 1960s and 1970s to a series of changes that ushered in a fourth major era in journalism. The corporate forms pioneered in the early twen-tieth century grew—according to economic logic—into giant publicly traded conglomerates. (see chapters 10–13). Since the 1920s, the major radio and televi-sion networks had been operating as big corporations; later, Henry Luce joined the trend when Time Inc. went public and started selling stock to the public. The Dow Jones Corporation was the first newspaper company to follow suit, in the 1960s; then the movement became a stampede. Family-owned newspapers sold out to chains such as Gannett and Knight-Ridder, and by the last decade of the twentieth century, independently owned media properties were an endan-gered species. As the scale of operations increased, the economic barriers to entry reached record levels, stifling innovation. Inside the giant corporations (especially in conglomerates, which included non-media interests as well), the paramount issue was financial performance. To meet ever-higher profit targets, many media outlets turned to inexpensive forms of "infotainment," coverage of celebrities and gossip, the use of "advertorials," or a rediscovery of the power of partisanship. On the business side, executives sought monopolies or strategic alliances wherever they could, crushing or buying out the competition whenever possible. All were strategies for reconciling the need for producing spectacular profits with present-ing the news. The result was a business environment and a newsroom climate that threatened the hard-won professional ethos of mid-century.

Journalism entered a new phase with the coming of the digital revolution, which is still transforming the field (see chapter 14). The dominant older business model (based on scarcity, monopoly, and high profit margins) that made media properties attractive to global conglomerates has collapsed, as revenues from both circulation and advertising have shriveled. Thanks to digital technology, the lines between media have dissolved, the notion of monopoly has become nearly irrelevant, and a new competition for news has opened that pits each against all. Barriers to entry have nearly vanished, allowing new ventures to sprout with-out the need for major financial backing. Top prizes in journalism go to digital enterprises that measure their lives in months or years rather than decades or centuries. Readers and users have adopted a more assertive stance toward the news, demanding not merely corrections but a chance to contribute. A new era of innovation, experimentation, and change is forcing fresh efforts to reconcile the culture of news with the culture of business. The digital era appears to be ushering in a set of changes that are as deep and transformative as those in the 1830s or the 1920s. In the earlier episodes, the practice of journalism emerged transformed, and there is no reason to think that we are anywhere near the "end of news" in the present transition. The historical pattern is one of recurring crises, followed by efforts of men and women of varying abilities, motives, and resources to devise new ways of adapting.

The long narrative of journalism in America suggests that the *practice* of journalism—as distinct from the *institutions* of journalism—is alive, if not always as well as we might wish. In *Covering America,* I have presented evidence that the news business is central to the economic life of the country and to the ongoing attempt to operate a constitutional democracy. Over three centuries, journalism has been changed, and it has caused change. When journalism has been comparatively robust, its practitioners have been in a position to bring change to other institutions. They do not always do so, but the potential is there. When journalism has been comparatively weak, outsiders (presidents, generals, political activists, corporate raiders) have been able to force change on the institutions of journalism. This appears to be an open-ended dynamic, with no obvious or inevitable endpoint. There is every reason to think that people will continue bringing changes to the techniques, forms, and practices of journalism. They may be impinged on by others, and they will have to create change within the prevailing set of social, technological, and legal arrangements, but I am confident that the practice of journalism will endure.

The evidence suggests that the two critical issues in the performance of the news media are resources and independence. Journalism seems to serve the rest of society best when it is independent—independent of parties, of sponsors, of advertisers, even (sometimes) of its audience. That is, journalism works best when it has some combination of millions of readers or viewers, all paying something, and hundreds or thousands of advertisers, all paying something. That way, no one is especially important. That way, the revenues are high enough to enable editors and reporters to be bold. These two issues are not just important; they are usually interdependent. That is, the news media are at their most robust when they have plenty of resources—either because they are very profitable or because they are well funded by some other means, such as a generous and benevolent patron or a reliable and generous form of subsidy. Without resources, the news media are vulnerable to pressure from those who have more. The news media need to have the wherewithal to tell others when to buzz off.[2]

What else does this long narrative suggest about the health of journalism?

It must be acknowledged that American journalism has problems. The field remains vulnerable to hoaxes, stunts, fakes, and fluff. Unprincipled insiders can wreak havoc by plagiarizing or by inventing news. Despite some high-profile incidents, which should have led to tighter quality control, news organizations appear more susceptible to error than ever. Many newsrooms are laying off their veteran reporters, those with the longest memories; many are trimming or scrapping their fact-checking departments; and every news site is under tremendous pressure to rush material to the Web first and verify it later. Moreover, journalism has a (probably congenital) weakness for hype, ballyhoo, and hucksterism. At the same time, the news business is locked in an arms race with the public relations and advertising fields which will probably never end. Celebrities seem to be more central to our culture than ever, and journalism is deeply implicated in their rise. Online presentation of the news has blurred the lines between original reporting and a host of other activities: copying, citing, linking, excerpting, aggregating, and outright stealing. Those issues remain to be sorted out. Journalism is probably more partisan and tendentious than it has been in a century, and there is growing evidence that what has been called a "journalism of assertion" is replacing the idea of journalism as an empirical enterprise seeking verification. Moreover, journalism in America has done almost nothing about one of its most persistent weaknesses: lack of coverage of other countries. Still, journalism has a relation to the public something like that of Congress. Many people say they despise the Congress, but they love their individual representative and keep returning their local member to Washington. Just so, many people like to complain about "the media," but they are quite attached to their personal favorites.

At the same time, it must also be said that American journalism in the early twenty-first century has emerged from its history with considerable strengths, which can be the basis for improvements. After more than three hundred years, the field boasts a roster of great journalists who are worthy of emulating—and who fill many of the pages of this book. Although there is no official canon of the "great works" of journalism, there is a growing repertoire of work by American journalists that is worth reading and that stands up to rereading.[3] There are also a few works that give contemporary reporting and newswriting something like a standard methodology.[4] Another strength lies in the emergence of press criticism in the last decade or so. Criticism of all news media has never been sharper, more pervasive, or more demanding. It now includes not only the traditional journals, academics, and experts, but also the growing number of ombudsmen at major media, a proliferation of blogs that engage in media criticism at least part of the time, the shrewd observations of humorists such as Jon Stewart and Stephen Colbert, along with regular programs on television and radio devoted to examining the performance of the news media. In addition, American journalism is blessed with a new set of tools (digital cameras, laptop computers, digital voice recorders, satellite telephones) that are better and cheaper than ever.

Above all, journalism continues to play a key role in the continuing experiment in self-government. Reporters and photographers remain indispensable in fulfilling John Adams's hope that Americans would have access to "that most dreaded and envied kind of knowledge, I mean of the characters and conduct of their rulers." That counterweight to power is important not just in terms of our elected officials and government officers. It extends as well to those who wield other forms of power—corporate, clerical, military, and scientific. Moreover, journalists are needed more than ever as the eyes and ears for the rest of us when it comes to understanding the wider arena of global news in a world where time and space are collapsing. We need more journalists, not fewer, and we need journalists who have expert knowledge and a wide range of new skills, along with the wit, nerve, and compassion needed to find great stories and tell them.

Fortunately, journalism is still an exciting enterprise, drawing bright, creative, and ambitious young people. The field has never been more open to new ideas, more vital to our public debate, or more essential in our attempt to keep democracy alive. The country and its journalism are so intertwined that they will rise, fall, or stumble sideways together, as they have for so long. For all those reasons and for as far ahead as we can see, it is my professional conviction, as well as my personal hope, that many, many more generations of journalists will go on covering America.

Appendix
Major Periods in the History of U.S. Journalism

—·—

1704–1832

The **politicization** of news. Printer-editors, using muscle-powered hand presses, turn to politics to survive, and journalism becomes increasingly political and partisan. (Chapters 1–2)

1833–1900

The **commercialization** of news. Finding a mass audience, journalism becomes big business with high capital requirements and an elaborate division of labor. (Chapters 3–5)

1900–1974

The **professionalization** of news. As the news "media" (now including broadcasting and weekly magazines) grow and become corporate, some journalists assert an ethos of public service, independence, and "objectivity." (Chapters 6–9)

1965–1995

The **conglomeration** of news. Most mainstream media become parts of giant leveraged companies, usually managed by non-journalists. Big Media become ever bigger, raising the cost of a startup to nearly $1 billion. (Chapters 10–13)

1995–

The **digitization** of news. The personal computer and the Internet disrupt all the old models. New forms arise and begin the process of defining a new philosophy of journalism that is compatible with the new economy. (Chapter 14)

Notes

INTRODUCTION

1. This account of Franklin's foray into printing draws primarily on his *Autobiography*, 1317–23, and on H. W. Brands's excellent biography, *The First American*, 19–34.
2. All quotations from Franklin are drawn from the 1987 Library of America edition of his *Writings* and follow that collection's style for spelling and punctuation.
3. According to the *Oxford English Dictionary*, the word "journalism" entered the English language in 1833, when a writer for the *Westminster Review* translated the title of a new book—*Du Journalisme*—from French. The reviewer commented that the term "journalism" filled a significant gap because such "a word was sorely wanted."

1. FOUNDATIONS OF THE AMERICAN PRESS, 1704–1763

1. Stephens, *History of News*, 148–49.
2. Nord, *Communities of Journalism*, chap. 1.
3. Stephens, *History of News*, 83.
4. Clark, "Newspapers of Provincial America," 367.
5. This familiar tale can be found, for example, in Emery, Emery, and Roberts, *The Press and America*.
6. Stephens, *History of News*, 167–69.
7. Mitchell Stephens, for example, in *History of News*, offers a sensible definition of a newspaper: it must be published frequently and regularly; it must address many topics per issue; and it must have a regular title and format. By these lights, Harris, with only a single edition, produced a curiosity or a piece of ephemera, not a true newspaper.
8. See Emery, Emery, and Roberts, *The Press and America*; Stephens, *History of News*; Clark, "Newspapers of Provincial America."
9. In presenting the news from the London papers, Campbell usually favored the official *Gazette* or else the *Flying Post*. He faced an obvious practical problem, which was that the newspapers he received were always at least six weeks old, given the minimum time required to cross the North Atlantic by ship (and in winter, no ships dared the crossing at all). Campbell took pains to try to reprint stories that pursued the same topic week after week. He wrote that he was trying to present his readers with a "Thread of Occurrences"—even if the news was late.
10. Clark, "Newspapers of Provincial America," 378.
11. David D. Hall, "The World of Print and Collective Mentality in Seventeenth-Century New England," in Folkerts, *Media Voices*, 5–16. Also see Clark, "Newspapers of Provincial America."
12. E. Jennifer Monaghan, "Literacy Instruction and Gender in Colonial New England," in Folkerts, *Media Voices*, 17–35.
13. A good description can be found in Burns, *Infamous Scribblers*, 69–72.
14. Nord, *Communities of Journalism*, chap. 1.
15. Franklin is the subject of several excellent recent biographies, including Brands, *The First American*; and Isaacson, *Benjamin Franklin*.
16. At the time of his birth, his birthday was reckoned as January 6, 1705; under the revised calendar

adopted during Franklin's life, his date of birth became January 17, 1706. See Brands, *The First American*, chap. 1, for Franklin's birth and childhood. Also worth consulting is Franklin's *Autobiography*, although it is not particularly reliable in matters of fact.

17. Brands, *The First American*, 16.

18. Franklin, *Autobiography*, 1313.

19. Ibid., 1317. Interestingly, in *Pilgrim's Progress* he would have encountered the allegorical character known as the Muckraker.

20. Ibid.

21. Ibid., 1317–18.

22. Brands, *The First American*, 26.

23. Franklin, *Writings*, 6.

24. In June 1722, James printed a letter criticizing the authorities in Massachusetts for not doing enough to battle the pirates operating offshore. Referring to the captain of the ship who had been deputized by the authorities to give chase, James wrote: " 'Tis thought he will sail sometime this month, if wind and weather permit," insinuating that the captain lacked enthusiasm for the chase. With those words, James Franklin was engaging in exactly the kind of "watchdog" journalism, involving an assessment of the performance of the government or other powerful institutions, that Americans would enshrine in the Bill of Rights and esteem as a bulwark of liberty. But in the 1720s journalists enjoyed no such protections. The Massachusetts legislature ordered James jailed, and his apprentice, Ben, suddenly found himself serving as the acting publisher and managing editor of the *New-England Courant* at the tender age of sixteen. About a month later James won his freedom, but the incident must have made quite an impression on the young Ben. See Brands, *The First American*, 30.

25. Franklin, *Writings*, 44–47. In counseling caution, Franklin may have been acknowledging that the *Courant* had, in its brief life, been almost constantly engaged in controversies. On its founding in 1721, Franklin and his friends waded into the great debate of the day—whether to try inoculation to prevent smallpox. (The *Courant* opposed the latest scientific thinking, which supported inoculation). It is also worth noting that while the *Courant* took a provocative approach to journalism, it depended on a number of sympathetic contributors, who were not paid. In this respect, the *Courant* stands as an important early experiment in journalism: it expressed a strong point of view and relied on the writing of people who were not dependent on the paper for their livelihood.

26. Ibid., 36–37.

27. Ibid., 132–36.

28. Ibid., 132–39.

29. Ibid., 136–37.

30. Ibid., 137. Oddly, in his list of credentials Franklin, the future man of science, neglects to mention the need for a knowledge of science or natural history.

31. Franklin and Deborah Read decided to move in together without benefit of marriage for what was then a common reason: Deborah's first husband had run off, and it was impossible to determine whether he was dead or alive. If he was dead, so much the better. But if he was still alive and Deborah married Ben, she would be guilty of bigamy. Franklin would have a long, difficult relationship with his bastard son, who became the colonial governor of New Jersey and chose the loyalist side in the Revolution.

32. Ibid., 171–77.

33. Milton, *Areopagitica*. We know that Franklin certainly read the widely known *Cato's Letters* (because he cribbed from them in some of his Dogood columns), but we do not know exactly which other books he had read by this point in his life, when he was all of twenty-five years old. Nevertheless, his views reflect the broad lines of thought shared by thinkers of the English Enlightenment, many of whose works Franklin surely would have been familiar with. See Bailyn, *Ideological Origins of the American Revolution*, chap. 2.

34. Perhaps the ultimate contemporary expression of Franklin's idea is in the "op-ed" pages of newspapers, where editors assemble a regular rotation of columnists representing different political points of view and invite conflicting arguments about new issues as they arise.

35. For more on the role of colonial-era women in the printing business, see Bradley, *Women and the Press*, chap. 1; and Beasley and Gibbons, *Taking Their Place*, part 1.

36. This account is based on several sources, including Nord, *Communities of Journalism*, chap. 2; and the handy *Brief Narrative of the Case and Tryal of John Peter Zenger*, edited by Paul Finkelman, which includes Zenger's own account of the case. Also see Sloan and Williams, *Early*

American Press, chap. 3. Hamilton's statement to the jury appears in Finkelman, *Brief Narrative,* 160–61.

37. While serving as a member of Parliament, Wilkes was charged with seditious libel in 1763 for comments he made that were critical of King George III. The king had Wilkes and forty-eight others arrested. Wilkes fought back, won the restoration of his seat in Parliament, and even sued those who had arrested him.
38. Brands, *The First American,* 124.
39. Quoted ibid., 125.
40. See Sloan and Williams, *Early American Press,* 66.
41. For a complete list, see ibid., 103.

2. PRINTERS TAKE SIDES, 1763–1832

1. In my view, the key to understanding the success of the rebellion lies precisely here. Others, such as Bernard Bailyn, have ably shown how the elites, after reading their Hume and Montesqieu, made the intellectual leap toward republicanism. But there were never enough wealthy lawyers, merchants, and gentleman planters to make a revolution. It is only by looking at the popular pamphleteers such as Paine that one can see how the far more numerous artisans and small farmers decided to join the cause. This argument is well made in Eric Foner's *Tom Paine and Revolutionary America.*
2. On the flight of loyalist printers from New England, see Humphrey, "*This Popular Engine,*" 55.
3. See Nerone, *Violence against the Press,* 42.
4. A prominent view of this development for more than a generation was that of Bernard Bailyn. See his landmark *Ideological Origins of the American Revolution,* as well as the collection of essays edited by Bailyn and John B. Hench, *The Press and the American Revolution.* More recently, other authors have stressed the social conflict in the revolutionary movement.
5. Pasley, "*Tyranny of Printers,*" appendix 1.
6. Bailyn, *Ideological Origins,* 1–2.
7. Ibid., 2.
8. Stephens, *History of News,* 157.
9. Like the bloggers of today, pamphleteers engaged in fierce invective, they enjoyed the cloak of anonymity, and they used a medium of expression that was nearly free.
10. Thomas, *History of Printing,* 150.
11. Richard Buel Jr., "Freedom of the Press in Revolutionary America: The Evolution of Libertarianism, 1760–1820," in Bailyn and Hench, *The Press and the American Revolution.* See also Nerone, *Violence against the Press,* chap. 2.
12. Foner, *Tom Paine and Revolutionary America,* 2. At the time, the family's name was spelled Pain, which seems apt for makers of bony undergarments. Tom added the "e" to his name in 1776.
13. Kaye, *Thomas Paine and the Promise of America,* 22.
14. Foner, *Tom Paine and Revolutionary America,* 3.
15. See the "Chronology" in Paine, *Collected Writings,* 833–53, for an excellent brief summary of his extraordinary life. For a fuller treatment, see Foner, *Tom Paine and Revolutionary America.* For a discussion of Paine's impact on American politics and journalism, see Kaye, *Thomas Paine and the Promise of America.*
16. Some historians disagree about the figures. For example, Thomas Slaughter, in his introduction to *Common Sense and Other Writings,* questions Paine's own estimate of 150,000 copies sold in America in 1776. He puts the figure in the range of 35,000 to 50,000 copies (see 29–33). Roger Streitmatter, however, in *Mightier Than the Sword,* claims that "more than 150,000 copies of 'Common Sense' were sold within three months" (16). The specific numbers are debatable, but the scale is not. It is also worth noting that Paine did not profit from the sales. According to Kaye (*Thomas Paine and the Promise of America,* 56), Paine directed that all proceeds from *Common Sense* should go to buy mittens for the rebel army.
17. Paine, *Collected Writings,* 45. The spelling of "independance" is Paine's.
18. See Wood, *Radicalism of the American Revolution.*
19. Unlike Franklin, Paine was strangely silent on the subject of slavery. He did not mention it in *Common Sense,* and he scarcely touched on the great issue in the rest of his voluminous writings on society.
20. Paine, *Collected Writings,* 16.
21. Ibid., 17.

22. Ibid., 20–36. Spellings are Paine's.
23. Foner makes this point in *Tom Paine and Revolutionary America,* chap. 3.
24. Paine, *Collected Writings,* 96.
25. Ibid.
26. For examples of an array of press tactics, see Sloan and Williams, *Early American Press,* chap. 7.
27. Paine, *Collected Writings,* 109.
28. For more on this process, see Stephen Botein, "Printers and the American Revolution," in Bailyn and Hench, *The Press and the American Revolution.*
29. Foner, *Tom Paine and Revolutionary America,* xix.
30. See Pasley, *"Tyranny of Printers,"* for a convincing argument about the role of printers in party politics.
31. Jefferson, *Writings,* 880.
32. For this reason, succeeding generations have had to depend primarily on the notes taken by a participant, James Madison, along with the incomplete recollections of some of the other framers.
33. See Humphrey, *"This Public Engine,"* 100. Humphrey makes the point that while pamphlets continued to be published, after the Revolution, the major debates on most political matters took place in newspapers.
34. John Adams, *A Dissertation on the Canon and Feudal Law,* in *Papers of John Adams,* 120–21. Adams first published his "Dissertation" in the pages of the *Boston Gazette* on August 12 and 19, September 30, and October 2, 1765.
35. Jefferson, *Writings,* 365.
36. These essays deserve their acclaim, but they are often abused by contemporary conservatives trying to invoke the "original intent" of the Founders on many constitutional issues. While it is true that *The Federalist Papers* reflect well the thinking of their authors, they represent only one side in what was a vigorous debate among the Founders. For a balancing view of many of the counterarguments, a good starting point is *The Antifederalist Papers,* edited by Morton Borden. Also see the website of the Constitution Society, www.constitution.org/afp/afp.htm.
37. See, for example, his letter from Paris to Madison dated December 20, 1787. After praising some provisions, Jefferson grew tart: "I will now add what I do not like. First the omission of a bill of rights." Jefferson, *Writings,* 915.
38. See Kelly, Harbison, and Belz, *American Constitution,* 142.
39. Originally, twelve amendments were bundled together and submitted to the states for ratification. The first two failed; they had to do with apportionment of the House (still unratified) and congressional pay raises (which finally passed in 1992 as the twenty-seventh and, at this writing, latest amendment). Thus it is a matter of historical happenstance that the Bill of Rights is headed by the amendment we call the First.
40. See, for example, Paine's "Of the Term 'Liberty of the Press,'" which appeared in *The American Citizen,* New York, October 20, 1806 (*Collected Writings,* 429–30).
41. Library of America, *Debates on the Constitution,* 826.
42. See Rosenfeld, *American Aurora,* 29–31.
43. Quoted in Daniel, *Scandal and Civility,* 109.
44. *Porcupine's Gazette,* March 17, 1798, quoted in Rosenfeld, *American Aurora,* 44.
45. This account of Callender's life is based primarily on Durey, "Callender."
46. Rosenfeld, *American Aurora,* 37.
47. See Pasley, *"Tyranny of Printers,"* passim.
48. See Rosenfeld, *American Aurora,* 32–33.
49. Cited ibid., 33.
50. For a good summary of the debate over its passage, see Stone, *Perilous Times,* 41–44.
51. The very first Republican targeted for prosecution was John Daly Burk (no relation to the author), a savagely partisan immigrant from Ireland, but he fled from authorities and took up an assumed name. Next up was another Irish immigrant, Matthew Lyon of Vermont, who was railroaded into prison by a Federalist judge, then won reelection to Congress from his jail cell. For details, see ibid., chap. 1.
52. See Pasley, *"Tyranny of Printers,"* chaps. 8–9.
53. Ibid., chap. 11.
54. Ibid., chap. 12, especially 295.
55. Reprinted in Gordon-Reed, *Thomas Jefferson and Sally Hemings,* 61.
56. See ibid. for a full discussion.

57. Jefferson, *Writings*, 521–22.
58. Ibid., 1177–78.
59. Schwarloze, *Nation's Newsbrokers*, 4–5.

3. PUTTING THE NEWS IN NEWSPAPERS, 1833–1850

1. Tocqueville, *Democracy in America*, 350.
2. Starr, *Creation of the Media*, 84–94.
3. Schudson, *Discovering the News*, 31–60.
4. The starting point remains George Rogers Taylor's essential work *The Transportation Revolution, 1815–1860*.
5. See E. Jennifer Monaghan, "Literacy Instruction and Gender in Colonial New England," in Folkerts, *Media Voices*, 17–35.
6. For the same reasons, radio and television would gravitate to New York City in the twentieth century.
7. See Hudson, *Journalism in the United States, from 1690 to 1872*, a remarkably useful book by a man who served as the managing editor of one of the *Sun*'s rivals, the *New York Herald*. See also Crouthamel, *Bennett's* New York Herald, 19.
8. In this pursuit, Day was greatly aided by decisions made by the Founders that were based on their familiarity with the Star Chamber and other forms of British power over subjects. The Founders adopted important protections for citizens, which are embodied in the Constitution. Among these are provisions that made the entire criminal justice system the most transparent in the world—from initial arrest and detention through to ultimate disposition and sentencing. To this day, few countries offer as much access at so many points.
9. *Sun*, September 5, 1833, quoted in Crouthamel, *Bennett's* New York Herald, 25.
10. Bleyer, *Main Currents*, 163.
11. The hiring of George Wisner, progenitor of the long chain of reporters to follow, is recounted in a history of the *Sun* that, regrettably, lacks footnotes or other documentation for this crucial moment. See O'Brien, *Story of the* Sun, 38.
12. Crouthamel, *Bennett's* New York Herald, 11.
13. Ibid., 23.
14. That is not to say that any group of editors had yet arrived at a self-conscious ideology of objectivity, either as a professional ideal or as a practical technique. Such a view was still a way off. But the earliest planks in the structure were being laid in the 1830s. For a thorough discussion, see Schiller, *Objectivity and the News;* Schudson, *Discovering the News;* and Mindich, *Just the Facts.*
15. Kluger, *The Paper*, 37.
16. Quoted ibid.
17. A full account of the crime and its coverage is found in Tucher, *Froth and Scum*. Tucher's title is drawn from a passage in the journals of Henry David Thoreau: "I know 2 species of men. The vast majority are men of society. They live on the surface, they are interested in the transient & fleeting—they are like drift wood on the flood—They ask forever & only the news—the froth & scum of the eternal sea." Thoreau, *Journal*, 4:486–87 (entry dated April 24, 1856).
18. Quoted in Tucher, *Froth and Scum*, 31.
19. Crouthamel, *Bennett's* New York Herald, 34–37.
20. Schudson, *Discovering the News*, 55.
21. Henretta, Brody, and Dumenil, *America: A Concise History*, 1:226.
22. Quotations are from Greeley's aptly titled autobiography *Recollections of a Busy Life*, 41, 45. Also see Kluger, *The Paper*, chap. 1.
23. Greeley, *Recollections*, 47.
24. Ibid., 54, 61.
25. My sketch of this period in Greeley's life is based on Kluger, *The Paper*, 21–46; Lunde, *Horace Greeley*, 1–45; and Greeley, *Recollections*, 124–40.
26. Greeley, *Recollections*, 137–38.
27. Ibid., 137.
28. See John, *Spreading the News;* and Starr, *Creation of the Media*, chap. 3.
29. Brisbane had a son, Arthur, who became a widely read columnist for William Randolph Hearst in the 1920s and 1930s, and was often derided as a crackpot. Arthur's grandson, Arthur S. Brisbane, after a career at the *Washington Post* and the Knight Ridder company, was appointed the "public editor" of the *New York Times* in June 2010.
30. Kluger, *The Paper*, 52.

31. Ibid., 54.

32. Greeley, *Recollections of a Busy Life,* 192.

33. But see the note in Kluger, *The Paper,* 53, which argues that Greeley popularized the phrase but did not coin it.

34. There Margaret Fuller covered several major stories for the *Tribune,* married, and was returning to New York with her husband when their ship, within sight of land, sank off Fire Island, and she drowned at age forty.

35. This description of Garrison's childhood is based on the first two chapters in the magisterial biography by Henry Mayer, *All on Fire: William Lloyd Garrison and the Abolition of Slavery.*

36. Ibid., 23.

37. Quoted ibid., 49–51.

38. *Liberator,* September 20, 1839.

39. Garrison, "Address to the American Colonization Society," reprinted in Cain, *William Lloyd Garrison and the Fight against Slavery,* 62.

40. Ibid., 4.

41. *Liberator,* January 1, 1831.

42. Cain, *William Lloyd Garrison and the Fight against Slavery,* 5.

43. 1 Corinthians 5:6. For Garrison's views on religion and journalism and on his role as editor of a paper serving a community, see Nord, *Communities of Journalism,* chap. 4.

44. For the overall development of the telegraph, see Blondheim, *News over the Wires;* as well as Standage, *Victorian Internet.* In addition, see Starr, *Creation of the Media,* chap. 5; and John, *Network Nation,* chaps. 1–3.

45. Standage, *Victorian Internet,* 1–24.

46. Starr, *Creation of the Media,* 161.

47. Ibid., 162–65.

48. *New York Herald,* August 12, 1866.

49. See Blondheim, *News over the Wires,* 210, n. 5.

50. Quoted ibid., 190.

51. Starr, *Creation of the Media,* 169–70.

52. Ibid., 176–77.

53. Crouthamel. "Beach, Moses Yale."

54. See Pyle, "19th-Century Papers," a news report citing documents left by the Beach family to the Associated Press, which were discovered when the wire service moved in 2005 from its longtime headquarters at Rockefeller Center to a new location on Manhattan's West Side. Also see Mears, "A Brief History of AP," which appears in *Breaking News,* the 2007 in-house history of the AP.

55. The dating of the exact origin of the AP is somewhat murky. Recent evidence points to 1846, although the AP itself long dated its origins to 1848 and officially celebrated its 150th anniversary in 1998. For a detailed discussion, see Schwarzlose, *The Nation's Newsbrokers,* vol. 1, chaps. 2–3. Also see Blondheim, *News over the Wires;* and Mears, "Brief History."

56. Throughout this book I use the name Associated Press, often for convenience, since the organization that emerged as the AP went through several reorganizations, combining the NYAP, the Western Associated Press, and other former rivals. This lengthy and complicated history of the AP as a business is well told in Blondheim, *News over the Wires;* as well as Schwarzlose, *The Nation's Newsbrokers.*

57. On the AP in general, see Blondheim, *News over the Wires;* and Schwarzlose, *The Nation's Newsbrokers.* Of some interest is the authorized company history by Oliver Gramling, *AP: The Story of News* (1940), although it is quite dated, as well as the 2007 update, *Breaking News.*

58. Quoted in Gramling, *AP: The Story of News,* 39.

59. Schwarzlose, *The Nation's Newsbrokers,* 180–81.

60. Crouthamel, *Bennett's* New York Herald, 2.

61. Kluger, *The Paper,* 17.

62. See Wilentz, *Chants Democratic,* for a thorough picture of how this process played out in New York City.

63. Quoted in Blondheim, *News over the Wires,* 190.

4. RADICALS ALL! 1830–1875

1. U.S. Census Bureau, "United States—Race and Hispanic Origin: 1790 to 1990."

2. Douglass, *Narrative of the Life of Frederick Douglass*(1845), 37–38. Also see Douglass's *My Bond-*

age and My Freedom (1855), 217–18. In this telling, Douglass makes it sound as if Auld is delivering a set of prepared remarks on the perils of slave literacy, but there is no reason to doubt that a master would have said or thought something very much like that.

3. Lionel C. Barrow Jr., "'Our Own Cause': *Freedom's Journal* and the Beginnings of the Black Press," in Folkerts, *Media Voices*, 54–60.

4. By one estimate, black readers made up 80 percent of the first 450 subscribers. See Pride and Wilson, *History of the Black Press*, 26.

5. *Liberator*, September 3, 1831.

6. Mayer, *All on Fire*, 122–23.

7. See, for example, "Declaration of Sentiments Adopted by the Peace Convention," *Liberator*, September 28, 1838.

8. In 1854, for example, on the Fourth of July, he burned a copy of the U.S. Constitution at a public gathering.

9. See, for example, *Liberator*, May 3, 1861.

10. This account is based on the well-researched version found in Mayer, *All on Fire*, 199–208; as well as Nerone, *Violence against the Press*, 101–2.

11. While in the jail, Garrison inscribed a message on the wall: "William Lloyd Garrison was put into this cell on Wednesday afternoon, October 21, 1835, to save him from the violence of a 'respectable and influential' mob, who sought to destroy him for preaching the abominable and dangerous doctrine that 'all men are created equal' and that all oppression is odious in the sight of God."

12. See Ratner and Teeter, *Fanatics and Fire-Eaters*, 25–27; and Dillon, "Lovejoy: Elijah Parish."

13. For details on many other cases, see Nerone, *Violence against the Press*, chaps. 4–5.

14. See Mayer, *All on Fire*, 305–7; and Douglass, *My Bondage and My Freedom*, 364–66.

15. Douglass, *My Bondage and My Freedom*, 362.

16. Mayer, *All on Fire*, 306.

17. Douglass, *My Bondage and My Freedom*, 368.

18. Fee, "'Intelligent Union of Black with White,'" 36. The name of the paper reflected the importance of Rochester as a way station on the Underground Railroad, helping runaway slaves escape to Canada, where they would be beyond the grasp of the Fugitive Slave Law. The slaves usually had no maps to guide them, and they often had to travel at night. Thus they had to navigate by the stars, ever following the North Star toward freedom.

19. Douglass, *My Bondage and My Freedom*, 392.

20. Nerone, *Violence against the Press*, chap. 4.

21. See, for example, Jackson's seventh annual message to Congress, on December 7, 1835, in which he said, "Peace depends upon the maintenance, in good faith, of those compromises of the Constitution upon which the Union is founded," then went on to call for legislation to prohibit the circulation of "incendiary publications intended to instigate the slaves to insurrection." Andrew Jackson, *Congressional Globe*, December 14, 1835, 10. Also see Nerone, *Violence against the Press*, chap. 4.

22. *Acts of the General Assembly of Virginia, 1835–36* (Richmond, 1836), chap. 66.

23. *New York Herald*, May 24, 1856.

24. *Richmond Enquirer*, June 3, 1856.

25. *Richmond Whig*, May 31, 1856.

26. *Charleston Mercury*, January 26, 1865.

27. Marx and Greeley had fundamental disagreements about capitalism, and in 1862 Greeley sacked Marx from "the only salaried position he held during his lifetime," according to Sally Taylor in her informative article "Marx and Greeley on Slavery and Labor," 122. See also Steele, *The Sun Shines for All*, 35.

28. Kluger, *The Paper*, 92. No newspaper today has anything like that reach.

29. Ibid., 90.

30. Quoted ibid., 91.

31. *Liberator*, November 12, 1860.

32. Ibid.

33. The honor of firing the first shot was awarded to Edmund Ruffin, a fire-eating newspaper editor.

34. *Tribune*, April 15, 1861.

35. Ratner and Teeter, *Fanatics and Fire-Eaters*, 103.

36. Schwarzlose, *Nation's Newsbrokers*, 241–43.

37. Andrews, *The North Reports the Civil War*, 359. See also Sears, *Chancellorsville*, 74–75. To be

sure, the byline did not begin with Hooker's edict, and it did not become universal overnight; the byline ruling was one step in a lengthy process. Hooker himself is the focus of a dispute in American lexicology. Although he could not tolerate reporters, General Hooker could apparently tolerate prostitutes. Popular belief has it that so many camp followers attached themselves to his army during the war that they became known as "Hooker's girls," later shortened to "hookers." Scholars note, however, that the term "hooker" predates the Civil War. See, for example, *The American Heritage Dictionary of the English Language*, 3rd ed.

38. Lincoln to Erastus Corning and others, June 12, 1863, reprinted in *New York Tribune*, June 15, 1863.
39. For cases, see Nelson, *Freedom of the Press*, 229–47. For an overview, see Blondheim, "'Public Sentiment Is Everything.'"
40. Andrews, *The North Reports the Civil War*, 32.
41. See Drew Gilpin Faust, "'Dread Void of Uncertainty.'"
42. Andrews, *The North Reports the Civil War*, 20–21.
43. Blondheim, *News over the Wires*, 130.
44. Schwarzlose, *Nation's Newsbrokers*, 242–43.
45. See Guelzo, *Lincoln's Emancipation Proclamation*, 133.
46. Kluger, *The Paper*, 96.
47. *New-York Times*, July 6, 1863.
48. McKay, *The Civil War and New York City*, 200.
49. Quoted in Kluger, *The Paper*, 110.
50. Cook, *Armies of the Streets*, 88.
51. Cain, *William Lloyd Garrison*, 53.
52. Ibid., 53.
53. Lawrence Gobright, *Recollection of Men and Things*, 348.
54. Gobright's story can be found in many papers on the following day. For example, see *New York Tribune*, April 15, 1865.
55. Knightley, *The First Casualty*, 21.
56. Quoted in Endres, "The Press and the Civil War, 161.
57. Andrews, *The North Reports the Civil War*, 115.
58. Kluger, *The Paper*, 98.
59. The chronology of this development is a matter of debate among specialists. My point is not that there were *no* examples of hard-news leads before the war. Nor is it my point that *every* story during the war carried such a lead. My point is that during the war, and because of the war, correspondents got better at writing such leads and used them somewhat more often. The practice did not become standard until after the war. See Mindich, "Edwin M. Stanton, the Inverted Pyramid, and Information Control."
60. For examples, see Mindich, *Just the Facts*, chap. 3.

5. CRUSADERS AND CONSERVATIVES, 1875–1912

1. Joseph Pulitzer is the subject of several full-length biographies, including James McGrath Morris, *Pulitzer: A Life in Politics, Print, and Power* (2010). All of his biographers benefited from the fact that Pulitzer's health and eyesight were so poor for so many years that he ended up dictating an enormous volume of letters and memos telling his editors how to run his newspapers. This vast correspondence is a treasure chest for historians. In addition, one of his close associates, Don Carlos Seitz, got into the Pulitzer biography business early and could draw on his own personal reminiscences as well as written records. For many years, the definitive biography was W. A. Swanberg, *Pulitzer*, but more recent works include, in addition to the biography by Morris, Denis Brian's *Pulitzer: A Life*. This chapter is based on all these works, as well as several others that shed considerable light on Pulitzer, his papers, and his times.
2. Wallace, "A Height Deemed Appalling."
3. Nast did such a fine job of portraying Tweed that one of his drawings served as the basis on which Spanish authorities arrested Tweed in 1876 and extradited him to the United States. Nast also deserves credit for devising the image of the donkey (1870) as an emblem for the Democrats and the elephant (1874) for the Republicans. In addition, he made a memorable series of sketches of Santa Claus as a jolly, pudgy elf.
4. Brian, *Pulitzer: A Life*, 29–30.
5. Quoted ibid., 64.

6. Pulitzer got Gould to agree to accept payment in installments, so he needed only a fraction in cash at the outset. Most of the purchase price came out of the earnings of the *World,* which began to make money almost immediately under Pulitzer. See Seitz, *Joseph Pulitzer: His Life and Letters,* 131.

7. Quoted in Morris, *Pulitzer: A Life in Politics, Print, and Power,* 209.

8. For a lavishly illustrated look at Pulitzer's Sunday papers, see Baker and Brentano, *The World on Sunday.* By most accounts, the first regularly published Sunday edition was created by Bennett at the *Herald* in 1841. Others followed, including many launched during the Civil War in response to the intense demand for the latest battlefield news. Still, by the time Pulitzer arrived in New York, only about one hundred newspapers out of about nine hundred in the United States had a Sunday edition.

9. Emery, Emery, and Roberts, *The Press and America,* 189–90.

10. Baldasty, *Commercialization of News,* 88.

11. See ibid. Indeed, this relationship is embodied in New York's Herald Square, where Macy's operates its giant flagship store across the street from what became the final home of James Gordon Bennett's *Herald.*

12. Figures for Bennett, Greeley, and Raymond are from Fellow, *American Media History,* 107.

13. Steele, *The Sun Shines for All,* 78.

14. Kluger, *The Paper* 131–35. Kluger concludes that the money for the purchase really came from Jay Gould, although no one has found any documentary evidence.

15. Fellow, *American Media History,* 157.

16. Nasaw, *The Chief,* 98.

17. Tifft and Jones, *The Trust,* 37–40. The authors note that Ochs raised an additional $1 million through shares of stock, which were kept closely held.

18. See Schwarzlose, *Nation's Newsbrokers,* 2:21–28, on the value of the AP franchise.

19. A. J. Liebling, the *New Yorker* magazine's pioneering press critic, brilliantly summed up the journalist's predicament by writing, "Freedom of the press is guaranteed only to those who own one." See *New Yorker,* May 14, 1960, 109.

20. Schudson, *Discovering the News,* 93–95.

21. Ibid., 93.

22. See Morris, *Pulitzer,* 245, and Brian, *Pulitzer: A Life,* 104–6.

23. See Kroeger, *Nellie Bly.*

24. Her account was published on the front pages of the *World,* then issued as a book. See Bly, *Ten Days in a Madhouse.*

25. Quoted in Fellow, *American Media History,* 161.

26. See Collins, *Scorpion Tongues,* chaps. 4 and 5. Gail Collins later became the editorial page editor of the *New York Times* and then a columnist.

27. Brian, *Pulitzer: A Life,* 144.

28. *The Journalist,* February 1, 1890, 5.

29. Brian, *Pulitzer: A Life,* 136. Sadly, the *World* building was torn down in 1955 to make way for a new approach to the Brooklyn Bridge.

30. *New York World,* April 13, 1884.

31. Kobre, *Yellow Press,* 52.

32. A few authorities dispute the connection between "The Yellow Kid" and the term "yellow journalism," but I rely on Pulitzer's own managing editor (Cockerill's successor) Don Carlos Seitz, who was present at the creation. See Seitz, *Joseph Pulitzer,* 231–32.

33. At the same time, several of these constituencies were busy building their own institutions to represent their interests. These included labor unions, some of which published their own newspapers.

34. Quoted in Brian, *Pulitzer: A Life,* 1.

35. Quoted ibid., 35.

36. Dunne, *Observations by Mr. Dooley,* 240. The quote is a cleaned-up version of Dunne's original, which was written in his exaggerated Irish dialect.

37. Pulitzer also managed to get elected to Congress from a safe Democratic seat in Manhattan, but he did not stay long. It did not suit him, and he resigned.

38. Kobre, *Yellow Press,* 56.

39. I am indebted throughout this section to David Nasaw for his masterly biography of Hearst, *The Chief.* Also helpful was Whyte, *The Uncrowned King,* which focuses on Hearst's rivalry with Pulitzer in the 1890s.

40. Nasaw, *The Chief*, 36.
41. Swanberg, *Citizen Hearst*, 35.
42. Nasaw, *The Chief*, 43.
43. Ibid., 77.
44. Swanberg, *Citizen Hearst*, 52.
45. Nasaw, *The Chief*, 80.
46. Ibid., 96.
47. Ibid., 98.
48. Hearst's biographer Kenneth Whyte argues that many of the defections were caused by Pulitzer himself, who was a demanding taskmaster. According to Whyte's version, Hearst snapped up talent rather than raiding it. See Whyte, *Uncrowned King*, chap. 3.
49. Seitz, *Joseph Pulitzer*, chaps. 7–9.
50. Nasaw, *The Chief*, 119.
51. See Campbell, *Yellow Journalism* and *The Year That Defined American Journalism;* as well as Hamilton, *Journalism's Roving Eye*, chap 8.
52. See, for example, Henretta, Brody, and Dumenil, *America: A Concise History,* chap. 21.
53. John Maxwell Hamilton and his coauthors call this "an enabling environment." See their essay in *Journalism Studies.*
54. Seitz, *Joseph Pulitzer*, 238.
55. Brian, *Pulitzer: A Life,* 240.
56. Poignantly, Arthur Lubow writes of Davis: "To be famous virtually all one's adult life and forgotten promptly at death: this is celebrity in its purest form" (*The Reporter Who Would Be King,* 1). It was Davis, already famous himself, who helped make the reputation of Theodore Roosevelt during the war in Cuba by describing the actions of T.R.'s Rough Riders in heroic terms.
57. Quoted in Knightley, *The First Casualty,* 55.
58. Creelman, *On the Great Highway,* 178. Unaccountably, Knightley accepts the Hearst telegram as authentic, while most others are more skeptical. For a full discussion, see Nasaw, *The Chief,* 127.
59. Also see Campbell, *Getting It Wrong,* chap. 1.
60. *New York Journal,* October 10, 1897.
61. Brian, *Pulitzer: A Life,* 230.
62. Ibid., 231.
63. Nasaw, *The Chief,* 37.
64. Creelman, *On the Great Highway,* 211–12. This passage gives a nice sense of the attitude many Americans shared during this war—that it was a dashing adventure for gentlemen. Elsewhere, Creelman hints at the presence of black U.S. troops, who did much of the fighting but shared little of the glory in contemporary newspaper accounts.
65. Quoted in Nasaw, *The Chief,* 141.
66. Quoted in Knightley, *The First Casualty,* 59.
67. E. L. Godkin, editorial, *The Nation* 66 (May 5, 1898): 336.
68. This discussion is based on the arguments in Schudson, *Discovering the News.*
69. A comprehensive history of the *Times* is *The Trust* by Susan E. Tifft and Alex S. Jones, published in 1999, which focuses on the Ochs-Sulzberger publishing dynasty. Many other histories are available; some focus more on the newspaper as an institution, others on various individuals. Some notable histories include those written by Elmer Davis (1921), Meyer Berger (1951), Gay Talese (1969), Harrison E. Salisbury (1980), Nan Robertson (1992), and Edwin Diamond (1994). Notable memoirs include those by Turner Catledge (1971), Russell Baker (1989), James Reston (1991), Max Frankel (1999), and Arthur Gelb (2003).
70. *New York Times,* September 18, 1851.
71. Tifft and Jones, *The Trust,* 31.
72. The name Ochs was a shortened version of the original German name, Ochsenhorn. It was changed by Adolph's father, Julius, when he immigrated. One branch of the family adopted the more anglicized spelling of Oakes. At times, some branches pronounced the name Ochs like "ox," but Adolph and most others pronounced it like "oaks."
73. Although it may seem irrelevant to note that the Ochses were Jewish, as are the Sulzbergers, who married into the family and run the paper today, from time to time, there are episodes in the history of the *Times* in which the religion of the owners is germane—as, for example, in the discussions of the paper's coverage of Nazism (see chapter 9) or Israel. For the most part, it is probably more accurate to observe that the *Times* was known as "a paper owned by Jews, edited by Catholics, and read by Protestants." See Halberstam, *The Powers That Be,* 213.

74. The most complete analysis of this transaction appears in Tifft and Jones, *The Trust*, 33–40.
75. The *Times* did not, however, invent the op-ed page, although it is often given credit for doing so. That was done in the 1920s at the *New York World* by editor Herbert Bayard Swope. See chapter 8.
76. In more than a hundred years, this system has not changed much, except that most newspapers now expect reporters to write their own articles, and stories are created in electronic form rather than on copy paper.
77. Emery, Emery and Roberts, *The Press and America*, 237.
78. This account is based on McMurry, *To Keep the Waters Troubled*.
79. Wells, *Southern Horrors and Other Writings*, 79. This quotation originally appeared in Wells's newspaper in Memphis, *The Free Speech*, in an editorial printed on May 21, 1892. She later incorporated the editorial into a pamphlet titled *A Red Record*, which is reprinted in *Southern Horrors and Other Writings*.
80. Ibid., 70.
81. See Hofstadter, *The Age of Reform*, 187.
82. Fitzpatrick, *Muckraking*, 1.
83. McClure, "Editorial," *McClure's Magazine*, January 1903, 336.
84. Tebbel and Zuckerman, *The Magazine in America*, chap. 10.
85. Sinclair, *The Brass Check*, 27.
86. Sinclair, *The Jungle*, 161.
87. Quoted in Fitzpatrick, *Muckraking*, 104.
88. See Nasaw, *The Chief*, 156–58, for a discussion of this fascinating issue.
89. Theodore Roosevelt's text can be found in Hofstadter, *The Progressive Movement*, 18.
90. Hofstadter, *Age of Reform*, 196–97.
91. Baker, *American Chronicle*, 226. Baker was comfortable enough with the status quo to serve a few years later as press secretary to President Woodrow Wilson.
92. See Lee, "Lee, Ivy Ledbetter."
93. For details, see Boylan, *Pulitzer's School*.

6. PROFESSIONALIZING THE NEWS IN PEACE AND WAR, 1900–1920

1. See Starr, *The Social Transformation of American Medicine*, chaps. 1–6. See also Mencken, *Newspaper Days*.
2. O'Dell, *History of Journalism Education*, 1–19, quotations on 5 and 14. Note that Lee proposed teaching journalists, not journalism. That is, he wanted to offer instruction to journalists, but in other fields. He was not proposing to teach the skills of reporting and editing. That idea would gather force in the next generation. Washington & Lee revived its journalism program in 1921 and remains a leader in the field.
3. See O'Dell, *History of Journalism Education*, 41–46, for a fascinating roundup of professional opinion as of 1888.
4. Hudson, *Journalism in the United States*, 713.
5. For a speculative account of mid-century stirrings in Missouri, see Banning, "Cradle of Professional Journalistic Education."
6. White, "School of Journalism," 25. This is a deeply rooted view in American journalism, even in the present age, when the older apprentice model has all but vanished from newsrooms under pressure to cut costs.
7. All quotations are from Pulitzer, "The College of Journalism," 641–80.
8. Quoted in Rucker, *Walter Williams*, 151. Among the six women was Mary Paxton, who was the first woman to graduate from a journalism school and went on to become the first woman on the staff of the *Kansas City Post*.
9. See the Missouri School of Journalism website, www.journalism.missouri.edu/about/creed.html.
10. See Boylan, *Pulitzer's School*, chap. 3. More specifically, Pulitzer pledged $1 million to begin with, followed by another $1 million if the journalism school survived its first three years.
11. Seitz, *Joseph Pulitzer*, 437.
12. In addition, hundreds of other degree-granting journalism programs exist without accreditation. See www.ku.edu/~acejmc/FULLINFO.HTML.
13. For Byrne's comment, see *The Journalist* 1, no. 1 (March 22, 1884): 7.
14. *The Journalist* 17, no. 7 (April 22, 1893): 4.
15. All the details about organizations that follow can be found on the websites maintained by the

current incarnation of each of these groups. For the most complete listing of groups, see the web page of the *American Journalism Review,* www.ajr.org/and follow the links to Resources and Journalism Organizations.

16. From time to time, interested parties have attempted to create nongovernmental, extrajudicial "news councils" that would provide a forum for readers or subjects of news accounts who believe that professional standards have not been met. All such efforts have ultimately foundered because the First Amendment makes it impossible to implement any effective enforcement mechanism. See Farrar, "News Councils and Libel Actions."

17. For more on the development of the black press between the founding of *Freedom's Journal* in 1827 and the rise of nationally distributed black-owned newspapers by the early twentieth century, see Hutton, *The Early Black Press in America;* Pride and Wilson, *History of the Black Press;* Vogel, *The Black Press;* Washburn, *The African American Newspaper;* and Wolseley, *The Black Press, U.S.A.*

18. See Wilkerson, *The Warmth of Other Suns;* and Lemann, *The Promised Land.*

19. *Chicago Defender,* August 15, 1914.

20. *Chicago Defender,* May 12, 1917.

21. W. E. B. Du Bois, "Close Ranks," *The Crisis,* July 1918, 111. For a fuller discussion, see Jordan, " 'The Damnable Dilemma.' "

22. The weekend after Debs lost the 1912 presidential race, Wayland committed suicide. See Shore, "Wayland, Julius Augustus."

23. *Appeal to Reason,* September, 11, 1915.

24. Nasaw, *The Chief,* chap. 13.

25. Quoted ibid., 241.

26. See ibid., chaps. 14–15. Hearst's opposition to U.S. intervention abroad was nothing if not consistent. He opposed U.S. efforts to roll back the Bolshevik Revolution in Russia, he undermined Wilson's campaign for a League of Nations, and he opposed U.S. entry into World War II, to the point of being accused of having Nazi sympathies.

27. *Congressional Record,* 65th Cong., 1st sess., April 4, 1917, 104.

28. See Ponder, *Managing the Press,* chaps. 1–5, for the years 1897–1912.

29. Ibid., 91.

30. Creel came from Missouri and got his start in journalism at the *Kansas City Independent,* a weekly. Later he worked at the *Denver Post* and became editor of the *Rocky Mountain News* before moving to New York, where he engaged in several muckraking exposés. The appointment of a journalist to regulate journalists was typical of Wilson's approach to other industries.

31. This account is based largely on the authoritative account in Vaughn, *Holding Fast the Inner Lines,* as well as Creel's own account, published after the war as a defense, *How We Advertised America.* Creel's main concern seems to have been to rebut his critics and deny that he was the nation's chief censor. Indeed, he makes a persuasive case that the CPI was primarily responsible for producing propaganda, and Creel himself should be recognized as the first master of public propaganda. His position is somewhat disingenuous, though, since he also served on the Censorship Board, which certainly censored aggressively, and he served in the Wilson administration, which, as a whole, censored heavily. Nevertheless, Creel's book is valuable for its insider's perspective.

32. While Daniels was serving as navy secretary, his assistant was a northerner, Franklin D. Roosevelt. Later Daniels supported FDR's 1932 presidential campaign, and the new president appointed Daniels U.S. ambassador to Mexico. Daniels eventually returned to the editor's desk, where he remained until his death in 1948 at age eighty-five.

33. Vaughn, *Holding Fast the Inner Lines,* 157.

34. Creel's apologia can be found throughout *How We Advertised America;* for quotations in this paragraph, see 3, 4, 25, 73. Creel, who later wrote a biography of Thomas Paine, may also have seen his role as similar to that of the great Revolutionary War advocate, at least in terms of mobilizing public support for a righteous military campaign. See Kaye, *Thomas Paine and the Promise of America,* 199.

35. Vaughn, *Holding Fast the Inner Lines,* 194.

36. Creel, *How We Advertised America,* 25.

37. A word of Latin origin meaning "spreading" (derived from Sacra Congregatio de Propaganda Fide, a division of the Roman Curia established in 1622 to spread the faith), *propaganda* refers to the deliberate dissemination of information or stories intended to shape public opinion. Accord-

ing to the *Oxford English Dictionary,* the term first began to take on sinister connotations in the nineteenth century as it became associated with political attempts to spread doctrines of dubious merit. Some authorities draw a distinction between types of propaganda: "white" propaganda is the deliberate spread of information that may be highly selective but is nonetheless basically true, while "black" propaganda is the dissemination of known falsehoods, also called "disinformation." All of these techniques became widespread during the great ideological battles of the twentieth century, and they continue to bedevil journalists to this day.

38. Bernays, *Propaganda,* 9, 20. See also Tye, *The Father of Spin.*

39. Vaughn, *Holding Fast the Inner Lines,* 142.

40. Ibid., 215.

41. Mock, *Censorship, 1917,* 80.

42. See Starr, *Creation of the Media,* chap. 10.

43. Ibid., 226.

44. See Stone, *Perilous Times,* 146–53; Chafee, *Freedom of Speech,* chap. 2.

45. The text of Title 1 of the Espionage Act of 1917 can be found in Nelson, *Freedom of the Press from Hamilton to the Warren Court,* 248–50. Stone, *Perilous Times,* 180.

46. Mock, *Censorship, 1917,* 59–60.

47. Moeller, *Shooting War,* chap. 4.

48. Mock, *Censorship, 1917,* 65.

49. Knightley, *The First Casualty,* 133.

50. It is useful to keep in mind a distinction between censorship and propaganda. Censorship can be defined as any effort to *withhold* material from the public, while propaganda is an effort to *disseminate* material to the public. They are flipsides of the same coin, that is, the attempt to shape public opinion.

51. There is another drawback to censorship that harms the military itself. With no reporters, there are no stories, and with no stories, there are no heroes. As later generations of military leaders would discover in Grenada, Panama, and Kuwait, when the military succeeds in imposing a news blackout, there is no chance for soldiers or officers to win public acclaim. They are practically invisible, which does not suit all military personnel by any means.

52. Knightley, *The First Casualty,* 129–30. Knightley makes a rare error in placing Broun on the staff of the *New York World,* which he joined later, rather than on the *Tribune,* where he worked during the war.

53. Mock, *Censorship, 1917,* 91.

54. Quoted in Stone, *Perilous Times,* 185.

55. Ibid., 186.

56. For a fascinating account of the Debs case, including the role of a *Cleveland Plain Dealer* reporter in his prosecution, see Sproule, *Propaganda and Democracy,* chap. 1.

57. Quoted in Stone, *Perilous Times,* 196–97.

58. For quotations from Debs's appeal to the jury, see Salvatore, *Eugene V. Debs,* 294–96.

59. Ibid., 297. To put Debs's conviction in a modern context, think of Ralph Nader. As an independent presidential candidate in 2000, Nader received almost 3 million votes—roughly comparable to Debs's showing in 1912. Nader went on to criticize President George W. Bush's invasion of Iraq, calling it unwise and unconstitutional and denouncing the president personally as "a judicially selected dictator" (www.counterpunch.org/nader03252003.html). If the United States had had a sedition law in effect in 2003, Attorney General John Ashcroft might have prosecuted Nader for such language.

60. Stone, *Perilous Times,* 170, citing annual reports of the U.S. attorney general.

61. See ibid., 192–220; also Chafee, *Freedom of Speech,* 88–94; and Nelson, *Freedom of the Press,* 60–62. Also well worth reading is a commentary on the case by Harvard Law professor Alan Dershowitz titled "Shouting 'Fire!' "; see *Atlantic Monthly* 263, no. 1 (January 1989): 72.

62. *Schenck v. U.S.,* 249 U.S. 47 (1919).

63. For the Court's opinions in the Pentagon Papers case, see chapter 12.

64. The text of Schenck's leaflet is available at http://faculty-web.at.northwestern.edu/commstud/ freespeech/cont/cases/schenck/pamphlet.html. In the leaflet Schenck also expressed serious doubts about the idea of waging a war to bring democracy to other nations. "Democracy," he wrote, "can not be shot into a nation. It must come spontaneously and purely from within. Democracy must come through liberal education." He hardly sounds like a dangerous revolutionary.

65. *Debs v. U.S.*, 249 U.S. 211 (1919).

66. The details are well told in Chafee, *Freedom of Speech,* chap. 3, which amounts to a devastating critique of the investigation, prosecution, and judicial conduct in this case. Chafee's analysis could also serve as a warning to all future generations of the recurring menace to free speech posed by war.

67. Stone, *Perilous Times,* 205.

68. Chafee, *Freedom of Speech,* 127, 134.

69. Holmes to Laski, quoted in Stone, *Perilous Times,* 203.

70. *Abrams v. U.S.*, 250 U.S. 616 (1919).

71. Bernays, *Biography of an Idea,* 194.

72. Stone, *Perilous Times,* 220–28; Chafee, *Freedom of Speech,* chap. 5.

73. According to news accounts, as recently as 2006 the Bush administration considered using the Espionage Act to prosecute journalists. *New York Times,* April 30, 2006.

7. JAZZ AGE JOURNALISM, 1920–1929

1. Kluger, *The Paper,* 210.

2. For the number of dailies, see Lee, *Daily Newspaper in America.* Total circulation reached a plateau of 62 to 63 million a day between about 1980 and 1990, then began to fall steeply, according to figures from the Newspaper Association of America; for details, see www.naa.org.

3. It was not always easy to tell them apart. I generally follow the nomenclature used by the people who produced the publications themselves. For much of the eighteenth century in particular, it could be very difficult to tell a weekly newspaper from a weekly magazine. Only later, when it became standard practice for newspapers to publish daily, did the distinction become a bit clearer. In general, you can recognize a newspaper because it prints a lot of news on cheap paper.

4. Tebell and Zuckerman, *The Magazine in America,* provides a brisk and detailed summary of the magazine trade, which I have relied on throughout this section. Also see Johanningsmeier, *Fiction and the American Literary Marketplace,* chap. 1.

5. For a detailed examination of the artisan readership of a leading magazine in 1790, see Nord, *Communities of Journalism,* chap. 8.

6. See the *Scientific American* website and the page "About *Scientific American,*" www.scientificamerican.com/pressroom/aboutus.cfm.

7. See the remarkable website HarpWeek, which contains access to the magazine's archives from 1857 to 1912 as well as a number of links to other sites documenting late-nineteenth-century America.

8. For a history of the magazine, see a talk given in 1994 by editor Cullen Murphy, "A History of *The Atlantic Monthly,*" www.theatlantic.com/past/docs/about/atlhistf.htm.

9. *The Nation,* July 6, 1865, 1.

10. The *Anglo-African* published one of the finest pieces of satire in the entire nineteenth century. Titled "What Shall We Do with the White People?" it was written by William J. Wilson, who signed the piece "Ethiop." He wrote: "This people, the white, must be saved; quiet and harmony must be restored. Plans for removal of these white people, as all such schemes are[,] . . . would be wrong in conception, and prove abortive in the attempt. . . . We give them also high credit for their material progress. Who knows, but that some day, when, after they shall have fulfilled their mission, carried arts and sciences to their highest point, they will make way for a milder, more genial race, or become so blended in it, as to lose their own peculiar and objectionable characteristics? In any case, in view of the existing state of things around us, let our constant thought be, 'What for the best good of all shall we do with the White people?'" *Anglo-African Magazine,* February 1860, 41–45.

11. Quoted in Tebell and Zuckerman, *The Magazine in America,* 34.

12. See ibid., chap. 12, on the rise of the agencies.

13. This account is based on several essential sources: Brinkley, *The Publisher;* Swanberg, *Luce and His Empire;* Halberstam, *The Powers That Be,* chaps. 2, 12, 17, 20, 28, 31, and 35; and the two-volume authorized history of *Time* magazine, Elson, *Time Inc.* An important corrective to the literature about Luce is the biography of his partner, Briton Hadden, by Isaiah Wilner, aptly titled *The Man Time Forgot.*

14. See Brinkley, *The Publisher,* chap. 2, for insight into their Hotchkiss years.

15. Hecht later co-wrote (with Charles MacArthur) a classic send-up of American journalism in the play *The Front Page,* which became the basis for the great screen comedy *His Girl Friday.*

16. Quoted in Swanberg, *Luce and His Empire,* 54.

17. Ibid., 55.

18. See Elson, *Time Inc.,* 14, for details on the incorporation of the company and allocation of the original fourteen thousand shares of stock.

19. Ibid., 75.

20. To save money in the early days, Luce moved *Time* to Cleveland for two years, then—at Hadden's insistence—moved the operation back to Manhattan. The printing of *Time* was done by R. R. Donnelley & Sons of Chicago, the nation's rail crossroads, to facilitate nationwide distribution.

21. The previous year Scottish scientist Alexander Fleming had discovered the antibiotic properties of a mold called *Penicillium notatum,* but it had not yet been developed into a practical medical treatment for bacterial infections. On Hadden's demise, see Wilner, *The Man That Time Forgot,* chap. 15.

22. Elson, *Time Inc.,* chap. 11. For the unofficial version, see Wilner, *The Man That Time Forgot,* chap. 16. Also see Brinkley, *The Publisher,* 141–48.

23. Brinkley, *The Publisher,* chap. 5.

24. *Time,* October 28, 1928, 20.

25. *Time,* March 10, 1930, International department.

26. Halberstam, *The Powers That Be,* 62.

27. Swanberg, *Luce and His Empire,* 142. Swanberg later quotes Luce: "I am a Protestant, a Republican and a free-enterpriser, which means I am biased in favor of God, Eisenhower and the stockholders of Time Inc.—and if anybody who objects doesn't know this by now, why the hell are they still spending 35 cents for the magazine?" (383).

28. See Elson, *Time Inc.,* 129–30.

29. Ibid., 278.

30. Tebbel and Zuckerman, *The Magazine in America,* 167–71.

31. Halberstam, *The Powers That Be,* 64–69.

32. This description of Ross's life is based on Thomas Kunkel's wonderful biography *Genius in Disguise,* the best of the many books about Ross and the magazine's founding.

33. The World War I series of *Stars and Stripes* is available online through the Library of Congress at http://memory.loc.gov/ammem/sgphtml/sashtml/. An earlier version appeared during the Civil War but produced only four issues. *Stars and Stripes* was revived in 1942 and has been published continuously ever since. It now produces print and online versions that circulate worldwide.

34. See Kunkel, *Genius in Disguise,* 88, for a very clear explanation.

35. For the full text, see ibid., appendix 1.

36. For a detailed examination of the *New Yorker'*s handling of libel suits and other reader complaints, see Forde, *Literary Journalism on Trial,* chap. 4.

37. See, for example, the memo from Ross to Fleischmann dated April 17, 1926, which appears in Kunkel, *Letters from the Editor,* 24, and another dated April 11, 1936, which appears ibid., 65.

38. Memorandum, Ross to Fleishmann, dated April 11, 1932. Reprinted in Kunkel, *Letters from the Editor,* 65–66.

39. Raoul Fleischmann, a benevolent figure, remained as publisher until he died in 1969 and was succeeded by his son Peter. In 1985 the Fleischmann family sold the magazine to Advance Publications Inc., a huge publishing conglomerate controlled by the Newhouse family, which folded the *New Yorker* into its Condé Nast division in 1999.

40. Wolcott Gibbs, "TIME . . . FORTUNE . . . LIFE . . . LUCE," *New Yorker,* November 28, 1936, 20–25.

41. Brinkley, *The Publisher,* 200.

42. John, *Network Nation,* chaps. 1 and 2.

43. This summary of the early development of radio is based on Tom Lewis's *Empire of the Air: The Men who Made Radio,* the companion volume to the 1990 Ken Burns video documentary by the same name. See also Starr, *Creation of the Media,* chaps. 6, 10, and 11; and Hilmes, *Only Connect,* chaps. 1–5; as well as Goodman and Gring, "The Ideological Fight over Creation of the Federal Radio Commission."

44. See Stephen Kern, "Wireless World," in Crowley and Heyer, *Communication in History,* 207–10.

45. Krattenmaker and Powe, *Regulating Broadcast Programming,* 6–7.

46. See Starr, *Creation of the Media,* chap. 6.

47. In this way, Sarnoff was among the ranks of American journalists who lacked a complete formal education—from Ben Franklin to Margaret Fuller, Lloyd Garrison, and Horace Greeley, from

Joseph Pulitzer and H. L. Mencken to Harold Ross. Even William Randolph Hearst never finished college. Properly educated journalists like Luce were, for a long time, the exception—a
pattern that contributed to the field's autodidactic ethos.

48. Stashower, *The Boy Genius and the Mogul*, 37. Sarnoff's 1916 memo has never been found. It is
possible he did not write down these thoughts until 1920.

49. Hilmes, *Only Connect*, 30.

50. Quoted ibid.

51. See Starr, *Creation of the Media*, 222–30.

52. Ibid., 327.

53. Ibid., 331.

54. Ibid., 336–37.

55. Ibid., 338.

56. Not everyone sees it that way, of course. For an argument in favor of allocating spectrum capacity through auction, see Krattenmaker and Powe, *Regulating Broadcast Programming*.

57. All quotations are from the Radio Act of 1927, 44 Stat. 1162–74. For a discussion, see Rivera-
Sanchez, "Origins of the Ban on 'Obscene, Indecent, or Profane' Language."

58. Starr, *Creation of the Media*, 352.

59. This sketch of Paley is based on the authoritative 1990 biography by Sally Bedell Smith, *In All
His Glory;* and on Halberstam, *The Powers That Be*, chaps. 1, 4, 7 10, 14, 16, 18, 23, 27, 32, and 36.
Additional details can be found in Bernays, *Biography of an Idea*, chap. 32.

60. Paley personally put up $417,000. When he retired from CBS in 1982, his shares of CBS stock
were worth over $115 million. See Smith, *In All His Glory*, appendix 1.

61. Starr, *Creation of the Media*, 354.

62. Ibid., 360.

63. Ibid., 377; Smith, *In All His Glory*, 165.

64. *New York Times*, Editorial, May 8, 1935.

8. HARD TIMES, 1929–1941

1. See Johanningsmeier, *Fiction and the American Literary Marketplace*, which discusses the economics of syndication in detail.

2. Neal Gabler quotes Heywood Broun: "I have said in all seriousness that a widely syndicated
writer has far more political power than any Senator." Gabler, *Winchell*, 267.

3. This discussion is based on Neal Gabler's fine biography *Winchell*, as well as on Winchell's own
autobiography, *Winchell Exclusive*.

4. Gabler, *Winchell*, xiii.

5. Some commentators find enormous significance in the Jewish ancestry of certain media figures, including Pulitzer, Ochs, Sarnoff, Paley, Winchell, and Lippmann, among others. These
same commentators rarely note the disproportionate number of media figures whose ancestors came from England, Scotland, or Ireland, or the fact that well over 90 percent of the
owners and other key decision makers in most news organizations are white, male, Christian,
and conservative. That is the social reality against which occasional exceptions who might
be nonwhite, non-Christian, female, or progressive stand out. It is a forest of very similar
species with a few exotics who get all the notice. As for the Jewish origins common to some
media figures, it may be worth noting that Pulitzer, Ochs, Sarnoff, and the others were highly
secular. In this they were of a mind with their non-Jewish counterparts in America media,
generally speaking. Indeed, I would venture to say that, on the whole, the top editors, writers, and on-air talent tend to be notably less observant regardless of their religion than most
Americans claim to be. Apart from this, I find it difficult to draw any further significance
from the subject.

6. Gabler, *Winchell*, 36.

7. Winchell helpfully supplied a "Glozzery of WWord WWeddings" at the end of his autobiography, *Winchell Exclusive*.

8. Gabler, *Winchell*, 106.

9. Not all the credit should go to Winchell. From an early stage in his career he was assisted by a
team of secretaries and ghostwriters. The gatekeeper for thirty-five years was his secretary, Rose
Bigman. The most important of the anonymous writers was probably Herman Klurfeld, who
toiled on Winchell's behalf for almost three decades. It was Klurfeld who came up with such lines
as "She's been on more laps than a napkin."

10. A small sample of his radio style can be heard through the website of the Radio Hall of Fame, www.radiohof.org/news/walterwinchell.html.

11. McKelway, "Gossip Writer," *New Yorker*, July 6, 1940, 28.

12. In the judgment of a panel of historians assembled in 2006 by the *Atlantic* magazine, of "The 100 Most Influential Americans of All Time," no fewer than eleven were journalists, the second-most numerous category after presidents. Those journalists were Ben Franklin (6), Mark Twain (16), Tom Paine (19), Rachel Carson (39), W. E. B. Du Bois (43), William Lloyd Garrison (46), Frederick Douglass (47), James Gordon Bennett (69), Betty Friedan (77), William Randolph Hearst (80), and, at number 89, Walter Lippmann.

13. Steffens, *Autobiography.*

14. Noteworthy too was the magazine's business model, such as it was. The venture had the financial backing of two of the greatest journalistic "angels" of all time, Willard and Dorothy Straight. He was a banker in the House of Morgan, but as a Whitney and thus an heir to the great the Standard Oil fortune, his wife had even more money. The Straights never interfered with the magazine's editorial operations and steadfastly stood by as the *New Republic* lost money year after year. By one reckoning, they subsidized the magazine by an average of $100,000 a year over forty years. See Steel, *Walter Lippmann and the American Century,* 62.

15. Ibid.

16. Ibid., 148.

17. Lippmann, *Public Opinion,* 25.

18. Ibid., 203.

19. Ibid., 215.

20. Ibid., 248.

21. Ibid., 273–74.

22. This prescription may sound vague and inadequate, but it is in fact quite widespread. In actual practice, journalists routinely call on experts of all sorts to help them understand data and draw conclusions, often without leaving any trace in their final reports of this kind of help. Some see this as the fundamental argument in favor of journalistic objectivity. See Blumenthal, "Journalism and Its Discontents." At the same time, certain reporters who work a regular "beat"— even on quite technical matters such as the federal tax code or military affairs—become experts themselves.

23. Dewey, "Review of *Public Opinion*," 286. Also see Sproule, *Propaganda and Democracy,* chap. 4; and John Morton Blum's introduction to Lippmann, *Public Philosopher: Selected Letters,* xx–xxi.

24. Steel, *Walter Lippmann and the American Century,* 199.

25. On Lippmann's move from the *World* to the *Herald Tribune,* see Kluger, *The Paper,* 256–61.

26. Figures are from Clinton Rossiter's introduction to *The Essential Lippmann,* and from Blum's preface to Lippmann, *Public Philosopher: Selected Letters.*

27. *New York Herald Tribune,* January 8, 1932. In the summer of 1932, when the Democrats gathered in Chicago for their presidential nominating convention, Roosevelt was the early leader in the balloting, but he could not pin down the required two-thirds majority. During the resulting deadlock, one of the names put forward for the nomination was none other than Walter Lippmann—proposed by his classmate and fellow columnist Heywood Broun. Nothing came of it.

28. *New York Herald Tribune,* April 6, 1933.

29. For a summary and analysis of his views, see Steel, *Walter Lippmann and the American Century,* chap. 26.

30. This discussion is based on Sanders, *Dorothy Thompson,* as well as articles about Thompson in *Time* and American National Biography Online. Thompson's columns are collected in several editions.

31. "Cartwheel Girl," *Time,* June 12, 1939, 47; Hamilton, *Journalism's Roving Eye,* chap 16.

32. Known legally and sometimes socially as "Mrs. Sinclair Lewis," she wrote under the byline Dorothy Thompson throughout her career.

33. Thompson, *I Saw Hitler!,* 13.

34. See Sanders, *Dorothy Thompson,* 199.

35. Quoted in Sanders, *Dorothy Thompson,* 223.

36. Quoted ibid., 251.

37. The figure comes from a two-part profile of Thompson by Margaret Case Harriman, "The It Girl," which appeared in the *New Yorker* in April 1940.

38. "Cartwheel Girl," 47.

39. Murrow's life is recounted in detail in A. M. Sperber's 1986 biography, *Murrow: His Life and Times*. Also see *The Murrow Boys* by Stanley Cloud and Lynne Olson, as well as the memoir written by Murrow's collaborator Fred Friendly, *Due to Circumstances beyond Our Control*. Dozens of memorable Murrow radio broadcasts can be heard on the CD that accompanies *World War II on the Air* by Mark Bernstein and Alex Lubertozzi, and many of his best television programs can be seen in a four-DVD set, *The Edward R. Murrow Collection* (CBS Television, 1991). A dramatization of Murrow's conflict with Senator Joseph McCarthy (and Paley) is presented in the 2005 feature film *Good Night and Good Luck*.

40. For insights into the world of Murrow's birth, see Hall et al., *Like a Family*, chaps. 1–3.

41. Quoted in Smith, *In All His Glory*, 164.

42. For many Americans, Shirer's was the first voice they heard warning of Nazism. In 1941, Shirer published a book, *Berlin Diary*, detailing the rise of Hitler. Later, after the war, Shirer was a target of red-baiting; he had to leave radio and turned to writing books. That was when he published his classic, *The Rise and Fall of the Third Reich* (1960), which has been in print ever since and has sold in the millions. Although no longer an essential reference for historians now that German and other sources are available, Shirer's work remains a popular touchstone.

43. Quoted in Sperber, *Murrow*, 119.

44. When Breckenridge married an official who served in the American Embassy, she left CBS on the grounds that her marriage created a conflict of interest. CBS executives in New York then laid down the law to Murrow: no more women. Murrow tried a few times to get around the edict but eventually gave up.

45. Quoted in Cloud and Olson, *The Murrow Boys*, 192.

46. Quoted in Sperber, *Murrow*, 127.

47. This account is based on Gilbert, *Kristallnacht;* Goebbels quote appears on page 29.

48. *New York Times,* November 11, 1938.

49. *Washington Post,* November 11, 1938.

50. Quoted in Sanders, *Dorothy Thompson*, 231.

51. Lippmann, *Liberty and the News*, 38.

52. This is one of the major points made by Deborah E. Lipstadt in her pathbreaking 1986 study *Beyond Belief: The American Press and the Coming of the Holocaust, 1933–1945*.

53. In an earlier era, journalists had a term for the presumption that most American readers have an aversion to tiresome, detailed reports about people far away: "Afghanistanism." That was before the United States invaded Afghanistan and tried to occupy it, forcing Americans to actually pay attention to Afghanistan.

54. Paradoxically, of course, the opposite is just as true. Government tends to oil the squeaky wheel, and it pays far more attention to issues that are the subject of sustained news coverage than it does to matters that are ignored by the media. But in foreign affairs, the initiative almost always belongs to the government.

55. Tifft and Jones, *The Trust,* 109–11.

56. Leff, *Buried by the Times,* 25; chap. 1 presents an excellent introduction to Sulzberger's views.

57. Laurel Leff presents an exhaustive analysis in *Buried by* The Times.

58. Lippmann to Dr. Lawrence J. Henderson, a member of Harvard's committee on the admission of Jews, October 27, 1922, in Lippmann, *Public Philosopher,* 148–54.

59. Steel, *Walter Lippmann and the American Century,* 373.

60. Quoted in Nasaw, *The Chief,* 553.

61. Stone, *Perilous Times,* 245–48.

62. *U.S. Code* (1940), Title 18, chap. 115, sec. 2385.

63. Stone, *Perilous Times,* 251.

64. Henry Luce, "The American Century," *Life,* February 17, 1941, 61–65. The artcicle is reprinted in Luce, *The American Century.*

65. Luce, "The American Century," 65.

66. Quoted in Brinkley, *The Publisher,* 271–73.

67. Ibid., 270.

68. For GDP figures, see Harrison, *The Economics of World War II,* 10.

69. Goralski, *World War II Almanac,* 89.

70. Pyle is the subject of a fine sympathetic biography by James Tobin, *Ernie Pyle's War* (1997). Also helpful is the biographical essay by David Nichols in his collection titled *Ernie's War*. Nichols collected Pyle's domestic writing in *Ernie's America*. Four collections of Pyle's wartime reporting

were published as books: *Ernie Pyle in England, Here Is Your War, Brave Men,* and *Last Chapter.* They remain eminently readable. In addition, some of his aviation columns are collected in *On a Wing and a Prayer,* and selected travel columns were published as *Home Country.*

71. Tobin, *Ernie Pyle's War,* chaps. 1 and 2.
72. Ibid., 17.
73. Ibid., 27.
74. Ibid., 38.
75. Quoted ibid., 32.
76. Quoted ibid., 48.
77. Cited in Seib, *Broadcasts from the Blitz,* 103.
78. This discussion is based primarily on Sperber, *Murrow;* Cloud and Olson, *The Murrow Boys;* Seib, *Broadcasts from the Blitz;* and Halberstam, *The Powers That Be,* chaps. 1 and 4; as well as transcripts and recordings of Murrow's broadcasts. See also Murrow, *This Is London.*
79. Quoted in Sperber, *Murrow,* 158.
80. Later Murrow used a similar tagline that became his signature: "Good night and good luck."
81. Tobin, *Ernie Pyle's War,* 53–54.
82. Reprinted in Nichols, *Ernie's War,* 42–43. Pyle's column is dated December 30, 1940.
83. "Tourist in the War Zone," *Time,* January 13, 1941, 50.
84. Tobin, *Ernie Pyle's War,* 57–58.
85. Murrow also made an offer around this time to a young UP reporter named Walter Cronkite, but Cronkite's bureau chief, Harrison Salisbury, came up with enough money to hang onto Cronkite for the duration of the war. Later Cronkite would jump to CBS.
86. Sperber, *Murrow,* 175.
87. Quoted ibid., 204.
88. Starr, *Creation of the Media,* 379.
89. Sperber, *Murrow,* 207.
90. Quoted in Sanders, *Dorothy Thompson,* 360.
91. *New York Times,* February 21, 1972.
92. Gabler, *Winchell,* 552.
93. This *New York Post* series ran from January 7 to March 16, 1952 (it spanned a period of suspension while Winchell was ill). The quotation is from the January 7 installment.

9. THE "GOOD WAR," 1941–1945

1. *New York Times,* October 15, 1941. Knox was a Republican with a background in journalism. He was a former newspaper publisher, having run the Manchester, New Hampshire, *Union-Leader,* the *Chicago Daily News,* and the Hearst papers in Boston.
2. Quoted in Emery, Emery, and Roberts, *The Press and America,* 341.
3. Emery, Emery, and Roberts, *The Press and America,* 345.
4. Bradley, *Women and the Press,* 220.
5. Sweeney, *The Military and the Press,* 94.
6. Barnouw, *History of Broadcasting,* vol. 2, *The Golden Web,* 166.
7. Ibid., 168–90.
8. Sproule, *Propaganda and Democracy,* 187–89. Many of these agencies were combined, recombined, and renamed, sometimes more than once.
9. Blum, *V Was for Victory,* 31.
10. Sproule, *Propaganda and Democracy,* 192.
11. Christie and Clark, "Framing Two Enemies," 56.
12. The entire series was an all-star effort. Most of the writing was done by Julius and Philip Epstein, the twin brothers who (along with Howard Koch) wrote the Oscar-winning 1942 drama *Casablanca.* Most of the narration of the "Why We Fight" series was supplied by Walter Huston, and the graphics were provided by Disney Studios. Capra is credited as co-director on each film, usually along with Anatole Litvak.
13. Weinberg, "What to Tell America." At war's end OWI was disbanded, and its overseas propaganda functions were assigned to the State Department. In August 1945, Secretary of State James Byrnes offered the job of running it to Walter Lippmann, who turned it down.
14. Cunningham, "The Battle of the Bulge."
15. Barnouw, *Golden Web,* 190–201.

16. The problem of finding an official source for everything would become an issue from time to time, especially in the case of German or Japanese attacks on the U.S. mainland. Reporters could see these with their own eyes, but no officials would confirm them, so reports could not be printed or broadcast. This may be part of the reason why most Americans still know little about this phase of World War II.

17. See Sweeney, *Secrets of Victory,* chap. 2; quote is from 42.

18. Stone, *Perilous Times,* 275–77; Marcus, *Father Coughlin,* 216; and Sweeney, *Secrets of Victory,* 74–79.

19. Sweeney, *Secrets of Victory,* 100–108.

20. See Washburn, *A Question of Sedition;* and Ritchie, *Reporting from Washington,* chap. 2.

21. Knightley, *The First Casualty,* 315–16, citing a letter from Middleton. As Middleton went on to observe, this relationship would break down by the time of the war in Vietnam. There, in the absence of censorship, many officers were reluctant to talk to reporters.

22. This account is based on Sweeney, *Secrets of Victory,* 79–83; and on Goren, "Communication Intelligence and the Freedom of the Press."

23. Brinkley, *The Publisher,* 224.

24. *Life,* November 30, 1942, 131.

25. Moeller, *Shooting War,* 204–7.

26. *New York Times Magazine,* August 16, 1942, 3, quoted in Leff, *Buried by* The Times; emphasis added.

27. This account is based on Knightley, *The First Casualty,* 349–51.

28. For his eyewitness account, see Grossman, *A Writer at War.*

29. Quoted in Leff, *Buried by* The Times, 285, note xi.

30. Pyle, "The God-Damned Infantry" (May 2, 1943), reprinted in Library of America, *Reporting World War II,* 1:556.

31. Knightley, *The First Casualty,* 357.

32. Pyle, *Here Is Your War,* 132.

33. Ibid., 173.

34. Reprinted in Library of America, *Reporting World War II,* 1:735–37.

35. Knightley, *The First Casualty,* 344.

36. White, "The Newspaper Reader Finds It Very Difficult to Get at the Truth."

37. Sherrod, *Tarawa,* 711.

38. This account is based on James Bradley (with Ron Powers), *Flags of Our Fathers;* as well as Moeller, *Shooting War,* 245–47. Moeller, who interviewed Rosenthal, reproduces much of the photographer's first-person account.

39. Moeller, *Shooting War,* 197.

40. *Life,* June 26, 1944, 13.

41. Moeller, *Shooting War,* 197–99.

42. A transcript of the broadcast can be found in Library of America, *Reporting World War II,* 2:681–85.

43. Sperber, *Murrow,* 252–53.

44. See Sweeney, *Secrets of Victory,* 197–206.

45. William L. Laurence, "Atomic Bombing of Nagasaki Told by a Flight Member," *New York Times,* September 9, 1945.

46. Homer Bigart, "In Hiroshima," *New York Herald Tribune,* September 5, 1945.

47. In the mythology surrounding this piece, it is often said that Ross cleared the entire magazine for Hersey's story. In fact Ross decided to rip out all the editorial matter but not the ads or entertainment listings. Thus Hersey's somber masterpiece appears disconcertingly alongside ads for "perma-lift" bras and the "latest hilarity" from S. J. Perelman, as well as full-page spreads offering civilian versions of such familiar items as the Willys Jeep.

48. In 1999 the journalism department at New York University invited a panel of judges to create a list of the one hundred best works of journalism of the twentieth century. Hersey's *Hiroshima* was ranked first. Wartime pieces by Murrow and Pyle were also in the top ten.

49. Figures on wartime casualties among journalists come from the Freedom Forum website, www.newseum.org/scripts/journalist/main.htm.

50. Moeller, *Shooting War,* 183.

51. Sproule, *Propaganda and Democracy,* 214.

52. Tobin, *Ernie Pyle's War,* 194–98.

10. CREATING BIG MEDIA, 1945–1963

1. Cloud and Olson, *The Murrow Boys,* 287.
2. For his assistance to Eisenhower's communications staff during World War II, Sarnoff was awarded a brigadier general's star. From that point on he preferred to be called General Sarnoff. Paley held the rank of colonel while working for the Office of War Information in London during the war.
3. Barnouw, *History of Broadcasting,* vol. 3, *The Image Empire,* 42–43.
4. Such decisions are what the scholar Paul Starr, writing about earlier media, calls "constitutive" decisions. See the introduction to Starr, *Creation of the Media.*
5. Barnouw, *Image Empire,* 280.
6. Mickelson, *The Decade That Shaped Television News,* xvi.
7. On the *Camel News Caravan,* the sponsor managed to impose detailed conditions. To encourage cigarette smoking, the company banned news film showing anyone smoking cigars (except Churchill), and it banned any film that happened to show a sign that said "No Smoking." See Barnouw, *Image Empire,* 43.
8. Halbertsam, *Powers That Be,* 130.
9. Quoted in Barnouw, *History of Broadcasting,* vol. 2, *The Golden Web,* 137. The doctrine derived its name from the Mayflower Broadcasting Corporation, which was trying to wrest a license away from station WAAB in Boston. The FCC sustained WAAB's license while giving the owners a stiff warning about advocacy.
10. Ibid.
11. Smith, *In All His Glory,* 361.
12. This account of *See It Now* is based on Barnouw, *Image Empire,* 40–58; Sperber, *Murrow,* chap. 12; Smith, *In All His Glory,* 300–307, 361–75; Cloud and Olson, *Murrow Boys,* 289–313; Halberstam, *Powers That Be,* chap. 4; as well as taped recordings of the *See It Now* programs.
13. Except for Jack O'Brian, the television columnist for the Hearst press, who looked for chances to criticize CBS and especially "Murrow and his partner in port-side reporting, Mr. Friendly." See Barnouw, *Image Empire,* 50.
14. One version of the derivation of the term "anchor" comes from CBS news director and, later, producer Don Hewitt, who writes in his memoir: "Sig Mickelson says it was he who coined the title 'anchorman,' at the 1952 Republican convention. I thought I had, but Sig could be right. At any rate, we both had a hand in it. In trying to explain what Cronkite's role would be vis-à-vis our other reporters, I said they would be a team—a relay team, if you will, and Sig, as best I remember, said Cronkite would run the final leg, the anchor leg. It had nothing to do with being 'anchored' to a desk." Hewitt, *Minute by Minute,* 83.
15. Cronkite, *A Reporter's Life,* 176.
16. O'Reilly, "Dies, Martin."
17. Oshinsky, *A Conspiracy So Immense,* 90.
18. Swanberg, *Luce and His Empire,* 267.
19. A. J. Liebling quotes no less an authority than Huey Long on the subject of bias in the Lucepress: "Mr. Luce is like a man who owns a shoestore and buys all the shoes to fit hisself." Liebling, *The Press,* 223.
20. Tragically, this kind of campaign had two negative outcomes: it drove almost anyone with any expertise in Asia out of the government, and it forced those who remained to prove continually that they were "tough" on communism. Both trends contributed to the eventual U.S. policy in Vietnam.
21. Oshinsky, *Conspiracy So Immense,* 109. Regrettably, the original broadcast of the event was not preserved. Actually, in contrast to what McCarthy famously said in Wheeling, there was no list. What McCarthy had was a copy of a letter, from Secretary of State James Byrnes to a congressman, stating that at the end of World War II, some three thousand government employees who had been in various agencies were transferred onto the State Department payroll in 1945; of those, a screening board had recommended against 284 on various grounds. Byrnes said that 79 of the people on the list had been let go, leaving 205 who might still be security risks—for whatever reasons, including not only membership in the Communist Party but also membership in the Nazi Party or any other undesirable qualities. For a detailed examination of the discrepancies in McCarthy's charges, see Bayley, *Joe McCarthy and the Press,* which provides an exhaustive empirical study of the coverage.
22. Bayley, *Joe McCarthy and the Press,* chap. 3, lays out this case well and supplies examples.

23. Of course, this is a very crude way of "scoring" what is hardly a game. A false charge followed by a denial is not the same as no charge at all. Even a person who mounts a vigorous defense is never the same after a public accusation, because some part of the audience can be counted on to remember the accusation and forget the rest. Not to mention that the target of the unfounded accusation suffers real anguish and loss of productive time while refuting the charges.

24. Meyer was a Republican, too, a businessman who made a fortune in corporate mergers and on Wall Street and then went on to serve presidents of both parties in high-profile appointive positions, usually trying to steer the U.S. economy. He was the father of Katharine Meyer, who became Katharine Graham when she married Phil. It was Kay Graham who eventually became publisher of the *Post* during the Watergate era (see chapter 11).

25. "Sewer Politics," *Washington Post*, February 14, 1950.

26. Graham, *Personal History*, 204.

27. Swanberg, *Luce and His Empire*, 297.

28. See Mickelson, *The Decade That Shaped Television News*, chap. 7.

29. Doherty, *Cold War, Cool Medium*, 7–8 and chap. 2.

30. Sperber, *Murrow*, 307.

31. This is the basic story line, for example, in the 2005 Hollywood hit film *Good Night and Good Luck*. It is also the theme of several books about Murrow. For example, see Streitmatter, *Mightier than the Sword*.

32. Friendly, *Due to Circumstances beyond Our Control*, 10.

33. Ibid., 34.

34. Ibid., 35.

35. This account is based on the memoirs of Friendly and Mickelson and on accounts in Sperber, *Murrow*; Halberstam, *Powers That Be*; Smith, *In All His Glory*; Cloud and Olson, *The Murrow Boys*; Oshinsky, *A Conspiracy So Immense*; Bayley, *Joe McCarthy and the Press*; Barnouw, *Image Empire*; and Persico, *Edward R. Murrow*; as well as viewing of the program, which is available on DVD in *The Edward R. Murrow Collection* (CBS Television, 1999).

36. Quoted in Friendly, *Due to Circumstances beyond Our Control*, 43, 53. Pegler was referring to Andrew Mellon, the Pittsburgh banker who became the richest man in America by investing in ALCOA, U.S. Steel, and Gulf Oil, among others. He also served three presidents as secretary of the U.S. Treasury and donated his vast art collection to the National Gallery. His fortune continues to shape American politics and journalism through the efforts of his great-grandnephew, the conservative billionaire Richard Mellon Scaife, who bankrolled the *American Spectator* magazine along with many other conservative media ventures.

37. *New York Times*, March 11, 1954.

38. *See It Now*, April 6, 1954.

39. Friendly, *Due to Circumstances beyond Our Control*, 59.

40. Barnouw, *Image Empire*, 54–55. The hearings were also televised by the Dumont network, but it was limited to ten stations. Dumont went out of business the following year.

41. The final version of the Senate resolution used the word "condemn" rather than "censure," but it was a distinction that made little difference. When the end came for McCarthy, most newspapers treated it as major news, with lengthy obituaries. The *New York Times* ran a news story but chose not to editorialize. Charles Merz, who ran the *Times* editorial page, said: "I don't think we need an editorial on this. Why dignify the bastard?" Salisbury, *Without Fear or Favor*, 470.

42. Friendly, *Due to Circumstances beyond Our Control*, 60.

43. Ibid., 75.

44. Ibid., 78.

45. Quoted in Smith, *In All His Glory*, 14.

46. Friendly, *Due to Circumstances beyond Our Control*, 92.

47. The text of Murrow's speech is available in Safire, *Lend Me Your Ears*, 771–78, and at www.rtdna.org/pages/media_items/edward-r.-murrow-speech998.php.

48. Sperber, *Murrow*, 542.

49. Smith, *In All His Glory*, Appendix 1, contains annual statements of Paley's stock holdings, 1928–1989.

50. For an overview, see Marzolf, *Civilizing Voices*.

51. Liebling, *The Press*, 22.

52. Ibid., 194–95.

53. Ibid., 23–24.
54. Ibid., 67.
55. Ibid., 32.
56. In recent years, many historians have established a new conceptualization of this broad social movement, often referring to it as "the long civil rights movement," a view that extends the period encompassed by the movement in both directions. For the purposes of this book, I have chosen to follow the chronology as suggested by the coverage of the civil rights movement rather than the movement itself.
57. For an illuminating discussion of the lengthy stories at either end of the "classical" civil rights era (1954–1965), see Hall, "The Long Civil Rights Movement and the Political Uses of the Past."
58. The union's main organizer, A. Philip Randolph, began his career as the co-founder of a magazine, the *Messenger,* which was labeled "dangerous" by the U.S. Justice Department during World War I. For much of his early career Randolph was primarily a journalist. Indeed, it has been argued that this was one of the keys to his success in organizing the porters' union. That is, because he did not work for the Pullman company, he could not be intimidated or fired.
59. Washburn, *The African American Newspaper,* 177.
60. *Chicago Defender,* June 2, 1945. More of Hughes's newspaper work can be found in two collections: *The Best of Simple,* and in a volume edited by Christopher B. De Santis, *Langston Hughes and the* Chicago Defender.
61. See, for example, comments by prominent journalists recorded in the 1987 documentary video *Dateline Freedom* (PBS), especially Jack Nelson, Claude Sitton, and John Chancellor.
62. Roberts and Klibanoff, *The Race Beat,* 194.
63. *New York Times,* March 29, 1960.
64. Roberts and Klibanoff, *The Race Beat,* 231.
65. Ibid., 239.
66. Ibid., 357.
67. *New York Times v. Sullivan,* 376 U.S. 254 (1964).
68. Because the starting point was so low, some of these early gains seemed statistically impressive. But in fact the process slowed to a crawl and still lags. According to the annual newsroom survey by the American Society of Newspaper Editors, the percentage of all minorities was less than 4 percent in 1978 and still had not reached 14 percent by 2007, while the percentage of all minorities in the general population was approximately 27 percent.
69. Washburn, *The African American Newspaper,* 190–94.
70. The change was triggered by broadcasters' exasperation over a Chicago man named Lar Daly (no relation to this author) who liked to dress up as Uncle Sam. Daly took a notion to run for mayor against the incumbent, Richard J. Daley, and demanded equal time, including all the minutes and seconds that television covered the sitting mayor at ceremonial events. See Barnouw, *Image Empire,* 160–62.
71. This account is based on Barnouw, *Image Empire,* 163–65.
72. Liebling, "The Wayward Press: The Big Decision," *New Yorker,* October 29, 1960, 146. Reprinted in Liebling, *The Press,* 37.
73. Smith, *In All His Glory,* 414.
74. Presupposing, of course, that all public officials are *men.* See Cronkite, *A Reporter's Life,* 220.
75. For an extensive litany of Kennedy's misdeeds, see the 1997 compilation by the prominent investigative reporter Seymour Hersh, *The Dark Side of Camelot.*
76. Most members of the media, of course, got the news that day—as they usually do—from "the wires." In this case, UPI scored a historic scoop over AP in an episode that deserves at least a footnote in journalism history. In that era before cell phones, the gathering of breaking news usually depended on finding and, if possible, monopolizing the nearest telephone. Here is a compact version of the famous incident, as told by William Prochnau: "Riding in a Secret Service car three cars behind the presidential limousine, Merriman Smith of UPI and Jack Bell of AP heard three shots ring out. Smith arm-wrestled the agent's car phone away from his rival, pinned Bell to the floorboards, dictated the first bulletin lead to his office, and then rolled over and smothered the phone with his body until the racing automobile reached Parkland Hospital. Bell, a distinguished reporter, never quite forgave Smith and never quite regained his reputation. Smith won the Pulitzer Prize." Prochnau, *Once Upon a Distant War,* 382.
77. Smith, *In All His Glory,* 420.

11. ROCKING THE ESTABLISHMENT, 1962–1972

1. Homer Bigart to David Halberstam, August 6, 1962, David Halberstam Collection, Howard Gotlieb Archival Research Center, Boston University (hereafter Halberstam Collection).
2. See Roberts and Klibanoff, *The Race Beat,* 226.
3. Later, while reporting from Saigon, Halberstam got in trouble with his draft board in a mix-up over his obligation to keep the board informed about his movements after he was assigned overseas. With help from the *Times,* he managed to placate the draft officials. He had joined the army under the Reserve Forces Act, which allowed the Pentagon to shrink the size of the active military while keeping a large reserve force on hand that could be mobilized rapidly. See Prochnau, *Once upon a Distant War,* 197–98.
4. See, for example, Halberstam's own oral history in Ferrari, *Reporting America at War.*
5. Cable, 1963 Halberstam Collection, box 2.
6. Sometimes these meetings would be at very high levels. When Walter Lippmann made his first visit to the Soviet Union in 1958, he was briefed by no less a figure than CIA director Allen Dulles at the agency's headquarters. See Steel, *Walter Lippmann and the American Century,* 510. Many other revelations about press-CIA cooperation tumbled out in 1975 when the Senate's Church Committee released its findings about U.S. intelligence agencies and their methods. Also see the lengthy *Rolling Stone* article by Carl Bernstein, "The CIA and the Media." These arrangements are partly to blame for the persistent belief in some parts of the world that all American journalists are spies.
7. Quotations are from a two-page, single-spaced memo Halberstam wrote in 1963 as guidance for the *Esquire* writer George Goodman, better known by his pen name, Adam Smith. The memo is in the Halberstam Collection, box 3.
8. For a detailed account of this group, see Prochnau, *Once upon a Distant War.* Also see memoirs by Malcolm Browne, *Muddy Boots and Red Socks;* and Peter Arnett, *Live from the Battlefield.* In addition, Neil Sheehan's masterpiece, *A Bright Shining Lie,* is indispensable. Also valuable is the foreword written by Halberstam to the 2007 in-house history of the Associated Press, *Breaking News,* in which he pays fond tribute to the AP's Saigon bureau.
9. Prochnau, *Once upon a Distant War,* 108.
10. For one thing, Arnett, Browne, Faas, Halberstam, and Sheehan would all eventually win Pulitzer Prizes for their work in or about Vietnam.
11. See Hallin, *The "Uncensored War."*
12. General William Westmoreland himself acknowledged that, except in a handful of cases, members of the news media acquitted themselves admirably in following the rules, which were meant to safeguard U.S. troops and plans. Ibid., 128. According to George Esper, who followed Browne as the AP bureau chief in Saigon, the Pentagon considered imposing censorship but ultimately rejected the idea "on the grounds that it would be a public relations black eye for the United States." Interview with the author, March 11, 2006, at "Vietnam and the Presidency," a conference sponsored by the National Archives and twelve presidential libraries, held at the Kennedy Library, Boston.
13. At the time and later, some conservatives and some military officials regretted this policy. Indeed, some held the unrestricted coverage responsible for the ultimate failure of the U.S. effort in Vietnam and "blamed the media." In military circles, one of the "lessons" of Vietnam was to make sure that U.S. forces never again engaged in combat under the scrutiny of an uncontrolled news media. This is the doctrine that informed censorship practices in the U.S. invasions of Grenada (1983) and Panama (1989) as well as the Persian Gulf war (1990–91).
14. Admiral Harry D. Felt, for example, gave a press conference shortly after the debacle at Ap Bac in 1963. At one point he glared at Mal Browne and asked, "Why can't you get on the team?" Browne, *Muddy Boots and Red Socks,* 163.
15. Ibid., 107–8.
16. This story is told in detail in Sheehan, *A Bright Shining Lie;* as well as in Halberstam, *The Making of a Quagmire;* and in Prochnau, *Once upon a Distant War.*
17. Quoted in Prochnau, *Once upon a Distant War,* 304.
18. Tallman and McKerns, " 'Press Mess.' "
19. Because Associated Press correspondents were outside the United States, they were beyond the jurisdiction of the AP's various unions, whose contracts required that reporters stick to writing stories and leave the taking of pictures to photographers.
20. Browne, *Muddy Boots and Red Socks,* 11–12.

21. Kennedy's remark was relayed to Browne later by Ambassador Henry Cabot Lodge, who heard it directly from Kennedy. Ibid., 12.

22. *New York Herald Tribune,* August 26–31, 1963.

23. David Halberstam to Nathaniel Gerstenzang, quoted in Prochnau, *Once upon a Distant War,* 398.

24. Arthur Sulzberger to David Halberstam, August 7, 1968, Halberstam Collection, box 3. Among his generation of the family, Punch Sulzberger (grandson of Adolph Ochs, son of Arthur Hays Sulzberger, and father of current publisher Arthur Ochs Sulzberger Jr.) was not expected to become the publisher of the *Times.* That job went first to his brother-in-law Orvill Dryfoos, who was a good bit older. But when Dryfoos died of a heart attack in 1963, Punch vaulted into the top spot.

25. Prochnau, *Once upon a Distant War,* 408.

26. "Foreign Correspondents: The View from Saigon," *Time,* September 20, 1963, 62.

27. Although he was not there, Halberstam describes the incident in his book on the media, *Powers That Be,* 445–46.

28. Ibid., 452. For a similar view from a *Washington Post* correspondent, see Just, "Saigon and Other Syndromes."

29. See Peter Arnett's oral history in Ferrari, *Reporting America at War,* 178–79.

30. Harwood, "The War Just Doesn't Add Up," reprinted in Library of America, *Reporting Vietnam,* 1:485.

31. Browne, *Muddy Boots and Red Socks,* 216.

32. See Barnouw, *Image Empire,* 301.

33. This account is based on Safer's oral history of the incident, which appears in Ferrari, *Reporting America at War,* 133–46.

34. Halberstam, *Powers That Be,* 490. For that book, Halberstam interviewed both Stanton and Safer.

35. Tifft and Jones, *The Trust,* 468.

36. The stock never made much money for the outside investors, a situation that has led to chronic unrest among the Class A stockholders and occasional threats to change the dual-stock arrangement. In recent years, as the stock's value has dropped sharply, the Sulzbergers agreed to offer non–family members more seats on the board while still retaining ultimate control.

37. For details, see Cranberg, Bezanson, and Soloski, *Taking Stock.*

38. Sarnoff retired from RCA in 1966. Luce began the process of retiring in 1964 but did not really leave Time Inc. until his sudden death in 1967. Paley held onto power at CBS until selling out to Laurence Tisch in 1986, but CBS had started to show signs much earlier of acting like a big public company, for example, becoming a conglomerate in the 1970s by acquiring publishing interests and even the New York Yankees baseball team, which CBS owned from 1964 to 1973.

39. For Luce, see Swanberg, *Luce and His Empire,* 481; for Paley, see Smith, *In All His Glory,* 611.

40. Quoted in Jane Howard, "A Six-Year Literary Vigil," *Life,* January 7, 1966, 70.

41. Her novel was published in July 1960 and won the Pulitzer Prize for fiction in 1961. She continued to help Capote with his work and was invited by the killers to witness their execution in 1965, but she declined. When *In Cold Blood* was published in 1966, Capote dedicated it to her (and to his lover, Jack Dunphy). After that point it appears that some sort of rift developed between Lee and Capote, although the details remain unclear. Lee has steadfastly avoided most interviews and avoided any autobiographical writing that might shed some light.

42. Perhaps the most extensive was a nine thousand–word Q-and-A that Capote did with the writer George Plimpton in the *New York Times Book Review* on January 16, 1966. Capote gives short shrift to anyone else, including John Hersey, and seeks to position himself as the promethean progenitor of a new genre, much as Tom Wolfe would also do.

43. Capote was quoted by *Life* magazine on the eve of the book's publication; see Howard, "A Six-Year Literary Vigil," 73.

44. See, for example, David Halberstam's comments in his introduction to the 1999 anthology *The Best American Sports Writing of the Century.*

45. Wolfe himself tried to define the movement in his influential 1973 essay "The New Journalism" in the anthology of the same name.

46. See Weingarten, *The Gang That Wouldn't Shoot Straight,* chap. 2.

47. Among the writers was Gail Sheehy, who wrote some fifty stories for *New York* and later married Felker. Felker's obituary appeared in the *New York Times* on July 2, 2008.

48. See Peck, *Uncovering the Sixties.*

49. McKeen, *Outlaw Journalist,* 34. I rely on McKeen's thorough account of Thompson's life and career throughout.

50. As she did in a wonderful piece that originally ran in *Show* magazine in 1963. The article appears in the 1983 anthology of her writings, *Outrageous Acts and Everyday Rebellions.*

51. See Giles and Snyder, *1968: Year of Media Decision;* and Gitlin, *The Whole World Is Watching.*

52. Hewitt, *Minute by Minute,* 27.

53. They were the first two of what turned into a revolving cast of talented TV journalists. The next to join, in 1970, was Morley Safer, the correspondent in the bush jacket who had reported from Vietnam about GIs using Zippos to burn down hootches.

54. Campbell, *60 Minutes and the News,* 2–3.

55. Johnson's remarks can be found on the website of the Corporation for Public Broadcasting, www.cpb.org/aboutpb/act/remarks.html.

56. According to a recent examination of the coverage, there was only a single documented report of bra-burning, a story that appeared in a nearby New Jersey newspaper. A few days after the event the humorist Art Buchwald seized on the image in his syndicated column, and thus was launched the myth that bra-burning was a widespread phenomenon. See Campbell, *Getting It Wrong.*

57. This discussion is based on Heilbrun, *The Education of a Woman;* Marcello, *Gloria Steinem;* Thom, *Inside Ms.;* Farrell, *Yours in Sisterhood;* Steinem, *Outrageous Acts and Everyday Rebellions* and *Revolution from Within;* and Fishel, *Sisters,* chap. 6.

58. "I Was a Playboy Bunny" originally appeared in *Show* magazine in 1963 and was later collected in Steinem's anthology *Outrageous Acts and Everyday Rebellions.*

59. Quoted in Thom, *Inside Ms.,* 9.

60. *New York Times Book Review,* August 11, 1968, 8.

61. Thom, *Inside Ms.,* 14.

12. THE ESTABLISHMENT HOLDS, 1967–1974

1. Schanberg, "The Military and the Press."

2. Hoffman, *On Their Own,* 3. Also see Beasley and Gibbons, *Taking Their Place,* chap. 21.

3. Johnson's assessment comes from *Post* publisher Katharine Graham (*Personal History,* 400). She may have been too modest. According to historian Donald A. Ritchie, Johnson valued the *Post* editorials at two divisions (*Reporting from Washington,* 255). LBJ's comment is reminiscent of Lincoln's observation about Horace Greeley: "Having him firmly behind me will be as helpful as an army of 100,000 men" (see chapter 4).

4. Quoted in "The War: Cards on the Table," *Time,* May 5, 1967.

5. Associated Press, *Breaking News,* 246. This famous quote has taken on a life of its own and is often invoked as an encapsulation of the futility of the war in Vietnam, and, in some cases, war itself. Oddly, no other reporter heard the same statement, and it was the source of some grumbling among other reporters, who considered the line too good to be true. In light of all the evidence (including a brief period working alongside Arnett myself at the AP), I have no reason to question it.

6. Hammond, *Reporting Vietnam,* 113–14. Also see Faas, "The Saigon Execution."

7. Quoted in Knightley, *The First Casualty,* 436.

8. According to Cronkite, there was no immediate reaction from the White House. In his version of the famous and often cited incident, "the explanation came many months later, when we learned that the President was actually stunned by the broadcast. George Christian, the President's news secretary, and his assistant Bill Moyers, later to win fame on television, were present as the President and some of his staff watched the broadcast. 'The President flipped off the set,' Moyers recalled, 'and said: "If I've lost Cronkite, I've lost middle America."'" Cronkite, *A Reporter's Life,* 258. The problem is, Bill Moyers was not present. According to Moyers himself, it was Christian and a White House aide, Tom Johnson, who were present. Moyers confirmed this through a research assistant in private correspondence (which is available at my website). The source of the quote, though much repeated and paraphrased, thus remains a bit of a mystery. Also see Dallek, *Flawed Giant,* 506.

9. Dallek, *Flawed Giant,* 519–32.

10. For Hersh's first-person account, see "How I Broke the Mylai 4 Story."

11. Eszterhaz later became prominent for his role as an editor at *Rolling Stone.* When the magazine moved to New York City, Eszterhaz turned to screenwriting so he could stay in California. He is best known for the screenplay of the hit movie *Basic Instinct* (1992).

12. Quoted in Knightley, *The First Casualty,* 431.

13. Hammond, *Reporting Vietnam,* 190.
14. Ritchie, *Reporting from Washington,* 204.
15. Porter, *Assault on the Media,* 49.
16. Ibid., 50.
17. See Lewis, "The Myth of Spiro Agnew's 'Nattering Nabobs of Negativism.'"
18. *Washington Post,* September 25, 1968.
19. Halberstam, *Powers That Be,* 662.
20. The little girl survived, after seventeen operations. She later left Vietnam for Cuba, then defected to Canada and settled in Ontario. In 1997 she was named a UNESCO goodwill ambassador. See the article by AP Photo editor Horst Faas and Marianne Fulton, "A Young Girl's Cry for Help." Also, Kim Phuc's own version, "The Long Road to Forgiveness," is available as a transcript of an essay she created for NPR in 2008. She is the subject of a biography, *The Girl in the Picture,* by Denise Chong.
21. See Earl Caldwell's oral history in Wallace Terry's *Missing Pages,* as well as Caldwell's book *Black American Witness;* also Caldwell's 2006 interview with PBS's *Frontline* series for the program "News War." In addition, his own account of his beginnings can be found at the Maynard Institute's history project page, www.mije.org/black_journalists_movement/earl_caldwell. Also see "The Caldwell Journals."
22. Gene Roberts went on to have one of the most distinguished careers in U.S. journalism of the twentieth century. He left the *Times* to become executive editor of the *Philadelphia Inquirer.* There he led a team of talented reporters, including Mark Bowden, Richard Ben Cramer, and the investigative team of Jim Steele and Don Bartlett. The paper won seventeen Pulitzer Prizes in Roberts's eighteen years there. He returned to the *New York Times* as managing editor from 1994 to 1998. After that he became a professor of journalism at the University of Maryland. He also co-wrote the 2006 book *The Race Beat,* a landmark study of the coverage of the civil rights movement, which won a Pulitzer Prize.
23. *New York Times,* April 5, 1968.
24. Caldwell quoted in Terry, *Missing Pages,* 267.
25. Amsterdam argued the case that resulted in the Supreme Court's decision to strike down the death penalty, known as *Furman v. Georgia.* He later became a law professor at NYU. See Toobin, "Comeback."
26. All quotations are from *Branzburg v. Hayes* 408 U.S. 665 (1972).
27. Those guidelines contained several key provisions. First, prosecutors should make "all reasonable attempts" to get information from nonjournalistic sources. Second, prosecutors should subpoena journalists only when the information being sought is "essential" to the case. And finally, prosecutors should subpoena reporters only as a last resort, after they have unsuccessfully tried all other sources. The guidelines also provided, however, that prosecutors could ignore all those provisions in "emergencies and other unusual situations"—which is tantamount to saying, "Just do your best." See *Branzburg v. Hayes,* majority opinion, footnote 41.
28. Adam Liptak has argued in the *New York Times* that Powell's notes at the time of the *Branzburg* decision indicate that Powell believed there should be *some* kind of journalistic privilege, just not a constitutional one. (See Liptak, "A Justice Scribbles on Journalists' Rights.")
29. For a perceptive discussion of that jeopardy as it pertains to more recent cases, see Freedman, "Reconstructing Journalists' Privilege." The same issue of *Cardozo Law Review* in which Freedman's article appears presents a very valuable roundtable discussion chaired by Dean David Rudenstine of Cardozo Law School with panelists Anthony Lewis, former correspondent and columnist for the *New York Times* as well as an author of two books on First Amendment topics; Max Frankel, former correspondent and senior editor of the *Times;* and Victor Kovner, a litigator who represents media clients.
30. It should be noted that not all journalists support the idea of shield laws (including Caldwell himself). Some argue that there is no need for a shield law because the entire government is enjoined from interfering with the operations of a free press. Furthermore, if Congress begins passing legislation that affects journalism, even by doing something considered favorable, then the camel's nose is under the tent. Following this reasoning, some reporters favor waiting until *Branzburg* is reversed. In the meantime, that will almost certainly mean that reporters who seek to protect their confidential sources will be held in contempt and jailed. Thus, prosecutors and judges will be abridging the freedom of the press and trampling on the people's right to be informed. As for Caldwell, after the Supreme Court case, he left the *Times* to become a columnist, first at the *Washington Star,* then at the *New York Post.* He also served as host of a long-

running weekly radio program on WBAI radio in New York. In 1977, Caldwell co-founded the Institute for Journalism Education, which trains minority journalists. It is now known as the Maynard Institute for its other co-founder, Robert C. Maynard.

31. This section is based on the masterly account of the Pentagon Papers by law professor David Rudenstine, *The Day the Presses Stopped*. Also essential are secondary sources including Halberstam, *Powers That Be*, 564–86; Stone, *Perilous Times*, 500–525; Tifft and Jones, *The Trust*, chap. 32; Ritchie, *Reporting from Washington*, 254–57; and Ungar, *The Papers and the Papers*. In addition, several of the principals have written memoirs of the case. The most detailed is Ellsberg's *Secrets*. Also valuable are the relevant portions of Graham, *Personal History*; Bradlee, *A Good Life*; and Frankel, *The Times of My Life*. In addition to the court rulings in the case, the briefs (including the "secret brief" made available by the National Security Archives) also proved indispensable. For an excellent collection of documents and analysis, see the National Security Archive website devoted to the case, edited by Tom Blanton, www.gwu.edu/~nsarchiv/NSAEBB/NSAEBB48/. Also see Abrams, "The Pentagon Papers a Decade Later."

32. Ellsberg, *Secrets*, 303.

33. Others included the main authors, Morton Halperin and Leslie Gelb.

34. Rudenstine, *The Day the Presses Stopped*, 2.

35. Ellsberg, *Secrets*, chap. 26.

36. Max Frankel, who was the Washington bureau chief at the time and thus Sheehan's immediate boss, recalls that the sum was $2,000. See Frankel, *The Times of My Life*, 325.

37. According to Max Frankel: "Neil was never *given* the material, and Ellsberg never *authorized* its duplication. This was not the kind of deal anticipated in Journalism 101, but it was hardly shocking to me and other reporters who had often trafficked in top secret military and diplomatic information." See Rudenstine, *The Day the Presses Stopped*, 53.

38. Halberstam, *Powers That Be*, 565–86.

39. At one meeting Loeb was accompanied by another of his firm's senior partners, Herbert Brownell, who had been attorney general under Eisenhower and who had drafted the executive order that established the federal system for classifying information. Brownell warned Sulzberger that he would probably go to jail.

40. When he retired in October 1997, after thirty-four years of publishing the *Times*, Sulzberger was asked what had been his toughest decision. Without hesitation, he said it had been the Pentagon Papers case.

41. Transcripts of Nixon's telephone conversations are available at www.gwu.edu/~nsarchiv/NSAEBB/NSAEBB48/transcript.pdf.

42. Quoted in Frankel, *The Times of My Life*, 335.

43. According to the tape recordings of Nixon's phone call to Mitchell on June 15, the attorney general and the president were feeling confident.

> MITCHELL: "We got a good judge on it—uh, Murray Gurfein. . . ."
> NIXON: "I know him well—smart as hell."
> MITCHELL: "Yeah, and—uh, he's new, and—he's appreciative, so . . . "
> NIXON: [laughing] "Good!"
> MITCHELL: "We ought to work it out."

44. For Ellsberg's account, see *Secrets*, chap. 32.

45. In the end, the stock offering went ahead, along lines similar to those used by the *Times* in 1969. The *Post* offered about 1 million Class A shares, which were all owned by members of the Graham family, and about 10 million Class B shares, which could be bought by the public. Two years later a big chunk of the Class B shares was bought by investor Warren Buffett, who became an important friend and adviser to Kay Graham. The date of the initial public offering was June 15, 1971, the day before Bagdikian got his copy of the Pentagon Papers.

46. Graham, *Personal History*, 450. In this trial by fire, many see the forging of an important bond of trust and mutual respect between Kay Graham and Ben Bradlee that would help them through the Watergate crisis a year later.

47. Quoted in Rudenstine, *The Day the Presses Stopped*, 143.

48. Quoted ibid., 172.

49. All references are to *New York Times v. United States*, 403 U.S. 713 (1971).

50. The most notable exception came in 1979, when the government attempted to stop a magazine called *The Progressive* from printing what the magazine called "the H-Bomb Secret." Citing the

standard for prior restraint articulated in the Pentagon Papers case, the federal judge in the *Progressive* case ruled that the government had met its burden of showing "grave, direct, immediate and irreparable harm to the United States" and granted a temporary restraining order. While the case was pending, however, others published details about H-bomb construction, forcing the government to drop its case against *The Progressive* on the grounds that it was now moot because the secrets were tumbling out in a variety of public forums. See De Volpi, *Born Secret*.

51. See Arthur Gelb, *City Room*, 563–64; Ellsberg, *Secrets*, 393–94. Zion had left the *Times* in 1970 to found *Scanlan's Monthly* magazine.

52. Quoted in Ellsberg, *Secrets*, 432.

53. Quoted ibid., 456.

54. Erwin Griswold, who, as the solicitor general of the United States in 1971, had argued the government's side in the Pentagon Papers before the Supreme Court, may deserve the last word. Writing an op-ed essay in 1989 (in, of all places, the *Washington Post*), Griswold observed:

> I have never seen any trace of a threat to the national security from the publication. Indeed, I have never seen it even suggested that there was such an actual threat. . . . It quickly becomes apparent to any person who has considerable experience with classified material that there is massive overclassification and that the principal concern of the classifiers is not with national security, but rather with governmental embarrassment of one sort or another. There may be some basis for short-term classification while plans are being made, or negotiations are going on, but apart from details of weapons systems, there is very rarely any real risk to current national security from the publication of facts relating to transactions in the past, even the fairly recent past. This is the lesson of the Pentagon Papers experience, and it may be relevant now. (*Washington Post*, February 15, 1989.)

55. The following section is based on Katharine Graham's memoir, *Personal History*, as well as Halberstam's *Powers That Be*, chaps. 5, 9, 13, 19, 22, 24, 26, 29 and 33. Also helpful was Chalmers Roberts' *The Washington Post: The First 100 Years*.

56. While Agnes was still deciding on her future, she announced to her parents that she planned to become a newspaper reporter. "My mother wept," she recalled later, "and my father said solemnly, 'I would rather see you dead.'" Graham, *Personal History*, 14.

57. See Graham, *Personal History*, 245–47.

58. Bradley, *Women and the Press*, chaps. 7–8.

59. Roberts, *The Washington Post*. 379.

60. Graham, *Personal History*, 391, 394.

61. *Washington Post*, August 9, 1968.

62. This discussion is based on Carl Bernstein and Bob Woodward, *All the President's Men;* Woodward and Bernstein, *The Final Days;* Woodward, *The Secret Man;* Graham, *Personal History*, chaps. 23–24; Bradlee, *A Good Life*, chap. 14; Halberstam, *Powers That Be*, chap. 24; Dean, *Blind Ambition;* as well as extensive tapes from the Nixon Oval Office, which can be found, inter alia, in Kutler, *Abuse of Power*. In addition, the *Post* has compiled the paper's complete coverage in a special report on its website, www.washingtonpost.com/national/special-reports.

63. Graham, *Personal History*, 460. Bradlee now held the title of executive editor.

64. Lewis knew his way around the police beat. He had been the *Post's* night police reporter since the 1930s—before Woodward was even born. The *Times* and other national publications with Washington bureaus had no one with comparable knowledge of Washington's local institutions. That would be a great advantage for the *Post* on the Watergate story.

65. Bernstein and Woodward, *All the President's Men*, 26.

66. This account is based on transcripts of conversations held in the Oval Office and taped by Nixon's secret recording system. See Kutler, *Abuse of Power*, 43–186.

67. Bernstein and Woodward, *All the President's Men*, 57.

68. Ibid., 105.

69. Henry Kissinger was a notorious leaker. Eventually, Nixon had Kissinger's phone tapped to try to catch him in the act. See Kutler, *Abuse of Power*, 191.

70. See Woodward's 2005 account, *The Secret Man*.

71. Ibid., 70–71. The line was probably written by the screenwriter William Goldman, who wrote such landmark films of the 1960s and 1970s as *Butch Cassidy and the Sundance Kid* and *Marathon Man,* as well as *All the President's Men.* He explicitly claimed credit for the line in 2005, at the time of the identification of Mark Felt as the real Deep Throat. Goldman called *New York Times* columnist Frank Rich to discuss it. See *New York Times,* "Week in Review" section, June 12, 2005.

72. For a detailed description of the political press corps during the 1972 election campaign, see Crouse, *The Boys on the Bus.*

73. They included a young Yale Law School grad, Hillary Rodham, who served on the House Judiciary Committee staff while it was considering impeachment.

74. Bradlee, *A Good Life,* 352. For Halberstam's version of how Bradlee engineered the final result, see Halberstam, *Powers That Be,* 709–10.

75. Bradlee, *A Good Life,* 362.

76. Set in 168-point type, it was the biggest headline the paper had run since the death of Stalin in 1953.

77. Graham, *Personal History,* 496.

78. Liebovich, *Richard Nixon, Watergate, and the Press,* Appendix 2.

13. BIG MEDIA GET BIGGER, 1980–1999

1. See the groundbreaking research by Kiku Adatto, summarized in "The Incredible Shrinking Sound Bite." On the origins of the phrase, see Safire, "On Language."

2. These comments are taken from Coll's testimony before the U.S. Senate Committee on Commerce, Science, and Transportation, May 6, 2009, http://commerce.senate.gov/public/?a=Files. Serve&File_id=0330b270-52b7-4938-9d81-c55318a4194d.

3. Quoted in Neuharth, *Confessions of an S.O.B.,* 178.

4. Ibid., 122.

5. Ibid., 130.

6. Bagdikian, *The New Media Monopoly,* 85.

7. Quoted in "At 25, 'McPaper' Is All Grown Up," *New York Times,* September 17, 2007.

8. The milestone can be found at the *Times'* own handy (if sanitized) timeline of company history, www.nytco.com/company/milestones/timeline_1971.html.

9. Neuharth, *Confessions of an S.O.B.,* 156.

10. Hartman, *The USA Today Way,* 8. The total of losses may have been even higher. Some analysts, including Hartman, assert that *USA Today* continued to lose several million dollars a year through the early 1990s, making it a continuing drag on Gannett.

11. That seems to be the real reason why Ted Turner left Brown, not the often-cited girl in his room. Turner says that once he knew he was leaving, he decided to break the 1950s-era no-girls rule, on the grounds that Brown could not punish him further. Turner, *Call Me Ted,* 40.

12. In researching CNN, I found the following sources useful: Auletta, *Media Man;* Whittemore, *CNN: The Inside Story;* Turner, *Call Me Ted;* Schonfeld, *Me and Ted against the World;* and Hack, *Clash of the Titans.* Also, there are of course numerous newspaper and magazine articles about CNN and profiles of Ted Turner. Regrettably, CNN, like all broadcast news organizations, has done a poor job of archiving its historical broadcasts.

13. Whittemore, *CNN: The Inside Story,* 27–28.

14. See Turner's own account in *Call Me Ted,* 159.

15. Whittemore, *CNN: The Inside Story,* 36.

16. See Matusow, *The Evening Stars.*

17. See Turner, *Call Me Ted,* especially chaps. 11–16.

18. Whittemore, *CNN: The Inside Story,* 231.

19. Ibid., 156.

20. Ibid., 260.

21. Ibid., 300.

22. Auletta, *Media Man,* 53.

23. It was then that he decided to leave reporting. Baker, *The Good Times,* 336.

24. Quoted in Whittemore, *CNN: The Inside Story,* 301.

25. *New York Times,* January 29, 1991.

26. For ownership figures, see the Project for Excellence in Journalism's annual report for 2010, "The State of the News Media," www.stateofthemedia.org/2010/media-ownership/sector_audio.php.

27. Cited in Seib, *Rush Hour,* 14.

28. Ibid., 53.

29. Ibid.

30. Quoted in Hack, *Clash of the Titans,* 9–10.

31. David Carr, "When Even Condé Nast Is in Retreat."

32. There are several versions of this encounter. See Auletta, *Backstory,* 264 (the source of the Nixon quote in the text); and Perlstein, *Nixonland,* 234–35.

33. Auletta, *Backstory,* 251.

34. Hack, *Clash of the Titans,* 9–10.

35. Quotes can be found at the website of Media Matters for America, http://mediamatters.org/research/200407140002. Also see the documentary film *Outfoxed* (dir. Robert Greenwald, 2004, Carolina Productions). I have edited the excerpts from Moody's memos slightly to make them more readable.

36. Brock, *Republican Noise Machine,* 343. No such rules appear to apply, however, when a Democrat is the commander in chief. President Obama pursued two wars launched by his predecessor, and O'Reilly routinely second-guessed and criticized the president, his top generals, and the overall war effort in Afghanistan and Iraq. For more on O'Reilly and his methods, see, for example, Conway et al., "Villains, Victims and the Virtuous in Bill O'Reilly's 'No-Spin Zone.'"

37. Full results of the study are available at the PIPA website, www.pipa.org/OnlineReports/Iraq/IraqMedia_Oct03/IraqMedia_Oct03_rpt.pdf. The study was also published, in expanded form, in *Political Science Quarterly* 118, no. 4 (Winter 2003–4): 569–98.

38. See http://historymatters.gmu.edu/d/6553.

39. See the ASNE annual newsroom census, http://asne.org/key_initiatives/diversity/newsroom_census.aspx.

40. See Johnson's obituary in the *New York Times,* August 9, 2005.

41. In November 2009, Winfrey, battling tears, announced that she had decided to terminate her television program as of September 2011, after twenty-five years on the air. She also announced that she planned to start a new talk show on the television channel OWN, the Oprah Winfrey Network, which she co-owns with Discovery Communication.

42. This sketch is based primarily on "Oprah Winfrey, the Tycoon," the chapter about Winfrey written by Juliet E. K. Walker for the book *Black Business and Economic Power,* as well as numerous profiles of Winfrey that have appeared in the popular press, as well as several articles in the trade press.

43. Quotation comes from an interview with Winfrey that appears on the Academy of Achievement website, www.achievement.org/autodoc/page/winoint-1.

44. Lowe, *Oprah Winfrey Speaks,* 32.

45. See Podhoretz, "The Old Time and the New Newsweek."

46. Actually, GE was *repurchasing* RCA, which GE had originally organized around the time of World War I. In the 1980s, GE split up the old RCA and sold off most divisions, except for NBC. In January 2011 the FCC approved a merger between NBC and Comcast (a major provider of cable television and internet service), giving Comcast majority ownership of the network.

47. For details, see Emery, Emery, and Roberts, *The Press and America,* 554.

48. See Auletta, *Media Man,* 109.

49. See Bagdikian, *New Media Monopoly,* 218–20.

50. Carr, "When Even Condé Nast Is in Retreat."

51. See the *New Yorker*'s own timeline, www.newyorker.com/magazine/timeline.

52. Details appear in the CPB annual reports, www.cpb.org/aboutpb/.

53. Bagdikian, *New Media Monopoly,* 185.

54. Klein, *No Logo,* 170–71.

55. According to *Ad Age,* the following five large newspaper companies all hit bottom in a four-month period at the end of 2008 and the start of 2009.

   - Tribune Company. Real estate mogul Sam Zell led a deal to buy Tribune Company, including the *Chicago Tribune, Los Angeles Times,* and other properties, for $13.8 billion in December 2007. Loaded with debt in a weak market, Tribune filed for Chapter 11 bankruptcy reorganization in December 2008.
   - Star Tribune Company. Avista Capital Partners, a private-equity firm, bought the Star Tribune Company of Minneapolis in March 2007 from McClatchy Co. for $530 million, a huge drop from the $1.2 billion McClatchy paid for the paper in 1998. The Avista deal left the *Star Tribune* with a pile of debt; a bad economy and the weak-

ening newspaper market made things worse. The newspaper filed for bankruptcy reorganization January 15, 2009.

- Journal Register Company. Owner of the *New Haven Register* and other papers, Journal Register went public in 1997 and grew through acquisitions. It too ended up laden with debt in a shrinking industry. Journal Register filed for Chapter 11 on February 21, 2009.

- Philadelphia Media Holdings. Led by local PR and advertising veteran Brian Tierney, Philadelphia Media bought the *Philadelphia Inquirer* and *Philadelphia Daily News* in June 2006 for $562 million from McClatchy, which sold the papers as part of McClatchy's acquisition of Knight Ridder. Burdened by $390 million in debt and shrinking revenue, Philadelphia Newspapers (Philadelphia Media Holdings) filed for Chapter 11 reorganization February 22, 2009.

- Sun-Times Media Group. Formerly Hollinger International, the Sun-Times group published the *Sun-Times* and community newspapers in Chicago. Former CEO Conrad Black was sentenced to prison in July 2007 for his role in defrauding shareholders and pocketing cash. The *Sun-Times* filed for Chapter 11 reorganization March 31, 2009.

- *Source:* Ad Age, *June 2009, http://adage.com/article/mediaworks/york-times-business -2012 /137628/.*

56. The *Christian Science Monitor* was one of the first to do so, in 2009.
57. The famous quotation from Stewart Brand (the visionary founder of *The Whole Earth Catalog,* and, later, the early Internet forum the WELL) that appears at the head of this chapter is often cited in a misleading way, as if Brand had said only that "information wants to be free." As can be seen from the full quote, that was only half of his meaning. See Brand, *The Media Lab,* 202.

14. GOING DIGITAL, 1995–

1. There is a distinction that is worth noting between the Internet and the Web. The Internet is a broader domain that encompasses all of the *inter*connected *net*works that link computers. It includes the Web as well as other functions such as e-mail, online chatting, and online gaming. The Web is that part of the Internet that uses hypertext to present linked, graphically rich pages. If you are using a browser, you are on the Web. For purposes of this discussion, however, the distinction is immaterial, so I use the terms interchangeably.
2. Quoted in Rosenberg, *Say Everything,* 51.
3. I am indebted for many of these ideas about the PC and the Internet to Jonathan Zittrain and his book *The Future of the Internet—And How to Stop It,* in which he argues that these are, crucially, what he calls "generative" technologies, whose end uses are not predetermined. Unlike what he calls "tethered appliances," the PC has a multitude of possible uses, including many that were never envisioned by its inventors or its manufacturers. It is also important to note that the "constitutive" decisions about the Internet resulted in an architecture that has no central administrator.
4. See Shirky, "Newspapers and Thinking the Unthinkable," on the smashing of the printing business model that prevailed from Gutenberg's time until about the year 2000.
5. See Wikipedia's "List of Defunct Department Stores of the United States," http://en.wikipedia. org/wiki/List_of_defunct_department_stores_of_the_United_States.
6. This phrase was coined by Jay Rosen in a famous essay posted on his website Pressthink in 2006; see http://journalism.nyu.edu/pubzone/weblogs/pressthink/2006/06/27/ppl_frmr.html.
7. See the NOAA website on lightning, www.lightningsafety.noaa.gov/medical.htm.
8. The word "blog" is a shortened form "weblog," which was coined by Jorn Barger in 1997. "Blog" itself was apparently first used (as a verb) by Peter Merholz on his site Peterme.com in 1999, and the noun form quickly followed. See Rosenberg, *Say Everything,* 101–2.
9. There is a debate over identifying the "first blog" that, ironically, recapitulates many of the features of the debate over the "first newspaper" about three centuries earlier. In both cases, much depends on definitions. Is "first" the same as "oldest," or does it mean the "oldest continuous"? What criteria are essential? Does a blog have to be organized by reverse chronology? Does it have to include links? Does it have to allow comments? Or, to go back a step, does a mass e-mail count? Isn't that the equivalent of the handwritten "newsletters" that some postmasters circulated among acquaintances before turning to printing? For a thorough discussion of the earliest bloggers, including the pioneering roles played by Justin Hall and Jorn Barger, see Rosenberg, *Say Everything,* chaps. 1–3.

10. Dave Winer, "Jay, I didn't ask if blogging is journalism," posting on the BloggerCon website, April 16, 2004, www.bloggercon.org/2004/04/16.

11. These can still be found online at http://scripting.com/davenet/index.html#y1994.

12. Winer explained his views in some detail, including a thorough technical discussion, in a forum hosted by the Berkman Center for Internet & Society in 2003. See http://blogs.law.harvard.edu/whatmakesaweblogaweblog.html. Later, Winer played a major role in the development of a technology intended to help users deal with the proliferation of websites, called "really simple syndication," or RSS. The idea was to allow anyone to designate certain blogs or websites as being of interest. The RSS software would note your list, then check those sites regularly and alert you when one of them had something new. That way you did not have to troll through each site every day looking for new postings.

13. For an account of the founding of Salon written by one of the original staffers, Gary Kamiya, see "Ten Years of Salon."

14. Under publisher Will Hearst, a descendant of William Randolph Hearst himself.

15. Kamiya, "Ten Years of Salon."

16. For quotation and this account in general, see Kinsley, "My History of Slate." Kinsley left Slate in 2002 and later became editor of the Los Angeles Times editorial page for a brief period, then became a contributor to Time. Microsoft spun Slate off, and it ended up in the Washington Post Company.

17. McAdams, "Inventing an Online Newspaper," 84.

18. See Carr, "Digital Ink Reboots." Also see McAdams's plan, www.helsinki.fi/science/optek/1995/n3/mcadams.txt. Essential as well is Gillmor, We the Media.

19. Now there is an online "museum" featuring artifacts from the Pathfinder era, www.disobey.com/ghostsites/pathfindermuseum/index.shtml. The actual screen can still be found at www.pathfinder.com/pathfinder/index.html.

20. For a different view, see Boczkowski, Digitizing the News, which documents dozens of early efforts by newspapers to migrate to the Web. Many of them bet on the wrong horses (either videotex or the proprietary online services like AOL or Compuserve). Also see Shafer, "How Newspapers Tried to Invent the Web, But Failed," which adds some analysis and other views to Boczkowski's analysis.

21. See Schumpeter's classic Capitalism, Socialism, and Democracy.

22. See Palfrey and Gasser, Born Digital, for a definition and discussion of the implications for mass media as well as other fields.

23. The rankings were based on findings by Nielsen Online, which measures "users"—that is, readers or viewers—in terms of the number of different human beings who visit a given website in a given period. The data are vital not only for measuring the reach of a particular website but also (in most cases) for determining advertising rates. Associated Press, April 26, 2010.

24. For background on Marshall, I am indebted to the following sources: Glenn, "The (Josh) Marshall Plan"; profiles in the New York Times and other media; articles at TPM about the organization; and the George Polk Awards site, www.brooklyn.liu.edu/polk/press/2007.html.

25. See Calderone, "Growing Pains for Talking Points Memo." The article cites figures from Google Analytics.

26. From Marshall's speech to the "Berkman @ 10" conference, Harvard Law School, May 16, 2008, http://cyber.law.harvard.edu/interactive/events/conferences/2008/05/joshuamarshall.

CONCLUSION

1. See, for example, Michael Hirschorn's essay "End Times" in the Atlantic (January/February 2009): 41–44. The idea of the end of journalism even merited an international conference at the University of Bedfordshire in England in October 2008. See http://theendofjournalism.wikidot.com.

2. As Michael Kinsley, the editor of the online magazine Slate, put it: "If you're self-supporting, you can say 'fuck you' to anyone, which is one important function of a magazine on almost any subject and in any medium." See Kinsley, "My History of Slate."

3. For a recent attempt by scholars to develop a consensus about a journalism canon, see Chapman and King, "A 'Dozen Best' Essential Readings in Journalism."

4. Books like The AP Stylebook, The Elements of Journalism by Bill Kovach and Tom Rosensteil, and The Elements of Style by Strunk and White are all nearly universal.

Bibliography

Abrams, Floyd. "The Pentagon Papers a Decade Later." *New York Times Magazine,* June 7, 1981, 22–25, 72–95.

Academy of Achievement. "Oprah Winfrey." www.achievement.org/autodoc/pagewinoint-1.

Adams, John. *Papers of John Adams.* Vols. 1 and 2. Cambridge: Belknap Press of Harvard University Press, 1977.

Adatto, Kiku. "The Incredible Shrinking Sound Bite." *New Republic,* May 28, 1990, 20–23.

American Society of Newspaper Editors. "Newsroom Census." http://asne.org/key_initiatives /diversity/newsroom_census.aspx.

Andrews, J. Cutler. *The North Reports the Civil War.* Pittsburgh: University of Pittsburgh Press, 1955.

Arnett, Peter. *Live from the Battlefield: From Vietnam to Baghdad, 35 Years in the World's War Zones.* New York: Simon & Schuster, 1995.

Associated Press. *Breaking News: How The Associated Press Has Covered War, Peace, and Everything Else.* New York: Princeton Architectural Press, 2007.

Auletta, Ken. *Backstory: Inside the Business of News.* New York: Penguin Press, 2003.

———. *Media Man: Ted Turner's Improbable Empire.* New York: Norton, 2004.

Bagdikian, Ben. *The New Media Monopoly.* Boston: Beacon Press, 2004.

Bailyn, Bernard. *The Ideological Origins of the American Revolution.* Cambridge: Harvard University Press, 1967.

Bailyn, Bernard, and John B. Hench, eds. *The Press and the American Revolution.* Worcester, Mass.: American Antiquarian Society, 1980.

Baker, Nicholson, and Margaret Brentano. *The World on Sunday: Graphic Art in Joseph Pulitzer's Newspaper, 1898–1911.* New York: Bulfinch Press, 2005.

Baker, Ray Stannard. *American Chronicle: The Autobiography of Ray Stannard Baker.* New York: Scribner's Sons, 1945.

Baker, Russell. *The Good Times.* New York: William Morrow, 1989.

Baldasty, Gerald. *The Commercialization of News in the Nineteenth Century.* Madison: University of Wisconsin Press, 1992.

Banning, Stephen A. "The Cradle of Professional Journalistic Education in the Mid-Nineteenth Century." *Media History Monographs* 4, no. 1 (2000–2001). www.scripps .ohiou.edu/mediahistory/mhmjour4-1.htm.

Barnouw, Erik. *A History of Broadcasting in the United States.* Vol. 1. *A Tower in Babel: To 1933.* New York: Oxford University Press, 1966.

———. *A History of Broadcasting in the United States.* Vol. 2. *The Golden Web: 1933–1953.* New York: Oxford University Press, 1968.

———. *A History of Broadcasting in the United States.* Vol. 3. *The Image Empire: From 1953.* New York: Oxford University Press, 1970.

Barton, C. V. "Speech." *The Journalist* 17, no. 7 (April 22, 1893): 4.

Bayley, Edwin R. *Joe McCarthy and the Press.* New York: Pantheon, 1981.

Beasley, Maurine H., and Sheila J. Gibbons. *Taking Their Place: A Documentary History of Women and Journalism.* 2nd ed. State College, Pa.: Strata Publishing, 2003.

Bernays, Edward. *Biography of an Idea: Memoirs of a Public Relations Counsel.* New York: Simon and Schuster, 1965.

———. *Propaganda.* New York: Liveright, 1928.

Bernstein, Carl. "The CIA and the Media." *Rolling Stone,* October 20, 1977, 55–77.

Bernstein, Carl, and Bob Woodward. *All the President's Men.* New York: Simon & Schuster, 1974.

Bernstein, Mark, and Alex Lubertozzi. *World War II on the Air: Edward R. Murrow and the Broadcasts That Riveted a Nation.* Naperville, Ill.: Sourcebooks, 2003.

Blanton, Tom, ed. "The Pentagon Papers: Secrets, Lies and Audiotapes." National Security Archive Electronic Briefing Book. www.gwu.edu/%7Ensarchiv/NSAEBB/NSAEBB48/.

Bleyer, Willard Grosvenor. *Main Currents in the History of American Journalism.* Boston: Houghton Mifflin, 1927.

Blondheim, Menahem. *News over the Wires: The Telegraph and the Flow of Public Information in America, 1844–1896.* Cambridge: Harvard University Press, 1994.

———. "'Public Sentiment Is Everything': The Union's Public Communications Strategy and the Bogus Proclamation of 1864." *Journal of American History* 89, no. 3 (2002): 869–99.

Blum, John Morton. Introduction. In *Public Philosopher: Selected Letters of Walter Lippmann.* New York: Ticknor & Fields, 1985. vii–xxi.

———. *V Was for Victory: Politics and American Culture during World War II.* New York: Harcourt, 1976.

Blumenthal, Sidney. "Journalism and Its Discontents." Afterword to Walter Lippmann, *Liberty and the News.* Princeton: Princeton University Press, 2007. 63–89.

Bly, Nellie. *Ten Days in a Madhouse.* http://digital.library.upenn.edu/women/bly/madhouse/madhouse.html.

Boczkowski, Pablo J. *Digitizing the News: Innovation in Online Newspapers.* Cambridge: MIT Press, 2004.

Borden, Morton, ed. *The Antifederalist Papers.* East Lansing: Michigan State University Press, 1965.

Boylan, James. *Pulitzer's School: Columbia University's School of Journalism, 1903–2003.* New York: Columbia University Press, 2003.

Bradlee, Ben. *A Good Life: Newspapering and Other Adventures.* New York: Simon & Schuster, 1995.

Bradley, James, with Ron Powers. *Flags of Our Fathers.* New York: Bantam Books, 2000.

Bradley, Patricia. *Women and the Press: The Struggle for Equality.* Evanston: Northwestern University Press, 2005.

Brand, Stewart. *The Media Lab: Inventing the Future at MIT.* New York: Viking, 1987.

Brands, H. W. *The First American: The Life and Times of Benjamin Franklin.* New York: Doubleday, 2000.

Brian, Denis. *Pulitzer: A Life.* New York: John Wiley, 2001.

Brinkley, Alan. *The Publisher: Henry Luce and His American Century.* New York: Alfred A. Knopf, 2010.

Brock, David. *The Republican Noise Machine: Right-Wing Media and How It Corrupts Democracy.* New York: Crown Publishers, 2004.

Browne, Malcolm. *Muddy Boots and Red Socks: A Reporter's Life.* New York: Times Books, 1993.

Burns, Eric. *Infamous Scribblers: The Founding Fathers and the Rowdy Beginnings of American Journalism.* New York: Public Affairs, 2006.

Byrne, C. A. Editorial. *The Journalist* 1, no. 1 (March 1884): 7.

Cain, William E., ed. *William Lloyd Garrison and the Fight against Slavery: Selections from The Liberator.* Boston: Bedford Books of St. Martin's Press, 1995.

Calderone, Michael. "Growing Pains for Talking Points." Politico.com. May 2, 2009. www.politico.com/news/stories/0409/21965.html.

Caldwell, Earl. *Black American Witness: Reports from the Front.* Washington, D.C.: Lion House Publishing, 1994.

———. "The Caldwell Journals." Maynard Institute Oral History Project. http://mije.org/historyproject/caldwell_journals.

———. Interview on *Frontline*. July 6, 2006. www.pbs.org/wgbh/pages/frontline/newswar/interviews/caldwell.html.

Campbell, Richard. *60 Minutes and the News: A Mythology for Middle America.* Chicago: University of Illinois Press, 1991.

Campbell, W. Joseph. *Getting It Wrong: Ten of the Greatest Misreported Stories in American Journalism.* Berkeley: University of California Press, 2010.

———. *The Year That Defined American Journalism: 1897 and the Clash of Paradigms.* New York: Routledge, 2006.

———. *Yellow Journalism: Puncturing the Myths, Defining the Legacies.* Westport, Conn.: Praeger, 2001.

Carey, James. *James Carey: A Critical Reader.* Edited by Eve Stryker Munson and Catherine A. Warren. Minneapolis: University of Minnesota Press, 1997.

Carr, David. "Digital Ink Reboots." *Washington City Paper,* February 16, 1996. www.washingtoncitypaper.com/articles/9814/digital-ink-reboots.

———. "When Even Condé Nast Is in Retreat." *New York Times,* February 2, 2009.

Chafee, Zechariah, Jr. *Freedom of Speech.* New York: Harcourt, Brace and Howe, 1920.

Chapman, Jane, and Elliot King, "A 'Dozen Best' Essential Readings in Journalism." *American Journalism* 26, no. 3 (Summer 2009): 168–83.

Chong, Denise. *The Girl in the Picture: The Story of Kim Phuc, the Photograph, and the Vietnam War.* New York: Viking, 2000.

Christie, Thomas B., and Andrew M. Clark. "Framing Two Enemies in Mass Media: A Content Analysis of U.S. Government Influence in American Film during World War II." *American Journalism* 25, no. 1 (2008): 55–72.

Clark, Charles E. "The Newspapers of Provincial America." In *Three Hundred Years of the American Newspaper.* Worcester, Mass.: American Antiquarian Society, 1991. 367–89.

———. *The Public Prints: The Newspaper in Anglo-American Culture, 1665–1740.* New York: Oxford University Press, 1994.

Cloud, Stanley, and Lynne Olson. *The Murrow Boys: Pioneers on the Front Lines of Broadcast Journalism.* New York: Mariner Books, 1996.

Collins, Gail. *Scorpion Tongues: Gossip, Celebrity, and American Politics.* New York: William Morrow, 1998.

The Complete New Yorker. 8 DVD set. New York: Random House, 2005.

Conway, Mike, et al. "Villains, Victims and the Virtuous in Bill O'Reilly's 'No-Spin Zone': Revisiting World War Propaganda Techniques." *Journalism Studies* 8, no. 2 (2007): 197–223.

Cook, Adrian. *The Armies of the Streets: The New York City Draft Riots of 1863.* Lexington: University Press of Kentucky, 1974.

Corporation for Public Broadcasting. "Annual Report." 2010. www.cpb.org/aboutpb/.

Cranberg, Gilbert, Randall Bezanson, and John Soloski. *Taking Stock: Journalism and the Publicly Traded Newspaper Company.* Ames: Iowa State University Press, 2001.

Creel, George. *How We Advertised America: The First Telling of the Amazing Story of the Committee on Public Information That Carried the Gospel of Americanism to Every Corner of the Globe.* New York: Harper & Bros., 1920.

Creelman, James. *On the Great Highway: The Wanderings and Adventures of a Special Correspondent*. Boston: Lothrop Publishing Co., 1901.

Cronkite, Walter. *A Reporter's Life*. New York: Knopf, 2006.

Crouse, Timothy. *The Boys on the Bus*. New York: Random House, 1972.

Crouthamel, James L. "Beach, Moses Yale." American National Biography Online. February 2000. www.anb.org.

———. *Bennett's* New York Herald *and the Rise of the Popular Press*. Syracuse: Syracuse University Press, 1989.

Crowley, David, and Paul Heyer, eds. *Communication in History: Technology, Culture, Society*. 5th ed. Boston: Pearson Education, 2007.

Cunningham, Ed. "The Battle of the Bulge." *Yank*, March 2, 1945.

Dallek, Robert. *Flawed Giant: Lyndon Johnson and His Times, 1961–1973*. New York: Oxford University Press, 1998.

Daniel, Marcus. *Scandal and Civility: Journalism and the Birth of American Democracy*. New York: Oxford University Press, 2009.

Dean, John. *Blind Ambition*. New York: Simon & Schuster, 1976.

Dershowitz, Alan. "Shouting 'Fire!'" *Atlantic Monthly*, January 1989, 72.

De Volpi, Alexander. *Born Secret: The H-Bomb, the Progressive Case, and National Security*. New York: Pergamon Press, 1981.

Dewey, John. "Review of *Public Opinion*." *New Republic*, May 3, 1922, 286–88.

Dillon, Merton L. "Lovejoy: Elijah Parish." American National Biography Online. February 2000. www.anb.org.

Doherty, Thomas. *Cold War, Cool Medium: Television, McCarthyism, and American Culture*. New York: Columbia University Press, 2003.

Douglass, Frederick. *Narrative of the Life of an American Slave* (1845), *My Bondage and My Freedom* (1855), *Life and Times of Frederick Douglass* (1893). Reprinted in one volume. New York: Library of America, 1994.

Dunne, Finley Peter. *Observations by Mr. Dooley*. New York: Harper & Brothers, 1902.

Durey, Michael J. "Callender, James Thomson." American National Biography Online. February 2000. www.anb.org.

Ellsberg, Daniel. *Secrets: A Memoir of Vietnam and the Pentagon Papers*. New York: Viking, 2002.

Elson, Robert T. *Time Inc.: The Intimate History of a Publishing Enterprise, 1923–1941*. 2 vols. New York: Atheneum, 1968.

Emery, Michael, Edwin Emery, and Nancy Roberts. *The Press and America: An Interpretive History of the Mass Media*. 9th ed. Needham Heights, Mass.: Allyn & Bacon, 2000.

Endres, Kathleen. "The Press and the Civil War, 1861–1865." In *The Media in America: A History*, ed. William David Sloan. 8th ed. Northport, Ala.: Vision Press, 2005. 159–74.

Faas, Horst. "The Saigon Execution." The Digital Journalist, October 2004. http://digital journalist.org/issue0410/faas.html.

Faas, Horst, and Marianne Fulton. "The Survivor: The Story of Kim Phuc and photographer Nick Ut." The Digital Journalist, August 2000. http://digitaljournalist.org/issue 0008/ngtext.htm.

Farrar, Ronald. "News Councils and Libel Actions." *Journalism Quarterly* 63, no. 3 (Autumn 1986): 509–16.

Farrell, Amy Erdman. *Yours in Sisterhood: Ms. Magazine and the Promise of Popular Feminism*. Chapel Hill: University of North Carolina Press, 1990.

Faust, Drew Gilpin. "'The Dread Void of Uncertainty': Naming the Dead in the American Civil War." *Southern Cultures* 11, no. 2 (Summer 2005): 7–32.

Fee, Frank E., Jr. "'Intelligent Union of Black with White': Frederick Douglass and the Rochester Press." *Journalism History* 31, no. 1 (Spring 2005): 32–45.

Fellow, Anthony R., with John Tebbel. *American Media History.* Belmont, Calif.: Wadsworth, 2005.

Ferrari, Michelle. *Reporting America at War: An Oral History.* New York: Hyperion, 2003.

Finkelman, Paul, ed. *A Brief Narrative of the Case and Tryal of John Peter Zenger.* St. James, N.Y.: Brandywine Press, 1997.

Fishel, Elizabeth R. *Sisters: Love and Rivalry Inside the Family and Beyond.* New York: William Morrow, 1979.

Fitzpatrick, Ellen F., ed. *Muckraking: Three Landmark Articles.* The Bedford Series in History and Culture. Boston: Bedford/St. Martin, 1994.

Folkerts, Jean, ed. *Media Voices: An Historical Perspective.* Upper Saddle River, N.J.: Prentice Hall, 1992.

Foner, Eric. *Tom Paine and Revolutionary America.* New York: Oxford University Press, 1976.

Forde, Kathy Roberts. *Literary Journalism on Trial: Masson v. New Yorker and the First Amendment.* Amherst: University of Massachusetts Press, 2008.

Frankel, Max. *The Times of My Life, and My Life with* The Times. New York: Random House, 1999.

Franklin, Benjamin. *The Autobiography.* In *Writings,* 1,305–1,469.

———. *Writings.* Library of America. New York: Literary Classics of the United States, 1987.

Freedman, Eric M. "Reconstructing Journalists' Privilege." *Cardozo Law Review* 29, no. 4 (March 2008): 1381–99.

Freedom Forum. Journalists Memorial. www.newseum.org/scripts/journalist/main.htm.

Friendly, Fred. *Due to Circumstances beyond Our Control.* New York: Vintage Books, 1967.

Gabler, Neal. *Winchell: Gossip, Power, and the Culture of Celebrity.* New York: Knopf, 1994.

Gelb, Arthur. *City Room.* New York: Putnam, 2003.

Gibbs, Wolcott. "A Very Active Type Man." *New Yorker,* May 2 and May 9, 1942, 21–30, 21–30.

Gilbert, Martin. *Kristallnacht: Prelude to Destruction.* New York: HarperCollins, 2006.

Giles, Robert, and Robert W. Snyder, eds. *1968: Year of Media Decision.* New Brunswick, N.J.: Transaction, 2001.

Gillmor, Dan. *We the Media: Grassroots Journalism by the People, for the People.* Sebastapol, Calif.: O'Reilly Media, 2004.

Gitlin, Todd. *The Whole World Is Watching: Mass Media in the Making and Unmaking of the New Left.* Berkeley: University of California Press, 2003.

Glenn, David. "The (Josh) Marshall Plan." *Columbia Journalism Review* 46, no. 3 (September–October 2007): 22–27.

Gobright, Lawrence A. *Recollection of Men and Things at Washington.* Philadelphia: Claxton, Remsen and Haffelfinger; Washington, D.C.: W. H. and O. H. Morrison, 1869.

Goodman, Mark, and Mark Gring. "The Ideological Fight over Creation of the Federal Radio Commission in 1927." *Journalism History* 26, no. 3 (2000): 117–24.

Goralski, Robert. *World War II Almanac: 1931–1945.* New York, Putnam, 1981.

Gordon-Reed, Annette. *Thomas Jefferson and Sally Hemings: An American Controversy.* Charlottesville: University Press of Virginia, 1997.

Goren, Dina. "Communication Intelligence and the Freedom of the Press: The *Chicago Tribune*'s Battle of Midway Dispatch and the Breaking of the Japanese Naval Code." *Journal of Contemporary History* 16, no. 4 (1981): 663–90.

Graham, Katharine. *Personal History.* New York: Knopf, 1997.

Gramling, Oliver. *AP: The Story of News.* New York: Farrar and Rinehart, 1940.

Greeley, Horace. *Recollections of a Busy Life.* New York: J. B. Ford and Company, 1868.

Griswold, Erwin N. "Secrets Not Worth Keeping: The Courts and Classified Information." *Washington Post,* February, 15, 1989.

Grossman, Vasily. *A Writer at War: Vasily Grossman with the Red Army, 1941–45.* 1st American ed. Edited and translated by Antony Beevor and Luba Vinogradova. New York: Pantheon Books, 2005.

Guelzo, Allen C. *Lincoln's Emancipation Proclamation.* New York: Simon & Schuster, 2004.

Hack, Richard. *Clash of the Titans: How the Unbridled Ambition of Ted Turner and Rupert Murdoch Has Created Global Empires That Control What We Read and Watch.* Beverly Hills: New Millennium Press, 2003.

Halberstam, David. *The Best and the Brightest.* New York: Random House, 1972.

———. Foreword. In Associated Press, *Breaking News,* 7–17.

———. Introduction. In *The Best American Sports Writing of the Century.* Boston: Houghton Mifflin, 1999. xix–xxxiii.

———. *The Making of a Quagmire: America and Vietnam during the Kennedy Era.* 1965. New York: Knopf, 1988.

———. *The Powers That Be.* New York: Knopf, 1975.

Hall, Jacquelyn Dowd. "The Long Civil Rights Movement and the Political Uses of the Past." *Journal of American History* 91, no. 4 (March 2005): 1233–64.

Hall, Jacquelyn, et al. *Like a Family: The Making of a Southern Cotton Mill World.* Chapel Hill: University of North Carolina Press, 1987.

Hallin, Daniel C. *The "Uncensored War": The Media and Vietnam.* New York: Oxford University Press, 1986.

Hamilton, Alexander, James Madison, and John Jay. *The Federalist Papers.* Upper Saddle River, N.J.: Prentice Hall, 2000.

Hamilton, John Maxwell. *Journalism's Roving Eye: A History of American Foreign Reporting.* Baton Rouge: Louisiana State University Press, 2009.

Hamilton, John Maxwell, et al. "An Enabling Environment: A Reconsideration of the Press and the Spanish-American War." *Journalism Studies* 7, no. 1 (2006): 78–93.

Hammond, William M. *Reporting Vietnam: Media and the Military at War.* Lawrence: University of Kansas Press, 1998.

Harriman, Margaret Case. "The It Girl." *New Yorker,* April 20 and 27, 1940, 24–30 and 23–29.

Harrison, Mark. *The Economics of World War II: Six Great Powers in International Comparison.* Cambridge: Cambridge University Press, 2004.

Hartman, John K. *The USA Today Way: A Candid Look at the National Newspaper's First Decade, 1992–1992.* Bowling Green, Ohio: John K. Hartman, 1992.

Harwood, Richard. "The War Just Doesn't Add Up." In Library of America, *Reporting Vietnam,* 1:484–89.

Hecht, Ben, and Charles MacArthur. *The Front Page.* New York: Samuel French, 2010.

Heilbrun, Carolyn. *The Education of a Woman: The Life of Gloria Steinem.* New York: Dial Press, 1995.

Henretta, James, David Brody, and Lynn Dumenil. *America: A Concise History.* 4th ed. 2 vols. Boston: Bedford/St. Martin's, 2009.

Hersh, Seymour M. *The Dark Side of Camelot.* New York: Little, Brown, 1997.

———. "How I Broke the Mylai 4 Story." *Saturday Review,* July 11, 1970, 46–49.

Hewitt, Don. *Minute by Minute.* New York: Random House, 1985.

Hilmes, Michele. *Only Connect: A Cultural History of Broadcasting in the United States.* Belmont, Calif.: Wadsworth, 2002.

Hoffman, Joyce. *On Their Own: Women Journalists and the American Experience in Vietnam.* Philadelphia: Da Capo Books, 2008.

Hofstadter, Richard. *The Age of Reform.* New York: Vintage, 1955.

———. *The Progressive Movement.* New York: Simon & Schuster, 1986.

Howard, Jane. "A Six-Year Literary Vigil." *Life,* January 7, 1966, 70–73.

Hudson, Frederic. *Journalism in the United States, from 1690–1872.* New York: Harper & Bros., 1872.

Hughes, Langston. *The Best of Simple.* New York: Hill and Wang, 1961.

———. *Langston Hughes and the Chicago Defender.* Edited by Christopher B. De Santis. Urbana: University of Illinois Press, 1995.

Humphrey, Carol Sue. *"This Popular Engine": New England Newspapers during the American Revolution, 1775–1789.* Newark: University of Delaware Press, 1992.

Hutton, Frankie. *The Early Black Press in America, 1827 to 1860.* Westport, Conn.: Greenwood Press, 1992.

Isaacson, Walter. *Benjamin Franklin: An American Life.* New York: Simon & Schuster, 2003.

Jefferson, Thomas. *Writings.* Library of America. New York: Literary Classics of the United States, 1984.

Johanningsmeier, Charles. *Fiction and the American Literary Marketplace.* Cambridge: Cambridge University Press, 1997.

John, Richard R. *Network Nation: Inventing American Telecommunications.* Cambridge: Belknap Press of Harvard University Press, 2010.

——. *Spreading the News: The American Postal System from Franklin to Morse.* Cambridge: Harvard University Press, 1995.

Johnson, Lyndon. "Remarks Upon Signing the Public Broadcasting Act of 1967." www.cpb.org/aboutpb/act/remarks.html.

Jordan, William. "'The Damnable Dilemma': African-American Accommodation and Protest during World War I." *Journal of American History* 81, no. 4 (March 1995): 1562–83.

Just, Ward. "Saigon and Other Syndromes." In Library of America, *Reporting Vietnam,* 1:348–70.

Kamiya, Gary. "Ten Years of Salon." *Salon.* http://dir.salon.com/story/special/10th/2005/11/14/salon_history/index.html.

Kaye, Harvey J. *Thomas Paine and the Promise of America.* New York: Hill and Wang, 2005.

Kelly, Alfred H., Winfred A. Harbison, and Herman Belz. *The American Constitution: Its Origins and Development.* 7th ed. New York: Norton, 1991.

Kinsley, Michael. "My History of Slate." *Slate.* June 18, 2006. www.slate.com/id/2143232/.

Klein, Naomi. *No Logo.* New York: Picador, 1999.

Kluger, Richard. *The Paper: The Life and Death of the* New York Herald Tribune. New York: Knopf, 1986.

Knightley, Phillip. *The First Casualty: From the Crimea to Vietnam; The War Correspondent as Hero, Propagandist, and Myth Maker.* 3rd ed. Baltimore: Johns Hopkins University Press, 2004.

Kobre, Sidney. *The Yellow Press and Gilded Age Journalism.* Gainesville: Florida State University Press, 1964.

Krattenmaker, Thomas G., and Lucas A. Powe Jr. *Regulating Broadcast Programming.* Washington, D.C.: AEI Press, 1994.

Kroeger, Brooke. *Nellie Bly: Daredevil, Reporter, Feminist.* New York: Times Books, 1994.

Kull, Steven, et al. "Misperceptions, the Media, and the Iraq War." *Political Science Quarterly* 118, no. 4 (Winter 2003–2004): 569–98.

Kunkel, Thomas. *Genius in Disguise: Harold Ross of* The New Yorker. New York: Random House, 1995.

——, ed. *Letters from the Editor: The New Yorker's Harold Ross.* New York: Modern Library, 2000.

Kutler, Stanley I., ed. *Abuse of Power: The New Nixon Tapes.* New York: Free Press, 1997.

Lee, Alfred McLung. *The Daily Newspaper in America: The Evolution of a Social Instrument.* New York: Macmillan, 1937.

Lee, Andrew H. "Lee, Ivy Ledbetter." American National Biography Online. February 2000. www.anb.org.

Leff, Laurel. *Buried by* The Times: *The Holocaust and America's Most Important Newspaper.* Cambridge: Cambridge University Press, 2005.

Lemann, Nicholas. *The Promised Land: The Great Black Migration and How It Changed America.* New York: Vintage, 1992.

Lewis, Norman P. "The Myth of Spiro Agnew's 'Nattering Nabobs of Negativism.'" *American Journalism* 27, no. 1 (2010): 89–115.

Lewis, Tom. *Empire of the Air: The Men Who Made Radio.* New York: Edward Burlingame Books, 1991.

Library of America. *Debates on the Constitution.* New York: Literary Classics of the United
        States, 1993.

———. *Reporting Civil Rights.* 2 vols. New York: Literary Classics of the United States, 2003.

———. *Reporting Vietnam.* 2 vols. New York: Literary Classics of the United States, 1998.

———. *Reporting World War II.* 2 vols. New York: Literary Classics of the United States, 1995.

Liebling, A. J. *The Press.* New York: Pantheon, 1961. (Also see 2nd revised edition with
        introduction by Jean Stafford.)

———. *The Wayward Pressman.* Garden City, N.Y.: Doubleday, 1948.

Liebovich, Louis W. *Richard Nixon, Watergate, and the Press: A Historical Retrospective.*
        Westport, Conn.: Praeger, 2003.

Lippmann, Walter. *Essays in the Public Philosophy.* Boston: Little, Brown, 1955.

———. *Liberty and the News.* New York: Harcourt, Brace and Howe, 1920.

———. *Public Opinion.* New York: Harcourt, Brace, 1922.

———. *Public Philosopher: Selected Letters of Walter Lippmann.* Edited by John Morton
        Blum. New York: Ticknor & Fields, 1985.

Lipstadt, Deborah E. *Beyond Belief: The American Press and the Coming of the Holocaust,
        1933–1945.* New York: Free Press, 1986.

Liptak, Adam. "A Justice Scribbles on Journalists' Rights." *New York Times,* October 7, 2007,
        Week in Review section.

Lowe, Janet. *Oprah Winfrey Speaks: Insight from the World's Most Influential Voice.* New
        York: John Wiley & Sons, 1998.

Lubow, Arthur. *The Reporter Who Would Be King: A Biography of Richard Harding Davis.*
        New York: Charles Scribner's Sons, 1992.

Luce, Henry Robinson. *The American Century.* New York: Farrar & Rinehart, 1941.

Lunde, Eric S. *Horace Greeley.* Boston: Twayne Publishers/G. K. Hall, 1981.

Marcello, Patricia Cronin. *Gloria Steinem: A Biography.* Westport, Conn.: Greenwood
        Press, 2004.

Marcus, Sheldon. *Father Coughlin: The Tumultuous Life of the Father of the Little Flower.*
        Boston: Little, Brown, 1973.

Marshall, Joshua Micah. Speech. Berkman @ 10 Conference. Berkman Center for Internet
        & Society, Harvard Law School, Cambridge, Mass. May 16, 2008. http://cyber.law
        .harvard.edu/interactive/events/conferences/2008/05/joshuamarshall.

Marzolf, Marion Tuttle. *Civilizing Voices: American Press Criticism, 1880–1950.* New York:
        Longman, 1991.

Matusow, Barbara. *The Evening Stars: The Making of the Network News Anchor.* Boston:
        Houghton Mifflin, 1983.

Mayer, Henry. *All on Fire: William Lloyd Garrison and the Abolition of Slavery.* New York:
        St. Martin's Press, 1998.

McAdams, Melinda. "Inventing an Online Newspaper." *Interpersonal Computing and Tech-
        nology* 3, no. 3 (July 1995): 64–90.

McKay, Ernest A. *The Civil War and New York City.* Syracuse: Syracuse University Press, 1990.

McKeen, William. *Outlaw Journalist: The Life and Times of Hunter S. Thompson.* New York:
        Norton, 2008.

McKelway, St. Clair. "Gossip Writer." *New Yorker,* June 15, 22, 29, July 6, 13, 20, 1940.

McMurry, Linda O. *To Keep the Waters Troubled: The Life of Ida B. Wells.* New York: Oxford
        University Press, 1998.

Mears, Walter R. "A Brief History of AP." In Associated Press, *Breaking News,* 402–14.

Media Matters for America. "33 Internal FOX Editorial Memos Reviewed by MMFA Reveal
        FOX News Channel's Inner Workings." July 14, 2004. http://mediamatters.org
        /research/200407140002.

Mencken, H. L. *Newspaper Days.* New York: Alfred A. Knopf, 1941.

Merholz, Peter. "Play with Your Words." May 17, 2002. www.peterme.com/archives
        /00000205.html.

Mickelson, Sig. *The Decade That Shaped Television News: CBS in the 1950s*. Westport, Conn.: Praeger, 1998.

Milton, John. *Areopagitica: A Speech for the Liberty of Unlicensed Printing to the Parliament of England*. London, 1644.

Mindich, David T. Z. "Edwin M. Stanton, the Inverted Pyramid, and Information Control." In *The Civil War and the Press*, ed. David Sachsman et al. New Brunswick, N.J.: Transaction, 2000. 179–208.

———. *Just the Facts: How "Objectivity" Came to Define American Journalism*. New York: New York University Press, 1998.

Mock, James R. *Censorship, 1917*. Princeton: Princeton University Press, 1941.

Moeller, Susan. *Shooting War: Photography and the American Experience of Combat*. New York: Basic Books, 1989.

Morris, James McGrath. *Pulitzer: A Life in Politics, Print, and Power*. New York: Harper-Collins, 2010.

Murphy, Cullen, "A History of *The Atlantic Monthly*." 1994. www.theatlantic.com/past/docs/about/atlhistf.htm.

Murrow, Edward R. *This Is London*. New York: Simon and Schuster, 1941.

Nasaw, David. *The Chief: The Life of William Randolph Hearst*. Boston: Houghton Mifflin, 2000.

Nelson, Harold L., ed. *Freedom of the Press from Hamilton to the Warren Court*. New York: Bobbs-Merrill, 1967.

Nerone, John. *Violence against the Press: Policing the Public Sphere in U.S. History*. New York: Oxford University Press, 1994.

Neuharth, Al. *Confessions of an S.O.B.* New York: Doubleday, 1989.

Nichols, David. Introduction. In *Ernie's War: The Best of Ernie Pyle's World War II Dispatches*. Edited by David Nichols. New York: Random House, 1986. xiii–xvi.

Nixon, Richard. Presidential tapes. www.gwu.edu/~nsarchiv/NSAEBB/NSAEB-B48/nixon.html.

Nord, David Paul. *Communities of Journalism: A History of American Newspapers and Their Readers*. Urbana: University of Illinois Press, 2001.

O'Brien, Frank M. *The Story of the Sun*. New York: George H. Doran, 1918.

O'Dell, De Forest. *The History of Journalism Education in the United States*. New York: Columbia University Teachers College Bureau of Publications, 1935.

O'Reilly, Kenneth. "Dies, Martin." American National Biography Online. February 2000. www.anb.org.

Oshinsky, David M. *A Conspiracy So Immense: The World of Joe McCarthy*. New York: Free Press, 1983.

Paine, Thomas. *Collected Writings*. Library of America. New York: Literary Classics of the United States, 1995.

Palfrey, John, and Urs Gasser. *Born Digital: Understanding the First Generation of Digital Natives*. New York: Basic Books, 2008.

Pasley, Jeffrey L. *"The Tyranny of Printers": Newspaper Politics in the Early American Republic*. Charlottesville: University Press of Virginia, 2001.

Peck, Abe. *Uncovering the Sixties: The Life and Times of the Underground Press*. New York: Pantheon, 1985.

Perlstein, Rick. *Nixonland: The Rise of a President and the Fracturing of America*. New York: Scribner, 2008.

Persico, Joseph E. *Edward R. Murrow: An American Original*. New York: McGraw-Hill, 1988.

Phuc, Kim. "The Long Road to Forgiveness." *This I Believe*. National Public Radio, June 30, 2008.

Plimpton, George. "Q + A with Truman Capote." *New York Times Book Review*, January 16, 1966, 2–3, 39–42.

Podhoretz, John. "The Old Time and the New Newsweek." *Contentions* (blog), *Commentary*,

May 19, 2009. www.commentarymagazine.com/2009/05/19/the-old-time-and-the
-new-newsweek/.

Ponder, Stephen. *Managing the Press: Origins of the Media Presidency, 1897–1933.* New York:
St. Martin's Press, 1998.

Porter, William E. *Assault on the Media: The Nixon Years.* Ann Arbor: University of Michigan Press, 1976.

Pride, Armistead S., and Clint C. Wilson II. *A History of the Black Press.* Washington, D.C.:
Howard University Press, 1997.

Prochnau, William. *Once upon a Distant War: Young War Correspondents and the Early
Vietnam Battles.* New York: Times Books, 1995.

Project for Excellence in Journalism. Annual Report. 2010. www.stateofthemedia.org/2010/
media-ownership/sector_audio.php.

Pulitzer, Joseph. "The College of Journalism." *North American Review* 178, no. 570 (May
1904): 641–80.

Pyle, Ernie. *Ernie's America: The Best of Ernie Pyle's 1930s Travel Dispatches.* Edited with an
introduction by David Nichols. New York: Random House, 1989.

———. *Ernie's War: The Best of Ernie Pyle's World War II Dispatches.* Edited with a biographical essay by David Nichols. New York: Random House, 1986.

———. *Here Is Your War.* New York: Henry Holt, 1943.

Pyle, Richard. "19th-Century Papers Shed New Light on Origins of The Associated Press."
AP dispatch. January 31, 2006.

Ratner, Lorman, and Dwight Teeter. *Fanatics and Fire-Eaters: Newspapers and the Coming
of the Civil War.* Champaign: University of Illinois Press, 2003.

Ritchie, Donald. *Reporting from Washington: The History of the Washington Press Corps.*
New York: Oxford, 2005.

Rivera-Sanchez, Milagros. "The Origins of the Ban on 'Obscene, Indecent or Profane' Language of the Radio Act of 1927." *Journalism Monographs* 149 (February 1995): 21.

Roberts, Chalmers. *The Washington Post: The First 100 Years.* Boston: Houghton Mifflin, 1977.

Roberts, Gene, and Hank Klibanoff. *The Race Beat: The Press, the Civil Rights Struggle, and
the Awakening of a Nation.* New York: Knopf, 2006.

Rosen, Jay. "The People Formerly Known as the Audience." Pressthink.org. June 27, 2006.
http://archive.pressthink.org/2006/06/27/ppl_frmr.html.

Rosenberg, Scott. *Say Everything: How Blogging Began, What It's Becoming, and Why It
Matters.* New York: Crown Publishers, 2009.

Rosenfeld, Richard N. *American Aurora: A Democratic-Republican Returns; The Suppressed
History of Our Nation's Beginnings and the Heroic Newspaper That Tried to Report
It.* New York: St. Martin's Press, 1997.

Rossiter, Clinton. Introduction. In *The Essential Lippmann.* Edited by Clinton Rossiter and
James Lare. New York: Random House, 1963. xi–xxi.

Rossiter, Clinton, and James Lare, eds. *The Essential Lippmann: A Political Philosophy for
Liberal Democracy.* New York: Random House, 1963.

Rucker, Frank W. *Walter Williams.* Columbia: Missourian Publishing Assn., 1964.

Rudenstine, David. *The Day the Presses Stopped: A History of the Pentagon Papers Case.*
Berkeley: University of California Press, 1996.

Safire, William, ed. *Lend Me Your Ears: Great Speeches in History.* 3rd ed. New York: Norton,
2004.

———. "On Language." *New York Times,* November 13, 1988.

Salisbury, Harrison E. *Without Fear or Favor:* The New York Times *and Its Times.* New
York: Times Books, 1980.

Salvatore, Nick. *Eugene V. Debs: Citizen and Socialist.* Urbana: University of Illinois Press,
1982.

Sanders, Marion K. *Dorothy Thompson: A Legend in Her Time.* Boston: Houghton Mifflin,
1973.

Schanberg, Sydney. "The Military and the Press." In Library of America, *Reporting Vietnam*, 2:394–407. Originally published in *New York Times Magazine*, November 12, 1972.

Schiller, Dan. *Objectivity and the News: The Public and the Rise of Commercial Journalism.* Philadelphia: University of Pennsylvania Press, 1981.

Schonfeld, Reese. *Me and Ted against the World: The Unauthorized Story of the Founding of CNN.* New York: HarperCollins, 2001.

Schudson, Michael. *Discovering the News: A Social History of American Newspapers.* New York: Basic Books, 1978.

———. *The Power of News.* Cambridge: Harvard University Press, 1996.

Schumpeter, Joseph. *Capitalism, Socialism, and Democracy.* New York: Harper, 1950.

Schwarzlose, Richard. *The Nation's Newsbrokers.* 2 vols. Evanston: Northwestern University Press, 1989–90.

Scientific American. "About Scientific American." www.scientificamerican.com/pressroom/aboutus.cfm.

Sears, Stephen W. *Chancellorsville.* New York: Houghton Mifflin, 1996.

Seib, Philip M. *Broadcasts from the Blitz: How Edward R. Murrow Helped Lead America into War.* Washington, D.C.: Potomac Books, 2006.

———. *Rush Hour: Talk Radio, Politics, and the Rise of Rush Limbaugh.* Fort Worth: Summit Group, 1993.

Seitz, Don Carlos. *Joseph Pulitzer: His Life and Letters.* New York: Simon & Schuster, 1924.

Stelter, Brian. "Finding Political News Online, the Young Pass It On." *New York Times,* March 27, 2008.

Shafer, Jack. "How Newspapers Tried to Invent the Web. But Failed." *Slate.* January 6, 2009. www.slate.com/id/2207912/.

Sheehan, Neil. *A Bright Shining Lie: John Paul Vann and America in Vietnam.* New York: Random House, 1988.

Sherrod, Robert. *Tarawa: The Story of a Battle.* 1944. Excerpted in Library of America, *Reporting World War II,* 1:683–712.

Shirer, William L. *Berlin Diary: The Journal of a Foreign Correspondent, 1934–1941.* New York: Alfred A. Knopf, 1941.

———. *The Rise and Fall of the Third Reich: A History of Nazi Germany.* New York: Simon & Schuster, 1960.

Shirky, Clay. "Newspapers and Thinking the Unthinkable." May 13, 2009. www.shirky.com/weblog/2009/03/newspapers-and-thinking-the-unthinkable/.

Shore, Elliott. "Wayland, Julius Augustus." American National Biography Online. February 2000. www.anb.org.

Sinclair, Upton. *The Brass Check: A Study of American Journalism.* Pasadena: Upton Sinclair, 1919.

———, *The Jungle.* New York: Doubleday, Page, 1906.

Slaughter, Thomas P. Introduction. In Thomas Paine, *"Common Sense" and Related Writings.* Edited by Thomas P. Slaughter. Boston: Bedford/St. Martin's, 2001. 1–26.

Sloan, William David, and Julie Hedgepeth Williams. *The Early American Press, 1690–1783.* Westport, Conn.: Greenwood Press, 1994.

Smith, Sally Bedell. *In All His Glory: The Life of William S. Paley.* New York: Simon and Schuster, 1990.

Sperber, A. M. *Murrow: His Life and Times.* New York: Freundlich Books, 1986.

Sproule, J. Michael. *Propaganda and Democracy: The American Experience of Media and Mass Persuasion.* New York: Cambridge University Press, 1997.

Standage, Tom. *The Victorian Internet: The Remarkable Story of the Telegraph and the Nineteenth Century's On-line Pioneers.* New York: Walker Publishing, 1998.

Starr, Paul. *The Creation of the Media: Political Origins of Modern Communications.* New York: Basic Books, 2004.

———. *The Social Transformation of American Medicine.* New York: Basic Books, 1982.

Stashower, Daniel. *The Boy Genius and the Mogul: The Untold Story of Television.* New York, Broadway Books, 2002.

Steel, Ronald. *Walter Lippmann and the American Century.* Boston: Little, Brown, 1980.

Steele, Janet E. *The Sun Shines for All: Journalism and Ideology in the Life of Charles A. Dana.* Syracuse: Syracuse University Press, 1993.

Steffens, Lincoln. *The Autobiography of Lincoln Steffens.* New York: Harcourt Brace, 1931.

Steinem, Gloria. *Outrageous Acts and Everyday Rebellions.* New York: Holt, Rinehart and Winston, 1983.

———. *Revolution from Within: A Book of Self-Esteem.* Boston: Little, Brown, 1992.

Stephens, Mitchell. *A History of News.* 3rd ed. New York: Oxford University Press, 2007.

———. "The Top 100 Works of Journalism in the United States in the 20th Century." www .nyu.edu/classes/stephens/Top%20100%20page.htm.

Stone, Geoffrey R. *Perilous Times: Free Speech in Wartime.* New York: Norton, 2004.

Streitmatter, Rodger. *Mightier Than the Sword: How the News Media Have Shaped American History.* Boulder, Colo.: Westview Press, 1997.

Swanberg, W. A. *Citizen Hearst.* New York: Charles Scribner's Sons, 1961.

———. *Luce and His Empire.* New York: Scribners, 1972.

———. *Pulitzer.* New York: Charles Scribner's Sons, 1967.

Sweeney, Michael S. *The Military and the Press: An Uneasy Truce.* Evanston: Northwestern University Press, 2006.

———. *Secrets of Victory: The Office of Censorship and the American Press and Radio in World War II.* Chapel Hill: University of North Carolina Press, 2001.

Talese, Gay. *The Kingdom and the Power.* Cleveland: World Publishing, 1966.

Tallman, Gary C., and Joseph P. McKerns. "'Press Mess': David Halberstam, the Buddhist Crisis, and U.S. Policy in Vietnam, 1963." *Journalism and Communication Monographs* 2, no. 3 (2000): 109–53.

Taylor, George Rogers. *The Transportation Revolution, 1815–1860.* New York, Rinehart and Co., 1951.

Taylor, Sally. ""Marx and Greeley on Slavery and Labor." *Journalism History* 6, no. 4 (Winter 1979–80): 103–6, 122.

Tebbel, John, and Mary Ellen Zuckerman. *The Magazine in America, 1741–1990.* New York: Oxford University Press, 1991.

Terry, Wallace. *Missing Pages: Black Journalists of Modern America; An Oral History.* New York: Carroll & Graf, 2007.

Thom, Mary. *Inside Ms.: 25 Years of the Magazine and the Feminist Movement.* New York: H. Holt, 1997.

Thomas, Isaiah. *The History of Printing in America.* Edited by Marcus A. McCorison. New York: Weathervane Books, 1970.

Thompson, Dorothy. *I Saw Hitler!* New York: Farrar & Rinehart, 1932.

Thompson, Hunter S. *Fear and Loathing in Las Vegas.* New York: Random House, 1971.

———. *Fear and Loathing on the Campaign Trail '72.* San Francisco: Straight Arrow Books, 1973.

———. *Hells Angels.* New York: Ballantine Books, 1967.

Thoreau, Henry. T*he Writings of Henry David Thoreau: Journal, Volume 4: 1851–1852.* Edited by Leonard N. Neufeldt and Nancy Craig Simmons. Princeton: Princeton University Press, 1992.

Thurber, James, and E. B. White. *Is Sex Necessary? Or, Why You Feel the Way You Do.* New York: Harper & Bros., 1929.

Tifft, Susan, and Alex S. Jones. *The Trust: The Private and Powerful Family behind* The New York Times. Boston: Little, Brown, 1999.

Tobin, James. *Ernie Pyle's War: America's Eyewitness to World War II.* New York: Free Press, 1997.

Tocqueville, Alexis de. *Democracy in America.* Library of America. New York: Literary Classics of the United States, 2004.

Toobin, Jeffrey, "Comeback." *New Yorker,* March 26, 2007, 33.

Tucher, Andie. *Froth and Scum: Truth, Beauty, Goodness, and the Ax Murder in America's First Mass Medium.* Chapel Hill: University of North Carolina Press, 1994.

Turner, Ted, with Bill Burke. *Call Me Ted.* New York: Grand Central Publishing, 2008.

Tye, Larry. *The Father of Spin: Edward L. Bernays and the Birth of Public Relations.* New York: Crown Publishers, 1998.

Ungar, Sanford J. *The Papers and the Papers: An Account of the Legal Battle over the Pentagon Papers.* New York: Columbia University Press, 1989.

U.S. Census Bureau. "United States—Race and Hispanic Origin: 1790 to 1990." www.census.gov/population/www/documentation/twps0056/tab01.pdf.

United States National Advisory Commission on Civil Disorders (the Kerner Commission). *Report of the National Advisory Commission on Civil Disorders.* New York: Bantam Books, 1968.

Vaughn, Stephen. *Holding Fast the Inner Lines: Democracy, Nationalism, and the Committee on Public Information.* Chapel Hill: University of North Carolina Press, 1980.

Vogel, Todd, ed. *The Black Press: New Literary and Historical Essays.* New Brunswick, N.J.: Rutgers University Press, 2001.

Walker, Juliet E. K. "Oprah Winfrey, the Tycoon: Contextualizing the Economics of Race, Class, and Gender in Black Business History in Post–Civil Rights America." In *Black Business and Economic Power,* ed. Alusine Jalloh and Toyin Falola. Rochester: University of Rochester Press, 2002. 484–525.

Wallace, Aurora. "A Height Deemed Appalling: Nineteenth-Century New York Newspaper Buildings." *Journalism History* 31, no. 4 (Winter 2006): 178–89.

Washburn, Patrick S. *The African American Newspaper: Voice of Freedom.* Evanston: Northwestern University Press, 2006.

———. *A Question of Sedition: The Federal Government's Investigation of the Black Press during World War II.* New York: Oxford University Press, 1986.

Weinberg, Sydney. "What to Tell America." *Journal of American History* 55 (June 1968): 73–89.

Weingarten, Marc. *The Gang That Wouldn't Shoot Straight: Wolfe, Thompson, Didion, and the New Journalism Revolution.* New York: Crown Publishers, 2006.

Wells, Ida B. *Southern Horrors and Other Writings.* Edited and introduced by Jaqueline Jones Royster. Bedford Series in History and Culture. Boston: Bedford/St. Martin's, 1997.

White, E. B. "The Newspaper Reader Finds It Very Difficult to Get at the Truth." In Library of America, *Reporting World War II,* 1:300–302. Excerpted from "One Man's Meat," *Harper's Magazine,* April 1942, 553–56.

White, Horace. "The School of Journalism," *North American Review* 178, no. 566 (January 1904): 25–32.

Whittemore, Hank. *CNN: The Inside Story.* Boston: Little, Brown, 1990.

Whyte, Kenneth. *The Uncrowned King: The Sensational Rise of William Randolph Hearst.* Berkeley: Counterpoint, 2009.

Wilentz, Sean. *Chants Democratic: New York City and the Rise of the American Working Class.* New York: Oxford University Press, 1984.

Wilkerson, Isabel. *The Warmth of Other Suns: The Epic Story of America's Great Migration.* New York: Random House, 2010.

Williams, Juan. "Dateline Freedom: Civil Rights and the Press." Public Broadcasting System. 1989.

Wilner, Isaiah. *The Man Time Forgot: A Tale of Genius, Betrayal, and the Creation of Time Magazine.* New York: HarperCollins, 2006.

Winchell, Walter. *Winchell Exclusive: Things That Happened to Me—And Me to Them.* London: Prentice-Hall, 1975.

Winer, David. Scripting News Weblog. http://scripting.com/.

———. "What Makes a Weblog a Weblog?" Weblogs at Harvard Law Conference. Hosted by Berkman Center for Internet & Society, Harvard Law School. May 23, 2003. http://blogs.law.harvard.edu/whatmakesaweblogaweblog.html.

Wolfe, Tom. *The New Journalism.* New York: Harper & Row, 1973.

Wolseley, Roland E. *The Black Press, U.S.A.* Ames: Iowa State University Press, 1990.

Wood, Gordon S. *The Radicalism of the American Revolution.* New York: Knopf, 1992.

Woodward, Bob. *The Secret Man: The Story of Watergate's Deep Throat.* New York: Simon & Schuster, 2005.

Woodward, Bob, and Carl Bernstein. *The Final Days.* New York: Simon and Schuster, 1976.

Zittrain, Jonathan. *The Future of the Internet—And How to Stop It.* New Haven: Yale University Press, 2008.

Acknowledgments

In a work of this scale, a writer accumulates many debts. My debts are certainly numerous and deep, and I want to acknowledge them. *Covering America* builds on many preceding studies, and I am the first to recognize that this book rests on decades of previous scholarship.

I also want to thank the many friends and colleagues who have contributed directly to the writing of this book. As Ben Franklin said when launching a new newspaper, it would be well if the author "could make up among his Friends what is wanting in himself."

First, I thank my father-in-law, Jim Fishel, who encouraged this project all along. As I came to topics in the twentieth century (most of which he lived through), I found him an invaluable guide. He supported me with his vast memory and his endless good cheer.

My neighbor and "tech guru" Dan Bricklin was an early and faithful supporter. His enthusiasm, his expertise, and his editing were invaluable.

I was also fortunate to enlist a number of family members at various stages of this project. I thank Nate Houghteling for his sharp insights about American history and literature. I am also indebted to Elizabeth Fishel, Will Houghteling, and Bob Houghteling, who all helped me to see further.

My work on this book has also benefited enormously from the generous efforts of two "teams" of readers—historians and journalists. Friends and colleagues from both fields have contributed much and kept me from error. Among the historians I thank Jim Green, who read the entire manuscript with great care and wisdom. Bruce Schulman, my colleague at Boston University, provided invaluable insight and warm support. I am also grateful to my old graduate school adviser, Leon Fink, who is still, I am happy to say, correcting me. Bob Korstad was greatly encouraging, and David Nord guided me through areas he knows best.

Among the journalists, who are also colleagues of mine at Boston University, I thank Mitch Zuckoff for our breakfasts and for his most encouraging words. Every writer should have such a reader. I am also grateful to Elizabeth Mehren for her sharp insights and her relentless enforcement of style matters. Thanks, too, to Nick Mills for his careful editing and to Elissa Papirno for her many thoughts and suggestions.

The members of the justly obscure Penultimate Society—Mark Starr, Howard Bauchner, Don Goff, and Michael Miller—lent me their support, their wit, and their monthly companionship. I owe a particular debt to Michael Miller, who also gave me many valuable suggestions away from the dinner table.

Boston University has supported this project in several ways. Dean Thomas Fiedler generously supported this work with a grant to help underwrite the cost of illustrations. The university granted me a sabbatical that allowed me to set the book on a firmer footing. I thank my B.U. colleagues for listening to drafts and suggesting many productive avenues. The university also supplied research assistants, who greatly increased my range. Thanks to Caitlin Tunney, Paul Crocetti, Neil St. Clair, Lauren Gniazdowski, John Eagan, Marc Lanza, Adam Tamburin, and Solomon Syed, and a special thanks to Ken Holmes. I also thank Peter Umans; every teacher should have such a student.

Boston University also provided invaluable aid through the Howard Gotlieb Archival Research Center, which houses the most important collection of papers relating to journalism in the country. I am especially grateful to archivist Charles Niles for his vast knowledge and his equally vast generosity. Thanks, too, to the incomparable Vita Paladino, the archive director, and her associate Sean Noel for many courtesies.

I have been fortunate in the writing of this book to have had several opportunities to try out drafts in various forums. Thanks to Dan Bricklin, I was able to post the draft chapters on my website (www.journalismprofessor.com), which allowed me to make the book-in-progress available to hundreds of my students at Boston University. In addition, I thank Christopher Callahan, dean of the Walter Cronkite School of Journalism and Mass Communication at Arizona State University, for deciding to adopt *Covering America* for classroom use while it was still in progress. The feedback from those students and from Kristin Gilger of the Walter Cronkite School was very helpful.

Some of the ideas in this book got public tryouts at various academic conferences, including the Organization of American Historians, the Association for

Education in Journalism and Mass Communication, and the American Journalism Historians Association, as well as conferences on journalism and writing. I particularly thank Adam Hochschild and Isabel Wilkerson for their masterly advice on narrative technique. I benefited immensely, too, from attendance and discussions at events arranged by the Berkman Center for Internet & Society at Harvard University.

In addition, I gratefully acknowledge the prompt, precise, and friendly help I received from many librarians and archivists around the country, including those at the Kennedy, Johnson, and Roosevelt presidential libraries, as well as the Columbia University library system and the Library of Virginia Archives. In addition, I thank the Library of Congress, as all Americans should, for preserving so much of our national heritage and for keeping it in the public domain.

I also thank my editor at University of Massachusetts Press, Clark Dougan, who shepherded this project through many tight passages. I am also grateful to the press's director, Bruce Wilcox, for his enthusiasm and to the diligent Amanda Heller for her intelligent and painstaking work, which saved me from many an error. Thanks also to Carol Betsch, Mary Bellino, Sally Nichols, and the whole UMass Press team for their cheerful and professional collaboration.

Above all, I want to thank my family. I thank "the boys"—Gabe and Joe, who actually were boys when this project began but are now grown into young men—who tolerated many absences, as well as those times when I was actually present but, shall we say, distracted. Their humor, their patience, and their support meant so much to me along the way.

Finally, and most important, I want to try to thank my wife, Anne Fishel, who has inspired me from the day we met. I am happy to have a chance to acknowledge her unstinting support, her wise judgment, and her great taste. At every step of this project she has been engaged, and my appreciation for her is boundless. She has saved me from countless lapses and pointed the way with many important suggestions. She has always been my best and most treasured reader. She has seen me through.

Index

CHRISTOPHER B. DALY is a professor of journalism at Boston University. Born in Boston, he was raised in Medford, Mass., and graduated from Harvard with a degree in American history and literature. While in graduate school at the University of North Carolina at Chapel Hill, he began work with several co-authors on the landmark social history *Like a Family: The Making of a Southern Cotton Mill World,* which won the Beveridge, Curti, and Taft awards for history. Daly spent ten years working for the Associated Press as a reporter and editor, and then covered New England for the *Washington Post* for nearly a decade before beginning his teaching career at Boston University. He has also contributed articles and book reviews to many publications, and he comments on journalism on his website, www.journalismprofessor.com. He lives near Boston with his wife, Dr. Anne K. Fishel. They have two sons.